SYSTEM
ANALYSIS AND
DESIGN

Fourth Edition

ALAN DENNIS

Indiana University

BARBARA HALEY WIXOM

University of Virginia

ROBERTA M. ROTH

University of Northern Iowa

WILEY

John Wiley & Sons, Inc.

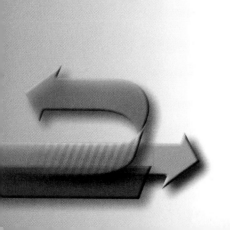

CREDITS

VICE PRESIDENT, & EXECUTIVE PUBLISHER	Don Fowley
EXECUTIVE EDITOR	Beth Lang Golub
ASSOCIATE EDITOR	Jen Devine
MARKETING MANAGER	Carly DeCandia
DESIGN DIRECTOR	Harry Nolan
SENIOR DESIGNER	Kevin Murphy
SENIOR PRODUCTION EDITOR	Patricia McFadden
SENIOR MEDIA EDITOR	Lauren Sapira
PRODUCTION MANAGEMENT SERVICES	Aptara®, Inc.

This book was set in 10.5/12 Times New Roman by Aptara®, Inc. and printed and bound by RRD/Von Hoffmann.

The cover was printed by RRD/Von Hoffmann.

This book is printed on acid-free paper. ∞

To order books or for Customer Service, please call 1-800-CALL WILEY (1-800-225-5945).

ISBN-13 978-0-470-22854-8

Printed in the United States of America
10 9 8 7 6 5 4 3 2 1

To Alec

To Chris, Haley, and Hannah

In memory of my mother, and, as always, to Rich and the boys

PREFACE

PURPOSE OF THIS BOOK

Systems Analysis and Design (SAD) is an exciting, active field in which analysts continually learn new techniques and approaches to develop systems more effectively and efficiently. However, there is a core set of skills that all analysts need to know no matter what approach or methodology is used. All information systems projects move through the four phases of planning, analysis, design, and implementation; all projects require analysts to gather requirements, model the business needs, and create blueprints for how the system should be built; and all projects require an understanding of organizational behavior concepts like change management and team building.

This book captures the dynamic aspects of the field by keeping students focused on doing SAD while presenting the core set of skills that we feel every systems analyst needs to know today and in the future. This book builds on our professional experience as systems analysts and on our experience in teaching SAD in the classroom.

This book will be of particular interest to instructors who have students do a major project as part of their course. Each chapter describes one part of the process, provides clear explanations on how to do it, gives a detailed example, and then has exercises for the students to practice. In this way, students can leave the course with experience that will form a rich foundation for further work as a systems analyst.

OUTSTANDING FEATURES

A Focus on Doing SAD

The goal of this book is to enable students to do SAD—not just read about it, but understand the issues so that they can actually analyze and design systems. The book introduces each major technique, explains what it is, explains how to do it, presents an example, and provides opportunities for students to practice before they do it in a real-world project. After reading each chapter, the student will be able to perform that step in the system development life cycle (SDLC) process.

Rich Examples of Success and Failure

The book includes a running case about a fictitious company called Tune Source. Each chapter shows how the concepts are applied in situations at Tune Source. Unlike running cases in other books, this text focuses examples on planning, managing, and executing the activities described in the chapter, rather than on detailed dialogue between fictitious actors. In this way, the running case serves as a template that students can apply to their own work. Each chapter also includes numerous Concepts in Action boxes that describe how real companies succeeded—and failed—in performing the activities in the chapter. Many of these examples are drawn from our own experiences as systems analysts.

Incorporation of Object-Oriented Concepts and Techniques

The field is moving toward object-oriented concepts and techniques, both through UML 2.0, the new standard for object-oriented analysts and design, as well as by gradually incorporating object-oriented concepts into traditional techniques. We have taken two approaches to incorporating object-oriented analysis and design into the book. First, we have integrated several object-oriented concepts into our discussion of traditional techniques, although this may not be noticed by the students because few concepts are explicitly labeled as object-oriented concepts. For example, we include the development of use cases as the first step in process modeling (i.e., data flow diagramming) in Chapter 4, and the use (and reuse) of standard interface templates and use scenarios for interface design in Chapter 9.

Second, and more obvious to students, we include a final chapter on the major elements of UML 2.0 that can be used as an introduction to object-oriented analysts and design. This chapter can be used at the end of a course—while students are busy working on projects—or can be introduced after or instead of Chapters 5 and 6.

Real-World Focus

The skills that students learn in a systems analysis and design course should mirror the work that they ultimately will do in real organizations. We have tried to make this book as "real" as possible by building extensively on our experience as professional systems analysts for organizations such as IBM, the U.S. Department of Defense, and the Australian Army. We have also worked with diverse industry advisory boards of IS professionals and consultants in developing the book and have incorporated their stories, feedback, and advice throughout. Many students who use this book will eventually apply the skills on the job in a business environment, and we believe that they will have a competitive edge by understanding what successful practitioners feel is relevant in the real world.

Project Approach

We have presented the topics in this book in the SDLC order in which an analyst encounters them in a typical project. Although the presentation necessarily is linear (because students have to learn concepts in the way in which they build on each other), we emphasize the iterative, complex nature of SAD as the book unfolds. The presentation of the material should align well with courses that encourage students to work on projects, because it presents topics as students need to apply them.

Graphic Organization

The underlying metaphor for the book is doing SAD through a project. We have tried to emphasize this graphically throughout the book so that students can better understand how the major elements in the SDLC are related to each other. First, at the start of every major phase of the system development life cycle, we present a graphic illustration showing the major deliverables that will be developed and added to the "project binder" during that phase. Second, at the start of each chapter, we present a checklist of key tasks or activities that will be performed to produce the deliverables associated with this chapter. These graphic elements—the binder of deliverables tied to each phase and the task checklist tied to each chapter—can help students better understand how the tasks, deliverables, and phases are related to and flow from one to another.

Finally, we have highlighted important practical aspects throughout the book by marking boxes and illustrations with a "push pin." These topics are particularly important in the practical day-to-day life of systems analysts and are the kind of topics that junior analysts should pull out of the book and post on the bulletin board in their office to help them avoid costly mistakes

WHAT'S NEW IN THE FOURTH EDITION

The fourth edition contains several important enhancements, including a new running case, new examples, many new Concepts in Action, and some reorganized material.

Part 1, Planning, has been substantially reorganized and streamlined. Students are introduced to project initiation immediately in the first chapter. The Tune Source running case is launched in Chapter 1 so that students can be involved in a project context from the outset of the book. The topic of project selection has been enhanced with a discussion of project portfolio management. The discussion of SDLC methodologies has been updated and shifted to Chapter 2. In this way, the review of alternative methodologies is placed within the context of planning a project and selecting the best methodology for it. Finally, some of the more technical concepts associated with economic feasibility financial calculations, function point analysis, and project management techniques have been moved to chapter appendices. This keeps the material available for those instructors who choose to include it, but streamlines the main chapter content for those instructors who exclude these topics due to time constraints.

In Part 2, Analysis, a new additional example case, Holiday Travel Vehicles, is introduced to provide additional illustrations of concepts, techniques, and deliverables. The topic of requirements determination is enhanced by a sample interview transcript that provides the basis for new requirements in the Holiday Travel Vehicles case. The discussion of data model normalization has been moved to a chapter appendix. Completed use cases, process models, and data models are included for both the Tune Source case and the Holiday Travel Vehicle cases, providing more extensive examples and illustrations for students and instructors.

Part 3, Design, includes some updated material on the use of packaged software and the use of offshore outsourcing. The n-tiered client-server architecture is explained through an e-commerce illustration. The role of external security requirements and standards is introduced as well. User interface examples and illustrations all have been updated to use Web-based forms or (Visual Basic) Windows-based forms to better reflect the environment with which students will be involved.

Throughout the book, the Concepts in Action material has been substantially revised and replaced with current examples and illustrations. Chapter references to outside sources have been updated to current resources wherever possible.

ORGANIZATION OF THIS BOOK

This book is organized by the phases of the systems development life cycle (SDLC). Each chapter has been written to teach students specific tasks that analysts need to accomplish over the course of a project, and the deliverables that will be produced from the tasks. As students complete the book, tasks will be "checked off" and deliverables will be completed and filed in a project binder. Along the way, students will be reminded of their progress by road maps that indicate where their current task fits into the larger context of SAD.

Part 1 covers the first phase of the SDLC, the planning phase. Chapter 1 introduces the SDLC, the roles and skills needed for a project team, project initiation, the systems request, and feasibility analysis. Chapter 2 discusses project selection, the selection of an SDLC methodology for the project, and project management, with emphasis on the work plan, staffing plan, project charter, risk assessment, and tools used to help manage and control the project.

Part 2 presents techniques needed during the analysis phase. In Chapter 3, students are introduced to requirements determination and are taught a variety of analysis techniques to help with business process automation, business process improvement, and business process reengineering. Chapter 4 focuses on use cases, Chapter 5 covers process models, and Chapter 6 explains data models and normalization.

The Design Phase is covered in Part 3 of the textbook. In Chapter 7, students create an alternative matrix that compares custom, packaged, and outsourcing alternatives. Chapter 8 focuses on designing the system architecture, which includes the architecture design, hardware/software specification, and security plan. Chapter 9 focuses on the user interface and presents interface design; in this chapter, students learn how to create use scenarios, the interface structure diagram, interface standards, and interface prototypes. Finally, data storage design and program design are discussed in Chapters 10 and 11, which contain information regarding the data storage design, the program structure chart, and program specifications.

The implementation phase is presented in Chapters 12 and 13. Chapter 12 focuses on system construction, and students learn how to build and test the system. It includes information about the test plan and user documentation. Conversion is covered in Chapter 13, where students learn about the conversion plan, the change management plan, the support plan, and the project assessment.

Chapter 14 provides a background of object orientation and explains several key object concepts supported by the standard set of object-modeling techniques used by systems analysts and developers. Then, we explain how to draw four of the most effective models in UML: the use case diagram, the sequence diagram, the class diagram, and the behavioral state machine diagram.

SUPPLEMENTS
(www.wiley.com/college/dennis)

Online Instructors Manual

The instructors manual provides resources to support the instructor both in and out of the classroom:

- Short experiential exercises can be used to help students experience and understand key topics in each chapter.
- Short stories have been provided by people working in both corporate and consulting environments for instructors to insert into lectures to make concepts more colorful and real.
- Additional mini-cases for every chapter allow students to perform some of the key concepts that were learned in the chapter.
- Answers to end-of-chapter questions and exercises are provided.

Online Instructor's Resources

- PowerPoint slides are provided that instructors can tailor to their classroom needs and that students can use to guide their reading and studying activities.
- Test Bank includes a variety of questions ranging from multiple choice to essay-style questions. A computerized version of the Test Bank is also available.

WebCT and Blackboard Courses

These online course management systems are tools that facilitate the organization and delivery of course materials on the Web. Easy to use, they provide powerful communication, loaded content, flexible course administration, and sophisticated online testing and diagnostic systems.

Student Web Site

- Web Resources provide instructors and students with Web links to resources that reinforce the major concepts in each chapter. See http://www.wiley.com/college/dennis.
- Web Quizzes help students prepare for class tests.

CASE Software

Two CASE (computer-aided software engineering) tools can be purchased with the text:
1. Visible Systems Corporation's Visible Analyst Student Edition.
2. Microsoft's Visio

Contact your local Wiley sales representative for details, including pricing and ordering information.

Project Management Software

A 60-day trial edition of Microsoft Project can be purchased with the textbook. Note that Microsoft has changed their policy and no longer offers the 120-day trial previously available. Contact your local Wiley sales representative for details.

Another option now available to education institutions adopting this Wiley textbook. is a free 3-year membership to the MSDN Academic Alliance. The

MSDN AA is designed to provide the easiest and most inexpensive way for academic departments to make the latest Microsoft software available in labs, classrooms, and on student and instructor PCs.

Microsoft Project 2007 software is available through this Wiley and Microsoft publishing partnership, free of charge with the adoption of any qualified Wiley textbook. Each copy of Microsoft Project is the full version of the software, with no time limitation, and can be used indefinitely for educational purposes. Contact your Wiley sales representative for details. For more information about the MSDN AA program, go to http://msdn.microsoft.com/academic/.

ACKNOWLEDGMENTS

We extend our thanks to the many people who contributed to the preparation of this fourth and past editions. We are indebted to the staff at John Wiley & Sons for their support, including Beth Lang Golub, Executive Editor, Jen Devine, Associate Editor, Marie Guarascio, Editorial Assistant, Carly DeCandia, Marketing Manager, Trish McFadden, Senior Production Editor, Kevin Murphy, Senior Designer.

We would like to thank the following reviewers and focus-group participants for their helpful and insightful comments:

Murugan Anandarajan	*Drexel University*
Lawrence Andrew	*Western Illinois University*
John Baron	*University of Illinois, Ph.D. Student*
Meral Binbasioglu	*Hofstra University*
Thomas Case	*Georgia Southern University*
Manoj Choudhary	*DeVry Institute of Technology, Scarborough, California*
Subhasish Dasgupta	*George Washington University*
Mark Dishaw	*University of Wisconsin, Oshkosh*
Terri Fox	*Baylor University*
Raol Freeman	*California State University*
Mark N. Frolick	*University of Memphis*
Yvonne Galusha	*University of Iowa*
Candace Garrod	*Red Rocks Community College*
Rick Gibson	*American University*
Peter C. Johnson	*California State University, Sacramento*
Bill Hardgrave	*University of Arkansas*
Fred G. Harold	*Florida Atlantic University*
Jeffrey S. Harper	*Indiana State University*
Albert Harris	*Appalachian State University*
Monica C. Holmes	*Central Michigan University*
Rebecca Horner	*University of Virginia*
Adam Huarng	*California State University Los Angeles*
Bushan Kapoor	*California State University Fullerton*
Ron Kelly	*Nova Scotia Community College, Burridge Campus*
Deepak Khazanchi	*Northern Kentucky University*
Elizabeth Kiggins	*University of Indianapolis*
Chung S. Kim	*Southwest Missouri State University*
Angela Klein	*Park University*
Craig Knight	*University of South Florida Lakeland*
Chang Koh	*University of North Texas*

George M. Marakas	*University of Kansas*
Vicki McKinney	*University of Arkansas*
Eric Meier	*University of Virginia*
Michael Morris	*University of Virginia*
Fred Niederman	*Saint Louis University*
Maggie O'Hara	*East Carolina University*
Richard O'Lander	*St. John's University-St. Vincent's College*
Elizabeth Perry	*SUNY Binghamton*
Tom Pettay	*DeVry Institute of Technology, Columbus, Ohio*
Robin Poston	*The University of Memphis*
Alan M. Przyworski	*DeVry Institute of Technology, Decatur, Georgia*
Thomas C. Richards	*University of North Texas*
Cynthia Ruppel	*University of Toledo*
Nancy L. Russo	*Northern Illinois University*
Linda Salchenberger	*Loyola University, Chicago*
Susan Sampson	*Bellevue University*
Stephen L. Shih	*Southern Illinois University*
Ulrike Schultze	*Southern Methodist University*
Tony Scime	*State University of New York, College at Brockport*
Arnold Schron	*Baruch College*
John B. Schwartz	*University of Maryland, Baltimore County*
Ken Shumate	*Chapman University College*
Anne Marie Smith	*LaSalle University*
Ted Strickland	*University of Louisville*
James Suleiman	*University of Colorado, Colorado Springs*
Ron Thompson	*Wake Forest University*
Jonathan Trower	*Baylor University*
Duane P. Truex III	*Georgia State University*
William J. Vachula	*University of Pennsylvania*
David Vance	*Southern Illinois University*
Bruce White	*Quinnipiac University*
Rosann Webb Collins	*University of South Florida*
Vincent Yen	*Wright State University*

We would like to thank the many practioners from private practice, public organizations, and consulting firms for helping us add a real-world component to this project. A special remembrance goes to Matt Anderson from Accenture, who was a role model for all who knew him—who demonstrated excellence in systems analysis and design and in life in general. Thanks also to Bruce White of Quinnipiac University for his contribution in updating the Concepts in Action material.

Thanks also to our families and friends for their patience and support along the way, especially to Christopher, Haley, and Hannah Wixom; Alec Dennis; and Richard Jones.

Alan Dennis
ardennis@indiana.edu

Barb Wixom
bwixom@mindspring.com

Robby Roth
Roberta.Roth@uni.edu

BRIEF CONTENTS

CONTENTS

PART THREE   DESIGN PHASE   245

CHAPTER 7   MOVING INTO DESIGN   247

CHAPTER 8   ARCHITECTURE DESIGN   269

CHAPTER 13   TRANSITION TO THE NEW SYSTEM   459

CHAPTER 14   THE MOVEMENT TO OBJECTS   491

SYSTEM
ANALYSIS AND
DESIGN

Fourth Edition

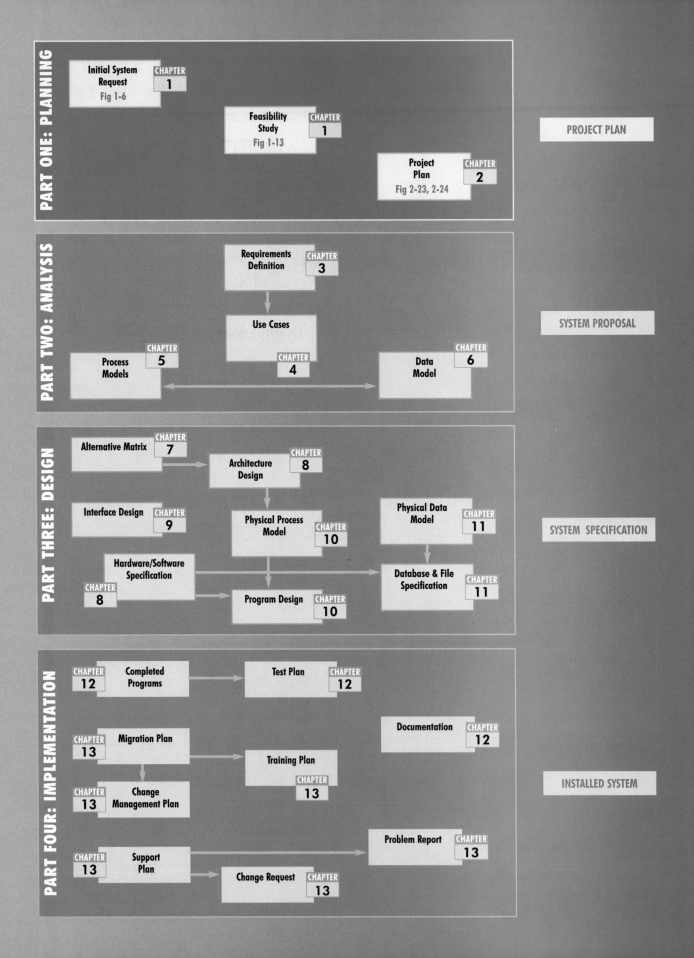

Initial System Request

Feasibility Analysis

Workplan

Staffing Plan

Standards

Risk Assessment

PART ONE
PLANNING PHASE

PROJECT BINDER

Project
Initiation

CHAPTER
1

The Planning Phase
is the fundamental two-step process
of understanding why
an information system should be developed
and creating a plan for how
the project team will develop it.

The deliverables from both steps
are combined into the project plan,
which is presented to the project sponsor and
approval committee at the end of the
Planning Phase. They decide whether it is
advisable to proceed with the system
development project.

Project
Management

CHAPTER
2

PLANNING

Task Checklist

- ☑ **Identify project.**
- ☑ **Develop systems request.**
- ☑ **Analyze technical feasibility.**
- ☑ **Analyze economic feasibility.**
- ☑ **Analyze organizational feasibility.**
- ☐ Perform project selection review.
- ☐ Estimate project time.
- ☐ Identify project tasks.
- ☐ Create work breakdown structure.
- ☐ Create PERT charts.
- ☐ Create Gantt charts.
- ☐ Manage scope.
- ☐ Staff project.
- ☐ Create project charter.
- ☐ Set up CASE repository.
- ☐ Develop standards.
- ☐ Begin documentation.
- ☐ Assess and manage risk.

PLANNING   ANALYSIS   DESIGN

CHAPTER 1

THE SYSTEMS ANALYST AND INFORMATION SYSTEMS DEVELOPMENT

T his chapter introduces the role of the systems analyst in information systems development projects. First, the fundamental four-stage systems development life cycle (planning, analysis, design, and implementation) is established as the basic framework for the IS development process. Next, ways in which organizations identify and initiate potential projects are discussed. The first steps in the process are to identify a project that will deliver value to the business and to create a system request that provides the basic information about the proposed system. Next, the analysts perform a feasibility analysis to determine the technical, economic, and organizational feasibility of the system.

OBJECTIVES

- Understand the role played in information systems development by the systems analyst.
- Understand the fundamental systems development life cycle and its four phases.
- Understand how organizations identify IS development projects.
- Understand the importance of linking the information system to business needs.
- Be able to create a system request.
- Understand how to assess technical, economic, and organizational feasibility.
- Be able to perform a feasibility analysis.

CHAPTER OUTLINE

IMPLEMENTATION

INTRODUCTION

The *systems development life cycle* (SDLC) is the process of understanding how an information system (IS) can support business needs, designing the system, building it, and delivering it to users. If you have taken a programming class or have programmed on your own, this probably sounds pretty simple. Unfortunately, it is not. In 2005, an estimated $1 trillion was spent by organizations and governments on IT hardware, software, and services worldwide. Of the initiated IT projects, some 5%–15% were abandoned as hopelessly inadequate, before or shortly after delivery.[1] Many of the systems that aren't abandoned are delivered to the users significantly late, cost far more than expected, and have fewer features than originally planned.

Most of us would like to think that these problems occur only to "other" people or "other" organizations, but they happen in most companies. See Figure 1-1 for a sampling of recent significant IT project failures. Even Microsoft has a history of failures and overdue projects (e.g., Windows 1.0, Windows 95).[2]

Although we would like to promote this book as a "silver bullet" that will keep you from experiencing failed IS projects, we must admit that such a silver bullet guaranteeing IS development success does not exist.[3] Instead, this book will provide you with several fundamental concepts and many practical techniques that you can use to improve the probability of success.

The key person in the SDLC is the systems analyst, who analyzes the business situation, identifies opportunities for improvements, and designs an information system to implement the improvements. A systems analyst is one of the most interesting, exciting, and challenging jobs around. As a systems analyst, you will work with a variety of people and learn how they conduct business. Specifically, you will work on a common mission with a team of systems analysts, programmers, and others. You will feel the satisfaction of seeing systems that you designed and developed make a significant business impact, while knowing that your unique skills helped make that happen.

It is important to remember that the primary objective of the systems analyst is not to create a wonderful system. The primary goal is to create value for the organization, which for most companies means increasing profits. (Government agencies and not-for-profit organizations measure value differently.) Many failed systems were abandoned because the analysts tried to build a wonderful system without clearly understanding how the system would support the organization's goals, current business processes, and other information systems to provide value. An investment in an information system is like any other investment, such as a new machine tool. The goal is not to acquire the tool, because the tool is simply a means to an end; the goal is to enable the organization to perform work better so that it can earn greater profits or serve its constituents more effectively.

---

[1] Charette, Robert N., "Why Software Fails," *IEEE Spectrum Online,* Sept. 2005.

[2] For more information on the problem, see Capers Jones, *Patterns of Software System Failure and Success,* London: International Thompson Computer Press, 1996; Capers Jones, *Assessment and Control of Software Risks,* Englewood Cliffs, NJ: Yourdon Press, 1994; Julia King, "IS Reins in Runaway Projects," *Computerworld.* February 24, 1997.

[3] The idea of using the silver bullet metaphor was first described in a paper by Frederick Brooks. See Frederick P. Brooks, Jr., "No Silver Bullet—Essence and Accident in Software Engineering," *Information Processing 1986, the Proceedings of the IFIP Tenth World Computing Conference,* H.-J. Kugler (ed.), 1986: 1069–76.

Company	Year	Project Outcome (in U.S. $)
Hudson Bay (Canada)	2005	Inventory system problems lead to $33.3 million loss.
UK Inland Revenue	2004–2005	$3.45 billion tax-credit overpayment caused by software errors.
Avis Europe PLC (UK)	2004	Enterprise resource planning (ERP) system cancelled after $54.5 million spent.
Ford Motor Co.	2004	Purchasing system abandoned after deployment costing approximately $400 million.
J Sainsbury (UK)	2004	Supply chain system abandoned after deployment costing approximately $527 million.
Hewlett-Packard Co	2004	ERP system problems contribute to $160 million loss.
AT&T Wireless	2003–2004	Customer relationship management (CRM) system upgrade problems lead to $100 million revenue loss.

Source: Charette, Robert N., "Why Software Fails," *IEEE Spectrum Online*, Sept. 2005.

FIGURE 1-1
Recent Significant IT Project Failures

This book will introduce you to the fundamental skills you will need to be a systems analyst. This is a pragmatic book that discusses best practices in systems development; it does not present a general survey of systems development that exposes you to everything about the topic. By definition, systems analysts *do things* and challenge the current way that an organization works. To get the most out of this book, you will need to actively apply the ideas and concepts in the examples and in the "Your Turn" exercises that are presented throughout to your own systems development project. This book will guide you through all the steps for delivering

CONCEPTS 1-A MANAGERIAL CAUSES OF IT FAILURES

IN ACTION

A significant proportion of IT projects fail to fulfill their original objectives, resulting in wasted resources and a damaged reputation for the responsible IT department. In many cases, the causes of the failure are organizational issues, not technical issues.

Qantas, the Australian national airline, has endured two high-profile IT failures in recent years. In 1995, Project eQ, a 10-year technology services contract with IBM, was cancelled after four years, at a cost of $200 million. Poor planning contributed to the failure to upgrade a complex and unwieldy IT infrastructure saddled with 700-odd applications written in older programming languages.

In 2008, Qantas canceled Jetsmart, a $40 million parts-management system implementation, due in part to a dispute with the unionized users (aircraft mechanics) of the system. The union advised its members not to assist with the implementation, claiming the software unnecessarily increased the members' workload.

An analysis of these IT failures reveals several contributing factors. First, Qantas faced the challenges of a complicated technical infrastructure and outdated legacy applications. More significantly, however, was the failure of company leadership to understand basic IT issues. In public statements, the company CFO seemed not to care about the user perspectives on new software, preferring instead to put in what management thought was appropriate. This attitude, in part, led to union problems and claims of poorly designed, hard-to-use software and inadequate training.

Aging applications and an unwieldy technical infrastructure are challenges faced by many organizations today. But the senior-management attitude that seemingly disregards the views of software users casts serious questions about Qantas' prospects for IT project success in the future.

Source: http:/blogs.zdnet.com/projectfailures/, February 29, 2008.

a successful information system. In the text, we illustrate how one organization, which we call Tune Source, applies the steps in one project, developing a Web-based digital music sales system. (Other illustrations of successful IS projects are provided on the course website.) By the time you finish the book, you won't be an expert analyst, but you will be ready to start building systems for real.

In this chapter, we first introduce the role of the systems analyst in information systems development projects. We discuss the wide range of skills needed to be successful in this role, and we explain various specialties that systems analysts may develop. We then introduce the basic SDLC that information systems projects follow. This life cycle is common to all projects and serves as a framework for understanding how information systems projects are accomplished. We discuss how projects are identified and initiated within an organization and how they are initially described in a system request. Finally, we describe the feasibility analysis that is performed, which drives the decision whether to proceed with the project.

THE SYSTEMS ANALYST

The systems analyst plays a key role in information systems development projects. The systems analyst assists and guides the project team so that the team develops the right system in an effective way. Systems analysts must understand how to apply technology to solve business problems. In addition, systems analysts may serve as *change agents* who identify the organizational improvements needed, design systems to implement those changes, and train and motivate others to use the systems.

Systems Analyst Skills

New information systems introduce change to the organization and its people. Leading a successful organizational change effort is one of the most difficult jobs that someone can do. Understanding what to change, knowing how to change it, and convincing others of the need for change require a wide range of skills. These skills can be broken down into six major categories: technical, business, analytical, interpersonal, management, and ethical.

Analysts must have the technical skills to understand the organization's existing technical environment, the new system's technology foundation, and the way in which both can be fit into an integrated technical solution. Business skills are required to understand how IT can be applied to business situations and to ensure that the IT delivers real business value. Analysts are continuous problem solvers at both the project and the organizational level, and they put their analytical skills to the test regularly.

Often, analysts need to communicate effectively, one-on-one with users and business managers (who often have little experience with technology) and with programmers (who often have more technical expertise than the analyst does). They must be able to give presentations to large and small groups and to write reports. Not only do they need to have strong interpersonal abilities, but they also need to manage people with whom they work, and they must manage the pressure and risks associated with unclear situations.

Finally, analysts must deal fairly, honestly, and ethically with other project team members, managers, and system users. Analysts often deal with confidential information or information that, if shared with others, could cause harm (e.g., dissent among employees); it is important for analysts to maintain confidence and trust with all people.

Specialization	Responsibilities
Business analyst	Analyzing the key business aspects of the system
	Identifying how the system will provide business value
	Designing the new business processes and policies
Systems analyst	Identifying how technology can improve business processes
	Designing the new business processes
	Designing the information system
	Ensuring that the system conforms to information systems standards
Infrastructure analyst	Ensuring that the system conforms to infrastructure standards
	Identifying infrastructure changes needed to support the system
Change management analyst	Developing and executing a change management plan
	Developing and executing a user training plan
Project manager	Managing the team of analysts, programmers, technical writers, and other specialists
	Developing and monitoring the project plan
	Assigning resources
	Serving as the primary point of contact for the project

FIGURE 1-2
Project Team Specializations

Systems Analyst Specialization

As organizations and technology have become more complex, most large organizations now build project teams that incorporate several analysts with different, but complementary, areas of specialization. Figure 1-2 presents a common list of project roles and specializations. Here we briefly describe these specialties and how they contribute to the project.

The *systems analyst* focuses on the IS issues surrounding the system. This person develops ideas and suggestions for ways that IT can improve business processes, helps design new business processes, designs the new information system, and ensures that all IS standards are maintained. The systems analyst will have significant training and experience in analysis and design and in programming.

YOUR TURN

1-1 BEING AN ANALYST

Suppose you decide to become an analyst after you graduate. What type of analyst would you most prefer to be? What type of courses should you take before you graduate? What type of summer job or internship should you seek?

QUESTION:
Develop a short plan that describes how you will prepare for your career as an analyst.

The *business analyst* focuses on the business issues surrounding the system. This person helps to identify the business value that the system will create, develops ideas for improving the business processes, and helps design new business processes and policies. The business analyst will have business training and experience, plus knowledge of analysis and design.

The *infrastructure analyst* focuses on technical issues surrounding the ways the system will interact with the organization's technical infrastructure (hardware, software, networks, and databases). This person ensures that the new information system conforms to organizational standards and helps to identify infrastructure changes that will be needed to support the system. The infrastructure analyst will have significant training and experience in networking, database administration, and various hardware and software products.

The *change management analyst* focuses on the people and management issues surrounding the system installation. This person ensures that adequate documentation and support are available to users, provides user training on the new system, and develops strategies to overcome resistance to change. The change management analyst will have significant training and experience in organizational behavior and specific expertise in change management.

The *project manager* is often a highly experienced systems analyst. This individual ensures that the project is completed on time and within budget and that the system delivers the expected value to the organization. More will be said about the project manager in the next chapter.

THE SYSTEMS DEVELOPMENT LIFE CYCLE

In many ways, building an information system is similar to building a house. First, the house (or the information system) starts with a basic idea. Second, this idea is transformed into a simple drawing that is shown to the customer and refined (often, through several drawings, each improving on the other) until the customer agrees that the picture depicts what he or she wants. Third, a set of blueprints is designed that presents much more detailed information about the house (e.g., the type of water faucets, where the telephone jacks will be placed). Finally, the house is built following the blueprints—and often with some changes and decisions made by the customer as the house is erected.

The SDLC has a similar set of four fundamental *phases:* planning, analysis, design, and implementation (Figure 1-3). Different projects may emphasize different parts of the SDLC or approach the SDLC phases in different ways, but all projects have elements of these four phases. Each phase is itself composed of a series of *steps,* which rely on *techniques* that produce *deliverables* (specific documents and files that provide understanding about the project).

For example, when you apply for admission to a university, there are several phases that you (and all students) go through: information gathering, applying, and being considered for acceptance. Each of these phases has steps: information gathering includes steps like searching for schools, requesting information, and reading brochures. Students then use techniques (e.g., Internet searching) that can be applied to steps (e.g., requesting information) to create deliverables (e.g., evaluations of different aspects of universities).

Figure 1-3 suggests that the SDLC phases and steps proceed in a logical path from start to finish. In some projects, this is true; but in many projects, the

Phase	Chapter	Step	Technique	Deliverable
Planning Focus: Why build this system? How to structure the project? Primary outputs: — System Request with feasibility study — Project plan	1 1 2 2 2	Identify opportunity Analyze feasibility Develop workplan Staff project Control and direct project	Project identification Technical feasibility Economic feasibility Organizational feasibility Time estimation Task identification Work breakdown structure PERT chart Gantt chart Scope management Project staffing Project charter CASE repository Standards Documentation Timeboxing Risk management	System request Feasibility study Project plan — work plan — Staffing plan — Standards list — Risk assessment
Analysis Focus: Who, what, where, and when for this system? Primary output — System proposal	3 3 4 5 6	Develop analysis strategy Determine business requirements Create use cases Model processes Model data	Business process automation Business process improvement Business process reengineering Interview JAD session Questionnaire Document analysis Observation Use case analysis Data flow diagramming Entity relationship modeling Normalization	System proposal — Requirements definition — Use cases — Process models — Data model
Design Focus: How will this system work? Primary output: — System specification	7 8 9 10 11	Design physical system Design architecture Design interface Design programs Design databases and files	Design strategy Architecture design Hardware & software selection Use scenario Interface structure Interface standards Interface prototype Interface evaluation Data flow diagramming Program structure chart Program specification Data format selection Entity relationship modeling Denormalization Performance tuning Size estimation	Alternative matrix System specification — Architecture report — Hardware & software specification — Interface design — Physical process model — Program design — Database & file specification — Physical data model
Implementation Focus: delivery and support of completed system Primary output: — Installed system	12 13 13 13	Construct system Install system Maintain system Post-implementation	Programming Software testing Performance testing Conversion strategy selection Training Support selection System maintenance Project assessment Post-implementation audit	Test plan Programs Documentation Migration plan — Conversion plan — Business contingency plan — Training plan Support plan Problem report Change request Post-implementation audit report

FIGURE 1-3
Systems Development Life Cycle Phases

project teams move through the steps consecutively, incrementally, iteratively, or in other patterns. In this section, we provide an overview of the phases, steps, and some of the techniques that are used to accomplish the steps. We should emphasize that, in practice, an organization may follow one or more of many variations on the overall SDLC.

For now, there are two important points to understand about the SDLC. First, you should get a general sense of the phases and steps that IS projects move through and some of the techniques that produce certain deliverables. Second, it is important to understand that the SDLC is a process of *gradual refinement*. The deliverables produced in the analysis phase provide a general idea of the shape of the new system. These deliverables are used as input to the design phase, which then refines them to produce a set of deliverables that describes in much more detailed terms exactly how the system will be built. These deliverables in turn are used in the implementation phase to produce the actual system. Each phase refines and elaborates on the work done previously.

Planning

The *planning phase* is the fundamental process of understanding *why* an information system should be built and determining how the project team will go about building it. It has two steps:

1. During *project initiation*, the system's business value to the organization is identified—how will it lower costs or increase revenues? Most ideas for new systems come from outside the IS area (from the marketing department, accounting department, etc.) in the form of a system request. A *system request* presents a brief summary of a business need, and it explains how a system that supports the need will create business value. The IS department works together with the person or department generating the request (called the *project sponsor*) to conduct a feasibility analysis. The *feasibility analysis* examines key aspects of the proposed project:

   - The technical feasibility (Can we build it?)
   - The economic feasibility (Will it provide business value?)
   - The organizational feasibility (If we build it, will it be used?)

   The system request and feasibility analysis are presented to an information systems *approval committee* (sometimes called a *steering committee*), which decides whether the project should be undertaken.
2. Once the project is approved, it enters *project management*. During project management, the *project manager* creates a *work plan*, staffs the project, and puts techniques in place to help the project team control and direct the project through the entire SDLC. The deliverable for project management is a *project plan* that describes how the project team will go about developing the system.

Analysis

The *analysis phase* answers the questions of *who* will use the system, *what* the system will do, and *where* and *when* it will be used. (See Figure 1-3.) During this phase, the project team investigates any current system(s), identifies improvement opportunities, and develops a concept for the new system. This phase has three steps:

1. An *analysis strategy* is developed to guide the project team's efforts. Such a strategy usually includes an analysis of the current system (called the *as-is system*) and its problems, and of proposed ways to design a new system (called the *to-be system*).
2. The next step is *requirements gathering* (e.g., through interviews or questionnaires). The analysis of this information—in conjunction with input from the project sponsor and many other people—leads to the development of a concept for a new system. The system concept is then used as a basis to develop a set of business *analysis models* that describes how the business will operate if the new system were developed. The set typically includes models that represent the data and processes necessary to support the underlying business process.
3. The analyses, system concept, and models are combined into a document called the *system proposal*, which is presented to the project sponsor and other key decision makers (e.g., members of the approval committee) who will decide whether the project should continue to move forward.

The system proposal is the initial deliverable that describes what business requirements the new system should meet. Because it is really the first step in the design of the new system, some experts argue that it is inappropriate to use the term *analysis* as the name for this phase; some argue a better name would be *analysis and initial design*. Because most organizations continue to use the name *analysis* for this phase, we will use it in this book as well. It is important to remember, however, that the deliverable from the analysis phase is both an analysis and a high-level initial design for the new system.

Design

The *design phase* decides *how* the system will operate in terms of the hardware, software, and network infrastructure that will be in place; the user interface, forms, and reports that will be used; and the specific programs, databases, and files that will be needed. Although most of the strategic decisions about the system are made in the development of the system concept during the analysis phase, the steps in the design phase determine exactly how the system will operate. The design phase has four steps:

1. The *design strategy* must be developed. This clarifies whether the system will be developed by the company's own programmers, whether its development will be outsourced to another firm (usually a consulting firm), or whether the company will buy an existing software package.
2. This leads to the development of the basic *architecture design* for the system that describes the hardware, software, and network infrastructure that will be used. In most cases, the system will add to or change the infrastructure that already exists in the organization. The *interface design* specifies how the users will move through the system (e.g., by navigation methods such as menus and on-screen buttons) and the forms and reports that the system will use.
3. The *database and file specifications* are developed. These define exactly what data will be stored and where they will be stored.

4. The analyst team develops the *program design*, which defines the programs that need to be written and exactly what each program will do.

This collection of deliverables (architecture design, interface design, database and file specifications, and program design) is the *system specification* that is handed to the programming team for implementation. At the end of the design phase, the feasibility analysis and project plan are reexamined and revised, and another decision is made by the project sponsor and approval committee about whether to terminate the project or continue. (See Figure 1-3.)

Implementation

The final phase in the SDLC is the *implementation phase*, during which the system is actually built (or purchased, in the case of a packaged software design). This is the phase that usually gets the most attention, because for most systems it is the longest and most expensive single part of the development process. This phase has three steps:

1. System *construction* is the first step. The system is built and tested to ensure that it performs as designed. Since the cost of fixing bugs can be immense, testing is one of the most critical steps in implementation. Most organizations spend more time and attention on testing than on writing the programs in the first place.
2. The system is installed. *Installation* is the process by which the old system is turned off and the new one is turned on. It may include a direct cutover approach (in which the new system immediately replaces the old system), a parallel conversion approach (in which both the old and new systems are operated for a month or two until it is clear that there are no bugs in the new system), or a phased conversion strategy (in which the new system is installed in one part of the organization as an initial trial and then gradually installed in others). One of the most important aspects of conversion is the development of a *training plan* to teach users how to use the new system and help manage the changes caused by the new system.
3. The analyst team establishes a *support plan* for the system. This plan usually includes a formal or informal post-implementation review, as well as a systematic way for identifying major and minor changes needed for the system.

PROJECT IDENTIFICATION AND INITIATION

Where do project ideas come from? A project is identified when someone in the organization identifies a *business need* to build a system. This could occur within a business unit or IT, be discovered by a steering committee charged with identifying business opportunities, or evolve from a recommendation made by external consultants. Examples of business needs include supporting a new marketing campaign, reaching out to a new type of customer, or improving interactions with suppliers. Sometimes, needs arise from some kind of "pain" within the organization, such as a drop in market share, poor customer service levels, or increased competition. Other times, new business initiatives and strategies are created and a system is required to enable them.

Business needs also can surface when the organization identifies unique and competitive ways of using IT. Many organizations keep an eye on *emerging technology*, which is technology that is still being developed and not yet viable for widespread business use. For example, if companies stay abreast of technology like smart cards or radio frequency identification (RFID) in its earliest stages, they can develop business strategies that leverage the capabilities of these technologies and introduce them into the marketplace as a *first mover.* Ideally, companies can take advantage of this first mover position by making money and continuing to innovate while competitors trail behind.

Both IT people (i.e., the experts in systems) and business people (i.e., the experts in business) should work closely together to find ways for technology to support business needs. In this way, organizations can leverage the exciting technologies available while ensuring that projects are based upon real business objectives such as increasing sales, improving customer service, and decreasing operating expenses. Ultimately, information systems need to affect the organization's bottom line (in a positive way!).

The *project sponsor* is someone who recognizes the strong business need for a system and has an interest in seeing the system succeed. He or she will work throughout the SDLC to make sure that the project is moving in the right direction from the perspective of the business. The project sponsor serves as the primary point of contact for the system. Usually, the sponsor of the project is from a business function such as marketing, accounting, or finance; however, members of the IT area also can sponsor or cosponsor a project.

The size or scope of the project determines the kind of sponsor that is needed. A small, departmental system may require sponsorship from only a single manager; however, a large, organizational initiative may need support from the entire senior management team and even the CEO. If a project is purely technical in nature (e.g., improvements to the existing IT infrastructure or research into the viability of an emerging technology), then sponsorship from IT is appropriate. When projects have great importance to the business, yet are technically complex, joint sponsorship by both the business and IT functions may be necessary.

The business need drives the high-level *business requirements* for the system. Requirements are what the information system will do or what *functionality* it will contain. They need to be explained at a high level so that the approval committee and, ultimately, the project team understand what the business expects from the final product. Business requirements are what features and capabilities the information system will have to include, such as the ability to collect customer orders online or the ability for suppliers to receive inventory information as orders are placed and sales are made.

The project sponsor also should have an idea of the *business value* to be gained from the system, in both tangible and intangible ways. *Tangible value* can be quantified and measured easily (e.g., 2% reduction in operating costs). An *intangible* value results from an intuitive belief that the system provides important, but hard-to-measure, benefits to the organization (e.g., improved customer service, a better competitive position).

Once the project sponsor identifies a project that meets an important business need and he or she can identify the business requirements and business value of the system, it is time to formally initiate the project. In most organizations, project initiation begins with a technique called a *system request.*

1-2 IMPLEMENTING A SATELLITE DATA NETWORK

A major retail store recently spent $24 million dollars on a large private satellite communication system that provides state-of-the-art voice, data, and video transmission between stores and regional headquarters. When an item gets sold, the scanner software updates the inventory system in real time. As a result, store transactions are passed on to regional and national headquarters instantly, which keeps inventory records up to date. One of the store's major competitors has an older system in which transactions are uploaded at the end of a business day. The first company feels that its method of instant communication and feedback allows it to react more quickly to changes in the market, giving the company a competitive advantage. For example, if an early winter snowstorm causes stores across the upper Midwest to start selling high-end (and high-profit) snow throwers quite quickly, the company's nearest warehouse can prepare next-day shipments to maintain a good inventory balance, while the competitor may not move quite as quickly and thus lose out on such quick inventory turnover.

QUESTIONS:

1. Do you think a $24 million investment in a private satellite communication system could be justified by a cost-benefit analysis? Could this be done with a standard communication line (with encryption)?
2. How might the competitor attempt to close the "information gap" in this example?

System Request

A *system request* is a document that describes the business reasons for building a system and the value that the system is expected to provide. The project sponsor usually completes this form as part of a formal system project selection process within the organization. Most system requests include five elements: project sponsor, business need, business requirements, business value, and special issues. (See Figure 1-4.) The *sponsor* describes the person who will serve as the primary contact for the project, and the *business need* presents the reasons prompting the project. The *business requirements* of the project refer to the business capabilities that the system will need to have, and the *business value* describes the benefits that the organization should expect from the system. *Special issues* are included on the document as a catchall category for other information that should be considered in assessing the project. For example, the project may need to be completed by a specific deadline. Project teams need to be aware of any special circumstances that could affect the outcome of the system.

The completed system request is submitted to the *approval committee* for consideration. This approval committee could be a company steering committee that meets regularly to make information systems decisions, a senior executive who has control of organizational resources, or any other decision-making body that governs the use of business resources. The committee reviews the system request and makes an initial determination, based on the information provided, of whether to investigate the proposed project or not. If so, the next step is to conduct a feasibility analysis.

Applying the Concepts at Tune Source

Throughout the book, we will apply the concepts in each chapter to a fictitious company called Tune Source. For example, in this section, we will illustrate the creation

Element	Description	Examples
Project Sponsor	The person who initiates the project and who serves as the primary point of contact for the project on the business side	Several members of the finance department Vice president of marketing IT manager Steering committee CIO CEO
Business Need	The business-related reason for initiating the system	Increase sales Improve market share Improve access to information Improve customer service Decrease product defects Streamline supply acquisition processes
Business Requirements	The business capabilities that the system will provide	Provide online access to information Capture customer demographic information Include product search capabilities Produce management reports Include online user support
Business Value	The benefits that the system will create for the organization	3% increase in sales 1% increase in market share Reduction in headcount by 5*FTEs $200,000 cost savings from decreased supply costs $150,000 savings from removal of existing system
Special Issues or Constraints	Issues that are relevant to the implementation of the system that need to be known by the approval committee	Government-mandated deadline for May 30 System needed in time for the Christmas holiday season Top-level security clearance needed by project team to work with data

* = Full-time equivalent

FIGURE 1-4
Elements of the System Request Form

CONCEPTS

IN ACTION

1-B INTERVIEW WITH DON HALLACY, PRESIDENT, TECHNOLOGY SERVICES, SPRINT CORPORATION

At Sprint, network projects originate from two vantage points—IT and the business units. IT projects usually address infrastructure and support needs. The business-unit projects typically begin after a business need is identified locally, and a business group informally collaborates with IT regarding how a solution can be delivered to meet customer expectations.

Once an idea is developed, a more formal request process begins, and an analysis team is assigned to investigate and validate the opportunity. This team includes members from the user community and IT, and they scope out at a high level what the project will do; create estimates for technology, training, and development costs; and create a business case. This business case contains the economic value added and the net present value of the project.

Of course, not all projects undergo this rigorous process. The larger projects require more time to be allocated to the analysis team. It is important to remain flexible and not let the process consume the organization. At the beginning of each budgetary year, specific capital expenditures are allocated for operational improvements and maintenance. Moreover, this money is set aside to fund quick projects that deliver immediate value without going through the traditional approval process. *Don Hallacy*

The South Dakota Department of Labor, Workers' Compensation division was sinking under a load of paper files. As a state agency which ascertains that employees are treated fairly when they are injured on the job, the agency had a plethora of paper files and filing cabinets. If a person (or company) called to see the status of an injury claim, the clerk who received the call would have to take a message, get the paper file, review the status, and call the person back. Files were stored in huge filing cabinets and were entered by year and case number (for example, the 415th person injured in 2008 would be in a file numbered 08-415). But most callers did not remember the file number and would give their name and address and the date of injury. The clerk would look in a spiral notebook for the last name around the date that was given—and then find the file number to retrieve the folder. Some folders were small—possibly documenting a minor cut or minor injury, and the employee was back to work after a brief treatment period. Other folders could be very large, with numerous medical reports from several doctors verifying the extent of a serious injury and treatment (such as an arm amputation). A digital solution was suggested—reports could be submitted online via a secure website. Medical reports could be submitted electronically, either as a pdf file or as a faxed digital file. This solution would also mean that the clerk taking the phone call could query the database by the person's name and access the information in a matter of seconds.

QUESTION:

Prepare a systems request for this project. Fill in as much as you can on the basis of the information provided.

of a system request. Tune Source is a company headquartered in southern California. Tune Source is the brainchild of three entrepreneurs with ties to the music industry: John Margolis, Megan Taylor, and Phil Cooper. Originally, John and Phil partnered to open a number of brick and mortar stores in southern California specializing in hard-to-find and classic jazz, rock, country, and folk recordings. Megan soon was invited to join the partnership because of her contacts and knowledge of classical music. Tune Source quickly became known as the place to go to find rare audio recordings. Annual sales last year were $40 million with annual growth at about 3%–5% per year.

Background   John, Megan, and Phil, like many others in the music industry, watched with alarm the rise of music-sharing websites like Napster, as music consumers shared digital audio files without paying for them, denying artists and record labels royalties associated with sales. Once the legal battle over copyright infringement was resolved and Napster was shut down, the partners set about establishing agreements with a variety of industry partners in order to offer a legitimate digital music download resource for customers in their market niche. Phil has asked Carly Edwards, a rising star in the Tune Source marketing department, to spearhead the digital music download project.

Tune Source currently has a website that enables customers to search for and purchase CDs. This site was initially developed by an Internet consulting firm and is hosted by a prominent local Internet Service Provider (ISP) in Los Angeles. The IT department at Tune Source has become experienced with Internet technology as it has worked with the ISP to maintain the site.

System Request   At Tune Source, new IT projects are reviewed and approved by a project steering committee that meets quarterly. The committee has representatives

System Request—Digital Music Download Project

Project Sponsor: Carly Edwards, Assistant Vice President, Marketing

Business Need: This project has been initiated to increase sales by creating the capability of selling digital music downloads to customers through kiosks in our stores, and over the Internet using our website.

Business Requirements: Using the Web or in-store kiosks, customers will be able to search for and purchase digital music downloads. The specific functionality that the system should have includes the following:

- Search for music in our digital music archive.
- Listen to music samples.
- Purchase individual downloads at a fixed fee per download.
- Establish a customer subscription account permitting unlimited downloads for a monthly fee.
- Purchase music download gift cards.

Business Value: We expect that Tune Source will increase sales by enabling existing customers to purchase specific digital music tracks and by reaching new customers who are interested in our unique archive of rare and hard-to-find music. We expect to gain a new revenue stream from customer subscriptions to our download services. We expect some increase in cross-selling, as customers who have downloaded a track or two of a CD decide to purchase the entire CD in a store or through our website. We also expect a new revenue stream from the sale of music download gift cards.

Conservative estimates of tangible value to the company include the following:

- $757,500 in sales from individual music downloads
- $950,000 in sales from customer subscriptions
- $205,000 in additional in-store or website CD sales
- $153,000 in sales from music download gift cards

Special Issues or Constraints:

- The marketing department views this as a strategic system. The ability to offer digital music downloads is critical in order to remain competitive in our market niche. Our music archive of rare and hard-to-find music is an asset that is currently underutilized.
- Many of our current loyal customers have been requesting this capability, and we need to provide this service or face the loss of these customers' business.
- Because customers have a number of music download options available to them elsewhere, we need to bring this system to market as soon as possible.

FIGURE 1-5
System Request for Tune Source

from IT as well as from the major areas of the business. Carly's first step was to prepare a system request for the committee.

Figure 1-5 shows the system request she prepared. The project sponsor is Carly, and the business needs are to increase sales and provide a music download capability demanded by a very competitive marketplace. Notice that the need does not focus on the technology associated with the project. The emphasis is on the business aspects: sales and maintaining a competitive position in the company's market.

In the system request, the project sponsor focuses on describing his or her vision of the business requirements at a very high level. Carly has expressed a clear vision of how this system will affect Tune Source: sales of individual music downloads, revenue from customer subscriptions, sales from cross-selling of CDs, and sales of music download gift cards. Carly acknowledges customer demand for

1-4 CREATE A SYSTEM REQUEST

Think about your own university or college and choose an idea that could improve student satisfaction with the course enrollment process. Currently, can students enroll for classes from anywhere? How long does it take? Are directions simple to follow? Is online help available?

Next, think about how technology can help support your idea. Would you need completely new technology? Can the current system be changed?

QUESTION:

Create a system request that you could give to the administration that explains the sponsor, business need, business requirements, and potential value of the project. Include any constraints or issues that should be considered.

this capability and also recognizes the need to respond to this demand in order to retain the business of its loyal customer base.

The estimates of tangible value were difficult to develop, since this venture is completely new to Tune Source. To prepare for this, Carly had several of her staff members conduct both an in-store customer survey and an online customer survey to assess the customers' interest in individual music downloads, subscription programs, and gift cards. The surveys also attempted to gauge the customers' price sensitivity for these offerings.

From the survey results, Carly and her staff developed a range of sales projections for the various revenue streams: a high-level estimate, a medium-level estimate, and low-level estimate. They also developed probability assessments for each of these outcomes, settling on a 25% likelihood for the high-level estimate, a 60% likelihood for the medium-level estimate, and a 15% likelihood for the low-level estimate. Based on the sales projections and the probability estimates, a weighted average estimated sales figure was computed for each revenue stream.

For example, for individual downloads,

$$\text{Expected sales} = (900{,}000 * .25) + (750{,}000 * .60) + (550{,}000 * .15)$$
$$= 225{,}000 + 450{,}000 + 82{,}500$$
$$= 757{,}500$$

These projections are summarized in Figure 1-6.

After analyzing the survey results, Carly and her staff were confident that the sales projections and probability estimates were as accurate as they could make them this early in the project. The completed system request is shown in Figure 1-5.

Steering Committee Approval   Carly Edwards presented the system request for the digital music download project to the Tune Source project steering committee at its next meeting. Response to the request was uniformly positive. The strong interest in the project by John, Megan, and Phil, the company's top executives, helped to spur the committee's rapid approval of the project. Following approval of the system request, Jason Wells, a senior systems analyst in the IT department, was assigned to work with Carly to develop a preliminary feasibility analysis for the project.

	Sales Projections			
	Individual Downloads	Subscriptions	Cross-Selling of CDs	Gift Cards
High-level estimate (prob. = 25%)	$900,000	$1,100,000	$250,000	$180,000
Medium-level estimate (prob. = 60%)	750,000	950,000	200,000	150,000
Low-level estimate (prob. = 15%)	550,000	700,000	150,000	120,000
Weighted average expected sales	$757,500	$950,000	$205,000	$153,000

FIGURE 1-6

Sales Projections for Tune Source Digital Music Download Project

FEASIBILITY ANALYSIS

Once the need for the system and its business requirements have been defined, the approval committee may authorize the systems analyst to create a more detailed business case to better understand the opportunities and limitations associated with the proposed project. *Feasibility analysis* guides the organization in determining whether to proceed with a project. Feasibility analysis also identifies the important *risks* associated with the project that must be addressed if the project is approved. As with the system request, each organization has its own process and format for the feasibility analysis, but most include techniques to assess three areas: technical feasibility, economic feasibility, and organizational feasibility. The results of these techniques are combined into a *feasibility study* deliverable that is given to the approval committee at the end of project initiation. See Figure 1-7.

Technical Feasibility: Can We Build It?

- Familiarity with application: Less familiarity generates more risk.
- Familiarity with technology: Less familiarity generates more risk.
- Project size: Large projects have more risk.
- Compatibility: The harder it is to integrate the system with the company's existing technology, the higher the risk will be.

Economic Feasibility: Should We Build It?

- Development costs
- Annual operating costs
- Annual benefits (cost savings and revenues)
- Intangible costs and benefits

Organizational Feasibility: If We Build It, Will They Come?

- Project champion(s)
- Senior management
- Users
- Other stakeholders
- Is the project strategically aligned with the business?

FIGURE 1-7

Feasibility Analysis Assessment Factors

Although we will discuss feasibility analysis now within the context of project initiation, most project teams will revise their feasibility study throughout the SDLC and revisit its contents at various checkpoints during the project. If at any point the project's risks and limitations outweigh its benefits, the project team may decide to cancel the project or make necessary improvements.

Technical Feasibility

The first technique in the feasibility analysis is to assess the *technical feasibility* of the project, the extent to which the system can be successfully designed, developed, and installed by the IT group. Technical feasibility analysis is, in essence, a *technical risk analysis* that strives to answer the question: "*Can* we build it?"[4]

Many risks can endanger the successful completion of the project. First and foremost is the users' and analysts' *familiarity with the application.* When analysts are unfamiliar with the business application area, they have a greater chance of misunderstanding the users or missing opportunities for improvement. The risks increase dramatically when the users themselves are less familiar with an application, such as with the development of a system to support a new business innovation (e.g., Microsoft starting up a new Internet dating service). In general, the development of new systems is riskier than extensions to an existing system, because existing systems tend to be better understood.

Familiarity with the technology is another important source of technical risk. When a system will use technology that has not been used before *within the organization*, there is a greater chance that problems will occur and delays will be incurred because of the need to learn how to use the technology. Risk increases dramatically when the technology itself is new (e.g., web development using Ajax).

Project size is an important consideration, whether measured as the number of people on the development team, the length of time it will take to complete the project, or the number of distinct features in the system. Larger projects present more risk, because they are more complicated to manage and because there is a greater chance that some important system requirements will be overlooked or misunderstood. The extent to which the project is highly integrated with other systems (which is typical of large systems) can cause problems, because complexity is increased when many systems must work together.

Finally, project teams need to consider the *compatibility* of the new system with the technology that already exists in the organization. Systems rarely are built in a vacuum—they are built in organizations that have numerous systems already in place. New technology and applications need to be able to integrate with the existing environment for many reasons. They may rely on data from existing systems, they may produce data that feed other applications, and they may have to use the company's existing communications infrastructure. A new CRM system, for example, has little value if it does not use customer data found across the organization in existing sales systems, marketing applications, and customer service systems.

The assessment of a project's technical feasibility is not cut and dried, because in many cases, some interpretation of the underlying conditions is needed (e.g., how large does a project need to grow before it becomes less feasible?). One approach is to compare the project under consideration with prior projects undertaken by the

---

[4] We use the words "build it" in the broadest sense. Organizations can also choose to buy a commercial software package and install it, in which case the question might be "Can we select the right package and successfully install it?"

organization. Another option is to consult with experienced IT professionals in the organization or with external IT consultants; often, they will be able to judge whether a project is feasible from a technical perspective.

Economic Feasibility

The second element of a feasibility analysis is to perform an *economic feasibility* analysis (also called a *cost–benefit analysis*) that identifies the financial risk associated with the project. This attempts to answer the question "*Should* we build the system?" Economic feasibility is determined by identifying costs and benefits associated with the system, assigning values to them, and then calculating the cash flow and return on investment for the project. The more expensive the project, the more rigorous and detailed the analysis should be. Figure 1-8 lists the steps to perform a cost–benefit analysis; each step will be described in the upcoming sections.

Identify Costs and Benefits   The first task when developing an economic feasibility analysis is to identify the kinds of costs and benefits the system will have and list them along the left-hand column of a spreadsheet. Figure 1-9 lists examples of costs and benefits that may be included.

The costs and benefits can be broken down into four categories: (1) development costs, (2) operational costs, (3) tangible benefits, and (4) intangibles. *Development costs* are those tangible expenses that are incurred during the creation of the system, such as salaries for the project team, hardware and software expenses, consultant fees, training, and office space and equipment. Development costs are usually thought of as one-time costs. *Operational costs* are those tangible costs that are required to operate the system, such as the salaries for operations staff, software licensing fees, equipment upgrades, and communications charges. Operational costs are usually thought of as ongoing costs.

1. Identify Costs and Benefits	List the tangible costs and benefits for the project. Include both one-time and recurring costs.
2. Assign Values to Costs and Benefits	Work with business users and IT professionals to create numbers for each of the costs and benefits. Even intangibles should be valued if at all possible.
3. Determine Cash Flow	Forecast what the costs and benefits will be over a certain period, usually, three to five years. Apply a growth rate to the values, if necessary.
4. Assess Project's Economic Value	Evaluate the project's expected returns in comparison to its costs. Use one or more of the following evaluation techniques:
• **Return on Investment (ROI)**	Calculate the rate of return earned on the money invested in the project, using the ROI formula.
• **Break-Even Point (BEP)**	Find the year in which the cumulative project benefits exceed cumulative project costs. Apply the breakeven formula, using figures for that year. This calculation measures how long it will take for the system to produce benefits that cover its costs.
• **Net Present Value (NPV)**	Restate all costs and benefits in today's dollar terms (present value), using an appropriate discount rate. Determine whether the total present value of benefits is greater than or less than the total present value of costs.

FIGURE 1-8

Steps to Conduct an Economic Feasibility Analysis

Development Costs	Operational Costs
Development team salaries	Software upgrades
Consultant fees	Software licensing fees
Development training	Hardware repairs
Hardware and software	Hardware upgrades
Vendor installation	Operational team salaries
Office space and equipment	Communications charges
Data conversion costs	User training

Tangible Benefits	Intangible Benefits
Increased sales	Increased market share
Reductions in staff	Increased brand recognition
Reductions in inventory	Higher quality products
Reductions in IT costs	Improved customer service
Better supplier prices	Better supplier relations

FIGURE 1-9
Example of Costs and Benefits
for Economic Feasibility

Tangible benefits include revenue that the system enables the organization to collect, such as increased sales. In addition, the system may enable the organization to avoid certain costs, leading to another type of tangible benefit: cost savings. For example, if the system produces a reduction in needed staff, lower salary costs result. Similarly, a reduction in required inventory levels due to the new system produces lower inventory costs. In these examples, the reduction in costs is a tangible benefit of the new system.

Of course, a project also can affect the organization's bottom line by reaping *intangible benefits* or incurring *intangible costs*. Intangible costs and benefits are more difficult to incorporate into the economic feasibility analysis because they are based on intuition and belief rather than on "hard numbers." Nonetheless, they should be listed in the spreadsheet along with the tangible items.

CONCEPTS   **1-C INTANGIBLE VALUE AT CARLSON HOSPITALITY**

IN ACTION

I conducted a case study at Carlson Hospitality, a global leader in hospitality services, encompassing more than 1300 hotel, resort, restaurant, and cruise ship operations in 79 countries. One of its brands, Radisson Hotels & Resorts, researched guest stay information and guest satisfaction surveys. The company was able to quantify how much of a guest's lifetime value can be attributed to his or her perception of the stay experience. As a result, Radisson knows how much of the collective future value of the enterprise is at stake, given the perceived quality of the stay experience. Using this model, Radisson can confidently show that a 10% increase in customer satisfaction among the 10% of highest quality customers will capture a one-point market share for the brand. Each point in market share for the Radisson brand is worth $20 million in additional revenue.   *Barbara Wixom*

QUESTION:
How can a project team use this information to help determine the economic feasibility of a system?

Assign Values to Costs and Benefits   Once the types of costs and benefits have been identified, you will need to assign specific dollar values to them. This may seem impossible—How can someone quantify costs and benefits that haven't happened yet? And how can those predictions be realistic? Although this task is very difficult, you have to do the best you can to come up with reasonable numbers for all of the costs and benefits. Only then can the approval committee make an educated decision about whether or not to move ahead with the project.

The most effective strategy for estimating costs and benefits is to rely on the people who have the best understanding of them. For example, costs and benefits that are related to the technology or the project itself can be provided by the company's IT group or external consultants, and business users can develop the numbers associated with the business (e.g., sales projections, order levels). The company also can consider past projects, industry reports, and vendor information, although these sources probably will be a bit less accurate. Likely, all of the estimates will be revised as the project proceeds.

If predicting a specific value for a cost or benefit is proving difficult, it may be useful to estimate a range of values for the cost or benefit and then assign a likelihood (probability) estimate to each value. With this information, an *expected value* for the cost or benefit can be calculated. Recall the calculations shown in Figure 1-6 in which the Tune Source marketing staff developed expected values for projected sales. As more information is learned during the project, the value estimates and the probability estimates can be revised, resulting in a revised expected value for the cost or benefit.

What about the *intangible* costs and benefits? Sometimes, it is acceptable to list intangible benefits, such as improved customer service, without assigning a dollar value. Other times, estimates have to be made regarding how much an intangible benefit is "worth." We suggest that you quantify intangible costs or benefits if at all possible. If you do not, how will you know if they have been realized? Suppose that a system claims to improve customer service. This benefit is intangible, but let's assume that the improvement in customer service will decrease the number of customer complaints by 10% each year over three years and that $200,000 is currently spent on phone charges and phone operators who handle complaint calls. Suddenly, we have some very tangible numbers with which to set goals and measure the originally intangible benefit.

Figure 1-10 shows costs and benefits along with assigned dollar values. In this example, for simplicity, all development costs are assumed to occur in the current year 2009, and all benefits and operational costs are assumed to begin when the system is implemented at the start of 2010, and continue through 2013. Notice that the customer service intangible benefit has been quantified, based on a decrease in customer complaint phone calls. The intangible benefit of being able to offer services that competitors currently offer was not quantified, but it was listed so that the approval committee will consider the benefit when assessing the system's economic feasibility.

Determine Cash Flow   A formal cost–benefit analysis usually contains costs and benefits over a selected number of years (usually, three to five years) to show cash flow over time. (See Figure 1-10.) With this *cash flow method*, the years are listed across the top of the spreadsheet to represent the period for analysis, and numeric values are entered in the appropriate cells within the spreadsheet's body. Sometimes, fixed amounts are entered into the columns. For example, Figure 1-10 lists the same amount for customer complaint calls, inventory costs, hardware, and software

	2009	2010	2011	2012	2013	Total
Benefits						
Increased sales		500,000	530,000	561,800	595,508	2,187,308
Reduction in customer complaint calls[a]		70,000	70,000	70,000	70,000	280,000
Reduced inventory costs		68,000	68,000	68,000	68,000	272,000
Total Benefits[b]		**638,000**	**668,000**	**699,800**	**733,508**	**2,739,308**
Development Costs						
2 servers @ $125,000	250,000	0	0	0	0	250,000
Printer	100,000	0	0	0	0	100,000
Software licenses	34,825	0	0	0	0	34,825
Server software	10,945	0	0	0	0	10,945
Development labor	1,236,525	0	0	0	0	1,236,525
Total Development Costs	**1,632,295**	**0**	**0**	**0**	**0**	**1,632,295**
Operational Costs						
Hardware		50,000	50,000	50,000	50,000	200,000
Software		20,000	20,000	20,000	20,000	80,000
Operational labor		115,000	119,600	124,384	129,359	488,343
Total Operational Costs		**185,000**	**189,600**	**194,384**	**199,359**	**768,343**
Total Costs	**1,632,295**	**185,000**	**189,600**	**194,384**	**199,359**	**2,400,638**
Total Benefits − Total Costs	**(1,632,295)**	**453,000**	**478,400**	**505,416**	**534,149**	**338,670**
Cumulative Net Cash Flow	**(1,632,295)**	**(1,179,295)**	**(700,895)**	**(195,479)**	**338,670**	
Return on Investment (ROI)	14.1%	(338,670/2,400,638)				
Break-even Point	3.37 years	(costs are fully recovered in year 4; [534,149 − 338,670]/534,149 = .37)				

[a] Customer service values are based on reduced costs of handling customer complaint phone calls.

[b] An important yet intangible benefit will be the ability to offer services that our competitors currently offer.

FIGURE 1-10
Cost–Benefit Analysis—Simple Cash Flow Method

for all four years. Often, amounts are augmented by some rate of growth to adjust for inflation or business improvements, as shown by the 6% increase that is added to the sales numbers in the sample spreadsheet. Similarly, labor costs are assumed to increase at a 4% rate each year. Finally, totals are added to determine what the overall benefits will be, and the higher the overall total, the more feasible the solution becomes in terms of its economic feasibility.

Determine Return on Investment   The return on investment (ROI) is a calculation that measures the average rate of return earned on the money invested in the project. A high ROI suggests that the project's benefits far outweigh the project's cost. ROI is a simple calculation that divides the project's net benefits (total benefits − total costs) by the total costs. (See Appendix 1A). Although ROI is commonly used in practice, it suffers from several important limitations and should not be used as the only measure of a project's worth. Figure 1-10 includes the ROI calculation for our example project.

Determine Break-Even Point   Another common approach to measuring a project's worth is the break-even point. The *break-even point* (also called the *payback method*) is defined as the number of years it takes a firm to recover its original investment in the project from net cash flows. As shown in Figure 1-10, the project's net cash flows "pay back" the initial investment during the fourth year; this is the year in which the cumulative cash flow figure becomes positive. Dividing the difference between that year's cash flow and its cumulative cash flow by that year's cash flow determines how far into the year the break-even will occur. See Appendix 1A for the break-even calculation.

The break-even point is easy to calculate and understand and does give an indication of a project's liquidity or the speed at which the project will generate cash returns. Also, projects that produce higher returns early in the project's life are thought to be less risky, since we can anticipate near-term events with more accuracy than we can long-term events. The break-even point does ignore cash flows that occur after the break-even point has been reached and therefore is biased against long-term projects.

Determine Net Present Value   The simple cash flow method, return on investment, and break-even point, as shown in Figure 1-10, all share the weakness of not recognizing the time value of money. In these analyses, the timing of cash flows is ignored. A dollar in year 3 of the project is considered equal to a dollar in year 1.

Net present value (*NPV*) is used to compare the present value of all cash inflows and outflows for the project in today's dollar terms. The key to understanding present values is to recognize that if you had a dollar today, you could invest it and receive some rate of return on your investment. Therefore, a dollar received in the future is worth less than a dollar received today, since you forgo that potential return. Appendix 1A shows the present value of a dollar received in the future for different numbers of years and rates of return. If you have a friend who owes you a dollar today, but instead gives you that dollar in three years—you've been had! Given a 10% rate of return on an investment, you'll be receiving the equivalent of 75 cents in today's terms.

The basic formula to convert a future cash flow to its present value is shown in Appendix 1A. In Figure 1-11, the present value of the costs and benefits has been calculated and added to our example spreadsheet, using a 6% rate of return. The NPV is simply the difference between the total present value of the benefits and the total present value of the costs. As long as the NPV is greater than zero, the project is considered economically feasible.

Organizational Feasibility

The final technique used for feasibility analysis is to assess the *organizational feasibility* of the system: how well the system ultimately will be accepted by its users and incorporated into the ongoing operations of the organization. There are many organizational factors that can have an impact on the project, and seasoned developers know that organizational feasibility can be the most difficult feasibility dimension to assess. In essence, an organizational feasibility analysis attempts to answer the question "If we build it, will they come?"

	2009	2010	2011	2012	2013	Total
Benefits						
Increased sales		500,000	530,000	561,800	595,508	
Reduction in customer complaint calls[a]		70,000	70,000	70,000	70,000	
Reduced inventory costs		68,000	68,000	68,000	68,000	
Total Benefits[b]		**638,000**	**668,000**	**699,800**	**733,508**	
Present Value Total Benefits		**601,887**	**594,518**	**587,566**	**581,007**	**2,364,978**
Development Costs						
2 Servers @ $125,000	250,000	0	0	0	0	
Printer	100,000	0	0	0	0	
Software licenses	34,825	0	0	0	0	
Server software	10,945	0	0	0	0	
Development labor	1,236,525	0	0	0	0	
Total Development Costs	**1,632,295**	**0**	**0**	**0**	**0**	
Operational Costs						
Hardware		50,000	50,000	50,000	50,000	
Software		20,000	20,000	20,000	20,000	
Operational labor		115,000	119,600	124,384	129,359	
Total Operational Costs		**185,000**	**189,600**	**194,384**	**199,359**	
Total Costs	**1,632,295**	**185,000**	**189,600**	**194,384**	**199,359**	
Present Value Total Costs	**1,632,295**	**174,528**	**168,743**	**163,209**	**157,911**	**2,296,686**
NPV (PV Total Benefits − PV Total Costs)						**68,292**

[a] Customer service values are based on reduced costs of handling customer complaint phone calls.

[b] An important yet intangible benefit will be the ability to offer services that our competitors currently offer.

FIGURE 1-11
Cost-Benefit Analysis—Present Value Method

CONCEPTS   **1-D RETURN ON INVESTMENT**

IN ACTION

Many companies are undergoing *server virtualization.* This is the concept of putting multiple "virtual" servers onto one physical device. The payoffs can be significant: fewer servers, less electricity, less generated heat, less air conditioning, less infrastructure and administration costs, increased flexibility, less physical presence (that is, smaller server rooms), faster maintenance of servers, and more. There are costs, of course, such as licensing the virtualization software, labor costs in establishing the virtual servers onto a physical device, labor costs in updating tables, and access. But determining the return on investment can be a challenge. Some companies have lost money on server virtualization, while most would say that they have gained a positive return on investment but have not really quantified the results.

QUESTIONS:

1. How might a company really determine the return on investment for server virtualization?
2. Is this a project that a systems analyst might be involved in? Why or why not?

	Role	To Enhance Organizational Feasibility
Champion	A champion: • Initiates the project • Promotes the project • Allocates his or her time to the project • Provides resources	• Make a presentation about the objectives of the project and the proposed benefits to those executives who will benefit directly from the system. • Create a prototype of the system to demonstrate its potential value.
Organizational Management	Organizational managers: • Know about the project • Budget enough money for the project • Encourage users to accept and use the system	• Make a presentation to management about the objectives of the project and the proposed benefits. • Market the benefits of the system, using memos and organizational newsletters. • Encourage the champion to talk about the project with his or her peers.
System Users	Users: • Make decisions that influence the project • Perform hands-on activities for the project • Ultimately determine whether the project is successful by using or not using the system	• Assign users official roles on the project team. • Assign users specific tasks to perform, with clear deadlines. • Ask for feedback from users regularly (e.g., at weekly meetings).

FIGURE 1-12
Important Stakeholders for Organizational Feasibility

One way to assess the organizational feasibility of the project is to understand how well the goals of the project align with business objectives. *Strategic alignment* is the fit between the project and business strategy—the greater the alignment, the less risky the project will be, from an organizational feasibility perspective. For example, if the marketing department has decided to become more customer focused, then a CRM project that produces integrated customer information would have strong strategic alignment with marketing's goal. Many IT projects fail when the IT department initiates them, because there is little or no alignment with business-unit or organizational strategies.

A second way to assess organizational feasibility is to conduct a *stakeholder analysis*.[5] *A stakeholder* is a person, group, or organization that can affect (or can be affected by) a new system. In general, the most important stakeholders in the introduction of a new system are the project champion, system users, and organizational management (see Figure 1-12), but systems sometimes affect other stakeholders as well. For example, the IS department can be a stakeholder of a system because IS jobs or roles may be changed significantly after the system's implementation. One key stakeholder—outside of the champion, users, and management—in Microsoft's project that embedded Internet Explorer as a standard part of Windows was the U.S. Department of Justice.

The *champion* is a high-level executive and is usually, but not always, the project sponsor who created the system request. The champion supports the project by providing time and resources (e.g., money) and by giving political support within the organization by communicating the importance of the system to other organizational decision makers. More than one champion is preferable because if the champion leaves the organization, the support could leave as well.

---

[5] A good book on stakeholder analysis that presents a series of stakeholder analysis techniques is R. O. Mason and I. I. Mittroff, *Challenging Strategic Planning Assumptions: Theory, Cases, and Techniques*, New York: John Wiley & Sons, 1981.

While champions provide day-to-day support for the system, *organizational management* also needs to support the project. Such management support conveys to the rest of the organization the belief that the system will make a valuable contribution and that necessary resources will be made available. Ideally, management should encourage people in the organization to use the system and to accept the many changes that the system will likely create.

A third important set of stakeholders is the *system users* who ultimately will use the system once it has been installed in the organization. Too often, the project team meets with users at the beginning of a project and then disappears until after the system is created. In this situation, rarely does the final product meet the expectations and needs of those who are supposed to use it, because needs change and users become savvier as the project progresses. User participation should be promoted throughout the development process to make sure that the final system will be accepted and used, by getting users actively involved in the development of the system (e.g., performing tasks, providing feedback, and making decisions).

The final feasibility study helps organizations make wiser investments regarding IS because it forces project teams to consider technical, economic, and organizational factors that can affect their projects. It protects IT professionals from criticism by keeping the business units educated about decisions and positioned as the leaders in the decision-making process. Remember—the feasibility study should be revised several times during the project at points where the project team makes critical decisions about the system (e.g., before the design begins). The final feasibility study can be used to support and explain the critical choices that are made throughout the SDLC.

Applying the Concepts at Tune Source

The steering committee met and placed the digital music download project high on its list of projects.

YOUR TURN

1-5 Too Much Paper, Part 2

Review the description of the South Dakota workers' compensation project in Your Turn 1-3. There were legal hurdles to implementing a digital solution to handle workers' compensation claims. One hurdle was that the previous paper method had physical signatures from employees signing off that they had received treatment or that the doctor had signed off on medical treatment performed. How could such permissions be preserved and duplicated digitally?

In addition, some clerks were afraid that the digital solution might not work. What if they could not find an electronic file on the computer? What if a hard drive crashed or the files were accidentally deleted? What if they could not retrieve the electronic file?

QUESTIONS:
1. What legal issues might arise from having only "digital signatures" or only electronic/paper copies of documents instead of physical documents? How do these issues affect the project's feasibility?
2. In terms of organizational feasibility and adoption, what might an analyst do to convince these clerks to adopt and use the new technology?

The next step was for Carly and Jason to develop the feasibility analysis. Figure 1-13 presents the executive summary page of the feasibility study: The report itself was about 10 pages long, and it provided additional detail and supporting documentation.

As shown in Figure 1-13, the project is somewhat risky from a technical perspective. Tune Source has minimal experience with the proposed application and

---

Digital Music Download Project Executive Summary

Carly Edwards and Jason Wells created the following feasibility analysis for the Tune Source Digital Music Download Project. The System Request is attached, along with the detailed feasibility study. The highlights of the feasibility analysis are as follows:

Technical Feasibility

The Digital Music Download system is feasible technically, although there is some risk.

Tune Source's risk regarding familiarity with music download applications is moderately high.

- The Marketing Department has little experience with a subscription-based business model.
- The IT department has strong knowledge of the company's existing Web-based CD sales system, but it has not worked with music downloads or customer subscriptions.
- Numerous music download sites exist on the Internet.

Tune Source's risk regarding familiarity with the technology is moderately low.

- The IT department has knowledge of the current Web-based order entry system and the databases and Internet technology it uses.
- The IT department has no direct knowledge of the technology required to store and deliver digital music downloads; however, many of the technical issues will be the responsibility of the ISP.
- Consultants are readily available to provide help in this area.

The project size is considered medium risk.

- The project team will likely consist of 10 or fewer people.
- Business user involvement will be required.
- The project time frame is somewhat critical, since the system is needed to maintain our competitive position in the market.

The compatibility with Tune Source's existing technical infrastructure should be good.

- An Internet infrastructure is already in place at the retail stores and corporate headquarters.
- The ISP should be able to scale its services to accommodate the new Digital Music Download system.

Economic Feasibility

A cost–benefit analysis was performed; see attached spreadsheet for details (provided in Appendix 1B). Conservative estimates show that the Digital Music Download system has a good chance of significantly enhancing the company's bottom line.

ROI over 3 years: 280%
NPV over 3 years: $4,180,431
Break-even occurs after 0.17 years

Intangible Costs and Benefits
Improved customer satisfaction.
Enhanced competitive position through expansion of our brand into the music download market.

Organizational Feasibility

From an organizational perspective, this project has low risk. The top executives of the company have a strong interest in the project, and the project champion, Carly Edwards, is a respected and knowledgeable marketing executive.

The users of the system, Internet consumers and in-store kiosk users, are expected to appreciate the entry of Tune Source into the music download arena. Management at the stores may have some concern about lost CD sales; however, since customers have so many other options available for music downloads, this system may prevent our losing those customers to other digital music sources and may provide us with the opportunity to cross-sell those customers from our CD inventory.

Additional comments:

- The Marketing Department views this as a strategic system. This system will allow us to leverage our music archive and our well-established market position to establish a presence in the digital music download business. Our customers have been requesting such a capability, and we believe it will be well accepted.
- We should consider hiring a consultant with expertise in similar applications to assist with the project.
- We will need new staff to operate the system and potentially to provide customer service for subscribers and gift-card holders.

FIGURE 1-13
Feasibility Analysis Executive Summary for Tune Source

YOUR

TURN

1-6 CREATE A FEASIBILITY ANALYSIS

Think about the idea that you developed in "Your Turn 1-4" to improve your university or college course enrollment process.

QUESTIONS:
1. List three things that influence the technical feasibility of the system.

2. List three things that influence the economic feasibility of the system.
3. List three things that influence the organizational feasibility of the system.
4. How can you learn more about the issues that affect the three kinds of feasibility?

the technology. One solution may be to hire a consultant to work with the IT department and to offer guidance.

The economic feasibility analysis includes the assumptions that Carly made in the system request. The summary spreadsheet that led to the values in the feasibility analysis has been included in Appendix 1B. Development costs are expected to be about $280,000. This is a very rough estimate, as Jason has had to make some assumptions about the amount of time it will take to design and program the system. Nonetheless, the digital music download system appears to be very strong economically.

The organizational feasibility is presented in Figure 1-13. There is a strong champion, well placed in the organization, to support the project. The project originated in the business or functional side of the company, not the IS department, and support for the project among the senior management team is strong.

Additional stakeholders in the project are the management team responsible for the operations of the traditional stores and the store managers. They should be quite supportive, given the added service that they now can offer. Carly and Jason need to make sure that they are included in the development of the system so that they can appropriately incorporate it into their business processes.

SUMMARY

Systems Analyst Skills and Specializations
The systems analyst is a key person in the development of information systems. The systems analyst helps to analyze the business situation, identify opportunities for improvements, and design an information system that adds value to the organization. The systems analyst serves as a change agent, and this complex responsibility requires a wide range of skills, including technical, business, analytical, interpersonal, management, and ethical. In some organizations, systems analysts may develop a specialization such as business analyst, infrastructure analyst, change management analyst, or project manager.

The System Development Life Cycle
All system development projects follow essentially the same fundamental process called the system development life cycle (SDLC). The SDLC starts with a planning phase in which the project team identifies the business value of the system, conducts

a feasibility analysis, and plans the project. The second phase is the analysis phase, in which the team develops an analysis strategy, gathers information, and builds a set of analysis models. In the next phase, the design phase, the team develops the design strategy, the physical design, architecture design, interface design, database and file specifications, and program design. In the final phase, implementation, the system is built, installed, and maintained.

Project Identification and Initiation

Projects are identified when someone recognizes a business need that can be satisfied through the use of information technology. Project initiation is the point at which an organization creates and assesses the original goals and expectations for a new system. The first step in the process is to identify the business value for the system by developing a system request that provides basic information about the proposed system. Next, the analysts perform a feasibility analysis to determine the technical, economic, and organizational feasibility of the system.

System Request

The business value for an information system is identified and then described in a system request. This form contains the project's sponsor, business need, business requirements, and business value of the information system, along with any other issues or constraints that are important to the project. The document is submitted to an approval committee who determines whether the project would be a wise investment of the organization's time and resources.

Feasibility Analysis

A feasibility analysis is then used to provide more detail about the risks associated with the proposed system, and it includes technical, economic, and organizational feasibilities. The technical feasibility focuses on whether the system *can* be built, by examining the risks associated with the users' and analysts' familiarity with the application, familiarity with the technology, project size, and compatibility with existing systems. The economic feasibility addresses whether the system *should* be built. It includes a cost–benefit analysis of development costs, operational costs, tangible benefits, and intangible costs and benefits. Finally, the organizational feasibility analysis assesses how well the system will be accepted by its users and incorporated into the ongoing operations of the organization. The strategic alignment of the project and a stakeholder analysis can be used to assess this feasibility dimension.

KEY TERMS

Analysis models	Business value	Design strategy
Analysis phase	Cash-flow method	Development costs
Analysis strategy	Champion	Economic feasibility
Approval committee	Change management analyst	Emerging technology
Architecture design	Compatibility	Familiarity with technology
As-is system	Construction	Familiarity with the application
Break-even analysis	Cost–benefit analysis	Feasibility analysis
Business analyst	Database and file specifications	Feasibility study
Business need	Deliverable	First mover
Business requirements	Design phase	Functionality

Gradual refinement
Implementation phase
Infrastructure analyst
Installation
Intangible benefits
Intangible costs
Intangible value
Interface design
Net present value (NPV)
Operation costs
Organizational feasibility
Organizational management
Payback method
Phase
Planning phase

Program design
Project initiation
Project management
Project manager
Project plan
Project size
Project sponsor
Requirements gathering
Special issues
Stakeholder
Stakeholder analysis
Steering committee
Step
Strategic alignment
Support plan

System proposal
System request
System specification
System users
Systems analyst
Systems development life cycle
   (SDLC)
Tangible benefits
Tangible value
Technical feasibility
Technique
To-be system
Training plan
Work plan

QUESTIONS

1. What are the six general skills all project team members should have?
2. What are the major roles on a project team?
3. Compare and contrast the role of a systems analyst, business analyst, and infrastructure analyst.
4. Compare and contrast phases, steps, techniques, and deliverables.
5. Describe the major phases in the systems development life cycle (SDLC).
6. Describe the principal steps in the planning phase. What are the major deliverables?
7. Describe the principal steps in the analysis phase. What are the major deliverables?
8. Describe the principal steps in the design phase. What are the major deliverables?
9. Describe the principal steps in the implementation phase. What are the major deliverables?
10. Which phase in the SDLC is the most important?
11. What does *gradual refinement* mean in the context of SDLC?
12. Give three examples of business needs for a system.
13. Describe the roles of the project sponsor and the approval committee.
14. What is the purpose of an approval committee? Who is usually on this committee?
15. Why should the system request be created by a businessperson as opposed to an IS professional?

16. What is the difference between intangible value and tangible value? Give three examples of each.
17. What are the purposes of the system request and the feasibility analysis? How are they used in the project selection process?
18. Describe two special issues that may be important to list on a system request.
19. Describe the three techniques for feasibility analysis.
20. What factors are used to determine project size?
21. Describe a "risky" project in terms of technical feasibility. Describe a project that would *not* be considered risky.
22. What are the steps for assessing economic feasibility? Describe each step.
23. List two intangible benefits. Describe how these benefits can be quantified.
24. List two tangible benefits and two operational costs for a system. How would you determine the values that should be assigned to each item?
25. Explain how an expected value can be calculated for a cost or benefit. When would this be done?
26. Explain the net present value and return on investment for a cost–benefit analysis. Why would these calculations be used?
27. What is the break-even point for the project? How is it calculated?
28. What is stakeholder analysis? Discuss three stakeholders that would be relevant for most projects.

EXERCISES

A. Look in the classified section of your local newspaper. What kinds of job opportunities are available for people who want analyst positions? Compare and contrast the skills that the ads solicit with the skills that were presented in this chapter.

B. Think about your ideal analyst position. Write a newspaper ad to hire someone for that position. What requirements would the job have? What skills and experience would be required? How would applicants demonstrate that they have the appropriate skills and experience?

C. Locate a news article in an IT trade magazine (e.g., *Computerworld*) about an organization that is implementing a new computer system. Describe the tangible and intangible values that the organization likely will realize from the new system.

D. Car dealers have realized how profitable it can be to sell automobiles by using the Web. Pretend that you work for a local car dealership that is part of a large chain such as CarMax. Create a system request that you might use to develop a Web-based sales system. Remember to list special issues that are relevant to the project.

E. Suppose that you are interested in buying yourself a new computer. Create a cost–benefit analysis that illustrates the return on investment that you would receive from making this purchase. Computer-related websites (www.dell.com, www.hp.com) should reveal real tangible costs that you can include in your analysis. Project your numbers out to include a three-year period and provide the net present value of the final total.

F. Consider the Amazon.com website. The management of the company decided to extend its Web-based system to include products other than books (e.g., wine, specialty gifts). How would you have assessed the feasibility of this venture when the idea first came up? How "risky" would you have considered the project that implemented this idea? Why?

G. Interview someone who works in a large organization, and ask him or her to describe the approval process that exists for proposed new development projects. What do they think about the process? What are the problems? What are the benefits?

H. Reread the "Your Turn 1-2" box (Implementing a Satellite Data Network). Create a list of the stakeholders that should be considered in a stakeholder analysis of this project.

MINICASES

1. Barbara Singleton, manager of western regional sales at the WAMAP Company, requested that the IS department develop a sales force management and tracking system that would enable her to better monitor the performance of her sales staff. Unfortunately, due to the massive backlog of work facing the IS department, her request was given a low priority. After six months of inaction by the IS department, Barbara decided to take matters into her own hands. Following the advice of friends, Barbara purchased a PC and simple database software and constructed a sales force management and tracking system on her own.

   Although Barbara's system has been "completed" for about six weeks, it still has many features that do not work correctly, and some functions are full of errors. Barbara's assistant is so mistrustful of the system that she has secretly gone back to using her old paper-based system, since it is much more reliable.

   Over dinner one evening, Barbara complained to a systems analyst friend, "I don't know what went wrong with this project. It seemed pretty simple to me. Those IS guys wanted me to follow this elaborate set of steps and tasks, but I didn't think all that really applied to a PC-based system. I just thought I could build this system and tweak it around until I got what I wanted without all the fuss and bother of the methodology the IS guys were pushing. I mean, doesn't that just apply to their big, expensive systems?"

   Assuming that you are Barbara's systems analyst friend, how would you respond to her complaint?

2. The Amberssen Specialty Company is a chain of 12 retail stores that sell a variety of imported gift items, gourmet chocolates, cheeses, and wines in the Toronto area. Amberssen has an IS staff of three people who have created a simple, but effective, information system of networked point-of-sale registers at the stores, and a

centralized accounting system at the company headquarters. Harry Hilman, the head of Amberssen's IS group, has just received the following memo from Bill Amberssen, Sales Director (and son of Amberssen's founder):

Harry—It's time Amberssen Specialty launched itself on the Internet. Many of our competitors are already there, selling to customers without the expense of a retail storefront, and we should be there too. I project that we could double or triple our annual revenues by selling our products on the Internet. I'd like to have this ready by Thanksgiving, in time for the prime holiday gift-shopping season. Bill

After pondering this memo for several days, Harry scheduled a meeting with Bill so that he could clarify Bill's vision of this venture. Using the standard content of a system request as your guide, prepare a list of questions that Harry needs to have answered about this project.

3. The Decker Company maintains a fleet of 10 service trucks and crews that provide a variety of plumbing, heating, and cooling repair services to residential customers. Currently, it takes on average about 6 hours before a service team responds to a service request. Each truck and crew averages 12 service calls per week, and the average revenue earned per service call is $150. Each truck is in service 50 weeks per year. Due to the difficulty in scheduling and routing, there is considerable slack time for each truck and crew during a typical week.

In an effort to more efficiently schedule the trucks and crews and improve their productivity, Decker management is evaluating the purchase of a prewritten routing and scheduling software package. The benefits of the system will include reduced response time to service requests and more productive service teams, but management is having trouble quantifying these benefits.

One approach is to make an estimate of how much service response time will decrease with the new system, which then can be used to project the increase in the number of service calls made each week. For example, if the system permits the average service response time to fall to 4 hours, management believes that each truck will be able to make 16 service calls per week on average—an increase of 4 calls per week. With each truck making 4 additional calls per week and the average revenue per call at $150, the revenue increase per truck per week is $600 (4 × $150). With 10 trucks in service 50 weeks per year, the average annual revenue increase will be $300,000 ($600 × 10 × 50).

Decker Company management is unsure whether the new system will enable response time to fall to 4 hours on average, or will be some other number. Therefore, management has developed the following range of outcomes that may be possible outcomes of the new system, along with probability estimates of each outcome occurring:

New Response Time	# Calls/Truck/Week	Likelihood
2 hours	20	20%
3 hours	18	30%
4 hours	16	50%

Given these figures, prepare a spreadsheet model that computes the expected value of the annual revenues to be produced by this new system.

4. Martin is working to develop a preliminary cost–benefit analysis for a new client-server system. He has identified a number of cost factors and values for the new system, summarized in the following tables:

Development Costs—Personnel

2 Systems Analysts	400 hours/ea @ $50/hour
4 Programmer Analysts	250 hours/ea @ $35/hour
1 GUI Designer	200 hours/ea @ $40/hour
1 Telecommunications Specialist	50 hours/ea @ $50/hour
1 System Architect	100 hours/ea @ $50/hour
1 Database Specialist	15 hours/ea @ $45/hour
1 System Librarian	250 hours/ea @ $15/hour

Development Costs—Training

4 Oracle training registration	$3500/student

Development Costs—New Hardware and Software

1 Development server	$18,700
1 Server software (OS, misc.)	$1500
1 DBMS server software	$7500
7 DBMS client software	$950/client

Annual Operating Costs—Personnel

2 Programmer Analysts	125 hours/ea @ $35/hour
1 System Librarian	20 hours/ea @ $15/hour

Annual Operating Costs—Hardware, Software, and Misc.

1 Maintenance agreement for server	$995
1 Maintenance agreement for server DBMS software	$525
Preprinted forms	15,000/year @ $.22/form

The benefits of the new system are expected to come from two sources: increased sales and lower inventory levels. Sales are expected to increase by $30,000 in the first year of the system's operation and will grow at a rate of 10% each year thereafter. Savings from lower inventory levels are expected to be $15,000 per year for each year of the project's life.

Using a format similar to the spreadsheets in this chapter, develop a spreadsheet that summarizes this project's cash flow, assuming a four-year useful life after the project is developed. Compute the present value of the cash flows, using an interest rate of 9%.

What is the NPV for this project? What is the ROI for this project? What is the break-even point? Should this project be accepted by the approval committee?

APPENDIX 1A: FINANCIAL CONCEPTS FOR COST–BENEFIT ANALYSIS

Performance Measure	Definition	Formula
Return on Investment (ROI)	The amount of revenue or cost saving return from a given investment	$\dfrac{\text{Total benefits} - \text{total costs}}{\text{Total costs}}$
Break-Even Point	The point in time at which the costs of the project equal the value it has delivered	$\dfrac{\text{Yearly Net Cash Flow} - \text{Cumulative Net Cash Flow}}{\text{Yearly Net Cash Flow}}$ Use the yearly net cash flow amount from the first year in which the project has a positive cash flow. Add the above amount to the year in which the project has a positive cash flow minus one.
Present Value (PV)	The value of a cash flow today compared with that same amount in the future, taking into account the time value of money	$\dfrac{\text{Cash flow amount}}{(1 + \text{interest rate})^n}$ n = number of years in the future
Net Present Value (NPV)	The total present value of benefits less the total present value of costs	Σ PV Benefits $- \Sigma$ PV Costs

FIGURE 1A-1
Common Cost–Benefit Financial Calculations

FIGURE 1A-2
The Present Value of a Dollar Received Some Years in the Future

Number of Years	6%	10%	15%
1	.943	.909	.870
2	.890	.826	.756
3	.840	.751	.572
4	.792	.683	.497

APPENDIX 1B—DETAILED ECONOMIC FEASIBILITY ANALYSIS FOR TUNE SOURCE

Figure 1B-1 contains the summary spreadsheet for the Tune Source digital music download project. As shown, Carly's original sales projections are used for the first year's revenues. Sales are expected to grow 4% in the second year and 3% in the third year.

Cost projections are based on Jason's assumptions about the time it will take to develop the system and the resources that will be required. Operating costs have a considerable new labor component because a new business unit is being created, requiring additional staff.*

---

* Some of the salary information may seem high to you. But keep in mind that most companies use a "full cost" model for estimating salary cost in which all benefits (e.g., health insurance, retirement, payroll taxes) are included in salaries when estimating costs.

Figure 1B-1 incorporates several of the financial analysis techniques we have discussed. The rows marked A and C summarize the annual benefits and costs, respectively. The row marked D shows the yearly net benefits (total benefits − total costs). The ROI calculation shows that this project is expected to return 280% on the investment, calculated by dividing the total benefits in row A by the total costs in row C.

Row E shows the cumulative cash flow for the project, and this is used to determine the break-even

	2009	2010	2011	2012	Total
Benefits					
Increased sales from individual music downloads		757,500	787,800	811,434	2,356,734
Increased sales from customer subscriptions		950,000	988,000	1,017,640	2,955,640
Increased sales from in-store or website CD sales		205,000	213,200	219,596	637,796
Increased sales from music download gift cards		153,000	159,120	163,894	476,014
Ⓐ **Total Benefits**		**2,065,500**	**2,148,120**	**2,212,564**	**6,426,184**
Ⓑ **Present Value Total Benefits**		**1,948,585**	**1,911,819**	**1,857,711**	**5,718,115**
Development Costs					
Labor: Analysis and design	42,000	0	0	0	42,000
Labor: Implementation	120,000	0	0	0	120,000
Consultant fees	50,000	0	0	0	50,000
Development training	5,000	0	0	0	5,000
Office space and equipment	2,000	0	0	0	2,000
In-store kiosks	25,000	0	0	0	25,000
Software	10,000	0	0	0	10,000
Hardware	25,000	0	0	0	25,000
Total Development Costs	**279,000**	**0**	**0**	**0**	**279,000**
Operational Costs					
Labor: Webmaster		85,000	87,550	90,177	262,727
Labor: Network technician		60,000	61,800	63,654	185,454
Labor: Computer operations		50,000	51,500	53,045	154,545
Labor: Business manager		60,000	61,800	63,654	185,454
Labor: Assistant manager		45,000	46,350	47,741	139,091
Labor: Three staff		90,000	92,700	95,481	278,181
Software upgrades		1,000	1,000	1,000	3,000
Software licenses		3,000	1,000	1,000	5,000
Hardware upgrades		5,000	3,000	3,000	11,000
User training		2,000	1,000	1,000	4,000
Additional ISP charges		15,000	17,000	18,500	50,500
Communications charges		20,000	20,000	20,000	60,000
Marketing expenses		25,000	25,000	25,000	75,000
Total Operational Costs		**461,000**	**469,700**	**483,251**	**1,413,951**
Ⓒ **Total Costs**	**279,000**	**461,000**	**469,700**	**483,251**	**1,692,951**
Ⓓ **Total Benefits − Total Costs**	**(279,000)**	**1,604,500**	**1,678,420**	**1,729,313**	**4,733,233**
Ⓔ **Cumulative Net Cash Flow**	**(279,000)**	**1,325,500**	**3,003,920**	**4,733,233**	
Ⓕ **Present Value Total Costs**	**279,000**	**434,906**	**418,031**	**405,747**	**1,537,684**
Return on Investment (ROI)	**280%**	**(6,426,184/1,692,951)**			
Break-Even Point	**0.17 years**	**(costs are fully recovered in the first year; [1,604,500 − 1,325,500]/1,604,500)**			
NPV (PV Total Benefits − PV Total Costs)	4,180,431	**(5,718,115 − 1,537,684)**			
Intangible Benefits:	Improved customer satisfaction Enhanced market position				

FIGURE 1B-1
Economic Feasibility Analysis for Tune Source

point. As seen in Figure 1B-1, the project fully recovers its costs in the first year, since the cumulative net cash flow is positive in the first year.

The row marked B computes the present value of each year's total benefits, and the row marked F computes the present value of each year's total costs. These values are used in the NPV calculation. The total present value of costs is subtracted from the total present value of benefits, and the result is a large positive number, indicating the high desirability of this investment.

This spreadsheet shows that this project can add significant business value even if the underlying assumptions prove to be overly optimistic.

PLANNING

- ☑ **Identify project.**
- ☑ **Develop systems request.**
- ☑ **Analyze technical feasibility.**
- ☑ **Analyze economic feasibility.**
- ☑ **Analyze organizational feasibility.**
- ☐ Perform project selection review.
- ☐ Estimate project time.
- ☐ Identify project tasks.
- ☐ Create work breakdown structure.
- ☐ Create PERT charts.
- ☐ Create Gantt charts.
- ☐ Manage scope.
- ☐ Staff project.
- ☐ Create project charter.
- ☐ Set up CASE repository.
- ☐ Develop standards.
- ☐ Begin documentation.
- ☐ Assess and manage risk.

TASK CHECKLIST

PLANNING   ANALYSIS   DESIGN

CHAPTER 2
PROJECT SELECTION AND MANAGEMENT

T his chapter discusses how organizations evaluate and select projects to undertake from the many available projects. Once a project has been selected, the project manager plans the project. Project management involves selecting a project methodology, creating the project work plan, identifying project staffing requirements, and preparing to manage and control the project. These steps produce important project management deliverables, including the work plan, staffing plan, standards list, project charter, and risk assessment.

OBJECTIVES

- Understand how projects are selected in some organizations.
- Understand various approaches to the SDLC that can be used to structure a development project.
- Understand how to select a project methodology based on project characteristics.
- Become familiar with project estimation.
- Be able to create a project work plan.
- Understand how to staff a project.
- Understand techniques to coordinate and manage the project.
- Understand how to manage risk on the project.

CHAPTER OUTLINE

IMPLEMENTATION

INTRODUCTION

Most IT departments face a demand for IT projects that far exceeds the department's ability to supply them. In the past 10 years, business application growth has exploded, and *chief information officers* (CIOs) are challenged to select projects that will provide the highest possible return on IT investments while managing project risk. In a recent analysis, AMR Research Inc. found that 2%–15% of projects taken on by IT departments are not strategic to the business.[1] In today's globally competitive business environment, the corporate IT department needs to carefully prioritize, select, and manage its portfolio of development projects.

Historically, IT departments have tended to select projects by ad hoc methods: first-in, first-out; political clout; or the squeaky wheel getting the grease. In recent years, IT departments have collected project information and mapped the projects' contributions to business goals, using a project portfolio perspective.[2] *Project portfolio management*, a process of selecting, prioritizing, and monitoring project results, has become a critical success factor for IT departments facing too many potential projects with too few resources.[3] Software for project portfolio management, such as Hewlett Packard's *Project and Portfolio Management*, Primavera Systems' *ProSight*, and open-source *Project.net*, has become a valuable tool for IT organizations.

Once selected, a systems development project undergoes a thorough process of *project management*, the process of planning and controlling the project within a specified time frame, at minimum cost, with the desired outcomes.[4] A *project manager* has the primary responsibility for managing the hundreds of tasks and roles that need to be carefully coordinated. Project management has evolved into an actual profession with many training options and professional certification (e.g., Project Management Professional, or PMP) available through the Project Management Institute (www.pmi.org). Dozens of software products are available to support project management activities.

Although training and software are available to help project managers, unreasonable demands set by project sponsors and business managers can make project management very difficult. Too often, the approach of the holiday season, the chance at winning a proposal with a low bid, or a funding opportunity pressures project managers to promise systems long before they are able to deliver them. These overly optimistic timetables are thought to be one of the biggest problems that projects face; instead of pushing a project forward faster, they result in delays.

Thus, a critical success factor for project management is to start with a realistic assessment of the work that needs to be accomplished and then manage the project according to the plan. This can be accomplished by carefully following the basic steps of project management as outlined in this chapter. First, the project manager chooses a system development methodology that fits the characteristics of the project. Based on the size of the system, estimates of a time frame are made. Then, a list of tasks to be performed is created that forms the basis of the project work plan. Staffing needs are determined, and the project manager sets in place mechanisms to coordinate the project team throughout the project. Finally, the project manager monitors the project and refines estimates as work proceeds.

[1] Tucci, Linda, "PPM Strategy a CIO's Must-Have in Hard Times," *SearchCIO.com*, March 5, 2008.

[2] Ibid.

[3] Tucci, Linda, "Project portfolio management takes flight at Sabre," *SearchCIO.com,* November 28, 2007.

[4] A good book on project management is by Robert K. Wysocki and Rudd McGary, *Effective Project Management: Traditional, Adaptive, Extreme,* 3rd Ed., New York: John Wiley & Sons, 2003. Also, the Project Management Institute (www.pmi.org) and the Information Systems Special Interest Group of the Project Management Institute (www.pmi-issig.org) have valuable resources on project management in information systems.

2-A PROJECT PORTFOLIO MANAGEMENT: AN ESSENTIAL TOOL FOR IT DEPARTMENTS

Information systems are at the core of Sabre Holdings Corporation. The Sabre reservation system is the booking system of choice for travel agencies worldwide. Sabre is also the parent company of Travelocity.com, the second largest online travel agency in the United States.

Like many companies, Sabre's IT department struggles with many more project requests than it has resources to accomplish—as many as 1500 proposals for 600 funded projects annually. Because of the volatile, competitive nature of the travel industry, Sabre is especially challenged to be certain that IT is doing the right projects under constantly changing conditions. While traditional project management techniques focus on getting individual projects done, Sabre needs to be able to rapidly change the entire set of projects it's working on as market conditions shift.

Project portfolio management software collects and manages information about all projects—those that are underway and those that are awaiting approval. The software helps prioritize projects, allocate employees, monitor projects in real time, flag cost and time variances, measure the ROI, and help the IT department objectively measure the efficiency and efficacy of IT investments.

Primavera Systems' PPM software has enabled Sabre Holdings to update its queue of projects regularly, and projects are now prioritized quarterly instead of annually. A study of users of Hewlett Packard's PPM Center software found that in all cases, the investment in the software paid for itself in a year. Other findings were an average 30% increase in on-time projects, a 12% reduction in budget variance, and a 30% reduction in the amount of time IT spent on project reporting.

Sources: Tucci, Linda, "Project portfolio management takes flight at Sabre," SearchCIO.com, November 28, 2007.

Tucci, Linda, "PPM strategy a CIO's must-have in hard times," SearchCIO.com, March 5, 2008.

PROJECT SELECTION

Investments in information systems projects today are evaluated in the context of an entire portfolio of projects. Decision makers look beyond project cost and consider a project's anticipated risks and returns in relation to other projects. Companies prioritize their business strategies and then assemble and assess project portfolios on the basis of how they meet those strategic needs.

The focus on a project's contribution to an entire portfolio of projects reinforces the need for the feasibility study as described in Chapter 1. The approval committee has the responsibility to evaluate not only the project's costs and expected benefits, but also the technical and organizational risks associated with the project. The feasibility analysis is submitted back to the approval committee, along with an updated system request. Using this information, the approval committee can examine the business need (found in the system request) and the project risks (described in the feasibility analysis).

Portfolio management takes into consideration the different kinds of projects that exist in an organization—large and small, high risk and low risk, strategic and tactical. (See Figure 2-1 for different ways of classifying projects.) A good project portfolio will have the most appropriate mix of projects for the organization's needs. The committee acts as a portfolio manager, with the goal of maximizing benefits versus costs and balancing other important factors of the portfolio. For example, an organization may want to keep high-risk projects to a level less than 20% of its total project portfolio.

The approval committee must be selective about where to allocate resources, because the organization has limited funds. This involves *trade-offs* in which the organization must give up something in return for something else in order to keep

Size	What is the size? How many people are needed to work on the project?
Cost	How much will the project cost the organization?
Purpose	What is the purpose of the project? Is it meant to improve the technical infrastructure? support a current business strategy? improve operations? demonstrate a new innovation?
Length	How long will the project take before completion? How much time will go by before value is delivered to the business?
Risk	How likely is it that the project will succeed or fail?
Scope	How much of the organization is affected by the system? a department? a division? the entire corporation?
Economic Value	How much money does the organization expect to receive in return for the amount the project costs?

FIGURE 2-1
Ways to Classify Projects

its portfolio well balanced. If there are three potentially high-payoff projects, yet all have very high risk, then maybe only one of the projects will be selected. Also, there are times when a system at the project level makes good business sense, but it does not at the organization level. Thus, a project may show a very strong ROI and support important business needs for a part of the company; however, it is not selected. This could happen for many reasons—because there is no money in the budget for another system, the organization is about to go through some kind of change (e.g., a merger, an implementation of a company-wide system like an ERP), projects that meet the same business requirements already are underway, or the system does not align well with current or future corporate strategy.

Applying the Concepts at Tune Source

The approval committee met and reviewed the Digital Music Download project along with two other projects—one that called for a new supply-chain portal and another that involved the enhancement of Tune Source's data warehouse. Unfortunately, the budget would allow for only one project to be approved, so the committee carefully examined the costs, expected benefits, risks, and strategic alignment of all three projects. Currently, top management is anxious to bring the digital music download capability to market in order to satisfy the demands of its existing customers and potentially expand its customer base. The Digital Music Download project is best aligned with that goal. Therefore, the committee decided to fund the Digital Music Download project.

YOUR TURN

2-1 To Select or Not to Select

It seems hard to believe that an approval committee would not select a project that meets real business needs, has a high potential ROI, and has a positive feasibility analysis. Think of a company that you have worked for or know about. Describe a scenario in which a project may be very attractive at the project level, but not at the organization level.

2-2 PROJECT SELECTION

In April 1999, one of Capital Blue Cross' health-care insurance plans had been in the field for three years, but hadn't performed as well as expected. The ratio of premiums to claims payments wasn't meeting historic norms. In order to revamp the product features or pricing to boost performance, the company needed to understand why it was underperforming. The stakeholders came to the discussion already knowing they needed better extraction and analysis of usage data in order to understand product shortcomings and recommend improvements.

After listening to input from the user teams, the stakeholders proposed three options. One was to persevere with the current manual method of pulling data from flat files via ad hoc reports and retyping it into spreadsheets.

The second option was to write a program to dynamically mine the needed data from Capital's customer information control system (CICS). While the system was processing claims, for instance, the program would pull out up-to-the-minute data at a given point in time for users to analyze.

The third alternative was to develop a decision-support system to allow users to make relational queries from a data mart containing a replication of the relevant claims and customer data.

Each of these alternatives was evaluated on cost, benefits, risks, and intangibles.

QUESTION:

1. What are three costs, benefits, risks, and intangibles associated with each project?
2. Based on your answer to question 1, which project would you choose?

Source: "Capital Blue Cross," *CIO Magazine,* February 15, 2000, by Richard Pastore.

2-B INTERVIEW WITH LYN MCDERMID, CIO, DOMINION VIRGINIA POWER

A CIO needs to have a global view when identifying and selecting projects for her organization. I would get lost in the trees if I were to manage on a project-by-project basis. Given this, I categorize my projects according to my three roles as a CIO, and the mix of my project portfolio changes depending on the current business environment.

My primary role is to **keep the business running**. That means every day when each person comes to work, they can perform his or her job efficiently. I measure this using various service level, cost, and productivity measures. Projects that keep the business running could have a high priority if the business were in the middle of a merger, or a low priority if things were running smoothly, and it were "business as usual."

My second role is to push **innovation that creates value for the business**. I manage this by looking at our lines of business and asking which lines of business create the most value for the company. These are the areas for which I should be providing the most value. For example, if we had a highly innovative marketing strategy, I would push for innovation there. If operations were running smoothly, I would push less for innovation in that area.

My third role is strategic, to look beyond today and find **new opportunities** for both IT and the business of providing energy. This may include investigating process systems, such as automated meter reading or looking into the possibilities of wireless technologies.

Lyn McDermid

CONCEPTS

2-C INTERVIEW WITH CARL WILSON, CIO, MARRIOTT CORPORATION

IN ACTION

At Marriott, we don't have IT projects—we have business initiatives and strategies that are enabled by IT. As a result the only time a traditional "IT project" occurs is when we have an infrastructure upgrade that will lower costs or leverage better functioning technology. In this case, IT has to make a business case for the upgrade and prove its value to the company.

The way IT is involved in business projects in the organization is twofold. First, senior IT positions are filled by people with good business understanding. Second, these people are placed on key business committees and forums where the real business happens, such as finding ways to satisfy guests. Because IT has a seat at the table, we are able to spot opportunities to support business strategy. We look for ways in which IT can enable or better support business initiatives as they arise.

Therefore, business projects are proposed, and IT is one component of them. These projects are then evaluated the same as any other business proposal, such as a new resort—by examining the return on investment and other financial measures.

At the organizational level, I think of projects as must-do's, should-do's, and nice-to-do's. The "must-do's" are required to achieve core business strategy, such as guest preference. The "should-do's" help grow the business and enhance the functionality of the enterprise. These can be somewhat untested, but good drivers of growth. The "nice-to-do's" are more experimental and look further out into the future.

The organization's project portfolio should have a mix of all three kinds of projects, with a much greater proportion devoted to the "must-do's."   *Carl Wilson*

CONCEPTS

2-D A PROJECT THAT DOES NOT GET SELECTED

IN ACTION

Hygeia Travel Health is a Toronto-based health insurance company whose clients are the insurers of foreign tourists to the United States and Canada. Its project selection process is relatively straightforward. The project evaluation committee, consisting of six senior executives, splits into two groups. One group includes the CIO, along with the heads of operations and research and development, and it analyzes the costs of every project. The other group consists of the two chief marketing officers and the head of business development, and they analyze the expected benefits. The groups are permanent, and to stay objective, they don't discuss a project until both sides have evaluated it. The results are then shared, both on a spreadsheet and in conversation. Projects are then approved, passed over, or tabled for future consideration.

Last year, the marketing department proposed purchasing a claims database filled with detailed information on the costs of treating different conditions at different facilities. Hygeia was to use this information to estimate how much money insurance providers were likely to owe on a given claim if a patient was treated at a certain hospital as opposed to any other. For example, a 45-year-old man suffering a heart attack may accrue $5000 in treatment costs at hospital A, but only $4000 at hospital B. This information

would allow Hygeia to recommend the less expensive hospital to its customer. That would save the customer money and help differentiate Hygeia from its competitors.

The benefits team used the same three-meeting process to discuss all the possible benefits of implementing the claims database. Members of the team talked to customers and made a projection by using Hygeia's past experience and expectations about future business trends. The verdict: The benefits team projected a revenue increase of $210,000. Client retention would rise by 2%, and overall, profits would increase by 0.25%.

The costs team, meanwhile, came up with large estimates: $250,000 annually to purchase the database and an additional $71,000 worth of internal time to make the information usable. Put it all together and it was a financial loss of $111,000 in the first year.

The project still could have been good for marketing—maybe even good enough to make the loss acceptable. But some of Hygeia's clients were also in the claims information business and, therefore, potential competitors. This, combined with the financial loss, was enough to make the company reject the project.

Source: "Two Teams Are Better Than One," *CIO Magazine,* July 15, 2001, by Ben Worthen.

CREATING THE PROJECT PLAN

Once the project is launched by being selected by the approval committee, it is time to carefully plan the project. In large organizations or on large projects, the role of project manager is commonly filled by a professional specialist in project management. In smaller organizations or on smaller projects, the systems analyst may fill this role. The project manager must make a myriad of decisions regarding the project, including determining the best project methodology, developing a work plan for the project, determine a staffing plan, and establishing mechanisms to coordinate and control the project.

Project Methodology Options

As we discussed in Chapter 1, the Systems Development Life Cycle (SDLC) provides the foundation for the processes used to develop an information system. A *methodology* is a formalized approach to implementing the SDLC (i.e., it is a list of steps and deliverables). There are many different systems development methodologies, and they vary in terms of the progression that is followed through the phases of the SDLC. Some methodologies are formal standards used by government agencies, while others have been developed by consulting firms to sell to clients. Many organizations have their own internal methodologies that have been refined over the years, and they explain exactly how each phase of the SDLC is to be performed in that company. Here we will review several of the predominant methodologies that have evolved over time.

Waterfall Development   With *waterfall development*, analysts and users proceed sequentially from one phase to the next. (See Figure 2-2.) The key deliverables for each phase are typically voluminous (often, hundreds of pages) and are presented to the approval committee and project sponsor for approval as the project moves from phase to phase. Once the work produced in one phase is approved, the phase ends and the next phase begins. As the project progresses from phase to phase, it moves forward in the same manner as a waterfall. While it is possible to go backward

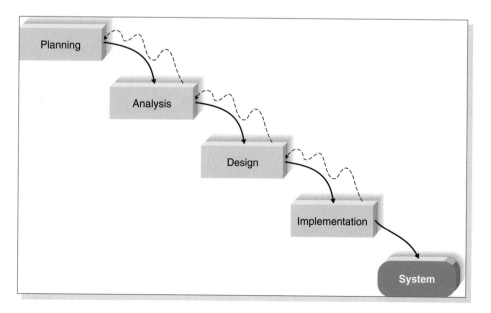

FIGURE 2-2
Waterfall Development

through the phases (e.g., from design back to analysis), it is quite difficult. (Imagine yourself as a salmon trying to swim upstream in a waterfall).

Waterfall development methodologies have the advantages of identifying requirements long before programming begins and limiting changes to the requirements as the project proceeds. The key disadvantages are that the design must be completely specified before programming begins, a long time elapses between the completion of the system proposal in the analysis phase and the delivery of system, and testing is treated almost as an afterthought in the implementation phase. In addition, the deliverables are often a poor communication mechanism, so important requirements may be overlooked in the volumes of documentation. If the project team misses an important requirement, expensive post-implementation programming may be needed. Users may forget the original purpose of the system, since so much time has elapsed between the original idea and actual implementation. Also, in today's dynamic business environment, a system that met the existing environmental conditions during the analysis phase may need considerable rework to match the environment when it is implemented. This rework requires going back to the initial phase and making needed changes through each of the subsequent phases in turn.

There are two important variants of waterfall development. The *parallel development* methodologies evolved to address the lengthy time frame of waterfall development. As shown in Figure 2-3, instead of doing the design and implementation in

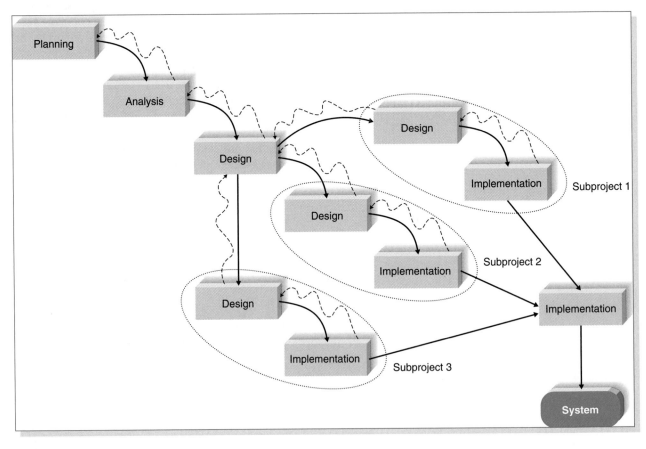

FIGURE 2-3
Parallel Development

sequence, a general design for the whole system is performed. Then the project is divided into a series of subprojects that can be designed and implemented in parallel. Once all subprojects are complete, there is a final integration of the separate pieces, and the system is delivered.

Parallel development reduces the time required to deliver a system, so changes in the business environment are less likely to produce the need for rework. The approach still suffers from problems caused by voluminous deliverables. It also adds a new problem: If the subprojects are not completely independent, design decisions in one subproject may affect another, and at the project end, integrating the subprojects may be quite challenging.

The **V-model** is another variation of waterfall development that pays more explicit attention to testing. As shown in Figure 2-4, the development process proceeds down the left-hand slope of the V, defining requirements and designing system components. At the base of the V, the code is written. On the upward-sloping right side of the model, testing of components, integration testing, and, finally, acceptance testing are performed. A key concept of this model is that as requirements are specified and components designed, testing for those elements is also defined. In this manner, each level of testing is clearly linked to a part of the analysis or design phase, helping to ensure high quality and relevant testing.

The V-model is simple and straightforward and improves the overall quality of systems through its emphasis on early development of test plans. It still suffers

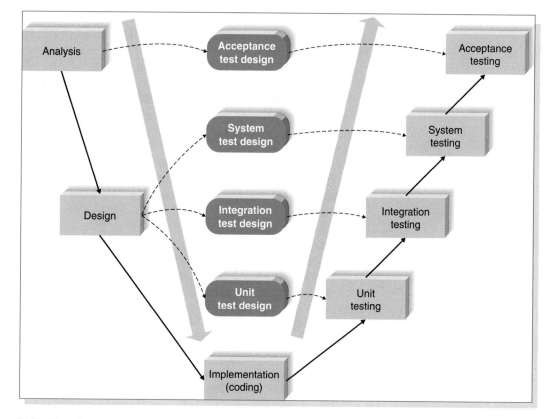

FIGURE 2-4
V-Model

from the rigidity of the waterfall development process, however, and is not always appropriate for the dynamic nature of the business environment.

Rapid Application Development (RAD)[5] *Rapid application development* is a collection of methodologies that emerged in response to the weaknesses of waterfall development and its variations. RAD incorporates special techniques and computer tools to speed up the analysis, design, and implementation phases in order to get some portion of the system developed quickly and into the hands of the users for evaluation and feedback. CASE (computer-aided software engineering) tools, JAD (joint application development) sessions, fourth-generation/visual programming languages (e.g., Visual Basic.NET), and code generators may all play a role in RAD. While RAD can improve the speed and quality of systems development, it may also introduce a problem in managing user expectations. As systems are developed more quickly and users gain a better understanding of information technology, user expectations may dramatically increase and system requirements may expand during the project (sometimes known as *scope creep* or *feature creep*).

RAD may be conducted in a variety of ways. ***Iterative development*** breaks the overall project into a series of *versions* that are developed sequentially. The most important and fundamental requirements are bundled into the first version of the system. This version is developed quickly by a mini-waterfall process, and once implemented, the users can provide valuable feedback to be incorporated into the next version of the system. (See Figure 2-5.) Iterative development gets a preliminary version of the system to the users quickly so that business value is provided. Since users are working with the system, important additional requirements may be identified and incorporated into subsequent versions. The chief disadvantage of iterative development is that users begin to work with a system that is intentionally incomplete. Users must accept that only the most critical requirements of the system will be available in the early versions and must be patient with the repeated introduction of new system versions.

System prototyping performs the analysis, design, and implementation phases concurrently in order to quickly develop a simplified version of the proposed system and give it to the users for evaluation and feedback. (See Figure 2-6). The system prototype is a "quick and dirty" version of the system and provides minimal features. Following reaction and comments from the users, the developers reanalyze, redesign, and reimplement a second prototype that corrects deficiencies and adds more features. This cycle continues until the analysts, users, and sponsor agree that the prototype provides enough functionality to be installed and used in the organization. System prototyping very quickly provides a system for users to evaluate and reassures users that progress is being made. The approach is very useful when users have difficulty expressing requirements for the system. A disadvantage, however, is the lack of careful, methodical analysis prior to making design and implementation decisions. System prototypes may have some fundamental design limitations that are a direct result of an inadequate understanding of the system's true requirements early in the project.

Throwaway prototyping[6] includes the development of prototypes, but uses the prototypes primarily to explore design alternatives rather than as the actual

---

[5] One of the best RAD books is that by Steve McConnell, *Rapid Development*, Redmond, WA: Microsoft Press, 1996.

[6] Our description of the throwaway prototyping is a modified version of the Spiral Development Model developed by Barry Boehm, "A Spiral Model of Software Development and Enhancement," *Computer,* May, 1988, 21(5):61–72.

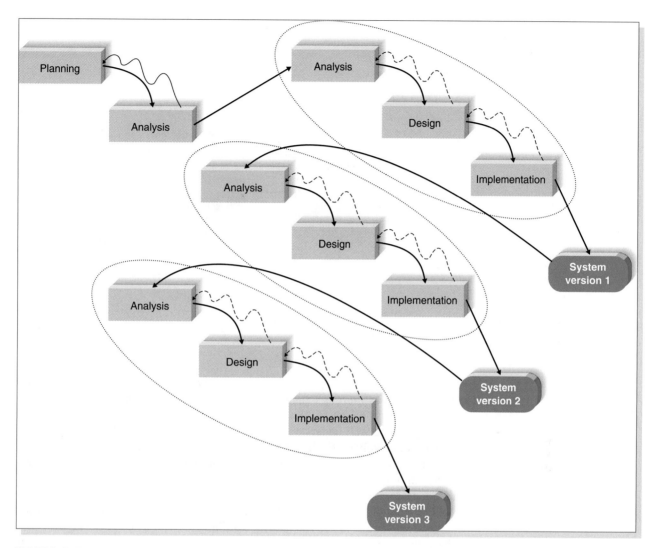

FIGURE 2-5
Iterative Development

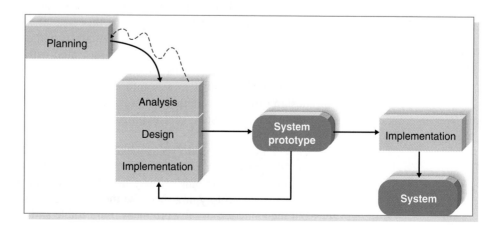

FIGURE 2-6
System Prototyping

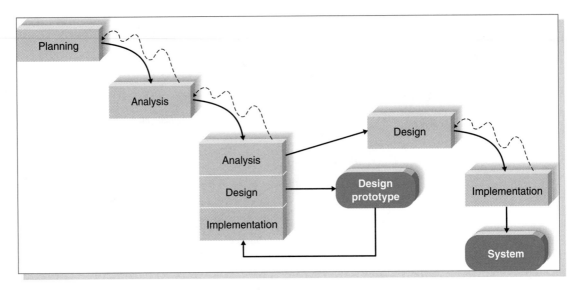

FIGURE 2-7
Throwaway Prototyping

new system (as in system prototyping). As shown in Figure 2-7, throwaway proto-typing has a fairly thorough analysis phase that is used to gather requirements and to develop ideas for the system concept. Many of the features suggested by the users may not be well understood, however, and there may be challenging techni-cal issues to be solved. Each of these issues is examined by analyzing, designing, and building a *design prototype*. A design prototype is not intended to be a work-ing system. It contains only enough detail to enable users to understand the issues under consideration.

For example, suppose that users are not completely clear on how an order entry system should work. The analyst team might build a series of HTML pages to be viewed on a Web browser to help the users visualize such a system. In this case, a series of mock-up screens *appear* to be a system, but they really do nothing. Or, suppose that the project team needs to develop a sophisticated graphics program in Java. The team could write a portion of the program with artificial data to ensure that they could create a full-blown program successfully.

A system that is developed by this type of methodology probably requires several design prototypes during the analysis and design phases. Each of the pro-totypes is used to minimize the risk associated with the system by confirming that important issues are understood before the real system is built. Once the issues are resolved, the project moves into design and implementation. At this point, the design prototypes are thrown away, which is an important difference between this approach and system prototyping, in which the prototypes evolve into the final system.

Throwaway prototyping balances the benefits of well-thought-out analysis and design phases with the advantages of using prototypes to refine key issues before a system is built. It may take longer to deliver the final system compared with system prototyping (because the prototypes do not become the final system), but the approach usually produces more stable and reliable systems.

Agile Development *Agile development*[7] is a group of programming-centric methodologies that focus on streamlining the SDLC. Much of the modeling and documentation overhead is eliminated; instead, face-to-face communication is preferred. A project emphasizes simple, iterative application development in which every iteration is a complete software project, including planning, requirements analysis, design, coding, testing, and documentation. (See Figure 2.8). Cycles are kept short (one to four weeks), and the development team focuses on adapting to the current business environment. There are several popular approaches to agile development, including extreme programming (XP)[8], Scrum[9], and dynamic systems development method (DSDM).[10] Here, we briefly describe extreme programming.

Extreme programming[11] emphasizes customer satisfaction and teamwork. Communication, simplicity, feedback, and courage are core values. Developers communicate with customers and fellow programmers. Designs are kept simple and clean. Early and frequent testing provides feedback, and developers are able to courageously respond to changing requirements and technology. Project teams are kept small.

An XP project begins with user stories that describe what the system needs to do. Then, programmers code in small, simple modules and test to meet those needs. Users are required to be available to clear up questions and issues as they arise. Standards are very important to minimize confusion, so XP teams use a common set of names, descriptions, and coding practices. XP projects deliver results sooner than even the RAD approaches, and they rarely get bogged down in gathering requirements for the system.

For small projects with highly motivated, cohesive, stable, and experienced teams, XP should work just fine. However, if the project is not small or the teams aren't jelled,[12] then the likelihood of success for the XP project is reduced. Consequently, the

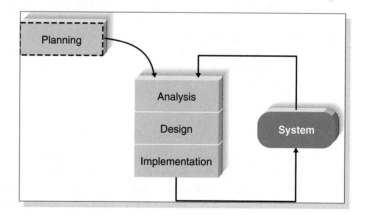

FIGURE 2-8
Extreme Programming

---

[7] For more information, see www.AgileAlliance.org.

[8] For more information, see www.extremeprogramming.org.

[9] For more information, see www.controlchaos.com.

[10] For more information, see www.dsdm.com

[11] For more information, see K. Beck, *Extreme Programming Explained: Embrace Change,* Reading, MA: Addison-Wesley, 2000, and M. Lippert, S. Roock, and H. Wolf, *Extreme Programming in Action: Practical Experiences from Real World Projects,* New York: John Wiley & Sons, 2002.

[12] A "jelled team" is one that has low turnover, a strong sense of identity, a sense of eliteness, a feeling that they jointly own the product being developed, and enjoyment in working together. For more information regarding jelled teams, see T. DeMarco and T. Lister, *Peopleware: Productive Projects and Teams,* New York: Dorsett House, 1987.

CONCEPTS   **2-E AGILE DEVELOPMENT AT TRAVELERS**

IN ACTION

Travelers Insurance Company of Hartford, Connecticut has adopted agile development methodologies. The insurance field can be competitive, and Travelers wanted to have the shortest "time to implement" in the field. Travelers set up development teams of six people—two systems analysts, two representatives from the user group (such as claim services), a project manager, and a clerical support person. In the agile approach, the users are physically assigned to the development team for the project. While at first it might seem that the users are just sitting around drinking coffee and not doing their regular jobs, that is not the case. The rapport that is developed within the team allows for

instant communication. The interaction is very deep and profound. The resulting software product is delivered quickly—and, generally, with all the features and nuances that the users wanted.

QUESTIONS:
1. Could this be done differently, such as through JAD sessions or having the users review the program on a weekly basis, rather than taking the users away from their real jobs to work on development?
2. What mind-set does an analyst need to work on such an approach?

use of XP in combination with outside contractors produces a highly questionable outcome, since the outside contractors may never "jell" with insiders.[13] XP requires a great deal of discipline to prevent projects from becoming unfocused and chaotic. Furthermore, it is recommended only for small groups of developers (not more than 10), and it is not advised for mission-critical applications. Since little analysis and design documentation is produced with XP, there is only code documentation; therefore, maintenance of large systems developed using XP may be impossible. Also, since mission-critical business information systems tend to exist for a long time, the utility of XP as a business information system development methodology is in doubt. Finally, the methodology requires considerable on-site user input, something that is frequently difficult to obtain.[14]

Selecting the Appropriate Development Methodology

As the previous section shows, there are many methodologies. The first challenge faced by project managers is to select which methodology to use. Choosing a methodology is not simple, because no one methodology is always best. (If it were, we'd simply use it everywhere!) Many organizations have standards and policies to guide the choice of methodology. You will find that organizations range from having one "approved" methodology to having several methodology options to having no formal policies at all.

---

[13] Considering the tendency for offshore outsourcing, this is a major obstacle for XP to overcome. For more information on offshore outsourcing, see P. Thibodeau, "ITAA panel debates outsourcing pros, cons," *Computerworld Morning Update,* September 25, 2003; and S. W. Ambler, "Chicken Little Was Right," *Software Development,* October 2003.

[14] Many of the observations described here on the utility of XP as a development approach are based on conversations with Brian Henderson-Sellers.

Usefulness in Developing Systems	Waterfall	Parallel	V-Model	Iterative	System Prototyping	Throwaway Prototyping	Extreme Programming
with unclear user requirements	Poor	Poor	Poor	Good	Excellent	Excellent	Excellent
with unfamiliar technology	Poor	Poor	Poor	Good	Poor	Excellent	Poor
that are complex	Good	Good	Good	Good	Poor	Excellent	Poor
that are reliable	Good	Good	Excellent	Good	Poor	Excellent	Good
with short time schedule	Poor	Good	Poor	Excellent	Excellent	Good	Excellent
with schedule visibility	Poor	Poor	Poor	Excellent	Excellent	Good	Good

FIGURE 2-9
Criteria for Selecting a Methodology

Figure 2-9 summarizes some important methodology selection criteria. One important item not discussed in this figure is the degree of experience of the analyst team. Many of the RAD and agile development methodologies require the use of new tools and techniques that have a significant learning curve. Often, these tools and techniques increase the complexity of the project and require extra time for learning. Once they are adopted and the team becomes experienced, the tools and techniques can significantly increase the speed in which the methodology can deliver a final system.

Clarity of User Requirements   When the user requirements for what the system should do are unclear, it is difficult to understand them by talking about them and explaining them with written reports. Users normally need to interact with technology to really understand what the new system can do and how to best apply it to their needs. System prototyping and throwaway prototyping are usually more appropriate when user requirements are unclear, because they provide prototypes for users to interact with early in the SDLC. Agile development may also be appropriate if on-site user input is available.

Familiarity with Technology   When the system will use new technology with which the analysts and programmers are not familiar (e.g., the first Web development project with Ajax), applying the new technology early in the methodology will improve the chance of success. If the system is designed without some familiarity with the base technology, risks increase because the tools may not be capable of doing what is needed. Throwaway prototyping is particularly appropriate for situations where there is a lack of familiarity with technology, because it explicitly encourages the developers to create design prototypes for areas with high risks. Iterative development is good as well, because opportunities are created to investigate the technology in some depth before the design is complete. While one might think that system prototyping would also be appropriate, it is much less so because the early prototypes that are built usually only scratch the surface of the new technology. Typically, it is only after several prototypes and several months that the developers discover weaknesses or problems in the new technology.

System Complexity Complex systems require careful and detailed analysis and design. Throwaway prototyping is particularly well suited to such detailed analysis and design, but system prototyping is not. The waterfall methodologies can handle complex systems, but without the ability to get the system or prototypes into users' hands early on, some key issues may be overlooked. Although iterative development methodologies enable users to interact with the system early in the process, we have observed that project teams who follow these methodologies tend to devote less attention to the analysis of the complete problem domain than they might if they were using other methodologies.

System Reliability System reliability is usually an important factor in system development. After all, who wants an unreliable system? However, reliability is just one factor among several. For some applications, reliability is truly critical (e.g., medical equipment, missile control systems), while for other applications it is merely important (e.g., games, Internet video). The V-model is useful when reliability is important, due to its emphasis on testing. Throwaway prototyping is most appropriate when system reliability is a high priority, because detailed analysis and design phases are combined with the ability for the project team to test many different approaches through design prototypes before completing the design. System prototyping is generally not a good choice when reliability is critical, due to the lack of careful analysis and design phases that are essential to dependable systems.

Short Time Schedules Projects that have short time schedules are well suited for RAD methodologies because those methodologies are designed to increase the speed of development. Iterative development and system prototyping are excellent choices when time lines are short because they best enable the project team to adjust the functionality in the system on the basis of a specific delivery date. If the project schedule starts to slip, it can be readjusted by removal of the functionality from the version or prototype under development. Waterfall-based methodologies are the worst choice when time is at a premium, because they do not allow for easy schedule changes.

Schedule Visibility One of the greatest challenges in systems development is knowing whether a project is on schedule. This is particularly true of the waterfall-based methodologies because design and implementation occur at the end of the project. The RAD methodologies move many of the critical design decisions to a position earlier in the project to help project managers recognize and address risk factors and keep expectations in check.

Estimating the Project Time Frame

As the previous section illustrated, some development methodologies have evolved in an attempt to accelerate the project through the SDLC as rapidly as possible while still producing a quality system. Regardless of whether time is a critical issue on a project or not, the project manager will have to develop a preliminary estimate of the amount of time the project will take. *Estimation*[15] is the process of assigning projected values for time and effort.

Estimation can be performed manually or with the help of an estimation software package like Construx Estimate,™ Costar,™ or KnowledgePLAN®—there are over 50 available on the market. The estimates developed at the start of a project are usually based on a range of possible values (e.g., the design phase will take three to four months) and gradually become more specific as the project moves forward (e.g., the design phase will be completed on March 22).

The numbers used to calculate these estimates can come from several sources. They can be provided with the methodology that is used, taken from projects with similar tasks and technologies, or provided by experienced developers. Generally speaking, the numbers should be conservative. A good practice is to keep track of the actual time and effort values during the SDLC so that numbers can be refined along the way, and the next project can benefit from real data. One of the greatest strengths of systems consulting firms is the past experience that they offer to a project; they have estimates and methodologies that have been developed and honed over time and applied to hundreds of projects.

There are two basic ways to estimate the time required to build a system. The simplest method uses the amount of time spent in the planning phase to predict the time required for the entire project. The idea is that a simple project will require little planning, and a complex project will require more planning; so using the amount of time spent in the planning phase is a reasonable way to estimate overall project time requirements.

With this approach, you take the time spent in (or estimated for) the planning phase and use industry standard percentages (or percentages from the organization's own experiences) to calculate estimates for the other SDLC phases. Industry standards suggest that a "typical" business application system spends 15% of its effort in the planning phase, 20% in the analysis phase, 35% in the design phase, and 30% in the implementation phase. This would suggest that if a project takes four months in the planning phase, then the rest of the project likely will take a total of 22.66 person-months ($4 \div .15 = 22.66$). These same industry percentages are then used to estimate the amount of time in each phase (Figure 2-10). The obvious limitation of this approach is that it can be difficult to take into account the specifics of your individual project, which may be simpler or more difficult than the "typical" project.

A more precise approach to estimation is called the *function point approach.* This approach is a more complex—and, it is hoped, more reliable—way of estimating time and effort for a project. The details of the function point approach are explained in Appendix 2A.

---

[15] Good books for further reading on software estimation are T. Capers Jones, *Estimation Software Costs,* New York: McGraw Hill, 1989; Coombs, *IT Project Estimation: A Practical Guide to the Costing of Software,* Cambridge University Press, 2003; and Steve McConnell, *Software Estimation: Demystifying the Black Art,* Microsoft Press, 2006.

	Planning	**Analysis**	**Design**	**Implementation**
Typical industry standards for business applications	15%	20%	35%	30%
Estimates based on actual figures for first stage of SDLC	Actual: 4 person-months	Estimated: 5.33 person-months	Estimated: 9.33 person-months	Estimated: 8 person-months

SDLC = systems development life cycle.

FIGURE 2-10
Estimating Project Time Using Industry Standards

Developing the Work Plan

Once a project manager has a general idea of the size and approximate schedule for the project, he or she creates a *work plan*, which is a dynamic schedule that records and keeps track of all of the tasks that need to be accomplished over the course of the project. The project manager first must assemble important details about each task to be completed. Figure 2-11 shows the type of task information needed, including when it needs to be completed, the person assigned to do the work, and any deliverables that will result. The level of detail and the amount of information captured by the work plan depend on the needs of the project (and the detail usually increases as the project progresses). Usually, the work plan is the main component of the project management software that we mentioned earlier.

To create a work plan, the project manager identifies the tasks that need to be accomplished and determines how long each one will take. Then the tasks are organized within a work breakdown structure.

Identify Tasks Remember that the overall objectives for the system were recorded on the system request, and the project manager's job is to identify all the tasks that will be needed to accomplish those objectives. This is a daunting task, certainly. The methodology that was selected by the project manager should be a valuable

Task Information	Example
Name of the task	Perform economic feasibility
Start date	Jan 05, 2010
Completion date	Jan 19, 2010
Person assigned to the task	Project sponsor Mary Smith
Deliverable(s)	Cost–benefit analysis
Completion status	Complete
Priority	High
Resources needed	Spreadsheet software
Estimated time	16 hours
Actual time	14.5 hours

FIGURE 2-11
Task Information

resource, however. The methodology that seems most appropriate for the project provides a list of steps and deliverables.

A project manager can take the methodology, select the steps and deliverables that apply to the current project, and add them to the work plan. If an existing methodology is not available within the organization, methodologies can be purchased from consultants or vendors, or books like this textbook can serve as guidance. Using an existing methodology is the most popular way to create a work plan, because most organizations have a methodology that they use for projects.

If a project manager prefers to begin from scratch, he or she can use a structured, top-down approach whereby high-level tasks are defined first and then broken down into subtasks. Each step is then broken down in turn and numbered in a hierarchical fashion. A list of tasks hierarchically numbered in this way is called a *work breakdown structure,* and it is the backbone of the project workplan. Figure 2-12 shows a portion of a work breakdown structure for the design phase of an actual data warehouse development project. Each of the main

Task ID	Task Name	Duration (days)	Dependency	Status
1	Design phase	30		Open
1.1	Develop database design document	9		Open
1.1.1	Staging database design	9		Open
1.1.2	Suspense database design	9		Open
1.2	Develop rejects-handling design document	9	1.1.1, 1.1.2	Open
1.2.1	Rejects-handling engine design	9		Open
1.3	Develop OLAP design document	9	1.1.1, 1.1.2	Open
1.3.1	Universe design	9		Open
1.4	Develop OLAP design part 1	8		Open
1.4.1	High-priority reports design	8		Open
1.5	Develop application design document	9		Open
1.5.1	Group consolidation and corporate reporting (GCCR) maintenance application design	9		Open
1.6	Extract, transform, load (ETL) design document	2		Open
1.6.1	Data export utility design	2		Open
1.7	Application design document	25		Open
1.7.1	Web entry application UI design	25		Open
1.7.2	Web entry application UI design sign-off	1		Open
1.7.3	Web entry forms and database model validation	11		Open
1.8	Functional requirements document	9		Open
1.8.1	Application design	9		Open
1.8.1.1	User authentication	4		Open
1.8.1.2	Call logging	2		Open
1.8.1.3	Search	3		Open

(Thanks to Priya Padmanhabhan for suggesting this example.)

FIGURE 2-12
Work Breakdown Structure

tasks focuses on one of the required design deliverables. Within each task, there are subtasks listed that detail the activities required to complete the main task.

The work breakdown structure can be organized in one of two ways: by SDLC phase or by product. For example, if a firm decided that it needed to develop a Web site, the firm could create a work breakdown structure based on the SDLC phases: planning, analysis, design, and implementation. In this case, a typical task that would take place during planning would be feasibility analysis. This task would be broken down into the different types of feasibility analysis: technical, economic, and organizational. Each of these would be further broken down into a series of subtasks. Alternatively, the firm could organize the work plan along the lines of the different products to be developed. In the case of a Web site, for example, the products could include applets, application servers, database servers, the various sets of Web pages, a site map, and so on. Each of these products could be decomposed into the different tasks associated with the phases of the SDLC. With either approach, once the overall structure is determined, tasks are identified and included in the work breakdown structure of the work plan.

The number of tasks and level of detail depend on the complexity and size of the project. The larger the project, the more important it becomes to define tasks in detail so that essential steps are not overlooked.

The Project Work Plan   The project work plan is the mechanism used to manage the tasks that are listed in the work breakdown structure. It is the project manager's primary tool for managing the project. Using it, the project manager can tell whether the project is ahead of or behind schedule, how well the project was estimated, and what changes need to be made to meet the project deadline.

Basically, the work plan is a table that lists all of the tasks in the work breakdown structure, along with important task information such as the people who are assigned to perform the tasks, the actual hours that the tasks took, and the variances between estimated and actual completion times. (See Figure 2-13). At a minimum, the information should include the duration of the task, the current statuses of the tasks (i.e., open, complete), and the *task dependencies,* which occur when one task cannot be performed until another task is completed. For example, Figure 2-13 shows that task 1.2 and task 1.3 cannot begin until task 1.1 is completed. Key *milestones,* or important dates, are also identified on the work plan. Presentations to the approval committee, the start of end-user training, a company retreat, and the due date of the system prototype are the types of milestones that may be important to track.

STAFFING THE PROJECT

Staffing the project includes determining how many people should be assigned to the project, matching people's skills with the needs of the project, motivating them to meet the project's objectives, and minimizing project team conflict that will occur over time. The deliverable for this part of project management is a staffing plan, which describes the number and kinds of people who will work on the pro-ject, the overall reporting structure, and the project charter, which describes the project's objectives and rules.

Staffing Plan

The first step to staffing is determining the average number of staff needed for the project. To calculate this figure, divide the total person-months of effort by the

Task ID	Task Name	Assigned To	Estimated				Actual			Dependency	Status
			Duration (days)	Start Date	Finish Date		Start Date	Finish Date	Duration variance		
1	Design Phase		31	Fri 11/19/10	Fri 12/31/10						Open
1.1	Develop database design document	Megan	9	Mon 12/6/10	Thurs 12/16/10						Open
1.1.1	Staging database design	Megan	9	Mon 12/6/10	Thurs 12/16/10						Open
1.1.2	Suspense database design	Megan	9	Mon 12/6/10	Thurs 12/16/10						Open
1.2	Develop rejects-handling design document	Megan	9	Fri 12/17/10	Wed 12/29/10					1.1.1, 1.1.2	Open
1.2.1	Rejects-handling engine design	Megan	9	Fri 12/17/10	Fri 12/29/10						Open
1.3	Develop OLAP design document	Joachim	9	Fri 12/17/10	Wed 12/29/10					1.1.1, 1.1.2	Open
1.3.1	Universe design	Joachim	9	Fri 12/17/10	Wed 12/29/10						Open
1.4	Develop OLAP design part 1	Kevin	8	Fri 12/10/10	Tues 12/21/10						Open
1.4.1	High-priority reports design	Kevin	8	Fri 12/10/10	Tues 12/21/10						Open
1.5	Develop application design document	Tomas	9	Fri 12/17/10	Wed 12/29/10						Open
1.5.1	Group consolidation and corporate reporting (GCCR) maintenance application design	Tomas	9	Fri 12/17/10	Wed 12/29/10						Open

(Continued)

FIGURE 2-13
Project Work Plan

Task ID	Task Name	Assigned To	Estimated Duration (days)	Estimated Start Date	Estimated Finish Date	Actual Start Date	Actual Finish Date	Duration Variance	Dependency	Status
1.6	Extract, transform, load (ETL) design document	Joachim	2	Thu 12/30/10	Fri 12/31/10					Open
1.6.1	Data export utility design	Joachim	2	Thu 12/30/10	Fri 12/31/10					Open
1.7	Application design document	Mei-ling	25	Fri 11/19/10	Fri 12/24/10					Open
1.7.1	Web entry application UI design	Mei-ling	25	Fri 11/19/10	Fri 12/24/10					Open
1.7.2	Web entry application UI design signoff	Mei-ling	1	Fri 12/3/10	Fri 12/3/10					Open
1.7.3	Web entry forms and database model validation	Kevin	11	Wed 11/24/10	Wed 12/8/10					Open
1.8	Functional requirements document	Chantelle	9	Mon 12/13/10	Thu 12/23/10					Open
1.8.1	Application design	Chantelle	9	Mon 12/13/10	Thu 12/23/10					Open
1.8.1.1	User authentication	Chantelle	4	Mon 12/13/10	Thu 12/16/10					Open
1.8.1.2	Call logging	Chantelle	2	Fri 12/17/10	Mon 12/20/10					Oper
1.8.1.3	Search	Chantelle	3	Tue 12/21/10	Thu 12/23/10					Open

(Thanks to Priya Padmanhabhan for suggesting this example.)

FIGURE 2-13
Project Work Plan

2-4 COMMUNICATION COMPLEXITY

Figure 2-14 shows the increasing number of communication channels that exist as a team grows from two members to four members. Using the figure as a guide, draw the number of communication channels that will be needed in a six-member team. Now, determine the number of communication channels that will be needed in an eight-person team.

QUESTIONS:

1. How many communication channels are there in the six-member team? The eight-member team?
2. From your results, how effective do you think a 12-member team would be? A 16-member team?

optimal schedule. So to complete a 40 person-month project in 10 months, a team should have an average of four full-time staff members, although this may change over time as different specialists enter and leave the team (e.g., business analysts, programmers, technical writers).

Many times, the temptation is to assign more staff to a project to shorten the project's length, but this is not a wise move. Adding staff resources does not translate into increased productivity; staff size and productivity share a disproportionate relationship, mainly because a large number of staff members is more difficult to coordinate. The more a team grows, the more difficult it becomes to manage. Imagine how easy it is to work on a two-person project team: the team members share a single line of communication. But adding two people increases the number of communication lines to six, and greater increases lead to more dramatic gains in communication complexity. Figure 2-14 and Your Turn 2-4 illustrate the impact of adding team members to a project team.

One way to reduce efficiency losses on teams is to understand the complexity that is created in numbers and to build in a *reporting structure* that tempers its effects. The rule of thumb is to keep team sizes under 8 to 10 people; therefore, if more people are needed, create subteams. In this way, the project manager can keep the communication effective within small teams, which in turn communicate to a contact at a higher level in the project.

After the project manager understands how many people are needed for the project, he or she creates a *staffing plan* that lists the roles that are required for the project and the proposed reporting structure for the project. Typically, a project will

FIGURE 2-14

Increasing Complexity with Larger Teams

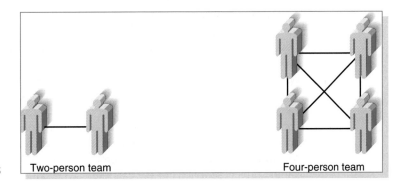

Two-person team

Four-person team

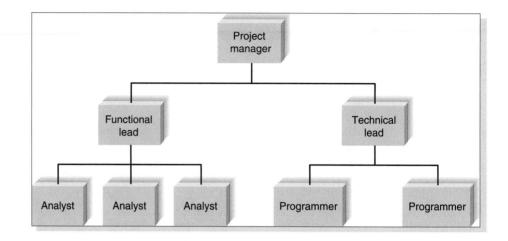

FIGURE 2-15
Possible Reporting Structure

have one project manager who oversees the overall progress of the development effort, with the core of the team composed of the various types of analysts described in Chapter 1. A *functional lead* usually is assigned to manage a group of analysts, and a *technical lead* oversees the progress of a group of programmers and more technical staff members.

There are many structures for project teams; Figure 2-15 illustrates one possible configuration of a project team. After the roles are defined and the structure is in place, the project manager needs to think about which people can fill each role. Often, one person fills more than one role on a project team.

When you make assignments, remember that people have *technical skills* and *interpersonal skills,* and both are important on a project. Technical skills are useful for working with technical tasks (e.g., programming in Java) and in trying to understand the various roles that technology plays in the particular project (e.g., how a Web server should be configured on the basis of a projected number of hits from customers).

Interpersonal skills, on the other hand, include interpersonal and communication abilities that are used when dealing with business users, senior management executives, and other members of the project team. They are particularly critical for performing the requirements-gathering activities and when addressing organizational feasibility issues. Each project will require unique technical and interpersonal skills. For example, a Web-based project may require Internet experience or Java programming knowledge, or a highly controversial project may need analysts who are particularly adept at managing political or volatile situations.

Ideally, project roles are filled with people who have the right skills for the job; however, the people who fit the roles best may not be available; they may be working on other projects, or they may not exist in the company. Therefore, assigning project team members really is a combination of finding people with the appropriate skill sets and finding people who are available. When the skills of the available project team members do not match those actually required by the project, the project manager has several options to improve the situation. First, people can be pulled off other projects, and resources can be shuffled around. This is the most disruptive approach from the organization's perspective. Another approach is to use outside help—such as a consultant or contractor—to train team members and start them off on the right foot. Training classes are usually available for both technical and interpersonal instruction, if time is available. Mentoring may also be an option; a project team member can be sent to work on another similar project so that he or she can return with skills to apply to the current job.

Don'ts	Reasons
Assign unrealistic deadlines	Few people will work hard if they realize that a deadline is impossible to meet.
Ignore good efforts	People will work harder if they feel that their work is appreciated. Often, all it takes is public praise for a job well done.
Create a low-quality product	Few people can be proud of working on a project that is of low quality.
Give everyone on the project a raise	If everyone is given the same reward, then high-quality people will believe that mediocrity is rewarded—and they will resent it.
Make an important decision without the team's input	Buy-in is very important. If the project manager needs to make a decision that greatly affects the members of her team, she should involve them in the decision-making process.
Maintain poor working conditions	A project team needs a good working environment, or motivation will go down the tubes. This includes lighting, desk space, technology, privacy from interruptions, and reference resources.

Source: Adapted from *Rapid Development,* Redmond, WA: Microsoft Press, 1996, by Steve McConnell.

FIGURE 2-16
Motivational Don'ts

Motivation   Assigning people to tasks isn't enough; project managers need to motivate the people to make the project a success. *Motivation* has been found to be the number-one influence on people's performance,[16] but determining how to motivate the team can be quite difficult. You may think that good project managers motivate their staff by rewarding them with money and bonuses, but most project managers agree that this is the last thing that should be done. The more often you reward team members with money, the more they expect it—and most times monetary motivation won't work.

Assuming that team members are paid a fair salary, technical employees on project teams are much more motivated by recognition, achievement, the work itself, responsibility, advancement, and the chance to learn new skills.[17] If you feel that you need to give some kind of reward for motivational purposes, try a pizza or free dinner, or even a kind letter or award. These often have much more effective results. Figure 2-16 lists some other motivational don'ts that you should avoid to ensure that motivation on the project is as high as possible.

Handling Conflict   The third component of staffing is organizing the project to minimize conflict among group members. *Group cohesiveness* (the attraction that members feel to the group and to other members) contributes more to productivity than do project members' individual capabilities or experiences.[18] Clearly defining the roles

[16] Barry W. Boehm, *Software Engineering Economics,* Englewood Cliffs, NJ: Prentice Hall, 1981. One of the best books on managing project teams is by Tom DeMarco and Timothy Lister, *Peopleware: Productive Projects and Teams,* New York: Dorset House, 1987.

[17] F. H. Hertzberg, "One More Time: How Do You Motivate Employees?" *Harvard Business Review,* 1968, January–February.

[18] B. Lakhanpal, "Understanding the Factors Influencing the Performance of Software Development Groups: An Exploratory Group-Level Analysis," *Information and Software Technology,* 1993, 35(8):468–473.

2-F RFID Promising technology

Some animals are extremely valuable. For centuries, horse thieves have stolen horses. Until now, most horses have identifying tattoos in their mouths. Likewise, purebred pets, such as dog show winners, are valuable animals. What if there was a better way to identify valuable animals?

Radio-frequency identification (or RFID) has been used in airplanes and on toll roads (consider EZPass and Sun Pass in the United States), as well as in libraries so that books and materials are not taken out of the library without being checked out. With RFID, when a low-frequency radio transmitter is bombarded with a radio wave, it replies with a unique signal. Some animal owners have inserted RFID chips into their pets' shoulders so that the animals can be identified. The code is unique and cannot be changed. If a racehorse is stolen, it could be tracked if it came within the range of an RFID device. Likewise, a pet shop or a veterinarian could identify a valuable pet.

QUESTIONS:
1. If you were working for a state consumer protection agency, what requirements might you place on pet shops to ensure that animals for sale have not been stolen?
2. What technological requirements might be needed in the proposed system?
3. What ethical issues might be involved?
4. If your system project team did not have the correct technical background, what might you do?

on the project and holding team members accountable for their tasks is a good way to begin mitigating potential conflict on a project. Some project managers develop a *project charter* that lists the project's norms and ground rules. For example, the charter may describe when the project team should be at work, when staff meetings will be held, how the group will communicate with each other, and the procedures for updating the work plan as tasks are completed. Figure 2-17 lists additional techniques that can be used at the start of a project to keep conflict to a minimum.

Coordinating Project Activities

Like all project management responsibilities, the act of coordinating project activities continues throughout the entire project until a system is delivered to the project sponsor and end users. This step includes putting efficient development practices in

---

- Clearly define plans for the project.
- Make sure the team understands how the project is important to the organization.
- Develop detailed operating procedures and communicate these to the team members.
- Develop a project charter.
- Develop schedule commitments ahead of time.
- Forecast other priorities and their possible impact on project.

Source: H. J. Thamhain and D. L. Wilemon, "Conflict Management in Project Life Cycles," *Sloan Management Review,* Spring 1975.

FIGURE 2-17
Conflict Avoidance Strategies

place and mitigating risk. These activities occur over the course of the entire SDLC, but it is at this point in the project that the project manager needs to put them in place. Ultimately, these activities ensure that the project stays on track and that the chance of failure is kept at a minimum. The rest of this section will describe each of these activities in more detail.

CASE Tools *Computer-aided software engineering* (*CASE*) is a category of software that automates all or part of the development process. Some CASE software packages are primarily used during the analysis phase to create integrated diagrams of the system and to store information regarding the system components (often called *upper CASE*), whereas others are design-phase tools that create the diagrams and then generate code for database tables and system functionality (often called *lower CASE*). *Integrated CASE,* or I-CASE, contains functionality found in both upper-CASE and lower-CASE tools in that it supports tasks that happen throughout the SDLC. CASE comes in a wide assortment of flavors in terms of complexity and functionality, and there are many good programs available in the marketplace, such as the Visible Analyst Workbench, Oracle Designer, Rational Rose, and the Logic Works suite.

The benefits of using CASE are numerous. With CASE tools, tasks are much faster to complete and alter; development information is centralized; and information is illustrated through diagrams, which typically are easier to understand. Potentially, CASE can reduce maintenance costs, improve software quality, and enforce discipline; and some project teams even use CASE to assess the magnitude of changes to the project.

Of course, like anything else, CASE should not be considered a silver bullet for project development. The advanced CASE tools are complex applications that require significant training and experience to achieve real benefits. Often, CASE serves only as a glorified diagramming tool that supports the practices described in Chapter 5 (process modeling) and Chapter 6 (data modeling). Our experience has shown that CASE is a helpful way to support the communication and sharing of project diagrams and technical specifications—as long as it is used by trained developers who have applied CASE on past projects.

The central component of any CASE tool is the *CASE repository*, otherwise known as the information repository or data dictionary. The CASE repository stores the diagrams and other project information, such as screen and report designs, and it keeps track of how the diagrams fit together. For example, most CASE tools will warn you if you place a field on a screen design that doesn't exist in your data model. As the project evolves, project team members perform their tasks by using CASE. As you read through the textbook, we will indicate when and how the CASE tool can be used so that you can see how CASE supports the project tasks.

Standards Members of a project team need to work together, and most project management software and CASE tools provide access privileges to everyone working on the system. When people work together, however, things can get pretty confusing. To make matters worse, people sometimes get reassigned in the middle of a project. It is important that their project knowledge does not leave with them and that their replacements can get up to speed quickly.

Standards are created to ensure that team members are performing tasks in the same way and following the same procedures. Standards can range from

2-5 COMPUTER-AIDED SOFTWARE ENGINEERING TOOL ANALYSIS

Select a computer-aided software engineering (CASE) tool—either one that you will use for class, a program that you own, or a tool that you can examine over the Web. Create a list of the capabilities that are offered by the CASE tool.

QUESTION:
Would you classify the CASE as upper CASE, lower CASE, or integrated CASE (I-CASE)? Why?

formal rules for naming files to forms that must be completed when goals are reached to programming guidelines. See Figure 2-18 for some examples of the types of standards that a project may include. When a team forms standards and then follows them, the project can be completed faster because task coordination becomes less complex.

Types of Standards	Examples
Documentation standards	The date and project name should appear as a header on all documentation.
	All margins should be set to 1 inch.
	All deliverables should be added to the project binder and recorded in its table of contents.
Coding standards	All modules of code should include a header that lists the programmer, last date of update, and a short description of the purpose of the code.
	Indentation should be used to indicate loops, if-then-else statements, and case statements.
	On average, every program should include one line of comments for every five lines of code.
Procedural standards	Record actual task progress in the work plan every Monday morning by 10 A.M.
	Report to project update meeting on Fridays at 3:30 P.M.
	All changes to a requirements document must be approved by the project manager.
Specification requirement standards	Name of program to be created
	Description of the program's purpose
	Special calculations that need to be computed
	Business rules that must be incorporated into the program
	Pseudocode
	Due date
User interface design standards	Labels will appear in boldface text, left-justified, and followed by a colon.
	The tab order of the screen will move from top left to bottom right.
	Accelerator keys will be provided for all updatable fields.

FIGURE 2-18
A Sampling of Project Standards

Standards work best when they are created at the beginning of each major phase of the project and well communicated to the entire project team. As the team moves forward, new standards are added when necessary. Some standards (e.g., file-naming conventions, status reporting) are applied to the entire SDLC, whereas others (e.g., programming guidelines) are appropriate only for certain tasks.

Documentation   Another technique that project teams put in place during the planning phase is good *documentation*, which includes detailed information about the tasks of the SDLC. Often, the documentation is stored in *project binder* (*s*) that contain all the deliverables and all the internal communication that takes place—the history of the project.

A poor project management practice is permitting the project team to wait until the last minute to create documentation. This typically leads to an undocumented system that no one understands. In fact, many problems that companies had in updating their systems to handle the year-2000 crisis were the result of the lack of documentation. Good project teams learn to document the system's history as it evolves, while the details are still fresh in their memory.

A simple way to set up your documentation is to get some binders and use dividers to separate content according to the major phases of the project. An additional divider should contain internal communication, such as the minutes from status meetings, written standards, letters to and from the business users, and a dictionary of relevant business terms. Then, as the project moves forward, place the deliverables from each task into the project binder with descriptions so that someone outside of the project will be able to understand it, and keep a table of contents up to date with the content that is added. Documentation takes time up front, but it is a good investment that will pay off in the long run.

MANAGING AND CONTROLLING THE PROJECT

The science (or art) of project management is in making *trade-offs* among three important concepts: the size of the system (in terms of what it does), the time to complete the project (when the project will be finished), and the cost of the project. Think of these three things as interdependent levers that the project manager controls throughout the SDLC. Whenever one lever is pulled, the other two levers are affected in some way. For example, if a project manager needs to readjust a deadline to an earlier date, then the only solution is to decrease the size of the system (by eliminating some of its functions) or to increase costs by adding more people or having team members work overtime. Often, a project manager will have to work with the project sponsor to change the goals of the project, such as developing a system with less functionality or extending the deadline for the final system, so that the project has reasonable goals that can be met.

Therefore, in the beginning of the project, the manager needs to estimate each of these levers and then continuously assess how to roll out the project in a way that meets the organization's needs.

Once the project begins, the project manager monitors the progress of the team on the project tasks. As the project team members make periodic status reports, the project manager updates the project work plan. As discussed in Appendix 2B, the Gantt chart and PERT chart are valuable tools for the project manager to use to evaluate project progress and, if necessary, redirect resources. As the project

CONCEPTS **2-G** TRADE-OFFS

IN ACTION

I was once on a project to develop a system that should have taken a year to build. Instead, the business need demanded that the system be ready within 5 months—impossible!

On the first day of the project, the project manager drew a triangle on a white board to illustrate some tradeoffs that he expected to occur over the course of the project. The corners of the triangle were labeled Functionality, Time, and Money. The manager explained, "We have too little time. We have an unlimited budget. We will not be measured by the bells and whistles that this system contains. So over the next several weeks, I want you as developers to keep this triangle in mind and do everything it takes to meet this 5-month deadline."

At the end of the 5 months, the project was delivered on time; however, the project was incredibly over budget, and the final product was "thrown away" after it was used because it was unfit for regular usage. Remarkably, the business users felt that the project was very successful because it met the very specific business needs for which it was built. They believed that the trade-offs that were made were worthwhile. *Barbara Wixom*

QUESTIONS:
1. What are the risks in stressing only one corner of the triangle?
2. How would you have managed this project? Can you think of another approach that might have been more effective?

proceeds, it may be necessary for the project manager to revise the original estimates made for the project. In addition, the manager must be on the watch for increases in project scope, which can make completing the project on time and under budget very difficult. Finally, the project manager should constantly assess the risk profile of the project and take steps to manage those risks.

Refining Estimates

The estimates that are produced during the planning phase will need to be refined as the project progresses. This does not necessarily mean that estimates were poorly done at the start of the project; it is virtually impossible to develop an exact assessment of the project's schedule before the analysis and design phases are conducted. A project manager should expect to be satisfied with broad ranges of estimates that become more and more specific as the project's product becomes better defined.

In the planning phase, when a system is first requested, the project sponsor and project manager attempt to predict how long the SDLC will take, how much it will cost, and what the system will ultimately do when it is delivered (i.e., its functionality). However, the estimates are based on very little knowledge of the system. As the project moves into the analysis phase, more information is gathered, the system concept is developed, and the estimates become even more accurate and precise. As the system moves closer to completion, the accuracy and precision increase until the final system is delivered.

According to one of the leading experts in software development,[19] a well-done project plan (prepared at the end of the planning phase) has a 100% margin

[19] Barry W. Boehm and colleagues, "Cost Models for Future Software Life Cycle Processes: COCOMO 2.0," in J. D. Arthur and S. M. Henry (eds), *Annals of Software Engineering: Special Volume on Software Process and Product Measurement,* Amsterdam: J. C. Baltzer AG Science Publishers, 1995.

Phase	Deliverable	Typical Margins of Error for Well-Done Estimates	
		Cost (%)	Schedule Time (%)
Planning phase	System request	400	60
	Project plan	100	25
Analysis phase	System proposal	50	15
Design phase	System specifications	25	10

Source: Barry W. Boehm and colleagues, "Cost Models for Future Software Life Cycle Processes: COCOMO 2.0," in J. D. Arthur and S. M. Henry (eds.) *Annals of Software Engineering Special Volume on Software Process and Product Measurement,* Amsterdam: J. C. Baltzer AG Science Publishers, 1995.

FIGURE 2-19
Margins of Error in Cost and Time Estimates

of error for project cost and a 25% margin of error for schedule time. In other words, if a carefully done project plan estimates that a project will cost $100,000 and take 20 weeks, the project will actually cost between $0 and $200,000 and take between 15 and 25 weeks. Figure 2-19 presents typical margins of error for other stages in the project. It is important to note that these margins of error apply only to well-done plans; a plan developed without much care has a much greater margin of error.

What happens if you overshoot an estimate (e.g., the analysis phase ends up lasting two weeks longer than expected)? There are a number of ways to adjust future estimates. If the project team finishes a step ahead of schedule, most project managers shift the deadlines sooner by the same amount but do not adjust the promised completion date. The challenge, however, occurs when the project team is late in meeting a scheduled date. Three possible responses to missed schedule dates are presented in Figure 2-20. We recommend that if an estimate proves too optimistic early in the project, do not expect to make up for lost time—very few projects end up working this way. Instead, change your future estimates to include an increase similar to the one that was experienced. For example, if the first phase was completed 10% over schedule, increase the rest of your estimates by 10%.

Managing Scope

You may assume that your project will be safe from scheduling problems because you carefully estimated and planned your project up front. However, the most common reason for schedule and cost overruns occurs after the project is underway—*scope creep.*

Scope creep happens when new requirements are added to the project after the original project scope was defined and "frozen." It can happen for many reasons: Users may suddenly understand the potential of the new system and realize new functionality that would be useful; developers may discover interesting capabilities to which they become very attached; a senior manager may decide to let this system support a new strategy that was developed at a recent board meeting.

Unfortunately, after the project begins, it becomes increasingly difficult to address changing requirements. The ramifications of change become more extensive, the focus is removed from original goals, and there is at least some impact on

Assumptions	Actions	Level of Risk
If you assume that the rest of the project is simpler than the part that was late and is also simpler than believed when the original schedule estimates were made, you can make up lost time.	Do not change schedule.	High risk
If you assume that the rest of the project is simpler than the part that was late and is no more complex than the original estimate assumed, you can't make up the lost time, but you will not lose time on the rest of the project.	Increase the entire schedule by the total amount of time that you are behind (e.g., if you missed the scheduled date by two weeks, move the rest of the schedule dates to two weeks later). If you included padded time at the end of the project in the original schedule, you may not have to change the promised system delivery date; you'll just use up the padded time.	Moderate risk
If you assume that the rest of the project is as complex as the part that was late (your original estimates were too optimistic), then all the scheduled dates in the future underestimate the real time required by the same percentage as the part that was late.	Increase the entire schedule by the percentage of weeks that you are behind (e.g., if you are two weeks late on part of the project that was supposed to take eight weeks, you need to increase all remaining time estimates by 25%). If this moves the new delivery date beyond what is acceptable to the project sponsor, the scope of the project must be reduced.	Low risk

FIGURE 2-20
Possible Actions When a Schedule Date
Is Missed

cost and schedule. Therefore, the project manager must actively work to keep the project tight and focused.

The keys are to identify the requirements as well as possible in the beginning of the project and to apply analysis techniques effectively. For example, if needs are fuzzy at the project's onset, a combination of intensive meetings with the users and prototyping could be used so that users "experience" the requirements and better visualize how the system could support their needs. In fact, the use of meetings and prototyping has been found to reduce scope creep to less than 5% on a typical project.

Of course, some requirements may be missed no matter what precautions you take, but several practices can help to control additions to the task list. First, the project manager should allow only absolutely necessary requirements to be added after the project begins. Even at that point, members of the project team should carefully assess the ramifications of the addition and present the assessment back to the users. For example, it may require two more person-months of work to create a newly defined report, which would throw off the entire project deadline by several weeks. Any change that is implemented should be carefully tracked so that an audit trail exists to measure the change's impact.

Sometimes, changes cannot be incorporated into the present system even though they truly would be beneficial. In this case, these additions to scope should be recorded as future enhancements to the system. The project manager can offer to provide functionality in future releases of the system, thus getting around telling someone no.

Timeboxing

Another approach to scope management is a technique called *timeboxing*. Up until now, we have described projects that are task oriented. In other words, we have described projects that have a schedule that is driven by the tasks that need to be accomplished, so the greater number of tasks and requirements, the longer the project will take. Some companies have little patience for development projects that take a long time, and these companies take a time-oriented approach that places meeting a deadline above delivering functionality.

Think about your use of word processing software. For 80% of the time, you probably use only 20% of the features, such as the spelling checker, boldfacing, and cutting and pasting. Other features, such as document merging and creation of mailing labels, may be nice to have, but they are not a part of your day-to-day needs. The same goes for other software applications; most users rely on only a small subset of their capabilities. Ironically, most developers agree that, typically, 75% of a system can be provided relatively quickly, with the remaining 25% of the functionality demanding most of the time.

To resolve this incongruency, a technique called timeboxing has become quite popular, especially when rapid application development (RAD) methodologies are used. This technique sets a fixed deadline for a project and delivers the system by that deadline no matter what, even if functionality needs to be reduced. Timeboxing ensures that project teams don't get hung up on the final "finishing touches" that can drag out indefinitely, and it satisfies the business by providing a product within a relatively fast time frame.

There are several steps to implementing timeboxing on a project (Figure 2-21). First, set the date of delivery for the proposed goals. The deadline should not be impossible to meet, so it is best to let the project team determine a realistic due date. Next, build the core of the system to be delivered; you will find that timeboxing helps create a sense of urgency and helps keep the focus on the most important features. Because the schedule is absolutely fixed, functionality that cannot be completed needs to be postponed. It helps if the team prioritizes a list of features beforehand to keep track of what functionality the users absolutely need. Quality cannot be compromised, regardless of other constraints, so it is important that the time allocated to activities is not shortened unless the requirements are changed (e.g., don't reduce the time allocated to testing without reducing features). At the end of the period, a high-quality system is delivered. Likely, future iterations will be needed to make changes and enhancements, and the timeboxing approach can be used once again.

1. Set the date for system delivery.
2. Prioritize the functionality that needs to be included in the system.
3. Build the core of the system (the functionality ranked as most important).
4. Postpone functionality that cannot be provided within the time frame.
5. Deliver the system with core functionality.
6. Repeat steps 3 through 5, to add refinements and enhancements.

FIGURE 2-21
Steps for Timeboxing

CONCEPTS   **2-H MANAGING A LATE PROJECT: WHEN TO SAY "WHEN"?**

IN ACTION

System projects are notorious for being late and over budget. When should management stop a project that is late or costing more than the intended budget? Consider this case:

Valley Enterprises opted to implement Voice over Internet Protocol (VoIP) service in its Phoenix, Arizona, service area. The company has 15 locations in the Phoenix area, all with local area networks and all with secure Wi-Fi connections. The company's current phone system was designed and implemented in the 1950s, when Valley operated in three locations. As more locations were added, standard telecommunications solutions were implemented, with little thought devoted to compatibility. Over the years, phone services were added as new buildings and facilities arose. Valley CEO Doug Wilson heard of VoIP at a trade show and contacted TMR Telecommunications Consultants, requesting a bid. TMR spent a week with the CIO of Valley Enterprises, gathering data, and submitted a bid for $50,000 in late 2007. The project was to be started by March 2008 and completed by January 2009. The bid was accepted.

TMR started the project in March 2008. In late July 2008, TMR was bought out by Advanced Communications of Scottsdale, Arizona. The merger delayed the project by over a month initially. In early September 2008, some of the same personnel from TMR, as well as a new project manager from Advanced Communications, went back to the project.

By March 2009, the project had already cost $150,000 and only 8 of the locations had implemented VoIP. Advanced Communications insisted that the local area networks were obsolete and were unable to carry the expanded load without major upgrades to the bandwidth, the routers, and other telecommunications equipment.

QUESTIONS:

1. Is it time to end this project? Why or why not?
2. What negotiations should have occured between TMR and Valley Enterprises prior to December 2008?
3. What should a project manager/project coordinator from Valley Enterprises have done when the project first started to slip?

Managing Risk

One final facet of project management is *risk management*, the process of assessing and addressing the risks that are associated with developing a project. Many things can cause risks: weak personnel, scope creep, poor design, and overly optimistic estimates. The project team must be aware of potential risks so that problems can be avoided or controlled well ahead of time.

Typically, project teams create a *risk assessment*, or a document that tracks potential risks along with an evaluation of the likelihood of the risk and its potential impact on the project (Figure 2-22). A paragraph or two is included that explains potential ways that the risk can be addressed. There are many options: A risk could be publicized, avoided, or even eliminated by dealing with its root cause. For example, imagine that a project team plans to use new technology, but its members have identified a risk in the fact that its members do not have the right technical skills. They believe that tasks may take much longer to perform because of a high learning curve. One plan of attack could be to eliminate the root cause of the risk— the lack of technical experience by team members—by finding time and resources that are needed to provide proper training to the team.

2-1 POOR NAMING STANDARDS

I once started on a small project (four people) in which the original members of the project team had not set up any standards for naming electronic files. Two weeks into the project, I was asked to write a piece of code that would be referenced by other files that had already been written. When I finished my piece, I had to go back to the other files and make changes to reflect my new work. The only problem was that the lead programmer decided to name the files using his initials (e.g., GG1.prg, GG2.prg, GG3.prg)—and there were over 200 files! I spent two days opening every one of those files because there was no way to tell what their contents were.

Needless to say, from then on, the team created a code for file names that provided basic information regarding the file's contents and they kept a log that recorded the file name, its purpose, the date of last update, and programmer for every file on the project.

Barbara Wixom

QUESTION:

Think about a program that you have written in the past. Would another programmer be able to make changes to it easily? Why or why not?

Most project managers keep abreast of potential risks, even prioritizing them according to their magnitude and importance. Over time, the list of risks will change as some items are removed and others surface. The best project managers, however, work hard to keep risks from having an impact on the schedule and costs associated with the project.

RISK ASSESSMENT

RISK #1: The development of this system likely will be slowed considerably because project team members have not programmed in Java prior to this project.

Likelihood of risk: High probability of risk

Potential impact on the project: This risk likely will increase the time to complete programming tasks by 50%.

Ways to address this risk:
It is very important that time and resources are allocated to up-front training in Java for the programmers who are used for this project. Adequate training will reduce the initial learning curve for Java when programming begins. Additionally, outside Java expertise should be brought in for at least some part of the early programming tasks. This person should be used to provide experiential knowledge to the project team so that Java-related issues (of which novice Java programmers would be unaware) are overcome.

RISK #2:
etc....

FIGURE 2-22
Sample Risk Assessment

APPLYING THE CONCEPTS AT TUNE SOURCE

Jason Wells was very excited about managing the Digital Music Download project at Tune Source, but he realized that his project team should move rapidly to deliver at least some parts of the system because of the company's desire to bring the application to market as quickly as possible. Therefore, he decided that the project should follow a RAD iterative development methodology, combined with the timeboxing technique. In this way, he could be sure that some version of the system would be operational within several months, even if the final system was delivered at a later date.

Jason knew that Carly Edwards and Tune Source's top managers wanted at least general ranges for a product delivery date. He expected to spend three weeks planning the project. Therefore, using industry standard percentages, he estimated that the entire project should be complete in 20 weeks (3 weeks/15%). Recall from Figure 2-10 that the planning phase typically takes 15% of the entire project. Jason's initial plan was to develop the basic music download purchase capability in the first version of the system. The second version will add the subscription purchase capability, and the third version will add the gift card purchase capability.

PRACTICAL TIP

2-1 AVOIDING CLASSIC PLANNING MISTAKES

As Seattle University's David Umphress has pointed out, watching most organizations develop systems is like watching reruns of *Gilligan's Island*. At the beginning of each episode, someone comes up with a cockamamie scheme to get off the island that seems to work for a while, but something goes wrong and the castaways find themselves right back where they started—stuck on the island. Similarly, most companies start new projects with grand ideas that seem to work, only to make a classic mistake and deliver the project behind schedule, over budget, or both. Here we summarize four classic mistakes in the planning and project management aspects of the project and discuss how to avoid them:

1. **Overly optimistic schedule:** Wishful thinking can lead to an overly optimistic schedule that causes analysis and design to be cut short (missing key requirements) and puts intense pressure on the programmers, who produce poor code (full of bugs).
   Solution: Don't inflate time estimates; instead, explicitly schedule slack time at the end of each phase to account for the variability in estimates, using the margins of error from Figure 2-19.
2. **Failing to monitor the schedule:** If the team does not regularly report progress, no one knows if the project is on schedule.

Solution: Require team members to honestly report progress (or the lack of progress) every week. There is no penalty for reporting a lack of progress, but there are immediate sanctions for a misleading report.

3. **Failing to update the schedule:** When a part of the schedule falls behind (e.g., information gathering uses all of the slack in item 1 above plus 2 weeks), a project team often thinks it can make up the time later by working faster. It can't. This is an early warning that the entire schedule is too optimistic.
   Solution: Immediately revise the schedule and inform the project sponsor of the new end date or use timeboxing to reduce functionality or to move it into future versions.
4. **Adding people to a late project:** When a project misses a schedule, the temptation is to add more people to speed it up. This makes the project take longer because it increases coordination problems and requires staff to take time to explain what has already been done.
   Solution: Revise the schedule, use timeboxing, throw away bug-filled code, and add people only to work on an isolated part of the project.

Source: Adapted from *Rapid Development*, Redmond, WA: Microsoft Press, 1996, pp. 29–50, by Steve McConnell.

With a general time frame determined, Jason began to identify the tasks that would be needed to complete the system. He used a RAD methodology that Tune Source had in-house, and he borrowed its high-level phases (e.g., analysis) and the major tasks associated with them (e.g., create requirements definition, gather requirements, analyze current system). These were recorded in a work plan created in Microsoft Project. Jason expected to define the steps in much more detail at the beginning of each phase (Figure 2-23).

Staffing the Project

Jason next turned to the task of how to staff his project. According to his earlier estimates, it appeared that about three people would be needed to deliver the system.

First, he created a list of the various roles that he needed to fill. He thought he would need several analysts to work with the analysis and design of the Digital Music Download system, as well as an infrastructure analyst to manage the integration of the system with Tune Source's existing technical environment. Jason also needed people who had good programming skills and who could be responsible for ultimately implementing the system. Kenji, Ming, and Maria are three analysts with strong technical and interpersonal skills (although Kenji is less balanced, having greater technical than interpersonal abilities), and Jason believed that they were available to bring onto this project. He wasn't certain whether they had experience with the actual Web technology that would be used on the project, but he decided to rely on vendor training or an external consultant to build those skills later when they were needed. Because the project was so small, Jason envisioned all of the team members reporting to him because he would be serving as the project's manager.

Jason created a staffing plan that captured this information, and he included a special incentive structure in the plan (Figure 2-24). Rapid implementation was very important to the project's success, so he decided to offer a day off to the team members who contributed to meeting that date. He hoped that this incentive would motivate the team to work very hard. Jason also planned to budget money for pizza and sodas for times when the team worked long hours.

Before he left for the day, Jason drafted a project charter, to be fine-tuned after the team got together for its *kick-off meeting* (i.e., the first time the project team gets together). The charter listed several norms that Jason wanted to put in place from the start to eliminate any misunderstanding or problems that could come up otherwise (Figure 2-25).

Coordinating Project Activities

Jason wanted the Digital Music Download project to be well coordinated, so he immediately put several practices in place to support his responsibilities. First, he acquired the CASE tool used at Tune Source and set up the product so that it could be used for the analysis-phase tasks (e.g., drawing the data flow diagrams). The team members would likely start creating diagrams and defining components of the system fairly early on. He pulled out some standards that he uses on all development projects and made a note to review them with his project team at the kick-off meeting for the system. He also had his assistant set up binders for the project deliverables that would start rolling in. Already, he was able to include the system request, feasibility analysis, initial work plan, staffing plan, project charter, standards list, and risk assessment.

ID	Task Name	Duration	Start	Finish	Predecessors	Resource Names
1	**Overall analysis**	10 days	Mon 2/1/10	Fri 2/12/10		
2	**Identify High-Level Requirements**	6 days	Mon 2/1/10	Mon 2/8/10		
3	JAD session	4 days	Mon 2/1/10	Thu 2/4/10		Jason, Carly, Ming
4	Informal benchmarking	2 days	Fri 2/5/10	Mon 2/8/10	3	Maria, Kenji
5	Prioritize requirements	2 days	Tue 2/9/10	Wed 2/10/10	2	Jason
6	Define Version 1 scope	2 days	Thu 2/11/10	Fri 2/12/10	5	Jason, Carly
7	**Version 1**	61 days	Mon 2/15/10	Mon 5/10/10		
8	**Detailed Requirements**	17 days	Mon 2/15/10	Tue 3/9/10		
9	Develop use cases	5 days	Mon 2/15/10	Fri 2/19/10	6	Ming
10	Develop process models	12 days	Mon 2/22/10	Tue 3/9/10	9	Ming
11	Develop data models	3 days	Mon 2/22/10	Wed 2/24/10	9	Maria
12	**Preliminary Design**	27 days	Mon 2/15/10	Tue 3/23/10		
13	System architecture	5 days	Mon 2/15/10	Fri 2/19/10	6	Kenji
14	User interface	7 days	Wed 3/10/10	Thu 3/18/10	10	Ming
15	Database	10 days	Thu 2/25/10	Wed 3/10/10	11	Maria
16	Programs	10 days	Wed 3/10/10	Tue 3/23/10	13,10	Kenji
17	**Implementation**	56 days	Mon 2/22/10	Mon 5/10/10		
18	Acquire HW & SW	10 days	Mon 2/22/10	Fri 3/5/10	13	Kenji
19	Construct database	7 days	Thu 3/11/10	Fri 3/19/10	15	Maria
20	Convert data	5 days	Mon 3/22/10	Fri 3/26/10	19	Maria
21	Write programs	20 days	Wed 3/24/10	Tue 4/20/10	16, 10	Ming, Kenji
22	Testing	10 days	Wed 4/21/10	Tue 5/4/10	20, 21	Maria, Kenji, Ming
23	Installation	4 days	Wed 5/5/10	Mon 5/10/10	22	Maria, Kenji, Ming
24	Version 2	42 days	Tue 5/11/10	Wed 7/7/10	23	Jason, Maria, Kenji, Ming
25	Version 3	28 days	Thu 7/8/10	Mon 8/16/10	24	Jason, Ming, Kenji, Maria

FIGURE 2-23
Gantt Chart

(Continued)

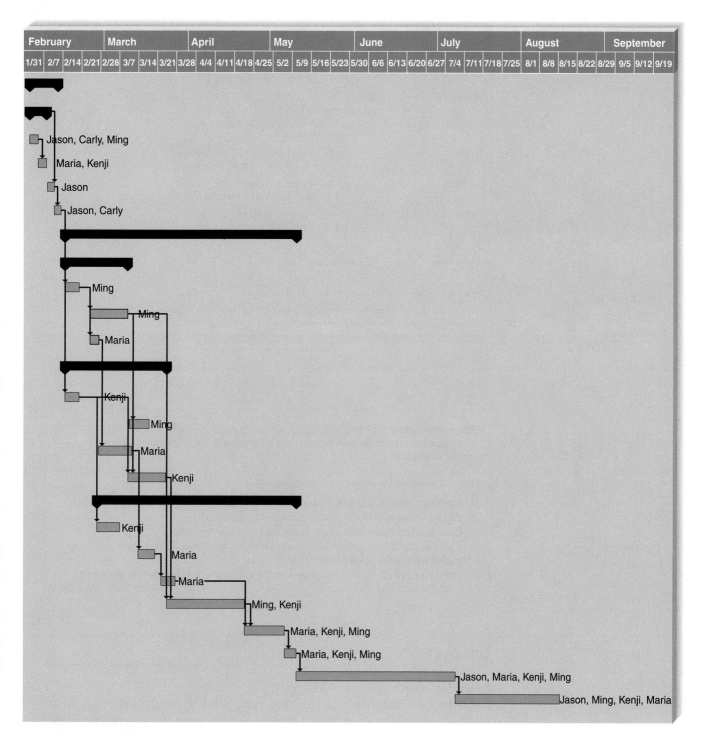

FIGURE 2-23
Gantt Chart

Role	Description	Assigned To
Project manager	Oversees the project to ensure that it meets its objectives on time and within budget	Jason
Infrastructure analyst	Ensures that the system conforms to infrastructure standards at Tune Source; ensures that the Tune Source infrastructure can support the new system	Kenji
Systems analyst	Designs the information system—with a focus on interfaces with the CD sales system	Kenji
Systems analyst	Designs the information system—with a focus on the process models and interface design	Ming
Systems analyst	Designs the information system—with a focus on the data models and system performance	Maria
Programmer	Codes system	Ming
Programmer	Codes system	Kenji

Reporting structure: All project team members will report to Jason.

Special incentives: If the deadline for the project is met, all team members who contributed to this goal will receive a free day off, to be taken over the holiday season.

FIGURE 2-24
Staffing Plan for the Digital Music Download System

Project objective: The Digital Music Download project team will create a working Web-based system to provide digital music downloads to Tune Source's customers as rapidly as possible.

The Digital Music Download team members will

1. Attend a staff meeting each Friday at 2 P.M. to report on the status of assigned tasks.
2. Update the work plan with actual data each Friday by 5 P.M.
3. Discuss all problems with Jason as soon as they are detected.
4. Agree to support each other when help is needed, especially for tasks that could hold back the progress of the project.
5. Post important changes to the project on the team bulletin board as they are made.

FIGURE 2-25
Project Charter for the Digital Music Download System

SUMMARY

Project Selection
Once the feasibility analysis has been completed, it is submitted back to the approval committee along with a revised system request. The committee then decides whether to approve the project, decline the project, or table it until additional information is available. The project selection process takes into account all of the projects in the organization, using portfolio management. The approval committee weighs many factors and makes trade-offs before a project is selected.

Creating the Project Plan

There are a number of different project methodologies that can be used to structure and guide systems development projects. Several of the key methodologies are waterfall development and its variations: parallel development and the V-model; rapid application development, including iterative development, system prototyping, and throwaway prototyping; and agile development, including extreme programming, Scrum, and others. The project manager evaluates characteristics of the project, including factors such as clarity of user requirements, familiarity with technology, complexity, reliability, time frame, and schedule visibility, to select the most appropriate methodology to use for the project.

The project manager then estimates the time frame for the project. Past experience, industry standards, and techniques such as function-point analysis, provide help in this task. The project methodology provides lists of tasks and deliverables for projects, which the project manager modifies, depending on the needs of the specific project. To create a work plan, the project manager refines the tasks into a work breakdown structure, and task time estimates and other information are entered into the work plan.

Staffing involves determining how many people should be assigned to the project, assigning project roles to team members, developing a reporting structure for the team, and matching people's skills with the needs of the project. Staffing also includes motivating the team to meet the project's objectives and minimizing conflict among team members. Both motivation and cohesiveness have been found to greatly influence performance of team members in project situations. Team members are motivated most by such nonmonetary things as recognition, achievement, and the work itself. Conflict can be minimized by clearly defining the roles on a project and holding team members accountable for their tasks. Some managers create a project charter that lists the project's norms and ground rules.

Coordinating project activities includes putting efficient development practices in place and mitigating risk, and these activities occur over the course of the entire SDLC. Three techniques are available to help coordinate activities on a project: computer-aided software engineering (CASE), standards, and documentation. CASE is a category of software that automates all or part of the development process; standards are formal rules or guidelines that project teams must follow during the project; and documentation includes detailed information about the tasks of the SDLC. Often, documentation is stored in project binder(s) that contain all the deliverables and all the internal communication that takes place—the history of the project.

Managing and Controlling the Project

As the project progresses, the project manager collects status reports from the team members and updates the work plan. Graphical tools such as Gantt and PERT charts help depict progress on tasks and clarify critical task dependencies. Project managers try to avoid introducing scope creep or feature creep into the schedule. As inevitable project changes arise, however, project managers try to balance the project size (number of features), time frame, and cost. Estimates may have to be revised as more is learned about the system. Timeboxing can be used to deal with shortened time frames. The project manager also keeps a close watch on the project risk. A risk assessment should be created and updated to evaluate the likelihood of various risks and their potential impact on the project.

KEY TERMS

Agile development
CASE repository
Chief information officer
Computer-aided software
  engineering (CASE)
Design prototype
Documentation
Estimation
Feature creep
Functional lead
Group cohesiveness
Integrated CASE
Interpersonal skills
Iterative development
Lower CASE

Methodology
Milestones
Motivation
Parallel development
Project binder
Project management
Project manager
Project portfolio management
Rapid application development
Reporting structure
Risk assessment
Risk management
Scope creep
Staffing plan
Standards

System prototyping
Task dependencies
Technical skills
Technical lead
Throwaway prototyping
Timeboxing
Trade-offs
Upper CASE
V-model
Versions
Work breakdown structure
Work plan
Waterfall development

QUESTIONS

1. Describe how projects are selected in organizations.
2. Describe how project portfolio management is used by IT departments.
3. Describe the major elements and issues with waterfall development.
4. Describe the major elements and issues with parallel development.
5. Describe the major elements and issues with the V-model.
6. Describe the major elements and issues with iterative development.
7. Describe the major elements and issues with system prototyping.
8. Describe the major elements and issues with throwaway prototyping.
9. Describe the major elements and issues with agile development.
10. Compare and contrast structured design methodologies in general with rapid application development (RAD) methodologies in general.
11. Compare and contrast extreme programming and throwaway prototyping.
12. What are the key factors in selecting a methodology?
13. Why do many projects end up having unreasonable deadlines? How should a project manager react to unreasonable demands?
14. Name two ways to identify the tasks that need to be accomplished over the course of a project.

15. What is the difference between a methodology and a work plan? How are the two terms related?
16. Some companies hire consulting firms to develop the initial project plans and manage the project, but use their own analysts and programmers to develop the system. Why do you think some companies do this?
17. Describe the differences between a technical lead and a functional lead. How are they similar?
18. Describe three technical skills and three interpersonal skills that would be very important to have on any project.
19. What are the best ways to motivate a team? What are the worst ways?
20. List three techniques to reduce conflict.
21. What is the difference between upper CASE (computer-aided software engineering) and lower CASE?
22. Describe three types of standards, and provide examples of each.
23. What belongs in the project binder? How is the project binder organized?
24. What are the trade-offs that project managers must manage?
25. What is scope creep, and how can it be managed?
26. What is timeboxing, and why is it used?
27. Create a list of potential risks that could affect the outcome of a project.
28. Describe the factors that the project manager must evaluate when a project falls behind schedule.

APPENDIX 2A QUESTIONS

1. What is a function point, and how is it used?
2. Describe the three steps of the function point approach.
3. What is the formula for calculating the effort for a project?

APPENDIX 2B QUESTIONS

1. Compare and contrast the Gantt chart and the PERT chart.
2. Of what value is the Gantt chart to the project manager? The PERT chart?

EXERCISES

A. Suppose that you are a project manager using the waterfall development methodology on a large and complex project. Your manager has just read the latest article in *Computerworld* that advocates replacing the waterfall methodology with prototyping and comes to your office requesting you to switch. What do you say?

B. Suppose that you are an analyst developing a new information system to automate the sales transactions and manage inventory for each retail store in a large chain. The system would be installed at each store and would exchange data with a mainframe computer at the company's head office. What methodology would you use? Why?

C. Suppose that you are an analyst developing a new executive information system (EIS) intended to provide key strategic information from existing corporate databases to senior executives to help in their decision making. What methodology would you use? Why?

D. Suppose that you are an analyst working for a small company to develop an accounting system. What methodology would you use? Why?

E. Visit a project management Web site, such as the Project Management Institute (www.pmi.org). Most have links to project management software products, white papers, and research. Examine some of the links for project management to better understand a variety of Internet sites that contain information related to this chapter.

F. Select a specific project management topic like computer-aided software engineering (CASE), project management software, or timeboxing, and use the Web search for information on that topic. The URL listed in question E or any search engine (e.g., Yahoo!, Google,) can provide a starting point for your efforts.

G. Pretend that the career services office at your university wants to develop a system that collects student résumés and makes them available to students and recruiters over the Web. Students should be able to input their résumé information into a standard résumé template. The information then is presented in a résumé format, and it also is placed in a database that can be queried through an online search form. You have been placed in charge of the project. Develop a plan for estimating the project. How long do you think it would take for you and three other students to complete the project? Provide support for the schedule that you propose.

H. Refer to the situation in question G. You have been told that recruiting season begins a month from today and that the new system must be used. How would you approach this situation? Describe what you can do as the project manager to make sure that your team does not burn out from unreasonable deadlines and commitments.

I. Consider the system described in question G. Create a work plan listing the tasks that will need to be completed to meet the project's objectives. Create a Gantt chart and a PERT chart in a project management tool (e.g., Microsoft Project), or use a spreadsheet package to graphically show the high-level tasks of the project.

J. Suppose that you are in charge of the project described in question G, and the project will be staffed by members of your class. Do your classmates have all of the right skills to implement such a project? If not, how will you go about making sure that the proper skills are available to get the job done?

K. Consider the application that is used at your school to register for classes. Complete a function point worksheet to determine the size of such an application. You will need to make some assumptions about the application's interfaces and the various factors that affect its complexity.

L. Read "Your Turn 2-5" in Appendix 2A of this chapter. Create a risk assessment that lists the potential risks associated with performing the project, along with ways to address the risks.

M. Pretend that your instructor has asked you and two friends to create a Web page to describe the course to potential students and provide current class information (e.g., syllabus, assignments, readings) to current students. You have been assigned the role of leader, so you will need to coordinate your activities and those of your classmates until the project is completed. Describe how you would apply the project management techniques that you have learned in this chapter to this situation. Include descriptions of how you would create a work plan, staff the project, and coordinate all activities—yours and those of your classmates.

N. Select two project management software packages and research them, using the Web or trade magazines. Describe the features of the two packages. If you were a project manager, which one would you use to help support your job? Why?

O. Select two estimation software packages and research them, using the Web or trade magazines. Describe the features of the two packages. If you were a project manager, which one would you use to help support your job? Why?

P. In 1997, Oxford Health Plans had a computer problem that caused the company to overestimate revenue and underestimate medical costs. Problems were caused by the migration of its claims processing system from the Pick operating system to a UNIX-based system that uses Oracle database software and hardware from Pyramid Technology. As a result, Oxford's stock price plummeted, and fixing the system became the number-one priority for the company. Pretend that you have been placed in charge of managing the repair of the claims processing system. Obviously, the project team will not be in good spirits. How will you motivate team members to meet the project's objectives?

MINICASES

1. Emily Pemberton is an IS project manager facing a difficult situation. Emily works for the First Trust Bank, which has recently acquired the City National Bank. Prior to the acquisition, First Trust and City National were bitter rivals, fiercely competing for market share in the region. Following the acrimonious takeover, numerous staff were laid off in many banking areas, including IS. Key individuals were retained from both banks' IS areas, however, and were assigned to a new consolidated IS department. Emily has been made project manager for the first significant IS project since the takeover, and she faces the task of integrating staffers from both banks on her team. The project they are undertaking will be highly visible within the organization, and the time frame for the project is somewhat demanding. Emily believes that the team can meet the project goals successfully, but success will require that the team become cohesive quickly and that potential conflicts are avoided. What strategies do you suggest that Emily implement in order to help ensure a successfully functioning project team?

2. Marcus Weber, IS project manager at ICAN Mutual Insurance Co., is reviewing the staffing arrangements for his next major project, the development of an expert system-based underwriters assistant. This new system will involve a whole new way for the underwriters to perform their tasks. The underwriters assistant system will function as sort of an underwriting supervisor, reviewing key elements of each application, checking for consistency in the underwriter's decisions, and ensuring that no critical factors have been overlooked. The goal of the new system is to improve the quality of the underwriters' decisions and to improve underwriter productivity. It is expected that the new system will substantially change the way the underwriting staff do their jobs.

Marcus is dismayed to learn that due to budget constraints, he must choose between one of two available staff members. Barry Filmore has had considerable experience and training in individual and organizational behavior. Barry has worked on several other projects in which the end users had to make significant adjustments to the new system, and Barry seems to have a knack for anticipating problems and smoothing the transition to a new work environment. Marcus had hoped to have Barry's involvement in this project.

Marcus's other potential staff member is Kim Danville. Prior to joining ICAN Mutual, Kim had considerable work experience with the expert system technologies that ICAN has chosen for this expert system project. Marcus was counting on Kim to help integrate the new expert system technology into ICAN's systems environment, and also to provide on-the-job training and insights to the other developers on this team.

Given that Marcus's budget will permit him to add only Barry or Kim to this project team, but not both, what choice do you recommend for him? Justify your answer.

3. Tom, Jan, and Julie are IS majors at Great State University. These students have been assigned to a class project by one of their professors, requiring them to develop a new Web-based system to collect and update information on the IS program's alumni. This system will be used by the IS graduates to enter job and address information as they graduate, and then make changes to that information as they change jobs and/or addresses. Their professor also has a number of queries that she is interested in being able to implement. Based on their preliminary discussions with their professor, the students have developed this list of system elements:

Inputs: 1 low complexity, 2 medium complexity, 1 high complexity
Outputs: 4 medium complexity
Queries: 1 low complexity, 4 medium complexity, 2 high complexity
Files: 3 medium complexity
Program interfaces: 2 medium complexity

Assume that an adjusted project complexity factor of 1.2 is appropriate for this project. Calculate the total adjusted function points for this project.

APPENDIX 2A—THE FUNCTION POINT APPROACH

The function point approach[20] is an estimating technique that can be used to estimate the size of the new system, the effort that will be required to complete the system, and the time the project will require. This approach requires detailed knowledge of system to be developed. When this knowledge is available, the function point approach produces a much more precise estimate for the project than the industry standard method mentioned earlier in Chapter 2.

The function point approach uses a three-step process (Figure 2A-1). First, the project manager estimates the size of the project in terms of the number of

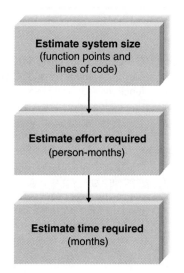

FIGURE 2A-1
Estimating Project Time, Using the Function Point Approach

[20] Two good books that focus on function points are J. Brian Dreger, *Function Point Analysis*, Englewood Cliffs, NJ: Prentice Hall, 1989; and C. R. Symons, *Software Sizing and Estimating: MK II FPA*, New York: John Wiley & Sons, 1991. Additional information on function point analysis can be found at www.ifpug.org.

lines of code the new system will require. This size estimate is then converted into the amount of effort required to develop the system in terms of the number of person-months. The estimated effort is then converted into an estimated schedule time in terms of the number of months from start to finish.

Step 1: Estimate System Size The first step is to estimate the size of a project by using function points, a concept developed in 1979 by Allen Albrecht of IBM. A *function point* is a measure of program size that is based on the system's number and complexity of inputs, outputs, queries, files, and program interfaces.

To calculate the function points for a project, components are listed on a worksheet to represent the major elements of the system. For example, data-entry screens are kinds of inputs, reports are outputs, and database queries are kinds of queries. (See Figure 2A-2.) The project manager records the total number of each component that the system will include, and then he or she breaks down the number to show the number of components that have low, medium, and high complexity. In Figure 2A-2, there are 19 outputs that need to be developed for the system, 4 of which have low complexity, 10 that have medium complexity, and 5 that are very complex. After each line is filled in, a total number of points are calculated per line by multiplying each number by a complexity index. The complexity index values are drawn from function point research and tell us, for example, that a low complexity input is "worth" three function points, while a high complexity output is "worth" seven function points. The line totals are added up to determine the *total unadjusted function points* (*TUFP*) for the project.

The *complexity* of the overall system is greater than the sum of its parts. Things like the familiarity of the project team with the business area and the technology that will be used to implement the project also may influence how complex a project will be. A project that is very complex for a team with little experience might have little complexity for a team with lots of experience. To create a more realistic size for the project, a number of additional system factors such as end-user efficiency, reusability, and data communications are assessed in terms of their effect on the project's complexity. (See Figure 2A-2.) These assessments are totaled and placed into a formula to calculate an *adjusted project complexity* (*APC*) factor. The APC factor has a baseline value of 0.65, and the total Processing Complexity (PC) score (converted to hundredths) is added to the baseline amount. The TUFP value is multiplied by the APC factor to determine the ultimate size of the project in terms of *total adjusted function points* (*TAFP*). This number should give the project manager a reasonable idea as to how big the project will be.

CONCEPTS
IN ACTION

2A-A FUNCTION POINTS AT NIELSEN

Nielsen Media used function point analysis (FPA) for an upgrade to the Global Sample Management System (GSMS) for Nielsen Media/NetRatings, which keeps track of the Internet rating sample, a group of 40,000 homes nationwide that volunteer to participate in ongoing ratings.

In late fall of 1998, Nielsen Media did an FP count based on the current GSMS. (FPA is always easier and more accurate when there is an existing system.) Nielsen Media had its counters—three quality assurance staff—do their FPA, and then input their count into Knowledge-Plan, a productivity modeling tool. In early 1999, seven programmers began writing code for the system, which they were expected to complete in 10 months. As November approached, the project was adding staff to try to meet the deadline. When it became evident that the deadline would not be met, a new FP count was conducted. The GSMS had grown to 900 FPs. Besides the original 500 plus 20%, there were 300 FPs attributable to features and functions that had crept into the project.

How did that happen? The way it always does: The developers and users had added a button here, a new feature there, and soon the project was much larger than it was originally. But Nielsen Media had put a stake in the ground at the beginning from which they could measure growth along the way.

The best practice is to run the FPA and productivity model at the project's launch and again when there is a full list of functional requirements. Then do another analysis anytime there is a major modification in the functional definition of the project.

Source: "Ratings Game," *CIO Magazine*, October 2000, by Bill Roberts.

System Components:

Description	Total Number	Complexity: Low	Complexity: Medium	Complexity: High	Total
Inputs	6	3 × 3	2 × 4	1 × 6	23
Outputs	19	4 × 4	10 × 5	5 × 7	101
Queries	10	7 × 3	0 × 4	3 × 6	39
Files	15	0 × 7	15 × 10	0 × 15	150
Program Interfaces	3	1 × 5	0 × 7	2 × 10	25
Total Unadjusted Function Points (TUFP):					338

Overall System:

Data communications	3
Heavy use configuration	0
Transaction rate	0
End-user efficiency	0
Complex processing	0
Installation ease	0
Multiple sites	0
Performance	0
Distributed functions	2
Online data entry	2
Online update	0
Reusability	0
Operational ease	0
Extensibility	0
Total Processing Complexity (PC):	7

(0 = no effect on processing complexity; 3 = great effect on processing complexity)

Adjusted Project Complexity (APC):

.65 + (0.01 x 7) = .72

Total Adjusted Function Points (TAFP):

.72 (APC) x 338 (TUFP) = 243 **(TAFP)**

FIGURE 2A-2
Function Point-Estimation Worksheet

2A-1 CALCULATE SYSTEM SIZE

Imagine that job hunting has been going so well that you need to develop a system to support your efforts. The system should allow you to input information about the companies with which you interview, the interviews and office visits that you have scheduled, and the offers that you receive. It should be able to produce reports, such as a company contact list, an interview schedule, and an office visit schedule, as well as generate thank-you letters to be brought into a word processor to customize. You also need the system to answer queries, such as the number of interviews by city and your average offer amount.

QUESTIONS:
1. Determine the number of inputs, outputs, interfaces, files, and queries that this system requires. For each element, determine whether the complexity is low,

medium, or high. Record this information on a worksheet similar to the one in Figure 2A-2.
2. Calculate the total function points for each line on your worksheet by multiplying the number of each element with the appropriate complexity score.
3. Sum up the total unadjusted function points.
4. Suppose that the system will be built by you using Visual Basic (VB). Given your VB skills, multiply the TUFP score by the APC score that best estimates how complex the system will be for you to develop (.65 = simple, 1 = average, 1.35 = complex), and calculate a TAFP value.
5. Using the table in Figure 2A-3, determine the number of lines of code that correspond to VB. Multiply this number by the TAFP to find the total lines of code that your system will require.

Sometimes a shortcut is used to determine the complexity of the project. Instead of calculating the exact APC score for the 14 factors listed in Figure 2A-2, project managers estimate an APC value that ranges from 0.65 for very simple systems to 1.00 for "normal" systems to as much as 1.35 for complex systems. This estimated APC score is then applied to the TUFP to compute the TAFP. For example, a very simple system that has 200 unadjusted function points would have a size of 130 adjusted function points (200 × .65 = 130). However, if the system with 200 unadjusted function points were very complex, its function point size would be 270 (200 × 1.35 = 270).

In the planning phase, the exact nature of the system has not yet been determined, so it is impossible to know *exactly* how many inputs, outputs, and so forth will be in the system. It is up to the project manager to make an intelligent guess. Some people feel that using function points this early in a project is not practical for this reason. We believe function points can be a useful tool for understanding a project's size at any point in the SDLC. Later in the project, once more is known about the system, the project manager will revise the estimates, using this better knowledge to produce more accurate results.

Once you have estimated the number of function points, you need to convert the number of function points into the lines of code that will be required to build the system. The number of lines of code depends on the programming language you choose to use. Figure 2A-3 presents a very rough conversion guide for some popular languages.

For example, the system in Figure 2A-2 has 243 function points. If you were to develop the system in COBOL, it would typically require approximately 26,730 lines of code to write it. Conversely, if you were to use Visual Basic, it typically would take 7290 lines of code. If you could develop the system by using a package such as Excel or Access, it would take between 2430 and 9720 lines of code. There is a great range for packages, because different packages enable you to do different things and not all systems can be built with certain packages. Sometimes you end up writing lots of extra code to do some simple function because the package does not have the capabilities you need.

There is also a very important message from the data in this figure. Since there is a direct relationship between lines of code and the amount of effort and time required to develop a system, the choice of development language has a significant impact on the time and cost of projects.

Language	Approximate Number of Lines of Code per Function Point
C	130
COBOL	110
Java	55
C++	50
Turbo Pascal	50
Visual Basic	30
PowerBuilder	15
HTML	15
Packages (e.g., Access, Excel)	10–40

Source: Capers Jones, Software Productivity Research, http://www.spr.com

FIGURE 2A-3
Converting from Function Points to Lines of Code

Step 2: Estimate Effort Required Once an understanding is reached about the size of the system, the next step is to estimate the effort that is required to build it. *Effort* is a function of the system size combined with production rates (how much work someone can complete in a given time). Much research has been done on software production rates. One of the most popular algorithms, the COCOMO model,[21] was designed by Barry W. Boehm to convert a lines-of-code estimate into a person-month estimate. There are different versions of the *COCOMO model* that vary with the complexity of the software, the size of the system, the experience of the developers, and the type of software that you are developing (e.g., business application software such as the registration system at your university; commercial software such as Word; or system software such as Windows). For small to moderate-size business software projects (i.e., 100,000 lines of code and 10 or fewer programmers), the model is quite simple:

effort (in person-months) = 1.4 × thousands of lines of code

For example, let's suppose that we were going to develop a business software system requiring 10,000 lines of code. This project would typically take 14 person-months of effort. If the system in Figure 2A-2 were developed in COBOL (which equates to 26,730 lines of code), it would require about 37.42 person-months of effort.

YOUR	**2A-2 CALCULATE EFFORT AND SCHEDULE TIME**
TURN	

Refer to the project size and lines of code that you calculated in "Your Turn 2A-1."

QUESTIONS:
1. Determine the effort of your project in person-months of effort by multiplying your lines of code (in thousands) by 1.4.

2. Calculate the schedule time in months for your project by using the formula 3.0 × person-months$^{1/3}$.
3. Based on your numbers, how much time will it take to complete the project if you are the developer?

---

[21] The original COCOMO model is presented by Barry W. Boehm in *Software Engineering Economics*, Englewood Cliffs, NJ: Prentice Hall, 1981. Since then, much additional research has been done. The latest version of COCOMO, COCOMO II, is described in B. W. Boehm, C. Abts, A. W. Brown, S. Chulani, B. K. Clark, E. Horowitz, R. Madachy, D. Reifer, and B. Steece, *Software Cost Estimation with COCOMO II*, Upper Saddle River, NJ: Prentice Hall PTR, 2000. For the latest updates, see http://sunset.use.edu/csse/research/COCOMOII/cocomo_main.html.

Step 3: Estimate Time Required Once the effort is understood, the optimal schedule for the project can be estimated. Historical data or estimation software can be used as aids, or one rule of thumb is to determine schedule by the following equation:

schedule time (months) $= 3.0 \times$ person-months$^{1/3}$

This equation is widely used, although the specific numbers vary (e.g., some estimators may use 3.5 or 2.5 instead of 3.0). The equation suggests that a project that has an effort of 14 person-months should be scheduled to take a little more than 7 months to complete. Continuing the Figure 2A-2 example, the 37.42 person-months would require a little over 10 months. It is important to note that this estimate is for the analysis, design, and implementation phases; it does not include the planning phase.

APPENDIX 2B-PROJECT MANAGEMENT TOOLS: THE GANTT CHART AND PERT CHART

Project managers utilize several tools to help manage projects. The project work plan, discussed previously, is a critical element of managing projects. In addition, two graphical tools are widely used to understand the relationship between project tasks and to monitor progress on the project.

Gantt Chart

A *Gantt chart* is a horizontal bar chart that shows the same task information as the project work plan, but in a graphical way. Sometimes a picture really is worth a thousand words, and the Gantt chart can communicate the high-level status of a project much faster and easier than the work plan. Creating a Gantt chart is simple and can be done with a spreadsheet package, graphics software (e.g., Microsoft VISIO), or a project management package.

First, tasks are listed as rows in the chart, and time is listed across the top in increments based on the needs of the projects. (See Figure 2B-1). A short project may be divided into hours or days, whereas a medium-sized project may be represented in weeks or months. Horizontal bars are drawn to represent the duration of each task; the bar's beginning and end mark exactly when the task will begin and end. As people work on tasks, the appropriate bars are filled in proportionately to how much of the task is finished. Too many tasks on a Gantt chart can become confusing, so it's best to limit the number of tasks to around 20 to 30. If there are more tasks, break them down into subtasks and create Gantt charts for each level of detail.

There are many things a project manager can see by looking quickly at a Gantt chart. In addition to seeing how long tasks are and how far along they are, the project manager also can tell which tasks are sequential, which tasks occur at the same time, and which tasks overlap in some way. He or she can get a quick view of tasks that are ahead of schedule and behind schedule by drawing a vertical line on today's date. If a bar is not filled in and appears to the left of the line, that task is behind schedule.

There are a few special notations that can be placed on a Gantt chart. Project milestones are shown by upside-down triangles or diamonds. Arrows are drawn between the task bars to show task dependencies. Sometimes, the names of people assigned to each task are listed next to the task bars to show what human resources have been allocated to each task.

PERT Chart

A second graphical way to look at the project work plan information is the *PERT chart*, which displays the project tasks in a flowchart. (See Figure 2B-2). *PERT (Program Evaluation and Review Technique)* is a network analysis technique that can be used when the individual task time estimates are fairly uncertain. Instead of assigning a specific value as the duration estimate, PERT uses three time estimates: optimistic, most likely, and pessimistic. It then combines the three estimates into a single weighted average estimate using the following formula:

$$\text{PERT weighted average} = \frac{\text{optimistic value} + (4 * \text{most likely value}) + \text{pessimistic value}}{6}$$

The PERT chart is drawn graphically with boxes (called *nodes*) representing each task and lines (called *arcs*) showing the dependency between tasks. The time estimates are shown in the nodes. Usually, the partially completed tasks are displayed with a diagonal line through the node, and completed tasks contain crossed lines.

Task Name	Duration	Start	Finish	Prede.	Nov 14, '10	21, '10	28, '10	Dec 5, '10	12, '10	19, '10	26, '10	Jan 2, '11
- Design Phase	31 days	Fri 11/19/10	Fri 12/31/10									
- Develop database design document	9 days	Mon 12/6/10	Thu 12/16/10									
Staging database design	9 days	Mon 12/6/10	Thu 12/16/10							Megan		
Suspense database design	9 days	Mon 12/6/10	Thu 12/16/10							Megan		
- Develop rejects-handling design document	9 days	Fri 12/17/10	Wed 12/29/10	3,4								
Rejects-handling engine design	9 days	Fri 12/17/10	Wed 12/29/10								Megan	
- Develop OLAP design document	9 days	Fri 12/17/10	Wed 12/29/10	3,4								
Universe design	9 days	Fri 12/17/10	Wed 12/29/10								Joachim	
- Develop OLAP design part 1	8 days	Fri 12/10/10	Tue 12/21/10									
High-priority reports design	8 days	Fri 12/10/10	Tue 12/21/10							Kevin		
- Develop application design document	9 days	Fri 12/17/10	Wed 12/29/10									
GCCR maintenance application design	9 days	Fri 12/17/10	Wed 12/29/10								Tomas	
- ETL design document	2 days	Thu 12/30/10	Fri 12/31/10									
Data export utility design	2 days	Thu 12/30/10	Fri 12/31/10								Joachim	
- Application design document	26 days	Fri 11/19/10	Fri 12/24/10									
Web entry application UI design	26 days	Fri 11/19/10	Fri 12/24/10								Mei-ling	
Web entry application UI design sign-off	1 day	Fri 12/3/10	Fri 12/3/10				♦					
Web entry forms and database model validation	11 days	Wed 11/24/10	Wed 12/8/10					Kevin				
- Functional requirements document	9 days	Mon 12/13/10	Thu 12/23/10									
- Application design	9 days	Mon 12/13/10	Thu 12/23/10									
User authentication	4 days	Mon 12/13/10	Thu 12/16/10							Chantelle		
Call logging	2 days	Fri 12/17/10	Mon 12/20/10								Chantelle	
Search	3 days	Tue 12/21/10	Thu 12/23/10								Chantelle	

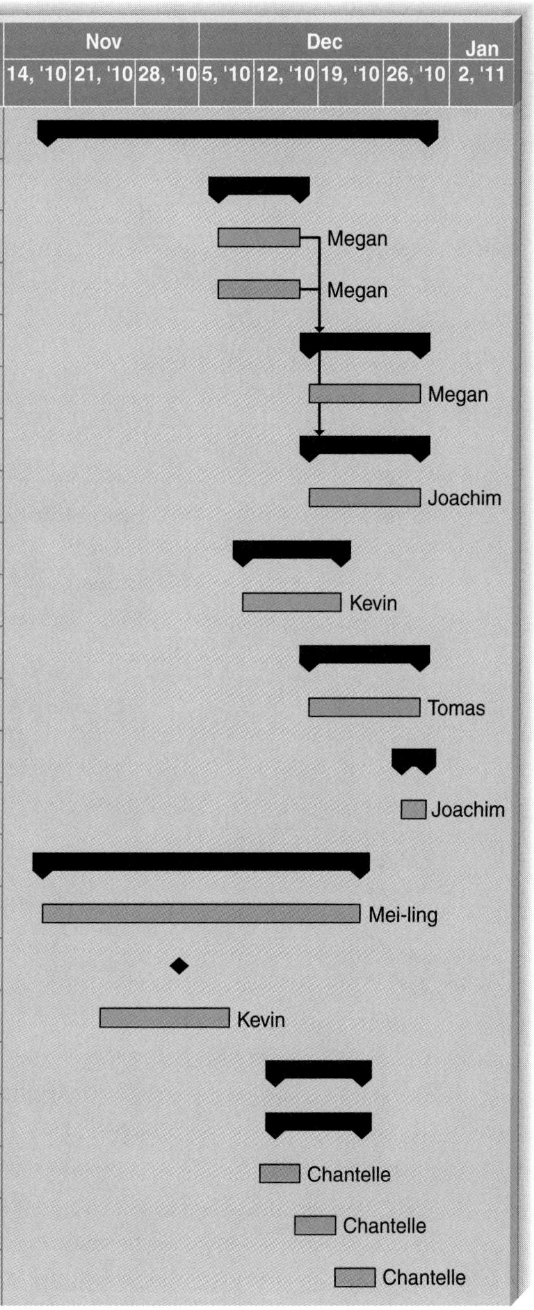

FIGURE 2B-1

Gantt Chart

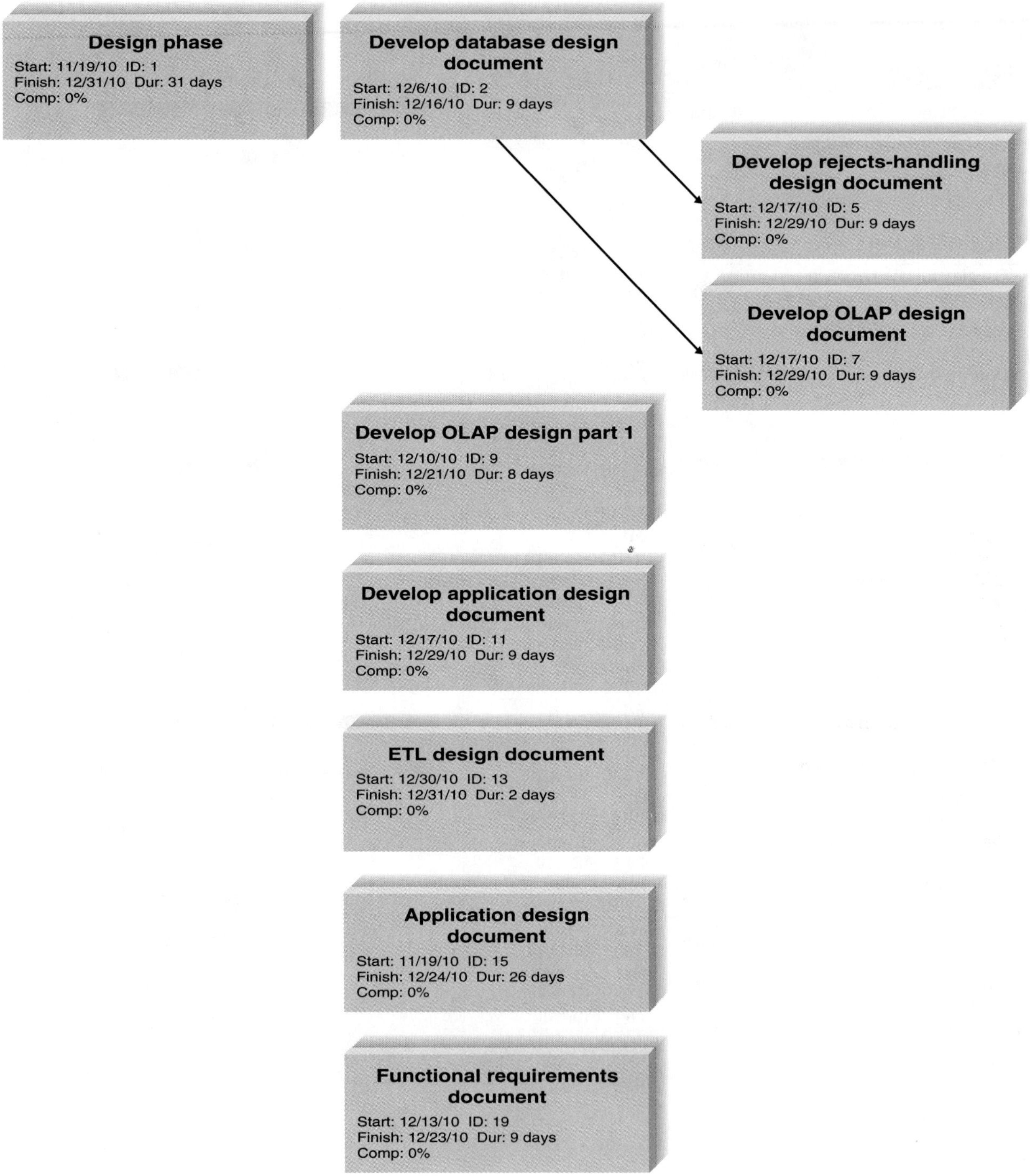

Design phase
Start: 11/19/10 ID: 1
Finish: 12/31/10 Dur: 31 days
Comp: 0%

Develop database design document
Start: 12/6/10 ID: 2
Finish: 12/16/10 Dur: 9 days
Comp: 0%

Develop rejects-handling design document
Start: 12/17/10 ID: 5
Finish: 12/29/10 Dur: 9 days
Comp: 0%

Develop OLAP design document
Start: 12/17/10 ID: 7
Finish: 12/29/10 Dur: 9 days
Comp: 0%

Develop OLAP design part 1
Start: 12/10/10 ID: 9
Finish: 12/21/10 Dur: 8 days
Comp: 0%

Develop application design document
Start: 12/17/10 ID: 11
Finish: 12/29/10 Dur: 9 days
Comp: 0%

ETL design document
Start: 12/30/10 ID: 13
Finish: 12/31/10 Dur: 2 days
Comp: 0%

Application design document
Start: 11/19/10 ID: 15
Finish: 12/24/10 Dur: 26 days
Comp: 0%

Functional requirements document
Start: 12/13/10 ID: 19
Finish: 12/23/10 Dur: 9 days
Comp: 0%

FIGURE 2B-2
PERT Chart

PERT charts are the best way to communicate task dependencies because they lay out the tasks in the order in which they need to be completed. The *critical path method* (*CPM*) allows the identification of the *critical path* in the network, the longest path from project inception to completion. The critical path shows all of the tasks that must be completed on schedule for the project as a whole to finish on schedule. If any of the tasks on the critical path (called *critical tasks*) takes longer than expected, the entire project will fall behind. CPM can be used with or without PERT.

Project management software packages like Microsoft Project enable the project manager to input the work plan once and then display the information in many different formats. You can toggle between the work plan, a Gantt chart, and a PERT chart, depending on your project management needs.

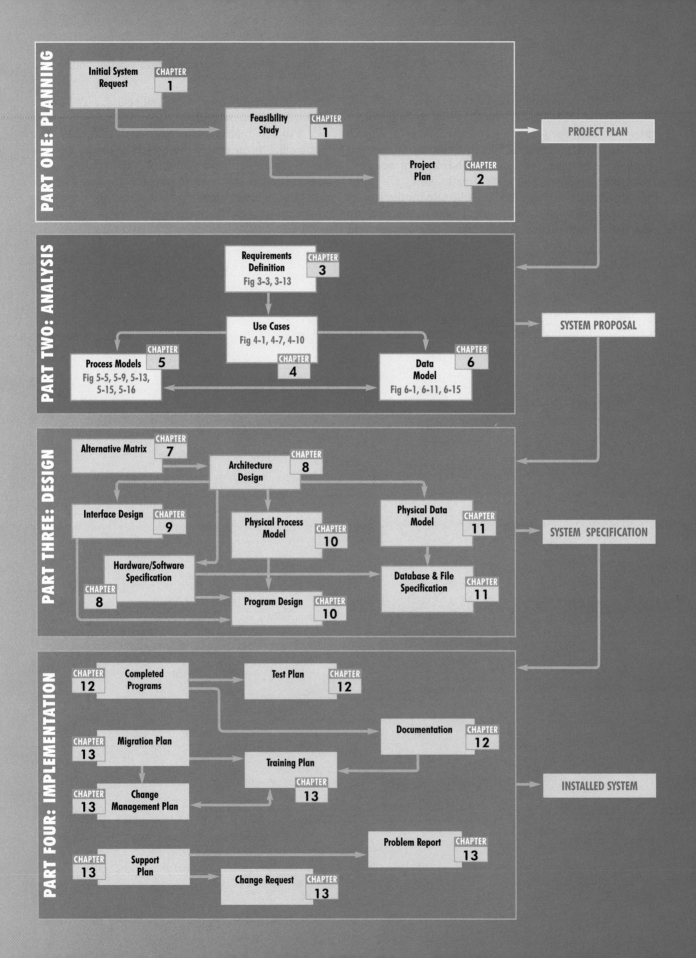

PART TWO
ANALYSIS PHASE

PROJECT BINDER

The analysis phase
answers the questions
of who will use the system,
what the system will do,
and
where and when it will be used.

All of the deliverables are combined
into a system proposal,
which is presented to management,
who decides whether the project should
continue to move forward.

Requirements
Determination

CHAPTER
3

Analysis
Plan

Requirements
Definition

Use Case
Analysis

CHAPTER
4

Use Cases

Process
Modeling

CHAPTER
5

Process
Model

Data
Modeling

CHAPTER
6

Data
Model

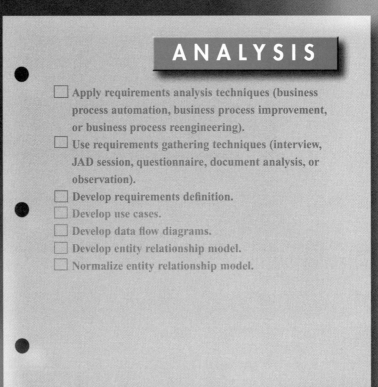

ANALYSIS

☐ Apply requirements analysis techniques (business process automation, business process improvement, or business process reengineering).

☐ Use requirements gathering techniques (interview, JAD session, questionnaire, document analysis, or observation).

☐ Develop requirements definition.

☐ Develop use cases.

☐ Develop data flow diagrams.

☐ Develop entity relationship model.

☐ Normalize entity relationship model.

TASK CHECKLIST

PLANNING   ANALYSIS   DESIGN

CHAPTER 3

REQUIREMENTS
DETERMINATION

During the analysis phase, the analyst determines the business requirements for the new system. This chapter begins by presenting the requirements definition, a document that lists the new system's capabilities. It then describes how to analyze requirements, using business process automation, business process improvement, and business process reengineering techniques, and how to gather requirements through interviews, JAD sessions, questionnaires, document analysis, and observation.

OBJECTIVES

- Become familiar with the analysis phase of the SDLC.
- Understand how to create a requirements definition.
- Become familiar with requirements analysis techniques.
- Understand when to use each requirements analysis technique.
- Understand how to gather requirements by using interviews, JAD sessions, questionnaires, document analysis, and observation.
- Understand when to use each requirements-gathering technique.

CHAPTER OUTLINE

IMPLEMENTATION

INTRODUCTION

The systems development life cycle (SDLC) is the process by which the organization moves from the current system (often called the *as-is system*) to the new system (often called the *to-be system*). The outputs of the planning phase that we discussed in Chapters 1 and 2 are the system request, feasibility study, and project plan, which provide general ideas for the to-be system, define the project's scope, assess project feasibility, and provide the initial work plan. We now begin the discussion of the analysis phase. Keep in mind that *analysis* refers to breaking a whole into its parts with the intent of understanding the parts' nature, function, and interrelationships. Therefore, the work of the analysis phase involves breaking the general request for a new system, outlined in the system request, into a more detailed understanding of exactly what the new system needs to do. These details will be expressed and documented in several ways, including a detailed requirements definition (this chapter), use cases (Chapter 4), process models (Chapter 5), and data models (Chapter 6). The final deliverable of the analysis phase is the *system proposal,* which contains all of the previously mentioned material along with a revised feasibility analysis (Chapter 1) and work plan (Chapter 2).

At the conclusion of the analysis phase, the system proposal is presented to the approval committee. Before moving into the design phase, the project should be reviewed to ensure that it continues to contribute business value to the organization. The system proposal presentation is usually in the form of a system *walk-through,* a meeting at which the concept for the new system is presented to the users, managers, and key decision makers. The goal of the walk-through is to explain the system in moderate detail so that the users, managers, and key decision makers clearly understand it, can identify needed improvements, and are able to make a decision about whether the project should continue. If approved, the system proposal moves into the design phase, and its elements (requirements definition, use cases, process models, and data model) are used as inputs to the steps in the design phase, which further refine them and define in much more detail how the system will be built.

The line between the analysis and design phases is very blurry, because the deliverables created in the analysis phase are really the first step in the design of the new system. Many of the major design decisions for the new system are found in the analysis deliverables. In fact, a better name for the analysis phase would really be "analysis and initial design," but because this name is rather long and because most organizations simply call this phase "analysis," we will, too. Nonetheless, it is important to remember that the deliverables from the analysis phase are really the first step in the design of the new system.

In many ways, the requirements determination step is the single most critical step of the entire SDLC. It is here that the major elements of the system first begin to emerge. During requirements determination, the system is easy to change because little work has been done yet. As the system moves through the subsequent phases in the SDLC, it becomes harder and harder to return to requirements determination and make major changes because of all of the rework that is involved. Although many factors contribute to the failure of systems development projects, failing to determine the correct requirements is a primary cause.[1] This is why the iterative approaches of many RAD and agile methodologies are so effective—small

---

[1] For example, see: Ewusi-Mensah, Kweku, *Software Development Failures: Anatomy of Abandoned Projects*, MIT Press, 2003.

batches of requirements can be identified and implemented in incremental stages, allowing the overall system to change and evolve over time.

In this chapter, we will focus on the requirements determination step of the analysis phase. We begin by explaining what a requirement is and the overall process of requirements analysis and requirements gathering. We then present a set of techniques that can be used to analyze and gather requirements.

REQUIREMENTS DETERMINATION

The *requirements determination* step is performed to expand the system request's high-level statement of business requirements into a more precise list. This detailed list of requirements can then be used as input into the other activities of the analysis phase: creating use cases, building process models, and building a data model. We first explain what a requirement is and discuss the process of creating a requirements definition.

What Is a Requirement?

A *requirement* is simply a statement of what the system must do or what characteristics it needs to have. During the analysis phase, requirements are written from the perspective of the businessperson, and they focus on *what* the system does. They focus on business user needs, so they usually are called *business requirements* (sometimes, user requirements). Later in the design phase, business requirements evolve to become more technical, and they describe *how* the system will be implemented. Requirements in the design phase are written from the developer's perspective, and they usually are called *system requirements.*

Before we continue, we want to stress that there is no black-and-white line dividing a business requirement and a system requirement—and some companies use the terms interchangeably. The important thing to remember is that a requirement is a statement of what the system must do, and requirements will change over time as the project moves from analysis to design to implementation. Requirements evolve from detailed statements of the business capabilities that a system should have to detailed statements of the technical way in which the capabilities will be implemented in the new system.

Requirements can be either functional or nonfunctional in nature. A *functional requirement* relates directly to a process the system has to perform or information it needs to contain. For example, a process-oriented functional requirement would be that the system must have the ability to search for available inventory. An information-oriented functional requirement would be that the system must include actual and budgeted expenses. (See Figure 3-1.) Functional requirements flow directly into the next steps of the analysis process (use cases, process models, data model) because they define the functions that the system needs to have.

Nonfunctional requirements refer to behavioral properties that the system must have, such as performance and usability. The ability to access the system through a Web browser would be considered a nonfunctional requirement. Nonfunctional requirements may influence the rest of the analysis process (use cases, process models, and data model), but often do so only indirectly; nonfunctional requirements are primarily used in the design phase when decisions are made about the user interface, the hardware and software, and the system's underlying architecture.

Functional Requirement	Description	Examples
Process-oriented	A process the system must perform; a process the system must do	■ The system must allow registered customers to review their own order history for the past three years. ■ The system must check incoming customer orders for inventory availability. ■ The system should allow students to view a course schedule while registering for classes.
Information-oriented	Information the system must contain	■ The system must retain customer order history for three years. ■ The system must include real-time inventory levels at all warehouses. ■ The system must include budgeted and actual sales and expense amounts for current year and three previous years.

FIGURE 3-1
Functional Requirements

Figure 3-2 lists different kinds of nonfunctional requirements and examples of each kind. Notice that the nonfunctional requirements describe a variety of characteristics regarding the system: operational, performance, security, and cultural and political. These characteristics do not describe business processes or information, but they are very important in understanding what the final system should be like. For example, the project team needs to know whether a system must be highly secure, requires subsecond response time, or has to reach a multilingual customer base. These requirements will affect design decisions that will be made in the design phase, particularly architecture design, so we will revisit them in detail in Chapter 8. The goal at this point is to identify any major issues.

YOUR TURN

3-1 IDENTIFYING REQUIREMENTS

One of the most common mistakes made by new analysts is to confuse functional and nonfunctional requirements. Pretend that you received the following list of requirements for a sales system:

Requirements for Proposed System:
The system should...

1. be accessible to Web users.
2. include the company standard logo and color scheme.
3. restrict access to profitability information.
4. include actual and budgeted cost information.
5. provide management reports.
6. include sales information that is updated at least daily.
7. have 2-second maximum response time for predefined queries and 10-minute maximum response time for ad hoc queries.
8. include information from all company subsidiaries.
9. print subsidiary reports in the primary language of the subsidiary.
10. provide monthly rankings of salesperson performance.

QUESTIONS:

1. Which requirements are functional business requirements? Provide two additional examples.
2. Which requirements are nonfunctional business requirements? What kind of nonfunctional requirements are they? Provide two additional examples.

Nonfunctional Requirement	Description	Examples
Operational	The physical and technical environments in which the system will operate	■ The system can run on handheld devices. ■ The system should be able to integrate with the existing inventory system. ■ The system should be able to work on any Web browser.
Performance	The speed, capacity, and reliability of the system	■ Any interaction between the user and the system should not exceed 2 seconds. ■ The system downloads new status parameters within 5 minutes of a change. ■ The system should be available for use 24 hours per day, 365 days per year. ■ The system supports 300 simultaneous users from 9–11 A.M.; 150 simultaneous users at all other times.
Security	Who has authorized access to the system under what circumstances	■ Only direct managers can see personnel records of staff. ■ Customers can see their order history only during business hours. ■ The system includes all available safeguards from viruses, worms, Trojan horses, etc.
Cultural and Political	Cultural and political factors and legal requirements that affect the system	■ The system should be able to distinguish between U.S. currency and currency from other nations. ■ Company policy is to buy computers only from Dell. ■ Country managers are permitted to authorize custom user interfaces within their units. ■ Personal information is protected in compliance with the Data Protection Act.

Source: The Atlantic Systems Guild, http://www.systemsguild.com

FIGURE 3-2
Nonfunctional Requirements

CONCEPTS
IN ACTION

3-A WHAT CAN HAPPEN IF YOU IGNORE NONFUNCTIONAL REQUIREMENTS

I once worked on a consulting project in which my manager created a requirements definition without listing nonfunctional requirements. The project was then estimated based on the requirements definition and sold to the client for $5,000. In my manager's mind, the system that we would build for the client would be a very simple stand-alone system running on current technology. It shouldn't take more than a week to analyze, design, and build.

Unfortunately, the client had other ideas. They wanted the system to be used by many people in three different departments, and they wanted the ability for any number of people to work on the system concurrently. The technology they had in place was antiquated, but nonetheless they wanted the system to run effectively on the existing equipment. Because we didn't set the project scope properly by including our assumptions about nonfunctional requirements in the requirements definition, we basically had to do whatever they wanted.

The capabilities they wanted took weeks to design and program. The project ended up taking four months, and the final project cost was $250,000. Our company had to pick up the tab for everything except the agreed upon $5,000. This was by far the most frustrating project situation I ever experienced. *Barbara Wixom*

Requirements Definition

The requirements definition report—usually just called the *requirements definition*—is a straightforward text report that simply lists the functional and nonfunctional requirements in an outline format. Figure 3-3 shows a sample requirements definition for Holiday Travel Vehicles, a recreational vehicle dealership.

The requirements are numbered in a legal or outline format so that each requirement is clearly identified. First, the requirements are grouped into functional

---

Functional Requirements

1. New Vehicle Management
1.1 The system will allow managers to view the current new vehicle inventory.
1.2 The system will allow the new vehicle manager to place orders for new vehicles.
1.3 The system will record the addition of new vehicles to inventory when they are received from the manufacturers.

2. Vehicle Sales Management
2.1 The system will enable salespersons to create a customer offer.
2.2 The system will allow salespeople to know whether an offer is pending on a specific vehicle.
2.3 The system will enable managers to record approval of a customer offer.
2.4 The system will prepare a sales contract.
2.5 The system will prepare a shop work order based on customer requested dealer options.
2.6 The system will record a customer deposit.
2.7 The system will record a customer payment.
2.8 The system will create a record of the customer's vehicle purchase.

3. Used Vehicle Management
3.1 The system will record information on a customer trade-in vehicle ... etc.

Nonfunctional Requirements

1. Operational
1.1 The system should run on tablet PCs to be used by salespeople.
1.2 The system should interface with the shop management system.
1.3 The system should connect to printers wirelessly.

2. Performance
2.1 The system should support a sales staff of 15 salespeople.
2.2 The system should be updated with pending offers on vehicles every 15 minutes.

3. Security
3.1 No salesperson can access any other salesperson's customer contacts.
3.2 Only the owner and sales manager may approve customer offers.
3.3 Use of each tablet PC should be restricted to the salesperson to whom it is assigned.

4. Cultural and Political
4.1 Company policy says that all computer equipment is purchased from Dell.
4.2 Customer personal information is protected in compliance with the Data Protection Act.
4.3 The system will conform to the state's "lemon law."

FIGURE 3-3
Sample Requirements Definition

and nonfunctional requirements. Then, within each of those headings, they are grouped further by the type of requirement or by function.

Sometimes, business requirements are prioritized on the requirements definition. They can be ranked as having "high," "medium," or "low" importance in the new system, or they can be labeled with the version of the system that will address the requirement (e.g., release 1, release 2, release 3). This practice is particularly important with RAD methodologies that deliver requirements in batches by developing incremental versions of the system.

The most *obvious* purpose of the requirements definition is to provide the information needed by the other deliverables in the analysis phase, which include use cases, process models, and data models, and to support activities in the design phase. The most *important* purpose of the requirements definition, however, is to define the scope of the system. The document describes to the analysts exactly what the final system needs to do. In addition, it serves to establish the users' expectations for the system. If and when discrepancies or misunderstandings arise, the document serves as a resource for clarification.

Determining Requirements

Both business and IT perspectives are needed to determine requirements for the requirements definition. Systems analysts may not understand the true business needs of the users. A recent study by the Standish Group found that the lack of user involvement is the top reason for IT project failure.[2] On the other hand, the business users may not be aware of the opportunities that a new technology may offer and may simply automate existing, inefficient procedures.

A good analogy is building a house or an apartment. We have all lived in a house or apartment, and most of us have some understanding of what we would like

---

YOUR

TURN

3-2 COLLECTING DATA FOR THE LONG TERM

Pharmaceutical companies are generally heavily regulated. It may take years for a new drug to make it to the marketplace, given the long development phase, highly monitored testing, and the necessity for final approval by the Food and Drug Administration (FDA). Once a drug is in the marketplace, other companies can try to produce generic drugs that seem to be compatible with the name-brand drug.

Occasionally, some years into its life span, an approved drug gets scrutiny for higher-than-expected side effects. For example, a drug that is effective in lowering cholesterol may also cause a side effect of an increased chance for cataract growth that was not discovered during the initial testing and approval cycle.

Data are collected on all aspects of clinical trials and from the marketplace, but some relationships are just harder to find.

QUESTIONS:
1. Is there a particular systems approach to being able to collect and analyze certain pieces of data from a mountain of data?
2. If you were building a strategic planning system for tracking a drug, from proposal through development and testing and into the marketplace, how would you approach the task?
3. What requirements might be necessary in building such a system?

---

[2] Frank Hayes, "Chaos is back," *Computerworld,* November 8, 2004.

to see in one. If we were asked to design one from scratch, however, it would be a challenge because we lack appropriate design skills and technical engineering skills. Likewise, an architect acting alone would probably miss some of our unique requirements.

Therefore, the most effective approach is to have both businesspeople and analysts working together to determine business requirements. Sometimes, however, the users neither know what they want nor understand what they need. It is important that the analyst ensures that the requirements list stays focused and does not become a bloated laundry list of user wishes. A variety of tools is available to help the analyst help the users discover their true needs. These tools are grouped into three broad techniques that are based on the degree of change anticipated in the to-be system. Business process automation (BPA) generally involves a small amount of change; business process improvement (BPI) involves a moderate amount of change, and business process reengineering (BPR) involves a substantial amount of change. According to the high-level business requirements stated in the systems request, the analyst can select the technique that seems to most closely fit the project at hand.

The three techniques work similarly. They help users critically examine the current state of systems and processes (the as-is system), identify exactly what needs to change, and develop a concept for a new system (the to-be system). All three techniques will be described in greater detail later in the chapter.

Although BPA, BPI, and BPR enable the analyst to help users create a vision for the new system, they are not sufficient for extracting information about the detailed business requirements that are needed to build it. Therefore, analysts use a portfolio of requirements-gathering techniques to acquire information from users. The analyst has many gathering techniques from which to choose: interviews, questionnaires, observation, joint application development (JAD), and document analysis. The information gathered by these techniques is critically analyzed and used to craft the requirements definition. The final section of this chapter describes each of the requirements-gathering techniques in greater depth.

Creating the Requirements Definition

Creating the requirements definition is an iterative and ongoing process whereby the analyst collects information with requirements-gathering techniques (e.g., interviews, document analysis), critically analyzes the information to identify appropriate business requirements for the system, and adds the requirements to the requirements definition report. The requirements definition is kept up to date so that the project team and business users can refer to it and get a clear understanding of the new system.

To create the requirements definition, the project team first determines the kinds of functional and nonfunctional requirements that they will collect about the system. (Of course, these may change over time.) These become the main sections of the document. Next, the analysts use a variety of requirement-gathering techniques (e.g., interviews, observation) to collect information, and they list the business requirements that were identified from that information. Finally, the analysts work with the entire project team and the business users to verify, change, and complete the list and to help prioritize the importance of the requirements that were identified.

This process continues throughout the analysis phase, and the requirements definition evolves over time as new requirements are identified and as the project moves into later phases of the SDLC. Beware: The evolution of the requirements definition must be carefully managed. Keeping the requirements list tight and focused is a key to project success. The project team cannot keep adding to the requirements definition, or the system will keep growing and growing and never get finished. Instead, the project team carefully identifies requirements and evaluates which ones fit within the system scope. When a requirement reflects a real business need, but is not within the scope of the current system or current release, it is added to a list of future requirements or given a low priority. The management of requirements (and system scope) is one of the hardest parts of managing a project!

REQUIREMENTS ANALYSIS TECHNIQUES

The basic process of *analysis* involves three steps:

- Understand the existing situation (the as-is system).
- Identify improvements.
- Define requirements for the new system (the to-be system).

The three requirements analysis techniques—business process automation, business process improvement, and business process reengineering—help the analysts lead users through the analysis steps so that the vision of the system can be developed.

Sometimes the first step (i.e., understanding the as-is system) is skipped or done in a limited manner. This happens when no current system exists, if the existing system and processes are irrelevant to the future system, or if the project team is using a RAD or agile development methodology in which the as-is system is not emphasized. Traditional methods such as waterfall and parallel development (see Chapter 2) typically allot significant time to understanding the as-is system and identifying improvements before moving to capture requirements for the to-be system. Newer RAD and agile methodologies, such as iterative development, system prototyping, throwaway prototyping, and extreme programming (see Chapter 2), focus almost exclusively on improvements and the to-be system requirements, and they allow little time for investigating the current as-is system.

To move the users "from here to there," an analyst needs strong *critical thinking skills*. Critical thinking is the ability to recognize strengths and weaknesses and recast an idea in an improved form and is needed in order for the analyst to understand issues and develop new business processes. These skills are essential in examining the results of requirements gathering, identifying business requirements, and translating those requirements into a concept for the new system.

As an example, let's say that a user expresses a requirement that the new system "eliminate inventory stock-outs." While this might be a worthy goal, the analyst needs to think about it critically. The analyst could first have the users think about circumstances leading to stock-outs (supplier orders are not placed in a timely way), and then describe the issues that lead to these circumstances (on-hand inventory levels are only updated once a week; delays occur in identifying the best supply source for the items). By focusing on these issues, the team is in a better position to develop new business processes that address these concerns.

We should note that requirements analysis techniques and requirements-gathering techniques go hand in hand. Analysts need to use requirements-gathering techniques to collect information; requirements analysis techniques drive the kind of information that is gathered and how it is ultimately analyzed. Although we focus now on the analysis techniques and then discuss requirements gathering at the end of the chapter, they happen concurrently and are complementary activities.

Business Process Automation

The business process automation (BPA) technique is used when the basic business requirements outlined in the system request focus on employing computer technology in some aspect of the business process, but leave the basic manner in which the organization operates unchanged. These types of projects can improve organizational efficiency, but have the least impact and value for the business. Projects in this category typically perform all three steps of the analysis process. Two popular activities used in the BPA technique are problem analysis and root cause analysis.

Problem Analysis The most straightforward (and probably the most commonly used) requirements analysis activity is *problem analysis*. Problem analysis means asking the users and managers to identify problems with the as-is system and to describe how to solve them in the to-be system. Most users have a very good idea of the changes they would like to see, and most will be quite vocal about suggesting them. Most changes tend to solve problems rather than capitalize on opportunities, but this is possible, too. Improvements from problem analysis tend to be small and incremental (e.g., add a field to store the customer's cell phone number; provide a new report that currently does not exist).

This type of improvement often is very effective at improving a system's efficiency or ease of use. However, it often provides only minor improvements in business value—the new system is better than the old, but it may be hard to identify significant monetary benefits from the new system.

Root Cause Analysis The ideas produced by problem analysis tend to be *solutions* to problems. All solutions make assumptions about the nature of the problem, assumptions that may or may not be valid. In our experience, users (and most people in general) tend to jump quickly to solutions without fully considering the nature of the problem. Sometimes the solutions are appropriate, but many times they address a *symptom* of the problem, not the true problem or *root cause* itself.[3]

For example, suppose that the users report that "inventory stock-outs happen frequently." Inventory stock-outs are not good, of course, and one obvious way to reduce their occurrence is to increase the quantity of items kept in stock. This action incurs costs, however, so it is worthwhile to investigate the underlying cause of the frequent stock-outs instead of jumping to a quick-fix solution. The solutions that users propose (or systems that analysts consider) may address either symptoms or causes, but without careful analysis, it is difficult to tell which one. Finding out later that you've just spent millions of dollars and have not fixed the *true* underlying problem is a horrible feeling!

Root cause analysis focuses on problems first rather than solutions. The analyst starts by having the users generate a list of problems with the current system, then prioritizes the problems in order of importance. Starting with the most important, the users and/or analysts generate all possible root causes for the problem.

---

[3] Two good books that discuss the problems in finding the root causes to problems are E. M. Goldratt and J. Cox, *The Goal,* Croton-on-Hudson, NY: North River Press, 1986; and E. M. Goldratt, *The Haystack Syndrome,* Croton-on-Hudson, NY: North River Press, 1990.

As shown in Figure 3-4, the problem of "too frequent stock-outs" has several potential root causes (inaccurate on-hand counts; incorrect reorder points; lag in placing supplier orders). Each possible root cause is investigated and additional root causes are identified. As Figure 3-4 shows, it is sometimes useful to display the potential root causes in a tree-like hierarchy. Ultimately, the investigation process reveals the true root cause or causes of the problem, enabling the team to design the system to correct the problem with the right solution. The key point in root cause analysis is to always challenge the obvious and dig into the problem deeply enough that the true underlying cause(s) is revealed.

Business Process Improvement

Business process improvement (*BPI*) means that the basic business requirements target moderate changes to the organization's operations. These changes take advantage of new opportunities offered by technology or copy what competitors are doing. BPI can improve efficiency (i.e., doing things right) and improve effectiveness (i.e., doing the right things). BPI projects also spend time understanding the as-is system, but much less time than BPA projects; their primary focus is on

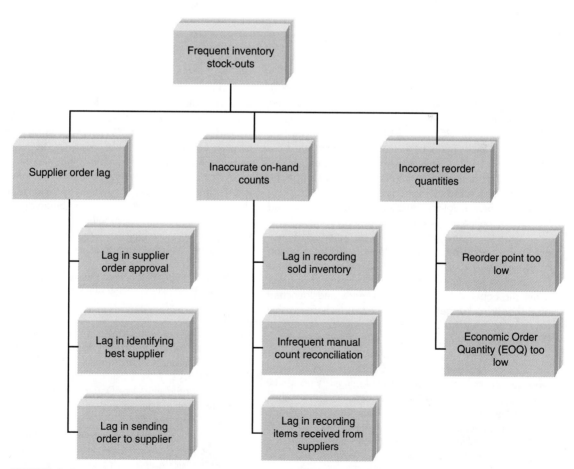

FIGURE 3-4
Root Cause Analysis for Inventory Stock Outs

improving business processes, so time is spent on the as-is system only to help with the improvement analyses and the to-be system requirements. Duration analysis, activity-based costing, and informal benchmarking are three popular BPI activities.

Duration Analysis *Duration analysis* requires a detailed examination of the amount of time it takes to perform each process in the current as-is system. The analysts begin by determining the total amount of time it takes, on average, to perform a set of business processes for a typical input. They then time each of the individual steps (or subprocesses) in the business process. The time to complete the basic steps are then totaled and compared with the total for the overall process. A significant difference between the two—and, in our experiences, the total time often can be 10 or even 100 times longer than the sum of the parts—indicates that this part of the process is badly in need of a major overhaul.

For example, suppose that the analysts arc working on a home mortgage system and discover that, on average, it takes 30 days for the bank to approve a mortgage. They then look at each of the basic steps in the process (e.g., data

---

CONCEPTS | **3-B SUCCESS FROM FAILURE**

IN ACTION

Few niches crashed more spectacularly during Web 1.0 than the pet sector. In 2000, over just nine months, Pets.com managed to raise a jaw-dropping $82.5 million in an IPO, air a $1.2 million Super Bowl ad starring its sock puppet mascot, land funding from Amazon.com build a network of cavernous warehouses ... and go out of business without making a penny in profit. When Pets.com rolled over and died in November 2000, it presaged scores of dot-com disasters to follow and slammed the door on online pet businesses, seemingly for good.

So when San Francisco Web designer Ted Rheingold co-founded Dogster.com in January 2004 as a kind of canine version of Friendster, the news drew smirks from the few who bothered to notice. How could Dogster, a pet site cobbled together on weekends and launched on a shoestring budget, expect to succeed where lavishly funded pet sites had flamed out? The consensus on Dogster was unanimous: It would fail.

And indeed, it has failed. Over and over. But, alas, each knock has been a boost. Dogster has discovered ways to turn its mistakes into better features. With pretty much no promotion, Dogster (and sister site Catster.com) has evolved into a premier pet lover's social network. Membership exceeds 275,000; the site features 340,000 photos and profiles of dogs and cats, and a blue-chip advertising list that includes Disney, Holiday Inn, and Target. Dogster, come to find out, has a good profit sheet.

In many ways, the site is a prime example of how a Web deployment fails, but fails well by quick feature launch, seeing what works, and fixing things fast. According to Rheingold, "When we roll out a new feature, we know we're probably not going to get it right the first time." Dogster and similar companies have discovered that continually reviewing user data—most importantly, the discouraging events—provides important direction for enhancements. Says Rheingold, "Instead of working on a feature for months trying to get it perfect, we'll work on something for two weeks and then spend two or three days listening to users and fine-tuning it."

Source: "A Startup's Best Friend? Failure," Tom McNichol, *Business 2.0.* San Francisco: March 2007, vol. 8, iss. 2, p. 39–41.

QUESTIONS:
1. Do you agree with Dogster's view, or should companies aim for "zero-defect" operations? Why or why not? What implications does this business model have for systems analysts?
2. Startup companies like Dogster are not the only companies that are implementing the "fail fast" strategy. Large companies like Google have used it and are still using it—in Google's case, with the implementation of the Google Toolbar. Cite another company that has used this strategy. Has it been successful?

entry, credit check, title search, appraisal, etc.) and find that the total amount of time actually spent on each mortgage is about 8 hours. This is a strong indication that the overall process is badly broken, because it takes 30 days to perform 1 day's work.

These problems likely occur because the process is badly fragmented. Many different people must perform different activities before the process is complete. In the mortgage example, the application probably sits on many peoples' desks for long periods of time before it is processed. Processes in which many different people work on small parts of the inputs are prime candidates for *process integration* or *parallelization.* Process integration means changing the fundamental process so that fewer people work on the input, which often requires changing the processes and retraining staff to perform a wider range of duties. Process parallelization means changing the process so that all the individual steps are performed at the same time. For example in the mortgage application example, there is probably no reason that the credit check cannot be performed at the same time as the appraisal and title check.

Activity-Based Costing   *Activity-based costing* is a similar analysis that examines the cost of each major process or step in a business process rather than the time taken.[4] The analysts identify the costs associated with each of the basic functional steps or processes, identify the most costly processes, and focus their improvement efforts on them.

Assigning costs is conceptually simple. You just examine the direct cost of labor and materials for each input. Materials costs are easily assigned in a manufacturing process, while labor costs are usually calculated on the basis of the amount of time spent on the input and the hourly cost of the staff. However, as you may recall from a managerial accounting course, there are indirect costs such as rent, depreciation, and so on that also can be included in activity costs.

CONCEPTS

IN ACTION

3-C A PROCESS IN NEED OF IMPROVEMENT

A group of executives from a Fortune 500 company used duration analysis to discuss their procurement process. Using a huge wall of Velcro and a handful of placards, a facilitator proceeded to map out the company's process for procuring a $50 software upgrade. Having quantified the time it took to complete each step, she then assigned costs based on the salaries of the employees involved. The 15-minute exercise left the group stunned. Their procurement process had gotten so convoluted that it took 18 days, countless hours of paperwork and nearly $22,000 in people time to get the product ordered, received, and up and running on the requester's desktop.

Source: "For Good Measure," *CIO* Magazine, March 1, 1999, by Debby Young.

---

[4] Many books have been written on activity-based costing. Useful ones include K. B. Burk and D. W. Webster, *Activity-Based Costing*, Fairfax, VA: American Management Systems, 1994; and D. T. Hicks, *Activity-Based Costing*: *Making It Work for Small and Mid-Sized Companies*, New York: John Wiley, 1998. The two books by Eli Goldratt mentioned previously (*The Goal* and *The Haystack Syndrome*) also offer unique insights into costing.

Informal Benchmarking   *Benchmarking* refers to studying how other organizations perform a business process in order to learn how your organization can do something better. Benchmarking helps the organization by introducing ideas that employees may never have considered, but that have the potential to add value.

Informal benchmarking is fairly common for "customer-facing" business processes (i.e., those processes that interact with the customer). With informal benchmarking, the managers and analysts think about other organizations, or visit them as customers to watch how the business process is performed. In many cases, the business studied may be a known leader in the industry or simply a related firm. For example, suppose that the team is developing a Web site for a car dealer. The project sponsor, key managers, and key team members would likely visit the Web sites of competitors, those of others in the car industry (e.g., manufacturers, accessories suppliers), and those of other industries that have won awards for their Web sites.

Business Process Reengineering

Business process reengineering (*BPR*) means changing the fundamental way in which the organization operates—"obliterating" the current way of doing business and making major changes to take advantage of new ideas and new technology. BPR projects allot little time to understanding the as-is system, because their goal is to focus on new ideas and new ways of doing business. Outcome analysis, technology analysis, and activity elimination are three popular BPR activities.

Outcome Analysis   *Outcome analysis* focuses on understanding the fundamental outcomes that provide value to customers. While these outcomes sound as though they should be obvious, they often aren't. For example, suppose that you are an insurance company and one of your customers has just had a car accident. What is the fundamental outcome from the *customer's* perspective? Traditionally, insurance companies have answered this question by assuming that the customer wants to receive the insurance payment quickly. To the customer, however, the payment is only a *means* to the real outcome: a repaired car. The insurance company might benefit by extending its view of the business process past its traditional boundaries to include, not simply paying for repairs, but performing the repairs or contracting with an authorized body shop to do them.

With this approach, the system analysts encourage the managers and project sponsor to pretend that they are customers and to think carefully about what the organization's products and services enable the customers to do—and what they *could* enable the customer to do.

Technology Analysis   Many major changes in business over the past decade have been enabled by new technologies. *Technology analysis* therefore starts by having the analysts and managers develop a list of important and interesting technologies. Then the group systematically identifies how each and every technology could be applied to the business process and identifies how the business would benefit.

For example, one useful technology might be the Internet. Saturn, the car manufacturer, took this idea and developed an extranet application for its suppliers. Rather than ordering parts for its cars, Saturn makes its production schedule available electronically to its suppliers, who ship the parts Saturn needs so that they arrive at the plant just in time. This saves Saturn significant costs because it eliminates the need for people to monitor the production schedule and issue purchase orders.

Activity Elimination *Activity elimination* is exactly what it sounds like. The analysts and managers work together to identify how the organization could eliminate each and every activity in the business process, how the function could operate without it, and what effects are likely to occur. Initially, managers are reluctant to conclude that processes can be eliminated, but this is a "force-fit" exercise in that they must eliminate each activity. In some cases the results are silly; nonetheless, participants must address each and every activity in the business process.

For example, in the home mortgage approval process discussed earlier, the managers and analysts would start by eliminating the first activity, entering the data into the mortgage company's computer. This leads to one of two obvious possibilities: (1) Eliminate the use of a computer system or (2) make someone else do the data entry (e.g., the customer, over the Web). They would then eliminate the next activity, the credit check. Silly, right? After all, making sure the applicant has good credit is critical in issuing a loan, isn't it? Not really. The real answer depends upon

---

YOUR TURN

3-3 IBM CREDIT

IBM Credit was a wholly owned subsidiary of IBM responsible for financing mainframe computers sold by IBM. While some customers bought mainframes outright or obtained financing from other sources, financing computers provided significant additional profit.

When an IBM sales representative made a sale, he or she would immediately call IBM Credit to obtain a financing quote. The call was received by a credit officer who would record the information on a request form. The form would then be sent to the credit department to check the customer's credit status. This information would be recorded on the form, which was then sent to the business practices department, which would write a contract (sometimes reflecting changes requested by the customer). The form and the contract would then go to the pricing department, which used the credit information to establish an interest rate and record it on the form. The form and contract was then sent to the clerical group, where an administrator would prepare a cover letter quoting the interest rate and send the letter and contract via Federal Express to the customer.

The problem at IBM Credit was a major one. Getting a financing quote took anywhere from four to eight days (six days, on average), giving the customer time to rethink the order or find financing elsewhere. While the quote was being prepared, sales representatives would often call to find out where the quote was in the process, so that they could tell the customer when to expect it. However, no one at IBM Credit could answer the question, because the paper forms could be in any department and

it was impossible to locate one without physically walking through the departments and going through the piles of forms on everyone's desk.

IBM Credit examined the process and changed it so that each credit request was logged into a computer system so that each department could record an application's status as soon as it was completed and sent it to the next department. In this way, sales representatives could call the credit office and quickly learn the status of each application. IBM used some sophisticated management science queuing theory analysis to balance workloads and staff across the different departments so that no applications would be overloaded. They also introduced performance standards for each department (e.g., the pricing decision had to be completed within one day after that department received an application).

However, process times got worse, even though each department was achieving almost 100 percent compliance on its performance goals. After some investigation, managers found that when people got busy, they conveniently found errors that forced them to return the credit request to the previous department for correction, thereby removing it from their time measurements.

QUESTIONS:

What techniques can you use to identify improvements? Choose one technique and apply it to this situation—what improvements did you identify?

Source: Reengineering the Corporation, New York: Harper Business, 1993, by M. Hammer and J. Champy.

how many times the credit check identifies bad applications. If all or almost all applicants have good credit and are seldom turned down by a credit check, then the cost of the credit check may not be worth the cost of the few bad loans it prevents. Eliminating it may actually result in lower costs, even with the cost of bad loans, unless the number of applicants with poor credit greatly increases.

Comparing Analysis Techniques

Each of the requirements analysis techniques discussed here has its own strengths and weaknesses, and no one technique is inherently better than the others. Remember that an organization will likely have a wide range of projects in its portfolio; the requirements analysis technique should be chosen to fit the nature of the project. As shown in Figure 3-5, projects using the three requirements analysis techniques will vary in terms of potential value to the business, cost, breadth of analysis, and risk.

Potential Business Value   The *potential business value* varies with analysis technique. While projects using BPA have the potential to improve the business, most of the benefits from BPA projects are tactical and small in nature. Since BPA projects do not seek to change the business processes, only process efficiency can be improved. BPI projects usually offer moderate potential benefits, depending on the scope, because they seek to change the business in some way. Both efficiency and effectiveness can be increased. BPR projects create large *potential* benefits because they seek to radically improve the nature of the business.

Project Cost   *Project cost* is always important. In general, BPA projects involve the lowest cost because of the narrow focus and few number of changes. BPI projects can be moderately expensive, depending on the scope. BPR projects are usually expensive, both because of the amount of time required of senior managers and the amount of business process redesign.

Breadth of Analysis   *Breadth of analysis* refers to the scope of analysis, or whether the analysis includes business processes within a single business function, processes that cross the organization, or processes that interact with those in customer or supplier organizations. BPR projects take a broad perspective, often spanning several major business processes, even across multiple organizations. BPI projects have a much narrower scope that usually includes one or several business functions. BPA projects typically examine a single process.

	Business Process Automation	Business Process Improvement	Business Process Reengineering
Potential business value	Low–moderate	Moderate	High
Project cost	Low	Low–moderate	High
Breadth of analysis	Narrow	Narrow–moderate	Very broad
Risk	Low–moderate	Low–moderate	Very high

FIGURE 3-5
Project Characteristics

3-4 ANALYSIS TECHNIQUE

Suppose that you are the analyst charged with developing a new Web site for a local car dealer who wants to be very innovative and try new things. What analysis technique would you recommend? What activities seem most promising? Why?

Risk   One final issue is *risk* of failure, which is the likelihood of failure due to poor design, unmet needs, or too much change for the organization to handle. BPA and BPI projects have low to moderate risk, because the to-be system is fairly well defined and understood and the project's potential impact on the business can be assessed before it is implemented. BPR projects, on the other hand, are less predictable. BPR is extremely risky and not something to be undertaken unless the organization and its senior leadership are committed to making significant changes. Mike Hammer, the father of BPR, estimates that 70% of BPR projects fail.

REQUIREMENTS-GATHERING TECHNIQUES

An analyst is very much like a detective (and business users sometimes are like elusive suspects). He or she knows that there is a problem to be solved and therefore must look for clues that uncover the solution. Unfortunately, the clues are not always obvious (and often are missed), so the analyst needs to notice details, talk with witnesses, and follow leads, just as Sherlock Holmes would have done. The best analysts will thoroughly gather requirements by a variety of techniques and make sure that the current business processes and the needs for the new system are well understood before moving into design. You don't want to discover later that you have key requirements wrong—surprises like this late in the SDLC can cause all kinds of problems.

Requirements-Gathering in Practice

Before discussing the five requirements-gathering techniques in detail, a few practical tips are in order. First, the analyst should recognize that important side effects of the requirements-gathering process include building political support for the project and establishing trust and rapport between the project team and the ultimate users of the system. Every contact and interaction between the analyst and a potential business user or manager is an opportunity to generate interest, enthusiasm, and commitment to the project. Therefore, the analyst should be prepared to make good use of these opportunities as they arise during the requirements-gathering process.

Second, the analyst should carefully determine who is included in the requirements-gathering process. The choice to include (or exclude) someone is significant; involving someone in the process implies that the analyst views that person as an important resource and values his or her opinions. You *must* include all of the key *stakeholders* (the people who can affect the system or who will be affected by the system). This might include managers, employees, staff members, and even some customers and suppliers. Also, be sensitive to the fact that some people may have significant influence within the organization even if they do not rank high in the formal organizational hierarchy. If you do not involve a key person, that individual may feel slighted, causing problems during implementation (e.g., saying "I could have told them this might happen, but they didn't ask *me*!").

Finally, do everything possible to respect the time commitment that you are asking the participants to make. The best way to do this is to be fully prepared and to make good use of all the types of requirements-gathering techniques. Although, as we will see, interviewing is the most commonly used technique, other indirect methods may help the analyst develop a basic understanding of the business domain so that the direct techniques are more productive. In general, a useful strategy for the analyst to employ is to begin requirements gathering by interviewing senior managers to gain an understanding of the project and get the "big picture." These preliminary interviews can then be followed by document analysis and, possibly, observation of business processes to learn more about the business domain, the vocabulary, and the as-is system. More interviews may then follow to gather the rest of the information needed to understand the as-is system.

In our experience, identifying improvements is most commonly done through JAD sessions because these sessions enable the users and key stakeholders to work together and create a shared understanding of the possibilities for the to-be system. Occasionally, these JAD sessions are followed by questionnaires sent to a much larger group of users or potential users to get a broad range of opinions. The concept for the to-be system is frequently developed through interviews with senior managers, followed by JAD sessions with users of all levels, to make sure that the key requirements of the new system are well understood.

In this chapter, we focus on the five most commonly used requirements-gathering techniques: interviews, JAD sessions, questionnaires, document analysis, and observation.

Interviews

The *interview* is the most commonly used requirements-gathering technique. After all, it is natural—usually, if you need to know something, you ask someone. In general, interviews are conducted one on one (one interviewer and one interviewee), but sometimes, due to time constraints, several people are interviewed at the same time. There are five basic steps to the interview process: selecting interviewees, designing interview questions, preparing for the interview, conducting the interview, and postinterview follow-up.[5]

Selecting Interviewees An *interview schedule* should be created, listing who will be interviewed, the purpose of the interview, and where and when it will take place. (See Figure 3-6.) The schedule can be an informal list that is used to help set up meeting times or a formal list that is incorporated into the work plan. The people who appear on the interview schedule are selected on the basis of the analyst's information needs. The project sponsor, key business users, and other members of the project team can help the analyst determine who in the organization can best provide important information about requirements. These people are listed on the interview schedule in the order in which they should be interviewed.

---

[5] A good book on interviewing is Brian James, *The Systems Analysis Interview*, Manchester: NCC Blackwell, 1989.

Name	Position	Purpose of Interview	Meeting
Andria McClellan	Director, Accounting	Strategic vision for new accounting system	Mon, March 1 8:00–10:00 A.M.
Jennifer Draper	Manager, Accounts Receivable	Current problems with accounts receivable process; future goals	Mon, March 1 2:00–3:15 P.M.
Mark Goodin	Manager, Accounts Payable	Current problems with accounts payable process; future goals	Mon, March 1 4:00–5:15 P.M.
Anne Asher	Supervisor, Data Entry	Accounts receivable and payable processes	Wed, March 3 10:00–11:00 A.M.
Fernando Merce	Data Entry Clerk	Accounts receivable and payable processes	Wed, March 3 1:00–3:00 P.M.

FIGURE 3-6
Sample Interview Schedule

People at different levels of the organization will have different viewpoints on the system, so it is important to include both managers who manage the processes and staff who actually perform the processes to gain both high-level and low-level perspectives on an issue. Also, the kinds of interview subjects that you need may change over time. For example, at the start of the project the analyst has a limited understanding of the as-is business process. It is common to begin by interviewing one or two senior managers to get a strategic view and then move to mid-level managers who can provide broad, overarching information about the business process and the expected role of the system being developed. Once the analyst has a good understanding of the big picture, lower-level managers and staff members can fill in the exact details of how the process works. Like most other things about systems analysis, this is an iterative process—starting with senior managers, moving to mid-level managers, then staff members, back to mid-level managers, and so on, depending upon what information is needed along the way.

It is quite common for the list of interviewees to grow, often by 50%–75%. As you interview people, you likely will identify more information that is needed and additional people who can provide the information.

CONCEPTS

IN ACTION

3-D SELECTING THE WRONG PEOPLE

In 1990, I led a consulting team for a major development project for the U.S. Army. The goal was to replace eight existing systems used on virtually every Army base across the United States. The as-is process and data models for these systems had been built, and our job was to identify improvement opportunities and develop to-be process models for each of the eight systems.

For the first system, we selected a group of mid-level managers (captains and majors) recommended by their commanders as being the experts in the system under construction. These individuals were the first and second line managers of the business function. The individuals were expert at managing the process, but did not know the exact details of how the process worked. The resulting to-be process model was very general and nonspecific. *Alan Dennis*

QUESTION:
Suppose you were in charge of the project. Create an interview schedule for the remaining seven projects.

Designing Interview Questions   There are three types of interview questions: closed-ended questions, open-ended questions, and probing questions. *Closed-ended questions* require a specific answer. You can think of them as being similar to multiple choice or arithmetic questions on an exam. (See Figure 3-7.) Closed-ended questions are used when the analyst is looking for specific, precise information (e.g., how many credit card requests are received per day). In general, precise questions are best. For example, rather than asking "Do you handle a lot of requests?" it is better to ask "How many requests do you process per day?"

Closed-ended questions enable analysts to control the interview and obtain the information they need. However, these types of questions don't uncover *why* the answer is the way it is, nor do they uncover information that the interviewer does not think to ask ahead of time.

Open-ended questions are those that leave room for elaboration on the part of the interviewee. They are similar in many ways to essay questions that you might find on an exam. (See Figure 3-7 for examples.) Open-ended questions are designed to gather rich information and give the interviewee more control over the information that is revealed during the interview. Sometimes the subjects the interviewee chooses to discuss uncover information that is just as important as the answer (e.g., if the interviewee talks only about other departments when asked for problems, it may suggest that he or she is reluctant to admit his or her own department's problems).

The third type of question is the *probing question.* Probing questions follow up on what has just been discussed in order for the interviewer to learn more, and they often are used when the interviewer is unclear about an interviewee's answer. They encourage the interviewee to expand on or to confirm information from a previous response, and they are a signal that the interviewer is listening and interested in the topic under discussion. Many beginning analysts are reluctant to use probing questions because they are afraid that the interviewee might be offended at being challenged or because they believe it shows that they didn't understand what the interviewee said. When done politely, probing questions can be a powerful tool in requirements gathering.

In general, you should not ask questions about information that is readily available from other sources. For example, rather than asking what information is used to perform to a task, it is simpler to show the interviewee a form or report (see document analysis later) and ask what information on it is used. This helps focus

Types of Questions	Examples
Closed-Ended Questions	• How many telephone orders are received per day?
	• How do customers place orders?
	• What information is missing from the monthly sales report?
Open-Ended Questions	• What do you think about the way invoices are currently processed?
	• What are some of the problems you face on a daily basis?
	• What are some of the improvements you would like to see in the way invoices are processed?
Probing Questions	• Why?
	• Can you give me an example?
	• Can you explain that in a bit more detail?

FIGURE 3-7
Three Types of Questions

the interviewee on the task and saves time, because he or she does not need to describe the information in detail—he or she just needs to point it out on the form or report.

Your interview questions should anticipate the type of information the interviewee is likely to know. Managers are often somewhat removed from the details of daily business processes and so might be unable to answer questions about them, whereas lower-level staff members could readily respond. Conversely, lower-level employees may not be able to answer broad, policy-oriented questions, while managers could. Since no one wants to appear ignorant, avoid confounding your interviewees with questions outside their areas of knowledge.

No type of question is better than another, and usually a combination of questions is used during an interview. At the initial stage of an IS development project the as-is process can be unclear, so the interview process begins with *unstructured interviews*, interviews that seek a broad and roughly defined set of information. In this case, the interviewer has a general sense of the information needed, but few closed-ended questions to ask. These are the most challenging interviews to conduct because they require the interviewer to ask open-ended questions and probe for important information "on the fly."

As the project progresses, the analyst comes to understand the business process much better, and he or she needs very specific information about how business processes are performed (e.g., exactly how a customer credit card is approved). At this time, the analyst conducts *structured interviews* in which specific sets of questions are developed prior to the interviews. There usually are more closed-ended questions in a structured interview than in the unstructured approach.

No matter what kind of interview is being conducted, interview questions must be organized into a logical sequence so that the interview flows well. For example, when trying to gather information about the current business process, the analyst will find it useful to move in logical order through the process or from the most important issues to the least important.

There are two fundamental approaches to organizing the interview questions: top-down or bottom-up; see Figure 3-8. With the *top-down interview*, the interviewer starts with broad, general issues and gradually works towards more specific

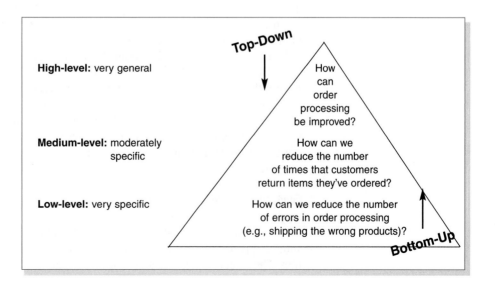

FIGURE 3-8
Top-Down and Bottom-Up Questioning Strategies

ones. With the *bottom-up interview*, the interviewer starts with very specific questions and moves to broad questions. In practice, analysts mix the two approaches, starting with broad general issues, moving to specific questions, and then back to general issues.

The top-down approach is an appropriate strategy for most interviews. (It is certainly the most common approach.) The top-down approach enables the interviewee to become accustomed to the topic before he or she needs to provide specifics. It also enables the interviewer to understand the issues before moving to the details, because the interviewer may not have sufficient information at the start of the interview to ask very specific questions. Perhaps most importantly, the top-down approach enables the interviewee to raise a set of big-picture issues before becoming enmeshed in details, so the interviewer is less likely to miss important issues.

One case in which the bottom-up strategy may be preferred is when the analyst already has gathered a lot of information about issues and just needs to fill in some holes with details. Or, bottom-up may be appropriate if lower-level staff members feel threatened or are unable to answer high-level questions. For example, "How can we improve customer service?" may be too broad a question for a customer service clerk, whereas a specific question is readily answerable (e.g., "How can we speed up customer returns?"). In any event, all interviews should begin with non-controversial questions first and then gradually move into more contentious issues after the interviewer has developed some rapport with the interviewee.

Preparing for the Interview   It is important to prepare for the interview in the same way that you would prepare to give a presentation. You should have a general interview plan which lists the questions that you will ask in the appropriate order; anticipates possible answers and provides how you will follow up with them; and identifies segues between related topics. Confirm the areas in which the interviewee has knowledge so you do not ask questions that he or she cannot answer. Review the topic areas, the questions, and the interview plan, and clearly decide which ones have the greatest priority in case you run out of time.

In general, structured interviews with closed-ended questions take more time to prepare than unstructured interviews. So, some beginning analysts prefer unstructured interviews, thinking that they can "wing it." This is very dangerous and often counterproductive, because any information not gathered in the first interview would have to be obtained by follow-up efforts, and most people do not like to be interviewed repeatedly about the same issues.

Be sure to prepare the interviewee as well. When you schedule the interview, inform the interviewee of the reason for the interview and the areas you will be discussing far enough in advance so that he or she has time to think about the issues and organize his or her thoughts. This is particularly important when you are an outsider to the organization and for interviewing lower-level employees who often are not asked for their opinions and who may be uncertain about why you are interviewing them.

Conducting the Interview   When you start the interview, the first goal is to build rapport with the interviewee so that he or she trusts you and is willing to tell you the whole truth, not just give the answers that he or she thinks you want. You should appear to be professional and an unbiased, independent seeker of information. The interview should start with an explanation of why you are there and why you have chosen to interview the person, and then move into your planned interview questions.

It is critical to carefully record all the information that the interviewee provides. In our experience, the best approach is to take careful notes—write down *everything* the interviewee says, even if it does not appear immediately relevant. Don't be afraid to ask the person to slow down or to pause while you write, because this is a clear indication that the interviewee's information is important to you. One potentially controversial issue is whether or not to tape-record the interview. Recording ensures that you do not miss important points, but it can be intimidating for the interviewee. Most organizations have policies or generally accepted practices about the recording of interviews, so find out what they are before you start an interview. If you are worried about missing information and cannot tape the interview, then bring along a second person to take detailed notes.

As the interview progresses, it is important that you understand the issues that are discussed. If you do not understand something, be sure to ask. Don't be afraid to ask "dumb questions," because the only thing worse than appearing "dumb" is to *be* "dumb" by not understanding something that you could have cleared up by questioning. If you don't understand something during the interview, you certainly won't understand it afterward. Try to recognize and define jargon, and be sure to clarify jargon you do not understand. One good strategy to increase your understanding during an interview is to periodically summarize the key points that the interviewee is communicating. This avoids misunderstandings and also demonstrates that you are listening.

Finally, be sure to separate facts from opinion. The interviewee may say, for example, "We process too many credit card requests." This is an opinion, and it is useful to follow this up with a probing question requesting support for the statement (e.g., "Oh, how many do you process in a day?"). It is helpful to check the facts because any differences between the facts and the interviewee's opinions can point out key areas for improvement. Suppose that the interviewee complains about a high or increasing number of errors, but the logs show that errors have been decreasing. This suggests that errors are viewed as a very important problem that should be addressed by the new system, even if they are declining.

As the interview draws to a close, be sure to give the interviewee time to ask questions or provide information that he or she thinks is important but was not part of your interview plan. In most cases, the interviewee will have no additional concerns or information, but in some cases this will lead to unanticipated, but important information. Likewise, it can be useful to ask the interviewee if there are other people who should be interviewed. Make sure that the interview ends on time. (If necessary, omit some topics or plan to schedule another interview.)

As a last step in the interview, briefly explain what will happen next. (See the next section.) You don't want to prematurely promise certain features in the new system or a specific delivery date, but you do want to reassure the interviewee that his or her time was well spent and very helpful to the project.

Beginning systems analysts may naively think that conducting an interview is as easy as conversing with a friend. Unfortunately, this is almost never true. Interviewees often are not able or willing to hand over the needed information in a neat, organized fashion. In some cases, they may not want to share what they know at all. Analysts should hone their interpersonal skills to improve their interviewing success. (See Practical Tip 3-1.)

3-1 DEVELOPING INTERPERSONAL SKILLS

Interpersonal skills are those that enable you to develop rapport with others, and they are very important for interviewing. They help you to communicate with others effectively. Some people develop good interpersonal skills at an early age; they simply seem to know how to communicate and interact with others. Other people are less "lucky" and need to work hard to develop their skills.

Interpersonal skills, like most skills, can be learned. Here are some tips:

- **Don't worry, be happy.** Happy people radiate confidence and project their feelings on others. Try interviewing someone while smiling and then interviewing someone else while frowning and see what happens!
- **Pay attention.** Pay attention to what the other person is saying (which is harder than you might think). See how many times you catch yourself with your mind on something other than the conversation at hand.
- **Summarize key points.** At the end of each major theme or idea that someone explains, you should repeat the key points back to the speaker (e.g., "Let me make sure I understand. The key issues are …"). This demonstrates that you consider the information important—and also forces you to pay attention. (You can't repeat what you didn't hear.)
- **Be succinct.** When you speak, be succinct. The goal in interviewing (and in much of life) is to learn, not to impress. The more you speak, the less time you give to others.
- **Be honest.** Answer all questions truthfully, and if you don't know the answer, say so.
- **Watch body language (yours and theirs).** The way a person sits or stands conveys much information. In general, a person who is interested in what you are saying sits or leans forward, makes eye contact, and often touches his or her face. A person leaning away from you or with an arm over the back of a chair is disinterested. Crossed arms indicate defensiveness or uncertainty, while "steepling" (sitting with hands raised in front of the body with fingertips touching) indicates a feeling of superiority.

Post-interview Follow-up   After the interview is over, the analyst needs to prepare an *interview report* that describes the information from the interview (Figure 3-9). The report contains *interview notes*, information that was collected over the course of the interview and is summarized in a useful format. In general, the interview report should be written within 48 hours of the interview, because the longer you wait, the more likely you are to forget information.

3-E THE RELUCTANT INTERVIEWEE

Early in my consulting career I was sent to a client organization with the goal of interviewing the only person in the organization who knew how the accounts receivable system worked, and developing documentation for that system (nonexistent at the time). The interviewee was on time, polite, and told me absolutely nothing of value about the accounts receivable system, despite my best efforts over several interview sessions. Eventually, my manager called me off this project, and our attempt to document this system was abandoned. *Roberta Roth*

QUESTIONS:
1. Why do you suppose the interviewee was so uncooperative?
2. Can you think of any ways to avoid this failed outcome?

Interview Notes Approved by: Linda Estey

Person Interviewed: Linda Estey,
   Director, Human Resources

Interviewer: Barbara Wixom

Purpose of Interview:

- Understand reports produced for Human Resources by the current system.
- Determine information requirements for future system.

Summary of Interview:
- Sample reports of all current HR reports are attached to this report. The information that is not used and missing information are noted on the reports.
- Two biggest problems with the current system are:
   1. The data are too old. (The HR Department needs information within 2 days of month end; currently information is provided to them after a 3-week delay.)
   2. The data are of poor quality. (Often, reports must be reconciled with the HR departmental database.)
- The most common data errors found in the current system include incorrect job-level information and missing salary information.

Open Items:
- Get current employee roster report from Mary Skudrna (extension 4355).
- Verify calculations used to determine vacation time with Mary Skudrna.
- Schedule interview with Jim Wack (extension 2337) regarding the reasons for data quality problems.

Detailed Notes: See attached transcript.

FIGURE 3-9
Interview Report

Often, the interview report is sent to the interviewee with a request to read it and inform the analyst of clarifications or updates. Make sure the interviewee is convinced that you genuinely want his or her corrections to the report. Usually, there are few changes, but the need for any significant changes suggests that a second interview will be required. Never distribute someone's information without prior approval.

Joint Application Development (JAD)

Joint application development (or *JAD* as it is more commonly known) is an information gathering technique that allows the project team, users, and management to work together to identify requirements for the system. IBM developed the JAD technique in the late 1970s, and it is often the most useful method for collecting information from users.[6] Capers Jones claims that JAD can reduce scope creep by 50%, and it prevents the requirements for a system from being too specific or too vague, both of which can cause trouble during later stages of the SDLC.[7] JAD is a structured process in which 10 to 20 users meet under the direction of a *facilitator* skilled in JAD techniques. The facilitator is a person who sets the meeting agenda and guides the discussion, but does not join in the discussion as a participant. He or she does not provide ideas or opinions on the topics under discussion

---

[6] More information on JAD can be found in J. Wood and D. Silver, *Joint Application Development*, New York: John Wiley & Sons, 1989; and Alan Cline, "Joint Application Development for Requirements Collection and Management," http://www.carolla.com/wp-jad.htm.

[7] See Kevin Strehlo, "Catching up with the Jones and 'Requirement' Creep," *InfoWorld*, July 29, 1996; and Kevin Strehlo, "The Makings of a Happy Customer: Specifying Project X," *Infoworld*, Nov 11, 1996.

and remains neutral during the session. The facilitator must be an expert in both group process techniques and systems analysis and design techniques. One or two *scribes* assist the facilitator by recording notes, making copies, and so on. Often, the scribes will use computers and CASE tools to record information as the JAD session proceeds.

The JAD group meets for several hours, several days, or several weeks until all of the issues have been discussed and the needed information is collected. Most JAD sessions take place in a specially prepared meeting room, away from the participants' offices, so that they are not interrupted. The meeting room is usually arranged in a U shape so that all participants can easily see each other. (See Figure 3-10.) At the front of the room (the open part of the "U"), there is a whiteboard, flip chart and/or overhead projector for use by the facilitator, who leads the discussion.

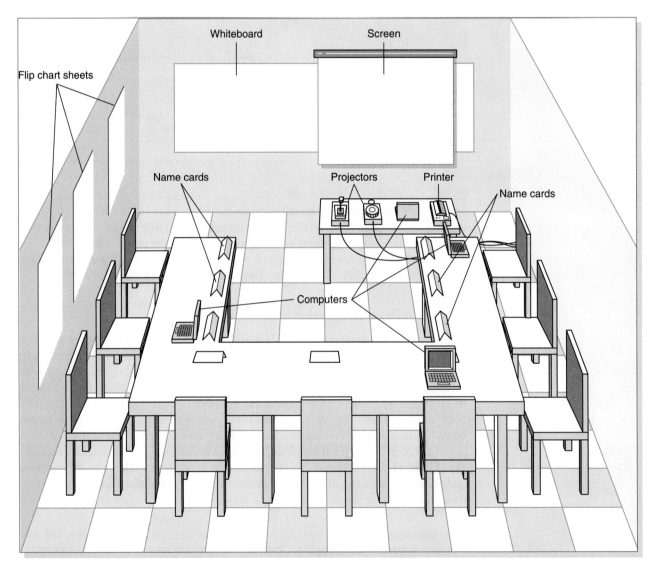

FIGURE 3-10
Joint Application Development Meeting Room

One problem with JAD is that it suffers from the traditional problems associated with groups: Sometimes people are reluctant to challenge the opinions of others (particularly their boss), a few people often dominate the discussion, and not everyone participates. In a 15-member group, for example, if everyone participates equally, then each person can talk for only 4 minutes each hour and must listen for the remaining 56 minutes—not a very efficient way to collect information.

A new form of JAD called *electronic JAD*, or *e-JAD*, attempts to overcome these problems by the use of groupware. In an e-JAD meeting room, each participant uses special software on a networked computer to send anonymous ideas and opinions to everyone else. In this way, all participants can contribute at the same time, without fear of reprisal from people with differing opinions. Initial research suggests that e-JAD can reduce the time required to run JAD sessions by 50%–80%.[8]

Selecting Participants Selecting JAD participants is done in the same basic way as selecting interview participants. Participants are selected on the basis of information they can contribute, to provide a broad mix of organizational levels, and to build political support for the new system. The need for all JAD participants to be away from their offices at the same time can be a major problem. The office may need to be closed or run with a skeleton staff until the JAD sessions are complete.

Ideally, the participants who are released from regular duties to attend the JAD sessions should be the very best people in that business unit. However, without strong management support, JAD sessions can fail, because those selected to attend the JAD session are people who are less likely to be missed (i.e., the least competent people).

The facilitator should be someone who is an expert in JAD or e-JAD techniques and, ideally, someone who has experience with the business under discussion. In many cases, the JAD facilitator is a consultant external to the organization because the organization may not have a regular day-to-day need for JAD or e-JAD expertise. Developing and maintaining this expertise in-house can be expensive.

Designing the JAD Session JAD sessions can run from as little as a half day to several weeks, depending upon the size and scope of the project. In our experience, most JAD sessions tend to last 5 to 10 days spread over a 3-week period. Most e-JAD

[8] For more information on e-JAD, see A. R. Dennis, G. S. Hayes, and R. M. Daniels, "Business Process Modeling with Groupware," *Journal of Management Information Systems*, 1999, 15(4); 115–142.

sessions tend to last 1 to 4 days in a 1-week period. JAD and e-JAD sessions usually move beyond the collection of information into producing analysis deliverables. For example, the users and the analysts collectively can create use cases, process models, or the requirements definition.

As with interviewing, JAD success depends upon a careful plan. JAD sessions usually are designed and structured along the same principles as interviews. Most JAD sessions are designed to collect specific information from users, and this requires the development of a set of questions prior to the meeting. A difference between JAD and interviewing is that all JAD sessions are structured—they *must* be carefully planned. In general, closed-ended questions are seldom used, because they do not spark the open and frank discussion that is typical of JAD. In our experience, it is better to proceed top-down in JAD sessions when gathering information. Typically, 30 minutes is allocated to each separate agenda item, and frequent breaks are scheduled throughout the day because participants tire easily.

Preparing for the JAD Session   As with interviewing, it is important to prepare the analysts and participants for the JAD session. Because the sessions can go beyond the depth of a typical interview and usually are conducted off-site, participants can be more concerned about how to prepare. It is important that the participants understand what is expected of them. If the goal of the JAD session, for example, is to develop an understanding of the current system, then participants can bring procedure manuals and documents with them. If the goal is to identify improvements for a system, then they can think about how they would improve the system prior to the JAD session.

Conducting the JAD Session   Most JAD sessions try to follow a formal agenda, and most have formal *ground rules* that define appropriate behavior. Common ground rules include following the schedule, respecting others' opinions, accepting disagreement, and ensuring that only one person talks at a time.

The role of the JAD facilitator can be challenging. Many participants come to the JAD session with strong feelings about the system being discussed. Channeling these feelings so that the session moves forward in a positive direction and getting participants to recognize and accept—but not necessarily agree on—opinions and situations different from their own requires significant expertise in systems analysis and design, JAD, and interpersonal skills. Few systems analysts attempt to facilitate JAD sessions without being trained in JAD techniques, and most apprentice with a skilled JAD facilitator before they attempt to lead their first session.

The JAD facilitator performs three key functions. First, he or she ensures that the group sticks to the agenda. The only reason to digress from the agenda is when it becomes clear to the facilitator, project leader, and project sponsor that the JAD session has produced some new information that is unexpected and requires the JAD session (and perhaps the project) to move in a new direction. When participants attempt to divert the discussion away from the agenda, the facilitator must be firm, but polite, in leading the discussion back to the agenda and getting the group back on track.

Second, the facilitator must help the group understand the technical terms and jargon that surround the system development process and help the participants understand the specific analysis techniques used. Participants are experts in their business area, but they probably are not experts in systems analysis. The facilitator must therefore minimize the learning required and teach participants how to effectively provide the right information.

Third, the facilitator records the group's input on a public display area, which can be a whiteboard, flip chart, or computer display. He or she structures the information that the group provides and helps the group recognize key issues and important solutions. Under no circumstance should the facilitator insert his or her opinions into the discussion. The facilitator *must* remain neutral at all times and simply help the group through the process. The moment the facilitator offers an opinion on an issue, the group will no longer see him or her as a neutral party, but rather as someone who could be attempting to sway the group into some predetermined solution.

However, this does not mean that the facilitator should not try to help the group resolve issues. For example, if two items appear to be the same to the facilitator, the facilitator should not say, "I think these may be similar." Instead, the facilitator should ask, "Are these similar?" If the group decides that they are, the facilitator can combine them and move on. However, if the group decides that they are not similar (despite what the facilitator believes), the facilitator should accept the decision and move on. The group is *always* right, and the facilitator has no opinion.

Post-JAD Follow-up   As with interviews, a JAD *post-session report* is prepared and circulated among session attendees. The post-session report is essentially the same as the interview report in Figure 3-9. Since the JAD sessions are longer and provide more information, it usually takes a week or two after the JAD session before the report is complete.

Questionnaires

A questionnaire is a set of written questions for obtaining information from individuals. Questionnaires often are used when there is a large number of people from whom information and opinions are needed. In our experience, questionnaires are commonly used for systems intended for use outside of the organization (e.g., by customers or vendors) or for systems with business users spread across many geographic locations. Most people automatically think of paper when they think of questionnaires, but today more questionnaires are being distributed in electronic form, either via e-mail or on the Web. Electronic distribution can save a significant amount of money, compared with distributing paper questionnaires.

Selecting Participants   As with interviews and JAD sessions, the first step is to select the individuals to whom the questionnaire will be sent. However, it is not usual to select every person who could provide useful information. The standard approach is to select a *sample,* or subset, of people who are representative of the entire group. Sampling guidelines are discussed in most statistics books, and most business schools include courses that cover the topic, so we will not discuss it here. The important point in selecting a sample, however, is to realize that not everyone who receives a questionnaire will actually complete it. On average, only 30%–50%

YOUR TURN

3-6 JAD Practice

Organize yourselves into groups of four to seven people, and pick one person in each group to be the JAD facilitator. Using a blackboard, whiteboard, or flip chart, gather information about how the group performs some process (e.g., working on a class assignment, making a sandwich, paying bills, getting to class). How did the JAD session go? Based on your experience, what are some pros and cons of using JAD in a real organization?

PRACTICAL	3-2 MANAGING PROBLEMS IN JAD SESSIONS
TIP	

I have run more than a hundred JAD sessions and have learned several standard "facilitator tricks." Here are some common problems and some ways to deal with them.

- **Reducing domination.** The facilitator should ensure that no one person dominates the group discussion. The only way to deal with someone who dominates is head on. During a break, approach the person, thank him or her for their insightful comments, and ask them to help you make sure that others also participate.
- **Encouraging noncontributors.** Drawing out people who have participated very little is challenging because you want to bring them into the conversation so that they will contribute again. The best approach is to ask a direct factual question that you are *certain* they can answer. And it helps to ask the question using some repetition to give them time to think. For example "Pat, I know you've worked shipping orders a long time. You've probably been in the Shipping Department longer than anyone else. Could you help us understand exactly what happens when an order is received in Shipping?"
- **Side discussions.** Sometimes participants engage in side conversations and fail to pay attention to the group. The easiest solution is simply to walk close to the people and continue to facilitate right in front of them. Few people will continue a side conversion when you are two feet from them and the entire group's attention is on you and them.
- **Agenda merry-go-round.** The merry-go-round occurs when a group member keeps returning to the same issue every few minutes and won't let go. One solution is to let the person have five minutes to ramble on about the issue while you carefully write down every point on a flip chart or computer file. This flip chart or file is then posted conspicuously on the wall. When the person brings up the issue again, you interrupt them,

walk to the paper and ask them what to add. If they mention something already on the list, you quickly interrupt, point out that it is there, and ask what other information to add. Don't let them repeat the same point, but write any new information.

- **Violent agreement.** Some of the worst disagreements occur when participants really agree on the issues but don't realize that they agree because they are using different terms. An example is arguing whether a glass is half empty or half full; they agree on the facts, but can't agree on the words. In this case, the facilitator has to translate the terms into different words and find common ground so the parties recognize that they really agree.
- **Unresolved conflict.** In some cases, participants don't agree and can't understand how to determine what alternatives are better. You can help by structuring the issue. Ask for criteria by which the group will identify a good alternative (e.g., "Suppose this idea really did improve customer service. How would I recognize the improved customer service?"). Then once you have a list of criteria, ask the group to assess the alternatives using them.
- **True conflict.** Sometimes, despite every attempt, participants just can't agree on an issue. The solution is to postpone the discussion and move on. Document the issue as an "open issue" and list it prominently on a flip chart. Have the group return to the issue hours later. Often the issue will resolve itself by then and you haven't wasted time on it. If the issue cannot be resolved later, move it to the list of issues to be decided by the project sponsor or some other more senior member of management.
- **Use humor.** Humor is one of the most powerful tools a facilitator has and thus must be used judiciously. The best JAD humor is always in context; never tell jokes but take the opportunity to find the humor in the situation.
Alan Dennis

of paper and e-mail questionnaires are returned. Response rates for Web-based questionnaires tend to be significantly lower (often, only 5%–30%).

Designing the Questionnaire   Developing good questions is critical for questionnaires because the information on a questionnaire cannot be immediately clarified for a confused respondent. Questions on questionnaires must be very clearly written and must leave little room for misunderstanding; therefore, closed-ended questions tend to be most commonly used. Questions must enable the analyst to clearly separate facts from opinions. Opinion questions often ask the respondent the extent to which they agree or

- Begin with nonthreatening and interesting questions.
- Group items into logically coherent sections.
- Do not put important items at the very end of the questionnaire.
- Do not crowd a page with too many items.
- Avoid abbreviations.
- Avoid biased or suggestive items or terms.
- Number questions to avoid confusion.
- Pretest the questionnaire to identify confusing questions.
- Provide anonymity to respondents.

FIGURE 3-11
Good Questionnaire Design

disagree (e.g., "Are network problems common?"), while factual questions seek more precise values (e.g., "How often does a network problem occur: once an hour, once a day, or once a week?"). See Figure 3-11 for guidelines on questionnaire design.

Perhaps the most obvious issue—but one that is sometimes overlooked—is to have a clear understanding of how the information collected from the questionnaire will be analyzed and used. You must address this issue before you distribute the questionnaire, because it is too late afterward.

Questions should be relatively consistent in style so that the respondent does not have to read instructions for each question before answering it. It is generally a good practice to group related questions together to make them simpler to answer. Some experts suggest that questionnaires should start with questions important to respondents, so that the questionnaire immediately grabs their interest and induces them to answer it. Perhaps the most important step is to have several colleagues review the questionnaire and then pretest it with a few people drawn from the groups to whom it will be sent. It is surprising how often seemingly simple questions can be misunderstood.

Administering the Questionnaire   The key issue in administering the questionnaire is getting participants to complete the questionnaire and send it back. Dozens of marketing research books have been written about ways to improve response rates. Commonly used techniques include clearly explaining why the questionnaire is being conducted and why the respondent has been selected; stating a date by which the questionnaire is to be returned; offering an inducement to complete the questionnaire (e.g., a free pen); and offering to supply a summary of the questionnaire responses. Systems analysts have additional techniques to improve responses rates inside the organization, such as personally handing out the questionnaire and personally contacting those who have not returned them after a week or two, as well as requesting the respondents' supervisors to administer the questionnaires in a group meeting.

Questionnaire Follow-up   It is helpful to process the returned questionnaires and develop a questionnaire report soon after the questionnaire deadline. This ensures that the analysis process proceeds in a timely fashion and that respondents who requested copies of the results receive them promptly.

Document Analysis

Project teams often use *document analysis* to understand the as-is system. Under ideal circumstances, the project team that developed the existing system will have produced documentation, which was then updated by all subsequent projects. In this case, the project team can start by reviewing the documentation and examining the system itself.

Unfortunately, most systems are not well documented, because project teams fail to document their projects along the way, and when the projects are over, there is no time to go back and document. Therefore, there may not be much technical documentation about the current system available, or it may not contain updated information about recent system changes. However, there are many helpful documents that do exist in the organization: paper reports, memorandums, policy manuals, user training manuals, organization charts, and forms.

But these documents (forms, reports, policy manuals, organization charts) only tell part of the story. They represent the *formal system* that the organization uses. Quite often, the "real," or *informal system* differs from the formal one, and these differences, particularly large ones, give strong indications of what needs to be changed. For example, forms or reports that are never used likely should be eliminated. Likewise, boxes or questions on forms that are never filled in (or are used for other purposes) should be rethought. See Figure 3-12 for an example of how a document can be interpreted.

The most powerful indication that the system needs to be changed is when users create their own forms or add additional information to existing ones. Such changes clearly demonstrate the need for improvements to existing systems. Thus, it is useful to review both blank and completed forms to identify these deviations. Likewise, when users access multiple reports to satisfy their information needs, it is a clear sign that new information or new information formats are needed.

Observation

Observation, the act of watching processes being performed, is a powerful tool for gathering information about the as-is system because it enables the analyst to see the reality of a situation, rather than listening to others describe it in interviews or JAD sessions. Several research studies have shown that many managers really do not remember how they work and how they allocate their time. (Quick, how many hours did you spend last week on each of your courses?) Observation is a good way to check the validity of information gathered from other sources such as interviews and questionnaires.

In many ways, the analyst becomes an anthropologist as he or she walks through the organization and observes the business system as it functions. The goal

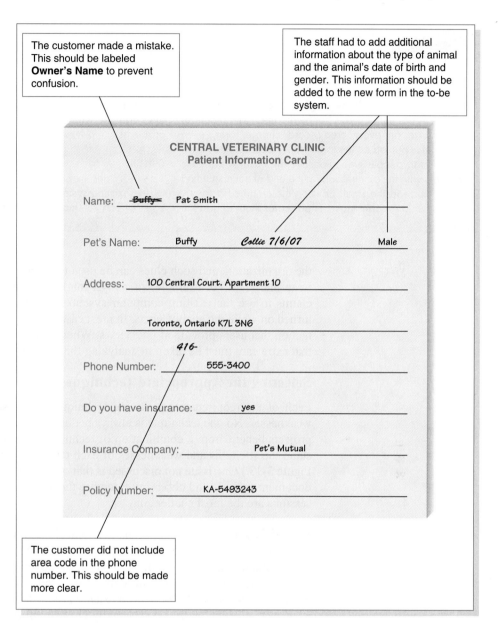

The customer made a mistake. This should be labeled **Owner's Name** to prevent confusion.

The staff had to add additional information about the type of animal and the animal's date of birth and gender. This information should be added to the new form in the to-be system.

The customer did not include area code in the phone number. This should be made more clear.

FIGURE 3-12
Performing a Document Analysis

is to keep a low profile, to not interrupt those working, and to not influence those being observed. Nonetheless, it is important to understand that what analysts observe may not be the normal day-to-day routine because people tend to be extremely careful in their behavior when they are being watched.[9] Even though normal practice may be to break formal organizational rules, the observer is unlikely to see this. (Remember how you drove the last time a police car followed you?) Thus, what you see may *not* be what you get.

Observation is often used to supplement interview information. The location of a person's office and its furnishings gives clues as to their power and influence in

[9] This illustrates the Hawthorne effect: an increase in worker productivity produced by the psychological stimulus of being singled out and made to feel important. See R. H. Frank and J. D. Kaul, "The Hawthorne Experiments: First Statistical Interpretation," *American Sociological Review*, 1978, 43: 623–643.

3-E Publix Credit Card Forms

At my neighborhood Publix grocery store, the cashiers always handwrite the total amount of the charge on every credit card charge form, even though it is printed on the form. Why? Because the "back office" staff people who reconcile the cash in the cash drawers with the amount sold at the end of each shift find it hard to read the small print on the credit card forms. Writing in large print makes it easier for them to add the values up. However, cashiers sometimes make mistakes and write the wrong amount on the forms, which causes problems.   *Barbara Wixom*

Questions:
1. What does the credit card charge form indicate about the existing system?
2. How can you make improvements with a new system?

the organization, and such clues can be used to support or refute information given in an interview. For example, an analyst might become skeptical of someone who claims to use the existing computer system extensively if the computer is never turned on while the analyst visits. In most cases, observation will support the information that users provide in interviews. When it does not, it is an important signal that extra care must be taken in analyzing the business system.

Selecting the Appropriate Techniques

Each of the requirements-gathering techniques just discussed has strengths and weaknesses. No one technique is always better than the others, and in practice most projects benefit from a combination of techniques. Thus, it is important to understand the strengths and weaknesses of each technique and when to use each. (See Figure 3-13.) One issue not discussed is that of the analysts' experience. In general, document analysis and observation require the least amount of training, while JAD sessions are the most challenging.

Type of Information   The first characteristic is type of information. Some techniques are more suited for use at different stages of the analysis process, whether understanding the as-is system, identifying improvements, or developing the to-be system. Interviews and JAD are commonly used in all three stages. In contrast, document analysis and observation usually are most helpful for understanding the as-is system, although they occasionally provide information about improvements.

3-8 Observation Practice

Visit the library at your college or university and observe how the book check-out process occurs. First, watch several students checking books out, and then check one out yourself. Prepare a brief summary report of your observations.

When you return to class, share your observations with others. You may notice that not all the reports present the same information. Why? How would the information be different had you used the interview or JAD technique?

	Interviews	Joint Application Design	Questionnaires	Document Analysis	Observation
Type of information	As-is, improvements, to-be	As-is, improvements, to-be	As-is, improvements	As-is	As-is
Depth of information	High	High	Medium	Low	Low
Breadth of information	Low	Medium	High	High	Low
Integration of information	Low	High	Low	Low	Low
User involvement	Medium	High	Low	Low	Low
Cost	Medium	Low–Medium	Low	Low	Low–Medium

FIGURE 3-13
Comparison of Requirements-Gathering Techniques

Questionnaires are often used to gather information about the as-is system, as well as general information about improvements.

Depth of Information   The depth of information refers to how rich and detailed the information is that the technique usually produces and the extent to which the technique is useful at obtaining not only facts and opinions, but also an understanding of *why* those facts and opinions exist. Interviews and JAD sessions are very useful at providing a good depth of rich and detailed information and helping the analyst to understand the reasons behind them. At the other extreme, document analysis and observation are useful for obtaining facts, but little beyond that. Questionnaires can provide a medium depth of information, soliciting both facts and opinions with little understanding of why.

Breadth of Information   Breadth of information refers to the range of information and information sources that can be easily collected by that technique. Questionnaires and document analysis both are easily capable of soliciting a wide range of information from a large number of information sources. In contrast, interviews and observation require the analyst to visit each information source individually and, therefore, take more time. JAD sessions are in the middle because many information sources are brought together at the same time.

Integration of Information   One of the most challenging aspects of requirements gathering is the integration of information from different sources. Simply put, different people can provide conflicting information. Combining this information and attempting to resolve differences in opinions or facts is usually very time consuming because it means contacting each information source in turn, explaining the discrepancy, and attempting to refine the information. In many cases, the individual wrongly perceives that the analyst is challenging his or her information, when in fact the source of conflict is another user in the organization. This can make the user defensive and make it hard to resolve the differences.

All techniques suffer integration problems to some degree, but JAD sessions are designed to improve integration because all information is integrated when it is collected, not afterward. If two users provide conflicting information, the conflict becomes immediately obvious, as does the source of the conflict. The immediate integration of information is the single most important benefit of JAD that distinguishes it from other techniques, and this is why most organizations use JAD for important projects.

User Involvement   User involvement refers to the amount of time and energy the intended users of the new system must devote to the analysis process. It is generally agreed that, as users become more involved in the analysis process, the chance of success increases. However, user involvement can have a significant cost, and not all users are willing to contribute valuable time and energy. Questionnaires, document analysis, and observation place the least burden on users, while JAD sessions require the greatest effort.

Cost   Cost is always an important consideration. In general, questionnaires, document analysis, and observation are low-cost techniques (although observation can be quite time consuming). The low cost does not imply that they are more or less effective than the other techniques. We regard interviews and JAD sessions as having moderate costs. In general, JAD sessions are much more expensive initially, because they require many users to be absent from their offices for significant periods, and they often involve highly paid consultants. However, JAD sessions significantly reduce the time spent in information integration and thus cost less in the long term.

APPLYING THE CONCEPTS AT TUNE SOURCE

Once the Tune Source approval committee approved the system request and feasibility analysis, the project team began performing analysis activities. These included gathering requirements by a variety of techniques and analyzing the requirements that were gathered. Some highlights of the project team's activities are presented next.

Requirements Analysis Techniques

Carly suggested that the project team conduct several JAD sessions with store managers, marketing analysts, and Web-savvy members of the IT staff. Together, the groups could brainstorm the features desired in the Digital Music Download system.

Jason facilitated three JAD sessions that were conducted over the course of a week. Jason's past facilitation experience helped the eight-person meetings run smoothly and stay on track. Because this project introduces a new business process, Jason used technology analysis and suggested several important Web technologies that could be used for the system. The JAD session generated ideas about how Tune Source could apply each of the technologies to the Digital Music Download system. Jason had the group categorize the ideas into three sets: "definite" ideas that would have a good probability of providing business value, "possible" ideas that might add business value, and "unlikely" ideas.

Next, Jason applied informal benchmarking by introducing the Web sites of several leading retailers and pointing out the features that they offered online. He selected some sites on the basis of their success with Internet sales, and others on the basis of their similarity to the vision for Tune Source's new system. The group discussed the features that were common across most retailers, versus unique functionality, and they created a list of suggested business requirements for the project team.

Requirements-Gathering Techniques

Jason believed that it would be important to understand the current Web-based sales processes and systems that already existed in the organization, because they would have to be closely integrated with the Digital Music Download system. Two requirements-gathering techniques proved to be helpful in understanding the current systems and processes—document analysis and interviews.

First, the project team collected existing reports (e.g., sales forms, screen shots of the online sales screens) and system documentation (data models, process models) that shed light on the as-is system. They were able to gather a good amount of information about the existing order processes and systems in this way. When questions arose, they conducted short interviews with the person who provided the documentation, for clarification.

Next, Jason interviewed the senior analysts for the current sales systems to get a better understanding of how those systems worked. He asked whether they had any ideas for the new system, as well as whether there were any integration issues that would need to be addressed. Jason also interviewed a contact from the ISP and the IT person who supported Tune Source's current Web site—both provided information about the existing communications infrastructure at Tune Source and its Web capabilities.

Requirements Definition

Throughout all of these activities, the project team collected information and tried to identify the business requirements for the system from the information. As the project progressed, requirements were added to the requirements definition and grouped by requirements type. When questions arose, they worked with Carly and Jason to confirm that requirements were in scope. The requirements that fell outside of the scope of the current system were typed into a separate document that would be saved for future use.

At the end of the analysis phase, the requirements definition was distributed to Carly, two marketing employees who would work with the system on the business side, and several retail store managers. This group then met for a two-day JAD session to clarify, finalize, and prioritize business requirements and to create use cases (Chapter 4) to show how the system would be used.

The project team also spent time creating process models (Chapter 5) and data models (Chapter 6) that depicted the processes and data in the future system. Members of marketing and IT reviewed the documents during interviews with the project team. Figure 3-14 shows a portion of the final requirements definition.

System Proposal

Jason reviewed the requirements definition and the other deliverables that the project team created during the analysis phase. Given Carly's desire to have the system in production as soon as possible, Jason decided to timebox the project. He had originally decided to approach the project in three versions (iterative development, see Chapter 2), and he is satisfied that this is a good way to structure the project. The first version, to be operational in the late spring, would implement a basic digital music download capability that will enable customers to download music on a fixed price per download basis. The second version, planned to be ready by midsummer, would incorporate a customer subscription program. The marketing department has yet to determine its preferred subscription program. It is considering a low fee, longer-term program or a higher fee, shorter-term program. By the time the project team is ready to begin version 2, however, the details should be

Functional Requirements:

1. Search and Browse
   1.1 The system will allow customers to browse music choices by predefined categories.
   1.2 The system will allow customers to search for music choices by title, artist, and genre.
   1.3 The system will allow customers to listen to a short sample of a music selection.
   1.4 The system will enable the customer to add music selections to a "favorites" list.

2. Purchase
   2.1 The system will enable the customer to create a customer account (if desired) that will store customer data and payment information.
   2.2 The system will enable the customer to specify the music choice for download.
   2.3 The system will collect and verify payment information. Once payment is verified, the music selection download process will begin.

3. Promote
   3.1 The system will keep track of the customer's interests on the basis of samples selected for listening and will use this information to promote music selections during future visits to the Web site.
   3.2 Marketing department can create promotions and specials on the Web site.
   3.3 Based on customer's previous purchases, music choices can be targeted to the customer on future visits to the Web site. (Customers who like X will also like Y.)
   3.4 On the basis of customer interests, customers can be notified of special offers on CDs that can be purchased at the regular Tune Source Web site or in a Tune Source store.

Nonfunctional Requirements:

1. Operational
   1.1 The digital music database will be constructed to facilitate searches by title, artist, and genre.
   1.2 The system will run on any Web browser and on in-store kiosks.
   1.3 In the event of a failure during a download, the customer will be able to restart the download.

2. Performance
   2.1 Download speeds will be monitored and kept at an acceptable level.

3. Security
   3.1 Customer information will be secured.
   3.2 Payment information will be encrypted and secured.

4. Cultural and political
   No special cultural and political requirements are expected.

FIGURE 3-14
Tune Source Requirements Definition

nailed down. The third version, expected to be ready by late summer, will add the gift card option, entitling the gift card holder to a fixed number of downloads over a limited time.

Jason reviewed the work plan and made some slight changes. He also conferred with Carly and the marketing department members to review the feasibility analysis. No major changes were made to it at this point; the project remains highly feasible overall. All of the deliverables from the project were then combined into a system proposal and submitted to the approval committee. Figure 3-15 shows the outline of the Tune Source system proposal. Carly and Jason met with the approval committee and presented the highlights of what was learned during the analysis phase and the final concept of the new system. On the basis of the proposal and presentation, the approval committee decided that it would continue to fund the Digital Music Download system.

1. **Table of Contents**

2. **Executive Summary**

   A summary of all the essential information in the proposal so that a busy executive can read it quickly and decide what parts of the plan to read in more depth.

3. **System Request**

   The revised system request form. (See Chapter 1.)

4. **Work plan**

   The original work plan, revised after having completed the analysis phase. (See Chapter 2.)

5. **Feasibility Analysis**

   A revised feasibility analysis, using the information from the analysis phase. (See Chapter 1.)

6. **Requirements Definition**

   A list of the functional and nonfunctional business requirements for the system (this chapter).

7. **Use Cases**

   A set of use cases that illustrate the basic processes that the system needs to support. (See Chapter 4.)

8. **Process Model**

   A set of process models and descriptions for the to-be system. (See Chapter 5.) This may include process models of the current as-is system that will be replaced.

9. **Data Model**

   A set of data models and descriptions for the to-be system. (See Chapter 6.) This may include data models of the as-is system that will be replaced.

Appendices

   These contain additional material relevant to the proposal, often used to support the recommended system. This might include results of a questionnaire survey or interviews, industry reports and statistics, etc.

FIGURE 3-15
Outline of the Tune Source
System Proposal

SUMMARY

Analysis

Analysis focuses on capturing the business requirements for the system. Analysis identifies the "what" of the system, and it leads directly into the design phase, during which the "how" of the system is determined. Many deliverables are created during the analysis phase, including the requirements definition, use cases, process models, and a data model. At the end of analysis, all of these deliverables, along with revised planning and project management deliverables, are combined into a system proposal and submitted to the approval committee for a decision regarding whether or not to move ahead with the project.

Requirements Determination

Requirements determination is the part of analysis in which the project team turns the very high level explanation of the business requirements stated in the system request into a more precise list of requirements. A requirement is simply a statement of what the system must do or what characteristic it needs to have. Business requirements describe the "what" of the system, and system requirements describe "how" the system will be implemented. A functional requirement relates directly to a process the system has to perform or information it needs to contain. Nonfunctional requirements refer to behavioral properties that the system must have, such as performance and usability. All of the functional and nonfunctional business requirements that fit within the scope of the system are written in the requirements definition, which is used to create other analysis deliverables and leads to the initial design for the new system.

Requirements Analysis Techniques

The basic process of analysis is divided into three steps: understanding the as-is system, identifying improvements, and developing requirements for the to-be system. Three requirements analysis techniques—business process automation, business process improvement, or business process reengineering—help the analyst lead users through the three (or two) analysis steps so that the vision of the system can be developed. Business process automation (BPA) means keeping basic business operations intact while incorporating computer technology to do some of the work. Problem analysis and root cause analysis are two popular BPA activities. Business process improvement (BPI) means making moderate changes to the way in which the organization operates to take advantage of new opportunities offered by technology or to copy what competitors are doing. Duration analysis, activity-based costing, and informal benchmarking are three popular BPI activities. Business process reengineering (BPR) means changing the fundamental way in which the organization operates. Outcome analysis, technology analysis, and activity elimination are three popular BPR activities.

Requirements-Gathering Techniques

Five techniques can be used to gather the business requirements for the proposed system: interviews, joint application development, questionnaires, document analysis, and observation. Interviews involve meeting one or more people and asking them questions. There are five basic steps to the interview process: selecting interviewees, designing interview questions, preparing for the interview, conducting the interview, and post-interview follow-up. Joint application development (JAD) allows the project team, users, and management to work together to identify requirements for the system. Electronic JAD attempts to overcome common problems associated with groups by using groupware. A questionnaire is a set of written questions developed for obtaining information from individuals. Questionnaires often are used when there is a large number of people from whom information and opinions are needed. Document analysis entails reviewing the existing documentation and examining the system itself. It can provide insights into the formal and informal system. Observation, the act of watching processes being performed, is a powerful tool for gathering information about the as-is system because it enables the analyst to see the reality of a situation firsthand.

KEY TERMS

Activity elimination
Activity-based costing
Analysis
As-is system
Benchmarking
Bottom-up interview
Breadth of analysis

Business process automation (BPA)
Business process improvement (BPI)
Business process reengineering (BPR)
Business requirement
Closed-ended question
Critical thinking skills

Document analysis
Duration analysis
Electronic JAD (e-JAD)
Facilitator
Formal system
Functional requirement
Ground rule

Informal benchmarking
Informal system
Interpersonal skill
Interview
Interview notes
Interview report
Interview schedule
Joint application development
  (JAD)
Nonfunctional requirements
Observation
Open-ended question
Outcome analysis

Parallelization
Postsession report
Potential business value
Probing question
Problem analysis
Process integration
Project cost
Questionnaire
Requirement
Requirements definition
Requirements determination
Risk
Root cause

Root cause analysis
Sample
Scribe
Stakeholder
Structured interview
Symptom
System proposal
System requirement
Technology analysis
To-be system
Top-down interview
Unstructured interview
Walk-through

QUESTIONS

1. What is the meaning of *analysis*? What is the purpose of the analysis phase of the SDLC?
2. What are the key elements of the system proposal?
3. A system development project may be approached in one of two ways: as a single, monolithic project in which all requirements are considered at once or as a series of smaller projects focusing on smaller sets of requirements. Which approach seems to be more successful? Why do you suppose that this is true?
4. Explain what is meant by a functional requirement. What are two types of functional requirements? Give two examples of each.
5. Explain what is meant by a nonfunctional requirement. What are the primary types of nonfunctional requirements? Give two examples of each.
6. What is the value of producing a requirements definition and having the project sponsor and key users review and approve it?
7. What are the three basic steps of the analysis process? Is each step performed in every project? Why or why not?
8. Three analysis techniques are discussed in this chapter: BPA, BPI, and BPR. What are the distinctions between these techniques?
9. Discuss problem analysis as a BPA activity. What are the strengths and limitations of this technique?
10. Discuss root cause analysis as a BPA activity. What are the strengths and limitations of this technique?
11. Compare and contrast duration analysis and activity-based costing. What role do these activities play in BPI?
12. In general, what is the purpose of the various activities that may be performed in BPR (e.g.,

outcome analysis, technology analysis, activity elimination)?
13. The analysis technique of BPA, BPI, or BPR is selected on the basis of several characteristics of the project. What are these characteristics and how do they influence the choice of analysis technique?
14. Discuss the appropriate way to set up and conduct interviews to gather requirements.
15. Give an example of a closed-ended question, an open-ended question, and a probing question. When would each type of question be used?
16. "Interviews should always be conducted as structured interviews." Do you agree with this statement? Why or why not?
17. Discuss the considerations that should be made when determining who to include in interviews and/or JAD sessions.
18. Is the primary purpose of requirements determination to gather facts or to gather opinions? Explain your answer.
19. Describe the five major steps in conducting JAD sessions.
20. Describe the primary roles involved in JAD sessions. What is the major contribution made by the person(s) fulfilling each role?
21. Discuss the reasons that question design for questionnaires is so difficult.
22. Why is document analysis useful? What insights into the organization can it provide?
23. Outline suggestions to make observation a useful, reliable information-gathering technique.
24. Describe a strategy for using the various information-gathering techniques in a project.

EXERCISES

A. Review the Amazon.com Web site. Develop the requirements definition for the site. Create a list of functional business requirements that the system meets. What different kinds of nonfunctional business requirements does the system meet? Provide examples for each kind.

B. Pretend that you are going to build a new system that automates or improves the interview process for the career services department of your school. Develop a requirements definition for the new system. Include both functional and nonfunctional system requirements. Pretend that you will release the system in three different versions. Prioritize the requirements accordingly.

C. Describe in very general terms the as-is business process for registering for classes at your university. What BPA technique would you use to identify improvements? With whom would you use the BPA technique? What requirements-gathering technique would help you apply the BPA technique? List some example improvements that you would expect to find.

D. Describe in very general terms the as-is business process for registering for classes at your university. What BPI technique would you use to identify improvements? With whom would you use the BPI technique? What requirements-gathering technique would help you apply the BPI technique? List some example improvements that you would expect to find.

E. Describe in very general terms the as-is business process for registering for classes at your university. What BPR technique would you use to identify improvements? With whom would you use the BPR technique? What requirements-gathering technique would help you apply the BPR technique? List some example improvements that you would expect to find.

F. Suppose that your university is having a dramatic increase in enrollment and is having difficulty finding enough seats in courses for students so that they can take courses required for graduation. Perform a technology analysis to identify new ways to help students complete their studies and graduate.

G. Suppose that you are the analyst charged with developing a new system for the university bookstore with which students can order books online and have them delivered to their dorms and off-campus housing. What requirements-gathering techniques will you use? Describe in detail how you would apply the techniques.

H. Suppose that you are the analyst charged with developing a new system to help senior managers make better strategic decisions. What requirements-gathering techniques will you use? Describe in detail how you would apply the techniques.

I. Find a partner and interview each other about what tasks you/they did in the last job held (full-time, part-time, past, or current). If you haven't worked before, then assume that your job is being a student. Before you do this, develop a brief interview plan. After your partner interviews you, identify the type of interview, interview approach, and types of questions used.

J. Find a group of students and run a 60-minute JAD session on improving alumni relations at your university. Develop a brief JAD plan, select two techniques that will help identify improvements, and then develop an agenda. Conduct the session, using the agenda, and write your post-session report.

K. Find a questionnaire on the Web that has been created to capture customer information. Describe the purpose of the survey, the way questions are worded, and how the questions have been organized. How can the questionnaire be improved? How will the responses be analyzed?

L. Develop a questionnaire that will help gather information regarding processes at a popular restaurant or the college cafeteria (e.g., ordering, customer service). Give the questionnaire to 10–15 students, analyze the responses, and write a brief report that describes the results.

M. Contact the career services department at your university and find all the pertinent documents designed to help students find permanent and/or part-time jobs. Analyze the documents and write a brief report.

MINICASES

1. The state firefighters' association has a membership of 15,000. The purpose of the organization is to provide some financial support to the families of deceased member firefighters and to organize a conference each year bringing together firefighters from all over the state. Annually, members are billed dues and calls.

"Calls" are additional funds required to take care of payments made to the families of deceased members. The bookkeeping work for the association is handled by the elected treasurer, Bob Smith, although it is widely known that his wife, Laura, does all of the work. Bob runs unopposed each year at the election, since no one wants to take over the tedious and time-consuming job of tracking memberships. Bob is paid a stipend of $8000 per year, but his wife spends well over 20 hours per week on the job. The organization, however, is not happy with their performance.

A computer system is used to track the billing and receipt of funds. This system was developed in 1984 by a computer science student and his father. The system is a DOS-based system written in dBase 3. The most immediate problem facing the treasurer and his wife is the fact that the software package no longer exists, and there is no one around who knows how to maintain the system. One query in particular takes 17 hours to run. Over the years, they have just avoided running this query, although the information in it would be quite useful. Questions from members concerning their statements cannot easily be answered. Usually, Bob or Laura just jots down the inquiry and returns a call with the answer. Sometimes it takes 3 to 5 hours to find the information needed to answer the question. Often, they have to perform calculations manually, since the system was not programmed to handle certain types of queries. When member information is entered into the system, each field is presented one at a time. This makes it very difficult to return to a field and correct a value that was entered. Sometimes a new member is entered, but disappears from the records. The report of membership used in the conference materials does not alphabetize members by city. Only cities are listed in the correct order.

What requirements analysis technique or techniques would you recommend for this situation? Explain your answer.

2. Brian Callahan, IS project manager, is just about ready to depart for an urgent meeting called by Joe Campbell, manager of manufacturing operations. A major BPI project, sponsored by Joe, recently cleared the approval hurdle, and Brian helped bring the project through project initiation. Now that the approval committee has given the go-ahead, Brian has been working on the project's analysis plan.

One evening, while playing golf with a friend who works in the manufacturing operations department, Brian learned that Joe wants to push the project's time frame up from Brian's original estimate of 13 months.

Brian's friend overheard Joe say, "I can't see why that IS project team needs to spend all that time 'analyzing' things. They've got two weeks scheduled just to look at the existing system! That seems like a real waste. I want that team to get going on building my system."

Because Brian has a little inside knowledge about Joe's agenda for this meeting, he has been considering how to handle Joe. What do you suggest that Brian tell Joe?

3. Barry has recently been assigned to a project team that will be developing a new retail store management system for a chain of submarine sandwich shops. Barry has several years of experience in programming, but has not done much analysis in his career. He was a little nervous about the new work he would be doing, but was confident that he could handle any assignment he was given.

One of Barry's first assignments was to visit one of the submarine sandwich shops and prepare an observation report on how the store operates. Barry planned to arrive at the store around noon, but he chose a store in an area of town he was unfamiliar with, and due to traffic delays and difficulty in finding the store, he did not arrive until 1:30 P.M. The store manager was not expecting him and refused to let a stranger behind the counter until Barry had him contact the project sponsor (the director of store management) back at company headquarters to verify who he was and what his purpose was.

After finally securing permission to observe, Barry stationed himself prominently in the work area behind the counter so that he could see everything. The staff had to maneuver around him as they went about their tasks; however, there were only occasional minor collisions. Barry noticed that the store staff seemed to be going about their work very slowly and deliberately, but he supposed that was because the store wasn't very busy. At first, Barry questioned each worker about what he or she was doing, but the store manager eventually asked him not to interrupt their work so much—he was interfering with their service to the customers.

By 3:30, Barry was a little bored. He decided to leave, figuring that he could get back to the office and prepare his report before 5:00 P.M. that day. He was sure that his team leader would be pleased with his quick completion of his assignment. As he drove, he reflected, "There really won't be much to say in this report. All they do is take the order, make the sandwich, collect the payment, and hand over the order. It's really simple!" Barry's confidence in his analytical skills soared as he anticipated his team leader's praise.

Back at the store, the store manager shook his head, commenting to his staff, "He comes here at the slowest time of day on the slowest day of the week. He never even looked at all the work I was doing in the back room while he was here—summarizing yesterday's sales, checking inventory on hand, making up resupply orders for the weekend ... plus he never even considered our store opening and closing procedures. I hate to think that the new store management system is going to be built by someone like that. I'd better contact Chuck (the director of store management) and let him know what went on here today." Evaluate Barry's conduct of the observation assignment.

4. Anne has been given the task of conducting a survey of sales clerks who will be using a new order entry system being developed for a household products catalog company. The goal of the survey is to identify the clerks' opinions on the strengths and weaknesses of the current system. There are about 50 clerks who work in three different cities, so a survey seemed like an ideal way of gathering the needed information from the clerks.

Anne developed the questionnaire carefully and pretested it on several sales supervisors who were available at corporate headquarters. After revising it according to their suggestions, she sent a paper version of the questionnaire to each clerk, asking that it be returned within one week. After one week, she had only three completed questionnaires returned. After another week, Anne received just two more completed questionnaires. Feeling somewhat desperate, Anne then sent out an e-mail version of the questionnaire, again to all the clerks, asking them to respond to the questionnaire by e-mail as soon as possible. She received two e-mail questionnaires and three messages from clerks who had completed the paper version expressing annoyance at being bothered with the same questionnaire a second time. At this point, Anne has just a 14% response rate, which she is sure will not please her team leader. What suggestions do you have that could have improved Anne's response rate to the questionnaire?

PLANNING

ANALYSIS

☑ **Apply Requirements Analysis Techniques (Business Process Automation, Business Process Improvement, or Business Process Reengineering)**

☑ **Use Requirements Gathering Techniques (Interview, JAD Session, Questionnaire, Document Analysis, or Observation)**

☑ **Develop Requirements Definition**

☐ Develop Use Cases

☐ Develop Data Flow Diagrams

☐ Develop Entity Relationship Model

☐ Normalize Entity Relationship Model

TASK CHECKLIST

PLANNING   ANALYSIS   DESIGN

CHAPTER 4

USE CASE

ANALYSIS

U se cases describe in more detail the key elements of the requirements definition. They explain the process by which the system will meet the functional require-ments defined in the previous chapter. The use cases are then used to build a process model, which defines the business processes in a more formal manner.

OBJECTIVES

- Understand the role of use cases.
- Understand the process used to create use cases.
- Be able to create use cases.

CHAPTER OUTLINE

IMPLEMENTATION

INTRODUCTION

The previous chapter discussed the process of requirements determination resulting in the requirements definition. The requirements definition defines what the system is to do. In this chapter, we discuss how these requirements are further refined into a set of use cases that provide more detail on the processes by which the system is to meet these requirements and the data the system needs to capture and store. Generally, each use case describes one or more system requirements. Once the use cases have been developed, the next steps are to use the requirements definition and the use cases to create even more detailed descriptions of the processes and data in the form of a process model and a data model for the new system.

A *use case* is a formal way of representing how a business system interacts with its environment. A use case illustrates the activities that are performed by the users of the system. As such, use case modeling is often thought of as an external or functional view of a business process, showing how the users view the process rather than the internal mechanisms by which the process and supporting mechanisms operate.

Use cases are a relatively new technique. For many years, systems analysts simply sat down with users and began drawing process and data models. However, users often found it difficult to learn the process and data modeling languages used by the analysts. In recent years, many organizations have begun employing the use case approach, in which the analysts first work with the users to create simple text descriptions of complex processes and then later apply these to build formal models. Since use cases describe the system's activities from the user's perspective in words, user involvement is essential in their development. Therefore, creating use cases helps ensure that users' insights are explicitly incorporated into the new system.

For complex processes, the approach of developing use cases first and process models second comes from two different parts of the systems analysis and design community, and thus there are two different views on how best to create the use cases. Organizations applying traditional techniques have begun to use what they call business scenarios to describe processes, while organizations applying object-oriented techniques (see Chapter 14) have begun to use what they call use cases. At present, there are no formal standards for either business scenarios or use cases, so we have tried to incorporate what we believe are the best elements of both approaches. We have adopted the term *use case* rather than *business scenario* because use case is gradually becoming more popular.[1] The use case approach is the same whether the project team is defining the as-is model or the to-be model, but obviously, the focus is different; the as-is model focuses on current business processes, whereas the to-be model focuses on desired business processes.

In this chapter, we first explain how to read use cases and describe their basic elements. Then we describe the process applied to build use cases.

---

[1] As you will see in Chapter 14, object-oriented techniques take the text-based use cases we describe in this chapter and create use case diagrams before moving to modeling structure and behavior (similar to the data and process models we describe in the next chapters). Use case diagrams are described in Chapter 14. We focus only on the text descriptions of the use cases in this chapter. For a more detailed description of business scenarios, see Karen McGraw and Karen Harbison, *User-Centered Requirements: The Scenario-Based Engineering Process*, Mahwah, NJ: Lawrence Erlbaum Associates, 1997. For a more detailed description of use cases, see I. Jacobson, M. Christerson, P. Jonsson, and G. Overgaard, *Object-Oriented Software Engineering: A Use Case Driven Approach*, Reading, MA: Addison-Wesley, 1992.

USE CASES

A use case depicts a set of activities performed to produce some output result. Each use case describes how an external user *triggers* an *event* to which the system must respond. For example, in a video store system, a customer might rent a video or return a video, or a video might become overdue. The acts of renting or returning videos and the passage of time are all events triggering a set of activities the system must perform. With this type of *event-driven modeling*, everything in the system can be thought of as a response to some trigger event. When there are no events, the system is at rest, patiently waiting for the next event to trigger it. When a trigger event occurs, the system (and the people using it) responds, performs the actions defined in the use case, and then returns to the waiting state.

In some situations, the process may be "small," such as the actions that are performed when a video is rented in the previous example. In more complex systems (such as the Tune Source example in this book), a use case may require several distinct activities, some of which are performed each time the use case is activated and some of which are performed only occasionally (e.g., consider the return of a rented video, which very rarely will be returned with damage). Simple use cases may have only one path through them, while complex use cases may have several possible paths.

We create use cases only when they are likely to help us better understand the situation and help simplify the modeling steps that follow. For very simple processes that are well explained in the requirements definition, we often do not bother to create a use case, but simply use the information in the requirements definition itself to build the process and data models.

It is important to create use cases whenever we are reengineering processes or making any changes to business processes that will significantly alter the way people work. Remember that the use case describes what the system will do from the user's perspective. Therefore, it is critical to involve the user in the creation of the use case so that the user understands the activities planned for the new system. Also, the user helps to ensure that no essential steps or tasks are omitted from the use case and that rare, special circumstances are included.

Creation of use cases is often done as a part of interview sessions with users and as a part of JAD sessions. Gathering the information needed for use cases is a relatively straightforward process—as we will see, use cases are fairly simple to understand and interpret. It does take considerable practice to create a meaningful and complete use case. Users work closely with the project team to create the use cases. In some instances, after some practice, experienced users are able to write the use cases themselves.

Elements of a Use Case

A use case contains a fairly complete description of all the activities that occur in response to a trigger event. To illustrate the components of a use case, we have created a sample describing a situation with which you are probably familiar, that of buying items at the supermarket. Refer to Figure 4-1 as we describe the sections of a use case. While there are numerous pieces of information in the use case, the information is organized into three main parts: basic information, inputs and outputs, and details.

Basic Information   Each use case has a name and number. The name should be as simple, yet descriptive, as possible. The number is simply a sequential number that serves to reference each use case (e.g., use case 3). The description provides a bit more information about the use case's purpose.

Use case name: **Customer Checkout**	ID: **1**	Importance level: **High**

Primary actor: **Customer**

Short description: **This use case describes how customers check out and purchase the items they have selected.**

Trigger: **Customer arrives at checkout lane with items to purchase**

Type: (**External**) / Temporal

Major Inputs		**Major Outputs**	
Description	Source	Description	Destination
Item UPC	Customer	Total due	Customer
Item details	Item data store	Purchase receipt	Customer
Payment details	Customer	Sales transaction	Sales data store
Payment validation	Clearinghouse	Sold item details	Sold inventory
Payment authorization	Customer		data store

Major Steps Performed

1. Determine total due
   1.1 Do for all items in cart
      1.1.1 Use UPC to find item price, description, — Item UPC
         and tax status — Item price, description, tax status
      1.1.2 Accumulate order cost subtotal
      1.1.3 Add item UPC to items purchased list
      End loop
   1.2 Calculate sales tax
   1.3 Display total due — Total due

   Subtotal due,   Items
   Sales tax   purchased

2. Process payment
   2.1 If cash payment, calculate change and print — Payment amount & type
      receipt
   2.2 If check, validate and print receipt — Payment validation
   2.3 If debit card, validate, authenticate customer
      with PIN, and print receipt — Payment authorization
   2.4 If credit card, validate, get customer
      authorization with signature, and print receipt — Purchase receipt

      Sales
   transaction

3. Record sales transaction — Purchase and payment detail

   Items
   purchased

4. Record sold inventory items — UPC and item quantity sold

Information for Steps

FIGURE 4-1
Supermarket Checkout Use Case

The *importance level* may be assigned to indicate the relative significance of the use case in the overall system. Some use cases will describe essential activities that the system must perform and hence will have a high importance level. Other use cases may describe activities that are less critical, having medium or low importance. Classifying the importance level is useful when a RAD methodology is used so that the most essential system features can be targeted first.

The *primary actor* refers to the external user that triggers the event to which the system responds. Often, the primary actor or external user will be someone external to the system, such as a customer or library patron. The primary actor does not always refer to a person or a role, however. A primary actor may also be an organization, another information system, or a device such as an alarm or sensor.

Another element of basic information is the trigger for the use case—the event that causes the use case to begin. A trigger can be an *external trigger*, such as a customer placing an order or the fire alarm ringing, or it can be *temporal trigger*, such as a video overdue at the video store or time to pay the rent.

Use cases are written from the bird's eye view of the system users. The use case in Figure 4-1, for example, is written from the perspective of an independent observer of the actions performed when the primary actor (the customer) triggers the event.

In our sample, the customer checkout use case is given an ID number of 1, has high importance, and describes the way that the customer checkout process is handled. The primary actor who triggers this external event is the customer, who arrives at the checkout lane with items to purchase.

Inputs and Outputs   The second major part of a use case is the set of major *inputs* and *outputs*. Each of the major inputs and outputs to the use case are described, along with their source or destination. These are all possible inputs and outputs, not just those that always or usually are part of the use case. The goal is to include everyone, but it is common for users and analysts to miss inputs and outputs when they first define use cases. This is not a major problem, because the process of building use cases is one of gradual refinement: As users and analysts work through the parts of the use case, they often return to previous parts to correct them.

In Figure 4-1, we see that in the input area, the customer provides the items to purchase as represented by the item UPC (Universal Product Code). The information that describes the item is important, not the physical item itself. Details about the item such as its description, price, and whether it is subject to sales tax are obtained from stored data—commonly, a database (referred to generically as a "data store"). The customer provides the payment and authorizes the payment if required. Electronic payments are validated through a generic clearinghouse. In the output area, we see that the customer is informed of the total due for the purchase and is provided a receipt. A sales transaction is written to a sales data store, and all items purchased are recorded in a sold inventory data store.

Details   The third major part of a use case is the description of the major steps that are performed to execute the response to the event, the inputs used for the steps, and the outputs produced by the steps. These steps are the activities performed during the use case, such as processing all items in the cart, accepting payment, and recording sales and inventory data. The steps are listed in the order in which they are performed. Any conditional steps (for example, the various payment types) and any repeated steps (for example, the repetitive process for all items in the shopping cart) are clearly noted.

Building Use Cases

Use cases can be used for both the as-is and the to-be systems; as-is use cases focus on the current system, whereas to-be use cases focus on the desired new system. When used for the to-be system, it is fairly common for the use cases to identify additional requirements that were not completely specified in the requirements definition. This, in fact, is one of the reasons use cases are important. After the use cases have been built, analysts often return to the requirements definition and revise it according to their improved understanding of the system.

The most common ways to gather information for the use cases are through the same requirement determination techniques discussed in the last chapter, especially interviews and JAD sessions. Observation also is sometimes used for as-is use cases. Regardless of whether interviews or JAD sessions are used, research shows that some ways to gather the information for use cases are better than others. The most effective process has four steps.[2] (See Figure 4-2.) These four steps are performed in order, but, of course, the analyst often cycles among them in an *iterative* fashion as he or she moves from use case to use case.

Step	Activities	Typical Questions Asked[a]
1. Identify the use cases.	Start a use case report form for each use case by filling in the name, description, trigger, and the easily identified major inputs and outputs. If there are more than nine use cases, group them into packages.	Ask *who*, *what*, *when*, and *where* about the use cases (or tasks) and their inputs and outputs (e.g., forms and reports). What are the major tasks that are performed? What triggers this task? What tells you to perform this task? What information/forms/reports do you need to perform this task? Who gives you these information/forms/reports? What information/forms/report does this produce and where do they go?
2. Identify the major steps within each use case.	For each use case, fill in the major steps needed to process the inputs and produce the outputs.	Ask *how* about each use case. How do you produce this report? How do you change the information on the report? How do you process forms? What tools do you use to do this step (e.g., paper, e-mail, phone)?
3. Identify elements within steps.	For each step, identify its triggers and its inputs and outputs.	Ask *how* about each step. How does the person know when to perform this step? What forms/reports/data does this step produce? What forms/reports/data does this step need? What happens when this form/report/data is not available?
4. Confirm the use case.	For each use case, validate that it is correct and complete.	Ask the user to execute the process, using the written steps in the use case—that is, have the user role-play the use case.

[a] We have used the typical questions for the as-is model (e.g., "What are the…"). These same questions can be used for the to-be model, but they would be phrased in the future tense (e.g., "What should be the…").

FIGURE 4-2
Steps for Writing for Use Cases

[2] The approach in this section is based on the work of George Marakas and Joyce Elam, "Semantic Structuring in Analyst Acquisition and Representation of Facts in Requirements Analysis," *Information Systems Research*, 1998, 9(1), 37–63, as well as our own: Alan Dennis, Glenda Hayes, and Robert Daniels, "Business Process Modeling with Group Support Systems," *Journal of Management Information Systems*, 1999, 15(4): 115–142.

Identify the Major Use Cases   As stated previously, use cases document one or more functional requirements outlined in the requirements definition. Therefore, identification of use cases begins with the requirements definition. The process-oriented functional requirements—things the system must do—suggest a direct action resulting from an external or temporal event. The information-oriented functional requirements—content the system must have—suggest things that happen involving information or time triggers to collect or produce information. Let's begin an example of building use cases by revisiting the Holiday Travel Vehicles scenario. We have already seen a requirements definition for this situation (Figure 3-3). How was this information obtained? Figure 4-3 contains a transcript of an initial interview between Hal, the owner of Holiday Travel Vehicles, and Sarah, a systems analyst who is working on a project to provide an improved information system for the dealership. This interview took place early in the project when Sarah was just getting familiar with the organization, and basically focuses on the as-is system. Take a moment and read the transcript now.

This interview gave Sarah quite a bit of information about the way the dealership operates. Following the meeting with Hal, Sarah began to draft the functional requirements section of the requirements definition shown in Figure 3-3. As she worked on this document, she also began to make a list of the major events that occur in the typical operations of Holiday Travel Vehicles and the responses made to the events. The events that Sarah listed encompass most of the requirements shown in Figure 3-3. The responses document the final result of the activities performed when the event occurs. Before looking at Sarah's event-response list in Figure 4-4, see if you can generate your own list of events and responses from the interview transcript in Figure 4-3.

Sarah studied the event-response list and decided that three of the events deserved to be expanded upon by using the use case format (events 3, 4, and 5). The other events (1, 2, and 6) seemed straightforward enough to go directly to process modeling and data modeling.

After the use cases are identified, the top parts of the use case form should be filled in with name, ID, primary actor, short description, and trigger—it may be too early to assign the importance level of the use case. The goal is to develop a set of major use cases with the major information about each, rather than jumping into one use case and describing it completely. This prevents the users and analysts from forgetting key use cases and helps the users explain the overall set of business processes that they are responsible for. It also helps users understand how to describe the use cases and reduces the chance of overlap between use cases. In this step, the analysts and users identify a set of major use cases that could benefit from additional definition beyond the requirements definition.

Identifying use cases is an iterative process, with users often changing their minds about what a use case is and what it includes. It is very easy to get trapped in the details at this point, so you need to remember that the goal at this step is to just identify the major use cases. For example, in the list of events shown in Figure 4-4, we have defined one event as "Customer makes an offer." This event includes offers from customers who have trade-in vehicles as well as those who don't have trade-in vehicles. We could describe these two situations as separate use cases, but this would create a larger set of smaller use cases. Therefore, these two possible variations of the event will be combined into a single use case. The trick is to select the right size so that you end up with the major use cases that need additional explanation beyond the requirements definition. Remember that

Interview transcript: Sarah (systems analyst) and Hal (owner, Holiday Travel Vehicles)

Sarah: Hal, the purpose of our discussion today is for you to give me an overview of your business. As you know, I head up a team that will be helping to develop plans for new information systems for your business. Initially, I am interested in learning about the major activities that are performed here as you go about your daily business. Later, I'll be asking more detailed questions about these activities.

Hal: Sounds good to me, Sarah. I know the recreational vehicle business pretty well, having taken over this business from my uncle over 15 years ago. Let's see ... well, things begin with our placing orders for new recreational vehicles and travel trailers with our five main suppliers. We try to keep a good balance of sizes, prices, and styles of RVs and trailers on hand. We keep our inventory fairly low during the winter, of course. Our peak selling seasons are spring and fall. After we place our orders, our suppliers send us the vehicles we've requested. When a vehicle that we've ordered arrives, we check it into our records by recording its VIN number, model, name, year, manufacturer, date of arrival, and invoice cost. We have a new vehicle form that we fill out with all of this information, and we keep these forms in a file cabinet in our main office.

Of course, the main activity of this business is selling those vehicles. We have a staff of knowledgeable salespeople who are here to determine our customers' needs and wants and find a vehicle or trailer that will fill the bill.

Sarah: Do you record any information about a customer while he's looking at vehicles?

Hal: No, nothing gets written down until the customer has decided on the vehicle he wants to buy. Then the salesperson and the customer fill out the offer form. This is pretty informal, but it does include the customer's name, the vehicle he wants to buy, the offer he is making, and a value for the trade-in vehicle if there is one.

Sarah: Who provides the trade-in value?

Hal: The salesperson goes to our used vehicle manager for that.

Sarah: Okay. Then what is done with the offer form?

Hal: Basically, the form contains all the details that I need to decide whether to accept the offer or not. The salesman brings the offer form in to me, and then I'll look up the new vehicle form if necessary to remind me of the vehicle's base cost. If there's a trade-in listed, then I'll check our Green Book that gives value estimates for older RVs and trailers to see if the trade-in value listed is reasonable. If I agree to all the terms, then I'll sign the offer form and give it back to the salesperson. If I don't agree to everything, then I tell the salesperson what I want changed, and he goes back to the customer to continue the negotiation.

Sarah: So then, does the salesperson make out a new offer form or does he just change the original one?

Hal: He usually writes out a new one if the customer agrees to modify his offer. It's less confusing that way.

Sarah: What happens to the original offer form?

Hal: It just gets torn up and thrown away. We don't want it floating around and someone accidentally finds out the details of a customer's offer.

Sarah: What if the customer doesn't want to change his offer? Does the form just get thrown away then, too?

Hal: No, in that case the salesperson usually keeps the offer form in his own customer file. That way, he has a record of the customer's offer and he can use that down the road when he follows up with the customer and tries to persuade him to submit another offer.

FIGURE 4-3
Holiday Travel Vehicles Interview Transcript

Sarah: So, let's say the customer finally gets his offer accepted. Then what happens?

Hal: Well, things get a lot more formal now. Once the offer is accepted, the salesperson fills out a sales contract. This sales contract form contains full customer information, a complete description of the purchase vehicle, complete details of the trade-in vehicle and trade-in allowance, and a full description of any dealer-installed options. Then we list ...

Sarah: (interrupting): Sorry, Hal, but that's the first time I've heard you mention dealer-installed options. Tell me about them.

Hal: Oh, right, I kind of skipped that, didn't I? Well, we sell base-model vehicles only. If customers want them fancied-up with extras and options, we can add them, for a price, of course! Any options that the customer wants should have been listed on the offer forms I mentioned earlier.

Sarah: Okay. So let's go back to when I interrupted. The sales contract is filled out with customer information, purchased vehicle information, trade-in information, dealer-installed options ... anything else?

Hal: Just the final negotiated price, taxes, and license fees, and the amount of the required customer deposit. Once we've received the deposit check, we settle on a delivery date that gives us the time we need to install the options, and then all parties sign the purchase contract, and we have ourselves a deal. Oh, and we make sure we list the salesperson's name so he can get his commission on the sale later.

Sarah: What happens then?

Hal: Well, the customer typically goes off to arrange financing for the balance due on the purchase. We don't provide financing ourselves in-house. If the customer needs help with that, we have a couple of local banks we direct him to that are interested in that kind of business.

         We pull the new vehicle form out of our files and staple it to a new form we call the vehicle purchase record. The vehicle purchase record is kind of a summary of the main points of the purchase: the customer info, the vehicle info, the options added, and the final price info. These forms go into our files, ordered by customer, so we have a record of every customer's vehicle purchase. At this point, we also write up a work order for the shop that lists all the work that needs to be done to get the vehicle ready for delivery to the customer.

Sarah: So, when it's time for a customer to take delivery on the vehicle, what happens?

Hal: The customer comes in with the money needed to finalize the sale and the trade-in vehicle, if there is one. We go through the new vehicle with him and make sure it is satisfactory. We then collect his money, get a final signature from him, and give him a copy of the sales contract form. He gets the keys and is on his way! We then staple the last copy of the sales contract with the vehicle purchase record, and it gets filed by customer name.

Sarah: What about the trade-in vehicle?

Hal: We fill out a form called the used vehicle form that describes the vehicle and the trade-in value. This is kind of like the new vehicle form we fill out when our new vehicles arrive in inventory. This gives the information we need on the trade-in so we know how we should price it. If it needs any work, we prepare a shop work order, the work gets done, and the vehicle is put on the lot.

Sarah: Is there anything else you can think of that's written down or recorded in these processes you've described?

Hal: Once the customer takes final delivery, we use a sales ledger to record the actual sale and the tax and license fees we've collected. Our bookkeeper needs that. Sarah, it looks like they need me on the sales floor. Can we talk again later?

Sarah: Sure, Hal. Let me absorb everything you've told me today and I'll get back in touch. This has been a great start. Thanks!

FIGURE 4-3 (*continued*)

Event	Response
1) New vehicles are needed for inventory.	Purchase order is placed with vehicle manufacturer.
2) New vehicles arrive from manufacturer.	Vehicle information is recorded on new vehicle record.
3) Customer makes an offer on a new vehicle.	Details of offer are recorded and presented to owner for acceptance decision.
4) Customer offer is accepted.	Details of accepted offer are recorded on a sales contract, and customer provides a deposit.
5) Customer takes delivery on new vehicle.	Customer pays for vehicle once offer is accepted, takes possession of the vehicle, and turns in trade-in. Details of the entire purchase are saved.
6) Trade-in is added to used vehicle inventory.	Used vehicle information is recorded on used vehicle form.

FIGURE 4-4

Sample Event-Response List

a use case is a set of end-to-end activities that starts with a trigger event and continues through many possible paths until some output has been produced and the system is again at rest.

If the project team discovers more than eight or nine major use cases, this suggests that the system is complex (or that the use cases are not defined at the right level of detail). If there really are more than eight or nine major use cases, the use cases are grouped together into *packages* of related use cases. For example, if we were to do a more thorough study of a recreational vehicle dealership, we would likely find more than the six events discussed in our example. The events leading to uses cases could be grouped logically together in packages, such as all use cases for inventory, all use cases for sales, all use cases for the shop, etc. These packages are then treated as the major processes for the top level of the process model, with the use cases appearing on lower levels, or are treated as separate systems and modeled as separate systems. (Process modeling will be described in the next chapter.)

Once the use cases have been identified, the users and analysts complete the second principle part of the use case: inputs and outputs (also called *data flows*), the major pieces of information that the use case needs or produces. Some use cases require physical inputs or produce physical outputs (e.g., a repair car use case would have a broken car as an input and a repaired car as an output). Since the use case is used to build an information system, information describing physical inputs and outputs is included, but the physical items themselves are not.

At this point, the analysts are not concerned with defining all the inputs and outputs—just the major ones that come to mind quickly. In later steps, they will return to this list to ensure that every single input and output is identified. However, it is important to understand and define acronyms and jargon so that the project team and others from outside the user group can clearly understand the use case. Typical questions asked by the analysts in this step are given in Figure 4-2. Figure 4-5 shows the Holiday Travel Vehicles use cases with the inputs and outputs section partially completed.

Identify the Major Steps for Each Use Case   At this point, the use cases and major inputs and outputs have been defined. In short, you have filled in the top two parts of the use case (basic information, and inputs and outputs). The next step is to

Use case name: Create an Offer		ID: 3	Importance level: High

Primary actor: Customer

Short description: This use case describes the process of handling customer offers.

Trigger: Customer decides to make an offer on a vehicle.

Type: (External) / Temporal

Major Inputs		Major Outputs	
Description	Source	Description	Destination
Customer name	Customer	Signed offer form	Accepted offer
Offer price	Customer		use case
New vehicle info	New vehicle	Rejected offer	Salesperson's
	record		personal file
Dealer options	Customer		
Trade-in-value	Used vehicle		
	manager		
Trade-in-value estimates	Green book		

Use case name: Accepted Offer		ID: 4	Importance level: High

Primary actor: Accepted offer use case

Short description: This use case describes how an accepted offer is handled.

Trigger: Customer's offer on a vehicle is accepted by dealership owner.

Type: (External) / Temporal

Major Inputs		Major Outputs	
Description	Source	Description	Destination
Signed offer	Create offer	Deposit check	Bookkeeper
	use case	Completed sales contract	Take delivery
Customer info	Customer		use case
Deposit check	Customer		

Use case name: Customer Takes Delivery		ID: 5	Importance level: High

Primary actor: Customer

Short description: This use case describes how the sales transaction is finalized and the customer takes delivery of the vehicle.

Trigger: When vehicle is ready, customer brings final payment and takes possession of vehicle.

Type: (External) / Temporal

Major Inputs		Major Outputs	
Description	Source	Description	Destination
Completed sales contract	Accepted offer	Final sales contract	Customer
	use case		
Payment	Customer		
Trade-in	Customer		

FIGURE 4-5
Sample Use Cases with Inputs
and Outputs

complete the third part: the detailed information. The users and analysts go back through the use cases to fill in the three to nine major *steps* within each use case. The steps focus on what an independent observer would see the system do in response to the event. In general, the steps should be listed in the order in which they are performed, from first to last, but there also may be steps that are performed only occasionally, have no formal sequence in which they are done, or loop back and forth. The order of steps implies a sequence, but does not require it. It is fine to list steps that have no sequence in any order you like, but if there is a sequence, you should list the steps in that way.

Each step should be about the same size as the others. For example, if we were writing steps for preparing a meal, steps such as "Take fork out of drawer" and "Put fork on table" are much smaller than "Prepare cake, using mix." If you end up with more than nine steps or steps that vary greatly in size, you must go back and adjust the steps. Recognizing the size of the steps takes practice, but will become natural in time.

One good approach to producing the steps for a use case is to have the users visualize themselves actually performing the use case and write down the steps as if they were writing a recipe for a cookbook. In most cases, the users will be able to quickly define what they do in as-is use cases. Defining the steps for to-be use cases may take a bit more coaching. In our experience, the descriptions of the steps change greatly as the users work through a use case. Our advice is to use a blackboard or whiteboard that easily can be erased (or paper with pencil) to develop the list of steps. Once the set of steps is fairly well defined, only then do you write it on the use case form. Use cases for Holiday Travel Vehicles with the major steps completed are shown in Figure 4-6.

Occasionally, a use case is so simple that further refinement is not needed. The analyst simply writes a brief description and does not bother to develop the steps within the use case. The information at the top of the use case form is sufficient, because the use case need not be explained in more detail. Some of the use cases presented in the exercises at the end of this chapter are simple enough that they do not need information beyond what is at the top of the use case form.

Identify Elements within Steps   At this point, the steps have been described, but not the elements that further define and link the steps. In other words, the use case form in Figure 4-6 requires further elaboration before it is complete. The last column ("Information for Steps") must be completed and arrows may be drawn between steps. We must delve more deeply into the steps within the use case to understand and describe their inputs and outputs. Each step should have at least one input and at least one output. See Figure 4-7 for the completed Holiday Travel Vehicles use cases.

The goal at this point is to identify the major inputs and outputs for each step. One could identify the inputs and outputs in great detail, but this would make it difficult to list them concisely at the top of the form. The solution is to identify details within the description of the steps, but to provide only general categories at the top of the use case form. For example, if a step needs the customer name, address, and phone number, we might note these in the step description but list only "customer information" as the major input at the top of the form. In Figure 4-7, for example, we list "customer info" at the top of the form but mention "name, address, and phone number" in step 1.

The users and analysts now return to the steps in the use case and begin linking the steps together. Typically, this means asking what inputs (e.g., information,

Use case name: Create an Offer   ID: 3   Importance level: High

Primary actor: Customer

Short description: This use case describes the process of handling customer offers.

Trigger: Customer decides to make an offer on a vehicle.

Type: (External) / Temporal

Major Inputs		Major Outputs	
Description	Source	Description	Destination
Customer name	Customer	Signed offer form	Accepted offer
Offer price	Customer		Use case
New vehicle info	New vehicle	Rejected offer	Salesperson's
	record		personal file
Dealer options	Customer		
Trade-in-value	Used vehicle		
	manager		
Trade-in-value estimates	Green book		

Major Steps Performed:

1) Record details of offer.
   If trade-in, get trade-in value.
2) Management reviews offer.
3) If offer accepted, perform accepted offer
   use case.
4) If customer wants to continue negotiation,
   discard rejected offer and repeat steps 1 & 2.

Information for Steps:

Use case name: Accepted Offer   ID: 4   Importance level: High

Primary actor: Accepted offer use case

Short description: This use case describes how an accepted offer is handled.

Trigger: Customer's offer on a vehicle is accepted by dealership owner.

Type: (External) / Temporal

Major Inputs		Major Outputs	
Description	Source	Description	Destination
Signed offer	Create offer	Deposit check	Bookkeeper
	use case	Completed sales contract	Take delivery
Customer info	Customer		use case
Deposit check	Customer		

Major Steps Performed:

1) Record sales details on sales contract.
2) Accept customer deposit and determine
   delivery date.
3) Prepare shop work order to prepare
   vehicle and install any dealer options.

Information for Steps:

Use case name: Customer Takes Delivery   ID: 5   Importance level: High

Primary actor: Customer

Short description: This use case describes how the sales transaction is finalized and the customer takes delivery of the vehicle.

Trigger: When vehicle is ready, customer brings final payment and takes possession of vehicle.

Type: (External) / Temporal

Major Inputs		Major Outputs	
Description	Source	Description	Destination
Completed sales contract	Accepted offer	Final sales contract	Customer
	use case		
Payment	Customer		
Trade-in	Customer		

Major Steps Performed

1) Customer inspects vehicle.
   If OK, customer signs sales contract.
   Otherwise, exit use case.
2) Payment is collected.
3) Record sales transaction details.
4) If trade-in, perform accept trade-in use
   case.

Information for Steps

FIGURE 4-6

Sample Use Cases with
Major Steps Added

Use case name: Create an Offer		ID: 3	Importance level: High
Primary actor: Customer			
Short description: This use case describes the process of handling customer offers.			
Trigger: Customer decides to make an offer on a vehicle.			
Type: (External) / Temporal			

Major Inputs		Major Outputs	
Description	Source	Description	Destination
Customer name	Customer	Signed offer form	Accepted offer
Offer price	Customer		use case
New vehicle info	New vehicle	Rejected offer	Salesperson's
	record		personal file
Dealer options	Customer		
Trade-in-value	Used vehicle		
	manager		
Trade-in-value estimates	Green book		

Major Steps Performed:	Information for Steps:
1) Record details of offer.	Customer name
If trade-in, get trade-in value.	New vehicle description
Offer	Dealer options
	Offer price
	Trade-in value
2) Management reviews offer.	New vehicle record
Rejected Accepted (signed)	Trade-in value estimates, green
offer offer	book
3) Perform accepted offer use case.	Signed offer
4) If customer wants to continue negotiation, discard rejected offer and repeat steps 1 & 2.	
Otherwise, store offer in salesperson's personal file.	Rejected offer

Use case name: Accepted Offer		ID: 4	Importance level: High
Primary actor: Accepted offer use case			
Short description: This use case describes how an accepted offer is handled.			
Trigger: Customer's offer on a vehicle is accepted by dealership owner.			
Type: (External) / Temporal			

Major Inputs:		Major Outputs:	
Description	Source	Description	Destination
Signed offer	Create offer	Deposit check	Bookkeeper
	use case	Completed sales contract	Take delivery
Customer info	Customer		use case
Deposit check	Customer	Shop work order	Shop
Delivery date	Shop manager	Completed sales contract	Customer
Customer acceptance	Customer	Completed sales contract	Pending sales

Major Steps Performed	Information for Steps
1) Record sales details on sales contract.	Customer name, address, phone number
Sales contract	Signed offer
2) Accept customer deposit and determine delivery date.	Deposit check
	Promised delivery date
	Customer acceptance
Completed Deposit	Recorded deposit check
sales contract check	Completed sales contract
3) Prepare shop work order to prepare vehicle and install any dealer options.	Shop work order
Completed sales contract	
4) Store completed sales contract	Completed sales contract

FIGURE 4-7

Sample Use Cases with Information for Steps Added

Use case name: **Customer Takes Delivery**   ID: __5__   Importance level: __High__

Primary actor: **Customer**

Short description: **This use case describes how the sales transaction is finalized and the customer takes delivery of the vehicle.**

Trigger: **When vehicle is ready, customer brings final payment and takes possession of vehicle.**

Type: (**External**) / Temporal

Major Inputs		Major Outputs	
Description	Source	Description	Destination
Completed sales contract	Pending sales	Final sales contract	Customer
Payment	Customer	Completed sales contract	Pending sales
Trade-in	Customer	Recorded payment	Bookkeeper
Customer acceptance	Customer	Sold vehicle record	Sold vehicle file
New vehicle record	New vehicle file	Trade-in details	Accept trade-in
			use case

Major Steps Performed	Information for Steps
1) Customer inspects vehicle. ◄———————	Completed sales contract
If OK, customer signs sales contract. ◄——	Customer acceptance
Otherwise, exit use case. ———————	
	——► Completed sales contract
Signed sales contract	
2) Payment is collected. ◄———————	Customer payment
	——► Recorded payment
Final sales contract	——► Final sales contract
	——— New vehicle record
3) Record sales transaction details. ◄———	
	——► Sold vehicle record
4) If trade-in, perform accept trade-in use case. ◄——	Trade-in description
	——► Trade-in details

FIGURE 4-7 (*continued*)

forms, reports) are used by each step and what outputs it produces. These are written in the last column on the use case form, with an arrow pointing into or out of a step (see Figure 4-7). Sometimes, forms, reports, and information will flow from one step to the next to the next; these are shown by arrows pointing from step to step.

Notice that these are some inputs and outputs in Figure 4-7 that were omitted from Figures 4-5 and 4-6. It is common at this point for users to discover that they forgot to list some major inputs and outputs during their first time through the use case. Sometimes users realize that they have forgotten entire steps in the description. These previously omitted inputs, outputs, and steps are simply added to the use case. Our experience has shown that users can forget to include seldom-used activities that occur in special cases (e.g., when data is not available or when something unexpected occurs), so it is useful to review the steps carefully to make sure that nothing has been omitted. Compare the use cases in Figures 4-6 and 4-7 and note the way additional details have been added as the use cases are gradually refined.

Confirm the Use Case   The final step is for the users to confirm that the use case is correct as written. Review the use case with the users to make sure that each step and each input and output are correct and that the final result of the use case is consistent with the final result in the event-action list. The most powerful approach is to ask the user to *role-play*, or execute the use case by using the written steps in the use case. The analyst will hand the user pieces of paper labeled as the major inputs to the use case. The user follows the written steps like a recipe to make sure that those steps and inputs really can produce the outputs and final result defined for the use case.

APPLYING THE CONCEPTS AT TUNE SOURCE

Identifying the Major Use Cases

The first step in creating the use cases is to identify the major use cases according to the requirements definition, which was developed in the last chapter and shown in Figure 3-14. Take a minute and carefully read the requirements definition. Identify the major use cases that you think need additional definition before you continue reading.

It is important that you think about the use cases before you read what we have to say about them. So, if you haven't tried to do this, take five minutes now and do it. We'll wait.

The information in the functional requirements definition sometimes just flows into the use cases, but it usually requires some thought as to how to structure the use cases. After you read the requirements definition, you may be tempted to identify use cases that correspond directly to the requirement categories, such as (1) search and browse, (2) purchase, and (3) promote. However, creating an event-response list helps to clarify the number and scope of the use cases. (See Figure 4-8.)

YOUR

TURN

4-1 CAMPUS HOUSING

Create a set of use cases for the following high-level requirements in a housing system run by the Campus Housing Service. The Campus Housing Service helps students find apartments. Owners of apartments fill in information forms about the rental units they have available (e.g., location, number of bedrooms, monthly rent), which are entered into a database. Students can search through this database via the Web to find apartments that meet their needs (e.g., a two-bed-room apartment for $800 or less per month within $1/2$ mile of campus). They then contact the apartment owners directly to see the apartment and possibly rent it. Apartment owners call the service to delete their listing when they have rented their apartment(s).

In building the major use cases, follow the four-step process: Identify the use cases, identify the steps within them, identify the elements within the steps, and confirm the use cases.

CONCEPTS   4-A BUILDING A BAD SYSTEM?

IN ACTION

Several years ago, a well-known national real estate company built a computer-based system to help its real estate agents sell houses more quickly. The system, which worked in many ways like an early version of realtor.com, enabled its agents to search the database of houses for sale to find houses matching the buyer's criteria using a much easier interface than the traditional system. The system also enabled the agent to show the buyer a virtual tour of selected houses listed by the company itself. It was believed that by more quickly finding a small set of houses more closely matching the buyer's desires, and by providing a virtual tour, the buyers (and the agent) would waste less time looking at unappealing houses. This would result in happier buyers and in agents who were able to close sales more quickly, leading to more sales for the company and higher commissions for the agent.

The system was designed with input from agents from around the country and was launched with great hoopla. The initial training of agents met with a surge of interest and satisfaction among the agents, and the project team received many congratulations.

Six months later, satisfaction with the system had dropped dramatically, absenteeism had increased by 300%, and agents were quitting in record numbers; turnover among agents had risen by 500%, and in exit interviews, many agents mentioned the system as the primary reason for leaving. The company responded by eliminating the system—with great embarrassment.

One of an agent's key skills was the ability to find houses that match the buyer's needs. The system destroyed the value of this skill by providing a system that could enable less skilled agents to perform almost as well as highly skilled ones. Worse still—from the viewpoint of the agent—the buyer could interact directly with the system, thus bypassing the "expertise" of the agent.

QUESTIONS:
1. How were the problems with the system missed?
2. How might these problems have been foreseen and possibly avoided?
3. In perfect hindsight, given the widespread availability of such systems on the Internet today, what should the company have done?

Source: "The Hidden Minefields in Sales Force Automation Technologies," *Journal of Marketing*, July 2002, by C. Speier and V. Venkatesh.

Thinking carefully about these requirements, we can see that there are three significant triggering events: A customer arrives at the site to search and/or browse music selections; a customer selects a tune to download and buy; and the marketing department wishes to create special promotions. Let's look at each event in turn.

When a customer arrives at the site, he or she will normally browse a predefined category of music (1.1) or enter a search for a particular title, artist, or genre of music (1.2). If the customer has visited the site and created entries on a Favorites list or has purchased any tunes in the past, the display of tunes on the site will be tailored to the customer's interests (3.1, 3.3). The customer may select one or more music samples to which to listen (1.3, 3.1). The customer may add tunes to his Favorites list at any time (1.4). As you can see, this event encompasses requirements from both category 1 and category 3.

The second event, a customer triggering the purchase process, is kept separate from the search and browse event, although both events involve the customer. Purchasing involves gathering information about the customer (2.1), the music selection (2.2), and the method of payment (2.1, 2.3) and verifies the payment information (2.4) before the download process is triggered.

Finally, on a periodic basis, customer Favorites lists and purchase records are reviewed by the marketing department so that promotions and Web specials can be

Event	Response	Requirements
Customer searches and browses Web site.	New entries in Favorites list and/or interests.	1.1, 1.2, 1.3, 1.4, 3.1, 3.3
Music is selected for purchase.	Purchase and download transaction is completed.	2.1, 2.2, 2.3, 2.4
Promotions are created.	Promotions are created for customers.	3.2, 3.4

FIGURE 4-8
Tune Source Event-Response List

developed (3.2). Targeted promotions are created for when customers revisit the site (3.3). Specific e-mails will be directed to customers, offering additional special promotions (3.4).

The project team felt satisfied that three use cases were sufficient to capture the major events associated with version 1 of the new system. These use cases were named *search and browse tunes*, *purchase tunes*, and *promote tunes*. The names were chosen because they describe how the system handles each of the events. Notice too that each use case name begins with a verb because the use case describes the act of doing something.

The project team then began to gather additional information to define each use case more completely. This was done on the basis of the results of the earlier analyses described in Chapter 3, as well as through the JAD sessions held with Carly, members of her marketing staff, plus some store managers and staff who are familiar with Tune Source's existing Web-based sales system.

For each use case, the primary actor, trigger, and major input and outputs were identified. For the Search and Browse Tunes use case, the primary input is the customer's request for tunes based on title, artist, or genre. Customers select tunes so that they can listen to samples, automatically adding those selected tunes to a file that tracks each customer's interests. Customers select tunes to add to their Favorites list as well. Finally, customers may select tunes to purchase and download.

For the Purchase Tunes use case, the tune selected to buy is a critical input. Following the selection of a tune, the customer is asked to enter a username and password if they have an account; otherwise, they may establish an account or just provide customer information for the current session only. If the customer chooses to create an account, customer details will be gathered from the customer and a new customer record will be created. The price of the selected tune(s) is obtained from stored tune data, and the total cost of the purchase is calculated. Payment information will be gathered from the customer and will be stored in the customer's account (if there is one) or just used for the current session. Once the payment information is verified, the customer authorizes the transaction, a new purchase record is written to the sales file, and the tune is downloaded to the customer.

Finally, for the Promote Tunes use case, the marketing staff regularly reviews the files of recent customer purchases and additions to the customer Favorites list. On the basis of this review, Web promotions are created. In addition, e-mails are created to promote sales and specials on the regular CD sales Web site and in the stores.

Note that, at this point, only the top half of each use case has been completed. Take a moment to review the use cases (see Figure 4-9) and make sure that you understand them. You will shortly discover (if you haven't already) that the inputs and outputs in the use cases in Figure 4-9 are incomplete; the users have overlooked several important inputs and outputs. This is not a problem, because this is typical of the way most use cases evolve.

Use case name: Search and Browse Tunes		ID: __1__	Importance level: __High__

Primary actor: Customer

Short description: This use case handles customers who search and browse the tunes on the Web site.

Trigger: Customer arrives at Web site to search and browse tune selections.

Type: (External)/ Temporal

Major Inputs		Major Outputs	
Description	Source	Description	Destination
Customer request	Customer	Tune sample	Customer
Web promotions	Targeted promotions file	New interests entry	Interests file
Customer tune selection	Customer	New favorites entry	Favorites file
		Selected tune to buy	Purchase Tune
			use case

Use case name: Purchase Tunes		ID: __2__	Importance level: __High__

Primary actor: Customer

Short description: This use case handles the purchase and download of tunes.

Trigger: Customer selects tune to buy and download.

Type: (External)/ Temporal

Major Inputs		Major Outputs	
Description	Source	Description	Destination
Selected tune to buy	Search and browse	New customer record	Customer file
	tunes use case	Total cost of purchase	Customer
Customer details	Customer	New purchase record	Sales file
Tune price	Tune information file	Downloaded tune	Customer
Payment details	Customer		

Use case name: Promote Tunes		ID: __3__	Importance level: __High__

Primary actor: Marketing Department Staff

Short description: This use case handles the periodic creation of targeted promotions.

Trigger: Time for marketing department to update current promotions/specials.

Type: External / (Temporal)

Major Inputs		Major Outputs	
Description	Source	Description	Destination
Customer favorites	Favorites file	New Web promotions	Targeted promotions file
Customer purchases	Sales file	Promotional e-mails	Customer

FIGURE 4-9
Tune Source Use Cases with Major Inputs and Outputs

Identifying the Major Steps for Each Use Case

The next step is to define the major steps for each use case. The goal at this point is to describe how the use case operates. In this example, we will elaborate on the two customer-oriented use cases: Search and Browse Tunes and Purchase Tunes. The best way to begin to understand how the customer works through these use cases is to visualize yourself browsing a sales-oriented Web site, searching for particular items, investigating specific items further, finally making a decision to buy, and completing the purchase. The techniques of visualizing your interaction with the process and thinking about how other systems work (informal benchmarking) are important techniques that help analysts and users understand how processes work and how to write the use cases. Both visualization and informal benchmarking are commonly used in practice.

After you connect to the Web site, you may browse through the categories of selections that are featured on the page. You also are likely to enter some kind of search based upon a search term for a specific artist, title, or genre. The site then displays a list of tunes matching your search, along with some basic information about the tune, including its download price. If one of the tunes is of interest, you may choose to listen to the sample. If you like what you hear, but are not ready to buy, you may add the tune to your Favorites list so that you don't lose track of it. If you are ready to buy, you signal that decision, usually by placing the item in a "shopping cart." You can continue to browse and search, adding more tunes to your shopping cart, or you may be ready to complete the purchase and "check out."

To actually purchase the tune(s) you have selected, you have several choices. If you are a regular Tune Source customer, you may want to create a customer account that keeps track of your name, address, phone, e-mail, etc., and (optionally) saves the credit card information you'd like to use for your purchases. If you have an account, the use case allows you to access it with your username and password. If you do not have an account, you can set one up. Alternatively, you can purchase your selected tune(s) without creating a customer account. The use case accommodates any of these options. Next, you can use the saved payment information or enter new payment information. Once you have confirmed the purchase, the use case validates the credit card information, charges your credit card, and releases the tune(s) for download.

Figure 4-10 shows these two use cases with the added steps we have just described. For completeness, use case 3 is also included.

Identifying the Elements within Steps

The next step is to add more detail to the steps by identifying their inputs and outputs. This means identifying what inputs are needed to complete the step (e.g., information, forms, reports) and what outputs are produced by each step. As we noted earlier, it is common for users to discover that there are major inputs and outputs that were forgotten on the first attempt to complete the use case, and Tune Source is no exception.

Look at the second step in the Search and Browse Tunes use case in Figure 4-10. We can see that a customer request initiates a search, but we didn't include as an input the list of tunes that we have available. Clearly, we need this list to search for matches to the customer request. In Figure 4-11, we have corrected this error and have completed the inflows and outflows from all the steps.

Use case name: Search and Browse Tunes		ID: 1	Importance level: High

Primary actor: Customer

Short description: This use case handles customer who search and browse the tunes on the Web site.

Trigger: Customer arrives at Web site to search and browse tune selections.

Type: (External) / Temporal

Major Inputs		Major Outputs	
Description	Source	Description	Destination
Customer request	Customer	Tune sample	Customer
Web promotions	Targeted promotions file	New interests entry	Interests file
		New favorites entry	Favorites file
Customer tune selection	Customer	Selected tune to buy	Purchase Tune
			Use case

Major Steps Performed:

1) Customer enters Web site, if not a first-time visitor,load Web customization, using Targeted Promotions.

2) Customer enters search request.

3) Customer selects tune
   3.1 to listen to sample
   3.2 to add to Favorites
   3.3 to buy

Information for Steps:

Use case name: Purchase Tunes		ID: 2	Importance level: High

Primary actor: Customer

Short description: This use case handles the purchase and download of tunes.

Trigger: Customer selects tune to buy and download.

Type: (External) / Temporal

Major Inputs		Major Outputs	
Description	Source	Description	Destination
Selected tune to buy	Search and browse	New customer record	Customer file
	Tune use case	Total cost of purchase	Customer
Customer details	Customer	New purchase record	Sales file
Tune price	Tune information file	Downloaded tune	Customer
Payment details	Customer		

Major Steps Performed:

1) Tune is selected to buy.
2) If returning customer, access account information.
3) If new customer, establish account if requested; otherwise, gather customer info.
4) Obtain tune price(s) and calculate total purchase cost.
5) Gather payment information.
6) Verify payment information.
7) Get customer purchase confirmation.
8) Release music download.

Information for Steps:

Use case name: Promote Tunes		ID: 3	Importance level: High

Primary actor: Marketing Department Staff

Short description: This use case handles the periodic creation of targeted promotions.

Trigger: Time for marketing department to update current promotions/specials

Type: External / (Temporal)

Major Inputs		Major Outputs	
Description	Source	Description	Destination
Customer favorites	Favorites file	New Web promotions	Targeted promotions file
Customer purchases	Sales file	Promotional e-mails	Customer

Major Steps Performed:

1) Search customer favorites and customer purchases to select promotions titles, artists, or genres
2) Create promotional choices
3) Create email messages for regular sales on Web site and in-stock specials

Information for Steps:

FIGURE 4-10
Tune Source Use Cases with
Major Steps Added

Take a moment to read through the steps listed for both of these customer-oriented use cases. Can you follow the steps? Do they seem logical? If you find something that you think may be missing, remember that use cases are created with gradual refinement, and errors and omissions can be corrected as they are discovered. Also, we have purposely tried to avoid getting lost in the details. Our goal is to include the major activities that are performed, but not necessarily every tiny detail at this point.

Confirming the Use Case

Once all the use cases had been defined, the final step in the JAD session was to confirm that they were accurate. The project team had the users role-play the use cases. A few minor problems were discovered and easily fixed. The final use cases are shown in Figure 4-11.

Use case name: **Search and Browse Tunes**	ID: **1**	Importance level: **High**

Primary actor: **Customer**

Short description: **This use case handles customers who search and browse the tunes on the Web site.**

Trigger: **Customer arrives at Web site to search and browse tune selections.**

Type: (**External**) / Temporal

Major Inputs		Major Outputs	
Description	Source	Description	Destination
Customer request	**Customer**	**Tune sample**	**Customer**
Web promotions	**Targeted promotions file**	**New interests entry**	**Interests file**
		New Favorites entry	**Favorites file**
Tunes matching request	**Available tunes**	**Selected tune to buy**	**Purchase Tune**
Customer tune selection	**Customer**		**use case**

Major Steps Performed:	Information for Steps:
1) Customer enters Web site. If not a first-time visitor, load Web customization, using targeted ← promotions.	─Targeted promotions
2) Customer enters search request. ←	─Search request ─Tunes matching request
│ Tunes matching request ↓	
3) Customer selects tune	→Tune sample
3.1 to listen to sample	→New interests record
3.2 to add to Favorites	→New Favorites record
3.3 to buy	→Selected tune to buy

FIGURE 4-11
Tune Source Use Cases—Elements within Steps Added

Use case name: Purchase Tunes		ID: __2__	Importance level: __High__

Primary actor: Customer

Short description: This use case handles the purchase and download of tunes.

Trigger: Customer selects tune to buy and download.

Type: (External) / Temporal

Major Inputs		Major Outputs	
Description	**Source**	**Description**	**Destination**
Selected tune to buy	Search and browse tune use case	New customer record	Customer file
		Total cost of purchase	Customer
Customer details	Customer	New purchase record	Sales file
Customer details	Customer file	Downloaded tune	Customer
Tune price	Tune information file	CC charge	CC company
Payment details	Customer		
CC authorization	CC clearinghouse		
Purchase confirmation	Customer		

Major Steps Performed **Information for Steps**

1) Tune is selected to buy. ◄——————— Selected tune

2) If returning customer, access account ◄——— Customer username and password
information.

    Tune to buy   Customer details ◄——— Customer details

3) If new customer, establish account if ◄——— Customer details
requested; otherwise, gather customer info.

   New customer detail ——————————► New customer record

4) Compute total purchase cost. ◄——————— Tune price

   Total purchase cost ——————————► Total purchase cost

5) Gather payment information. ◄——————— Payment details

  Tune to   purchase   customer   payment
  buy   cost   details   details

6) Verify payment information ◄——————— CC authorization

  Tune to   purchase   customer   payment
  buy   cost   details   details

7) Get customer purchase confirmation. ◄——— Customer purchase confirmation

  Tune to   purchase   customer   verified
  buy   cost   details   payment

8) Release music download. ——————————► New purchase record
                            ——————————► Downloaded tune
                            ——————————► CC charge

FIGURE 4-11 (*continued*)

YOUR	4-2 TUNE SOURCE DIGITAL MUSIC DOWNLOAD SYSTEM
TURN	

Complete the Promote Tunes use case by adding the inputs and outputs for each step.

SUMMARY

Use Cases

A use case contains all the information needed to build one part of a process model, expressed in an informal, simple way. A use case has a name, number, importance level, brief description, primary actor, trigger(s), major inputs and outputs, and a list of the major steps required to perform it. Use cases can be identified by reviewing the functional requirements. An event-action list also is useful in identifying the significant events that should be described in a use case.

Creating Use Cases

When writing a use case, first identify the triggering event (external or temporal) and the primary actor. List the major inputs and outputs associated with responding to the event. Next, develop a list of the major steps involved in using the input(s) to produce the needed output(s) and desired response(s) to the event. Now, think more deeply about each step and identify the specific input(s) and output(s) for every step. This may lead to the discovery of additional inputs and outputs to include on the top of the use case form. Finally, have the users role-play the use case to verify that it is correct as written.

KEY TERMS

Business scenario	Input	Temporal trigger
Data flow	Iteration	Trigger
Event	Output	Use case
Event-driven modeling	Primary actor	use case package
External trigger	Role-play	Viewput
Importance level	Step	Visualization

QUESTIONS

1. What is the purpose of developing use cases during systems analysis?
2. How do use cases relate to the requirements stated in the requirements definition?
3. Describe the elements of the use case's basic information section.
4. What is the purpose of the inputs and outputs section of the use case?
5. What is the purpose of stating the primary actor for the use case?
6. Why is it important to state the importance level for a use case?
7. What is the distinction between an external trigger and a temporal trigger Give two examples of each.
8. Why do we outline the major steps performed in the use case?

9. What is the purpose of an event-action list in the process of developing use cases?
10. Should a use case be prepared for every item on the event-action list? Why or why not?
11. Describe two ways to handle a situation in which there are a large number of use cases.
12. What role does iteration play in developing use cases?
13. Describe the best way to validate the content of the use cases.

EXERCISES

A. Create a set of use cases for the process of buying glasses from the viewpoint of the patient, but do not bother to identify the steps within each use case. (Just complete the information at the top of the use case form.) The first step is to see an eye doctor who will give you a prescription. Once you have a prescription, you go to a glasses store, where you select your frames and place the order for your glasses. Once the glasses have been made, you return to the store for a fitting and pay for the glasses.

B. Create a set of use cases for the accompanying dentist office system, but do not bother to identify the steps within each use case. (Just complete the information at the top of the use case form.) When new patients are seen for the first time, they complete a patient information form that asks for their name, address, phone number, and brief medical history, which are stored in the patient information file. When a patient calls to schedule a new appointment or change an existing appointment, the receptionist checks the appointment file for an available time. Once a good time is found for the patient, the appointment is scheduled. If the patient is a new patient, an incomplete entry is made in the patient file; the full information will be collected when the patient arrives for the appointment. Because appointments are often made far in advance, the receptionist usually mails a reminder postcard to each patient two weeks before the appointment.

C. Complete the use cases for the dentist office system in exercise B by identifying the steps and the data flows within the use cases.

D. Create a set of use cases for an online university registration system. The system should enable the staff of each academic department to examine the courses offered by their department, add and remove courses, and change the information about them (e.g., the maximum number of students permitted). It should permit students to examine currently available courses, add and drop courses to and from their schedules, and examine the courses for which they are enrolled. Department staff should be able to print a variety of reports about the courses and the students enrolled in them. The system should ensure that no student takes too many courses and that students who have any unpaid fees are not permitted to register. (Assume that a fees data store is maintained by the university's financial office, which the registration system accesses but does not change).

E. Create a set of use cases for the following system: A Real Estate, Inc. (AREI), sells houses. People who want to sell their houses sign a contract with AREI and provide information on their house. This information is kept in a database by AREI, and a subset of this information is sent to the citywide multiple listing service used by all real estate agents. AREI works with two types of potential buyers. Some buyers have an interest in one specific house. In this case, AREI prints information from its database, which the real estate agent uses to help show the house to the buyer (a process beyond the scope of the system to be modeled). Other buyers seek AREI's advice in finding a house that meets their needs. In this case, the buyer completes a buyer information form that is entered into a buyer database, and AREI real estate agents use its information to search AREI's database and the multiple listing service for houses that meet their needs. The results of these searches are printed and used to help the real estate agent show houses to the buyer.

F. Create a set of use cases for the following system: A Video Store (AVS) runs a series of fairly standard video stores. Before a video can be put on the shelf, it must be catalogued and entered into the video database. Every customer must have a valid AVS customer card in order to rent a video. Customers rent videos for three days at a time. Every time a customer rents a video, the system must ensure that this customer does not have any overdue videos. If so, the overdue videos must be returned and an overdue fee paid before the customer can rent more videos. Likewise, if the customer has returned overdue videos, but has not paid the overdue fee, the fee must be paid before new videos can be rented. Every morning, the store manager prints a report that lists overdue videos; if a video is two or more days overdue, the manager calls the customer to remind him or her to return the video. If a video is returned in damaged condition, the manager removes it from the video database and may sometimes charge the customer.

G. Create a set of use cases for the following health club membership system: When members join the health club, they pay a fee for a certain length of time. Most memberships are for one year, but memberships as short as two months are available. Throughout the year, the health club offers a variety of discounts on its regular membership prices (e.g., two memberships for the price of one for Valentine's Day). It is common for members to pay different amounts for the same length of membership. The club wants to mail out reminder letters to members asking them to renew their memberships one month before their memberships expire. Some members have become angry when asked to renew at a much higher rate than their original membership contract, so that the club wants to track the price paid so that the manager can override the regular prices with special prices when members are asked to renew. The system must track these new prices so that renewals can be processed accurately. One of the problems in the health club industry is the high turnover rate of members. While some members remain active for many years, about half of the members do not renew their memberships. This is a major problem because the health club spends a lot in advertising to attract each new member. The manager wants the system to track each time a member comes into the club. The system will then identify the heavy users and generate a report so that the manager can ask them to renew their memberships early, perhaps offering them a reduced rate for early renewal. Likewise, the system should identify members who have not visited the club in more than a month so that the manager can call them and attempt to reinterest them in the club.

H. Create a set of use cases for the following system: Picnics R Us (PRU) is a small catering firm with five employees. During a typical summer weekend, PRU caters 15 picnics with 20 to 50 people each. The business has grown rapidly over the past year, and the owner wants to install a new computer system for managing the ordering and buying process. PRU has a set of 10 standard menus. When potential customers call, the receptionist describes the menus to them. If the customer decides to book a picnic, the receptionist records the customer information (e.g., name, address, phone number, etc.) and the information about the picnic (e.g., place, date, time, which one of the standard menus, total price) on a contract. The customer is then faxed a copy of the contract and must sign and return it along with a deposit (often by credit card or check) before the picnic is officially booked. The remaining money is collected when the picnic is delivered. Sometimes, the customer wants something special (e.g., birthday cake). In this case, the receptionist takes the information and gives it to the owner who determines the cost; the receptionist then calls the customer back with the price information. Sometimes the customer accepts the price; other times, the customer requests some changes, which have to go back to the owner for a new cost estimate. Each week, the owner looks through the picnics scheduled for that weekend and orders the supplies (e.g., plates) and food (e.g., bread, chicken) needed to make them. The owner would like to use the system for marketing as well. It should be able to track how customers learned about PRU and identify repeat customers so that PRU can mail special offers to them. The owner also wants to track the picnics on which PRU sent a contract, but the customer never signed the contract or actually booked a picnic.

I. Create a set of use cases for the following system: Of-the-Month Club (OTMC) is an innovative young firm that sells memberships to people who have an interest in certain products. People pay membership fees for one year and each month receive a product by mail. For example, OTMC has a coffee-of-the-month club that sends members one pound of special coffee each month. OTMC currently has six memberships (coffee, wine, beer, cigars, flowers, and computer games), each of which costs a different amount. Customers usually belong to just one, but some belong to two or more. When people join OTMC, the telephone operator records the name, mailing address, phone number, e-mail address, credit card information, start date, and membership service(s) (e.g., coffee). Some customers request a double or triple membership (e.g., two pounds of coffee, three cases of beer). The computer game membership operates a bit differently from the others. In this case, the member must also select the type of game (action, arcade, fantasy/science fiction, educational, etc.) and age level. OTMC is planning to greatly expand the number of memberships it offers (e.g., video games, movies, toys, cheese, fruit, vegetables), so the system needs to accommodate this future expansion. OTMC is also planning to offer three-month and six-month memberships.

J. Create a set of use cases for a university library borrowing system. (Do not worry about catalogue searching, etc.) The system will record the books owned by the library and will record who has borrowed what books. Before someone can borrow a book, he or she must show a valid ID card that is checked to ensure that it is still valid against the student database maintained by the registrar's office (for student borrowers), the faculty/staff database maintained by the personnel office (for faculty/staff borrowers), or against the library's own guest database (for individuals issued a "guest" card by the library). The system must also check to ensure that the borrower does not have any overdue books or unpaid fines before he or she can borrow another book. Every Monday, the library prints and mails postcards to those people with overdue books. If a book is overdue by more than two weeks, a fine will be imposed and a librarian will telephone the borrower to remind him or her to return the book(s). Sometimes books are lost or are returned in damaged condition. The manager must then remove them from the database and will sometimes impose a fine on the borrower.

MINICASES

1. Williams Specialty Company is a small printing and engraving organization. When Pat Williams, the owner, brought computers into the business office eight years ago, the business was very small and very simple. Pat was able to utilize an inexpensive PC-based accounting system to handle the basic information processing needs of the firm. As time has gone on, however, the business has grown and the work being performed has become significantly more complex. The simple accounting software still in use is no longer adequate to keep track of many of the company's sophisticated deals and arrangements with its customers.

Pat has a staff of four people in the business office who are familiar with the intricacies of the company's record-keeping requirements. Pat recently met with her staff to discuss her plan to hire an IS consulting firm to evaluate their information system needs and recommend a strategy for upgrading their computer system.

The staff are excited about the prospect of a new system, since the current system causes them much aggravation. No one on the staff has ever done anything like this before, however, and they are a little wary of the consultants who will be conducting the project.

Assume that you are a systems analyst on the consulting team assigned to the Williams Specialty Co. engagement. At your first meeting with the Williams staff, you want to be sure that they understand the work that your team will be performing and how they will participate in that work.

a. Explain, in clear, nontechnical terms, the goals of the analysis phase of the project.

b. Explain, in clear, nontechnical terms, how use cases will be used by the project team. Explain what these models are, what they represent in the system, and how they will be used by the team.

ANALYSIS

☑ **Apply Requirements Analysis Techniques (Business Process Automation, Business Process Improvement, or Business Process Reengineering)**

☑ **Use Requirements Gathering Techniques (Interview, JAD Session, Questionnaire, Document Analysis, or Observation)**

☑ **Develop Requirements Definition**

☑ **Develop Use Cases**

☐ **Develop Data Flow Diagrams**

☐ **Develop Entity Relationship Model**

☐ **Normalize Entity Relationship Model**

TASK CHECKLIST

PLANNING   ANALYSIS   DESIGN

CHAPTER 5

PROCESS MODELING

A process model describes business processes—the activities that people do. Process models are developed for the as-is system and/or the to-be system. This chapter describes data flow diagramming, one of the most commonly used process modeling techniques.

OBJECTIVES

- Understand the rules and style guidelines for data flow diagrams.
- Understand the process used to create data flow diagrams.
- Be able to create data flow diagrams.

CHAPTER OUTLINE

IMPLEMENTATION

INTRODUCTION

The previous chapters discussed requirements activities, such as interviewing and JAD, and how to transform those requirements into more detailed use cases. In this chapter, we discuss how the requirements definition and use cases are further refined into a process model. A *process model* is a formal way of representing how a business system operates. It illustrates the processes or activities that are performed and how data move among them. A process model can be used to document the current system (i.e., as-is system) or the new system being developed (i.e., to-be system), whether computerized or not.

There are many different process modeling techniques in use today. In this chapter, we focus on one of the most commonly used techniques:[1] data flow diagramming. Data flow diagramming is a technique that diagrams the business processes and the data that pass among them. In this chapter, we first describe the basic syntax rules and illustrate how they can be used to draw simple one-page data flow diagrams (DFDs). Then we describe how to create more complex multipage diagrams.

Although the name *data flow diagram* (DFD) implies a focus on data, this is not the case. The focus is mainly on the processes or activities that are performed. Data modeling, discussed in the next chapter, presents how the data created and used by processes are organized. Process modeling—and creating DFDs in particular—is one of the most important skills needed by systems analysts.

In this chapter, we focus on *logical process models*, which are models that describe processes, without suggesting how they are conducted. When reading a logical process model, you will not be able to tell whether a process is computerized or manual, whether a piece of information is collected by paper form or via the Web, or whether information is placed in a filing cabinet or a large database. These physical details are defined during the design phase when these logical models are refined into *physical models*, which provide information that is needed to ultimately build the system. (See Chapter 10.) By focusing on logical processes first, analysts can focus on how the business should run, without being distracted by implementation details.

In this chapter, we first explain how to read DFDs and describe their basic syntax. Then we describe the process used to build DFDs that draws information from the use cases and from additional requirements information gathered from the users.

DATA FLOW DIAGRAMS

Reading Data Flow Diagrams

Figure 5-1 shows a DFD for the process of buying goods at the supermarket. By examining the DFD, an analyst can understand the process by which customers checkout at the supermarket. Take a moment to examine the diagram before reading on. How much do you understand?

---

[1] Another commonly used process modeling technique is IDEF0. IDEF0 is used extensively throughout the U.S. Government. For more information about IDEF0, see FIPS 183: *Integration Definition for Function Modeling (IDEF0)*, Federal Information Processing Standards Publications, Washington, DC: U.S. Department of Commerce, 1993.

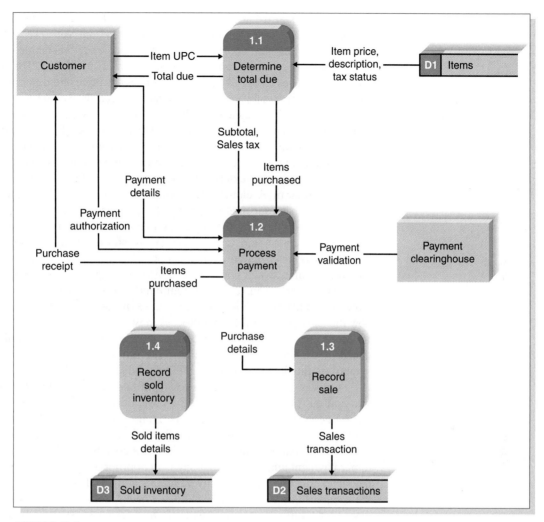

FIGURE 5-1
Supermarket Checkout DFD

You may recognize this scenario as the use case in the previous chapter (Figure 4-1), which described the supermarket checkout process. Most people start reading in the upper left corner of the DFD, so this is where most analysts try to make the DFD begin, although this is not always possible. The first item in the upper left corner of Figure 5-1 is the "Customer" external entity, which is a rectangle that represents individual customers who are buying things at the supermarket. This symbol has three arrows pointing away from it to rounded rectangular symbols. These arrows represent data flows and show that the external entity (Customer) provides three "bundles" of data to processes that use the data. Now look again at Figure 4-1 and notice that these same data bundles are listed as Major Inputs in the use case, with the source listed as the Customer. Also, there are two arrows coming in to the Customer external entity from the rounded rectangles, representing bundles of data that the processes produce to flow back to the customer. These data bundles are listed under Major Outputs in the use case (Figure 4-1), with the destination listed as the Customer.

Now look at the arrow that flows in to the "Determine total due" process from the right side. In order to determine the total amount you owe, the process has to retrieve some information from storage. The open-ended rectangle labeled "Items" is called a data store, and it represents a collection of stored data. The "Determine total due" process uses an item's UPC to find the item's price and description and to determine whether it is subject to sales tax from stored data about the item. Notice that "Item details" is listed as a Major Input on the use case (Figure 4-1), with the source listed as the Item data store. Now, still referring to Figure 4-1, notice that every Major Input listed in the use case flows in to a process from an external entity or stored data (noted by the source). Also notice that every Major Output listed in the use case flows out to a destination (an external entity or data storage) on the data flow diagram.

Now look more closely at the Major Steps Performed section of the use case. You can see that four major steps are listed in the use case, and you can also see four process symbols on the data flow diagram. On the DFD (Figure 5-1), as you follow the arrow "Item UPC" from the Customer to the "Determine total due" process, imagine each item in your shopping cart, at the checkout lane, being passed over the scanner, which reads the UPC. After all items are scanned, the "Total due" data flow informs you of the total amount you owe for the items you are buying. Now look at the description on the use case (Figure 4-1) for the first step and notice how the use case describes that process in words. Notice also how the "Information for Steps" section of the use case lists the data elements that are either used or produced by each step, corresponding to the inflows and outflows from each process symbol on the data flow diagram (Figure 5-1).

Look at the other three process symbols in the DFD and examine the flows into and out of each process. On the basis of the data flowing in and flowing out, try to understand what the process is doing. Check your understanding by looking at the Major Steps Performed and Information for Steps in the use case.

You probably recognized that the "Process payment" process receives the customer payment and handles that payment appropriately, according to its type. Some payments must be electronically validated, and a "Clearinghouse" entity represents the agencies that electronically validate checks, debit cards, and credit cards. Some payments require additional customer authorization, such as entering a personal identification number (PIN), showing an ID, or signing a form. Then, along with the facts about the purchase and a confirmed payment, the receipt can be printed and handed to the customer to conclude the customer's interaction with the system. You can also see that two additional processes are performed by the system: A record of the entire sales transaction is created to keep track of all the facts of the sale, and the details on the sold items are recorded in a data store so that the supermarket's inventory on hand can be reduced by the items that were just purchased.

Finally, you can see on the data flow diagram that sometimes a process sends a data flow directly to another process. This is also illustrated on the use case as you see data elements flowing between one step and another in the Major Steps Performed section.

The relationships described here between the use case and the data flow diagram are not accidental. A well-constructed use case makes developing a data flow diagram quite straightforward. The Major Inputs and Major Outputs listed on the use case provide a list of the sources and destinations, respectively, of the inflows and outflows of the processes. The processes themselves on the data flow diagram correspond to the Major Steps Performed section of the use case. The Information for Steps section shows the data flowing in or produced by each step of the use case, and these correspond to the data flows that enter or leave each process on the data flow diagram.

Data Flow Diagram Element	Typical Computer-Aided Software Engineering Fields	Gane and Sarson Symbol	DeMarco and Yourdon Symbol
Every *process* has a number a name (verb phase) a description at least one output data flow at least one input data flow	Label (name) Type (process) Description (what is it) Process number Process description (structured English) Notes	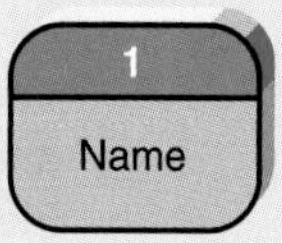 1 Name	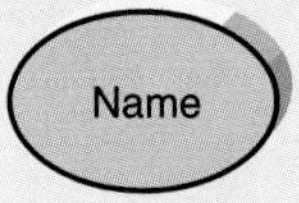 Name
Every *data flow* has a name (a noun) a description one or more connections to a process	Label (name) Type (flow) Description Alias (another name) Composition (description of data elements) Notes	 Name →	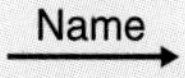 Name →
Every *data store* has a number a name (a noun) a description one or more input data flows one or more output data flows	Label (name) Type (store) Description Alias (another name) Composition (description of data elements) Notes	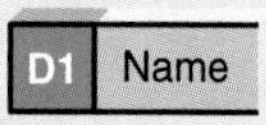 D1 Name	 D1 Name
Every *external entity* has a name (a noun) a description	Label (name) Type (entity) Description Alias (another name) Entity description Notes	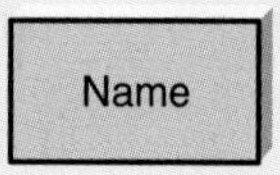 Name	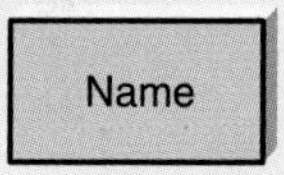 Name

FIGURE 5-2
Data Flow Diagram Elements

Elements of Data Flow Diagrams

Now that you have had a glimpse of a DFD, we will present the language of DFDs, which includes a set of symbols, naming conventions, and syntax rules. There are four symbols in the DFD language (processes, data flows, data stores, and external entities), each of which is represented by a different graphic symbol. There are two commonly used styles of symbols, one set developed by Chris Gane and Trish Sarson and the other by Tom DeMarco and Ed Yourdon[2] (Figure 5-2). Neither is better than the other; some organizations use the Gane and Sarson style of symbols, and others use the DeMarco/Yourdon style. We will use the Gane and Sarson style in this book.

Process   A *process* is an activity or a function that is performed for some specific business reason. Processes can be manual or computerized. Every process should be named starting with a verb and ending with a noun (e.g., "Determine total due").

[2] See Chris Gane and Trish Sarson, *Structured Systems Analysis: Tools and Techniques*, Englewood Cliffs, NJ: Prentice Hall, 1979; Tom DeMarco, *Structured Analysis and System Specification*, Englewood Cliffs, NJ: Prentice-Hall, 1979; and E. Yourdon and Larry L. Constantine, *Structured Design: Fundamentals of a Discipline of Computer Program and Systems Design*, Englewood Cliffs, NJ: Prentice-Hall, 1979.

Names should be short, yet contain enough information so that the reader can easily understand exactly what they do. In general, each process performs only one activity, so most system analysts avoid using the word "and" in process names because it suggests that the process performs several activities. In addition, every process must have at least one input data flow and at least one output data flow.

Figure 5-2 shows the basic elements of a process and how they are usually named in CASE tools. Every process has a unique identification number, a name, and a description, all of which are noted in the CASE repository. Descriptions clearly and precisely describe the steps and details of the processes; ultimately, they are used to guide the programmers who need to computerize the processes (or the writers of policy manuals for noncomputerized processes). The process descriptions become more detailed as information is learned about the process through the analysis phase. Many process descriptions are written as simple text statements about what happens. More complex processes use more formal techniques such as structured English, decision tables, or decision trees, which are discussed in a later section.

Data Flow   A *data flow* is a single piece of data (e.g., item UPC) (sometimes called a data element), or a logical collection of several pieces of information (e.g., purchase receipt). Every data flow should be named with a noun. The description of a data flow lists exactly what data elements the flow contains. For example, the payment details data flow can list the payment type, payment amount, and account number as its data elements.

Data flows are the glue that holds the processes together. One end of every data flow will always come from or go to a process, with the arrow showing the direction into or out of the process. Data flows show what inputs go into each process and what outputs each process produces. Every process must create at least one output data flow, because if there is no output, the process does not do anything. Likewise, each process has at least one input data flow, because it is difficult, if not impossible, to produce an output with no input.

Data Store   A *data store* is a collection of data that is stored in some way (which is determined later when creating the physical model). Every data store is named with a noun and is assigned an identification number and a description. Data stores form the starting point for the data model (discussed in the next chapter) and are the principal link between the process model and the data model.

Data flows coming out of a data store indicate that information is retrieved from the data store, and data flows going into a data store indicate that information is added to the data store or that information in the data store is changed. Whenever a process updates a data store (e.g., by retrieving a record from a data store, changing it, and storing it back), we document both the data coming from the data store and the data written back into the data store.

All data stores must have at least one input data flow (or else they never contain any data), unless they are created and maintained by another information system or on another page of the DFD. Likewise, they have at least one output data flow on some page of the DFD. (Why store data if you never use it?) In cases in which the same process both stores data and retrieves data from a data store, there is a temptation to draw one data flow with an arrow on both ends. This practice is incorrect, however. The data flow that stores data and the data flow that retrieves data should always be shown as two separate data flows.

External Entity   An *external entity* is a person, organization, or system that is external to the system, but interacts with it (e.g., customer, clearinghouse, government organization, accounting system). The external entity typically corresponds to the primary actor identified in the use case. External entities provide data to the system or receive data from the system, and serve to establish the system boundaries. Every external entity has a name and a description. The key point to remember about an external entity is that it is external to the system, but may or may not be part of the organization.

A common mistake is to include people who are part of the system as external entities. The people who execute a process are part of the process and are not external to the system (e.g., data-entry clerks, order takers). The person who performs a process is often described in the process description, but never on the DFD itself. However, people who use the information from the system to perform other processes or who decide what information goes into the system are documented as external entities (e.g., managers, staff).

Using Data Flow Diagrams to Define Business Processes

Most business processes are too complex to be explained in one DFD. Most process models are therefore composed of a set of DFDs. The first DFD provides a summary of the overall system, with additional DFDs providing more and more detail about each part of the overall business process. Thus, one important principle in process modeling with DFDs is the decomposition of the business process into a series of DFDs, each representing a lower level of detail. Figure 5-3 shows how one business process can be decomposed into several levels of DFDs.

Context Diagram   The first DFD in every business process model, whether a manual system or a computerized system, is the *context diagram* (see Figure 5-3). As the name suggests, the context diagram shows the entire system in context with its environment. All process models have one context diagram.

The context diagram shows the overall business process as just one process (i.e., the system itself) and shows the data flows to and from external entities. Data stores usually are not included on the context diagram, unless they are "owned" by systems or processes other than the one being documented. For example, an information system used by the university library that records who has borrowed books would likely check the registrar's student information database to see whether a student is currently registered at the university. In this context diagram, the registrar's student information data store could be shown on the context diagram because it is external to the library system, but used by it. Many organizations, however, would show this not as a data store, but as an external entity called "Registrar's Student Information System."

Level 0 Diagram   The next DFD is called the *level 0 diagram* or *level 0 DFD.* (See Figure 5-3.) The level 0 diagram shows all the processes at the first level of numbering (i.e., processes numbered 1 through 3), the data stores, external entities, and data flows among them. The purpose of the level 0 DFD is to show all the major high-level processes of the system and how they are interrelated. All process models have one and only one level 0 DFD.

Another key principle in creating sets of DFDs is *balancing.* Balancing means ensuring that all information presented in a DFD at one level is accurately represented

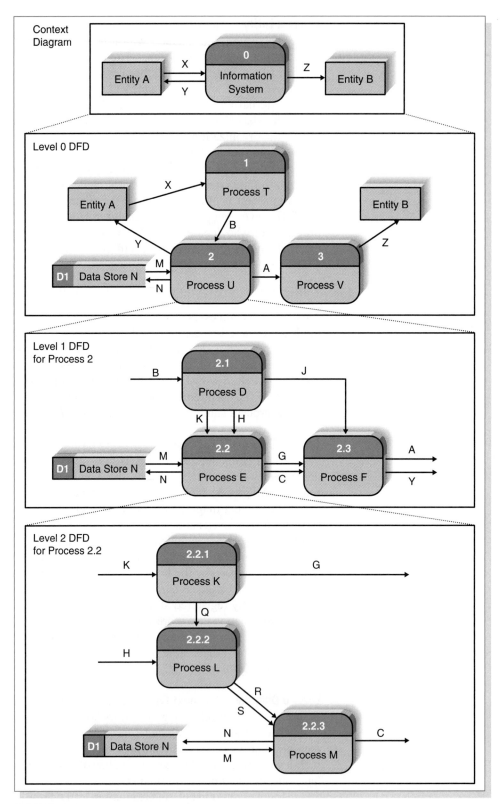

FIGURE 5-3
Relationships among Levels of Data Flow Diagrams (DFDs)

in the next-level DFD. This doesn't mean that the information is identical, but that it is shown appropriately. There is a subtle difference in meaning between these two words that will become apparent shortly, but for the moment, let's compare the context diagram with the level 0 DFD in Figure 5-3 to see how the two are balanced. In this case, we see that the external entities (A, B) are identical between the two diagrams and that the data flows to and from the external entities in the context diagram (X, Y, Z) also appear in the level 0 DFD. The level 0 DFD replaces the context diagram's single process (always numbered 0) with three processes (1, 2, 3), adds a data store (D1), and includes two additional data flows that were not in the context diagram (data flow B from process 1 to process 2; data flow A from process 2 to process 3).

These three processes and two data flows are contained within process 0. They were not shown on the context diagram because they are the internal components of process 0. The context diagram deliberately hides some of the system's complexity in order to make it easier for the reader to understand. Only after the reader understands the context diagram does the analyst "open up" process 0 to display its internal operations by decomposing the context diagram into the level 0 DFD, which shows more detail about the processes and data flows inside the system.

Level 1 Diagrams   In the same way that the context diagram deliberately hides some of the system's complexity, so, too, does the level 0 DFD. The level 0 DFD shows only how the major high-level processes in the system interact. Each process on the level 0 DFD can be decomposed into a more explicit DFD, called a *level 1 diagram*, or *level 1 DFD*, which shows how it operates in greater detail. The DFD illustrated in Figure 5-1 is a level 1 DFD.

In general, all process models have as many level 1 diagrams as there are processes on the level 0 diagram; every process in the level 0 DFD would be *decomposed* into its own level 1 DFD, so the level 0 DFD in Figure 5-3 would have three level 1 DFDs (one for process 1, one for process 2, one for process 3). For simplicity, we have chosen to show only one level 1 DFD in this figure, the DFD for process 2. The processes in level 1 DFDs are numbered on the basis of the process being decomposed. In this example, we are decomposing process 2, so the processes in this level 1 DFD are numbered 2.1, 2.2, and 2.3.

Processes 2.1, 2.2, and 2.3 are the *children* of process 2, and process 2 is the *parent* of processes 2.1, 2.2, and 2.3. These three children processes wholly and completely make up process 2. The set of children and the parent are identical; they are simply different ways of looking at the same thing. When a parent process is decomposed into children, its children must completely perform all of its functions, in the same way that cutting up a pie produces a set of slices that wholly and completely make up the pie. Even though the slices may not be the same size, the set of slices is identical to the entire pie; nothing is omitted by slicing the pie.

Once again, it is very important to ensure that the level 0 and level 1 DFDs are balanced. The level 0 DFD shows that process 2 accesses data store D1, has two input data flows (B, M), and has three output data flows (A, N, and Y). A check of the level 1 DFD shows the same data store and data flows. Once again, we see that five new data flows have been added (C, G, H, J, K) at this level. These data flows are contained within process 2 and therefore are not documented in the level 0 DFD. Only when we decompose or open up process 2 via the level 1 DFD do we see that they exist.

The level 1 DFD shows more precisely which process uses the input data flow B (process 2.1) and which produces the output data flows A and Y (process 2.3). Note, however, that the level 1 DFD does not show where these data flows come from or go to. To find the source of data flow B, for example, we have to move up to the level 0 DFD, which shows data flow B coming from external entity B. Likewise, if we follow the data flow from A up to the level 0 DFD, we see that it goes to process 3, but we still do not know exactly which process within process 3 uses it (e.g., process 3.1, 3.2). To determine the exact source, we would have to examine the level 1 DFD for process 3.

This example shows one downside to the decomposition of DFDs across multiple pages. To find the exact source and destination of data flows, one often must follow the data flow across several DFDs on different pages. Several alternatives to this approach to decomposing DFDs have been proposed, but none is as commonly used as the "traditional" approach. The most common alternative is to show the source and destination of data flows to and from external entities (as well as data stores) at the lower level DFDs. The fact that most data flows are to or from data stores and external entities, rather than processes on other DFD pages, can significantly simplify the reading of multiple page DFDs. We believe this to be a better approach, so when we teach our courses, we show external entities on all DFDs, including level 1 DFDs and below.

Level 2 Diagrams   The bottom of Figure 5-3 shows the next level of decomposition: a *level 2 diagram*, or *level 2 DFD*, for process 2.2. This DFD shows that process 2.2 is decomposed into three processes (2.2.1, 2.2.2, and 2.2.3). The level 1 diagram for process 2.2 shows interactions with data store D1, which we see in the level 2 DFD as occurring in process 2.2.3. Likewise, the level 2 DFD for 2.2 shows two input data flows (H, K) and two output data flows (C, G), which we also see on the level 2 diagram, along with several new data flows (Q, R, S). The two DFDs are therefore balanced.

It is sometimes difficult to remember which DFD level is which. It may help to remember that the level numbers refer to the number of decimal points in the process numbers on the DFD. A level 0 DFD has process numbers with no decimal points (e.g., 1, 2), whereas a level 1 DFD has process numbers with one decimal point (e.g., 2.3, 5.1), a level 2 DFD has numbers with two decimal points (e.g., 1.2.5, 3.3.2), and so on.

Alternative Data Flows   Suppose that a process produces two different data flows under different circumstances. For example, a quality-control process could produce a quality-approved widget or a defective widget, or our credit card authorization request could produce an "approved" or a "rejected" result. How do we show these alternative paths in the DFD? The answer is that we show both data flows and use the process description to explain that they are alternatives. Nothing on the DFD itself shows that the data flows are mutually exclusive. For example, process 2.1 on the level 1 DFD produces three output data flows (H, J, K). Without reading the text description of process 2.1, we do not know whether these are produced simultaneously or whether they are mutually exclusive.

Process Descriptions

The purpose of the process descriptions is to explain what the process does and provide additional information that the DFD does not provide. As we move through the SDLC, we gradually move from the general text descriptions of requirements into more and more precise descriptions that are eventually translated into very precise programming languages. In most cases, a process is straightforward enough that the requirements definition, a use case, and a DFD with a simple text description together provide sufficient detail to support the activities in the design phase. Sometimes, however, the process is sufficiently complex that it can benefit from a more detailed process description that explains the logic which occurs inside the process. Three techniques are commonly used to describe more complex processing logic: structured English, decision trees, and decision tables. Very complex processes may use a combination of structured English and either decision trees or decision tables.

Structured English uses short sentences to describe the work that a process performs. *Decision trees* display decision logic (IF statements) as a set of nodes (questions) and branches (answers). *Decision tables* represent complex policy decisions as rules that link various conditions with actions. Since these techniques are commonly discussed in programming texts, we will not elaborate on them here. They are useful to the systems analyst in conveying the proper understanding of what goes on "inside" a process.

CREATING DATA FLOW DIAGRAMS

Data flow diagrams start with the information in the use cases and the requirements definition. Although the use cases are created by the users and project team working together, the DFDs typically are created by the project team and then reviewed by the users. Generally speaking, the set of DFDs that make up the process model simply integrates the individual use cases (and adds in any processes in the requirements definition not selected as use cases). The project team takes the use cases and rewrites them as DFDs. However, because DFDs have formal rules about symbols and syntax that use cases do not, the project team sometimes has to revise some of the information in the use cases to make them conform to the DFD rules. The most common types of changes are to the names of the use cases that become processes and the inputs and outputs that become data flows. The second most common type of change is to combine several small inputs and outputs in the use cases into larger data flows in the DFDs (e.g., combining three separate inputs, such as "customer name," "customer address," and "customer phone number," into one data flow, such as "customer information").

Project teams usually use process modeling tools or CASE tools to draw process models. Simple tools such as Visio are just fancy drawing tools that work like PowerPoint in that they do not understand the syntax or the meaning of DFD elements. Other process modeling tools such as BPWin understand the DFD and can perform simple syntax checking to make sure that the DFD is at least somewhat correct. A full CASE tool, such as Visible Analyst Workbench, provides many capabilities in addition to process modeling (e.g., data modeling as discussed in the next chapter). CASE tools tend to be complex, and while they are valuable for large and complex projects, they often cost more than they add for simple projects. Figure 5-4 shows a sample screen from the Visible Analyst CASE tool.

Building a process model that has many levels of DFDs usually entails several steps. Some analysts prefer to begin process modeling by focusing first on the level 0 diagram. We have found it useful to first build the context diagram showing all the external entities and the data flows that originate from or terminate in them. Second, the team creates a DFD fragment for each use case that shows how the use case exchanges data flows with the external entities and data stores. Third, these

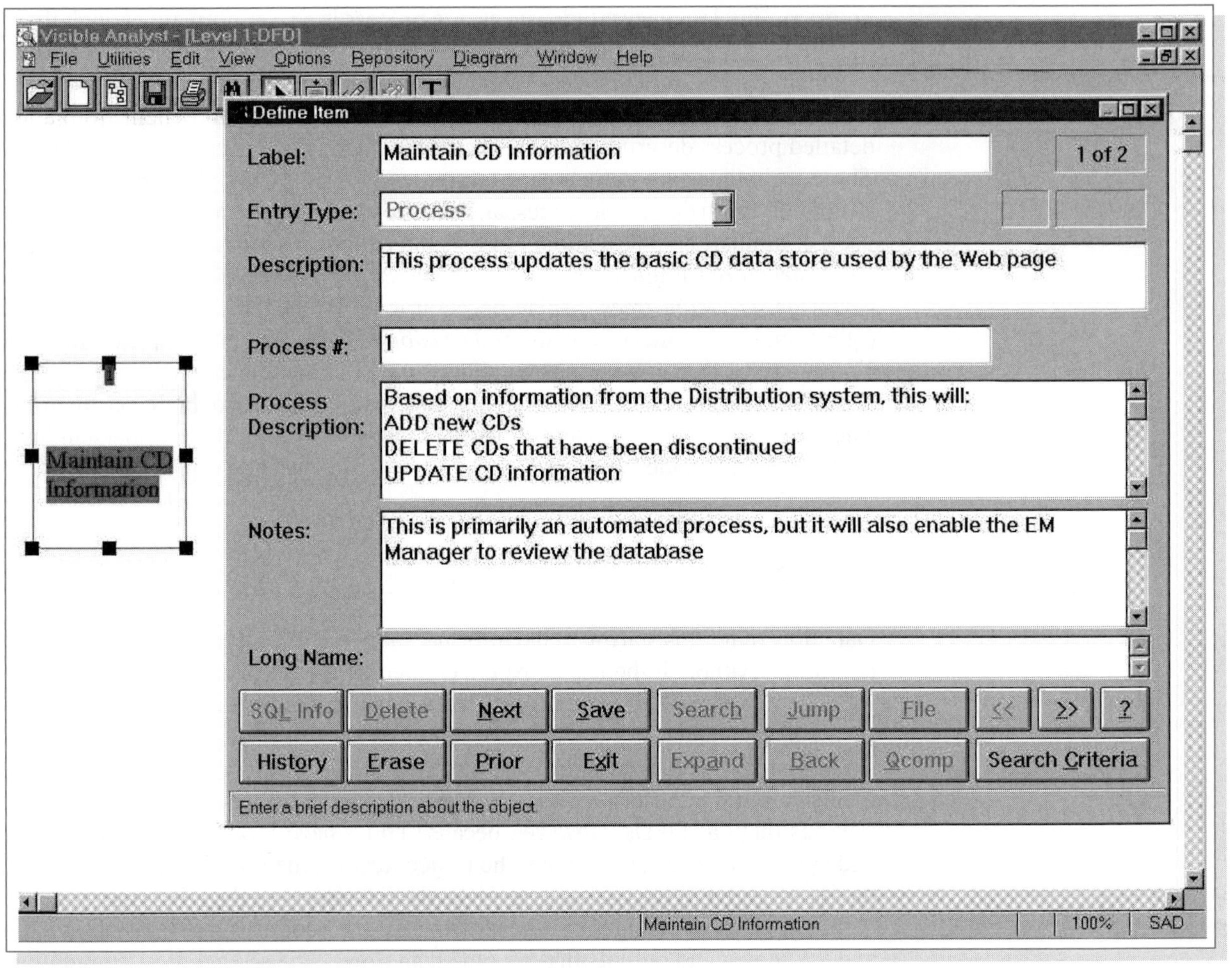

FIGURE 5-4
Entering Data Flow Diagram Processes in a Computer-Aided Software Engineering Tool

DFD fragments are organized into a level 0 DFD. Fourth, the team develops level 1 DFDs, based on the steps within each use case, to better explain how they operate. In some cases, these level 1 DFDs are further decomposed into level 2 DFDs, level 3 DFDs, level 4 DFDs, and so on. Fifth, the team validates the set of DFDs to make sure that they are complete and correct.

In the following sections, process modeling is illustrated with the Holiday Travel Vehicles information system.

Creating the Context Diagram

The context diagram defines how the business process or computer system interacts with its environment—primarily the external entities. To create the context diagram, you simply draw one process symbol for the business process or system being modeled (numbered 0 and named for the process or system). You read through the use cases and add the inputs and outputs listed at the top of the form, as well as their sources and destinations. Usually, all the inputs and outputs will come from or go to external entities such as a person, organization, or other information system. If any inputs and outputs connect directly to data stores in an external system, it is best practice to create an external entity which is named for the system that owns the data store. None of the data stores inside the process/system that are created by the process or system itself are included in the context diagram, because they are "inside" the system. Because there are sometimes so many inputs and outputs, we often combine several small data flows into larger data flows.

Figure 5-5 shows the context diagram for the Holiday Travel Vehicles system. Take a moment to review this system as described in Chapter 4 and review the use cases in Figure 4-7. You can see from the Major Inputs and Outputs sections in the Figure 4-7 use cases that the system has many interactions with the Customer external entity. We have simplified these inflows and outflows to just four primary data flows on the context diagram. If we had included each small data flow, the context diagram would become too cluttered. The smaller data flows will become evident as we decompose the context diagram into more detailed levels. Notice that we have established three external entities to represent parts of the Holiday Travel Vehicle organization which receive information from or supply information to this system. Payments flow to the bookkeeping department, and shop work orders flow to the shop. The company owner or manager provides information to the system. Finally, we place orders for new vehicles with our vehicle manufacturers, who then supply the dealership with the requested vehicles.

Creating Data Flow Diagram Fragments

A *DFD fragment* is one part of a DFD that eventually will be combined with other DFD fragments to form a DFD diagram. In this step, each use case is converted into

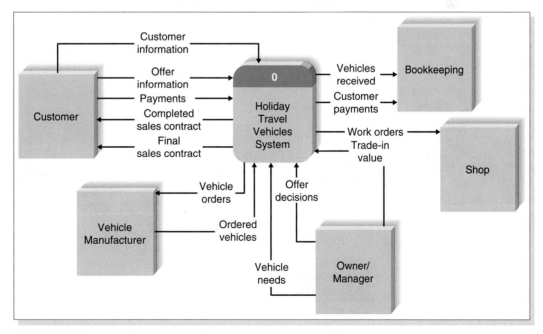

FIGURE 5-5
Holiday Travel Vehicles Context Diagram

one DFD fragment. You start by taking each use case and drawing a DFD fragment, using the information given on the top of the use case: the name, ID number, and major inputs and outputs. The information about the major steps that make up each use case is ignored at this point; it will be used in a later step. Figure 5-6 shows a use case and the DFD fragment that was created from it.

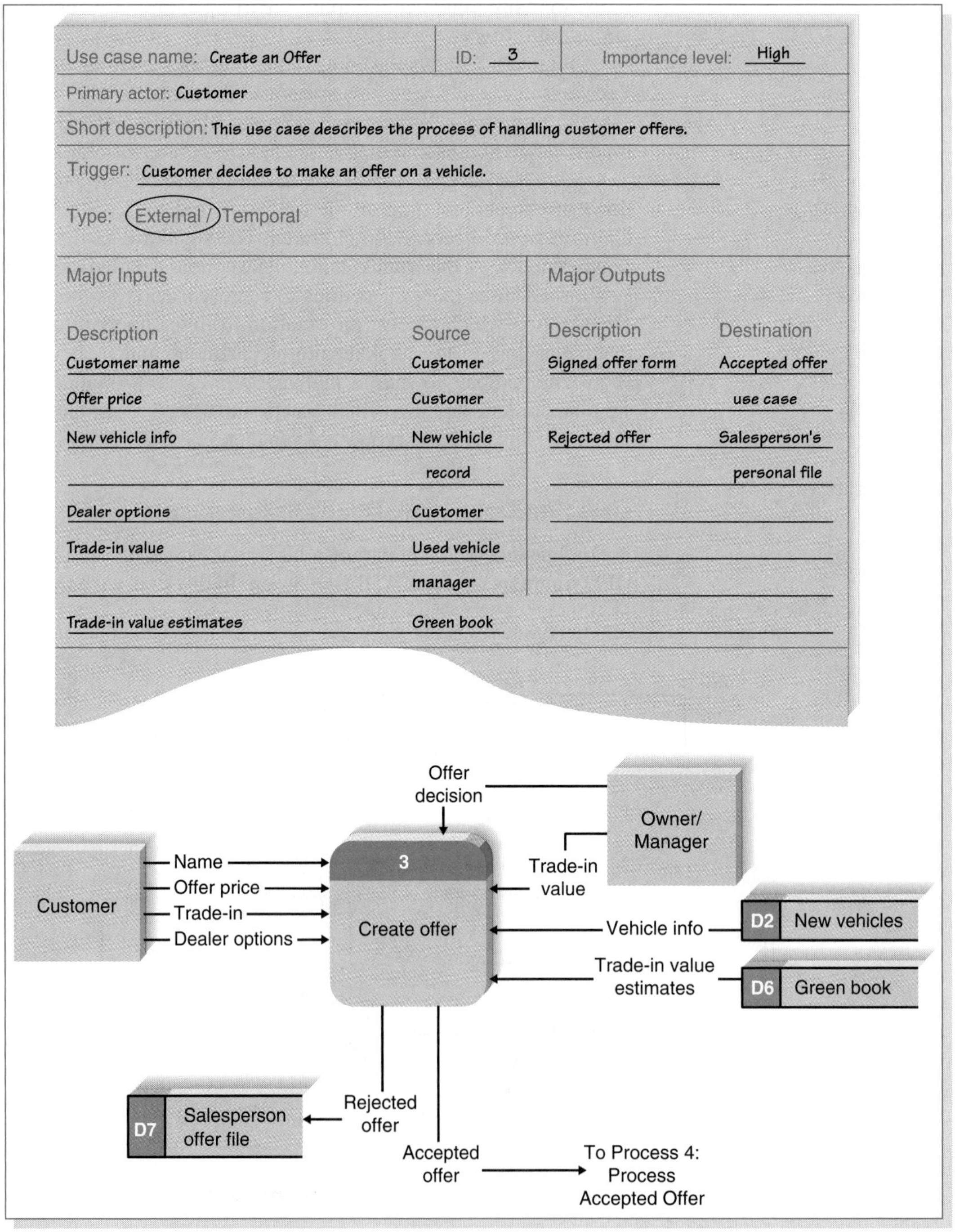
Use case name: Create an Offer
ID: 3
Importance level: High
Primary actor: Customer
Short description: This use case describes the process of handling customer offers.
Trigger: Customer decides to make an offer on a vehicle.
Type: External / Temporal
Major Inputs
Description
Source
Customer name
Customer
Offer price
Customer
New vehicle info
New vehicle record
Dealer options
Customer
Trade-in value
Used vehicle manager
Trade-in value estimates
Green book
Major Outputs
Description
Destination
Signed offer form
Accepted offer use case
Rejected offer
Salesperson's personal file
Offer decision
Owner/ Manager
Trade-in value
Customer
Name
Offer price
Trade-in
Dealer options
3
Create offer
Vehicle info
D2
New vehicles
Trade-in value estimates
D6
Green book
D7
Salesperson offer file
Rejected offer
Accepted offer
To Process 4: Process Accepted Offer

FIGURE 5-6
Holiday Travel Vehicles Process 3 DFD Fragment

Once again, some subtle, but important changes are often made in converting the use case into a DFD. The two most common changes are modifications to the process names and the addition of data flows. There were no formal rules for use case names, but there are formal rules for naming processes on the DFD. All process names must be a verb phrase—they must start with a verb and include a noun. (See Figure 5-2.) Not all of our use case names are structured in this way, so we sometimes need to change them. It is also important to have a consistent *viewpoint* when naming processes. For example, the DFD in Figure 5-6 is written from the viewpoint of the dealership, not of the customer. All the process names and descriptions are written as activities that the staff performs. It is traditional to design the processes from the viewpoint of the organization running the system, so this sometimes requires some additional changes in names.

The second common change is the addition of data flows. Use cases are written to describe how the system interacts with the user. Typically, they do not describe how the system obtains data, so the use case often omits data flows read from a data store. When creating DFD fragments, it is important to make sure that any information given to the user is obtained from a data store. The easiest way to do this is to first create the DFD fragment with the major inputs and outputs listed at the top of the use case and then verify that all outputs have sufficient inputs to create them.

There are no formal rules covering the *layout* of processes, data flows, data stores, and external entities within a DFD. They can be placed anywhere you like on the page; however, because we in Western cultures tend to read from top to bottom and left to right, most systems analysts try to put the process in the middle of the DFD fragment, with the major inputs starting from the left side or top entering the process and outputs leaving from the right or the bottom. Data stores are often written below the process.

Take a moment and draw a DFD fragment for the two other use cases shown in Figure 4-7 (Accepted Offer and Customer Takes Delivery). We have included possible ways of drawing these fragments in Figure 5-7. (Don't look until you've attempted the drawings on your own!) For completeness, we have also included fragments for the more simple events of this system in Appendix A of this chapter. Remember that we did not elaborate on the events of Ordering New Vehicles, Receiving New Vehicles, or Accepting Trade-Ins with use cases, because these are not complex events. Even so, they will need to be incorporated into our system, and we have drawn the DFD fragments for them now.

Creating the Level 0 Data Flow Diagram

Once you have the set of DFD fragments (one for each of the major use cases), you simply combine them into one DFD drawing that becomes the level 0 DFD. As mentioned earlier, there are no formal layout rules for DFDs. However, most systems analysts try to put the process that is first chronologically in the upper left corner of the diagram and work their way from top to bottom, left to right (e.g., Figure 5-1). Generally speaking, most analysts try to reduce the number of times that data flow lines cross or to ensure that when they do cross, they cross at right angles so that there is less confusion. (Many give one line a little "hump" to imply that one data flow jumps over the other without touching it.) Minimizing the number of data flows that cross is challenging.

Iteration is the cornerstone of good DFD design. Even experienced analysts seldom draw a DFD perfectly the first time. In most cases, they draw it once to understand the pattern of processes, data flows, data stores, and external entities and then draw it a second time on a fresh sheet of paper (or in a fresh file) to make

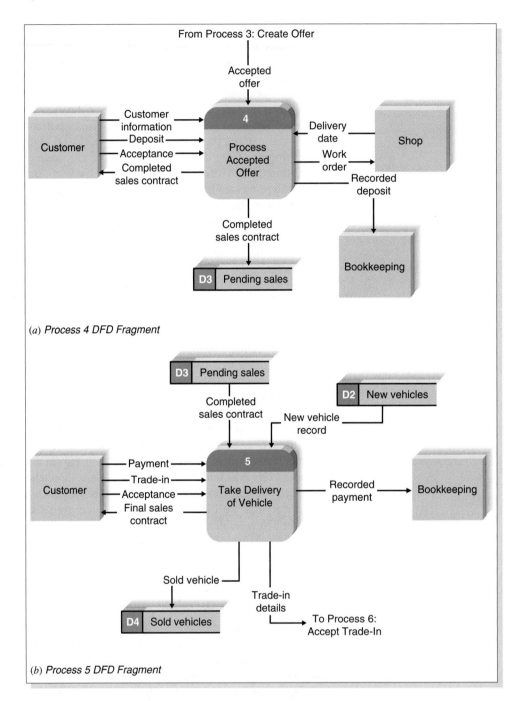

(a) *Process 4 DFD Fragment*

(b) *Process 5 DFD Fragment*

FIGURE 5-7
Additional DFD Fragments for
Holiday Travel Vehicles

it easier to understand and to reduce the number of data flows that cross. Often, a DFD is drawn many times before it is finished.

Figure 5-8 combines the DFD fragments in Figures 5-6 and 5-7. Take a moment to examine Figure 5-8 and find the DFD fragments from Figures 5-6 and 5-7 contained within it. You will note as you examine Figure 5-8 that there is a data flow (Accepted Offer) shown that flows between Process 3 and Process 4. A direct flow between processes is uncommon on a level 0 diagram, since at this level the data produced by one event-handling process normally would be stored, at least temporarily,

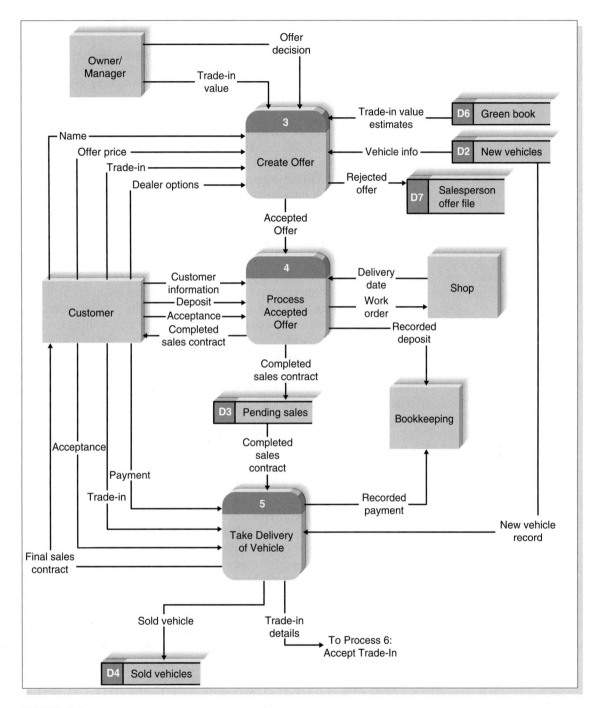

FIGURE 5-8
Holiday Travel Vehicles Partial Level 0 DFD

before it is processed by another event-handling process. This issue should be evaluated by the analyst and, if necessary, a new data store created that holds Accepted Offers until process 4, Process Accepted Offer, is performed. This issue again illustrates the evolving nature of data flow diagrams. In Appendix 5A, we have included a complete level 0 diagram with all six main processes incorporated into the diagram.

Creating Level 1 Data Flow Diagrams (and Below)

The team now begins to create lower-level DFDs for each process in the level 0 DFD that needs a level 1 DFD. Each one of the use cases is turned into its own DFD. The process for creating the level 1 DFDs is to take the steps as written on the use cases and convert them into a DFD in much the same way as for the level 0 DFD. Usually, each step in the use case becomes a process on the level 1 DFD, with the inputs and outputs becoming the input and output data flows. Once again, however, sometimes subtle changes are required to go from the informal descriptions in the use case to the more formal process model, such as adding input data flows that were not included in the use case. And because the analysts are now starting to think more deeply about how the processes will be supported by an information system, they sometimes slightly change the use case steps to make the process easier to use.

In some approaches to creating DFDs, no source and destination are given on the level 1 DFD (and lower) for the inputs that come and go between external entities (or other processes outside of this process). But the source and destination of data flows for data stores and data flows that go to processes within this DFD are included (i.e., from one step to another in the same use case, such as "Items Purchased" from process 1.1 to 1.2 in Figure 5-1). This is because the information is redundant; you can see the destination of data flows by reading the level 0 DFD.

The problem with these approaches is that in order to really understand the level 1 DFD, you must refer back to the level 0 DFD. For small systems that only have one or two level 1 DFDs, this is not a major problem. But for large systems that have many levels of DFDs, the problem grows; in order to understand the destination of a data flow on a level 3 DFD, you have to read the level 2 DFD, the level 1 DFD, and the level 0 DFD—and if the destination is to another activity, then you have to trace down in the lower-level DFDs in the other process.

We believe that including external entities in level 1 and lower DFDs dramatically simplifies the readability of DFDs, with very little downside. In our work in several dozen projects with the U.S. Department of Defense, several other federal agencies, and the military of two other countries, we came to understand the value of this approach and converted the powers that be to our viewpoint. Because DFDs are not completely standardized, each organization uses them slightly differently. So, the ultimate decision of whether or not to include external entities on level 1 DFDs is yours—or your instructor's! In this book, we will include them.

Ideally, we try to keep the data stores in the same general position on the page in the level 1 DFD as they were in the level 0 DFD, but this is not always possible. We try to draw input data flows arriving from the left edge of the page and output data flows leaving from the right edge. For example, see the level 1 DFD in Figure 5-1.

One of the most challenging design questions is when to decompose a level 1 DFD into lower levels. The decomposition of DFDs can be taken to almost any level, so for example, we could decompose process 1.2 on the level 1 DFD into processes 1.2.1, 1.2.2, 1.2.3, and so on in the level 2 DFD. This can be repeated to any level of detail, so one could have level 4 or even level 5 DFDs.

There is no simple answer to the "ideal" level of decomposition, because it depends on the complexity of the system or business process being modeled. In general, you decompose a process into a lower-level DFD whenever that process is sufficiently complex that additional decomposition can help explain the process. Most experts believe that there should be at least three, and no more than seven to nine, processes on every DFD, so if you begin to decompose a process and end up with only two processes on the lower-level DFD, you probably don't need to decompose it. There seems little point in decomposing a process and creating another lower-level

DFD for only two processes; you are better off simply showing two processes on the original higher level DFD. Likewise, a DFD with more than nine processes becomes difficult for users to read and understand, because it is very complex and crowded. Some of these processes should be combined and explained on a lower-level DFD.

One guideline for reaching the ideal level of decomposition is to decompose until you can provide a detailed description of the process in no more than one page of process descriptions: structured English, decision trees, or decision tables. Another helpful rule of thumb is that each lowest level process should be no more complex than what can be realized in about 25–50 lines of code.

We have provided level 1 DFDs for two of the processes in the Holiday Travel Vehicle system—Process 4, Process Accepted Offer; and Process 5, Take Delivery of Vehicle—in Figures 5-9 and 5-10, respectively. Take a moment to compare these diagrams with the Major Steps sections of their use cases in Figure 4-7.

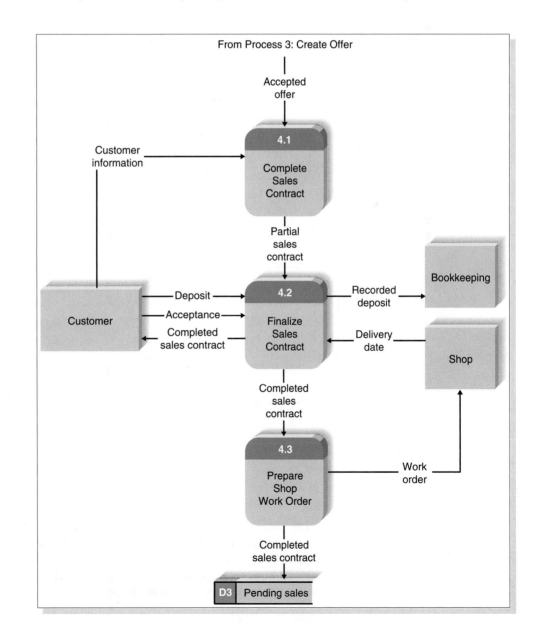

FIGURE 5-9
Level 1 DFD for Process Accepted Offer

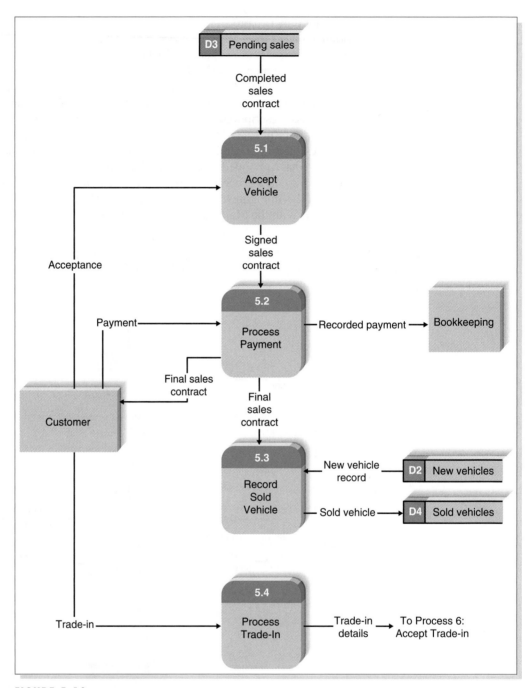

FIGURE 5-10
Level 1 DFD for Take Delivery of Vehicle

The process model is more likely to be drawn to the lowest level of detail for a to-be model if a traditional development process is used (i.e., not rapid application development [RAD]; see Chapter 2) or if the system will be built by an external contractor. Without the complete level of detail, it may be hard to specify in a contract exactly what the system should do. If a RAD approach,

CONCEPTS   5-A U.S. ARMY AND MARINE CORPS BATTLEFIELD LOGISTICS

IN ACTION

Shortly after the Gulf War in 1991 (Desert Storm), the U.S. Department of Defense realized that there were significant problems in its battlefield logistics systems that provided supplies to the troops at the division level and below. During the Gulf War, it had proved difficult for army and marine units fighting together to share supplies back and forth because their logistics computer systems would not easily communicate. The goal of the new system was to combine the army and marine corps logistics systems into one system to enable units to share supplies under battlefield conditions.

The army and marines built separate as-is process models of their existing logistics systems that had 165 processes for the army system and 76 processes for the marines. Both process models were developed over a 3-month time period and cost several million dollars to build, even though they were not intended to be comprehensive.

I helped them develop a model for the new integrated battlefield logistics system that would be used by both services (i.e., the to-be model). The initial process model contained 1,500 processes and went down to level 6 DFDs in many places. It took 3,300 pages to print. They realized that this model was too large to be useful. The project leader decided that level 4 DFDs was as far as the model would go, with additional information contained in the process descriptions. This reduced the model to 375 processes (800 pages) and made it far more useful.   *Alan Dennis*

QUESTIONS:
1. What are the advantages and disadvantages to setting a limit for the maximum depth for a DFD?
2. Is a level 4 DFD an appropriate limit?

which involves a lot of interaction with the users and, quite often, prototypes, is being used, we would be less likely to go to as low a level of detail, because the design will evolve through interaction with the users. In our experience, most systems go to only level 2 at most.

There is no requirement that all parts of the system must be decomposed to the same level of DFDs. Some parts of the system may be very complex and require many levels, whereas other parts of the system may be simpler and require fewer.

Validating the Data Flow Diagrams

Once you have created a set of DFDs, it is important to check them for quality. Figure 5-11 provides a quick checklist for identifying the most common errors. There are two fundamentally different types of problems that can occur in DFDs: *syntax errors* and *semantics errors*. "Syntax," refers to the structure of the DFDs and whether the DFDs follow the rules of the DFD language. Syntax errors can be thought of as grammatical errors made by the analyst when he or she creates the DFD. "Semantics" refers to the meaning of the DFDs and whether they accurately describe the business process being modeled. Semantics errors can be thought of as misunderstandings by the analyst in collecting, analyzing, and reporting information about the system.

In general, syntax errors are easier to find and fix than are semantics errors, because there are clear rules that can be used to identify them (e.g., a process must have a name). Most CASE tools have syntax checkers that will detect errors within one page of a DFD in much the same way that word processors have spelling checkers and grammar checkers. Finding syntax errors that span several pages of a DFD (e.g., from a level 1 to a level 2 DFD) is slightly more challenging, particularly for consistent viewpoint, decomposition, and balance. Some CASE tools can detect balance errors, but that is about all. In most cases, analysts must carefully and

Syntax	
Within DFD	
Process	• Every process has a unique name that is an action-oriented verb phrase, a number, and a description.
	• Every process has at least one input data flow.
	• Every process has at least one output data flow.
	• Output data flows usually have different names than input data flows because the process changes the input into a different output in some way.
	• There are between three and seven processes per DFD.
Data Flow	• Every data flow has a unique name that is a noun, and a description.
	• Every data flow connects to at least one process.
	• Data flows only in one direction (no two-headed arrows).
	• A minimum number of data flow lines cross.
Data Store	• Every data store has a unique name that is a noun, and a description.
	• Every data store has at least one input data flow (which means to add new data or change existing data in the data store) on some page of the DFD.
	• Every data store has at least one output data flow (which means to read data from the data store) on some page of the DFD.
External Entity	• Every external entity has a unique name that is a noun, and a description.
	• Every external entity has at least one input or output data flow.
Across DFDs	
Context diagram	• Every set of DFDs must have one context diagram.
Viewpoint	• There is a consistent viewpoint for the entire set of DFDs.
Decomposition	• Every process is wholly and completely described by the processes on its children DFDs.
Balance	• Every data flow, data store, and external entity on a higher level DFD is shown on the lower-level DFD that decomposes it.
Semantics	
Appropriate Representation	• User validation
	• Role-play processes
Consistent Decomposition	• Examine lowest-level DFDs
Consistent Terminology	• Examine names carefully

FIGURE 5-11
Data Flow Diagram Quality Checklist

painstakingly review every process, external entity, data flow, and data store on all DFDs by hand to make sure that they have a consistent viewpoint and that the decomposition and balance are appropriate.

Each data store is required to have at least one input and one output on some page of the DFD. In Figure 5-10, data store D2, New Vehicles, has only outputs and data store D4, Sold Vehicles, has only inputs. This situation is not necessarily an error. The analyst should check elsewhere in the DFDs to find where data is written to data store D2 or read from data store D4. All data stores should have at least one inflow and one outflow, but the flows may not be on the same diagram, so check other parts of the system. Another issue that arises is when the data store is utilized by other systems. In that case, data may be added to or used by a separate system. This is perfectly fine, but the analyst should investigate to verify that the required flows in and out of data stores exist somewhere.

In our experience, the most common syntax error that novice analysts make in creating DFDs is violating the law of conservation of data.[3] The first part of the law states the following:

1. *Data at rest stays at rest until moved by a process.*

In other words, data cannot move without a process. Data cannot go to or come from a data store or an external entity without having a process to push it or pull it.

The second part of the law states the following:

2. *Processes cannot consume or create data.*

In other words, data only enters or leaves the system by way of the external entities. A process cannot destroy input data; all processes must have outputs. Drawing a process without an output is sometimes called a "black hole" error. Likewise, a process cannot create new data; it can transform data from one form to another, but it cannot produce output data without inputs. Drawing a process without an input is sometimes called a "miracle" error (because output data miraculously appear). There is one exception to the part of the law requiring inputs, but it is so rare that most analysts never encounter it.[4] Figure 5-12 shows some common syntax errors.

Generally speaking, semantics errors cause the most problems in system development. Semantics errors are much harder to find and fix because doing so requires a good understanding of the business process. And even then, what may be identified as an error may actually be a misunderstanding by the person reviewing the model. There are three useful checks to help ensure that models are semantically correct. (See Figure 5-11.)

The first check to ensure that the model is an appropriate representation is to ask the users to validate the model in a walk-through (i.e., the model is presented to the users, and they examine it for accuracy). A more powerful technique is for the users to role-play the process from the DFDs in the same way in which they role-played the use case. The users pretend to execute the process exactly as it is described in the DFDs. They start at the first process and attempt to perform it by using only the inputs specified and producing only the outputs specified. Then they move to the second process, and so on.

One of the most subtle forms of semantics error occurs when a process creates an output, but has insufficient inputs to create it. For example, in order to create water (H_2O), we need to have both hydrogen (H) and oxygen (O) present. The same is true of computer systems, in that the outputs of a process can be only combinations and transformations of its inputs. Suppose, for example, that we want to record an order; we need the customer name and mailing address and the quantities and prices for the items the customer is ordering. We need information from the customer data store (e.g., address) and information from the items data store (e.g., price). We cannot draw a process that produces an output order data flow without inputs from these two data stores. Role-playing with strict adherence to the inputs and outputs in a model is one of the best ways to catch this type of error.

A second semantics error check is to ensure consistent decomposition, which can be tested by examining the lowest-level processes in the DFDs. In most

---

[3] This law was developed by Prof. Dale Goodhue at the University of Georgia.

[4] The exception is a temporal process that issues a trigger output based on an internal time clock. Whenever some predetermined period elapses, the process produces an output. The timekeeping process has no inputs because the clock is internal to the process.

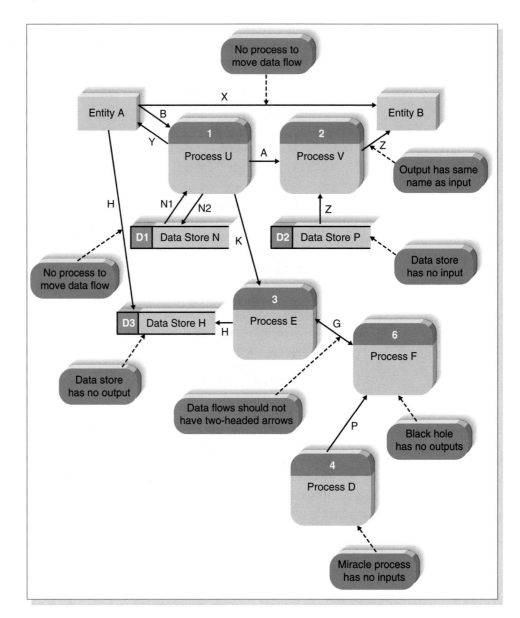

FIGURE 5-12
Some Common Errors

circumstances, all processes should be decomposed to the same level of detail—which is not the same as saying the same number of levels. For example, suppose that we were modeling the process of driving to work in the morning. One level of detail would be to say the following: (1) Enter car; (2) start car; (3) drive away. Another level of detail would be to say the following: (1) Unlock car; (2) sit in car; (3) buckle seat belt; and so on. Still another level would be to say the following: (1) Remove key from pocket; (2) insert key in door lock; (3) turn key; and so on. None of these is inherently better than another, but barring unusual circumstances, it is usually best to ensure that all processes at the very bottom of the model provide the same consistent level of detail.

Likewise, it is important to ensure that the terminology is consistent throughout the model. The same item may have different names in different parts of the organization, so one person's "sales order" may be another person's "customer order." Likewise, the same term may have different meanings; for example, "ship date" may mean one thing to the sales representative taking the order (e.g., promised date) and something else to the warehouse (e.g., the actual date shipped). Resolving these differences before the model is finalized is important in ensuring that everyone who reads the model or who uses the information system built from the model has a shared understanding.

APPLYING THE CONCEPTS AT TUNE SOURCE

Creating the Context Diagram

The project team began by creating the context diagram. They read through the top part of the three major use cases in Figure 4-10 to find the major inputs and outputs.

The team noticed that the majority of data flow interactions are with the customers who are using the Web site to browse music selections and make download purchases. There will be an interaction with the credit card clearinghouse entity that will handle payment verification and processing of purchases. Finally, although it is not obvious from the use cases, the marketing managers will be using sales information from the system to design and implement promotional campaigns. The team used the major inflows and outflows from the use cases and developed the context diagram shown in Figure 5-13.

Creating Data Flow Diagram Fragments

The next step was to create one DFD fragment for each use case. This was done by drawing the process in the middle of the page, making sure that the process number and name were appropriate, and connecting all the input and output data flows to it. Unlike the context diagram, the DFD fragment includes data flows to external entities and to internal data stores.

The completed DFD fragments are shown in Figure 5-14. Before looking at the figure, take a minute and draw them on your own. There are many good ways to draw these fragments. In fact, there are many "right" ways to create use cases and DFDs. Notice that on the DFD fragment for process 3 we have shown a dotted line

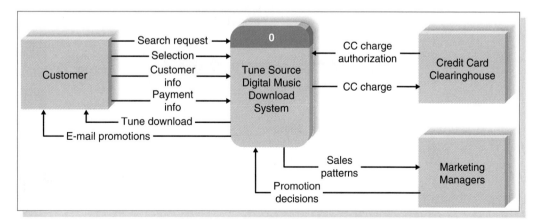

FIGURE 5-13
Tune Source Context Diagram

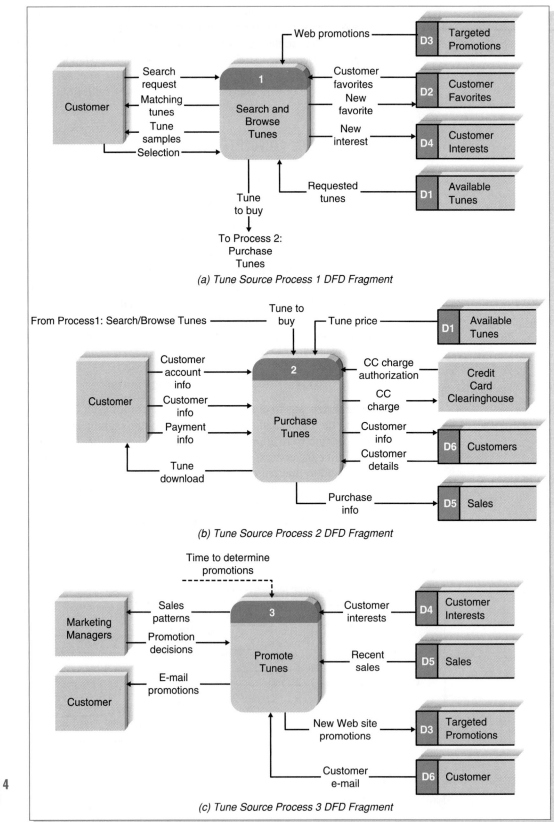

(a) Tune Source Process 1 DFD Fragment

(b) Tune Source Process 2 DFD Fragment

(c) Tune Source Process 3 DFD Fragment

FIGURE 5-14
Tune Source DFD
Fragments

inflow labeled "Time to determine promotions" into the process. Recall that we specified that the use case, Promote Tunes, was a temporal use case, triggered when it was time to update promotions and specials. The dotted line flow into process 3 in Figure 5-14 is sometimes referred to as a *control flow* and is commonly used to represent a time-based trigger for an event.

Creating the Level 0 Data Flow Diagram

The next step was to create the level 0 DFD by integrating the DFD fragments, which proved to be anticlimactic. The team simply took the DFD fragments and drew them together on one piece of paper. Although it sometimes is challenging to arrange all the DFD fragments on one piece of paper, it was primarily a mechanical exercise (Figure 5-15). Compare the level 0 diagram with the context diagram

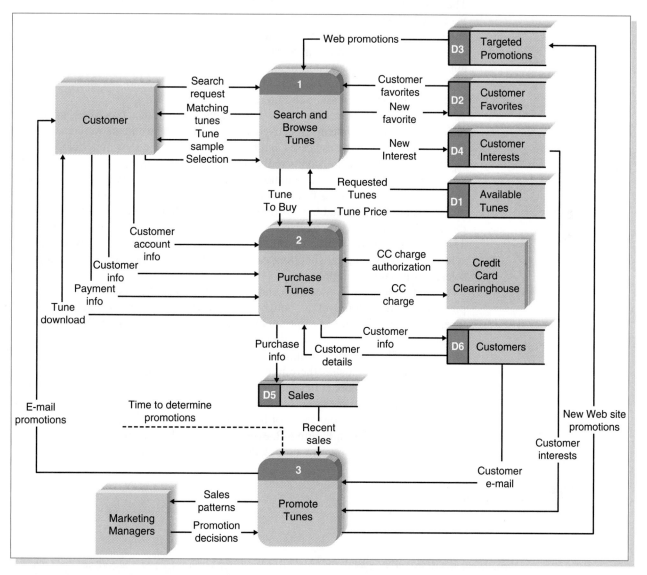

FIGURE 5-15
Tune Source Level 0 DFD

in Figure 5-13. Are the two DFDs balanced? Notice the additional detail contained in the level 0 diagram.

A careful review of the data stores in Figure 5-15 reveals that every one has both an inflow and an outflow, with one exception, D1:Available Tunes. D1:Available Tunes is read by two processes, but is not written to by any process shown. This violation of DFD syntax needs to be investigated by the team because it may be a serious oversight. As we will explain later, in this situation we need to create a process specifically for adding, modifying, and deleting data in D1:Available Tunes. "Administrative" processes such as this are often overlooked, as we initially focus on business requirements only, but will need to be added before the system is complete.

Creating Level 1 Data Flow Diagrams (and Below)

The next step was to create the level 1 DFDs for those processes that could benefit from them. The analysts started with the first use case (search and browse tunes) and started to draw a DFD for the individual steps it contained. The steps in the use case were straightforward, but as is common, the team had to choose names and numbers for the processes and to add input data flows from data stores not present in the use case. The team also discovered the omission of a data flow, customer interests, from the use case. See Figure 5-16.

The team also developed level 1 diagrams for the other processes, using the major steps outlined in their respective use cases. Some adjustments were made from the steps as shown in the use cases, but the team followed the steps fairly closely. See Figures 5-17 and 5-18, and compare them with their use cases shown in Figure 4-11.

An issue that required some thought was the transition between process 1 and process 2, shown as a data flow called "Tune to Buy." This flow represents one or more music selections that the customer has decided to purchase. In thinking about this transition, the team recognized a logical place to use a shopping cart approach. The customer, while searching and browsing music in process 1, would place selected tunes in a digital shopping cart. Actually paying for and downloading the selections is handled in process 2.

A close look at Figures 5-16 and 5-17 shows no explicit mention of the shopping cart as a data store; yet, obviously, we do need to store the selected tunes somewhere. It would be quite appropriate to include another data store called D7: Shopping Cart, to store the tunes selected as an output from process 1.3 and an input to process 2.3. This data store would be a temporary data store that contains data only until the customer finishes the purchase process. Once the purchase is completed, the temporary data store is deleted. By tradition, we do not include temporary data stores that do not survive a transaction on the DFDs. While it is not incorrect to do so, it is just not the standard way of handling temporary storage requirements.

As we specified in Figure 5-2, every data store should have one or more input data flows and one or more output data flows. A careful look at Figure 5-16,

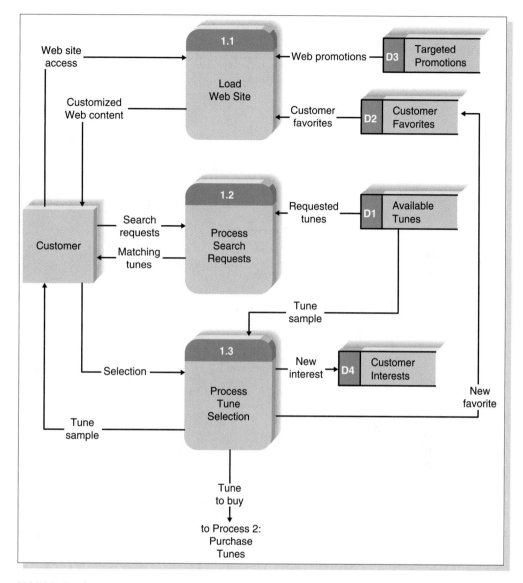

FIGURE 5-16
Level 1 DFD for Tune Source Process 1: Search and Browse Tunes

however, reveals that D1: Available Tunes has output data flows, but no input data flows. This data store is the main repository for the digital music library, so, clearly, it has a central role in our system. The team will need to be sure to create an administrative process for maintaining this data store: adding new information to it, modifying its existing contents, and removing information from it. These administrative tasks are sometimes omitted from the business-oriented tasks listed in the use cases, so it is up to the team to ensure that processes are included to add, modify, and delete the contents of data stores somewhere in the system. Simply checking the DFD syntax (all data stores must have at least one input data flow and at least one output data flow) helped discover this omission in the process model.

Although it would have been possible to decompose several of the processes on the level 1 DFDs into more detail on a level 2 diagram, the project team decided

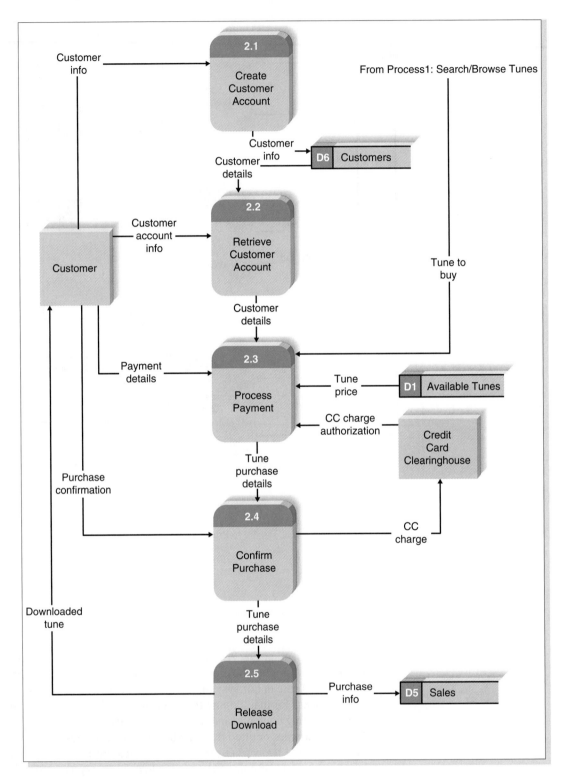

FIGURE 5-17
Level 1 DFD for Tune Source Process 2: Purchase Tunes

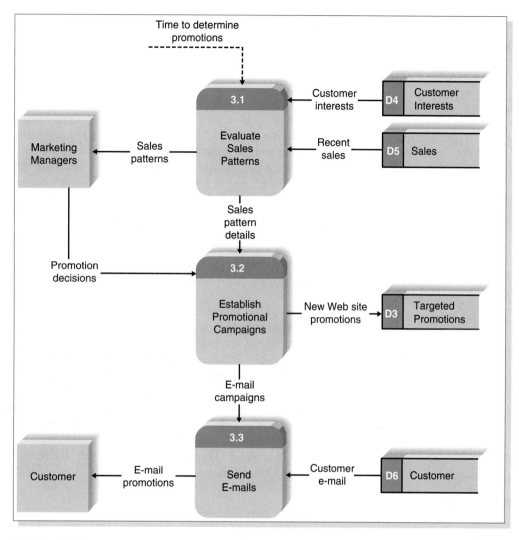

FIGURE 5-18
Level 1 DFD for Tune Source Process 3: Promote Tunes

that that step was not necessary. Instead, they made sure that the process descriptions they created in the CASE repository for each of the processes was very detailed. This detail would be critical in developing the data models and designing the user interface and programs during the design phase.

Validating the Data Flow Diagrams

The final set of DFDs was validated by the project team and then by Carly and her marketing team in a final JAD meeting. There was general approval of the customer-facing processes (process 1 and process 2) and considerable discussion of the specific information that would be required to help the marketing team make its promotional campaign decisions (process 3). This information was recorded in the CASE repository so that it could be recalled during the development of the system's data model, the subject of our next chapter.

SUMMARY

Data Flow Diagram Syntax

Four symbols are used on data flow diagrams (processes, data flows, data stores, and external entities). A process is an activity that does something. Each process has a name (a verb phrase), a description, and a number that shows where it is in relation to other processes and to its children processes. Every process must have at least one output and usually has at least one input. A data flow is a piece of data or an object and has a name (a noun) and a description and either starts or ends at a process (or both). A data store is a manual or computer file, and it has a number, a name (a noun), and at least one input data flow and one output data flow (unless the data store is created by a process external to the data flow diagram [DFD]). An external entity is a person, organization, or system outside the scope of the system and has a name (a noun) and a description. Every set of DFDs starts with a context diagram and a level 0 DFD and has numerous level 1 DFDs, level 2 DFDs, and so on. Every element on the higher-level DFDs (i.e., data flows, data stores, and external entities) must appear on lower-level DFDs, or else they are not balanced.

Creating Data Flow Diagrams

The DFDs are created from the use cases. First, the team builds the context diagram that shows all the external entities and the data flows into and out of the system from them. Second, the team creates DFD fragments for each use case that show how the use case exchanges data flows with the external entities and data stores. Third, these DFD fragments are organized into a level 0 DFD. Fourth, the team develops level 1 DFDs on the basis of the steps within each use case to better explain how they operate. Fifth, the team validates the set of DFDs to make sure that they are complete and correct and contain no syntax or semantics errors. Analysts seldom create DFDs perfectly the first time, so iteration is important in ensuring that both single-page and multipage DFDs are clear and easy to read.

KEY TERMS

Action statement
Balancing
Bundle
Case statement
Children
Context diagram
Data flow
Data flow diagram (DFD)
Data store
Decision table
Decision tree

Decomposition
DFD fragment
External entity
For statement
If statement
Iteration
Layout
Level 0 DFD
Level 1 DFD
Level 2 DFD
Logical process model

Parent
Physical model
Process model
Process
Semantics error
Structured English
Syntax error
Viewpoint
While statement

QUESTIONS

1. What is a process model? What is a data flow diagram? Are the two related? If so, how?
2. Distinguish between logical process models and physical process models.

3. Define what is meant by a *process* in a process model. How should a process be named? What information about a process should be stored in the CASE repository?

4. Define what is meant by a *data flow* in a process model. How should a data flow be named? What information about a data flow should be stored in the CASE repository?

5. Define what is meant by a *data store* in a process model. How should a data store be named? What information about a data store should be stored in the CASE repository?

6. Define what is meant by an *external entity* in a process model. How should an external entity be named? What information about an external entity should be stored in the CASE repository?

7. Why is a process model typically composed of a set of DFDs? What is meant by decomposition of a business process?

8. Explain the relationship between a DFD context diagram and the DFD level 0 diagram.

9. Explain the relationship between a DFD level 0 diagram and DFD level 1 diagram(s).

10. Discuss how the analyst knows how to stop decomposing the process model into more and more levels of detail.

11. Suppose that a process on a DFD is numbered 4.3.2. What level diagram contains this process? What is this process's parent process?

12. Explain the use of structured English in process descriptions.

13. Why would one use a decision tree and/or decision table in a process description?

14. Explain the process of balancing a set of DFDs.

15. How are mutually exclusive data flows (i.e., alternative paths through a process) depicted in DFDs?

16. Discuss several ways to verify the correctness of a process model.

17. Identify three typical syntax errors commonly found in DFDs.

18. What is meant by a DFD semantic error? Provide an example.

19. Creating use cases when working with users is a recent development in systems analysis practice. Why is the trend today to employ use cases in user interviews or JAD sessions?

20. How can you make a DFD easier to understand? (Think first about how to make one difficult to understand.)

21. Suppose that your goal is to create a set of DFDs. How would you begin an interview with a knowledgeable user? How would you begin a JAD session?

EXERCISES

A. Draw a level 0 data flow diagram (DFD) for the process of buying glasses in Exercise A, Chapter 4.

B. Draw a level 0 data flow diagram (DFD) for the dentist office system in Exercise B, Chapter 4.

C. Draw a level 0 data flow diagram (DFD) for the university system in Exercise D, Chapter 4.

D. Draw a level 0 data flow diagram (DFD) for the real estate system in Exercise E, Chapter 4.

E. Draw a level 0 data flow diagram (DFD) for the video store system in Exercise F, Chapter 4.

F. Draw a level 0 data flow diagram (DFD) for the health club system in Exercise G, Chapter 4.

G. Draw a level 0 data flow diagram (DFD) for the Picnics R Us system in Exercise H, Chapter 4.

H. Draw a level 0 data flow diagram (DFD) for the Of-the-Month Club system in Exercise I, Chapter 4.

I. Draw a level 0 data flow diagram (DFD) for the university library system in Exercise J, Chapter 4.

MINICASES

1. The Hatcher Company is in the process of developing a new inventory management system. One of the event handling processes in that system is Receive Supplier Shipments. The (inexperienced) systems analyst on the project has spent time in the warehouse observing this process and developed the following list of activities that are performed: getting the new order in the warehouse, unpacking the boxes, making sure that all the ordered items were actually received, putting the items on the correct shelves, dealing with the supplier to reconcile any discrepanices, adjusting the inventory quantities on hand, and passing along the shipment information to the accounts payable office. He also created the accompanying Level 1 data flow diagram for this process. Unfortunately, this DFD has numerous syntax and semantic errors. Identify the errors. Redraw the

DFD to more correctly represent the Receive Supplier Shipments process.

2. Professional and Scientific Staff Management (PSSM) is a unique type of temporary staffing agency. Many organizations today hire highly skilled technical employees on a short-term, temporary basis to assist with special projects or to provide a needed technical skill. PSSM negotiates contracts with its client companies in which it agrees to provide temporary staff in specific job categories for a specified cost. For example, PSSM has a contract with an oil and gas exploration company, in which it agrees to supply geologists with at least a master's degree for $5000 per week. PSSM has contracts with a wide range of companies and can place almost any type of professional or scientific staff members, from computer programmers to geologists to astrophysicists.

When a PSSM client company determines that it will need a temporary professional or scientific employee, it issues a staffing request against the contract it had previously negotiated with PSSM. When a staffing request is received by PSSM's contract manager, the contract number referenced on the staffing request is entered into the contract database. Using information from the database, the contract manager reviews the terms and conditions of the contract and determines whether the staffing request is valid. The staffing request is valid if the contract has not expired, the type of professional or scientific employee requested is listed on the original contract, and the requested fee falls within the negotiated fee range. If the staffing request is not valid, the contract manager sends the staffing request back to the client with a letter stating why the staffing request cannot be filed, and a copy of the letter is filed. If the staffing request is valid, the contract manager enters the staffing request into the staffing request database, as an outstanding staffing request. The staffing request is then sent to the PSSM placement department.

In the placement department, the type of staff member, experience, and qualifications requested on the staffing request are checked against the database of available professional and scientific staff. If a qualified individual is found, he or she is marked "reserved" in the staff database. If a qualified indi-

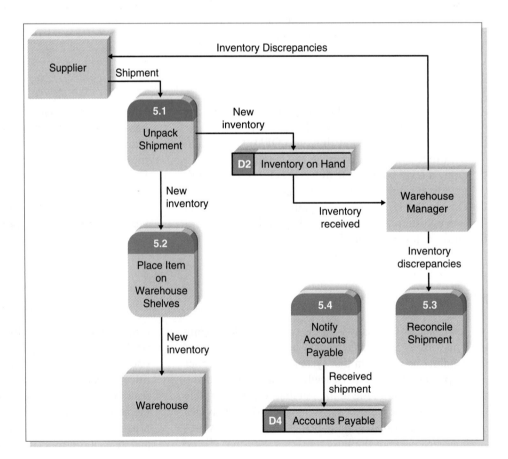

Hatcher Company Inventory Management System Level 1 DFD

vidual cannot be found in the database or is not immediately available, the placement department creates a memo that explains the inability to meet the staffing request and attaches it to the staffing request. All staffing requests are then sent to the arrangements department.

In the arrangement department, the prospective temporary employee is contacted and asked to agree to the placement. After the placement details have been worked out and agreed to, the staff member is marked "placed" in the staff database. A copy of the staffing request and a bill for the placement fee is sent to the client. Finally, the staffing request, the "unable to fill" memo (if any), and a copy of the placement fee bill is sent to the contract manager. If the staffing request was

filled, the contract manager closes the open staffing request in the staffing request database. If the staffing request could not be filled, the client is notified. The staffing request, placement fee bill, and "unable to fill" memo are then filed in the contract office.

a. Develop a use case for each of the major processes just described.
b. Create the context diagram for the system just described.
c. Create the DFD fragments for each of the four use cases outlined in part a, and then combine them into the level 0 DFD.
d. Create a level 1 DFD for the most complicated use case.

APPENDIX 5A: SUPPLEMENTAL DFDs FOR HOLIDAY TRAVEL VEHICLES

In this appendix, we have included several additional DFDs for the Holiday Travel Vehicle scenario. First, in Figure 5A-1, we repeat the Holiday Travel Vehicle Context Diagram from Figure 5-5. Next, Figure 5A-2 includes three DFD fragments for process 1, Order New Vehicles; process 2, Receive New Vehicles; and process 6, Accept Trade-In Vehicles. Recall that the other three DFD fragments were shown in Figure 5-6 and 5-7.

We also have merged all six DFD fragments into one level 0 diagram in Figure 5A-3. This diagram shows how all six processes interact with the external environment, with each other, and with shared stored data. As you can see, the level 0 diagrams can get fairly complex.

In order to avoid crossing data flow lines, we have duplicated the D2:New Vehicles data store and the Shop external entity on the diagram. This is certainly permissible. Usually, the duplicated objects are drawn with a small slanted line in the corner, as shown in Figure 5A-3.

Once again, we see in the level 0 diagram that not all the data stores shown have both input and output data flows—specifically, D4:Sold Vehicles, D5:Used Vehicles, and D7:Salesperson Offer File. Keep in mind that it is very likely that these data stores will be used to provide inputs into other processes that are part of other systems. The development team should verify this assumption, however.

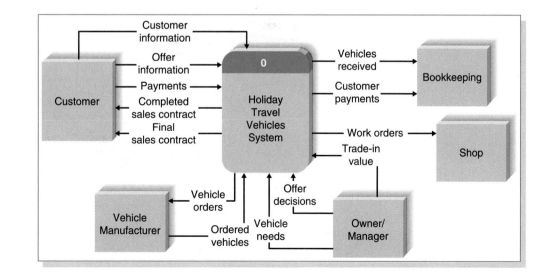

FIGURE 5A-1
Holiday Travel Vechiles Context Diagram

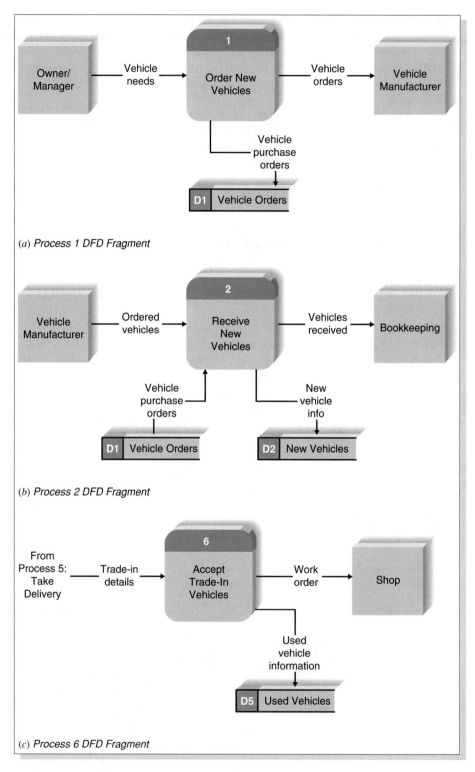

(a) *Process 1 DFD Fragment*

(b) *Process 2 DFD Fragment*

(c) *Process 6 DFD Fragment*

FIGURE 5A-2
Additional DFD Fragments for Holiday Travel Vehicles

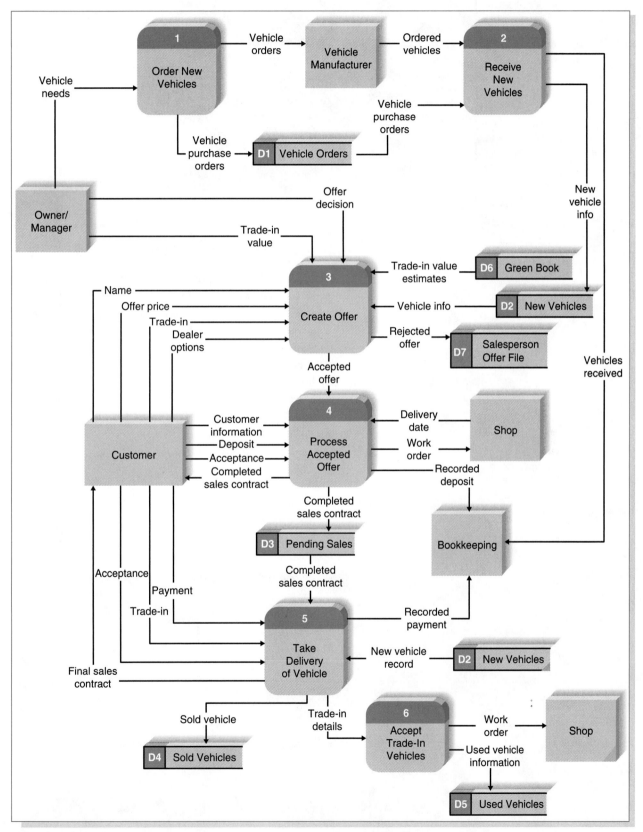

FIGURE 5A-3
Holiday Travel Vehicles Level 0 DFD

PLANNING

ANALYSIS

☑ Apply Requirements Analysis Techniques (Business
    Process Automation, Business Process
    Improvement, or Business Process Reengineering)

☑ Use Requirements Gathering Techniques (Interview,
    JAD Session, Questionnaire, Document Analysis,
    or Observation)

☑ Develop Requirements Definition

☑ Develop Use Cases

☑ Develop Data Flow Diagrams

☐ Develop Entity Relationship Model

☐ Normalize Entity Relationship Model

TASK CHECKLIST

PLANNING ANALYSIS DESIGN

CHAPTER 6

DATA

MODELING

A data model describes the data that flow through the business processes in an organization. During the analysis phase, the data model presents the logical organization of data without indicating how the data are stored, created, or manipulated so that analysts can focus on the business without being distracted by technical details. Later, during the design phase, the data model is changed to reflect exactly how the data will be stored in databases and files. This chapter describes entity relationship diagramming, one of the most common data modeling techniques used in industry.

OBJECTIVES

- Understand the rules and style guidelines for creating entity relationship diagrams.
- Be able to create an entity relationship diagram.
- Become familiar with the data dictionary and metadata.
- Understand how to balance between entity relationship diagrams and data flow diagrams.
- Become familiar with the process of normalization.

CHAPTER OUTLINE

IMPLEMENTATION

INTRODUCTION

During the analysis phase, analysts create process models to represent how the business system will operate. At the same time, analysts need to understand the information that is used and created by the business system (e.g., customer information, order information). In this chapter, we discuss how the data that flow through the processes are organized and presented.

A *data model* is a formal way of representing the data that are used and created by a business system; it illustrates people, places, or things about which information is captured and how they are related to each other. The data model is drawn by an iterative process in which the model becomes more detailed and less conceptual over time. During analysis, analysts draw a logical data model, which shows the logical organization of data without indicating how data are stored, created, or manipulated. Because this model is free of any implementation or technical details, the analysts can focus more easily on matching the diagram to the real business requirements of the system.

In the design phase, analysts draw a *physical data model* to reflect how the data will physically be stored in databases and files. At this point, the analysts investigate ways to store the data efficiently and to make the data easy to retrieve. The physical data model and performance tuning are discussed in Chapter 11.

Project teams usually use CASE tools to draw data models. Some of the CASE tools are data modeling packages, such as ER*win* by Platinum Technology, that help analysts create and maintain logical and physical data models; they have a wide array of capabilities to aid modelers, and they can automatically generate many different kinds of databases from the models that are created. Other CASE tools (e.g., Oracle Designer) come bundled with database management systems (e.g., Oracle), and they are particularly good for modeling databases that will be built in their companion database products. A final option is to use a full-service CASE tool, such as Visible Analyst Workbench, in which data modeling is one of many capabilities, and the tool can be used with many different databases. A benefit of the full-service CASE tool is that it integrates the data model information with other relevant parts of the project.

In this chapter, we focus on creating a logical data model. Although there are several ways to model data, we will present one of the most commonly used techniques: entity relationship diagramming, a graphic drawing technique developed by Peter Chen[1] that shows all the data components of a business system. We will first describe how to create an entity relationship diagram (ERD) and discuss some style guidelines. Then, we will present a technique called normalization that helps analysts validate the data models that they draw. The chapter ends with a discussion of how data models balance, or interrelate, with the process models that you learned about in Chapter 5.

THE ENTITY RELATIONSHIP DIAGRAM

An *entity relationship diagram* (*ERD*) is a picture which shows the information that is created, stored, and used by a business system. An analyst can read an ERD to discover the individual pieces of information in a system and how they are organized

---

[1] P. Chen, "The Entity-Relationship Model—Toward a Unified View of Data," *ACM Transactions on Database Systems*, 1976, 1:9–36.

and related to each other. On an ERD, similar kinds of information are listed together and placed inside boxes called entities. Lines are drawn between entities to represent relationships among the data, and special symbols are added to the diagram to communicate high-level business rules that need to be supported by the system. The ERD implies no order, although entities that are related to each other are usually placed close together.

For example, consider the supermarket checkout system that was described in Chapter 5. Although this system is just a small part of the information system for an entire grocery store, we will use it for our discussion on how to read an entity relationship diagram. First, go back and look at the sample DFD for the checkout process in Figure 5-1. Although we understand how the system works from studying the data flow diagram, we have very little detailed understanding of the information itself that flows through the system. What exactly is "items purchased"? What pieces of data are captured in "purchase details"? How is an item related to the sales transaction?

Reading an Entity Relationship Diagram

The analyst can answer these questions and more by using an entity relationship diagram. We have included an ERD for the supermarket checkout scenario in Figure 6-1. First, we can see that the data to support the checkout process can be organized into four main categories: Item, Sold Item, Sale, and Payment. The Item data describe every product available for sale in the store. The Sale data capture information about every sale event, and the Payment data describe the payment(s) made for the sale. The Sold Item data describe every item involved in a specific sale. For example, if you buy a 14-oz. bag of tortilla chips, there will be Sold Item data that associate the UPC for that product and the Sale ID for that sale event.

We can also see the specific facts that describe each of the four categories. For example, an Item is described by its UPC (Universal Product Code), price, description, category, and tax status. We can also see what can be used to uniquely identify an item, a sale, a payment, and so on, by looking for the asterisks next to the data elements. For example, the item UPC is used to uniquely identify every item sold by the store. A unique ID has been created to identify every sale and every payment. A sold item is uniquely identified by a combination of the item UPC and the sale ID in which the item was involved.

The lines connecting the four categories of information communicate the relationships that the categories share. By reading the relationship lines, the analyst understands that a sale is paid for by a payment(s); a sale involves sold item(s); and items may be included in sold item(s).

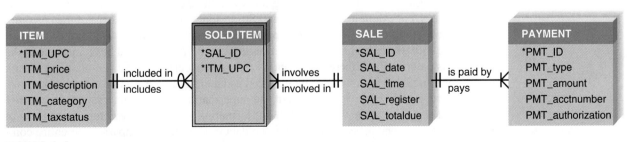

FIGURE 6-1
Supermarket ERD

The ERD also communicates high-level business rules. Business rules are constraints or guidelines that are followed during the operation of the system; they are rules such as "A payment can be cash, check, debit card, credit card, coupon(s), or food stamps", "A sale is paid for by one or more payments", or "A payment pays for only one sale." Over the course of a workday, people are constantly applying business rules to do their jobs, and they know the rules through training or knowing where to look them up. If a situation arises where the rules are not known, workers may have to refer to a policy guide or written procedure to determine the proper business rules.

On a data model, business rules are communicated by the kinds of relationships that the entities share. From the ERD, for example, we know from the "crow's foot" placed on the line closest to the Sold Item that a Sale may include many Sold Items. We can see by the two bars placed on the line closest to Sale that a Payment pays for exactly one Sale. Ultimately, the new system should support the business rules we just described, and it should ensure that users don't violate the rules when performing the processes of the system. Therefore, in our example, the system should not permit a Sale with no Sold Items. Similarly, the system should not allow a payment to pay for more than one Sale.

Now that you've seen an ERD, let's step back and learn the ERD basics. In the following sections, we will first describe the syntax of the ERD, using the diagram in Figure 6-1. Then we will teach you how to create an ERD by using an example from Tune Source.

Elements of an Entity Relationship Diagram

There are three basic elements in the data modeling language (entities, attributes, and relationships), each of which is represented by a different graphic symbol. There are many different sets of symbols that can be used on an ERD. No one set of symbols dominates industry use, and none is necessarily better than another. We will use crow's foot in this book. Figure 6-2 summarizes the three basic elements of ERDs and the symbols we will use.

Entity   The *entity* is the basic building block for a data model. It is a person, place, event, or thing about which data is collected—for example, an employee, an order, or a product. An entity is depicted by a rectangle, and it is described by a singular noun spelled in capital letters. All entities have a name, a short description that explains what they are, and an *identifier* that is the way to locate information in the entity (which is discussed later). In Figure 6-1, the entities are Item, Sold Item, Sale, and Payment.

Entities represent something for which there exist multiple *instances*, or occurrences. For example, John Smith and Susan Jones could be instances of the customer entity (Figure 6-3). We would expect the customer entity to stand for all of the people with whom we have done business, and each of them would be an instance in the customer entity. If there is just one instance, or occurrence, of a person, place, event, or thing, then it should not be included as an entity in the data model. For example, think a little more broadly about the supermarket information system. Figure 6-1 focuses on just a small part of that information system. If the company consists of more than one grocery store, then the data model that encompasses the entire company would include a Store entity so that specific facts about each store could be captured. If the company owned just one grocery store, however, there would be no need

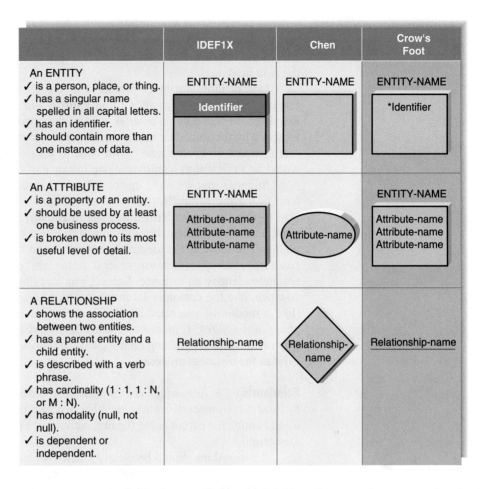

FIGURE 6-2
Data Modeling Symbol Sets

to set up a store entity in the overall data model. There is no need to capture data in the system about something having just a single instance.

Attribute   An *attribute* is some type of information that is captured about an entity. For example, last name, home address, and e-mail address are all attributes of a customer. It is easy to come up with hundreds of attributes for an entity (e.g., a customer has an eye color, a favorite hobby, a religious affiliation), but only those that actually will be used by a business process should be included in the model.

Attributes are nouns that are listed within an entity. Usually, some form of the entity name is appended to the beginning of each attribute to make it clear as to what entity it belongs (e.g., CUS_lastname, CUS_address). Without doing this,

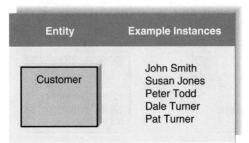

FIGURE 6-3
Entities and Instances

you can get confused by multiple entities that have the same attributes—for example, a customer and an employee both can have an attribute called "lastname." CUS_lastname and EMP_lastname are much clearer ways to name attributes on the data model.

One or more attributes can serve as the identifier—the attribute(s) that can uniquely identify one instance of an entity—and the attributes that serve as the identifier are noted by an asterisk next to the attribute name. If there are no customers with the same last name, then last name can be used as the identifier of the customer entity. In this case, if we need to locate John Brown, the name Brown would be sufficient to identify the one instance of the Brown last name.

Suppose that we add a customer named Sarah Brown. Now we have a problem: Using the name Brown would not uniquely lead to one instance—it would lead to two (i.e., John Brown and Sarah Brown). You have three choices at this point, and all are acceptable solutions. First, you can use a combination of multiple fields to serve as the identifier (last name and first name). This is called a *concatenated identifier* because several fields are combined, or concatenated, to uniquely identify an instance. Second, you can find a field that is unique for each instance, like the customer ID number. Third, you can wait to assign an identifier (like a randomly generated number that the system will create) until the design phase of the SDLC (Figure 6-4). Many data modelers don't believe that randomly generated identifiers belong on a logical data model, because they do not logically exist in the business process.

Relationship   *Relationships* are associations between entities, and they are shown by lines that connect the entities together. Every relationship has a *parent entity* and a *child entity,* the parent being the first entity in the relationship, and the child being the second.

Relationships should be clearly labeled with active verbs so that the connections between entities can be understood. If one verb is given to each relationship, it is read in two directions. For example, we could write the verb *pays* alongside the relationship for the *sale* and *payment* entities, and this would be read as "a payment pays a sale" and "a sale is paid for by a payment." In Figure 6.1, we have included words for both directions of the relationship line; the top words are read from parent to child, and the bottom words are read from child to parent. Notice that the *item* entity is the parent entity in the *item–sold item* relationship. In addition, some CASE tools require that every relationship name be unique on the ERD, so we select unique descriptive verbs for each relationship.

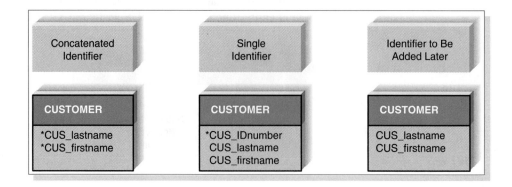

FIGURE 6-4
Choices for Identifiers

Cardinality Relationships have two properties. First, a relationship has cardinality, which is the ratio of parent instances to child instances. To determine the cardinality for a relationship, we ask ourselves: "How many instances of one entity are associated with an instance of the other?" (Remember that an instance is one occurrence of an entity, such as customer John Brown or item 14-oz. Nacho Cheese Doritos™.) For example, a payment pays for how many sales? A sale includes how many sold items? The cardinality for binary relationships (i.e., relationships between two entities) is 1:1, 1:N, or M:N, and we will discuss each in turn.

The 1:1 (read as "one to one") relationship means that one instance of the parent entity is associated with one instance of the child entity. There are no examples of 1:1 relationships in Figure 6-1. So, imagine for a moment that, as a reward, a company assigns a specific reserved parking place to every employee who is honored as an "employee of the month." One reserved parking place is assigned to each honored employee, and each honored employee is assigned one reserved parking place. If we were to draw these two entities, we would place a bar next to the Employee entity and a bar next to the Reserved Parking Place entity. The cardinality is clearly 1:1 in this case, because each honored employee is assigned exactly one reserved parking place, and a reserved parking place is assigned to exactly one employee.

More often, relationships are 1:N (read as "one to many"). In this kind of relationship, a single instance of a parent entity is associated with many instances of a child entity; however, the child entity instance is related to only one instance of the parent. For example, a Sale (parent entity) can be paid for by many Payments (child entity), but a particular Payment pays for only one Sale, suggesting a 1:N relationship between Sale and Payment. A character resembling a crow's foot is placed closest to the Payment entity to show the "many" end of the relationship. The parent entity is always on the "1" side of the relationship; hence, a bar is placed next to the Sale entity. Can you identify other 1:N relationships in Figure 6-1? Identify the parent and child entities for each relationship.

A third kind of relationship is the M:N (read as "many to many") relationship. In this case, many instances of a parent entity can relate to many instances of a child entity. There are no M:N relationships shown in Figure 6-1, but take a look at Figure 6-5. This figure shows an early draft version of the Supermarket ERD. In this version, an M:N relationship does exist between Sale and Item. As we can see, one Sale (parent entity) can include many Items (e.g., tortilla chips, salsa, and cheese), and an Item (child entity) can be included in many Sales. M:N relationships are depicted on an ERD by having crow's feet at both ends of the relationship line. As we will learn later, there are advantages to eliminating M:N relationships from an ERD, so that is why it was removed from Figure 6-1 by creating the Sold Item entity between Sale and Item. The process of "resolving" an M:N relationship will be explained later in the chapter.

FIGURE 6-5
M:N Relationships

YOUR

TURN

6-1 Understanding the Elements of an ERD

A wealthy businessman owns a large number of paintings that he loans to museums all over the world. He is interested in setting up a system that records what he loans to whom so that he doesn't lose track of his investments. He would like to keep information about the paintings that he owns as well as the artists who painted them. He also wants to track the various museums that reserve his art, along with the actual reservations. Obviously, artists are associated with paintings, paintings are associated with reservations, and reservations are associated with museums.

Questions:
1. Draw the four entities that belong on this data model.

2. Provide some basic attributes for each entity, and select an identifier, if possible.
3. Draw the appropriate relationships between the entities and label them.
4. What is the cardinality for each relationship? Depict this on your drawing.
5. What is the modality for each relationship? Depict this on your drawing.
6. List two business rules that are communicated by your ERD.

Modality   Second, relationships have a *modality* of null or not null, which refers to whether or not an instance of a child entity can exist without a related instance in the parent entity. Basically, the modality of a relationship indicates whether the child-entity instance is required to participate in the relationship. It forces you to ask questions like, Can you have a sale without a sold item? and Can you have a payment without a sale? Modality is depicted by placing a zero on the relationship line next to the parent entity if nulls are allowed. A bar is placed on the relationship line next to the parent entity if nulls are not allowed.

In the two questions we just asked, the answer is no: Of course you need a sale to have a sold item, and of course you can't have a payment without an associated sale. The modality is "not null," or "required," for both of these relationships in Figure 6-1. Notice, however, that a zero has been placed on the relationship line between Item and Sold Item next to the Sold Item entity. This means that items can exist in our system without requiring that a sold item exists. Said another way, instances of sold items are optional for an item. The modality is "null."

The Data Dictionary and Metadata

As we described earlier, a CASE tool is used to help build ERDs. Every CASE tool has something called a *data dictionary*, which quite literally is where the analyst goes to define or look up information about the entities, attributes, and relationships on the ERD. Even Visio 2007, primarily known as a drawing tool, has some elementary data dictionary capabilities. Figures 6-6, 6-7, and 6-8 illustrate common data dictionary entries for an entity, an attribute, and a relationship; notice the kinds of information the data dictionary captures about each element.

The information you see in the data dictionary is called *metadata*, which, quite simply, is data about data. Metadata is anything that describes an entity, attribute, or relationship, such as entity names, attribute descriptions, and relationship cardinality, and it is captured to help designers better understand the system that

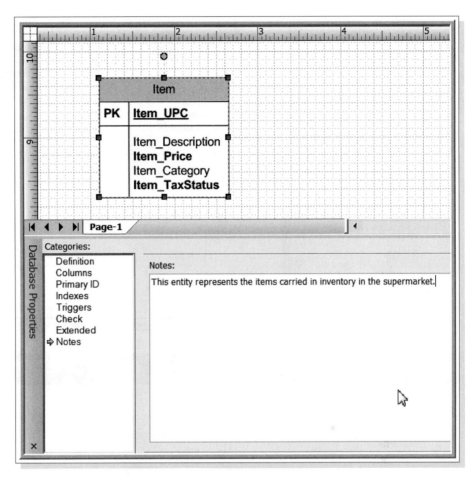

FIGURE 6-6
Data Dictionary Description for Item
Entity (in Visio 2007)

they are building and to help users better understand the system that they will use. Figure 6-9 lists typical metadata that are found in the data dictionary. Notice that the metadata can describe an ERD element (like entity name) and also information that is helpful to the project team (like the user contact, the analyst contact, and special notes).

FIGURE 6-7
Data Dictionary Description for Item
Attributes (in Visio 2007)

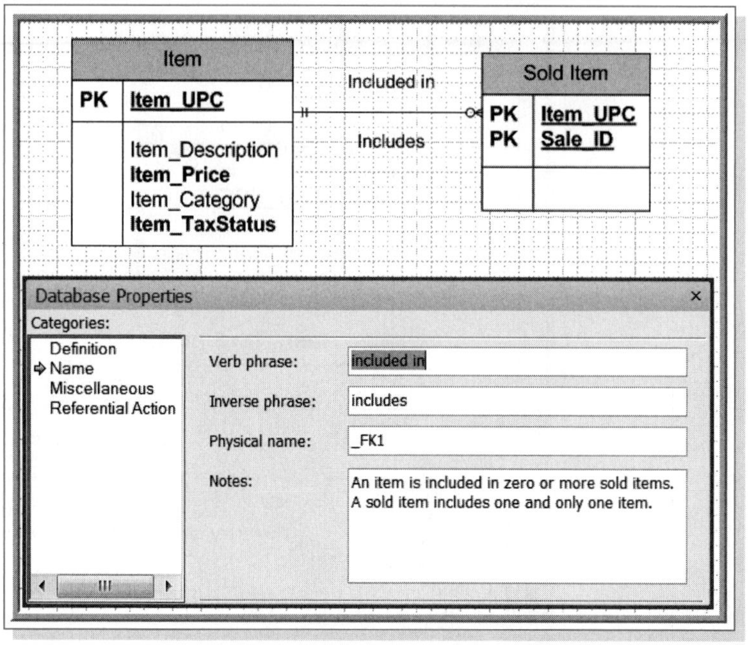

FIGURE 6-8
Data Dictionary Description for
Relationship (in Visio 2007)

ERD Element	Kinds of Metadata	Example
Entity	Name	Item
	Definition	Represents any item carried in inventory in the supermarket
	Special notes	Includes produce, bakery, and deli items
	User contact	Nancy Keller (x6755) heads up the item coding department
	Analyst contact	John Michaels is the analyst assigned to this entity
Attribute	Name	Item_UPC
	Definition	The standard Universal Product Code for the item based on Global Trade Item Numbers developed by GS1
	Alias	Item Bar Code
	Sample values	036000291452; 034000126453
	Acceptable values	Any 12-digit set of numerals
	Format	12 digit, numerals only
	Type	Stored as alphanumeric values
	Special notes	Values with the first digit of 2 are assigned locally, representing items packed in the store, such as meat, bakery, produce, or deli items. See Nancy Keller for more information.
Relationship	Verb phrase	Included in
	Parent entity	Item
	Child entity	Sold item
	Definition	An item is included in zero or more sold items. A sold item includes one and only one item.
	Cardinality	1:N
	Modality	Null
	Special notes	

FIGURE 6-9
Types of Metadata Captured by the Data Dictionary

Metadata are stored in the data dictionary so that they can be shared and accessed by developers and users throughout the SDLC. The data dictionary allows you to record the standard pieces of information about your elements in one place, and it makes that information accessible to many parts of a project. For example, the data attributes in a data model also appear on the process models as elements of data stores and data flows, and on the user interface as fields on an input screen. When you make a change in the data dictionary, the change ripples to the relevant parts of the project that are affected.

When metadata are complete, clear, and shareable, the information can be used to integrate the different pieces of the analysis phase and ultimately lead to a much better design. It becomes much more detailed as the project evolves through the SDLC.

CREATING AN ENTITY RELATIONSHIP DIAGRAM

Drawing an ERD is an iterative process of trial and revision. It usually takes considerable practice. ERDs can become quite complex—in fact, there are systems that have ERDs containing hundreds or thousands of entities. The basic steps in building an ERD are these: (1) Identify the entities, (2) add the appropriate attributes to each entity, and then (3) draw relationships among entities to show how they are associated with one another. First, we will describe the three steps in creating ERDs, using the data model example from Figure 6-1. We will then discuss several advanced concepts of ERD's. Finally, we will present an ERD for Tune Source.

Building Entity Relationship Diagrams

Step 1: Identify the Entities   As we explained, the most popular way to start an ERD is to first identify the entities for the model, and their attributes. The entities should represent the major categories of information that you need to store in your system. If the process models (e.g., DFDs) have been prepared, the easiest way to start is with them: The data stores on the DFDs, the external entities, and the data flows indicate the kinds of information that are captured and flow through the system. If you begin your data model by using a use case, look at the major inputs to the use case, the major outputs, and the information used for the use case steps.

Examine the complete level 0 process model (Figure 5A-3) and the use cases (Figure 4-7) for the Holiday Travel Vehicle system. As you look at the level 0 diagram, you see that there are a number of data stores: vehicle orders, new vehicles, offers, pending sales, sold vehicles, used vehicles, and the Green Book. Each of these unique collections of data has the potential to become an entity on our data model.

YOUR

TURN

6-2 EVALUATE YOUR CASE TOOL

Examine the CASE tool that you will be using for your project, or find a CASE tool on the Web that you are interested in learning about. What kind of metadata does its data dictionary capture? Does the CASE tool integrate data model information with other parts of a project? How?

As a next step, you should examine the external entities and ask yourself, "Will the system need to capture information about any of these entities?" It is clear that the system will need to capture information about customers, since customers play such an important role in the system. We may want to consider creating an entity with manufacturer information as well. The interview transcript told us that there were just five manufacturers that the company orders from, but the vehicle ordering process will be improved if information about the manufacturers is readily available in data storage. We do not set up an entity for the shop, however, since there is only one instance of the shop for this company.

It is a good practice to look at the data flows themselves to see whether there is any more information that should be captured in the data model. A review of the level 0 diagram and rereading the interview transcript suggests that there are multiple salespeople involved in the system who assist in the process and earn commissions on the vehicle sales. Therefore, an entity that captures salesperson information will be added to the data model.

Finally, we review the entities to verify that they should be included in the data model. There seems to be a lot of similarity between the new vehicle entity, the sold vehicle entity, and the used vehicle entity. Careful consideration suggests that the new vehicle and used vehicle are essentially the same, so we will create a single vehicle entity in the data model. The sold vehicle entity, however, is a little different, since it captures the selling event for the vehicle, so we will leave it in the data model for now. We also looked carefully at the Green Book, a reference publication listing used vehicle values. Since this publication is not currently available in electronic form, we have decided to exclude that from the data model. Finally, we examine Pending Sale and realize that this represents temporary storage that will be deleted as soon as the sale is complete, so we will remove this from our list of entities as well. Therefore, our list of entities at this point consists of vehicle order, vehicle, offer, sold vehicle, manufacturer, and salesperson.

Step 2: Add Attributes and Assign Identifiers   The information that describes each entity becomes its attributes. It is likely that you identified a few attributes if you read the Holiday Travel Vehicle system use cases and paid attention to the information flows on their DFDs. For example, a customer has a name and address, and a vehicle has a make and model. Unfortunately, much of the information from the process models and use cases is at too high a level to identify the exact attributes that should exist in each of our six entities.

On a real project, there are a number of places you can go to figure out what attributes belong in your entity. For one, you can check in the CASE tool—often, an analyst will describe a process model data flow in detail when he or she enters the data flow into the CASE repository. For example, an analyst may create an entry for the customer information data flow like the one shown in Figure 6-10 which lists 10 data elements that make up customer information. The elements of the data flow should be added to the ERD as attributes in your entities. A second approach is to check the requirements definition. Often, there is a section under functional requirements called data requirements. This section describes the data needs for the

FIGURE 6-10

Elements of the Customer Information Data Flow

Data flow name:	Customer information
Data elements:	identification number + first name + last name + address + city + state + zip code + home phone number + cell phone number + e-mail address

system that were identified while requirements were gathered. A final approach to identifying attributes is to use requirements-gathering techniques. The most effective techniques would be interviews (e.g., asking people who create and use reports about their data needs) or document analysis (e.g., examining existing forms, reports, or input screens).

Once the attributes are identified, one or more of them will become the entity's identifier. The identifier must be an attribute(s) that is able to uniquely identify a single instance of the entity. Look at Figure 6-1 and notice the identifiers that were selected for each entity. Three of the entities had some attribute that could identify an instance by itself (e.g., item UPC, sale ID, and payment ID).

Step 3: Identify Relationships

The last step in creating ERDs is to determine how the entities are related to each other. Lines are drawn between entities that have relationships, and each relationship is labeled and assigned both a cardinality and a modality. The easiest approach is to begin with one entity and determine all the entities with which it shares relationships. For example, there likely are relationships between vehicle and order, offer, and sold vehicle. We know that a vehicle may be ordered from a manufacturer, may be included in an offer, and may become a sold vehicle. The same exercise is done with each entity until all of the relationships have been identified. Each relationship should be labeled with a descriptive word or phrase as it is added. See Figure 6-11.

When you find a relationship to include on the model, you need to determine its cardinality and modality. For cardinality, ask how many instances of each entity participate in the relationship. You know that a manufacturer can receive many orders, but a specific order is sent to only one manufacturer. Therefore, we place a crow's foot next to the order entity and a single bar closest to the manufacturer entity. This suggests that there is a 1:N relationship in which the manufacturer is the parent entity (the "1") and the order is the child entity (the "many"). Next, we examine the relationship's modality. Can a manufacturer exist without an associated order? For Holiday Travel Vehicles, the answer to that question is "no," because the dealership stores information only about manufacturers from whom vehicles have been ordered. Therefore, the modality of that relationship is "not null," or required, and we place a bar next to the crow's foot to indicate that a manufacturer receives one or more orders. Now, can an order exist without an associated manufacturer? This answer is "no," so we place another single bar next to the manufacturer entity to indicate that an order must be related to one and only one manufacturer.

Let's examine some of the other relationships shown in the model. The vehicle entity is related to several other entities. We see that a vehicle may or may not have an associated order and can have a maximum of one associated order. The reason for this is that a vehicle may have been acquired as a result of being traded in rather than ordered, so an order is not required for every vehicle. We also see that an order requests one and only one vehicle. This reflects the practice that Holiday Travel Vehicles has of ordering one vehicle at a time from a manufacturer. Remember that our relationships should correspond to the actual business rules that underlie the model. We also see that a vehicle may or may not be involved in any offers, reflecting the fact that a vehicle may not have had any offers made for it. Also, a vehicle could be involved in many offers, because it is possible that several offers might be made on a vehicle before a deal can be struck. An offer, however, lists exactly one vehicle. In addition, a vehicle may become a sold vehicle (but may not be), and a sold vehicle includes exactly one vehicle. The same type of thinking is

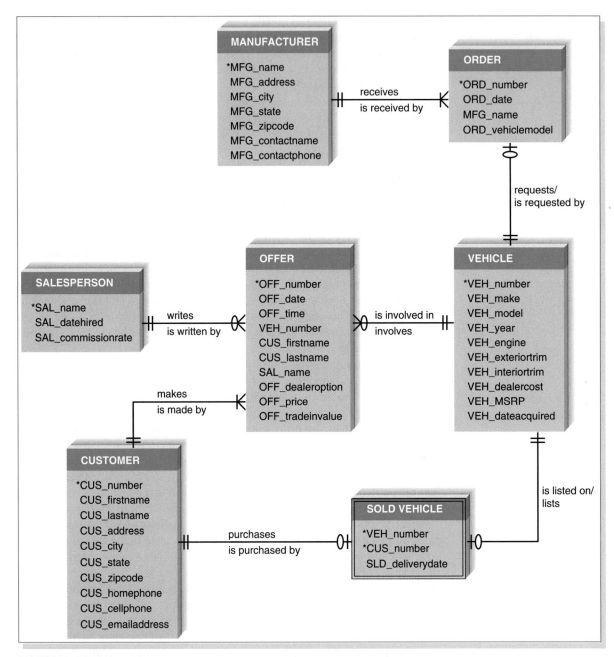

FIGURE 6-11
Holiday Travel Vehicles ERD

applied to each entity until all of the relationships have been labeled appropriately. Review the cardinality and modality of each relationship in Figure 6-11.

Again, remember that data modeling is an iterative process. Often, the assumptions you make and the decisions you make change as you learn more about the business requirements and as changes are made to the use cases and process models. But you have to start somewhere—so do the best you can with the three steps we just described and keep iterating until you have a model that works. Later in this chapter, we will show you a few ways to validate the ERDs that you draw.

Advanced Syntax

Now that we have created a data model according to the basic syntax that was presented earlier, we can move to several advanced concepts. We will explain three special types of entities and show how they can be used in our RV dealership system.

Independent Entity   An independent entity is an entity that can exist without the help of another entity, such as manufacturer, vehicle, salesperson, and customer. These entities all have identifiers that were created from their own attributes (vehicle number, customer number, manufacturer name). Attributes from other entities were not needed to uniquely identify instances of these entities. As shown in Figure 6-11, the vehicle number is sufficient to uniquely identify vehicles. Information from the order, offer, or sold vehicle entities is not needed to identify a vehicle, even though these entities share relationships with the vehicle entity. Independent entities are drawn as rectangles with a single border line.

When a relationship includes an independent child entity, it is called a *nonidentifying relationship*. This name is derived from the fact that parent entity attributes are not needed as part of the child entity's identifier. The customer-offer relationship is an example of a nonidentifying relationship in Figure 6-11.

Dependent Entity   There are situations when a child entity does require attributes from the parent entity to uniquely identify an instance. In these cases, the child entity is called a *dependent entity*, and its identifier consists of at least one attribute from the parent entity.

A good example of a dependent entity is the Sold Vehicle entity shown in Figure 6-11. A sold vehicle is a specific vehicle that has been sold to a specific customer. To fully identify the Sold Vehicle entity, we use the vehicle number from the Vehicle entity and the customer number from the Customer entity as the sold vehicle identifiers. Since attributes from both parent entities are used as identifier attributes in the Sold Vehicle entity, Sold Vehicle is considered a dependent entity and is shown as a rectangle with a double border line.

When relationships have a dependent child entity, they are called *identifying relationships*. This name is derived from the fact that parent entity attributes are needed as part of the child entity's identifier.

Intersection Entity   A third kind of entity is the *intersection entity*. It exists in order to capture some information about the relationship between two other entities. Typically, intersection entities are added to a data model to store information about two entities sharing an M:N relationship. These entities are also called Associative Entities. Think back to the M:N relationship between Sale and Item shown in Figure 6-5. In that figure, one instance of an Item (tortilla chips) could occur with many Sales, and a Sale can include many Items (tortilla chips, salsa, cheese). A difficulty arises if we want to capture the date on which a particular item was included in a sale. We cannot put the date in the Item entity, because the Item is involved in many Sales. We also cannot put the date in the Sale entity, because there are many items involved in the Sale. Therefore, we need another entity that enables us to associate a specific item with a specific sale. Recall that the version of the supermarket ERD shown in Figure 6-1 did include such an entity (Sold Item).

The process of adding an intersection entity is called "resolving an M:N relationship" because it eliminates the M:N relationship and its associated problems from the data model. There are three steps involved in adding an intersection entity. Step 1: Remove the M:N relationship line and insert a new entity in between the two existing ones. Step 2: Add two 1:N relationships to the model. The two original entities should serve as the parent entities for each 1:N, and the new intersection entity becomes the child entity in both relationships. Step 3: Name the intersection entity. Intersection entities are often named by a concatenation of the two entities that created it (e.g., Sold Item), making its meaning clear. Alternatively, the entity can be given another appropriate name. Figure 6-12 shows the M:N Item-Sale relationship and how it was resolved with the use of an intersection entity.

Are intersection entities dependent or independent? Actually, it depends. Sometimes an intersection entity has a logical identifier that can uniquely identify its instances. For example, an intersection entity between a student and a course (a student may take many courses and a course is taken by many students) may be called a *transcript*. If transcripts have unique transcript numbers, then the entity would be considered independent. In contrast, the Sold Item intersection entity in Figure 6-12 requires the identifiers from both Sale and Item for an instance to be uniquely identified. Thus, Sold Item is a dependent entity.

Applying the Concepts at Tune Source

Let's go through one more example of creating a data model by using the context of Tune Source. For now, review the use cases that were presented in Figure 4-11 and the final level 0 process model presented in Figure 5-15.

Identify the Entities   When you examine the Tune Source level 0 DFD, you see that there are six data stores: customer, sale, available tunes, customer interests, customer favorites, and targeted promotions. Each of these unique types of data likely will be represented by entities on a data model.

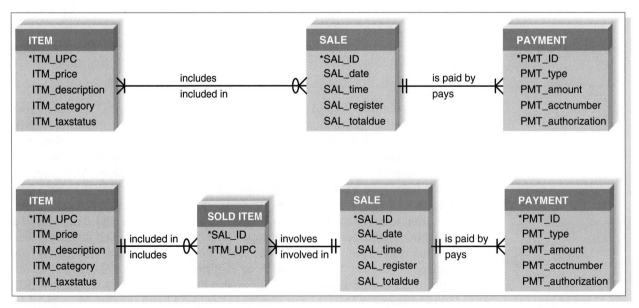

FIGURE 6-12
Resolving an M:N Relationship

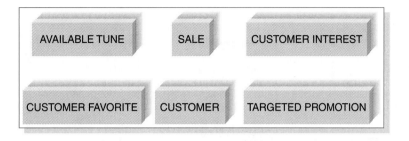

FIGURE 6-13
Entities for Tune Source ERD

As a next step, you should examine the external entities and ask yourself, "Will the system need to capture information about any of these entities?" You may be tempted to include marketing managers, but there really is no need to track information about these in our system. Later, we may want to track system users, passwords, and data access privileges, but this information has to do with the *use* of the new system and would not be added until the physical data model is created in the design phase.

It is good practice to also look at the data flows on your process model and make sure that all of the information that flows through the system has been covered by your ERD. Unlike the situation in Holiday Travel Vehicle, the example (which found an additional entity by looking at the data flows), it appears that the main entities for Tune Source have been identified after an examination of the data stores and external entities. See Figure 6-13 for the beginning of our data model.

Identify the Attributes   The next step is to select which attributes should be used to describe each entity. It is likely that you identified a handful of attributes if you read the Tune Source use cases and examined the DFDs. For example, an available tune has an artist, title, genre, and length, and some attributes of customer are name and contact information, which likely includes address, phone number, and e-mail address.

The two entities customer favorite and customer interest might seem similar at first glance, but they are used to capture different types of information about the customer's music preferences. A customer favorite is a tune that the customer specifically adds to his/her Favorites list in order to monitor tunes as the Web site is searched and browsed. In a sense, it's like a future shopping list, so we just record the customer's ID, the tune's ID, and the date the tune was added to the list. The customer's Favorites are available each time the customer revisits the site to help in recalling tunes previously discovered and to (hopefully) purchase them. On the other hand, the customer interest is created automatically as the customer investigates tunes and listens to samples. Customer interests are used by the marketing department to help design promotions for the customer that will be tailored to the types of music the customer has explored. Slightly different attributes are associated with these two entities because of their different purposes in the system.

Targeted promotions are special offers that will be created for a customer on the basis of his or her interests and with regard to sales patterns. A promotion will include a sale price for a specific tune if it is purchased within a specific time frame. Attributes for the targeted promotions are listed in Figure 6-14. Finally, we also see that several attributes associated with a tune sale have been listed in the ERD.

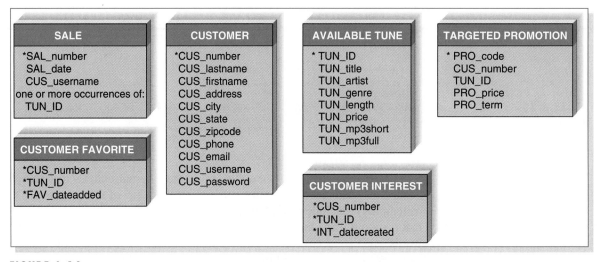

FIGURE 6-14
Attributes and Identifiers for Tune Source ERD

To determine the entity identifiers, we consider the attribute or attributes that will uniquely identify each entity. We will establish a customer number for each customer in the system. Each available tune that we have will be assigned a unique tune ID. Each targeted promotion will be given a unique promotion code, and each sale will be given a unique sale number. Finally, each customer favorite and each customer interest can be uniquely identified by the customer number, tune ID, and the date created.

The customer, sale, available tune, and targeted promotion entities are independent entities; attributes from other entities are not needed to uniquely identify instances. The identifiers for customer interests and customer favorites, however, do rely on attributes from their parent entities: customer and available tune. This is because a customer favorite (or a customer interest) is uniquely identified by the customer who created it, the tune involved, and the date it was created. Therefore, since these two entities draw part of their primary keys from their parent entities, they are considered dependent entities.

Identify the Relationships   The last step in creating ERDs is to determine how the entities are related to each other. Lines are drawn between entities that have relationships, and each relationship is labeled and assigned a cardinality and modality. A shown in Figure 6-15, a customer may make many sales, but a sale is made by one customer. A sale is not required for a particular customer instance, but a customer is required for a sale. A customer may be targeted by many targeted promotions, but a targeted promotion is for one customer. A targeted promotion is not required for a customer, but a customer is required for a targeted promotion. A customer creates many favorites, but a favorite is created by only one customer. A favorite is not required for a customer, but a customer is required for a favorite. An available tune may be included in many customers' favorites, but a favorite includes only one tune. A favorite is not required for an available tune, but a tune is required for a favorite. (The same relationships apply to customer–interest–available tune). We can also see that an available tune may

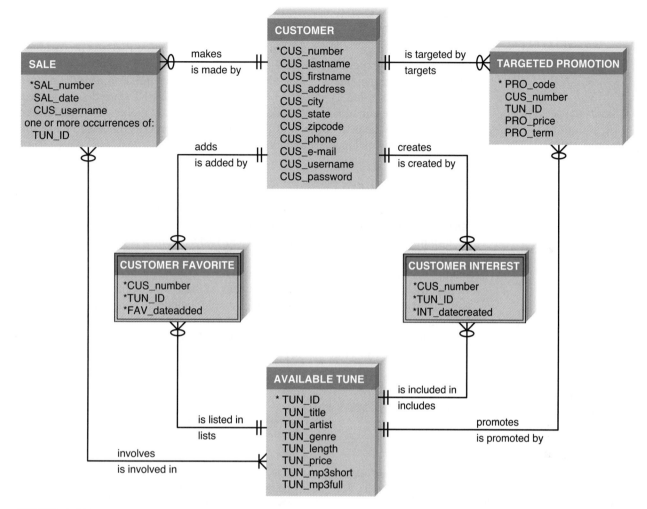

FIGURE 6-15
Relationships for Tune Source ERD

be promoted by many targeted promotions, but a targeted promotion promotes only one tune. An available tune is not required to have a targeted promotion, but a targeted promotion must be associated with an available tune. Finally, we see that customers may place many sales, but a sale is not required for a customer. A sale belongs to one and only one customer. A sale may include many tunes, and a tune may be included on many sales. A tune is required on a sale, but a sale is not required for a tune.

The customer–customer favorite, customer favorite–available tune, customer–customer interest, and customer interest–available tune relationships are identifying relationships. All other relationships are nonidentifying relationships.

As a final step in the creation of the Tune Source ERD, we should resolve any M:N relationships in the data model. A look at Figure 6-15 shows one such relationship, between sale and available tune. See Your Turn 6-6 and resolve this relationship on your own.

VALIDATING AN ERD

As you probably guessed from the previous section, creating ERDs is pretty tough. It takes a lot of experience to draw ERDs well, and there are not many black-and-white rules to help guide you. Luckily, there are some general design guidelines that you can keep in mind as you build ERDs, and once the ERDs are drawn, you can use a technique called *normalization* to validate that your models are well formed. Another technique is to check your ERD against your process models to make sure that both models balance each other.

Design Guidelines

Design guidelines are not rules that must be followed; rather, they are "best practices" that often lead to better quality diagrams. For example, labels and naming conventions are important for creating clear ERDs. Names should not be ambiguous (e.g., name, number); instead, they should clearly communicate what the model component represents. These names should be consistent across the model and reflect the terminology used by the business. If Tune Source refers to people who order music as *customers*, the data model should include an entity called customer, not client or stakeholder.

There are no rules covering the layout of ERD components. They can be placed anywhere you like on the page, although most systems analysts try to put the

---

CONCEPTS **6-A The User's Role in Data Modeling**

IN ACTION

I have two very different stories regarding data models. First, when I worked with First American Corporation, the head of Marketing kept a data model for the marketing systems hanging on a wall in her office. I thought this was a little unusual for a high-level executive, but she explained to me that data was critical for most of the initiatives that she puts in place. Before she can approve a marketing campaign or new strategy, she likes to confirm that the data exists in the systems and that it's accessible to her analysts. She has become very good at understanding ERDs over the years because they had been such an important communications tool for her to use with her own people and with IT.

On a very different note, here is a story I received from a friend of mine who heads up an IT department:

"We were working on a business critical, time dependent development effort, and VERY senior management decided that the way to ensure success was to have the various teams do technical design walkthroughs to senior management on a weekly basis. My team was responsible for the data architecture and database design. How could senior management, none of whom probably had ever designed an Oracle architecture, evaluate the soundness of our work?

So, I had my staff prepare the following for the one (and only) design walkthrough our group was asked to do. First, we merged several existing data models and then duplicated each one . . . that is, every entity and relationship printed twice (imitating, if asked, the redundant architecture). Then we intricately color coded the model and printed the model out on a plotter and printed one copy of every inch of model documentation we had. On the day of the review, I simply wheeled in the documentation and stretched the plotted model across the executive boardroom table. 'Any questions,' I asked? 'Very impressive,' they replied. That was it! My designs were never questioned again." *Barbara Wixom*

QUESTIONS:

1. From these two stories, what do you think is the user's role in data modeling?
2. When is it appropriate to involve users in the ERD creation process?
3. How can users help analysts create better ERDs?

YOUR TURN

6-3 CAMPUS HOUSING SYSTEM

Consider the accompanying system, which was described in Chapter 4. Use the use cases and process models that you created in Chapters 4 and 5 to help you answer the questions that follow.

The Campus Housing Service helps students find apartments. Owners of apartments fill in information forms about the rental units they have available (e.g., location, number of bedrooms, monthly rent). Students who register with the service can search the rental information to find apartments that meet their needs (e.g., a two-bedroom apartment for $800 or less per month within $1/2$ mile of campus). They then contact the apartment owners directly to see the apartment and, possibly, rent it. Apartment owners call the service to delete their listing when they have rented their apartment(s).

QUESTIONS:

1. What entities would you include on a data model?
2. What attributes would you list for each entity? Select an identifier for each entity, if possible.
3. What relationships exist between the entities that you identified? Label the relationships appropriately, and denote the cardinality and modality of each relationship.

entities together that are related to each other. If the model becomes too complex or busy (some companies have hundreds of entities on a data model), the model can be broken down into *subject areas*. Each subject area would contain related entities and relationships, and the analyst can work with one group of entities at a time to make the modeling process less confusing.

In general, data modeling can be quite tricky, mainly because the data model is heavily based on interpretation; therefore, when business rules change, the relationships or other data model components will have to be altered. *Assumptions* are an important part of data modeling. It is important that we verify all assumptions about business rules so that our data model is correct.

YOUR TURN

6-4 INDEPENDENT ENTITIES

Locate the independent entities on Figure 6-15. How do you know which of the entities are independent? Locate the nonidentifying relationships. How did you find them? Can you create a rule that describes the association between independent entities and nonidentifying relationships?

YOUR TURN

6-5 DEPENDENT ENTITIES

Locate the dependent entities on Figure 6-15. Locate the identifying relationships. How did you find them? Can you create a rule that describes the association between dependent entities and identifying relationships?

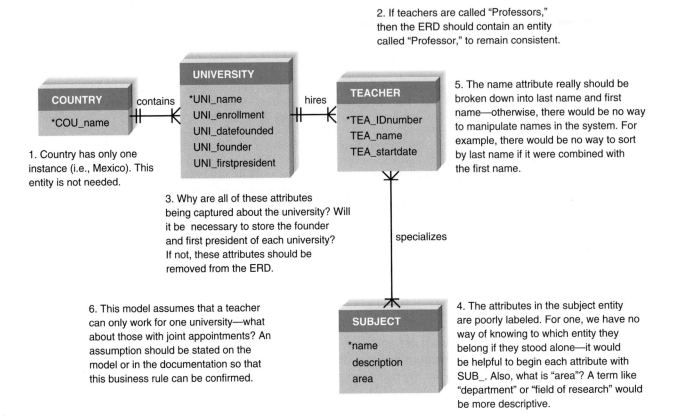

2. If teachers are called "Professors," then the ERD should contain an entity called "Professor," to remain consistent.

1. Country has only one instance (i.e., Mexico). This entity is not needed.

5. The name attribute really should be broken down into last name and first name—otherwise, there would be no way to manipulate names in the system. For example, there would be no way to sort by last name if it were combined with the first name.

3. Why are all of these attributes being captured about the university? Will it be necessary to store the founder and first president of each university? If not, these attributes should be removed from the ERD.

6. This model assumes that a teacher can only work for one university—what about those with joint appointments? An assumption should be stated on the model or in the documentation so that this business rule can be confirmed.

4. The attributes in the subject entity are poorly labeled. For one, we have no way of knowing to which entity they belong if they stood alone—it would be helpful to begin each attribute with SUB_. Also, what is "area"? A term like "department" or "field of research" would be more descriptive.

FIGURE 6-16
Data Modeling Guidelines Summary

Therefore, when you model data, don't panic or become overwhelmed by details. Rather, add components to the diagram slowly, knowing that they will be changed and rearranged many times. Make assumptions along the way and then confirm these assumptions with the business users. Work iteratively and constantly challenge the data model with business rules and exceptions to see whether the diagram is communicating the business system appropriately. Figure 6-16 summarizes the guidelines presented in this chapter to help you evaluate your data model.

YOUR

TURN

6-6 INTERSECTION ENTITIES

Resolve the M:N relationship between the sale and available tune that is shown in Figure 6-15. What kinds of information could you capture about this relationship? What would the new ERD look like? Would the intersection entity be considered dependent or independent?

Can you think of other kinds of M:N relationships that exist in the real world? How would you resolve these M:N relationships if you were to include them on an ERD?

6-B IMPLEMENTING AN EIM SYSTEM

A large direct health and insurance medical provider needed an enterprise information management (EIM) system to enable enterprisewide information management and to support the effective use of data for critical cross-functional decision making. In addition, the company needed to resolve issues related to data redundancy, inconsistency, and unnecessary expenditure. The company faced several information challenges: The company data resided in multiple locations, the data were developed for department-specific use, and there was limited enterprise access. In addition, data definitions were created by individual departments and were not standardized, and data were being managed by multiple departments within the company.

Source: http://www.deloitte.com/dtt/case_study/o,1005, sid%253D26562%2526cid%253D132760,00.html

QUESTIONS:
1. What solution would you propose for this company?
2. Discuss the role that data modeling would play in a project to solve this problem.

Normalization

Once you have created your ERD, there is a technique called *normalization* that can help analysts validate the models that they have drawn. It is a process whereby a series of rules are applied to a logical data model or a file to determine how well formed it is. Normalization rules help analysts identify entities that are not represented correctly in a logical data model, or entities that can be broken out from a file. The result of the normalization process is that the data attributes are arranged to form stable, yet flexible, relations for the data model. In Appendix 6A, we describe three normalization rules that are applied regularly in practice.

Balancing Entity Relationship Diagrams with Data Flow Diagrams

All the analysis activities of the systems analyst are interrelated. For example, the requirements analysis techniques are used to determine how to draw both the

6-7 BOAT CHARTER COMPANY

A charter company owns boats that are used for charter trips to islands. The company has created a computer system to track the boats it owns, including each boat's ID number, name, and seating capacity. The company also tracks information about the various islands, such as their names and populations. Every time a boat is chartered, it is important to know the date that the trip is to take place and the number of people on the trip. The company also keeps information about each captain, such as Social Security number, name, birthdate, and contact information for next of kin. Boats travel to only one island per visit.

QUESTIONS:
1. Create a data model. Include entities, attributes, identifiers, and relationships.
2. Which entities are dependent? Which are independent?
3. [Optional] Use the steps of normalization to put your data model in 3NF. Describe how you know that it is in 3NF.

process models and data models, and the CASE repository is used to collect information that is stored and updated throughout the entire analysis phase. Now we will see how the process models and data models are interrelated.

Although the process model focuses on the processes of the business system, it contains two data components—the data flow (which is composed of data elements) and the data store. The purposes of these are to illustrate what data are used and created by the processes and where those data are kept. These components of the DFD need to *balance* with the ERD. In other words, the DFD data components need to correspond with the ERD's data stores (i.e., entities) and the data elements that comprise the data flows (i.e., attributes) depicted on the data model.

Many CASE tools offer the feature of identifying problems with balance between DFDs and ERDs; however, it is a good idea to understand how to identify problems on your own. This involves examining the data model you have created and comparing it with the process models that have been created for the system. Check your data model and see whether there are any entities you have created that do not appear as data stores on your process models. If there are, you should add them to your process models to reflect your decision to store information about that entity in your system.

Similarly, the bits of information that are contained in the data flows (these are usually defined in the CASE entry for the data flow) should match up to the attributes found in entities in the data models. For example, if the customer information data flow that goes from the *customer* entity to the *purchase tunes* process were defined as having customer name, e-mail address, and home address, then each of these pieces of information should be recorded as attributes in the *customer* entity on the data model. We must verify that all the data items included in the data stores and data flows in the process model have been included somewhere as an entity attribute in the data model. We want to ensure that the data model fully incorporates all the data identified in the process model. If it does not, then the data model is incomplete. In addition, all the data elements in the data model should appear as a part of a data store and data flow(s) in the process model. If some data elements have been omitted from the process model, then we need to investigate whether those data items are truly needed in the processing of the system. If they are needed, they must be added to the process model data stores and data flows; otherwise, they should be deleted from the data model as extraneous data items.

A useful tool to clearly depict the interrelationship between process and data models is the *CRUD matrix*. The CRUD (create, read, update, delete) matrix is a table that depicts how the system's processes use the data within the system. It is helpful to develop the CRUD matrix on the basis of the logical process and data models and then revise it later in the design phase. The matrix also provides important information for program specifications, because it shows exactly how data are created and used by the major processes in the system.

To create a CRUD matrix, a table is drawn listing all the system processes along the top, and all the data entities (and entity attributes) along the left-hand side of the table. Then, from the information presented in the process model, the analyst fills in each cell with a C, R, U, D, (or nothing) to describe the process's interaction with each data entity (and its attributes). Figure 6-17 shows a portion of a data flow diagram and the CRUD matrix that can be derived from it. As you can see, if a process reads information from a data store, but does not update it, there should be a data flow coming out of the data store only. When a process

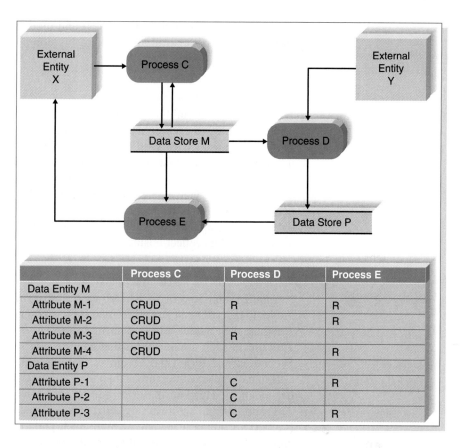

FIGURE 6-17
Partial Process Model and CRUD Matrix

	Process C	Process D	Process E
Data Entity M			
Attribute M-1	CRUD	R	R
Attribute M-2	CRUD		R
Attribute M-3	CRUD	R	
Attribute M-4	CRUD		R
Data Entity P			
Attribute P-1		C	R
Attribute P-2		C	
Attribute P-3		C	R

updates a data store in some way, there should be a data flow going from the process to the data store.

Thinking carefully about the content of the data flows in the process models, we can identify places where attributes may have been omitted from the data stores/entities. In addition, we can verify that every attribute is created, read, updated, and deleted somewhere in the process model. If it is not read by some process, then the attribute is probably not needed. If it is not created or updated, the attribute probably needs to be added to a data flow(s) in the process model.

SUMMARY

Basic Entity Relationship Diagram Syntax

The entity relationship diagram (ERD) is the most common technique for drawing a data model, a formal way of representing the data that are used and created by a business system. There are three basic elements in the data modeling language, each of which is represented by a different graphic symbol. The entity is the basic building block for a data model. It is a person, place, or thing about which data are collected. An attribute is some type of information that is captured about an entity.

The attribute that can uniquely identify one instance of an entity is called the identifier. The third data model component is the relationship, which conveys the associations between entities. Relationships have cardinality (the ratio of parent instances to child instances) and modality (a parent needs to exist if a child exists). Information about all of the components is captured by metadata in the data dictionary.

Creating an Entity Relationship Diagram

The basic steps in building an ERD are (1) identify the entities, (2) add the appropriate attributes to each entity, and (3) draw relationships among entities to show how they are associated with one another. There are three special types of entities that ERDs contain. Most entities are independent, because one (or more) attribute can be used to uniquely identify an instance. Entities that rely on attributes from other entities to identify an instance are dependent. An intersection entity is placed between two entities to capture information about their relationship. In general, data models are based on interpretation; therefore, it is important to clearly state assumptions that reflect business rules.

Validating an Entity Relationship Diagram

Normalization, the process whereby a series of rules is applied to the logical data model to determine how well formed it is, is described in the Chapter 6 Appendix. A logical data model is in first normal form (1NF) if it does not contain repeating attributes, which are attributes that capture multiple values for a single instance. Second normal form (2NF) requires that all entities are in 1NF and contain only attributes whose values are dependent on the whole identifier (i.e., no partial dependency). Third normal form (3NF) occurs when a model is in both 1NF and 2NF and none of the resulting attributes is dependent on nonidentifier attributes (i.e., no transitive dependency). With each violation, additional entities should be created to remove the repeating attributes or improper dependencies from the existing entities. Finally, ERDs should be balanced with the data flow diagrams (DFDs)—which were presented in Chapter 5—by making sure that data model entities and attributes correspond to data stores and data flows on the process model. The CRUD matrix is a valuable tool to use when balancing process and data models.

KEY TERMS

1:1 relationship	Derived attribute	Nonidentifying relationship
1:N relationship	Entity	Normalization
Assumption	Entity relationship diagram (ERD)	Parent entity
Attribute	First normal form (1NF)	Partial dependency
Balance	IDEF1X	Physical data model
Business rule	Identifier	Relationship
Cardinality	Identifying relationship	Repeating attributes
Child entity	Independent entity	Repeating groups
Concatenated identifier	Instance	Second normal form (2NF)
CRUD matrix	Intersection entity	Subject area
Data dictionary	Logical data model	Third normal form (3NF)
Data model	M:N relationship	Transcript
Dependent	Metadata	Transitive dependency
Dependent entity	Modality	

QUESTIONS

1. Provide three different options that are available for selecting an identifier for a student entity. What are the pros and cons of each option?
2. What is the purpose of developing an identifier for an entity?
3. What type of high-level business rule can be stated by an ERD? Give two examples.
4. Define what is meant by an *entity* in a data model. How should an entity be named? What information about an entity should be stored in the CASE repository?
5. Define what is meant by an *attribute* in a data model. How should an attribute be named? What information about an attribute should be stored in the CASE repository?
6. Define what is meant by a *relationship* in a data model. How should a relationship be named? What information about a relationship should be stored in the CASE repository?
7. A team of developers is considering including "warehouse" as an entity in its data model. The company for whom they are developing the system has just one warehouse location. Should "warehouse" be included? Why or why not?
8. What is meant by a concatenated identifier?
9. Describe, in terms a businessperson could understand, what are meant by the cardinality and modality of a relationship between two entities.
10. What are metadata? Why are they important to system developers?
11. What is an independent entity? What is a dependent entity? How are the two types of entities differentiated on the data model?
12. Explain the distinction between identifying and nonidentifying relationships.
13. What is the purpose of an intersection entity? How do you know whether one is needed in an ERD?
14. Describe the three-step process of creating an intersection entity.
15. Is an intersection entity dependent or independent? Explain your answer.
16. What is the purpose of normalization?
17. Describe the analysis that is applied to a data model in order to place it in first normal form (1NF).
18. Describe the analysis that is applied to a data model in order to place it in second normal form (2NF).
19. Describe the analysis that is applied to a data model in order to place it in third normal form (3NF).
20. Describe how the data model and process model should be balanced against each other.
21. What is a CRUD matrix? How does it relate to process models and data models?

EXERCISES

A. Draw data models for the following entities:
   - Movie (title, producer, length, director, genre)
   - Ticket (price, adult or child, showtime, movie)
   - Patron (name, adult or child, age)
B. Draw a data model for the following entities, considering the entities as representing a system for a patient billing system and including only the attributes that would be appropriate for this context:
   - Patient (age, name, hobbies, blood type, occupation, insurance carrier, address, phone)
   - Insurance carrier (name, number of patients on plan, address, contact name, phone)
   - Doctor (specialty, provider identification number, golf handicap, age, phone, name)
C. Draw the relationships that follow. Would the relationships be identifying or nonidentifying? Why?

   - A patient must be assigned to only one doctor, and a doctor can have many patients.
   - An employee has one phone extension, and a unique phone extension is assigned to an employee.
   - A movie theater shows many different movies, and the same movie can be shown at different movie theaters around town.
D. Draw an entity relationship diagram (ERD) for the following situations:
   1. Whenever new patients are seen for the first time, they complete a patient information form that asks their name, address, phone number, and insurance carrier, all of which are stored in the patient information file. Patients can be signed up with only one carrier, but they must be signed up

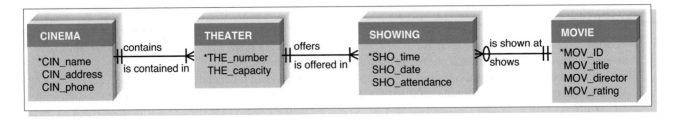

to be seen by the doctor. Each time a patient visits the doctor, an insurance claim is sent to the carrier for payment. The claim must contain information about the visit, such as the date, purpose, and cost. It would be possible for a patient to submit two claims on the same day.

2. The state of Georgia is interested in designing a database that will track its researchers. Information of interest includes researcher name, title, position; university name, location, enrollment; and research interests. Each researcher is associated with only one institution, and each researcher has several research interests.

3. A department store has a bridal registry. This registry keeps information about the customer (usually the bride), the products that the store carries, and the products for which each customer registers. Customers typically register for a large number of products, and many customers register for the same products.

4. Jim Smith's dealership sells Fords, Hondas, and Toyotas. The dealership keeps information about each car manufacturer with whom it deals so that employees can get in touch with manufacturers easily. The dealership also keeps information about the models of cars that it carries from each manufacturer. It keeps such information as list price, the price the dealership paid to obtain the model, and the model name and series (e.g., Honda Civic LX). The dealership also keeps information about all sales that it has made. (For instance, employees will record the buyer's name, the car the buyer bought, and the amount the buyer paid for the car.) To allow employees to contact the buyers in the future, contact information is also kept (e.g., address, phone number, e-mail).

E. Examine the data models that you created for Exercise D. How would the respective models change

(if at all) on the basis of these corresponding new assumptions?
- Two patients have the same first and last names.
- Researchers can be associated with more than one institution.
- The store would like to keep track of purchased items.
- Many buyers have purchased multiple cars from Jim over time because he is such a good dealer.

F. Visit a Web site that allows customers to order a product over the Web (e.g., Amazon.com). Create a data model that the site needs to support its business process. Include entities to show what types of information the site needs. Include attributes to represent the type of information the site uses and creates. Finally, draw relationships, making assumptions about how the entities are related.

G. Create metadata entries for the following data model components and, if possible, input the entries into a computer-aided software engineering (CASE) tool of your choosing:
- Entity—product
- Attribute—product number
- Attribute—product type
- Relationship—company makes many products, and any one product is made by only one company.

H. Describe the assumptions that are implied from the data model shown at the top of this page.

I. Create a data model for one of the processes in the end-of-chapter Exercises for Chapter 4. Explain how you would balance the data model and process model.

J. Apply the steps of normalization to validate the models you drew in Exercise D.

K. You have been given a file that contains fields relating to CD information. Using the steps of normalization, create a logical data model that represents this file in third normal form. The fields include the following:
- Musical group name
- Musicians in group
- Date group was formed

- Group's agent
- CD title 1
- CD title 2
- CD title 3
- CD 1 length
- CD 2 length
- CD 3 length

The assumptions are as follows:
- Musicians in group contains a list of the members of the people in the musical group.
- Musical groups can have more than one CD, so both group name and CD title are needed to uniquely identify a particular CD.

MINICASES

1. West Star Marinas is a chain of 12 marinas that offer lakeside service to boaters; service and repair of boats, motors, and marine equipment; and sales of boats, motors, and other marine accessories. The systems development project team at West Star Marinas has been hard at work on a project that eventually will link all the marina's facilities into one unified, networked system.

   The project team has developed a logical process model of the current system. This model has been carefully checked for syntax errors. Last week, the team invited a number of system users to role-play the various data flow diagrams, and the diagrams were refined to the users' satisfaction. Right now, the project manager feels confident that the as-is system has been adequately represented in the process model.

   The director of operations for West Star is the sponsor of this project. He sat in on the role-playing of the process model and was very pleased by the thorough job the team had done in developing the model. He made it clear to you, the project manager, that he was anxious to see your team begin work on the process model for the to-be system. He was a little skeptical that it was necessary for your team to spend any time modeling the current system in the first place, but grudgingly admitted that the team really seemed to understand the business after going through that work.

   The methodology that you are following, however, specifies that the team should now turn its attention to developing the logical data model for the as-is system. When you stated this to the project sponsor, he seemed confused and a little irritated. "You are going to spend even more time looking at the current system? I thought you were done with that! Why is this necessary? I want to see some progress on the way things will work in the future!"
   a. What is your response to the director of operations?
   b. Why do we perform data modeling?

   c. Is there any benefit to developing a data model of the current system at all?
   d. How does the process model help us develop the data model?

2. The system development team at the Wilcon Company is working on developing a new customer order entry system. In the process of designing the new system, the team has identified the following data entity attributes:

   Inventory Order
   Order Number (identifier)
   Order Date
   Customer Name
   Street Address
   City
   State
   Zip
   Customer Type
   Initials
   District Number
   Region Number
   1 to 22 occurrences of:
     Item Name
     Quantity Ordered
     Item Unit
     Quantity Shipped
     Item Out
     Quantity Received
   a. State the rule that is applied to place an entity in first normal form. Revise this data model so that it is in first normal form.
   b. State the rule that is applied to place an entity into second normal form. Revise the data model (if necessary) to place it in second normal form.
   c. State the rule that is applied to place an entity into third normal form. Revise the data model to place it in third normal form.
   d. What other guidelines and rules can you follow to validate that your data model is in good form?

APPENDIX 6A: NORMALIZING THE DATA MODEL

In this Appendix, we describe the rules of normalization that help analysts improve the quality of the data model. These rules help identify entities that are not represented correctly in the logical data model and entities that can be broken out from a file. The result of the normalization process is that the data attributes are arranged to form stable yet flexible relations for the data model. Typically, three rules of normalization are applied regularly in practice. (See Figure 6A-1.) We describe these rules and illustrate them with an example here.

First Normal Form   A logical data model is in first normal form (1NF) if it does not contain attributes that have repeating values for a single instance of an entity.

Often, this problem is called repeating attributes, or repeating groups. Every attribute in an entity should have only one value per instance for the model to "pass" 1NF.

Let's pretend that the Tune Source project team was given the layout for the CD purchase file that is used by the existing CD sales system. The team members are anxious to incorporate the data from this file into their own system, and they decide to put the file into third normal form to make the information easier to understand and, ultimately, easier for them to add to the data model for the new Digital Music Download system. See Figure 6A-2 for the file layout that the project team received.

	0 Normal Form
Do any attributes have multiple values for a single instance of an entity?	Yes: Remove the repeating attributes and repeating groups. Create an entity that describes the attributes. Usually, you will need to add a relationship to connect the old and new entities. No: The data model is in 1NF.
	1 Normal Form
Is the identifier composed of more than one attribute? If so, are any attribute values dependent on just part of the identifier?	Yes: Remove the partial dependency. Move the attributes to an entity in which their values are dependent on the entire identifier. Usually, you will need to create a new entitiy and add a relationship to connect the old and new entities. No: The data model is in 2NF.
	2 Normal Form
Do any attribute values depend on an attribute that is not the entity's identifier?	Yes: Remove the transitive dependency or derived attribute. Move the attributes to an entity in which their values are dependent on the identifier. Usually, you will need to create a new entity and add a relationship to connect the old and new entities. No: The data model is in 3NF.
	3 Normal Form

FIGURE 6A-1
Normalization Steps

```
┌─────────────────────────────────┐
│ CD Purchase                     │
│                                 │
│ *Purchase date                  │
│ *Customer last name             │
│ *Customer first name            │
│  Phone                          │
│  Address                        │
│  E-mail                         │
│  Birthdate                      │
│  Music preferences              │
│  One or more occurrences of:    │
│        CD UPC                   │
│        Title                    │
│        Artist                   │
│        Label                    │
│        Category                 │
│        Price                    │
│  Totoal due                     │
│  Sale authorization             │
│  Ship date                      │
│  Payment number                 │
│  Payment type                   │
│  Payment account number         │
│  Payment authorization          │
│  Payment amount                 │
└─────────────────────────────────┘
```

FIGURE 6A-2
Initial CD Sales System File

If you examine the file carefully, you should notice that there are two cases in which multiple values are captured for one or more attributes. The most obvious example is the multiple occurrences of CDs that are included in the purchase, a clear violation of 1NF. The repeated group of attributes about each CD included in the purchase should be removed by creating a new entity called CD and placing all of the CD attributes into it. The relationship between purchase and CD is M:N, since a purchase can include many CDs and a CD can be included in many purchases.

The second violation of 1NF may not be as readily noticed. The music preferences attribute includes the kinds of music the customer prefers (e.g., classical, rock, jazz). The fact that the attribute name is plural is a clue that many different preferences may be captured for each instance of a sale and that music preferences is a repeating attribute. This can be resolved by creating a new entity that contains preference information, and a relationship is added between CD purchase and preference. The new relationship is M:N, because a CD purchase can be associated with many music preferences and a music preference can be found on many CD purchases. See Figure 6A-3a for the current data model in 1NF.

Since we normally resolve M:N relationships as the ERD develops, we have done so now in Figure 6A-3b.

Note that a new intersection entity was inserted between CD Purchase and Preference to associate an instance of CD Purchase with specific instances of preference. Also, the intersection entity Purchased CD was inserted between CD Purchase and CD. This intersection entity associates a CD purchase instance with specific CD instances. The attribute ship date was moved to Purchased CD because the various CDs in a purchase may ship at different dates; therefore, this attribute describes a specific purchased CD, not the entire CD purchase.

Second Normal Form *Second normal form (2NF)* requires first that the data model is in 1NF and second that the data model leads to entities containing attributes that are *dependent* on the whole identifier. This means that the value of all attributes that serve as identifier can determine the value for all of the other attributes for an instance in an entity. Sometimes, nonidentifier attributes are dependent on only part of the identifier (i.e., *partial dependency*), and these attributes belong in another entity.

Figure 6A-4 shows the CD purchase data model placed in 2NF. Notice that originally, the *CD purchase* entity had three attributes that were used as identifiers: purchase date, customer last name, and customer first name. The problem was that some of the

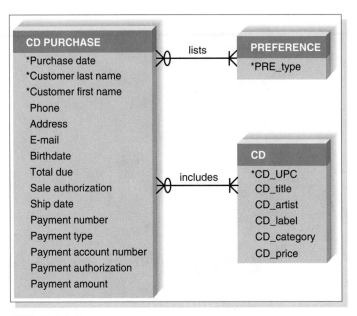

FIGURE 6A-3a
First Normal Form

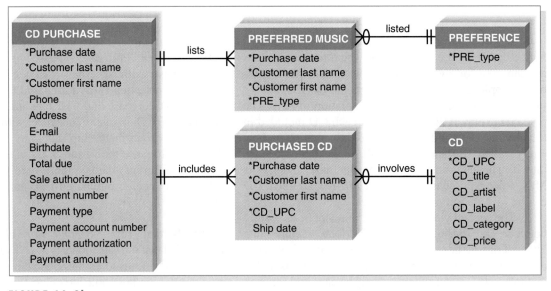

FIGURE 6A-3b
First Normal Form with M:N Relationships Resolved

attributes were dependent on the customer last name and first name, but had no dependency on purchase date. These attributes were those that describe a customer: phone, address, e-mail, and birth date. To resolve this problem, a new entity called *customer* was created, and the customer attributes were moved

into the new entity. A 1:N relationship exists between customer and CD purchase because a customer can purchase many CDs, but a CD purchase is associated with only one customer.

Remember that the customer last name and first name are still used in the *CD Purchase* entity—we know

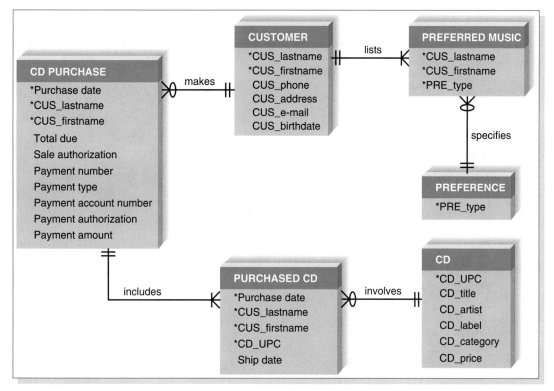

FIGURE 6A-4
Second Normal Form

this because of the identifying 1:N relationship between *customer* and *CD purchase.* The identifying relationship implies that the customer identifier (i.e., last name and first name) are used in CD Purchase as a part of its identifier.

Notice that we moved the relationship with Preferred Music to the new Customer entity. Logically, a preference should be associated with a customer, not a particular CD purchase.

Third Normal Form   *Third normal form (3NF)* occurs when a model is in both 1NF and 2NF and when, in the resulting entities, none of the attributes is dependent on a nonidentifier attribute (i.e., *transitive dependency*). A violation of 3NF can be found in the CD Purchase entity in Figure 6A-4.

The problem with the CD Purchase entity is that there are attributes in the entity that depend on the payment number, not the CD purchase date and customer first and last names. The payment type, account number, authorization, and amount depend on the payment number, a nonidentifying attribute. Therefore, we create a separate *payment* entity and move the payment attributes to it. The 1:1 relationship assumes that there is one

payment for every CD purchase, and every CD purchase has one payment. Also, a payment is required for every CD purchase, and every CD purchase requires a payment.

Third normal form also addresses issues of *derived,* or calculated, *attributes.* By definition, derived attributes can be calculated from other attributes and do not need to be stored in the data model. As an example, a person's age would not be stored as an attribute if birthdate were stored, because, by knowing the birthdate and current date, we can always calculate the age. You might legitimately question whether total due should be stored as an attribute of CD purchase, since its value can be calculated by summing the prices of all the CDs included in the purchase. Like much of data modeling, there is no hard-and-fast rule about this. Many times, values such as total due are included to serve as a control value. In order to verify that no purchased CDs are omitted from the entire purchase, the total due is stored as an attribute of CD purchase, and the sum of the individual CD prices is also computed to ensure that they match. We will leave the total due in the data model and show the final ERD in 3NF in Figure 6A-5.

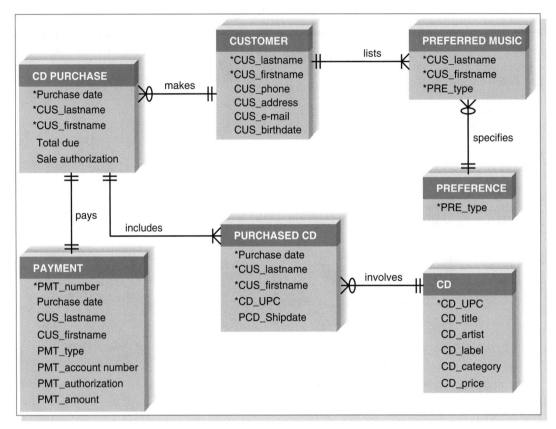

FIGURE 6A-5
Third Normal Form

YOUR TURN

6A-1 NORMALIZING A STUDENT ACTIVITY FILE

Pretend that you have been asked to build a system that tracks student involvement in activities around campus. You have been given a file with information that needs to be imported into the system, and the file contains the following fields:

- Student Social Security number (identifier)
- Activity 1 code (identifier)
- Activity 1 description
- Activity 1 start date
- Activity 1 years with activity
- Activity 2 code
- Activity 2 description
- Activity 2 start date

- Activity 3 code
- Activity 3 description
- Activity 3 start date
- Activity 3 years with activity
- Student last name
- Student first name
- Student birthdate
- Student age
- Student advisor name
- Student advisor phone

Normalize the file. Show how the logical data model would change as you move from 1NF to 2NF to 3NF.

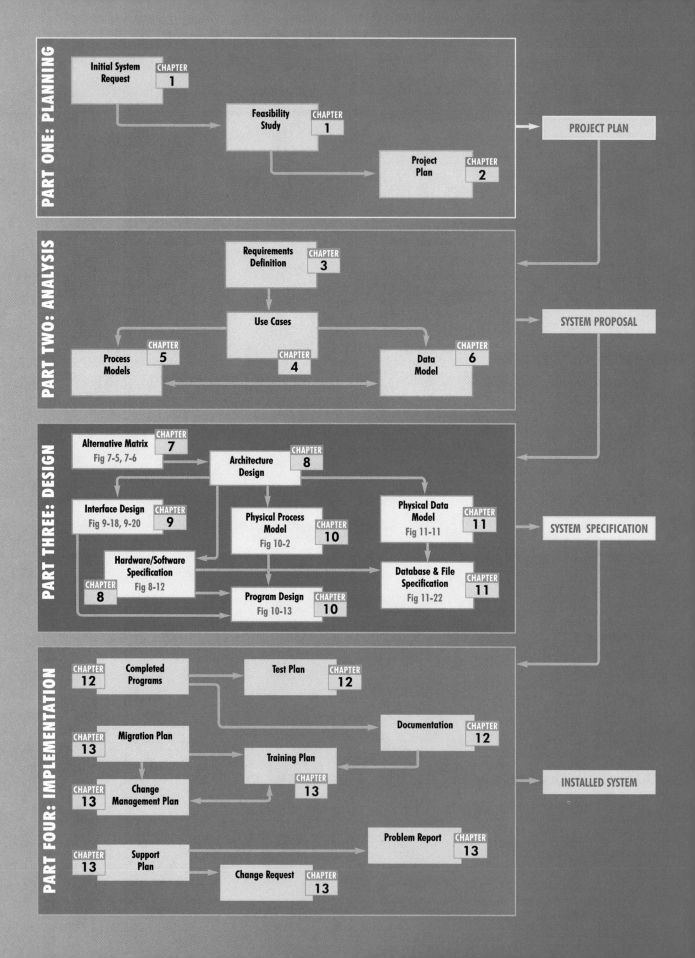

PART THREE
DESIGN PHASE

PROJECT BINDER

The design phase
decides how the system will operate.
This collection of deliverables
is the system specification
that is handed to the programming team
for implementation.

At the end of the design phase,
the feasibility analysis and project plan
are reexamined and revised,
and another decision is made by the project
sponsor and approval committee
about whether to terminate the project
or continue.

Moving into Design — **CHAPTER 7**

Architecture Design — **CHAPTER 8**

User Interface Design — **CHAPTER 9**

Program Design — **CHAPTER 10**

Data Storage Design — **CHAPTER 11**

PLANNING

ANALYSIS

DESIGN

- [ ] **Select Design Strategy**
- [ ] **Design Architecture**
- [ ] **Select Hardware and Software**
- [ ] **Develop Use Scenarios**
- [ ] **Design Interface Structure**
- [ ] **Develop Interface Standards**
- [ ] **Design Interface Prototype**
- [ ] **Evaluate User Interface**
- [ ] **Design User Interface**
- [ ] **Develop Physical Data Flow Diagrams**
- [ ] **Develop Program Structure Charts**
- [ ] **Develop Program Specifications**
- [ ] **Select Data Storage Format**
- [ ] **Develop Physical Entity Relationship Diagrams**
- [ ] **Denormalize Entity Relationship Diagram**
- [ ] **Performance Tune Data Storage**
- [ ] **Size Data Storage**

TASK CHECKLIST

PLANNING   ANALYSIS   DESIGN

CHAPTER 7

MOVING INTO DESIGN

The design phase of the SDLC uses the requirements that were gathered during analysis to create a blueprint for the future system. A successful design builds on what was learned in earlier phases and leads to a smooth implementation by creating a clear, accurate plan of what needs to be done. This chapter describes the initial transition from analysis to design and presents three ways to accomplish the design for the new system.

OBJECTIVES

- Understand the initial transition from analysis to design.
- Understand how to create a system specification.
- Be familiar with three ways to acquire a system: custom, packaged, and outsourced alternatives.
- Be able to create an alternative matrix.

CHAPTER OUTLINE

IMPLEMENTATION

INTRODUCTION

The design phase decides *how* the new system will operate. Many activities will be involved as the development team develops the system requirements. This chapter provides an outline of those design phase activities, which culminates in the creation of the system specification. We also describe three alternative strategies for acquiring the system that are available to the development team.

TRANSITION FROM REQUIREMENTS TO DESIGN

The purpose of the analysis phase is to figure out what the business needs. The purpose of the *design phase* is to decide how to build it. System design is the determination of the overall system architecture—consisting of a set of physical processing components, hardware, software, people, and the communication among them—that will satisfy the system's essential requirements.[1]

During the initial part of design, the project team converts the business requirements for the system into *system requirements* that describe the technical details for building the system. Unlike business requirements, which are listed in the requirements definition and communicated through use cases and *logical* process and data models, system requirements are communicated through a collection of design documents and *physical* process and data models. Together, the design documents and physical models make up the blueprint for the new system.

The design phase has a number of activities that lead to the system blueprint. (See Figure 7-1.) An important initial part of the design phase is the examination of

Activities in the Design Phase	Deliverables	Chapter
✓ Determine preferred system acquisition strategy (make, buy, or outsource).	– Alternative matrix	7
✓ Design the architecture for the system.	– Architecture design	8
✓ Make hardware and software selections.	– Hardware and software specification	
✓ Design system navigation, inputs, and outputs.	– Interface design	9
✓ Convert logical process model to physical process model.	– Physical process model	10
✓ Update CASE repository with additional system details.	– Updated CASE repository	
✓ Design the programs that will perform the system processes.	– Program design specifications	
✓ Convert logical data model to physical data model.	– Physical data model	11
✓ Update CASE repository with additional system details.	– Updated CASE repository	
✓ Revise CRUD matrix.	– CRUD matrix	
✓ Design the way in which data will be stored.	– Data storage design	
✓ Compile final system specification.	– System specification: all of the above deliverables combined and presented to approval committee	7

FIGURE 7-1
Activities of the Design Phase

[1] Ken Shumate and Marilyn Keller, *Software Specification and Design*, New York: John Wiley & Sons, 1992.

several system acquisition strategies to decide which will be used to build the system. Systems can be built from scratch, purchased and customized, or outsourced to others, and the project team needs to investigate the viability of each alternative. The decision to make, to buy, or to outsource influences the design tasks that are performed throughout the rest of the phase.

The project team carefully considers the nonfunctional business requirements that were identified during analysis. The nonfunctional business requirements influence the system requirements that drive the design of the system's architecture. Major considerations of the "how" of a system are operational, performance, security, cultural, and political in nature. For example, the project team needs to plan for the new system's performance: how fast the system will operate, what its capacity should be, and its availability and reliability. The team needs to create a secure system by specifying access restrictions and by identifying the need for encryption, authentication, and virus control. The nonfunctional requirements are converted into system requirements that are described in the *architecture design* document (Chapter 8).

At the same time, architecture decisions are made regarding the hardware and software that will be purchased to support the new system (Chapter 8). These decisions are documented in the *hardware and software specification*, which is a document that describes what hardware and software are needed to support the new application. The actual acquisition of hardware and software is sometimes the responsibility of the purchasing department or the area in the organization that handles capital procurement; however, the project team uses the hardware and software specification to communicate the hardware and software needs to the appropriate people.

The user's interactions with the system also must be designed. The system inputs and outputs will be designed along with a plan or roadmap of the way the system's features will be navigated. Chapter 9 describes these activities in detail, along with techniques, such as storyboarding and prototyping, that help the project team design a system that meets the needs of its users and is satisfying to use. Design decisions made regarding the interface are communicated through the design document called the interface design.

The processes described in the logical process model provide the foundation for the system's functionality. Chapter 10 describes how these logical DFDs are converted into physical DFDs that document physical design decisions about how the system will be built. CASE repository entries are updated to reflect specific technology decisions as they are made. Program specifications are prepared to provide the final design details and ensure that programmers have sufficient information to build the right system efficiently. The program design document contains all of the information about new system's programs.

The data component of the system, described in the logical data model, also must be designed prior to implementation. Chapter 11 discusses the development of the physical data model, updates to the CASE repository, and describes how the CRUD matrix should be updated to verify the consistency between the process and data models. Design decisions regarding data storage are written up in the data storage design document.

Although a textbook such as this must present information sequentially, the many activities of the design phase are highly interrelated. As with the steps in the analysis phase, analysts often go back and forth between them. For example, prototyping in the interface design step often uncovers additional information that is

- Recommended System Acquisition Strategy
- System Acquisition Weighted Alternative Matrix
- Architecture Design
- Hardware and Software Specification
- Interface Design
- Physical Process Model
- Program Design Specifications
- Physical Data Model
- Data Storage Design
- Updated CRUD Matrix
- Updated CASE Repository Entries

FIGURE 7-2
System Specification Outline

needed in the system, leading to a revision of the physical DFDs or ERDs. Alternatively, a system that is being designed for an organization with centralized systems may require substantial hardware and software investments if the project team decides to change to a system in which all the processing is distributed.

At the end of the design phase, the project team creates the final deliverable for the phase called the *system specification*. This document contains all of

---

PRACTICAL **7-1 AVOIDING CLASSIC DESIGN MISTAKES**

TIP

In Chapters 2 and 3, we discussed several classic mistakes and how to avoid them. Here, we summarize four classic mistakes in the design phase and discuss how to avoid them:

1. **Reducing design time:** If time is short, there is a temptation to reduce the time spent in such "unproductive" activities as design so that the team can jump into "productive" programming. This results in missing important details that have to be investigated later at a much higher time cost (usually, at least 10 times longer).
   Solution: If time pressure is intense, use rapid application development (RAD) techniques and timeboxing to eliminate functionality or move it into future versions.

2. **Feature creep:** Even if you are successful at avoiding scope creep, about 25% of system requirements will still change. Changes—big and small—can significantly increase time and cost.
   Solution: Ensure that all changes are vital and that the users are aware of the impact on cost and time. Try to move proposed changes into future versions.

3. **Silver bullet syndrome:** Analysts sometimes believe the marketing claims that some design tools solve all problems and magically reduce time and costs. No one tool or technique can eliminate overall time or costs by more than 25% (although some can reduce individual steps by this much).
   Solution: If a design tool has claims that appear too good to be true, just say no.

4. **Switching tools in midproject:** Sometimes, analysts switch to what appears to be a better tool during design in the hopes of saving time or costs. Usually, any benefits are outweighed by the need to learn the new tool. This also applies to even "minor" upgrades to current tools.
   Solution: Don't switch or upgrade unless there is a compelling need for specific features in the new tool, and then explicitly increase the schedule to include learning time.

Source: Adapted from *Professional Software Developmnt*, Redmond, WA: Microsoft Press, 2003, by Steve McConnell.

the design documents just described: physical process models, physical data model, architecture design, hardware and software specification, interface design, data storage design, and program design. Collectively, the system specification conveys exactly what system the project team will implement during the implementation phase of the SDLC. See Figure 7-2 for an outline of the system specification content.

SYSTEM ACQUISITION STRATEGIES

Until now, we have assumed that the system will be built and implemented by the project team. However, there are actually three ways to approach the creation of a new system: (1) Develop a custom application in-house; (2) buy a packaged system and customizing it; and (3) rely on an external vendor, developer, or service provider to build the system. Each of these choices has its strengths and weaknesses, and each is more appropriate in different situations. The following sections describe each acquisition choice in turn, and then we present criteria you can use to select one of the three approaches for your project:

Custom Development

Many project teams assume that *custom development*, or building a new system from scratch, is the best way to create a system. For one, teams have complete control over the way the system looks and functions. Let's consider the purchasing process for Tune Source. If the company wants a Web-based feature that links tightly with its existing CD sales system, the project may involve a complex, highly specialized program. Alternatively, Tune Source might have a technical environment in which all information systems are built from standard technology and interface designs so that they are consistent and easier to update and support. In both cases, it could be very effective to create a new system from scratch that meets these highly specialized requirements.

In some situations, the challenges being addressed with the new system are so significant and demanding that serious systems engineering is required to solve them. In these cases, the developers really cannot find a packaged solution that is capable of meeting the project requirements, and a custom development project is the only real viable choice. (See Concepts in Action 7-A.)

Custom development also allows developers to be flexible and creative in the way they solve business problems. Tune Source may envision the Web interface that

---

CONCEPTS

IN ACTION

7-A OUT OF THE BOX . . . ?

A consultant I know is currently (2008) leading a very large project revising the financial systems of a major global financial services company. The company had a successful, well-defined program of software standards in place. Therefore, initially, the project team attempted to employ software from one of the major ERP software vendors in the project. After experiencing dismal (and unacceptable) processing speed during tests of the ERP software, the CIO and team concluded, "Out of the Box is out of the question." *Roberta Roth*

CONCEPTS

IN ACTION

7-B BUCKING CONVENTIONAL WISDOM WITH CUSTOM DEVELOPMENT

Bonhams 1793 Ltd. is a London-based auctioneering house, ranked number three globally behind Christie's International PLC and Sotheby's. After embarking on a series of acquisitions in 2000, the firm recognized the need to standardize its IT system. The requirements that Bonhams 1793 faced included ERP functions, customer relationship management, and auction catalog production, among others. Rather than follow the lead of its larger competitors and acquire a software package from SAP AG or Siebel Systems Inc., Bonhams 1793 instead developed a system from scratch. By carefully planning the system architecture, selecting powerful and integrated development tools, employing open source software when possible, and empowering its in-house developers, Bonhams 1793 developed a custom system rapidly and at lower cost than it could have by using a packaged solution. Bonhams 1793 avoided purchasing an expensive package and then spending a significant amount to tailor and implement it. The result is a successful custom system that provides exactly the functions that Bonhams 1793 sought.

Source: Anthes, Gary, "Best in Class 2007, Bonhams 1793," *Computerworld*, August 14, 2007.

takes customer digital music purchases as an important strategic enabler. The company may want to use the information from the system to better understand its customers who buy digital music over the Web, and it may want the flexibility to evolve the system to incorporate technology such as data-mining software and geographic information systems to perform marketing research. A custom application would be easier to change to include components that take advantage of current technologies that can support such strategic efforts.

Building a system in-house also builds technical skills and functional knowledge within the company. As developers work with business users, their understanding of the business grows and they become better able to align information systems with strategies and needs. These same developers climb the technology learning curve so that future projects applying similar technology become much easier.

Custom application development, however, requires a dedicated effort that includes long hours and hard work. Many companies have a development staff that is already overcommitted. Facing huge backlogs of systems requests, the staff just does not have time for another project. Also, a variety of skills—technical, interpersonal, functional, project management, modeling—all have to be in place for the project to move ahead smoothly. IS professionals, especially highly skilled individuals, are quite difficult to hire and retain.

The risks associated with building a system from the ground up can be quite high, and there is no guarantee that the project will succeed. Developers could be pulled away to work on other projects, technical obstacles could cause unexpected delays, and the business users could become impatient with a growing timeline.

Packaged Software

Many business needs are not unique, and because it makes little sense to reinvent the wheel, many organizations buy *packaged software* that has already been written, rather than developing their own custom solution. In fact, there are thousands of commercially available software programs that have already been written to serve a multitude of purposes. Think about your own need for a word processor—did you ever consider writing your own word processing software? That would be very silly, considering the number of good software packages available for a relatively inexpensive cost.

Similarly, most companies have needs, such as payroll or accounts receivable, that can be met quite well by packaged software. It can be much more efficient to buy programs that have already been created, tested, and proven, and a packaged system can be bought and installed quickly compared with a custom system. Plus, packaged systems incorporate the expertise and experience of the vendor who created the software.

Let's think about the needs that Tune Source will have in its Digital Music Download system. One requirement is to have a simple, fast, and flexible process in place to deliver the purchased tunes over the Internet to the purchaser. Server-side download management software programs are available that are designed to optimize the delivery of file downloads. Some of these products are available for free, and in some products, these tools are incorporated into a overall shopping-cart capability as well. Tune Source will certainly need to consider this type of option as it considers alternatives for the Digital Music Download system.

Packaged software can range from small single-function tools, such as the server-side download manager, to huge all-encompassing systems, such as *enterprise resource planning* (*ERP*) applications that are installed to automate an entire business. Implementing ERP systems is a popular practice in which large organizations spend millions of dollars installing packages by such companies as SAP, Oracle, and Infor and then change their businesses accordingly. Installing ERP software is much more difficult than installing small application packages, because benefits can be harder to realize and problems are much more serious.

One problem is that companies utilizing packaged systems must accept the functionality that is provided by the system, and rarely is there a perfect fit. If the packaged system is large in scope, its implementation could mean a substantial change in the way the company does business. Letting technology drive the business can be a dangerous way to go.

Most packaged applications allow for some customization or for the manipulation of system parameters to change the way certain features work. For example, the package might have a way to accept information about your company or the company logo that would then appear on input screens. An accounting software package could offer a choice of various ways to handle cash flow or inventory control so that it could support the accounting practices in different organizations. If the amount of customization is not enough and the software package has a few features that don't quite work the way the company needs them to work, the project team can create a *workaround*. A workaround is a custom-built add-on program that interfaces with the packaged application to handle special needs. It can be a nice way to create needed functionality that does not exist in the software package. However, workarounds should be a last resort, for several reasons. First, workarounds are not supported by the vendor who supplied the packaged software, so when upgrades are made to the main system, they may make the workaround ineffective. Also, if problems arise, vendors have a tendency to blame the workaround as the culprit and refuse to provide support.

Although choosing a packaged software system is simpler than going with custom development, it also can benefit from following a formal methodology, just as if you were building a custom application. The search for a software package should be based on the detailed requirements identified during analysis.

Systems integration refers to the process of building new systems by combining packaged software, existing legacy systems, and new software written to integrate these. Many consulting firms specialize in systems integration, so it is not uncommon for companies to select the packaged software option and then outsource the integration of a variety of packages to a consulting firm. (Outsourcing is discussed in the next section.)

The key challenge in systems integration is finding ways to integrate the data produced by the different packages and legacy systems. Integration often hinges on taking data produced by one package or system and reformatting it for use in another package or system. The project team starts by examining the data produced by and needed by the different packages and systems and identifying the transformations that must occur to move the data from one to the other. In many cases, this involves fooling the different packages or systems into thinking that the data were produced by an existing program module that the package or system expects to produce the data, rather than by the new package or system that is being integrated.

For example, Tune Source might want to integrate its new Digital Music Download system with its existing Web-based CD sales system. The CD sales system enables customers to purchase CDs over the Web, and it interfaces with Tune Source's accounting and inventory management systems. The new Digital Music Download system will not require integration with the inventory management system, but it will need to interface with the accounting system and perhaps could share customer data with the CD sales system. The Digital Music Download project team will need to consider these areas of system integration as it evaluates its development options.

Outsourcing

The acquisition choice that requires the least in-house resources is *outsourcing*, which means hiring an external vendor, developer, or service provider to create or supply the system. Outsourcing has become quite popular in recent years, with both U.S. and non-U.S. (offshore) service providers available.

The term *outsourcing* has come to include a variety of ways to obtain IT services and products. Outsourcing firms called *application service providers* (ASPs) supply software applications and/or software-related services over the Internet. In this approach to obtaining software, the ASP owns and operates a software application, and owns, operates, and maintains the servers that run the application. The ASP also employs the people needed to maintain the application.

Organizations wishing to use a software application contract with the ASP, who makes it available to the customer via the Internet, either in a browser or through some sort of "thin client." The customer is billed by the ASP for the application either on a per-use basis or on a monthly or annual fee basis.

Obtaining access to a software package through an application service provider has many advantages. There is a low cost of entry and, in most cases, an extremely short setup time. The pay-as-you-go model is often significantly less expensive for all but the most frequent users of the service. Investments in IT staff can be reduced, and investments in specialized IT infrastructure often can be avoided.

Outsourcing firms are also available that will develop a custom system on behalf of the customer. There can be great benefit to having others develop your system. They may be more experienced in the technology or have more resources, such as experienced programmers. Many companies embark on outsourcing deals

CONCEPTS

7-C BUILDING A CUSTOM SYSTEM—WITH SOME HELP

IN ACTION

I worked with a large financial institution in the southeast that suffered serious financial losses several years ago. A new chief executive officer was brought in to change the strategy of the organization to being more customer-focused. The new direction was quite innovative, and it was determined that custom systems, including a data warehouse, would have to be built to support the new strategic efforts. The problem was that the company did not have the in-house skills for these kinds of custom projects.

The company now has one of the most successful data warehouse implementations because of its willingness to use outside skills and its focus on project management. To supplement skills within the company, eight sets of external consultants, including hardware vendors, system integrators, and business strategists, were hired to take part and transfer critical skills to internal employees. An in-house project manager coordinated the data warehouse implementation full time, and her primary goals were to clearly set expectations, define responsibilities, and communicate the interdependencies that existed among the team members.

This company showed that successful custom development can be achieved even when the company may not start off with the right skills in-house. However, this kind of project is not easy to pull off—it takes a talented project manager to keep the project moving along and to transition the skills to the right people over time.
Barbara Wixom

QUESTIONS:
1. What are the risks in building a custom system without having the right technical skills available within the organization?
2. Why did the company select a project manager from within the organization?
3. Would it have been better to hire an external professional project manager to coordinate the project? Why or why not?

to reduce costs, whereas others see it as an opportunity to add value to the business. For example, instead of creating a program that handles the purchasing process or buying a preexisting package, Tune Source may decide to let a Web service provider provide commercial services for them.

For whatever reason, outsourcing can be a good alternative for a new system; however, it does not come without costs. If you decide to leave the creation of a new system in the hands of someone else, you could compromise confidential information or lose control over future development. In-house professionals are not benefiting from the skills that could be learned from the project; instead, the expertise is transferred to the outside organization. Ultimately, important skills can walk right out the door at the end of the contract.

Most risks can be addressed if you decide to outsource, but two are particularly important. First, assess the requirements for the project thoroughly—you should never outsource what you don't understand. If you have conducted rigorous planning and analysis, then you should be well aware of your needs. Second, carefully choose a vendor, developer, or service with a proven track record with the type of system and technology that your system needs.

There are three primary types of contracts that can be drawn to control the outsourcing deal. A *time and arrangements* deal is very flexible because you agree to pay for whatever time and expenses are needed to get the job done. Of course, this agreement could result in a large bill that exceeds initial estimates. This arrangement works best when you and the outsourcer are unclear about what it is going to take to finish the job.

FIGURE 7-3
Outsourcing Guidelines

- Keep the lines of communication open between you and your outsourcer.
- Define and stabilize requirements before signing a contract.
- View the outsourcing relationship as a partnership.
- Select the vendor, developer, or service provider carefully.
- Assign a person to manage the relationship.
- Don't outsource what you don't understand.
- Emphasize flexible requirements, long-term relationships, and short-term contracts.

You will pay no more than expected with a *fixed-price contract* because if the outsourcer exceeds the agreed-on price, he or she will have to absorb the costs. Outsourcers are very careful about clearly defining requirements up front, and there is little flexibility for change.

The type of contract gaining in popularity is the *value-added contract*, whereby the outsourcer reaps some percentage of the completed system's benefits. You have very little risk in this case, but expect to share the wealth once the system is in place.

Creating fair contracts is an art because you need to carefully balance flexibility with clearly defined terms. Needs often change over time, so you don't want the contract to be so specific and rigid that alterations can't be made. Think about how quickly technology like the World Wide Web changes. It is difficult to foresee how a project may evolve over a long period. Short-term contracts leave room for reassessment if needs change or if relationships are not working out the way both parties expected. In all cases, the relationship with the outsourcer should be viewed as a partnership in which both parties benefit and communicate openly.

Managing the outsourcing relationship is a full-time job. Thus, someone needs to be assigned full time to manage the outsourcer, and the level of that person should be appropriate for the size of the job. (A multimillion-dollar outsourcing engagement should be handled by a high-level executive.) Throughout the relationship, progress should be tracked and measured against predetermined goals. If you do embark on an outsourcing design strategy, be sure to get more information. Many books have been written that provide much more detailed information on the topic.[2] Figure 7-3 summarizes some guidelines for outsourcing.

INFLUENCES ON THE ACQUISITION STRATEGY

Each of the system acquisition strategies just discussed has its strengths and weaknesses, and no one strategy is inherently better than the others. Thus, it is important to understand the strengths and weaknesses of each strategy and when to use each. Figure 7-4 summarizes the project characteristics that influence the choice of acquisition strategy.

Business Need

If the business need for the system is common and technical solutions already exist in the marketplace that can fulfill the system requirements, it is usually appropriate to select a packaged software solution. Packaged systems are good alternatives for

---

[2] For more information on outsourcing, we recommend M. Lacity and J. Rottman, *Offshore Outsourcing of IT Work: Client and Supplier Perspectives*, Palgrave Macmillan, 2008.

	When to Use Custom Development	When to Use a Packaged System	When to Use Outsourcing
Business need	The business need is unique.	The business need is common.	The business need is not core to the business.
In-house experience	In-house functional and technical experience exists.	In-house functional experience exists.	In-house functional or technical experience does not exist.
Project skills	There is a desire to build in-house skills.	The skills are not strategic.	The decision to outsource is a strategic decision.
Project management	The project has a highly skilled project manager and a proven methodology.	The project has a project manager who can coordinate vendor's efforts.	The project has a highly skilled project manager at the level of the organization that matches the scope of the outsourcing deal.
Time frame	The time frame is flexible.	The time frame is short.	The time frame is short or flexible.

FIGURE 7-4
Selecting a System Acquisition Strategy

common business needs. The widespread availability and usefulness of packaged software has caused many larger companies to develop a recommended list of packaged solutions for use throughout the organization. By limiting the selection of software packages from the list of standard options, the organization is able to ensure consistency across the organizational units, streamline decision making, and ultimately reduce costs.

Packaged software is not suitable for every situation, however. A custom solution should be explored when the business need is unique, when there are especially difficult or demanding requirements that cannot be addressed successfully with a package, or when the organization is unable to change enough to adapt to the way of doing business that is embodied in a software package.

Outsourcing can be used to assist a company with custom development projects and to acquire software packages. The specialization and expertise of an outsourcing firm can be very valuable. Because outsourcing brings an outside third party into the development process, it is usually used in situations where the business need is not a critical element of company strategy. If the business need is central to the company strategy, then it is usually better for the company to retain exclusive control over the project if possible.

Many organizations are using or are considering using offshore outsourcing as a way of "exporting" IT-related work to countries that have lower labor costs. Two-thirds of companies on the InformationWeek 500 list of business technology innovators say they engage in offshore IT outsourcing. Good quality IT skills are available in a number of countries, but companies considering this option in order to save money need to carefully manage the risks of this way of obtaining IT services.[3]

In-House Experience

If in-house experience exists for all the functional and technical needs of the system, it will be easier to build a custom application than if these skills do not exist. A packaged system may be a better alternative for companies that do not have the

---

[3] Weier, Mary Hayes, "The Second Decade of Offshore Outsourcing: Where We're Headed," *InformationWeek*, Nov. 3, 2007.

CONCEPTS | **7-D** ELECTRONIC DATA SYSTEM'S VALUE-ADDED CONTRACT

IN ACTION

Value-added contracts can be quite rare—and very dramatic. They exist when a vendor is paid a percentage of revenue generated by the new system, which reduces the up-front fee, sometimes to zero. The landmark deal of this type was signed three years ago by the City of Chicago and EDS (a large consulting and systems integration firm), which agreed to reengineer the process by which the city collects the fines on 3.6 million parking tickets per year. At the time, because of clogged courts and administrative problems, the city collected on only about 25% of all tickets issued. It had a $60 million backlog of uncollected tickets.

Dallas-based EDS invested an estimated $25 million in consulting and new systems in exchange for the right to up to 26% of the uncollected fines, a base pro-cessing fee for new tickets, and software rights. To date, EDS has taken in well over $50 million on the deal, analysts say. The deal has come under some fire from various quarters as an example of an organization giving away too much in a risk/reward–sharing deal. City officials, however, counter that the city has pulled in about $45 million in previously uncollected fines and has improved its collection rate to 65% with little up-front investment.

QUESTION:
Do you think the city of Chicago got a good deal from this arrangement? Why or why not?

Source: "Outsourcing? Go out on a Limb Together," *Datamation*, February 1, 1999, 41(2): 58–61, by Jeff Moad.

technical skills to build the desired system. For example, a project team that does not have Web commerce technology skills may want to acquire a Web commerce package that can be installed without many changes. Outsourcing is a good way to bring in outside experience that is missing in-house so that skilled people are in charge of building the system.

Project Skills

The skills that are applied during projects are either technical (e.g., Java, Structured Query Language [SQL]) or functional (e.g., electronic commerce), and different design alternatives are more viable, depending on how important the skills are to the company's strategy. For example, if certain functional and technical expertise that relates to Internet sales applications and Web commerce application development is important to the organization because the company expects the Internet to play an important role in sales over time, then it makes sense for the company to develop Web commerce applications in-house, using company employees so that the skills can be developed and improved. On the other hand, some skills, such as network security, may be either beyond the technical expertise of employees or not of interest to the company's strategists—it is just an operational issue that needs to be handled. In this case, packaged systems or outsourcing should be considered so that internal employees can focus on other business-critical applications and skills.

Project Management

Custom applications require excellent project management and a proven methodology. There are so many things that can push a project off track, such as funding obstacles, staffing holdups, and overly demanding business users. Therefore, the project team should choose to develop a custom application only if it is certain that the underlying coordination and control mechanisms will be in place. Packaged and outsourcing alternatives also must be managed; however, they are more shielded from internal obstacles because the external parties have their own objectives and priorities (e.g., it may be easier for an outside contractor to say no to a user than for a person within the company to do so). The latter alternatives typically have their own methodologies, which can benefit companies that do not have an appropriate methodology to use.

Time Frame

When time is a factor, the project team should probably start looking for a system that is already built and tested. In this way, the company will have a good idea of how long the package will take to put in place and what the final result will contain. Of course, this assumes that the package can be installed as-is and does not need many workarounds to integrate it into the existing business processes and technical environment. The time frame for custom applications is hard to pin down, especially when you consider how many projects end up missing important deadlines. If you must choose the custom development alternative and the time frame is very short, consider using techniques like timeboxing to manage this problem. The time to produce a system through outsourcing really depends on the system and the outsourcer's resources. If a service provider has services in place that can be used to support the company's needs, then a business need could be met quickly. Otherwise, an outsourcing solution could take as long as a custom development initiative.

SELECTING AN ACQUISITION STRATEGY

Once the project team has a good understanding of how well each acquisition strategy fits with the project's needs, it must begin to understand exactly how to implement these strategies. For example, what tools and technology would be used if a custom alternative were selected? What vendors make packaged systems that address the project needs? What service providers would be able to build this system if the application were outsourced? This information can be obtained by talking to people working in the IS Department and getting recommendations from business users by contacting other companies with similar needs and investigating the types of systems that they have put in place. Vendors and consultants are usually willing to provide information about various tools and solutions in the form of brochures, product demonstrations, and information seminars.

Project teams employ several approaches to gather additional information that is needed. One helpful tool is the *request for proposal* (*RFP*), a document that solicits a formal proposal from a potential vendor, developer, or service provider. RFPs describe in detail the system or service that is needed, and vendors respond by describing in detail how they could supply those needs.

Although there is no standard way of writing an RFP, it should include certain key facts that the vendor requires, such as a detailed description of needs, any special technical needs or circumstances, evaluation criteria, procedures to follow, and timetable. In a large project, the RFP can be hundreds of pages long, since it is essential that all required project details are included.

The RFP is not just a way to gather information. Rather, it results in a vendor proposal that is a binding offer to accomplish the tasks described in the RFP. The vendor proposal includes a schedule and a price for which the work is to be performed. Once the winning vendor proposal is chosen, a contract for the work is entered into.

YOUR

TURN

7-1 SELECT A DESIGN STRATEGY

Suppose that your university were interested in creating a new course registration system that could support Web-based registration.

QUESTION:
What should the university consider when determining whether to invest in a custom, packaged, or outsourced system solution?

For smaller projects with smaller budgets, the *request for information* (*RFI*) may be sufficient. An RFI is a shorter, less detailed request that is sent to potential vendors to obtain general information about their products and services. Sometimes, the RFI is used to determine which vendors have the capability to perform a service. It is often then followed up with an RFP to the qualified vendors.

When a list of equipment is so complete that the vendor need only provide a price, without any analysis or description of what is needed, the *request for quote* (*RFQ*) may be used. For example, if 20 long-range RFID tag readers are needed from the manufacturer on a certain date at a certain location, the RFQ can be used. If an item is described, but a specific manufacturer's product is not named, then extensive testing will be required to verify fulfillment of the specifications.

After evaluating the acquisition strategy options and seeking additional information, the design team will likely have several viable choices to use to obtain the system. For example, the project team may find three vendors who make packaged systems that could meet the project's needs; or the team may be debating over whether to develop a system by using Visual Basic as a development tool and the database management system from Sybase; or the team may think it worthwhile to outsource the development effort to a consulting firm like Accenture or American Management Systems. Each alternative will have pros and cons associated with it that must be considered, and only one solution can be selected in the end.

Alternative Matrix

An alternative matrix can be used to organize the pros and cons of the design alternatives so that the best solution will be chosen in the end. (See Figure 7-5.) This matrix is created by the same steps as the feasibility analysis, which was presented in Chapter 1. The only difference is that the alternative matrix combines several feasibility analyses into one matrix so that the alternatives can be easily compared. The alternative matrix is a grid that contains the technical, economical, and organizational feasibilities for each system candidate, pros and cons associated with adopting each solution, and other information that is helpful when making comparisons. Sometimes, weights are provided for different parts of the matrix to show when some criteria are more important to the final decision.

To create the alternative matrix, draw a grid with the alternatives across the top and different criteria (e.g., feasibilities, pros, cons, and other miscellaneous criteria) along the side. Next, fill in the grid with detailed descriptions about each

Evaluation Criteria	Relative Importance (Weight)	Alternative 1: Custom Application Using VB.NET	Score (1–5)*	Weighted Score	Alternative 2: Custom Application Using Java	Score (1–5)*	Weighted Score	Alternative 3: Packaged Software Product ABC	Score (1–5)*	Weighted Score
Technical Issues:										
Criterion 1	20		5	100		3	60		3	60
Criterion 2	10		3	30		3	30		5	50
Criterion 3	10		2	20		1	10		3	30
Economic Issues:										
Criterion 4	25	Supporting	3	75	Supporting	3	75	Supporting	5	125
Criterion 5	10	Information	3	30	Information	1	10	Information	5	50
Organizational Issues										
Criterion 6	10		5	50		5	50		3	30
Criterion 7	10		3	30		3	30		1	10
Criterion 8	5		3	15		1	5		1	5
TOTAL	100			350			270			360

* This denotes how well the alternative meets the criteria. 1 = poor fit; 5 = perfect fit.

FIGURE 7-5
Sample Alternative Matrix Using Weights

alternative. This becomes a useful document for discussion because it clearly presents the alternatives being reviewed and comparable characteristics for each one.

Sometimes, weights and scores are added to the alternative matrix to create a weighted alternative matrix that communicates the project's most important criteria and the alternatives that best address them. A scorecard is built by adding a column labeled "weight" that includes a number depicting how much each criterion matters to the final decision. Typically, analysts take 100 points and spread them out across the criteria appropriately. If five criteria were used and all mattered equally, each criterion would receive a weight of 20. However, if cost were the most important criterion for choosing an alternative, it may receive 60 points, and the other four criteria may get only 10 points each.

Then, the analysts add to the matrix a column called "Score" that communicates how well each alternative meets the criteria. Usually, number ranges like 1 to 5 or 1 to 10 are used to rate the appropriateness of the alternatives by the criteria. So, for the cost criterion, the least expensive alternative may receive a 5 on a 1-to-5 scale, whereas a costly alternative would receive a 1. Weighted scores are computed with each criterion's weight multiplied by the score it was given for each alternative. Then, the weighted scores are totaled for each alternative. The highest weighted score achieves the best match for our criteria. When numbers are used in the alternative matrix, project teams can make decisions quantitatively and on the basis of hard numbers.

It should be pointed out, however, that the score assigned to the criteria for each alternative is nothing more than a subjective assignment. Consequently, it is entirely possible for an analyst to skew the analysis according to his or her own biases. In other words, the weighted alternative matrix can be made to support

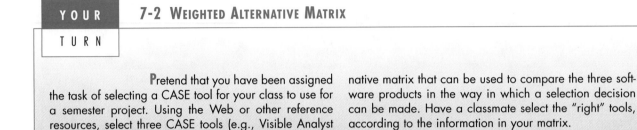

whichever alternative you prefer and yet retains the appearance of an objective, rational analysis. To avoid the problem of a biased analysis, each analyst on the team could develop ratings independently; then, the ratings could be compared and discrepancies resolved in an open team discussion.

The final step, of course, is to decide which solution to design and implement. The approval committee should make the decision after the issues involved with the different alternatives are well understood. Remember that the line between the analysis and design is quite fuzzy. Sometimes alternatives are described and selected at the end of analysis, and sometimes this is done at the beginning of design. The bottom line is that at some point before moving into the heart of the design phase, the project team and the approval committee must understand all of the feasible ways in which the system can be created, and they must select the way that makes the most sense for the organization. The acquisition strategy selection that is made will then drive many of the remaining activities in the design phase.

Applying the Concepts at Tune Source

Jason Wells, senior systems analyst and project manager for Tune Source's Digital Music Download system, had three different approaches that he could take with the new system: He could develop the entire system, using development resources from Tune Source; he could buy a packaged software program (or a set of different pack- ages and integrate them); or he could hire a consulting firm or service provider to create the system. Immediately, Jason ruled out the third option. Building Internet applications, especially e-commerce systems, was becoming increasingly important to the Tune Source business strategy. By outsourcing the Internet system, Tune Source would not develop Internet application development skills and business skills within the organization.

Instead, Jason decided that a custom development project using the com- pany's standard Web development tools would be the best choice for Tune Source. In this way, the company would be developing critical technical and business skills in-house, and the project team would be able to have a high level of flexibility and control over the final product. Also, Jason wanted the new music download system to interface with the existing Internet-based CD sales system, and there was a chance that a packaged solution would not integrate as well into the Tune Source environment. Finally, Jason knew that additional features were planned for sub- sequent versions of this system, so he knew that having control over each version was important.

There was one part of the project that might be handled by packaged software: the purchasing portion of the application. Jason realized that a multitude of programs have been written and are available (at low prices) to handle customer transactions over the Web. These programs, called shopping-cart programs, usually allow customers to select items for an order form, input basic information, and finalize the purchase transaction. Jason believed that the project team should at least consider some of these packaged alternatives so that less time had to be spent writing a program that handled basic Web tasks and more time could be devoted to innovative marketing ideas and custom interfaces with the CD sales system.

To help better understand some of the shopping cart programs that were available in the market and how their adoption could benefit the project, Jason created a weighted alternative matrix that compared three different shopping-cart programs against one another (Figure 7-6). Although all three alternatives had positive points, Jason saw alternative 2 (WebShop) as the best alternative for handling the shopping cart functionality for the new music download system. WebShop was written in Java, the tool that Tune Source selected as its standard Web development language; the expense was reasonable, with no hidden or recurring costs; and there was an in-house person who had some positive experience with the program. Jason made a note to look into acquiring WebShop as the shopping-cart program for the Digital Music Download system.

Evaluation Criteria	Relative Importance (Weight)	Alt 1: Shop With Me	Score (1–5)*	Wtd Score	Alt 2: WebShop	Score (1–5)*	Wtd Score	Alt 3: Shop-N-Go	Score (1–5)*	Wtd Score
Technical Issues:										
Develops desirable in-house skills	15	Developed in C; little interest in developing C skills in-house	1	15	Developed in C and Java; would like to develop in-house Java skills	3	45	Developed in Java; would like to develop in-house Java skills	5	75
Integration with existing systems	15	Orders sent as e-mail files	3	45	Flexible export features for passing order information to other systems	4	60	Orders saved to a number of file formats	5	75
Experience with product	10	None	1	10	Tom in IS Support has had limited, but positive experience with this program.	5	50	None	1	10
Economic Issues:										
Cost	25	$150 initial charge	5	125	$700 initial charge; no yearly fees	4	100	$200 per year fee	3	75
Organizational Issues										
Demonstrated product in market	15	Program used by other retail music companies	5	75	Program used by other retail music companies	5	75	Brand-new product; few companies have experience.	2	30
Customizable interface	20	No	1	20	Yes, easy to do	5	100	Yes, but not easy	3	60
TOTAL	100			290			430			325

* This denotes how well the alternative meets the criteria. 1 = poor fit; 5 = perfect fit.

FIGURE 7-6
Alternative Matrix for Shopping Cart Program

SUMMARY

Transition from Requirements to Design

The design phase is the phase of the SDLC in which the blueprint for the new system is developed, and it contains many steps that guide the project team through planning exactly how the system needs to be constructed. The requirements that were identified in the analysis phase serve as the primary inputs for design activities. The main deliverable from the design phase is the system specification, which includes the physical process and data models, architecture design, hardware and software specifications, interface design, data storage design, and program design.

System Acquisition Strategies

During the design phase, the project team also needs to consider three approaches to creating the new system, including developing a custom application in-house; buying a packaged system and customizing it; and relying on an external vendor, developer, or system provider to build and/or support the system. Custom development allows developers to be flexible and creative in the way they solve business problems, and it builds technical and functional knowledge within the organization. Many companies have a development staff that is already over-committed to filling huge backloads of systems requests, however, and they just don't have time to devote to a project for which a system is built from scratch. It can be much more efficient to buy programs that have been created, tested, and proven; and a packaged system can be bought and installed in a relatively short period of time, when compared with a custom solution. Workarounds can be used to meet the needs that are not addressed by the packaged application. The third design strategy is to outsource the project and pay an external vendor, developer, or service provider to create the system. It can be a good alternative for how to approach the new system; however, it does not come without costs. If a company does decide to leave the creation of a new system in the hands of someone else, the organization could compromise confidential information or lose control over future development.

Influences on Acquisition Strategy

Each of the acquisition strategies just discussed has its strengths and weaknesses, and no one strategy is inherently better than the others. Thus, it is important to consider such issues as the uniqueness of business need for the system, the amount of in-house experience that is available to build the system, and the importance of the project skills to the company. Also, the existence of good project management and the amount of time available to develop the application play a role in the selection process.

Selecting an Acquisition Strategy

Ultimately, the decision must be made regarding the specific acquisition strategy for the system. An alternative matrix can help the design team make this decision by presenting feasibility information for several candidate solutions in a way in which they can be compared easily. The request for proposal, request for information, and request for quote are ways to gather accurate details regarding the alternatives. At this point, the team decides exactly who will perform each part of the design phase and what packages will be used.

KEY TERMS

Alternative matrix
Application service provider (ASP)
Custom development
Design phase
Enterprise resource planning (ERP)
Fixed-price contract

Outsourcing
Packaged software
Request for information (RFI)
Request for proposal (RFP)
Request for quote (RFQ)
System requirement

System specification
Systems integration
Time and arrangements deal
Value-added contract
Weighted alternative matrix
Workaround

QUESTIONS

1. Summarize the distinctions between the analysis phase and the design phase of the SDLC.
2. Describe the primary activities of the design phase of the SDLC.
3. List and describe the contents of the system specification.
4. Describe the three primary strategies that are available to obtain a new system.
5. What circumstances favor the custom design strategy?
6. What circumstances favor the use of packaged software?
7. What circumstances favor using outsourcing to obtain the new system?
8. What are some problems associated with using packaged software? How can these problems be minimized?
9. What is meant by customizing a software package?
10. What is meant by creating a workaround for a software package? What are the disadvantages of workarounds (if any)?
11. What is involved with systems integration? When is it necessary?
12. Describe the role of application service providers (ASPs) in obtaining new systems. What are their advantages and disadvantages?
13. Explain the distinctions between time and arrangements, fixed-price, and value-added outsourcing contracts. What are the pros and cons of each?
14. What is the purpose of a request for proposal (RFP)? How does it differ from the RFI?
15. What information is typically conveyed in an RFP?
16. What is the purpose of the weighted alternative matrix? Describe its typical content.
17. Should the analysis phase be eliminated or reduced when we intend to use a software package instead of custom development or outsourcing?

EXERCISES

A. Assume that you are developing a new system for a local real estate agency. The agency wants to keep a database of its own property listings and also wants to have access to the citywide multiple listings service used by all real estate agents. Which design strategy would you recommend for the construction of this system? Why?
B. Assume that you are developing a new system for a multistate chain of video stores. Each store will run a fairly standardized set of video store processes (cataloging video inventory, customer registration, video rentals, video returns, overdue fees, etc.). In

addition, each store's system will be networked to the corporate offices for sales and expense reporting. Which design strategy would you recommend for the construction of this system? Why?
C. Assume that you are part of a development team that is working on a new warehouse management system. You have the task of investigating software packages that are available through application service providers. Using the World Wide Web, identify at least two potential sources of such software. What are the pros and cons of this approach to obtaining a software package?

D. Assume that you are leading a project that will implement a new course registration system for your university. You are thinking about using either a packaged course registration application or outsourcing the job to an external consultant. Create a request for proposal (RFP) to which interested vendors and consultants could respond.

E. Assume that you and your friends are starting a small business painting houses in the summertime. You need to buy a software package that handles the financial transactions of the business. Create an alternative matrix that compares three packaged systems (e.g., Quicken, Microsoft Money, QuickBooks). Which alternative appears to be the best choice?

MINICASES

1. Susan, president of MOTO, Inc., a human resources management firm, is reflecting on the client management software system her organization purchased four years ago. At that time, the firm had just gone through a major growth spurt, and the mixture of automated and manual procedures that had been used to manage client accounts became unwieldy. Susan and Nancy, her IS department head, researched and selected the package that is currently used. Susan had heard about the software at a professional conference she attended, and at least initially, it worked fairly well for the firm. Some of their procedures had to change to fit the package, but they expected that and were prepared for it.

Since that time, MOTO, Inc. has continued to grow, not only through an expansion of the client base, but through the acquisition of several smaller employment-related businesses. MOTO, Inc. is a much different business than it was four years ago. Along with expanding to offer more diversified human resource management services, the firm's support staff has also expanded. Susan and Nancy are particularly proud of the IS department they have built up over the years. Using strong ties with a local university, an attractive compensation package, and a good working environment, the IS department is well staffed with competent, innovative people, plus a steady stream of college interns keeps the department fresh and lively. One of the IS teams pioneered the use of the Internet to offer MOTO's services to a whole new market segment, an experiment that has proven very successful.

It seems clear that a major change is needed in the client management software, and Susan has already begun to plan financially to undertake such a project. This software is a central part of MOTO's operations, and Susan wants to be sure that a quality system is obtained this time. She knows that the vendor of their current system has made some revisions and additions to its product line. There are also a number of other software vendors who offer products that may be suitable. Some of these vendors did not exist when the purchase was made four years ago. Susan is also considering Nancy's suggestion that the IS department develop a custom software application.

a. Outline the issues that Susan should consider which would support the development of a custom software application in-house.

b. Outline the issues that Susan should consider which would support the purchase of a software package.

c. Within the context of a systems development project, when should the decision of "make-versus-buy" be made? How should Susan proceed? Explain your answer.

DESIGN

☑ **Select Design Strategy**
☐ Design Architecture
☐ Select Hardware and Software
☐ Develop Use Scenarios
☐ Design Interface Structure
☐ Develop Interface Standards
☐ Design Interface Prototype
☐ Evaluate User Interface
☐ Design User Interface
☐ Develop Physical Data Flow Diagrams
☐ Develop Program Structure Charts
☐ Develop Program Specifications
☐ Select Data Storage Format
☐ Develop Physical Entity Relationship Diagram
☐ Denormalize Entity Relationship Diagram
☐ Performance Tune Data Storage
☐ Size Data Storage

T A S K C H E C K L I S T

PLANNING   ANALYSIS   DESIGN

CHAPTER 8

ARCHITECTURE DESIGN

A n important component of the design phase is the architecture design, which describes the system's hardware, software, and network environment. The architecture design flows primarily from the nonfunctional requirements, such as operational, performance, security, cultural, and political requirements. The deliverables from architecture design include the architecture design and the hardware and software specification.

OBJECTIVES

- Understand the fundamental components of an information system.
- Understand server-based, client-based, and client–server architectures.
- Understand how operational, performance, security, cultural, and political requirements affect the architecture design.
- Be familiar with how to create an architecture design.
- Be familiar with how to create a hardware and software specification.

CHAPTER OUTINE

IMPLEMENTATION

INTRODUCTION

In today's environment, most information systems are spread across two or more computers. A Web-based system, for example, will run in the browser on your desktop computer, but will interact with the Web server (and possibly other computers) over the Internet. A system that operates completely inside a company's network may have a Visual Basic program installed on your computer, but interact with a database server elsewhere on the network. Therefore, an important step of the design phase is the creation of the *architecture design*, the plan for how the system will be distributed across the computers and what hardware and software will be used for each computer (e.g., Windows, Linux).

Designing an architecture can be quite difficult, and therefore, many organizations hire expert consultants or assign very experienced analysts to the task.[1] In this chapter, we will examine the key factors in architecture design, but it is important to remember that it takes lots of experience to do it well. The nonfunctional requirements developed early in the analysis phase (see Chapter 3) play a key role in architecture design. These requirements are reexamined and refined into more detailed requirements that influence the system's architecture. In this chapter, we first explain how the designers think about application architectures and describe the three primary architectures: server-based, client-based, and client–server. Then we examine how the very general nonfunctional requirements from the analysis phase are refined into more specific requirements, and the implications that they have for architecture design. Finally, we consider how the requirements and architecture can be used to develop the hardware and software specifications that define exactly what hardware and other software (e.g., database systems) are needed to support the information system being developed.

ELEMENTS OF AN ARCHITECTURE DESIGN

The objective of architecture design is to determine what parts of the application software will be assigned to what hardware. In this section, we first discuss the major architectural elements of the software to understand how the software can be divided into different parts. Then we briefly discuss the major types of hardware onto which the software can be placed. Although there are numerous ways in which the software components can be placed on the hardware components, there are three principal application architectures in use today: server-based architectures, client-based architectures and client–server architectures. The most common architecture is the client–server architecture, so we focus on it here.

Architectural Components

The major *architectural components* of any system are the software and the hardware. The major software components of the system being developed have to be identified and then allocated to the various hardware components on which the system will operate. Each of these components can be combined in a variety of different ways.

---

[1] For more information on architecture design, see the Zachman Institute at www.zifa.com.

All software systems can be divided into four basic *functions*. The first is *data storage*. Most information systems require data to be stored and retrieved, whether a small file, such as a memo produced by a word processor, or a large database, such as one that stores an organization's accounting records. These are the data entities documented in ERDs. The second function is the *data access logic*, the processing required to access data, which often means database queries in Structured Query Language (SQL). The third function is the *application logic*, which is the logic documented in the DFDs, use cases, and functional requirements. The fourth function is the *presentation logic*, the display of information to the user and the acceptance of the user's commands (the user interface). These four functions (data storage, data access logic, application logic, and presentation logic) are the basic building blocks of any information system.

The three primary hardware components of a system are *client computers*, *servers*, and the *network* that connects them. Client computers are the input–output devices employed by the user and are usually desktop or laptop computers, but can also be handheld devices, cell phones, special purpose terminals, and so on. Servers typically are larger computers used to store software and data that can be accessed by anyone who has permission. Servers can come in several "flavors": *mainframes* (very large, powerful computers usually costing millions of dollars), *minicomputers* (large computers costing hundreds of thousands of dollars), and *microcomputers* (small desktop computers like the one you use to ones costing $10,000 or more). The network that connects the computers can vary in speed from slow cell phones or modem connections that must be dialed, to medium-speed always-on frame relay networks, to fast always-on broadband connections such as cable modem, DSL, or T1 circuits, to high-speed always-on Ethernet, T3, or ATM circuits.[2]

Server-Based Architectures

The very first computing architectures were *server based,* with the server (usually, a central mainframe computer) performing all four application functions. The clients (usually, *terminals*) enabled users to send and receive messages to and from the server computer. The clients merely captured keystrokes and sent them to the server for processing, accepting instructions from the server on what to display (Figure 8-1).

This very simple architecture often works very well. Application software is developed and stored on one computer, and all data are on the same computer. There is one point of control because all messages flow through the one central server. The fundamental problem with server-based networks is that the server must process all messages. As the demands for more and more applications grow, many server computers become overloaded and unable to quickly process all the users' demands. Response time becomes slower, and network managers are required to spend increasingly more money to upgrade the server computer. Unfortunately, upgrades come in large increments and are expensive (e.g., $500,000); it is difficult to upgrade "a little."

Client-Based Architectures

With *client-based architectures*, the clients are microcomputers on a local area network, and the server computer is a server on the same network. The application software on the client computers is responsible for the presentation logic,

[2] For more information on networks, see Alan Dennis, *Networking in the Internet Age*, New York: John Wiley & Sons, 2002.

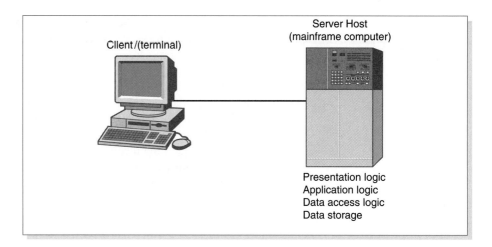

FIGURE 8-1
Server-Based Architecture

the application logic, and the data access logic; the server simply stores the data (Figure 8-2).

This simple architecture often works very well. However, as the demands for more and more network applications grow, the network circuits can become overloaded. The fundamental problem in client-based networks is that all data on the server must travel to the client for processing. For example, suppose that the user wishes to display a list of all employees with company life insurance. All the data in the database must travel from the server, where the database is stored, over the network to the client, which then examines each record to see whether it matches the data requested by the user. This can overload both the network and the power of the client computers.

Client–Server Architectures

Most organizations today are moving to *client–server architectures*, which attempt to balance the processing between the client and the server. In these architectures, the client is responsible for the presentation logic, whereas the server is responsible for the data access logic and data storage. The application logic may either reside on the client, reside on the server, or be split between both (Figure 8-3). If the client shown in Figure 8-3 contains all or most of the application logic, it is referred to as a *thick* or *fat* client. Currently, *thin* clients, containing just a small portion of the

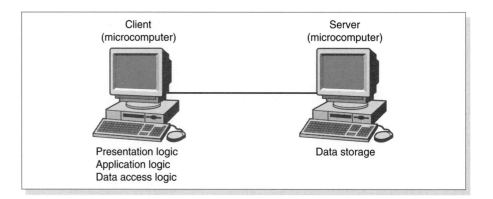

FIGURE 8-2
Client-Based Architecture

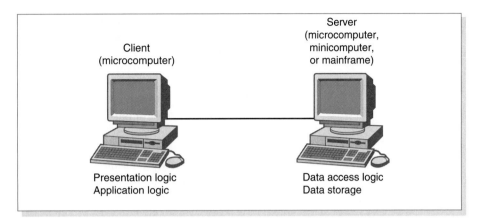

FIGURE 8-3
Client–Server Architecture.   *Source:* Jerry FitzGerald and Alan Dennis, *Business Data Communications and Networking,* 6th ed., p.75. Copyright © 1999 by John Wiley & Sons, Inc. Used with permission.

application logic, are popular because of lower overhead and easier maintenance. For example, many Web-based systems are designed with the Web browser performing presentation and only minimal application logic using such programming languages as JavaScript, while the Web server has most of the application logic, all of the data access logic, and all of the data storage.

Client–server architectures have four important benefits. First and foremost, they are *scalable.* That means it is easy to increase or decrease the storage and processing capabilities of the servers. If one server becomes overloaded, you simply add another server so that many servers are used to perform the application logic, data access logic, or data storage. The cost to upgrade is much more gradual, and you can upgrade in smaller steps (e.g., $5000) rather than spending hundreds of thousands to upgrade a mainframe server.

Second, client–server architectures can support many different types of clients and servers. It is possible to connect computers that use different operating systems so that users can choose which type of computer they prefer (e.g., combining both Windows computers and Apple Macintoshes on the same network). You are not locked into one vendor, as is often the case with server-based networks. *Middleware* is a type of system software designed to translate between different vendors' software. Middleware is installed on both the client computer and the server computer. The client software communicates with the middleware, which can reformat the message into a standard language that can be understood by the middleware, which assists the server software.

Third, for thin client–server architectures that use Internet standards, it is simple to clearly separate the presentation logic, the application logic, and the data access logic and design each to be somewhat independent. For example, the presentation logic can be designed in HTML or XML to specify how the page will appear on the screen (e.g., the colors, fonts, order of items, specific words used, command buttons, type of selection lists, and so on; see Chapter 9). Simple program statements are used to link parts of the interface to specific application logic modules that perform various functions. These HTML or XML files defining the interface can be changed without affecting the application logic. Likewise, it is possible to change the application logic without changing the presentation logic or the data, which are stored in databases and accessed by SQL commands.

Finally, because no single server computer supports all the applications, the network is generally more reliable. There is no central point of failure that will halt the entire network if it fails, as there is with server-based architectures. If any one server fails in a client-server architecture, only the applications requiring that server will fail; the network will continue to function with all the other servers.

Client–server architectures also have some critical limitations, the most important of which is their complexity. All applications in client–server computing have two parts, the software on the client and the software on the server. Writing this software is more complicated than writing the traditional all-in-one software used in server-based architectures. Updating the network with a new version of the software is more complicated, too. In server-based architectures, there is one place in which application software is stored; to update the software, you simply replace it there. With client–server architectures, you must update all clients and all servers.

Much of the debate about server-based versus client–server architectures has centered on cost. Certainly, the dramatic cost decreases and performance increases of microcomputers over the last two decades have made them an important element of today's computer architectures. The *total cost of ownership*, however, comprises factors beyond just the hardware and software costs. For example, many cost comparisons overlook the increased complexity associated with developing application software for client–server networks. Most experts believe that it costs four to five times more to develop and maintain application software for client–server computing than it does for server-based computing.

Client–Server Tiers

There are many ways in which the application logic can be partitioned between the client and the server. The example in Figure 8-3 is one of the most common. In this case, the server is responsible for the data and the client is responsible for the application and presentation. This is called a *two-tiered architecture* because it uses only two sets of computers—clients and servers.

A *three-tiered architecture* uses three sets of computers, as shown in Figure 8-4. In this case, the software on the client computer is responsible for presentation logic, an application server(s) is responsible for the application logic, and a separate database server(s) is responsible for the data access logic and data storage.

An *n-tiered architecture* distributes the work of the application among multiple layers of more specialized server computers. This type of architecture is common in today's Web-based e-commerce systems. See Figure 8-5. The browser software on

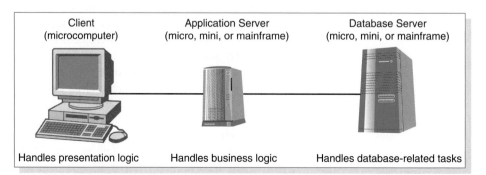

FIGURE 8-4
Three-Tiered Client–Server Architecture

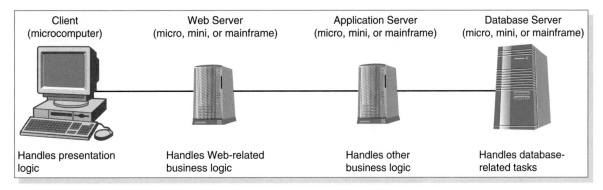

FIGURE 8-5
n-Tiered Client–Server Architecture

client computers makes HTTP requests to view pages from the Web server(s), and the Web server(s) enable the user to view merchandise for sale by responding with HTML documents. As the user shops, components on the application server(s) are called as needed to allow the user to put items in a shopping cart; determine item pricing and availability; compute purchase costs, sales tax, and shipping costs; authorize payments, etc. These elements of business logic, or detailed processing, are stored on the application server(s) and are accessible to any application. For example, the cash register application that requires item price look-ups could use the same price determination business logic used by the e-commerce Web site. The database server(s) manage the data components of the system. Each of these four components is separate, which makes it easy to spread the different components on different servers and to partition the application logic on a Web-oriented server and a business-oriented server.

The primary advantage of an n-tiered client–server architecture compared with a two-tiered architecture (or a three-tiered with a two-tiered) is that it separates out the processing that occurs to better balance the load on the different servers; it is more scalable. In Figure 8-5, we have three separate servers, a configuration that provides more power than if we had used a two-tiered architecture with only one server. If we discover that the application server is too heavily loaded, we can simply replace it with a more powerful server or just put in several more application servers. Conversely, if we discover that the database server is underused, we could store data from another application on it.

There are two primary disadvantages to an n-tiered architecture compared with a two-tiered architecture (or a three-tiered with a two-tiered). First, the configuration puts a greater load on the network. If you compare Figures 8-3, 8-4, and 8-5, you will see that the n-tiered model requires more communication among the servers; it generates more network traffic, so you need a higher-capacity network. Second, it is much more difficult to program and test software in n-tiered architectures than in two-tiered architectures, because more devices have to communicate to complete a user's transaction.

Comparing Architecture Options

Most systems are built to use the existing infrastructure in the organization, so often the current infrastructure restricts the choice of architecture. For example, if the new system will be built for a mainframe-centric organization, server-based

	Server-Based	Client-Based	Client-Server
Cost of infrastructure	Very high	Medium	Low
Cost of development	Medium	Low	High
Difficulty of development	High	Low	Low-medium
Interface capabilities	Low	High	High
Control and security	High	Low	Medium
Scalability	Low	Medium	High

FIGURE 8-6
Characteristics of Computing Architectures

architecture may be the best option. Other factors like corporate standards, existing licensing agreements, and product/vendor relationships also can mandate the project team's architecture choice. Many organizations now have a variety of infrastructures in use, however, or are actively looking for pilot projects to test new architectures and infrastructures, enabling the project team to select an architecture on the basis of other important factors.

Each of the architectures just discussed has its strengths and weaknesses, and no architecture is inherently better than the others. Thus, it is important to understand the strengths and weaknesses of the various computing architectures and when to use each. Figure 8-6 presents a summary of important characteristics of each of the architectural options.

Cost of Infrastructure Client–server architectures are strongly favored on the basis of the cost of infrastructure (the hardware, software, and networks that will support the application system). Since the personal computer of today has such impressive performance capabilities and such low costs, the cost of client–server architectures is low compared with served-based architectures that rely on mainframes. Client–server architectures also tend to be cheaper than client-based architectures because they place less of a load on networks and thus require less network capacity.

Cost of Development Developing applications for client-based architectures is low cost, due to the availability of many *graphical user interface* (*GUI*) development tools for this environment (e.g., Visual Basic, Access). On the other hand, most experts believe that developing and maintaining client–server applications is four to five times more expensive than server-based applications due to their high complexity. This cost differential may change as more companies gain experience with client–server applications, new client–server products are developed and refined, and client–server standards mature. Given the inherent complexity of client–server software, however, and the need to coordinate the interactions of software on different computers, a difference in development cost is likely to remain.

Difficulty of Development The tools used to create mainframe-based systems are often not very user friendly and require specialized skills that are difficult to acquire. Therefore, server-based systems are difficult to develop. By contrast, the GUI development tools used to create applications for the client-based and client-server architectures can be intuitive and easy to use. The development of applications for these architectures can be fast and painless. Keep in mind, however, that client–server architectures do involve the added complexity of several layers of hardware (e.g., database servers, Web servers, client workstations) that must communicate effectively with each other. Project teams often underestimate the difficulty associated with creating secure, efficient client–server applications.

Interface Capabilities   Server-based applications typically present a plain, character-based interface to the user. This interface can be quite powerful for the skilled user, but requires the average user to have significant training in order to use the many commands and codes that are needed to navigate through the system. Today, system users expect a GUI or a Web-based interface incorporating mouse-driven commands and graphical objects (buttons, icons, etc.). GUI and Web development tools are used to create client-based or client-server applications; rarely can server-based environments support these types of applications.

Control and Security   The server-based architecture was originally developed to control and secure data and has the significant advantage of having all the data stored in a single location. In contrast, the tools available for security in client-based systems are minimal. Also, the client-server architecture requires a high degree of coordination among many components, and the chance for security holes or control problems is fairly high. The hardware and software used in client-based and client-server systems are still maturing in terms of security. When an organization has a system that absolutely must be secure (e.g., an application used by the U.S. Department of Defense), then the project team is more likely to accomplish this goal with the server-based architecture option.

Scalability   Scalability refers to the ability to increase or decrease the capacity of the computing infrastructure in response to changing capacity needs. The most scalable architecture is client-server because servers can be added to (or removed from) the infrastructure when processing needs change. Also, the types of hardware that are used in client-server (e.g., minicomputers) typically can be upgraded at a pace that most closely matches the growth of the applications. In contrast, server-based architectures rely primarily on mainframe hardware that must be scaled up in large, expensive increments. Client-based architectures have ceilings above which the application cannot grow, because increases in use and data can result in unacceptable increases in network traffic.

CREATING AN ARCHITECTURE DESIGN

The architecture design specifies the overall architecture and the placement of software and hardware that will be used. Architecture design is very complex process that is often left to experienced architecture designers and consultants, but we will give a sense of the process here.

Each of the computing architectures discussed earlier has its strengths and weaknesses. Most organizations are moving to client–server architectures for cost and scalability reasons, so, in the event that there is no reason other than cost, client–server is generally used today.

Creating an architecture design begins with the nonfunctional requirements. The first step is to refine the nonfunctional requirements into more detailed requirements that are then employed to help select the architecture to be used (server-based, client-based, or client–server) and the software components to be placed on each device. In a client–server architecture, one also has to decide whether to use a two-tier, three-tier, or n-tier architecture. Then the nonfunctional requirements and the architecture design are used to develop the hardware and software specification.

There are four primary types of nonfunctional requirements that can be important in designing the architecture: operational requirements, performance requirements, security requirements, and cultural and political requirements. We describe each in turn and then explain how they may affect the architecture design.

Operational Requirements

Operational requirements specify the operating environment(s) in which the system must perform and how those may change over time. This usually refers to operating systems, system software, and information systems with which the system must interact, but will on occasion also include the physical environment if the environment is important to the application (e.g., in a noisy factory floor where no audible alerts can be heard). Figure 8-7 summarizes four key operational requirement areas and provides some examples of each.

Technical Environment Requirements *Technical environment requirements* specify the type of hardware and software on which the system will work. These requirements usually focus on the operating system software (e.g., Windows, Linux), database

Type of Requirement	Definition	Examples
Technical Environment Requirements	Special hardware, software, and network requirements imposed by business requirements	• The system will work over the Web environment with Internet Explorer. • All office locations will have an always-on network connection to enable real-time database updates. • A version of the system will be provided for customers connecting over the Internet via a small-screen PDA.
System Integration Requirements	The extent to which the system will operate with other systems	• The system must be able to import and export Excel spreadsheets. • The system will read and write to the main inventory database in the inventory system.
Portability Requirements	The extent to which the system will need to operate in other environments	• The system must be able to work with different operating systems (i.e., Linux; Windows Vista). • The system may need to operate with handheld devices such as a Blackberry.
Maintainability Requirements	Expected business changes to which the system should be able to adapt	• The system will be able to support more than one manufacturing plant upon six months advance notice. • New versions of the system will be released every six months.

FIGURE 8-7
Operational Requirements

system software (e.g., Oracle), and other system software (e.g., Internet Explorer). Occasionally, there may be specific hardware requirements that impose important limitations on the system, such as the need to operate on a PDA or cell phone with a very small display.

System Integration Requirements   *System integration requirements* are those that require the system to operate with other information systems, either inside or outside the company. These typically specify interfaces through which data will be exchanged with other systems.

Portability Requirements   Information systems never remain constant. Business needs and operating technologies change, so the information systems that support them and run on them must change, too. *Portability requirements* define how the technical operating environments may evolve over time and how the system must respond (e.g., the system may currently run on Windows XP, but in the future may have to run on Windows Vista and Linux). Portability requirements also refer to potential changes in business requirements that will drive technical-environment changes. For example, in the future, users may want to access a Web site from their cell phones.

Maintainability Requirements   *Maintainability requirements* specify the business requirement changes that can be anticipated. Not all changes are predictable, but some are. For example, suppose that a small company has only one manufacturing plant, but is anticipating the construction of a second plant in the next five years. All information systems must be written to make it easy to track each plant separately, whether for personnel, budgeting, or inventory management. The maintainability requirement attempts to anticipate future requirements so that the systems designed today will be easy to maintain if and when those future requirements appear. Maintainability requirements may also define the update cycle for the system, such as the frequency with which new versions will be released.

Performance Requirements

Performance requirements focus on performance issues such as response time, capacity, and reliability. As analysts define the performance requirements for the system, the testability of those requirements is a key issue. Each requirement must be measurable so that a benchmark comparison can be made. Only in that way can the achievement of a performance requirement be verified. In fact, many systems analysts write a test specification containing a well-defined test for each requirement, at the same time that they create the requirements. Such attention to testability prevents the creation of a poor performance requirement, such as "The system must have a response time fast enough to allow staff to effectively accomplish their work." Figure 8-8 summarizes three key performance requirement areas and provides some examples.

Speed Requirements   *Speed requirements* are exactly what they say: how fast the system must operate. First and foremost, this is the *response time* of the system: How long does it take the system to respond to a user request? While everyone would prefer low response times with the system responding immediately to each user request, this is not practical. We could design such a system, but it would be

Type of Requirement	Definition	Examples
Speed Requirements	The time within which the system must perform its functions	• Response time must be 4 seconds or less for any transaction over the network. • The inventory database must be updated in real time. • Orders will be transmitted to the factory floor every 3 minutes.
Capacity Requirements	The total and peak number of users and the volume of data expected	• There will be a maximum of 2000 simultaneous users at peak use times. • A typical transaction will require the transmission of 300 K of data. • The system will store data on approximately 50,000 customers for a total of about 2 GB of data.
Availability and Reliability Requirements	The extent to which the system will be available to the users and the permissible failure rate due to errors	• The system should be available 24/7, with the exception of scheduled maintenance. • Scheduled maintenance shall not exceed one 6-hour period each month. • The system will have 99% uptime performance.

FIGURE 8-8
Performance Requirements

expensive. Most users understand that certain parts of a system will respond quickly, while others are slower. Those actions that are performed locally on the user's computer must be almost immediate (e.g., typing, dragging and dropping), while others that require communicating across a network can have higher response times (e.g., a Web request). In general, response times less than 7 seconds are considered acceptable when they require communication over a network.

The second aspect of speed requirements is how long it takes transactions in one part of the system to be reflected in other parts. For example, how soon after an order is placed will the items it contains be shown as no longer available for sale to someone else? If the inventory is not updated immediately, then someone else could place an order for the same item, only to find out later that it is out of stock. Or, how soon after an order is placed is it sent to the warehouse to be picked from inventory and shipped? In this case, some time delay might have little impact.

Capacity Requirements   *Capacity requirements* attempt to predict how many users the system will have to support, both in total and simultaneously. Capacity requirements are important in understanding the size of the databases, the processing power needed, and so on. The most important requirement is usually the peak number of simultaneous users, because this has a direct impact on the processing power of the computer(s) needed to support the system.

It is often easier to predict the number of users for internal systems designed to support an organization's own employees than it is to predict the number of users for customer-facing systems, especially those on the Web. How does weather.com estimate the peak number of users who will simultaneously seek weather information? This is as much an art as a science, so the team often provides a range of estimates, with wider ranges used to signal a less accurate estimate.

CONCEPTS

IN ACTION

8-A WHEN PERFORMANCE COUNTS

A global financial services company's new financial system (multi-hundred million dollar program) posed a major challenge in terms of processing performance. Tests of an ERP package resulted in dismal and unacceptable processing performance. (See Concepts in Action 7-A.) The project team determined that custom development was required for a system capable of providing acceptable performance, given the huge transaction volume associated with this system. "Modern" programming languages involve so much resource overhead in the systems developed with them that they were incapable of adequate processing speed. Ultimately, the project team settled on implementation with COBOL and assembly language, with the bulk of the processing being done on IBM z-series mainframe computers. These languages enabled the developers to work much closer to the machine, and they were able to develop systems capable of processing the huge transaction volume very rapidly. Transaction throughput rates for the package were in the range of 50,000 per hour. Throughput for the custom solution came out in the range of 2 million per minute.

Availability and Reliability Requirements *Availability and reliability requirements* focus on the extent to which users can assume that the system will be available for them to use. While some systems are intended to be used just during the 40-hour work week, other systems are designed to be used by people around the world. For such systems, project team members need to consider how the application can be operated, supported, and maintained 24/7 (i.e., 24 hours a day, 7 days a week). This 24/7 requirement means that users may need help or may have questions at any time and a support desk available 8 hours a day will not be sufficient. It is also important to consider what reliability is needed in the system. A system that requires high reliability (e.g., a medical device or telephone switch) needs far greater planning and testing than one that does not have such high reliability needs (e.g., personnel system, Web catalog).

It is more difficult to predict the peaks and valleys in usage of a system with a global audience. Typically, applications are backed up on weekends or late evenings when users are no longer accessing the system. Such maintenance activities will have to be rethought with global initiatives. The development of Web interfaces in particular has escalated the need for 24/7 support; by default, the Web can be accessed by anyone at any time. For example, the developers of a Web application for U.S. outdoor gear and clothing retailer Orvis were surprised when the first order after going live came from Japan.

Security Requirements

Security is the ability to protect the information system from disruption and data loss, whether caused by an intentional act (e.g., a hacker or a terrorist attack) or a random event (e.g., disk failure, tornado).[3] Security is primarily the responsibility of the operations group—the staff responsible for installing and operating security *controls* such as firewalls, intrusion detection systems, and routine backup and recovery operations. Nonetheless, developers of new systems must ensure that the

---

[3] For more information, see Brett C. Tjaden, *Fundamentals of Secure Computer Systems*, Wilsonville, OR: Franklin, Beedle, and Associates, 2004.

8-B THE IMPORTANCE OF CAPACITY PLANNING

At the end of 1997, Oxford Health Plans posted a $120 million loss to its books. The company's unexpected growth was its undoing because the system, which was originally planned to support the company's 217,000 members, had to meet the needs of a membership that exceeded 1.5 million.

System users found that processing a new-member sign-up took 15 minutes instead of the proposed 6 seconds. Also, the computer problems left Oxford unable to send out bills to many of its customer accounts and rendered it unable to track payments to hundreds of doctors and hospitals. In less than a year, uncollected payments from customers tripled to more than $400 million, and the payments owed to caregivers amounted to more than $650 million. Mistakes in infrastructure planning can cost far more than the cost of hardware, software, and network equipment alone.

Source: "Management: How New Technology was Oxford's Nemesis," *The Wall Street Journal*, December 11, 1997, page A.1, by Ron Winslow and George Anders.

QUESTION:
If you had been in charge of the Oxford project, what things would you have considered when planning the system capacity?

system's *security requirements* produce reasonable precautions to prevent problems; system developers are responsible for ensuring security within the information systems themselves.

System developers must know the security standards that are applicable to their organizations. Some industries are subject to various restrictions imposed by law. For example, the Sarbanes–Oxley Act is well known for the responsibilities it places on publicly traded companies to protect their financial systems from fraud and abuse. The Health Insurance Portability and Accountability Act (HIPAA) applies to health-care providers, health insurers, and health information data processors, while the financial industry must conform to the requirements of the Graham–Leach–Bliley (GLB) Act. There are also voluntary security standards that companies may choose to benchmark against, such as the standards adopted by the International Standards Organization (ISO). ISO 17799 is a generally accepted standard for information security, and organizations can become ISO 17799 compliant by engaging an accredited outside auditor to examine their security practices and operations. Retailers will focus on complying with the Payment Card Industry Data Security Standards (PCI DSS), which were established by the major credit card companies to ensure the privacy of stored customer information.

Security is an ever-increasing problem in today's Internet-enabled world. Historically, the greatest security threat has come from inside the organization itself. Ever since the early 1980s when the FBI first began keeping computer crime statistics and security firms began conducting surveys of computer crime, organizational employees have perpetrated the majority of computer crimes.

Although external threats became a more significant problem in the early 2000's, today, surveys show that internal security threats are a bigger problem than external threats. Many organizations are struggling with liability concerns following the theft of confidential records, making hundreds or thousands of employees and customers vulnerable to identify theft.

Developing security requirements usually starts with some assessment of the value of the system and its data. This helps pinpoint extremely important systems so that the operations staff are aware of the risks. Security within systems usually focuses on specifying who can access what data, identifying the need for encryption and authentication, and ensuring that the application prevents the spread of viruses. (See Figure 8-9.)

Adding security requirements to the system obviously adds cost. How much should be spent to ensure security in a system? A good rule of thumb is to estimate the amount of the expected loss and then estimate the probability of that loss occurring. Multiplying these values provides an estimate of how much to spend on security measures. So, a $100,000,000 expected loss with a 10% probability means that $100 million $\times$ 10%, or up to $10 million, should be spent on security.

System Value   The most important computer asset in any organization is not the equipment; it is the organization's data. For example, suppose that someone destroyed a mainframe computer worth $10 million. The mainframe could be replaced simply by buying a new one. It would be expensive, but the problem would be solved in a few weeks. Now suppose that someone destroyed all the student records at your university so that no one knew what courses anyone had taken or their grades. The cost of this destruction would far exceed the cost of replacing a $10 million computer. The lawsuits alone would easily exceed $10 million, and the cost of staff to find and reenter paper records would be enormous and certainly would take more than a few weeks.

In some cases, the information system itself has value that far exceeds the cost of the equipment as well. For example, for an Internet bank that has no brick-and-mortar branches, the Web site is a *mission critical system*. If the Web site crashes, the bank cannot conduct business with its customers. A mission critical application is an information system that is literally critical to the survival of the organization. It is an application that cannot be permitted to fail, and if it does fail, the operations staff drops everything else to fix it. Mission critical applications are usually clearly identified so that their importance is not overlooked.

Type of Requirement	Definition	Examples
System Value Estimates	Estimated business value of the system and its data	• The system is not mission critical, but a system outage is estimated to cost $150,000 per hour in lost revenue. • A complete loss of all system data is estimated to cost $20 million.
Access Control Requirements	Limitations on who can access what data	• Only department managers will be able to change inventory items within their own department. • Telephone operators will be able to read and create items in the customer file, but cannot change or delete items.
Encryption and Authentication Requirements	Defines what data will be encrypted where and whether authentication will be needed for user access	• Data will be encrypted from the user's computer to the Web site to provide secure ordering. • Users logging in from outside the office will be required to authenticate.
Virus Control Requirements	Controls the spread of viruses	• All uploaded files will be checked for viruses before being saved in the system.

FIGURE 8-9
Security Requirements

CONCEPTS 8-C Securing the Environment

IN ACTION

Quinnipiac University is a four-year university in Hamden, Connecticut, with about 7400 students. The IT staff has to support academic functions—but, since the university has residence halls, the IT staff has to be an "Internet service provider" (ISP) for students as well. The IT staff can shape much of the academic usage of the Internet, but students living in residence halls can cause havoc. Students (and faculty) inadvertently open the campus to all kind of attacks from viruses, malware, worms, spybots, and other intruders, as they access various Web sites. A particularly trying time is after the semester break in late January when students return to campus and plug in their laptops that have been corrupted with other viruses from home networks. These viruses try to infect the entire campus.

Quinnipiac University installed an intrusion prevention system (IPS) by Tipping Point Technology in August 2006. On a daily basis, this IPS detects and drops thousands of destructive messages and packets. But the real proof was in late January 2007 when students returned to campus from semester break. In the previous year, the viruses and spyware virtually took the campus network down for three days. But in January 2007, there were no outages and the network remained strong and functioning at full speed. Brian Kelly, Information Security Officer at Quinnipiac University, said, "Without the IPS solution, this campus would have struggled under this barrage of malicious packets and may have shut down. With the IPS system, we were able to function at full speed without any problems."

Questions:
1. What is the value of the network on a college campus? Consider students, faculty, and staff perspectives in your answer.
2. What might be some of the tangible and intangible costs of having the Internet down for three days on a busy college campus?
3. What benefits would an intruction prevention system offer to the end users on campus (e.g., faculty, staff, and students)?

Even temporary disruptions in service can have significant costs. The cost of disruptions to a company's primary Web site or to the LANs and backbones that support telephone sales operations often measures in the millions of dollars. Amazon.com, for example, has average revenues of more than $1.8 million per hour, so if its Web site was unavailable for an hour or two, it would cost them millions of dollars in lost revenue if customers took their business elsewhere. Companies that do less e-business or telephone sales have lower costs, but recent surveys suggest that losses of $100,000 to $200,000 per hour are not uncommon for major customer-facing information systems.

Access Control Requirements Some of the data stored in the system need to be kept confidential; some data need special controls on who is allowed to change or delete them. Personnel records, for example, should be readable only by the personnel department and the employee's supervisor; changes should be permitted to be made only by the personnel department. *Access control requirements* state who can access what data and what type of access is permitted—whether the individual can create, read, update, and/or delete the data. The requirements reduce the chance that an authorized user of the system can perform unauthorized actions.

Encryption and Authentication Requirements One of the best ways to prevent unauthorized access to data is *encryption*, which is a means of disguising information by the use of mathematical algorithms (or formulas). Encryption can be used to protect data stored in databases or data that are in transit over a network from a

CONCEPTS

IN ACTION

8-D POWER OUTAGE COSTS A MILLION DOLLARS

Lithonia Lighting, located just outside of Atlanta, Georgia, is the world's largest manufacturer of light fixtures, with more than $1 billion in annual sales. One afternoon, the power transformer at its corporate headquarters exploded, leaving the entire office complex, including the corporate data center, without power. The data center's backup power system immediately took over and kept critical parts of the data center operational. However, it was insufficient to power all systems, so the system supporting sales for all of Lithonia Lighting's North American agents, dealers, and distributors had to be turned off.

The transformer was quickly replaced and power was restored. However, the 3-hour shutdown of the sales system cost $1 million in potential sales lost. Unfortunately, it is not uncommon for the cost of a disruption to be hundreds or thousands of times the cost of the failed components.

QUESTION:
What would you recommend to avoid similar losses in the future?

database to a computer. There are two fundamentally different types of encryption: symmetric and asymmetric. A *symmetric encryption algorithm* (such as Data Encryption Standard [DES] or Advanced Encryption Standard [AES]) is one in which the key used to encrypt a message is the same as the one used to decrypt it. With symmetric encryption, it is essential to protect the key, and a separate key must be used for each person or organization with whom the system shares information (or else everyone can read all the data).

In an *asymmetric encryption algorithm* (such as *public key encryption*), the key used to encrypt data (called the *public key*) is different from the one used to decrypt it (called the *private key*). Even if everyone knows the public key, once the data are encrypted, they cannot be decrypted without the private key. Public key encryption greatly reduces the key management problem. Each user has a public key that is used to encrypt incoming messages. These public keys are widely publicized (e.g., listed in a telephone book-style directory)—that's why they're called "public" keys. The private key, in contrast, is kept secret (that's why it's called a "private" key).

Public key encryption also permits *authentication* (or digital signatures). When one user sends a message to another, it is difficult to legally prove who actually sent the message. Legal proof is important in many communications, such as bank transfers and buy/sell orders in currency and stock trading, which normally require legal signatures. Public key encryption algorithms are *invertible*, meaning that text encrypted with either key can be decrypted by the other. Normally, we encrypt with the public key and decrypt with the private key. However, it is possible to do the inverse: encrypt with the private key and decrypt with the public key. Since the private key is secret, only the real user could use it to encrypt a message. Thus, a digital signature or authentication sequence is used as a legal signature on many financial transactions. This signature is usually the name of the signing party plus other unique information from the message (e.g., date, time, or dollar amount). This signature and the other information are encrypted by the sender using the private key. The receiver uses the sender's public key to decrypt the signature block and compares the result with the name and other key contents in the rest of the message to ensure a match.

The only problem with this approach lies in ensuring that the person or organization who sent the document with the correct private key is actually the person or organization they claim to be. Anyone can post a public key on the Internet, so there is no way of knowing for sure who they actually are. For example, it would be possible for persons other than "Organization A" in this example to claim to be Organization A when in fact they are an imposter.

This is where the Internet's public key infrastructure (PKI) becomes important.[4] The PKI is a set of hardware, software, organizations, and policies designed to make public key encryption work on the Internet. PKI begins with a *certificate authority* (*CA*), which is a trusted organization that can vouch for the authenticity of the person or organization using authentication (e.g., VeriSign). A person wanting to use a CA registers with the CA and must provide some proof of identity. There are several levels of certification, ranging from a simple confirmation from valid e-mail address to a complete police-style background check with an in-person interview. The CA issues a digital certificate that is the requestor's public key encrypted, using the CA's private key as proof of identify. This certificate is then attached to the user's e-mail or Web transactions, in addition to the authentication information. The receiver then verifies the certificate by decrypting it with the CA's public key—and must also contact the CA to ensure that the user's certificate has not been revoked by the CA.

The *encryption and authentication requirements* state what encryption and authentication requirements are needed for what data. For example, will sensitive data such as customer credit card numbers be stored in the database in encrypted form, or will encryption be used to take orders over the Internet from the company's Web site? Will users be required to use a digital certificate in addition to a standard password?

Virus Control Requirements   The single most common security problem comes from *viruses*. Recent studies have shown that over 50% of organizations suffer a virus infection each year. Viruses cause unwanted events—some harmless (such as nuisance messages), some serious (such as the destruction of data). Any time a system permits data to be imported or uploaded from a user's computer, there is the potential for a virus infection. Many systems require that all information systems permitting the import or upload of user files check those files for viruses before they are stored in the system.

Cultural and Political Requirements

Cultural and political requirements are specific to the countries in which the system will be used. In today's global business environment, organizations are expanding their systems to reach users around the world. Although this can make great business sense, its impact on application development should not be underestimated. Yet another important part of the design of the system's architecture is understanding the global cultural and political requirements for the system; see Figure 8-10.

Multilingual Requirements   The first and most obvious difference between applications used in one region and those designed for global use is language. Global applications often have *multilingual requirements*, which means that they have to

---

[4] For more on the PKI, http://csrc.nist.gov/groups/ST/crypto_apps_infra/pki/index.html.

Type of Requirement	Definition	Examples
Multilingual Requirements	The language in which the system will need to operate	• The system will operate in English, French, and Spanish.
Customization Requirements	Specification of what aspects of the system can be changed by local users	• Country managers will be able to define new fields in the product database in order to capture country-specific information. • Country managers will be able to change the format of the telephone-number field in the customer database.
Making Unstated Norms Explicit	Explicitly stating assumptions that differ from country to country	• All date fields will be explicitly identified as using the month-day-year format. • All weight fields will be explicitly identified as being stated in kilograms.
Legal Requirements	The laws and regulations that impose requirements on the system	• Personal information about customers cannot be transferred out of European Union countries into the United States. • It is against U.S. federal law to divulge information on who rented what videotape, so access to a customer's rental history is permitted only to regional managers.

FIGURE 8-10
Cultural and Political Requirements

support users who speak different languages and write with non-English letters (e.g., those with accents, Cyrillic, Japanese). Even systems used exclusively in the United States, for example, may be used in regions with high populations of non–English-speaking immigrants. One of the most challenging aspects in designing multilingual systems is getting a good translation of the original-language messages into a new language. Words often have similar meanings, but can convey subtly different ideas when they are translated, so it is important to use translators skilled in translating technical words.

The other challenge often is screen space. In general, English-language messages usually take 20%–30% fewer letters than their French or Spanish counterparts. Designing global systems requires allocating more screen space to messages than might be used in the English-language version.

Some systems are designed to handle multiple languages on the fly so that users in different countries can use different languages concurrently; that is, the same system supports several different languages simultaneously (a *concurrent multilingual system*). Other systems contain separate parts that are written in each language and must be reinstalled before a specific language can be used; that is, each language is provided by a different version of the system so that any one installation will use only one language (i.e., a *discrete multilingual system*). Either approach can be effective, but this functionality must be designed into the system well in advance of implementation.

Customization Requirements   For global applications, the project team will need to give some thought to *customization requirements:* How much of the application will be controlled by a central group and how much of the application will be managed locally? For example, some companies allow subsidiaries in some countries to

CONCEPTS   **8-E DEVELOPING MULTILINGUAL SYSTEMS**

IN ACTION

I've had the opportunity to develop two multilingual systems. The first was a special-purpose decision support system to help schedule orders in paper mills called BCW-Trim. The system was installed by several dozen paper mills in Canada and the United States, and it was designed to work in either English or French. All messages were stored in separate files (one set English, one set French), with the program written to use variables initialized either to the English or French text. The appropriate language files were included when the system was compiled to produce either the French or English version.

The second program was a groupware system called GroupSystems, for which I designed several modules. The system has been translated into dozens of different languages, including French, Spanish, Portuguese,

German, Finnish, and Croatian. This system enables the user to switch between languages at will by storing messages in simple text files. This design is far more flexible because each individual installation can revise the messages at will. Without this approach, it is unlikely that there would have been sufficient demand to warrant the development of versions to support less commonly used languages (e.g., Croatian). *Alan Dennis*

QUESTIONS:
1. How would you decide how much to support users who speak languages other than English?
2. Would you create multilingual capabilities for any application that would be available to non-English speaking people? Think about Web sites that exist today.

customize the application by omitting or adding certain features. This decision has trade-offs between flexibility and control because customization often makes it more difficult for the project team to create and maintain the application. It also means that training can differ between different parts of the organization, and customization can create problems when staff move from one location to another.

Unstated Norms   Many countries have *unstated norms* that are not shared internationally. It is important for the application designer to make these assumptions explicit, because they can lead to confusion otherwise. In the United States, the unstated norm for entering a date is the date format MM/DD/YY; however, in Canada and most European countries, the unstated norm is DD/MM/YY. When you are designing global systems, it is critical to recognize these unstated norms and make them explicit so that users in different countries do not become confused. Currency is the other item sometimes overlooked in system design; global application systems must specify the currency in which information is being entered and reported.

Legal Requirements   *Legal requirements* are imposed by laws and government regulations. System developers sometimes forget to think about legal regulations, but unfortunately, ignorance of the law is no defense. For example, in 1997, a French court convicted the Georgia Institute of Technology of violating French language law. Georgia Tech operated a small campus in France that offered summer programs for American students. The information on the campus Web server was primarily in English because classes are conducted in English, which violated the law requiring French to be the predominant language on all Internet servers in France. By formally considering legal regulations, analysts can ensure that they are less likely to be overlooked.

Designing the Architecture

In many cases, the technical environment requirements as driven by the business requirements may simply define the application architecture. In this case, the choice is simple: Business requirements dominate other considerations. For example, the business requirements may specify that the system needs to work over the Web, using the customer's Web browser. In this case, the application architecture must be thin client–server. Such business requirements most likely occur in systems designed to support external customers. Internal systems may also impose business requirements, but usually they are not as restrictive.

In the event that the technical environment requirements do not require the choice of a specific architecture, then the other nonfunctional requirements become important. Even in cases when the business requirements drive the architecture, it is still important to work through and refine the remaining nonfunctional requirements, because they are important in later stages of the design and implementation phases. Figure 8-11 summarizes the relationship between requirements and recommended architectures.

Requirements	Server-Based	Client-Based	Thin Client-Server	Thick Client-Server
Operational Requirements				
System Integration Requirements	✓		✓	✓
Portability Requirements			✓	
Maintainability Requirements	✓		✓	
Performance Requirements				
Speed Requirements			✓	✓
Capacity Requirements			✓	✓
Availability/Reliability Requirements	✓		✓	✓
Security Requirements				
High System Value	✓		✓	
Access Control Requirements	✓			
Encryption/Authentication Requirements			✓	✓
Virus Control Requirements	✓			
Cultural/Political Requirements				
Multilingual Requirements			✓	
Customization Requirements			✓	
Making Unstated Norms Explicit			✓	
Legal Requirements	✓		✓	✓

FIGURE 8-11
Nonfunctional Requirements and Their Implications for Architecture Design

Operational Requirements   System integration requirements may lead to one architecture over another, depending upon the architecture and design of the system(s) with which the system needs to integrate. For example, if the system must integrate with a desktop system (e.g., Excel), then this may suggest a thin or thick client–server architecture, while if it must integrate with a server-based system, then a server-based architecture may be indicated. Systems that have extensive portability requirements tend to be best suited for a thin client–server architecture because it is simpler to write for Web-based standards (e.g., HTML, XML) that extend the reach of the system to other platforms than to write and rewrite extensive presentation logic for different platforms in the server-based, client-based, or thick client–server architectures. Systems with extensive maintainability requirements may not be well suited to client-based or thick client–server architectures because of the need to reinstall software on the desktops.

Performance Requirements   Generally speaking, information systems that have high performance requirements are best suited to client–server architectures. Client–server architectures are more scalable, which means that they respond better to changing capacity needs and thus enable the organization to better tune the hardware to the speed requirements of the system. Client–server architectures that have multiple servers in each tier should be more reliable and have greater availability, because if any one server crashes, requests are simply passed to other servers and users may not even notice (although response time may be worse). In practice, however, reliability and availability depend greatly on the hardware and operating system, and Windows-based computers tend to have lower reliability and availability than Linux or mainframe computers.

Security Requirements   Generally speaking, server-based architectures tend to be more secure because all software is in one location and because mainframe operating systems are more secure than microcomputer operating systems. For this reason, high-value systems are more likely to be found on mainframe computers, even if the mainframe is used as a server in a client–server architecture. In today's Internet-dominated world, authentication and encryption tools for Internet-based client–server architectures are more advanced than those for mainframe-based server-based architectures. Viruses are potential problems in all architectures because they spread easily on desktop computers. If server-based systems can reduce the functions needed on desktop systems, then they may be more secure.

Cultural and Political Requirements   As the cultural and political requirements become more important, the ability to separate the presentation logic from the application logic and the data becomes important. Such separation makes it easier to develop the presentation logic in different languages while keeping the application logic and data the same. It also makes it easier to customize the presentation logic for different users and to change it to better meet cultural norms. To the extent that the presentation logic provides access to the application and data, it also makes it easier to implement different versions that enable or disable different features required by laws and regulations in different countries. This separation is the easiest in thin client–server architectures, so systems with many cultural and political requirements often use thin client–server architectures. As with system integration requirements, the impact of legal requirements depends upon the specific nature of the requirements, but in general, client-based systems tend to be less flexible.

HARDWARE AND SOFTWARE SPECIFICATION

The design phase is also the time to begin selecting and acquiring the hardware and software that will be needed for the future system. In many cases, the new system will simply run on the existing equipment in the organization. Other times, however, new hardware and software (usually, for servers) must be purchased. The *hardware and software specification* is a document that describes what hardware and software are needed to support the application. There are several steps involved in creating the document. Figure 8-12 shows a sample hardware and software specification.

First, you will need to define the software that will run on each component. This usually starts with the operating system (e.g., Windows, Linux) and includes any special purpose software on the client and servers (e.g., Oracle database). Here, you should consider any additional costs such as technical training, maintenance, extended warranties, and licensing agreements (e.g., a site license for a software package). Again, the needs that you list are influenced by decisions that are made in the other design phase activities.

Next, you must create a list of the hardware needed to support the future system. In general, the list can include such things as database servers, network servers, peripheral devices (e.g., printers, scanners), backup devices, storage components, and any other hardware component needed to support an application. At this time, you also should note the quantity of each item that will be needed.

Finally, you need to describe, in as much detail as possible, the minimum requirements for each piece of hardware. Many organizations have standard lists of approved hardware and software that must be used, so, in many cases, this step simply involves selecting items from the lists. Other times, however, the team is operating in new territory and is not constrained by the need to select from an approved list. In these cases, the project team must convey such requirements as the amount of processing capacity, the amount of storage space, and any special features that should be included.

	Standard Client	Standard Web Server	Standard Application Server	Standard Database Server
Operating System	• Windows • Mozilla	• Linux	• Linux	• Linux
Special Software	• Real Audio • Adobe Acrobat Reader	• Apache	• Java	• Oracle
Hardware	• 40-GB disk drive • Dual-core Pentium • 17-inch Monitor	• 80-GB disk drive • Dual-core Xeon	• 80-GB disk drive • Dual-core Xeon	• 250-GB disk drive • RAID • Quad core Xeon
Network	• Always-on Broadband, preferred • Dial-up at 56 Kbps, possible with some performance loss	• Dual 100 Mbps Ethernet	• Dual 100 Mbps Ethernet	• Dual 100 Mbps Ethernet

FIGURE 8-12

Sample Hardware and Software Specification

YOUR

TURN

8-1 University Course Registration System

Think about the course registration system in your university. First, develop a set of nonfunctional requirements as if the system were to be developed today. Consider the operational requirements, perform- ance requirements, security requirements, and cultural and political requirements. Then create an architecture design to satisfy these requirements.

YOUR

TURN

8-2 Global e-Learning System

Many multinational organizations pro- vide global Web-based e-learning courses to their employ- ees. First, develop a set of nonfunctional requirements for such a system. Consider the operational requirements, performance requirements, security requirements, and cultural and political requirements. Then create an archi- tecture design to satisfy these requirements.

This step will become easier for you with experience; however, there are some hints that can help you describe hardware needs (see Figure 8-13). For example, consider the hardware standards within the organization or those recommended by vendors. Talk with experienced system developers or other companies with similar systems. Finally, think about the factors that affect hardware performance, such as the response-time expectations of the users, data volumes, software memory requirements, the number of users accessing the system, the number of external connections, and growth projections.

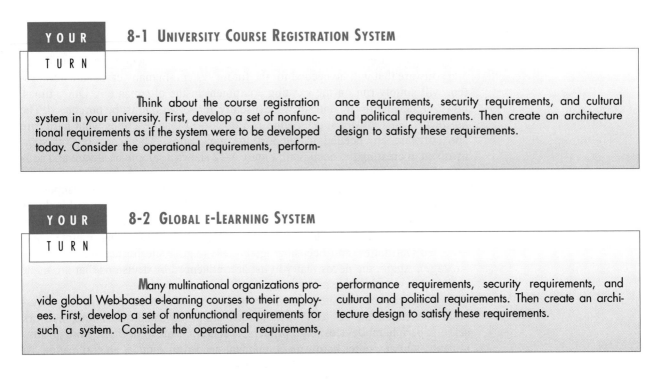

1. **Functions and Features** What specific functions and features are needed (e.g., size of moni- tor, software features)?

2. **Performance** How fast do the hardware and software operate (e.g., processor, number of database writes per second)?

3. **Legacy Databases and Systems** How well do the hardware and software interact with legacy systems (e.g., can it write to this database)?

4. **Hardware and OS Strategy** What are the future migration plans (e.g., the goal is to have all of one vendor's equipment)?

5. **Cost of Ownership** What are the costs beyond purchase (e.g., incremental license costs, annual maintenance, training costs, salary costs)?

6. **Political Preferences** People are creatures of habit and are resistant to change, so changes should be minimized.

7. **Vendor Performance** Some vendors have reputations or future prospects that are different from those of a specific hardware or software system that they currently sell.

FIGURE 8-13
Factors in Hardware and Software Selection

After preparing the hardware and software specification, the project team works with the purchasing department to acquire the hardware and software. The project team prepares an RFP based on legal and organizational policies provided by the purchasing department, which then issues the RFP. The project team then selects the most desirable vendor for the hardware and software on the basis of the proposals received, perhaps using a weighted alternative matrix. On a large project, this evaluation may take months and involves extensive testing and benchmarking of the projects offered by the vendors. The purchasing department is actively involved in the vendor selection, again ensuring that organizational policies are followed. Finally, the purchasing department negotiates final terms with the vendor, issues a contract, and accepts delivery of the items, subject to approval of the project team.

APPLYING THE CONCEPTS AT TUNE SOURCE

Creating an Architecture Design

Jason Wells, senior systems analyst and project manager for Tune Source's Digital Music Download system, realized that the hardware, software, and networks that would support the new application would need to be integrated into the current infrastructure at Tune Source. He began using the high-level nonfunctional requirements developed in the analysis phase (see Figure 3-14 in Chapter 3) and conducted a JAD session and a series of interviews with managers in the marketing department and three store managers in order to refine the nonfunctional requirements into more detail. Figure 8-14 shows some of the results. The clear business need for a Web-based architecture required a thin client–server architecture.

Tune Source had a formal architecture group responsible for managing its architecture and its hardware and software infrastructure. Therefore, Jason set up a meeting with the project team and the architecture group. During the meeting, he confirmed that Tune Source was still moving toward a target client–server architecture,

YOUR | **8-3 UNIVERSITY COURSE REGISTRATION SYSTEM**

TURN

Develop a hardware and software specification for the university course registration system described in "Your Turn 8-1."

YOUR | **8-4 GLOBAL E-LEARNING SYSTEM**

TURN

Develop a hardware and software specification for the global e-learning system described in "Your Turn 8-2."

1. Operational Requirements	
Technical Environment	1.1 The system will work over the Web environment with Mozilla and Real Audio.
	1.2 Customers will need only Mozilla and RA on their desktops.
System Integration	1.3 The Internet system will read information from the main music information database, which contains basic information about tunes (e.g., title, artist, ID number, price). The Internet system will not write information to the main music information database.
	1.4 The Internet system will read and write to the main customer database.
Portability	1.5 The system will need to remain current with evolving Web standards, especially those pertaining to music formats.
Maintainability	1.6 No special maintainability requirements are anticipated.
2. Performance Requirements	
Speed	2.1 Response times must be less than 7 seconds.
	2.2 Download speeds must be maintained above the industry norm.
	2.3 Customers must be able to specify the type of Internet connection used for the download.
Capacity	2.4 There will be a maximum of 100 simultaneous users at peak use times.
	2.5 The system will support streaming audio to up to 50 simultaneous users.
Availability and Reliability	2.6 The system should be available 24/7.
	2.7 The system shall have 99% uptime performance.
3. Security Requirements	
System Value	3.1 No special system value requirements are anticipated.
Access Control	3.2 Customers can access their accounts with username and password.
Encryption/Authentication	3.3 Customer payment information must be transmitted securely.
Virus Control	3.4 Downloads must be verified as virus free.
4. Cultural and Political Requirements	
Multilingual	4.1 No special multilingual requirements are anticipated.
Customization	4.2 No special customization requirements are anticipated.
Unstated Norms	4.3 No special unstated norms requirements are anticipated.
Legal	4.4 No special legal requirements are anticipated.

FIGURE 8-14
Selected Nonfunctional Requirements for Tune Source

although the central mainframe still existed as the primary server for many server-based applications.

They discussed the Digital Music Download system and decided that it should be built according to a three-tier thin client–server architecture. Everyone believed that it was hard to know at this point exactly how much traffic this Web site would get and how much power the system would require, but a client–server architecture would allow Tune Source to easily scale up the system as needed. Customers would use their personal computers running a Web browser as the client. A database server would store the system's databases, whereas an application server would have Web server software and the application software to run the system.

A second two-tier client–server system would enable staff in the marketing department to develop promotional campaign material. This system would have an application for the microcomputers of the staff working in the Internet sales group that would communicate directly with the database server. The database server would have a separate program to enable it to exchange data with Tune Source's Web server and e-mail server.

Given that the Web interface could reach a geographically dispersed group, the project team realized that it needed to plan for 24/7 system support. Jason met with the Tune Source systems operations group and discussed how they might be able to support the system outside of standard working hours.

Hardware and Software Specification

The architecture group and the Internet project team decided that the only components that needed to be acquired for the project were a database server, a Web server, and five new client computers for the marketing group who will create the promotional campaigns. They developed a hardware and software specification for these components, prepared an RFP, and worked with the purchasing department to acquire the hardware and software.

SUMMARY

Application Architectures

All software systems can be divided into four basic functions: data storage, data access logic (e.g., SQL), application logic (which is the logic that is documented in the DFDs, use cases, and functional requirements), and the presentation logic (the user interface). There are three fundamental computing architectures that place these functions on different computers. In server-based architectures, the server performs all the functions. In client-based architectures, the client computers are responsible for presentation logic, application logic, and data access logic, with data stored on a file server. In client–server architectures, the client is responsible for the presentation logic and the server is responsible for the data access logic and data storage. In thin client–server architectures, the server performs the application logic, while in thick client–server architectures, the application logic is shared between the servers and clients. In a two-tiered client–server architecture, there are two groups of computers: one client and a set of servers. In a three-tiered client–server architecture, there are three groups of computers: a client, a set of application servers, and a set of database servers.

Architecture Design

Creating architecture designs begins with the nonfunctional requirements. Operational requirements specify the operating environment(s) in which the system must perform and how those may change over time (i.e., technical environment, system integration, portability, and maintainability). Performance requirements focus on performance issues such as system speed, capacity, and availability and reliability. Security requirements attempt to protect the information system from disruption and data loss (e.g., system value, access control, encryption and authentication, and virus control). Cultural and political requirements are those that are specific to the countries in which the system will be used (e.g., multilingual, customization, unstated norms, and legal).

Hardware and Software Specification

The hardware and software specification is a document that describes what hardware and software are needed to support the application. When a specification document is created, the hardware needed to support the future system is listed and then described in as much detail as possible. Next, the software to run on each hardware component is written down, along with any additional associated costs, such as technical training, maintenance, extended warranties, and licensing agreements. The project team will work in conjunction with the purchasing department to acquire the hardware and software.

KEY TERMS

24/7
Access control requirements
Application logic
Architectural component
Architecture design
Asymmetric encryption algorithm
Authentication
Availability and reliability
  requirements
Capacity requirements
Certificate authority (CA)
Client-based architecture
Client computer
Client–server architecture
Concurrent multilingual system
Control
Cultural and political requirements
Customization requirements
Data access logic
Data storage
Discrete multilingual system
Encryption

Encryption and authentication
  requirements
Fat client
Functions
Graphical user interface (GUI)
Hardware and software
  specification
Legal requirements
Mainframe
Maintainability requirements
Microcomputer
Middleware
Minicomputer
Mission critical system
Multilingual requirements
Network
n-tiered architecture
Operational requirements
Performance requirements
Portability requirements
Presentation logic
Private key

Public key
Public key encryption
Response time
Scalable
Security requirements
Server
Server-based architecture
Speed requirements
Symmetric encryption algorithm
System integration requirements
System value
Technical environment
  requirements
Terminal
Thick client
Thin client
Three-tiered architecture
Total cost of ownership
Two-tiered architecture
Unstated norms
Virus
Virus control requirements

QUESTIONS

1. List and describe the four primary functional components of a software application.
2. List and describe the three primary hardware components of a system.
3. Explain the server-based architecture.
4. Explain the client-based architecture.
5. Explain the client–server architecture.
6. Compare and contrast the server-based, client-based, and client–server architectures.
7. Distinguish between the two-tier, three-tier, and n-tier client–server architectures.
8. What is meant by the term *scalable*? What is its importance in architecture selection?
9. Explain the six criteria that distinguish the computing architecture options.

10. What is meant by total cost of ownership? How does this factor affect the choice of architecture?
11. Describe the types of operational requirements and how they may influence architecture design.
12. Describe the types of performance requirements and how they may influence architecture design.
13. Describe the types of security requirements and how they may influence architecture design.
14. What is meant by system value? Explain how various systems can have a different value to the organization.
15. Explain the difference between a symmetric encryption algorithm and an asymmetric encryption algorithm.
16. What is meant by authentication? What is its role in securing transactions?

17. Describe the usefulness of the Internet's public key infrastructure (PKI).
18. Describe the types of cultural and political requirements and how they may influence architecture design.
19. Explain the difference between concurrent multilingual systems and discrete multilingual systems.
20. Why is it useful to define the nonfunctional requirements in more detail even if the technical environment requirements dictate a specific architecture?
21. What is the purpose of the hardware and software specification?
22. What do you think are three common mistakes that novice analysts make in developing the architecture design and hardware/software specification?
23. Are some nonfunctional requirements more important than others in influencing the architecture design and hardware/software specification?
24. What do you think are the most important security issues for a system?

EXERCISES

A. Using the Web (or past issues of computer industry magazines, such as *Computerworld*), locate a system that runs in a server-based environment. On the basis of your reading, why do you think the company chose that computing environment?

B. Using the Web (or past issues of computer industry magazines, such as *Computerworld*), locate a system that runs in a client–server environment. On the basis of your reading, why do you think the company chose that computing environment?

C. Using the Web, locate examples of a mainframe component, a minicomputer component, and a microcomputer component. Compare the components in terms of price, speed, available memory, and disk storage. Do you find large differences in prices when the performances of the components are considered?

D. You have been selected to find the best client–server computing architecture for a Web-based order entry system that is being developed for L.L. Bean. Write a short memo that describes to the project manager your reason for selecting an n-tiered architecture over a two-tiered architecture. In the memo, give some idea of the different components of the architecture that you would include.

E. Think about the system that your university currently uses for career services and pretend that you are in charge of replacing the system with a new one. Describe how you would decide on the computing architecture for the new system, using the criteria presented in this chapter. What information will you need to find out before you can make an educated comparison of the alternatives?

F. Locate a consumer products company on the Web and read its company description (so that you get a good understanding of the geographic locations of the company). Pretend that the company is about to create a new application to support retail sales over the Web. Create an architecture design that depicts the locations that would include components that support this application.

G. Pretend that your mother is a real estate agent and that she has decided to automate her daily tasks by using a laptop computer. Consider her potential hardware and software needs and create a hardware and software specification that describes them. The specification should be developed to help your mother buy her hardware and software on her own.

H. Pretend that the admissions office in your university has a Web-based application so that students can apply for admission online. Recently, there has been a push to admit more international students into the university. What do you recommend that the application include to ensure that it supports this global requirement?

MINICASES

1. The system development project team at Birdie Masters golf schools has been working on defining the architecture design for a new system. The major focus of the project is a networked school location operations system allowing each school location to easily record and retrieve all school location transaction data. Another system element is the use of the Internet to enable current and prospective students to view class offerings at any of the Birdie Masters' locations, schedule lessons and enroll in classes at any Birdie Masters' location, and maintain a student progress profile—a confidential analysis of the student's golf skill development.

The project team has been considering the globalization issues that should be factored into the architecture design. The school's plan for expansion into the golf-crazed Japanese market is moving ahead. The first Japanese school location is tentatively planned to open about six months after the target completion date for the system project. Therefore, it is important that issues related to the international location be addressed now during design.

Prepare a set of nonfunctional requirements, including operational requirements, performance requirements, security requirements, and cultural and political requirements. Much information is incomplete, but do your best.

2. Jerry is the project manager for a team developing a retail store management system for a chain of sporting goods stores. Company headquarters is in Las Vegas, and the chain has 27 locations throughout Nevada, Utah, and Arizona. Several cities have multiple stores. Stores will be linked to one of three regional servers, and the regional servers will be linked to corporate headquarters in Las Vegas. The regional servers also link to each other. Each retail store will be outfitted with similar configurations of two PC-based point-of-sale terminals networked to a local file server. Jerry has been given the task of developing the architecture design and hardware and software specification for a network model that will document the geographic structure of this system. He has not faced a system of this scope before and is a little unsure of how to begin. What advice would you give?

3. Java Masters is an employment exchange agency that has offices in Northern California. Java Masters operates as a broker that links its client companies with independent software experts (commonly called contractors) with advanced Java and Web-development skills for short-term contracts. They are developing a Web-based system that will enable client companies to list job needs and search the database of independent contractors. The independent contractors also can post résumés and availabilities, and search the database of available jobs. Both contractors and companies pay fees to join the service. Some contractors and companies prefer to remain anonymous until they meet face-to-face. Develop the nonfunctional requirements and architecture design for the system.

PLANNING

ANALYSIS

DESIGN

- ☑ **Select Design Strategy**
- ☑ **Design Architecture**
- ☑ **Select Hardware and Software**
- ☐ Develop Use Scenarios
- ☐ Design Interface Structure
- ☐ Develop Interface Standards
- ☐ Design Interface Prototype
- ☐ Evaluate User Interface
- ☐ Design User Interface
- ☐ Develop Physical Data Flow Diagrams
- ☐ Develop Program Structure Charts
- ☐ Develop Program Specifications
- ☐ Select Data Storage Format
- ☐ Develop Physical Entity Relationship Diagram
- ☐ Denormalize Entity Relationship Diagram
- ☐ Performance Tune Data Storage
- ☐ Size Data Storage

TASK CHECKLIST

PLANNING   ANALYSIS   DESIGN

CHAPTER 9

USER INTERFACE DESIGN

A user interface is the part of the system with which the users interact. It includes the screen displays that provide navigation through the system, the screens and forms that capture data, and the reports that the system produces (whether on paper, on the Web, or via some other media). This chapter introduces the basic principles and processes of interface design and discusses how to design the interface structure and standards.

OBJECTIVES

- Understand several fundamental user interface design principles.
- Understand the process of user interface design.
- Understand how to design the user interface structure.
- Understand how to design the user interface standards.
- Be able to design a user interface.

CHAPTER OUTLINE

IMPLEMENTATION

INTRODUCTION

Interface design is the process of defining how the system will interact with external entities (e.g., customers, suppliers, other systems). In this chapter, we focus on the design of *user interfaces*, but it is also important to remember that sometimes there are *system interfaces* that exchange information with other systems. System interfaces are typically designed as part of a systems integration effort. They are defined in general terms as part of the physical entity relationship diagram (ERD) and in the nonfunctional requirements (operational requirements), and are designed in detail during program design (see Chapter 10) and data storage design (see Chapter 11).

The user interface design defines the way in which the users will interact with the system and the nature of the inputs and outputs that the system accepts and produces. The user interface includes three fundamental parts. The first is the *navigation mechanism*, the way in which the user gives instructions to the system and tells it what to do (e.g., *buttons*, *menus*). The second is the *input mechanism*, the way in which the system captures information (e.g., *forms* for adding new customers). The third is the *output mechanism*, the way in which the system provides information to the user or to other systems (e.g., *reports*, *Web pages*). Each of these is conceptually different, but all are closely intertwined: All computer displays contain navigation mechanisms, and most contain input and output mechanisms. Therefore, navigation design, input design, and output design are tightly coupled.

The study of human-computer *interaction* (HCI) focuses on improving the interactions between users and computers by making computers more usable and receptive to the user's needs. Some organizations employ professional HCI designers, who specialize in applying design processes to the creation of graphical user interfaces and Web interfaces.

This chapter first introduces several fundamental user interface design principles. Second, it provides an overview of the user interface design process. It then provides an overview of the navigation, input, and output components that are used in interface design. This chapter focuses on the design of Web-based interfaces and *graphical user interfaces* (*GUI*) that use windows, menus, icons, and a mouse (e.g., Windows, Macintosh).[1] Although text-based interfaces are still commonly used on mainframes and UNIX systems, GUIs are probably the most common type of interfaces that you will use, with the possible exception of printed reports.[2]

PRINCIPLES FOR USER INTERFACE DESIGN

In many ways, user interface design is an art. The goal is to make the interface pleasing to the eye and simple to use, while minimizing the effort users expend to accomplish their work. The system is never an end in itself; it is merely a means to accomplish the business of the organization.

---

[1] Many people attribute the origin of GUI interfaces to Apple or Microsoft. Some people know that Microsoft copied from Apple, which in turn "borrowed" the whole idea from a system developed at the Xerox Palo Alto Research Center (PARC) in the 1970s. Very few know that the Xerox system was based on one developed by Doug Englebart that was first demonstrated at the Western Computer Conference in 1968. Around the same time, Doug also invented the mouse, desktop videoconferencing, groupware, and a host of other things we now take for granted. Doug is a legend in the computer science community and has won too many awards to count, but is relatively unknown by the general public.

[2] A good book on GUI design is Susan Fowler, *GUI Design Handbook*, New York: McGraw-Hill, 1998.

Principle	Description
Layout	The interface should be a series of areas on the screen that are used consistently for different purposes—for example, a top area for commands and navigation, a middle area for information to be input or output, and a bottom area for status information.
Content awareness	Users should always be aware of where they are in the system and what information is being displayed.
Aesthetics	Interfaces should be functional and inviting to users through careful use of white space, colors, and fonts. There is often a trade-off between including enough white space to make the interface look pleasing and losing so much space that important information does not fit on the screen.
User experience	Although ease of use and ease of learning often lead to similar design decisions, there is sometimes a trade-off between the two. Novice users or infrequent users of software will prefer ease of learning, whereas frequent users will prefer ease of use.
Consistency	Consistency in interface design enables users to predict what will happen before they perform a function. It is one of the most important elements in ease of learning, ease of use, and aesthetics.
Minimize user effort	The interface should be simple to use. Most designers plan on having no more than three mouse clicks from the starting menu until users perform work.

FIGURE 9-1
Principles of User Interface Design

We have found that the greatest problem facing experienced designers is using space effectively. Simply put, there is more information to present than room to present it. Analysts must balance the need for simplicity and pleasant appearance against the need to present the information across multiple pages or screens, which decreases simplicity. In this section, we discuss some fundamental interface design principles, which are common for navigation design, input design, and output design[3] (Figure 9-1).

Layout

The first principle of user interface design deals with the *layout* of the *screen*, *form*, or *report*. Layout refers to organizing areas of the screen or document for different purposes and using those areas consistently throughout the user interface. Most software designed for personal computers follows the standard Windows or Macintosh approach for screen layout. This approach divides the screen into three main areas: The top area provides the user with ways to navigate through the system; the middle (and largest) area is for display of the user's work; and the bottom area contains status information about what the user is doing.

In many cases (particularly on the Web), multiple layout areas are used. Figure 9-2 shows a screen with five navigation areas, each of which is organized to provide different functions and navigation within different parts of the system.

---

[3] Good books on the design of interfaces include Susan Weinschenk, Pamela Jamar, and Sarah Yeo, *GUI Design Essentials*, New York: John Wiley & Sons, 1997; Jenifer Tidwell, *Designing Interfaces,* O'Reilly Media, 2005; Alan Cooper, Robert Reimann, and David Cronin, *About Face 3.0: The Essentials of Interaction Design,* New York: Wiley, 2007.

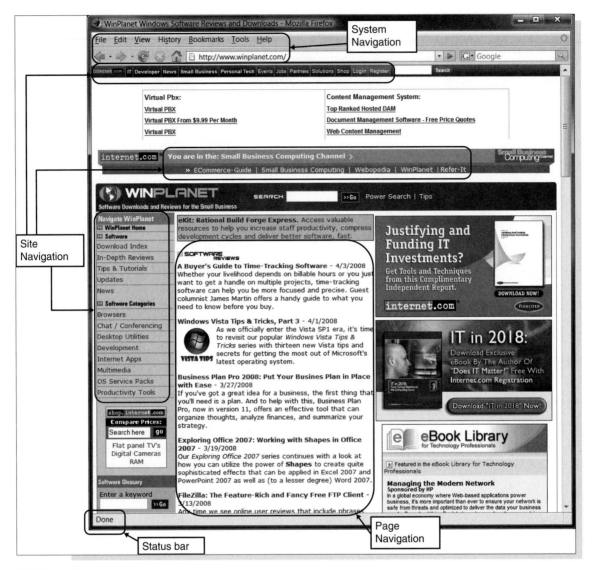

FIGURE 9-2
Web Page Layout with Multiple Navigation Areas

The top area provides the standard web browser navigation and command controls that change the contents of the entire system. The navigation area on the left edge maneuvers between sections and changes all content to its right. The other two section navigation areas at the top and bottom of the page provide other ways to navigate between sections. The content in the middle of the page displays the results (i.e., software review articles) and provides additional navigation within the page about these reviews.

This use of multiple layout areas for navigation also applies to inputs and outputs. Data areas on reports and forms are often subdivided into subareas, each of which is used for different types of information. These areas are almost always rectangular in shape, although sometimes space constraints will require odd shapes. Nonetheless, the margins on the edges of the screen should be consistent. Each of

obvious. Likewise, all printed forms and software should provide version numbers so that users, analysts, and programmers can identify outdated materials.

Figure 9-4, a form from the University of Georgia, illustrates the logical grouping of fields into areas with an explicit box (top left), as well as an implied area with no box (lower left). The address fields within the address area follow a clear, natural order. Field labels are short where possible (see the top left), but long where more information is needed to prevent misinterpretation (see the bottom left).

Aesthetics

Aesthetics refers to designing interfaces that are pleasing to the eye. Interfaces do not have to be works of art, but they do need to be functional and inviting to use. In most cases, "less is more," meaning that a simple, minimalist design is the best.

Space usually is at a premium on forms and reports, and often there is the temptation to squeeze as much information as possible onto a page or a screen. Unfortunately, this can make a form or report so unpleasant that users do not want to complete it. In general, all forms and reports need at least a minimum amount of white space that is intentionally left blank.

What was your first reaction when you looked at Figure 9-4? This is the most unpleasant form at the University of Georgia, according to staff members. Its *density* is too high; it has too much information packed into too small a space with too little white space. Although it may be efficient in saving paper by being one page instead of two, it is not effective for many users.

In general, novice or infrequent users of an interface, whether on a screen or on paper, prefer interfaces with low density, often one with a density of less than 50% (i.e., less than 50% of the interface occupied by information). More experienced users prefer higher densities, sometimes approaching 90% occupied, because they know where information is located and high densities reduce the amount of physical movement through the interface. We suspect that the form in Figure 9-4 was designed for the experienced staff in the personnel office, who use it daily, rather than for the clerical staff in academic departments, who have less personnel experience and use the form only a few times a year.

The design of text is equally important. In general, there should be one font for the entire form or report and no more than two sizes of that font on the form or report. A larger font size may be used for titles, section headings, etc., and a smaller font for the report or form content. If the form or report will be printed, the smaller font should be at least 8 points in size. A minimum of 10 points is preferred if the users will be older people. For forms or reports displayed on the screen, consider a minimum of a 12-point font size if the display monitor is set for a high screen resolution. Italics and underlining should be avoided because they make text harder to read.

Serif fonts (i.e., those having letters with serifs, or "tails," such as Times Roman or the font you are reading right now) are the most readable for printed reports, particularly for small letters. Sans serif fonts (i.e., those without serifs, such as Tahoma or Arial or the ones used for the chapter titles in this book) are the most readable for computer screens and are often used for headings in printed reports. Never use all capital letters, except possibly for titles—all-capitals text "shouts" and is harder to read.

Color and patterns should be used carefully and sparingly and only when they serve a purpose. (About 10% of men are color blind, so the improper use of color

EMPLOYEE PERSONNEL REPORT

UNIVERSITY OF GEORGIA

PAY TYPE

| DOCUMENT NO. | PAGE | DATE | FY | DEPARTMENT PHONE | COLLEGE OR DIVISION |

UGA EMPLOYMENT HISTORY
☐ (C) CURRENT ☐ (P) PREVIOUS
DATE __|__|__

| DEPARTMENT/PROJECT | PRI DEPT | HIGH DEGREE | INSTITUTION | YEAR |

| SOC.SEC.NUM. | LAST NAME | FIRST NAME/INITIAL | MIDDLE INITIAL/NAME | SUF |

☐ (1) REGULAR ☐ (3) TEMPORARY
☐ (2) UGA STUDENT ☐ (4) NR-ALIEN

UGA % TIME | ACTION MO DA YR

| STREET OR ROUTE NO. (LINE 1) | NON-WORK PHONE | BIRTH DATE | SPOUSE'S NAME | CHAIR |

☐ (E) EXEMPT ☐ (N) NON-EXEMPT ☐ (T) TIPPED
☐ (M) MALE ☐ (S) SINGLE ☐ (Y) FACULTY-RANK
☐ (F) FEMALE ☐ (M) MARRIED ☐ (N) NON-FACULTY

| STREET OR ROUTE NO. (LINE 2) | UNIVERSITY PHONE | CITIZEN OF | I-9 VISA COUNTY |

☐ (1) WHITE ☐ (3) ORIENTAL/ASIAN ☐ (5) HISPANIC
☐ (2) BLACK ☐ (4) AMERICAN INDIAN ☐ (6) MULTIRACIAL
☐ (9)

| CITY | STATE | ZIP + 4 | UNIVERSITY BUILDING NAME | BLDG.NO/FLOOR/ROOM |

FOR PAYROLL DEPT USE ONLY

| FED EXM | STATE EXM |

OASDI _____ RETIRE _____ GDCP _____
HI _____ EIC _____

COUNTY MONEY (PER PAY PERIOD)

COOP. EXT. EMPLOYEES ONLY
UGA SALARY _____
COUNTY MONEY _____
TOTAL _____

PAYROLL PAYMENT DISTRIBUTION
☐ (1) SEND TO DEPT (DIST CODE) _____
☐ (2) DIRECT DEPOSIT(SEND PR105 TO PAYROLL
☐ (3) PICK UP AT PAYROLL WINDOW

TRX	HOME DEPT	SHORT TITLE	POSN NO.	APPT. BEGIN MO DA YR HR	APPT. END MO DA YR HR	JOBCLASS CODE	POSITION TITLE	POS % TIME	C N	FULL TIME ANNUAL SALARY	S C	SUPPLEMENT AMOUNT

PAYROLL AUTHORIZATION

TRX	HOME DEPT	SHORT TITLE	POSN NO	ACCOUNT	FISCAL YEAR EFT	BUDGET		MO DA YR HR	MO DA YR HR	MO DA YR HR	MO DA YR HR	MO DA YR HR
							FROM					
							THRU					
							AMOUNT PER PAY PERIOD OR HOURLY RATE					

TOTALS

☐ (A) NEW UGA EMPLOYEE ☐ (B) LATERAL TRANSFER ☐ (C) PROMOTION
☐ (D) REPLACEMENT POSN-NAME OF LAST INCUMBENT _____
☐ (E) APPOINTMENT TO NEW POSITION
☐ (F) CHANGE % TIME EMPLOYED FROM _____ TO _____
☐ (G) CONTINUATION WITHIN EXISTING BUDGET POSITION
☐ (H) REVISE DISTRIBUTION OF SALARY
☐ (I) TRANSFER FROM DEPT _____ TO _____
☐ (J) CHANGE PAY TYPE FROM _____ TO _____

☐ (K) CHANGE TITLE FROM _____ TO _____
☐ (L) CHANGE NAME FROM _____ TO _____
☐ (M) CHANGE SSN FROM _____ TO _____
☐ (N) LEAVE W/O PAY FROM _____ TO _____
☐ (O) CHG COUNTY $ FROM _____ TO _____
☐ (P) TERMINATION-REASON _____
☐ (Q) OTHER (SPECIFY) _____

REMARKS

| DEPARTMENT HEAD | DATE | VICE PRESIDENT | DATE | BUDGET REVIEW | DATE | BUDGET OFFICE | DATE |

FIGURE 9-4
Form Example

can impair their ability to read information.) A quick trip around the Web will demonstrate the problems caused by indiscriminate use of colors and patterns. Remember, the goal is pleasant readability, not art; colors and patterns should be used to strengthen the message, not overwhelm it. Color is best used to separate and categorize items, such as showing the difference between headings and regular text, or to highlight important information. Therefore, colors with high contrast should be used (e.g., black and white). In general, black text on a white background is the most readable, with blue on red the least readable. (Most experts agree that background patterns on Web pages should be avoided.) Color has been shown to affect emotion, with red provoking intense emotion (e.g., anger) and blue provoking lowered emotions (e.g., drowsiness).

User Experience

User experience refers to designing the user interface with the users' level of computer experience in mind. A computer system will be used by people with experience and by people with no experience; the user interface should be designed for both types. Novice users usually are most concerned with *ease of learning*—how quickly and easily they can learn to use the system. Expert users are typically more concerned with *ease of use*—how quickly and easily they can complete a task with the system once they have learned how to use it. Often, these two objectives are complementary and lead to similar design decisions, but sometimes, there are trade-offs. Novices, for example, often prefer menus that show all available system functions, because these promote ease of learning. Experts, on the other hand, sometimes prefer fewer menus that are organized around the most commonly used functions.

Systems that will end up being used by many people on a daily basis are more likely to have a majority of expert users (e.g., order entry systems). Although interfaces should try to balance ease of use and ease of learning, these types of systems should put more emphasis on ease of use rather than on ease of learning. Users should be able to access the commonly employed functions quickly, with few keystrokes or a small number of menu selections.

In many other systems (e.g., decision support systems), most people will remain occasional users for the lifetime of the system. In this case, greater emphasis may be placed on ease of learning rather than on ease of use.

Although ease of use and ease of learning often go hand in hand, sometimes they don't. Research shows that expert and novice users have different requirements and behavior patterns in some cases. For example, novices virtually never look at the bottom area of a screen that presents status information, but experts refer to the status bar when they need information. Most systems should be designed to support frequent users, except for systems that are to be used infrequently or those for which many new users or occasional users are expected (e.g., the Web). Likewise, systems that contain functionality that is used only occasionally must contain a highly intuitive interface, or an interface that contains explicit guidance regarding its use.

The balance between quick access to commonly used and well-known functions and guidance through new and less-well-known functions is challenging to the interface designer, and this balance often requires elegant solutions. Microsoft Office, for example, addresses this issue through the use of the "show me" functions that demonstrate the menus and buttons for specific functions. These features remain in the background until they are needed by novice users (or even experienced users when they use an unfamiliar part of the system).

Consistency

Consistency in design is probably the single most important factor in making a system simple to use, because it enables users to predict what will happen. When interfaces are consistent, users can interact with one part of the system and then know how to interact with the rest—aside, of course, from elements unique to those parts. Consistency usually refers to the interface within one computer system, so that all parts of the same system work in the same way. Ideally, however, the system also should be consistent with other computer systems in the organization and with whatever commercial software is used (e.g., Windows). For example, many users are familiar with the Web, so the use of Web-like interfaces can reduce the amount of learning required by the user. In this way, the user can reuse Web knowledge, thus significantly reducing the learning curve for a new system.

Consistency occurs at many different levels. Consistency in the navigation controls conveys how actions in the system should be performed. For example, using the same icon or command to change an item clearly communicates how changes are made throughout the system. Consistency in terminology is also important. This refers to using the same words for elements on forms and reports (e.g., not "customer" in one place and "client" in another). We also believe that consistency in report and form design is important, although one study suggests that being too consistent can cause problems.[4] When reports and forms are very similar except for minor changes in titles, users sometimes mistakenly use the wrong form and either enter incorrect data or misinterpret its information. The implication for design is to make the reports and forms similar, but give them some distinctive elements (e.g., color, size of titles) that enable users to immediately detect differences.

Minimize User Effort

Finally, interfaces should be designed to minimize the amount of effort needed to accomplish tasks. This means using the fewest possible mouse clicks or keystrokes to move from one part of the system to another. Most interface designers follow the *three-clicks rule*: Users should be able to go from the start or main menu of a system to the information or action they want in no more than three mouse clicks or three keystrokes.

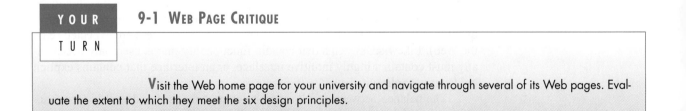

YOUR TURN **9-1 WEB PAGE CRITIQUE**

Visit the Web home page for your university and navigate through several of its Web pages. Evaluate the extent to which they meet the six design principles.

---

[4] John Satzinger and Lorne Olfman, "User Interface Consistency Across End-User Application: The Effects of Mental Models," *Journal of Management Information Systems*, Spring 1998, 14(4): 167–193.

USER INTERFACE DESIGN PROCESS

User interface design[5] is a five-step process that is iterative—analysts often move back and forth between steps rather than proceed sequentially from step 1 to step 5 (Figure 9-5). First, the analysts examine the DFDs and use cases developed in the analysis phase (see Chapters 4 and 5) and interview users to develop *use scenarios* that describe users' commonly employed patterns of actions so that the interface can enable users to quickly and smoothly perform these scenarios. Second, the analysts develop the *interface structure diagram* (*ISD*) that defines the basic structure of the interface. This diagram (or set of diagrams) shows all the interfaces (e.g., screens, forms, and reports) in the system and how they are connected. Third, the analysts design *interface standards*, which are the basic design elements on which interfaces in the system are based. Fourth, the analysts create an *interface design prototype* for each of the individual interfaces in the system, such as navigation controls, input screens, output screens, forms (including preprinted paper forms), and reports. Finally, the individual interfaces are subjected to *interface evaluation* to determine whether they are satisfactory and how they can be improved.

Interface evaluations almost always identify improvements, so the interface design process is repeated in a cyclical process until no new improvements are identified. In practice, most analysts interact closely with the users during the interface design process, so that users have many chances to see the interface as it evolves rather than waiting for one overall interface evaluation at the end of the interface design process. It is better for all concerned (both analysts and users) if

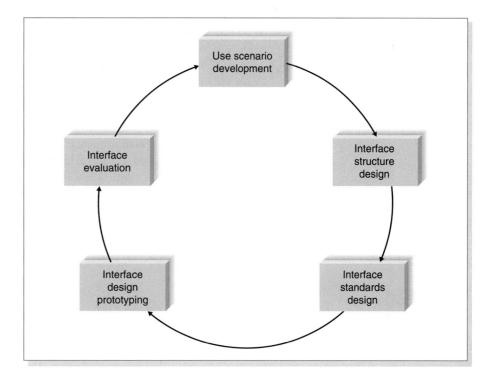

FIGURE 9-5
User Interface Design Process

---

[5] One of the best books on user interface design is Ben Schneiderman, *Designing the User Interface: Strategies for Effective Human-Computer Interaction*, 3d ed., Reading, MA: Addison-Wesley, 1998.

changes are identified sooner rather than later. For example, if the interface structure or standards need improvement, it is better to identify changes before most of the screens that use the standards have been designed.

Use Scenario Development

A *use scenario* is an outline of the steps that the users perform to accomplish some part of their work. A use scenario is one commonly used path through a use case. Recall that use cases and data flow diagrams may include multiple ways in which the response to the event can be completed. For example, think back to the Search and Browse Tunes use case from Figure 4-11 in Chapter 4 that was modeled in a level 1 DFD shown in Figure 5-16 in Chapter 5. This figure shows process 1.2 (Process Search Requests) as being distinct from process 1.3 (Process Tune Selection). We model the two processes separately and write the programs separately because they are separate processes within process 1 (Search and Browse Tunes).

The DFD was designed to model all possible uses of the system—that is, its complete functionality or all possible paths through the use case. But use scenarios are just one path through the use case. In one use scenario, for example, a user will browse through many tunes, much like someone browsing through a real music store looking for interesting music. He or she will search for a tune, listen to a sample, perhaps add it to the shopping cart, browse for more, and so on. Eventually, the user will want to purchase the download(s), perhaps removing some things from the shopping cart beforehand.

In another use scenario, a user will want to buy one specific tune. He or she will go directly to the tune, price it, and buy it immediately, much like someone running into a store, making a beeline for the one item he or she wants, and immediately paying and leaving the store. This user will enter the tune information in the search portion of the system, look at the resulting cost information, and immediately buy the download or leave. Anything that slows him or her down will risk loss of the sale. For this use scenario, we need to ensure that the path through the DFD as presented by the interface is short and simple, with very few menus and mouse clicks.

Use scenarios are presented in a simple narrative description that is tied to the DFD. Figure 9-6 shows the two use scenarios just described. The key point in using use scenarios for interface design is not to document all possible use scenarios within a use case, because then you end up just repeating the DFD in a different form. The goal is to describe the handful of most commonly occurring use scenarios so that the interface can be designed to enable the most common uses to be performed simply and easily.

YOUR   **9-2 USE SCENARIO DEVELOPMENT FOR THE WEB**

TURN

    Visit the Web site for your university and navigate through several of its Web pages. Develop two use scenarios for it.

Use Scenario: The Browsing Shopper
User is not sure what they want to buy and will browse through several tunes.

1. User may search for a specific artist or browse through a music category (1.2).
2. User will likely read the basic information for several tunes, as well as the marketing material for some. He or she will likely listen to music samples and browse related tunes (1.3).
3. User will put the tune in the shopping cart (1.3) and will continue browsing (1.2).
4. Eventually, the user will want to purchase the download, but will probably want to look through the shopping cart, possibly discarding some tunes first (1.3).

Use Scenario: The Hurry-up Shopper
User knows exactly what he or she wants and wants it quickly.

1. User will search for a specific artist or tune (1.2).
2. User will look at the price and enough other information to confirm that the tune is the desired tune (1.3).
3. User will want to buy the download (process 2) or move on to other Web sites.

The numbers in parentheses refer to process numbers in the DFD.

FIGURE 9-6
Two Use Scenarios for the Search and Browse Tunes Use Case

Interface Structure Design

The *interface structure design* defines the basic components of the interface and how they work together to provide functionality to users. An interface structure diagram (ISD) is used to show how all the screens, forms, and reports used by the system are related and how the user moves from one to another. Most systems have several ISDs, one for each major part of the system.

An ISD is somewhat similar to a DFD in that it uses boxes and lines to show structure. However, unlike DFDs, there are no commonly used rules or standards for their development. With one approach, each interface element (e.g., screen, form, report) on an ISD is drawn as a box and is given a unique number (at the top) and a unique name (in the middle). The numbers usually follow a tree-type structure, although this is not always done. Unlike the DFDs, however, the numbers do not mean that all the screens belong to "parents" higher in the tree; instead, they usually imply relationships between a menu and a submenu. The lines denote the ability to navigate from one menu to another.

Each box on the ISD also shows (at the bottom) the DFD process that is supported by the interface (Figure 9-7). Sometimes, there is more than one interface for a given process (e.g., in Figure 9-7, interfaces 1.1 through 1.3 support process 1.1.1); in other cases, there is only one interface for each process (e.g., interfaces 3.1 through 3.3 support processes 1.1.3.1 through 1.1.3.3).

YOUR TURN

9-3 USE SCENARIO DEVELOPMENT FOR AN AUTOMATED TELLER MACHINE

Pretend that you have been charged with the task of redesigning the interface for the ATM at your local bank. Develop two use scenarios for it.

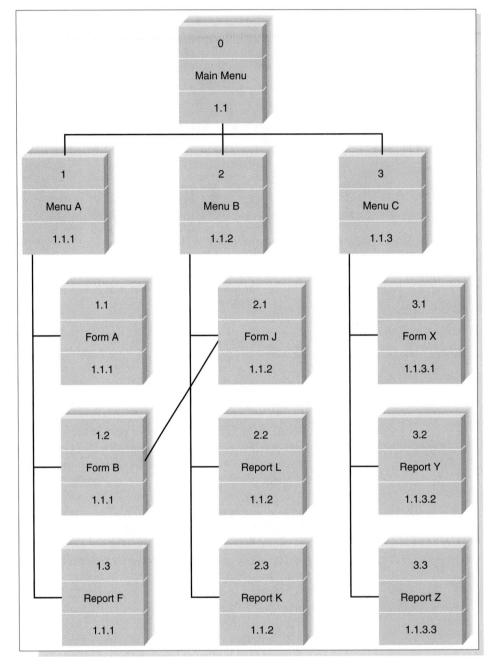

FIGURE 9-7
Example Interface Structure Diagram

Each interface is linked to other interfaces by lines that show how users can transition from one interface to the next. In most cases, the interfaces form a hierarchy, or a tree; but sometimes, an interface is linked to one outside of the hierarchy, as shown by the link from Form J to Form B (e.g., the ability to update a customer address while entering a new order).

The basic structure of the interface follows the basic structure of the business process itself as defined in the process model or object model. The analyst starts with the DFD and develops the fundamental flow of control of the system as it moves from process to process. There are usually several major parts to an information system, each of them distinct, in the same way that there are several high-level processes in a DFD. In general—but not always—there is one ISD for each process on the level 0 DFD.

The analyst then examines the use scenarios to see how well the ISD supports them. Quite often, the use scenarios identify paths through the ISD that are more complicated than they should be. The analyst then reworks the ISD to simplify the ability of the interface to support the use scenarios, sometimes by making major changes to the menu structure, sometimes by adding shortcuts.

Interface Standards Design

The interface standards are the basic design elements that are common across the individual screens, forms, and reports within the system. Depending on the application, there may be several sets of interface standards for different parts of the system (e.g., one for Web screens, one for paper reports, one for input forms). For example, the part of the system used by data-entry operators may mirror other data-entry applications in the company, whereas a Web interface for displaying information from the same system may adhere to some standardized Web format. Likewise, each individual interface may not contain all the elements in the standards (e.g., a report screen may not have an "edit" capability), and they may contain additional characteristics beyond the standard ones, but the standards serve as the touchstone which ensures that the interfaces are consistent across the system.

Interface Metaphor First of all, the analysts must develop the fundamental *interface metaphor*(s) that defines how the interface will work. An interface metaphor is a concept from the real world that is used as a model for the computer system. The metaphor helps the user to understand the system and enables the user to predict what features the interface might provide, even without actually using the system. Sometimes systems have one metaphor, whereas in other cases there are several metaphors in different parts of the system.

In many cases, the metaphor is explicit. Quicken, for example, uses a checkbook metaphor for its interface, even to the point of having the users type information into an on-screen form that looks like a real check. In other cases, the metaphor is implicit, or unstated, but it is there nonetheless. Many Windows systems use the paper form or table as a metaphor.

In some cases, the metaphor is so obvious that it requires no thought. The Tune Source Digital Music Download system, for example, will use the retail music store as the metaphor (e.g., shopping cart). In other cases, a metaphor is hard to identify. In general, it is better not to force a metaphor that really doesn't fit a system, because an ill-fitting metaphor will confuse users by promoting incorrect assumptions.

Interface Templates The *interface template* defines the general appearance of all screens in the information system and the paper-based forms and reports that are

---

YOUR

TURN

9-4 INTERFACE STRUCTURE DESIGN

Pretend that you have been charged with the task of redesigning the interface for the ATM at your local bank. Design an ISD that shows how a user would navigate among the screens.

used. The template design, for example, specifies the basic layout of the screens (e.g., where the navigation area[s], status area, and form/report area[s] will be placed) and the color scheme(s) that will be applied. It defines whether windows will replace one another on the screen or will cascade on top of each other. The template defines a standard placement and order for common interface actions (e.g., "File, Edit, View" rather than "File, View, Edit"). In short, the template draws together the other major interface design elements: metaphors, objects, actions, and icons.

Interface Objects   The template specifies the names that the interface will use for the major *interface objects*, the fundamental building blocks of the system such as the entities and data stores. In many cases, the object names are straightforward, such as calling the shopping cart the "shopping cart." In other cases, it is not simple. For example, Tune Source has chosen to call its digital music downloads "tunes." Some people may refer to individual music selections as "tracks" or "cuts." Obviously, the object names should be easily understood and should help promote the interface metaphor.

In general, in cases of disagreements between the users and the analysts over names, whether for objects or actions (discussed later), the users should win. A more understandable name always beats a more precise or more accurate name.

Interface Actions   The template also specifies the navigation and command language style (e.g., menus) and grammar (e.g., object–action order; see "Navigation Design" later in this chapter). The template gives names to the most commonly used *interface actions* in the navigation design (e.g., "buy" versus "purchase," or "modify" versus "change").

Interface Icons   The interface objects and actions, and also their status (e.g., deleted, overdrawn), may be represented by *interface icons*. Icons are pictures that will appear on command buttons as well as in reports and forms to highlight important information. Icon design is very challenging because it means developing a simple picture less than half the size of a postage stamp that needs to convey an often-complex meaning. The simplest and best approach is to adopt icons developed by others (e.g., a blank page to indicate "create a new file," a diskette to indicate "save"). This has the advantage of quick icon development, and the icons may already be well understood by users because users have seen them in other software.

Commands are actions that are especially difficult to represent with icons because they are in motion, not static. Many icons have become well known from widespread use, but icons are not as well understood as it was at first believed that they would be. The use of icons can sometimes cause more confusion than insight. (For example, did you know that a picture of a sweeping paintbrush in Microsoft Word means "format painter"?) Icon meanings become clearer with use, but because they are often cryptic, many applications now provide text *tool tips* that appear when the pointer hovers over an icon. This feature explains the purpose of the icon in words.

YOUR TURN

9-5 INTERFACE STANDARDS DEVELOPMENT

Pretend that you have been charged with the task of redesigning the interface for the ATM at your local bank. Develop an interface standard that includes metaphors, objects, actions, icons, and a template.

Interface Design Prototyping

An interface design prototype is a mock-up or a simulation of a computer screen, form, or report. A prototype is prepared for each interface in the system to show the users and the programmers how the system will perform. In the "old days," an interface design prototype was usually specified on a paper form that showed what would be displayed on each part of the screen. Paper forms are still used today, but more and more interface design prototypes are being built with computer tools instead of on paper. The three most common approaches to interface design prototyping are storyboarding, HTML prototyping, and language prototyping.

Storyboard At its simplest, an interface design prototype is a paper-based *storyboard*. The storyboard shows hand-drawn pictures of what the screens will look like and how they will flow from one screen to another, in the same way that a storyboard for a cartoon shows how the action will flow from one scene to the next (Fig. 9-8). Storyboards are the simplest technique because all they require is paper (often on a flip chart) and a pen—and someone with some artistic ability.

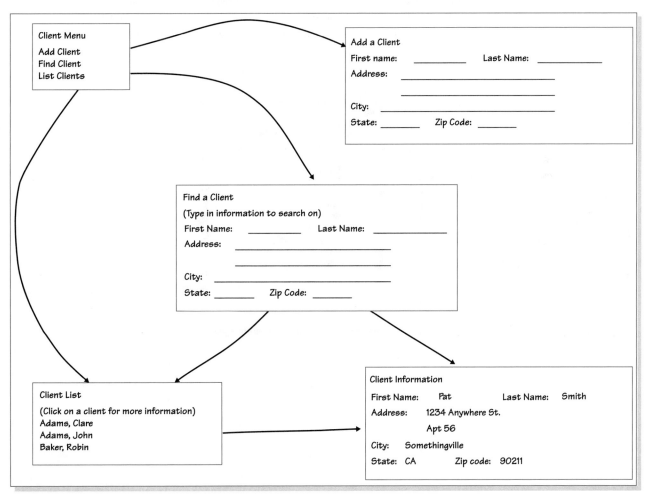

FIGURE 10-8
An Example Storyboard

HTML Prototype One of the most common types of interface design prototypes used today is the *HTML prototype*. As the name suggests, an HTML prototype is built with the use of Web pages created in HTML (hypertext mark-up language). The designer uses HTML to create a series of Web pages that show the fundamental parts of the system. The users can interact with the pages by clicking on buttons and entering pretend data into forms (but because there is no system behind the pages, the data are never processed). The pages are linked together so that, as the user clicks on buttons, the requested part of the system appears. HTML prototypes are superior to storyboards in that they enable users to interact with the system and gain a better sense of how to navigate among the different screens. However, HTML has limitations—the screens shown in HTML will never appear exactly like the real screens in the system (unless, of course, the real system will be a Web system in HTML).

Language Prototype A *language prototype* is an interface design prototype built in the actual language or by the actual tool that will be used to build the system. Language prototypes are designed in the same ways as HTML prototypes. (They enable the user to move from screen to screen, but they perform no real processing). For example, in Visual Basic, it is possible to create and view screens without actually attaching program code to the screens. See Figure 9-9 for a sample Visual Basic Language prototype. Language prototypes take longer to develop

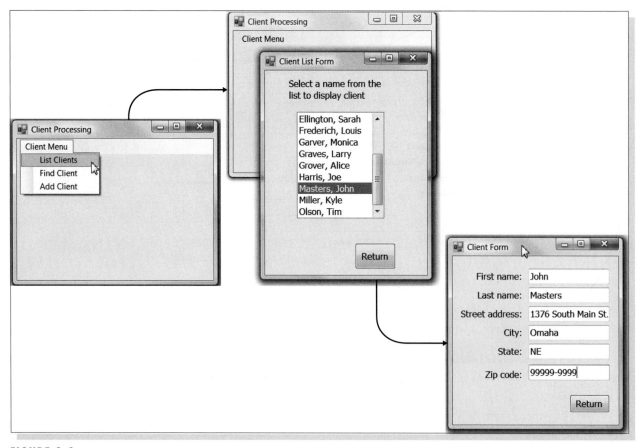

FIGURE 9-9
Sample Language Prototype—Part A

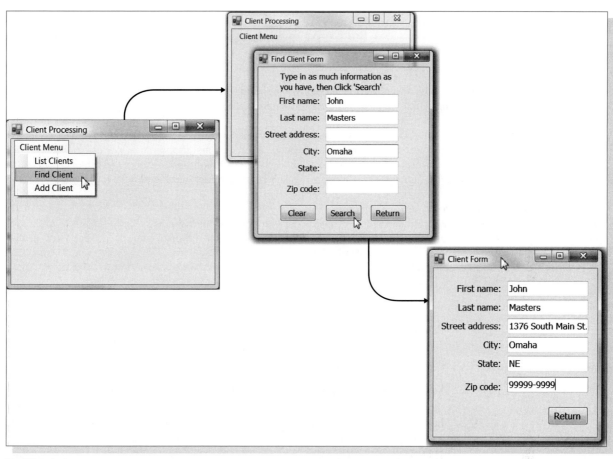

FIGURE 9-9
Sample Language Prototype — Part B

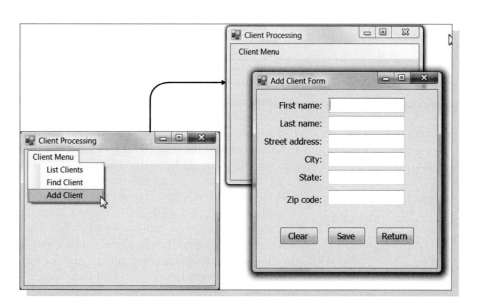

FIGURE 9-9
Sample Language Prototype — Part C

CONCEPTS IN ACTION

9-A INTERFACE DESIGN PROTOTYPES FOR A DSS APPLICATION

I was involved in the development of several decision support systems (DSS) while working as a consultant. On one project, a future user was frustrated because he could not imagine what a DSS looked like and how one would be used. He was a key user, but the project team had a difficult time involving him in the project because of his frustration. The team used SQL Windows (one of the most popular development tools at the time) to create a language prototype that demonstrated the future systems appearance, proposed menu system, and screens (with fields, but no processing).

The team was amazed at the user's response to the prototype. He appreciated being given a context with which to visualize the DSS, and he soon began to recommend improvements to the design and flow of the system, and to identify some important information that was overlooked during the analysis phase. Ultimately, the user became one of the strongest supporters of the system, and the project team felt sure that the prototype led to a much better product in the end. *Barbara Wixom*

QUESTIONS:
1. Why do you think the team chose to use a language prototype rather than a storyboard or HTML prototype?
2. What trade-offs were involved in the decision?

than do storyboards or HTML prototypes, but they have the distinct advantage of showing exactly what the screens will look like. The user does not have to guess about the shape or position of the elements on the screen.

Selecting the Appropriate Techniques   Projects often use a combination of different interface design prototyping techniques for different parts of the system. Storyboarding is the fastest and least expensive, but provides the least amount of detail. Language prototyping is the slowest, most expensive, and most detailed approach. HTML prototyping falls between the two extremes. Therefore, storyboarding is used for parts of the system in which the interface is well understood and when more expensive prototypes are thought to be unnecessary. HTML prototypes and language prototypes are used for parts of the system that are critical, yet not well understood.

Interface Evaluation

The objective of interface evaluation is to understand how to improve the interface design. Interface design is subjective; there are no formulas that guarantee a great user interface. Most interface designers intentionally or unintentionally design an interface that meets their personal preferences, which may or may not match the preferences of the users. The key message, therefore, is to have as many people as possible evaluate the interface—and the more users, the better. Most experts recommend involving at least 10 potential users in the evaluation process.

Many organizations save interface evaluation for the very last step in the SDLC before the system is installed. Ideally, however, interface evaluation should be performed while the system is being designed—before it is built—so that any major design problems can be identified and corrected before the time and cost of programming have been spent on a weak design. It is not uncommon for the system to undergo one or two major changes after the users see the first interface design prototype, because they identify problems that are overlooked by the project team.

As with interface design prototyping, interface evaluation can take many different forms, each with different costs and different levels of detail. Four common approaches are heuristic evaluation, walk-through evaluation, interactive evaluation, and formal usability testing. As with interface design prototyping, the different parts of a system can be evaluated by different techniques.

Heuristic Evaluation   A *heuristic evaluation* examines the interface by comparing it to a set of heuristics, or principles, for interface design. The project team develops a checklist of interface design principles—from the list at the start of this chapter, for example, as well as the lists of principles in the navigation, input, and output design sections. At least three members of the project team then individually work through the interface design prototype, examining each interface to ensure that it satisfies each design principle on the formal checklist. After each member has gone through the prototype separately, they all meet as a team to discuss their evaluation and identify specific improvements that are required. Because this technique does not involve the users, it is considered the weakest type of evaluation.

Walk-through Evaluation   An interface design *walk-through evaluation* is a meeting conducted with the users who will ultimately have to operate the system. The project team presents the prototype to the users and walks them through the various parts of the interface. The project team shows the storyboard or actually demonstrates the HTML or language prototype and explains how the interface will be used. The users identify improvements to each of the interfaces that are presented.

Interactive Evaluation   With an *interactive evaluation*, the users themselves actually work with the HTML or language prototype in one-on-one sessions with members of the project team. (An interactive evaluation cannot be used with a storyboard.) As the user works with the prototype (often by going through the use scenarios or just navigating at will through the system), he or she tells the project team members what he or she likes and doesn't like and what additional information or functionality is needed. As the user interacts with the prototype, team members record the situation when the user appears to be unsure of what to do, makes mistakes, or misinterprets the meaning of an interface component. If the pattern of uncertainty, mistakes, or misinterpretations recurs across several evaluation sessions with several users, it is a clear indication that those parts of the interface need improvement.

Formal Usability Testing   Formal *usability testing* is commonly done with commercial software products and products developed by large organizations that will be widely used through the organization. As the name suggests, it a very formal—almost scientific—process that can be used only with language prototypes (and systems that have been completely built and are awaiting installation or shipping).[6] As with interactive evaluation, usability testing is done in one-on-one sessions in which a user works directly with the software. However, it is typically done in a special lab equipped with video cameras and special software that records each and every keystroke and mouse operation so that they can be replayed to help in understanding exactly what the user did.

---

[6] A good source for usability testing is Jakob Nielsen and Robert Mack, eds. *Usability Inspection Methods*, New York: John Wiley & Sons, 1994. See also www.useit.com/papers.

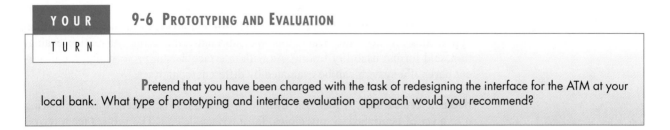

Pretend that you have been charged with the task of redesigning the interface for the ATM at your local bank. What type of prototyping and interface evaluation approach would you recommend?

The user is given a specific set of tasks to accomplish (usually the use scenarios), and after some initial instructions the project teams member(s) are not permitted to interact with the user to provide assistance. The user must work with the software without help, which can be hard on the user if he or she becomes confused with the system. It is critical that users understand that the goal is to test the interface, not their abilities, and if they are unable to complete the task, the interface—not the user—has failed the test. Several performance measures are used, such as time to complete the task, error rate, and user satisfaction.

Formal usability testing is very expensive, because each one-user session (which typically lasts one to two hours) can take one to two days to analyze due to the volume of detail collected in the computer logs and videotapes. Most usability testing involves 5 to 10 users because fewer than 5 users makes the results depend too much on the specific individual users who participated, and more than 10 users is often too expensive to justify (unless you work for a large commercial software developer).

NAVIGATION DESIGN

The navigation component of the interface enables the user to enter commands to navigate through the system and perform actions to enter and review information it contains. The navigation component also presents messages to the user about the success or failure of his or her actions. The goal of the navigation system is to make the system as simple as possible to use. A good navigation component is one that the user never really notices. It simply functions the way the user expects, and thus the user gives it little thought.

Basic Principles

One of the hardest things about using a computer system is learning how to manipulate the navigation controls to make the system do what you want. Analysts usually must assume that users have not read the manual, have not attended training, and do not have external help readily at hand. All controls should be clear and understandable and placed in an intuitive location on the screen. Ideally, the controls should anticipate what the user will do and simplify his or her efforts. For example, many set-up programs are designed so that, for a typical installation, the user can simply keep pressing the "Next" button.

Prevent Mistakes   The first principle of designing navigation controls is to prevent the user from making mistakes. A mistake costs time and creates frustration. Worse still, a series of mistakes can cause the user to discard the system. Mistakes can be reduced by labeling commands and actions appropriately and by limiting choices. Too many choices can confuse the user, particularly when they are similar and hard to describe in the short space available on the screen. When there are many similar choices on a menu, consider creating a second level of menu or a series of options for basic commands.

Never display a command that cannot be used. For example, many Windows applications gray-out commands that cannot be used; they are displayed on pull-down menus in a very light-colored font, but they cannot be selected. This shows that they are available, but that they cannot be used in the current context. It also keeps all menu items in the same place.

When the user is about to perform a critical function that is difficult or impossible to undo (e.g., deleting a file), it is important to confirm the action with the user (and make sure the selection was not made by mistake). This is usually done by having the user respond to a confirmation message that explains what the user has requested and asks the user to confirm that this action is correct.

Simplify Recovery from Mistakes   No matter what the system designer does, users will make mistakes. The system should make it as easy as possible to correct these errors. Ideally, the system will have an "Undo" button that makes mistakes easy to override; however, writing the software for such buttons can be very complicated.

Use Consistent Grammar Order   One of the most fundamental decisions is the *grammar order.* Most commands require the user to specify an object (e.g., file, record, word) and the action to be performed on that object (e.g., copy, delete). The interface can require the user to first choose the object and then the action (an *object–action order*) or first choose the action and then the object (an *action–object order*). Most Windows applications use an object–action grammar order (e.g., think about copying a block of text in your word processor).

The grammar order should be consistent throughout the system, both at the data element level and at the overall menu level. Experts debate about the advantages of one approach over the other, but because most users are familiar with the object–action order, most systems today are designed with that approach.

Types of Navigation Controls

There are two traditional hardware devices that can be used to control the user interface: the keyboard and a pointing device, such as a mouse, trackball, or touch screen. In recent years, voice recognition systems have made an appearance, but they are not yet common. There are three basic software approaches for defining user commands: languages, menus, and direct manipulation.

Languages   With a *command language,* the user enters commands in a special language developed for the computer system (e.g., UNIX and SQL both use command languages). Command languages sometimes provide greater flexibility than do other approaches, because the user can combine language elements in ways not predetermined by developers. However, they put a greater burden on users because users must learn syntax and type commands rather than select from a well-defined, limited number of choices. Systems today use command languages sparingly, except in cases in which there are an extremely large number of command combinations, making it impractical to try to build all combinations into a menu (e.g., SQL queries for databases).

| YOUR | **9-7 DESIGN A NAVIGATION SYSTEM** |
| TURN | |

Design a navigation system for a form into which users must enter information about customers, products, and orders. For all three information categories, users will want to change, delete, find one specific record, and list all records.

Natural language interfaces are designed to understand the user's own language (e.g., English, French, Spanish). These interfaces attempt to interpret what the user means, and often they present back to the user a list of interpretations from which to choose. Many "help" systems today enable the user to ask free-form questions to get help.

Menus The most common type of navigation system today is the menu. A *menu* presents the user with a list of choices, each of which can be selected. Menus are easier to learn than languages because the user sees an organized, but limited, set of choices. Clicking on an item with a pointing device or pressing a key that matches the menu choice (e.g., a function key) takes very little effort. Therefore, menus are usually preferred to languages.

Menus should be designed with care, because the submenus behind a main menu are hidden from users until they click on the menu item. It is better to make menus broad and shallow (i.e., with each menu containing many items and each item containing only one or two layers of menus) rather than narrow and deep (i.e., with each menu containing only a few items, but each item leading to three or more layers of menus). A broad and shallow menu presents the user with the most information initially, so that he or she can see many options, and requires only a few mouse clicks or keystrokes to perform an action. A narrow and deep menu makes users hunt and seek for items hidden behind menu items and requires many more clicks or keystrokes to perform an action.

Research suggests that in an ideal world, any one menu should contain no more than eight items and it should take no more than two mouse clicks or keystrokes from any menu to perform an action (or three from the main menu that starts a system).[7] However, analysts sometimes must break this guideline in the design of complex systems. In this case, menu items are often grouped together and separated by a horizontal line (Fig. 9-10). Often, menu items have *hot keys* that enable experienced users to quickly invoke a command with keystrokes in lieu of a menu choice (e.g., Control-F in Word invokes the Find command, whereas Alt-F opens the File menu).

Menus should put together similar categories of items so that the user can intuitively guess what each menu contains. Most designers recommend grouping menu items by interface objects (e.g., Customers, Purchase Orders, Inventory) rather than by interaction actions (e.g., New, Update, Format), so that all actions pertaining to one object are in one menu, all actions for another object are in a different menu, and so on. However, this is highly dependent on the specific interface. As Figure 9-10 shows, Microsoft Visual Studio groups menu items by interface

---

[7] Kent L. Norman, *The Psychology of Menu Selection*, Norwood, NJ: Ablex Publishing, 1991.

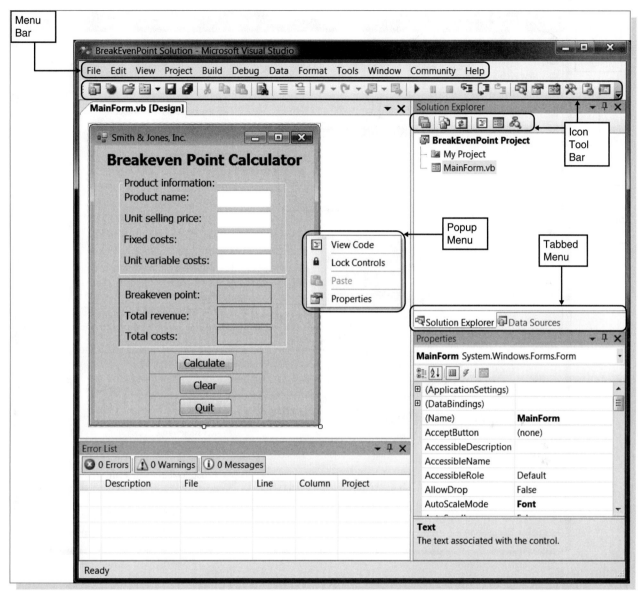

FIGURE 9-10
Common Types of Menus—Part A

objects (e.g., File, Project, Window) *and* by interface actions (e.g., Edit, View, Build) on the same menu. Some of the more common types of menus include *menu bars*, *drop-down menus*, *pop-up menus*, *tab menus*, *tool bars*, and *image maps*. (See Figure 9-11.)

Direct Manipulation   With *direct manipulation*, the user enters commands by working directly with interface objects. For example, users can change the size of objects in Microsoft PowerPoint by clicking on objects and moving the sides, or they can move files in Windows Explorer by dragging the file names from one folder to another. Direct manipulation can be simple, but it suffers from two problems. First,

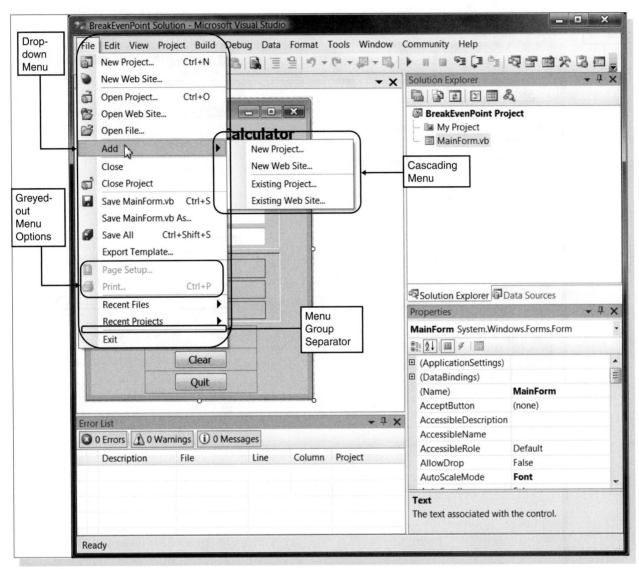

FIGURE 9-10
Common Types of Menus—Part B

users familiar with language- or menu-based interfaces don't always expect it. Second, not all commands are intuitive. (For example, how do you copy [not move] files in Windows Explorer?)

Messages

Messages are the way in which the system responds to a user and informs him or her of the status of the interaction. There are many different types of messages, such as *error messages*, *confirmation messages*, *acknowledgment messages*, *delay messages*, and *help messages* (Figure 9-12). In general, messages should be clear, concise, and complete, which are sometimes conflicting objectives. All messages should be grammatically correct and free of jargon and abbreviations (unless they

Type of Menu	When to Use	Notes
Menu Bar List of commands at the top of the screen. Always on screen.	Main menu for system	• Use the same organization as the operating system and other packages (e.g., File, Edit, View). • Menu items are always one word, never two. • Menu items lead to other menus, rather than performing action. • Never allow users to select actions they can't perform. (Instead, use grayed-out items).
Drop-down Menu Menu that drops down immediately below another menu. Disappears after one use.	Second-level menu, often from menu bar	• Menu items are often multiple words. • Avoid abbreviations. • Menu items perform action or lead to another cascading drop-down menu, pop-up menu, or tab menu.
Hyperlink Menu A set of items arranged as a menu, usually along one edge of the screen.	Main menu for Web-based system	• Most users are familiar with hyperlink menus on the left edge of the screen, although they can be placed along any edge. • Menu items are usually only one or two words.
Embedded Hyperlinks A set of items embedded and underlined in text.	As a link to ancillary, optional information	• Used sparingly to provide additional information, because they can complicate navigation. • Usually open a new window that is closed once the action is complete so that the user can return to the original use scenario.
Pop-up Menu Menu that pops up and floats over the screen. Disappears after one use.	As a shortcut to commands for experienced users	• Often (not always) invoked by a right click in Windows-based systems. • Menu choices vary depending on pointer position. • Often overlooked by novice users, so usually should duplicate functionality provided in other menus.
Tab Menu Multipage menu with one tab for each page that pops up and floats over the screen. Remains on screen until closed.	When user needs to change several settings or perform several related commands	• Menu items should be short to fit on the tab label. • Avoid more than one row of tabs because clicking on a tab to open it can change the order of the tabs, and in virtually no other case does selecting from a menu rearrange the menu itself.
Tool Bar Menu of buttons (often with icons) that remains on the screen until closed.	As a shortcut to commands for experienced users	• All buttons on the same tool bar should be the same size. • If the labels vary dramatically in size, then use two different sizes (small and large). • Buttons with icons should have a tool tip—an area that displays a text phrase explaining the button when the user pauses the pointer over it.
Image Map Graphical image in which certain areas are linked to actions or other menus.	Only when the graphical image adds meaning to the menu	• Image should convey meaning to show which parts perform an action when clicked. • Tool tips can be helpful.

FIGURE 9-11
Types of Menus

are users' jargon and abbreviations). Avoid negatives, because they can be confusing (e.g., replace "Are you sure you do not want to continue?" with "Do you want to quit?"). Likewise, avoid humor, because it wears off quickly after the same message appears dozens of times.

Messages should require the user to acknowledge them (by clicking, for example), rather than being displayed for a few seconds and then disappearing. The exceptions are messages that inform the user of delays in processing, which should disappear once the delay has passed. In general, messages are text, but sometimes standard icons are used. For example, Windows Vista displays a revolving circle when the system is busy.

Type of Messages	When to Use	Notes
Error message Informs the user that he or she has attempted to do something to which the system cannot respond.	When user does something that is not permitted or not possible	Always explain the reason and suggest corrective action. Traditionally, error messages have been accompanied by a beep, but many applications now omit it or permit users to remove it.
Confirmation message Asks the user to confirm that he or she really wants to perform the action selected.	When user selects a potentially dangerous choice, such as deleting a file	Always explain the cause and suggest possible action. Often include several choices other than "OK" and "cancel."
Acknowledgment message Informs the user that the system has accomplished what it was asked to do.	Seldom or never; users quickly become annoyed with all the unnecessary mouse clicks	Acknowledgment messages are typically included because novice users often like to be reassured that an action has taken place. The best approach is to provide acknowledgment information without a separate message on which the user must click. For example, if the user is viewing items in a list and adds one, then the updated list on the screen showing the added item is sufficient acknowledgment.
Delay message Informs the user that the computer system is working properly.	When an activity takes more than seven seconds	This message should permit the user to cancel the operation in case he or she does not want to wait for its completion. The message should provide some indication of how long the delay may last.
Help message Provides additional information about the system and its components.	In all systems	Help information is organized by table of contents and/or keyword search. Context-sensitive help provides information that is dependent on what the user was doing when help was requested. Help messages and online documentation are discussed in Chapter 12.

FIGURE 9-12
Types of Messages

All messages should be carefully crafted, but error messages and help messages require particular care. Messages (and especially error messages) should always explain the problem in polite, succinct terms (e.g., what the user did incorrectly) and explain corrective action as clearly and as explicitly as possible so that the user knows exactly what needs to be done. In the case of complicated errors, the error message should display what the user entered, suggest probable causes for the error, and propose possible user responses. When in doubt, provide either more information than the user needs or the ability to get additional information. Error messages should provide a message number. Message numbers are not intended for users, but their presence makes it simpler for those staffing help desks and customer support lines to identify problems and help users, because many messages use similar wording.

INPUT DESIGN

Input mechanisms facilitate the entry of data into the computer system, whether highly structured data, such as order information (e.g., item numbers, quantities, costs), or unstructured information (e.g., comments). Input design means designing the screens used to enter the information, as well as any forms on which users write or type information (e.g., time cards, expense claims).

Basic Principles

The goal of input design is to capture accurate information for the system simply and easily. The fundamental principles for input design reflect the nature of the inputs (whether batch or online) and ways to simplify their collection.

Use Online and Batch Processing Appropriately   There are two general formats for entering inputs into a computer system: online processing and batch processing. With *online processing* (sometimes called *transaction processing*), each input item (e.g., a customer order, a purchase order) is entered into the system individually, usually at the same time as the event or transaction prompting the input. For example, when you borrow a book from the library, buy an item at the store, or make an airline reservation, the computer system that supports each process uses online processing to immediately record the transaction in the appropriate database(s). Online processing is most commonly used when it is important to have *real-time information* about the business process. For example, when you reserve an airline seat, the seat is no longer available for someone else to use, so that piece of information must be recorded immediately.

With *batch processing*, all the inputs collected over some period are gathered together and entered into the system at one time in a batch. Some business processes naturally generate information in batches. For example, most hourly payrolls are done by batch processing because time cards are gathered together in batches and processed at once. Batch processing also is used for transaction processing systems that do not require real-time information. For example, most stores send sales information to district offices so that new replacement inventory can be ordered. This information could be sent in real time as it is captured in the store, so that the district offices are aware within a second or two that a product is sold. If stores do not need up-to-the-second real-time data, they will collect sales data throughout the day and transmit the data every evening in a batch to the district office. This batching simplifies the data communications process and often cuts communications costs. It does mean, however, that inventories are not accurate in real time, but rather are accurate only at the end of the day after the batch has been processed.

Capture Data at the Source   Perhaps the most important principle of input design is to capture the data in an electronic format at the original source or as close to the original source as possible. In the early days of computing, computer systems replaced traditional manual systems that were based on paper forms. As these business processes were automated, many of the original paper forms remained, either because no one thought to replace them or because it was too expensive to do so. Instead, the business process continued to contain manual forms that were taken to the computer center in batches to be typed into the computer system by a *data-entry operator.*

Many business processes still operate this way today. For example, many organizations have expense claim forms that are completed by hand and submitted to an accounting department, which approves them and enters them into the system in batches. There are three problems with this approach. First, it is expensive because it duplicates work. (The form is filled out twice, once by hand and once by keyboard.) Second, it increases processing time because the paper forms must be physically moved through the process. Third, it increases the cost and the probability of error, because it separates the entry from the processing of information; someone may misread the handwriting on the input form, data could be entered incorrectly, or the original input may contain an error that invalidates the information.

Most transaction processing systems today are designed to capture data at its source. *Source data automation* refers to using special hardware devices to automatically capture data without requiring anyone to type it. Stores commonly use *bar code readers* that automatically scan products and enter data directly into the computer system. No intermediate formats, such as paper forms, are used. Similar technologies include *optical character recognition*, which can read printed numbers and text (e.g., on checks); *magnetic stripe readers*, which can read information encoded on a stripe of magnetic material similar to a diskette (e.g., credit cards); and *smart cards* that contain microprocessors, memory chips, and batteries (much like credit card-size calculators). A recent development is the *RFID* (*radio frequency identification*) *tag*, combining a microprocessor chip with an antenna to broadcast its information to electronic readers. Information can be read from or written to the RFID tag. As well as reducing the time and cost of data entry, these systems reduce errors because they are far less likely to capture data incorrectly. Today, portable computers and scanners allow data to be captured at the source even in mobile settings (e.g., air courier deliveries, use of rental cars).

A lot of information, however, cannot be collected by these automatic systems, so the next-best option is to capture data immediately from the source by using a trained entry operator. Many airline and hotel reservations, loan applications, and catalog orders are recorded directly into a computer system while the customer provides the operator with answers to questions. Some systems eliminate the operator altogether and allow users to enter their own data. For example, many universities no longer accept paper-based applications for admissions; all applications are typed by students into electronic forms.

The forms for capturing information (on a screen, on paper, etc.) should support the data source. That is, the order of the information on the form should match the natural flow of information from the data source, and data-entry forms should match paper forms used to initially capture the data.

Minimize Keystrokes   Another important principle is to minimize keystrokes. Keystrokes cost time and money, whether they are performed by a customer, user, or trained data-entry operator. The system should never ask for information that can be obtained in another way (e.g., by retrieving it from a database or by performing a calculation). Likewise, a system should not require a user to type information that can be selected from a list; selecting reduces errors and speeds entry.

In many cases, data have values that often recur. These frequent values should be used as the *default value* for the data so that the user can simply accept the value and not have to retype it time and time again. Examples of default values are the current date, the area code held by the majority of a company's customers, and a

CONCEPTS

9-B PUBLIC SAFETY DEPENDS ON A GOOD USER INTERFACE

IN ACTION

Police officers in San Jose, California, experienced a number of problems with a new mobile dispatch system that included a Windows-based touch-screen computer in every patrol car. Routine tasks were difficult to perform, and the essential call for asssistance was considered needlessly complicated.

The new system, costing $4.7 million, was an off-the-shelf system purchased from Intergraph Corp. It replaced a 14-year-old text-based system that was custom developed. Initially, the system was unstable, periodically crashing a day or two after installation and down for the next several days.

At the request of the San Jose police union, a user-interface design consulting firm was brought in to evaluate the new system. A number of errors were discovered in the system, including inaccurate map information, screens cluttered with unnecessary information, difficult-to-read on-screen type, and difficult-to-perform basic tasks, such as license plate checks. In addition, the police officers themselves were not consulted about the design of the interface. Many users felt that the Windows desktop GUI with its complex hierarchical menu structure was not suitable for in-vehicle use. While driving, officers found that the repeated taps on the screen required to complete tasks were very distracting, and one officer crashed his vehicle into a parked car because of the distraction of working with the system.

Further complicating the transition to the new system was the bare-bones training program. Just three hours of training were given on a desktop system, using track pads on the keyboards, not the 12-inch touch screen that would be found in the patrol cars.

After the rocky start, the software vendor worked closely with the city of San Jose to fix bugs and smooth out work flows. It seems clear, however, that the rollout could have been much easier if the officers and dispatchers had been involved in planning the system in the first place.

Source: "Wanted by the Police: A Good Interface," *The New York Times*, November 11, 2004, by Katie Hafner.

QUESTION:

If you were involved in the acquisition of a new system for the police force in your community, what steps could you take to ensure the success of the project?

billing address that is based on the customer's residence. Most systems permit changes to default values to handle data entry exceptions as they occur.

Types of Inputs

Each data item that has to be input is linked to a field, on the form into which its value is typed. Each field also has a field label, which is the text beside, above, or below the field, that tells the user what type of information belongs in the field. Often, the field label is similar to the name of the data element, but the two do not have to have identical wording. In some cases, a field will display a template over the entry box to show the user exactly how data should be typed. There are many different types of inputs, in the same way that there are many different types of fields. (See Fig. 9-13.)

Text As the name suggests, a *text box* is used to enter text. Text boxes can be defined to have a fixed length or can be scrollable and accept a virtually unlimited amount of text. In either case, boxes can contain single or multiple lines of textual information. Never use a text box if you can use a selection box.

Text boxes should have field labels placed to the *left* of the entry area, with their size clearly delimited by a box (or a set of underlines in a non-GUI interface). If there are multiple text boxes, their field labels and the left edges of their entry boxes should be aligned. Text boxes should permit standard GUI functions such as cut, copy, and paste.

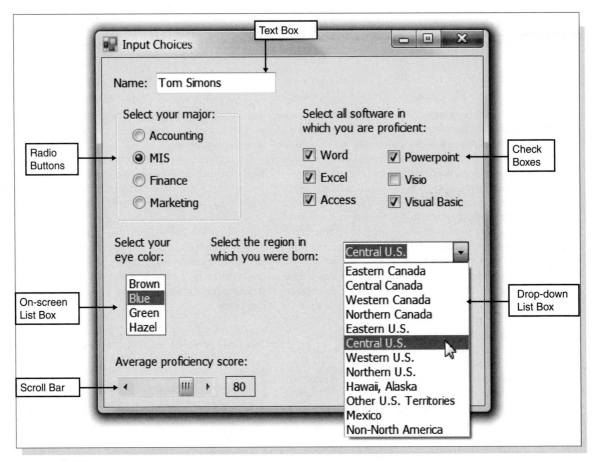

FIGURE 9-13
User Input Options

Numbers   A *number box* is used to enter numbers. Some software can automatically format numbers as they are entered, so that 3452478 becomes $34,524.78. Dates are a special form of numbers that sometimes have their own type of number box. Never use a number box if you can use a selection box.

Selection Box   A *selection box* enables the user to select a value from a predefined list. The items in the list should be arranged in some meaningful order, such as alphabetical for long lists, or in order of most frequently used. The default selection value should be chosen with care. A selection box can be initialized as "unselected" or, better still, start with the most commonly used item already selected.

There are six commonly used types of selection boxes: *check boxes*, *radio buttons*, *on-screen list boxes*, *drop-down list boxes*, *combo boxes*, and *scroll bars* (Figs. 9-13, 9-14). The choice among the types of text selection boxes generally comes down to one of screen space and the number of choices the user can select. If screen space is limited and only one item can be selected, then a drop-down list box is the best choice, because not all list items need to be displayed on the screen. If screen space is limited, but the user can select multiple items, an on-screen list box that displays only a few items can be used. Check boxes (for multiple selections) and radio buttons (for single selections) both require all list items to be displayed at all times, thus requiring more screen space, but since they display all choices, they are often simpler for novice users.

Type of Box	When to Use	Notes
Check box Presents a complete list of choices, each with a square box in front.	When several items can be selected from a list of items	Check boxes are not mutually exclusive. Do not use negatives for box labels. Check-box labels should be placed in some logical order, such as that defined by the business process, or failing that, alphabetically or most commonly used first. Use no more than 10 check boxes for any particular set of options. If you need more boxes, group them into subcategories.
Radio button Presents a complete list of mutually exclusive choices, each with a circle in front.	When only one item can be selected from a set of mutually exclusive items	Use no more than six radio buttons in any one list; if you need more, use a drop-down list box. If there are only two options, one check box is usually preferred to two radio buttons, unless the options are not clear. Avoid placing radio buttons close to check boxes to prevent confusion between different selection lists.
On-screen list box Presents a list of choices in a box.	Seldom or never—only if there is insufficient room for check boxes or radio buttons	This box can permit only one item to be selected (in which case it is an ugly version of radio buttons). This box can also permit many items to be selected (in which case it is an ugly version of check boxes), but users often fail to realize that they can choose multiple items. This box permits the list of items to be scrolled, thus reducing the amount of screen space needed.
Drop-down list box Displays selected item in one-line box that opens to reveal list of choices.	When there is insufficient room to display all choices	This box acts like radio buttons, but is more compact. This box hides choices from users until it is opened, which can decrease ease of use; conversely, because it shelters novice users from seldom-used choices, it can improve ease of use. This box simplifies design if the number of choices is unclear, because it takes only one line when closed.
Combo box A special type of drop-down list box that permits user to type as well as scroll the list.	Shortcut for experienced users	This box acts like a drop-down list, but is faster for experienced users when the list of items is long.
Scroll Bar (Vertical or horizontal) Graphic scale with a sliding pointer to select a number.	When entering an approximate numeric value from a large continuous scale	The slider makes it difficult for the user to select a precise number. Some sliders also include a number box to enable the user to enter a specific number.

FIGURE 9-14
Types of Selection Boxes

Input Validation

All data entered into the system must be validated in order to ensure accuracy. Input *validation* (also called *edit checks*) can take many forms. Ideally, to prevent invalid information from entering the system, computer systems should not accept data that fail any important validation check. However, this can be very difficult, and invalid data often slip by data-entry operators and the users providing the information. It is up the system to identify invalid data and either make changes or notify someone who can resolve the information problem.

There are six different types of validation checks: *completeness check, format check, range check, check digit check, consistency check*, and *database check*. (See Figure 9-15.) Every system should use at least one validation check on all entered data and, ideally, will perform all appropriate checks where possible.

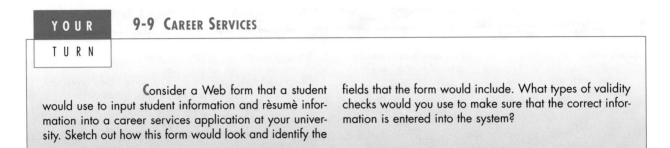

Consider a Web form that a student would use to input student information and rèsumè information into a career services application at your university. Sketch out how this form would look and identify the fields that the form would include. What types of validity checks would you use to make sure that the correct information is entered into the system?

Type of Validation	When to Use	Notes
Completeness check Ensures that all required data have been entered.	When several fields must be entered before the form can be processed	If required information is missing, the form is returned unprocessed to the user.
Format check Ensures that data are of the right type (e.g., numeric) and in the right format (e.g., month, day, year).	When fields are numeric or contain coded data	Ideally, numeric fields should not permit users to type text data, but if this is not possible, the entered data must be checked to ensure that it is numeric. Some fields use special codes or formats (e.g., license plates with three letters and three numbers) that must be checked.
Range check Ensures that numeric data are within correct minimum and maximum values.	With all numeric data, if possible	A range check permits only numbers between correct values. Such a system can also be used to screen data for "reasonableness"—e.g., rejecting birthdates prior to 1890 because people do not live to be a great deal over 100 years old (most likely, *1990* was intended).
Check digit check Check digits are added to numeric codes.	When numeric codes are used	Check digits are numbers added to a code as a way of enabling the system to quickly validate correctness. For example, U.S. Social Security Numbers and Canadian Social Insurance Numbers assign only eight of the nine digits in the number. The ninth number—the check digit—is calculated by a mathematical formula from the first eight numbers. When the identification number is typed into a computer system, the system uses the formula and compares the result with the check digit. If the numbers don't match, then an error has occurred.
Consistency checks Ensure that combinations of data are valid.	When data are related	Data fields are often related. For example, someone's birth year should precede the year in which he or she was married. Although it is impossible for the system to know which data are incorrect, it can report the error to the user for correction.
Database checks Compare data against a database (or file) to ensure that they are correct.	When data are available to be checked	Data are compared against information in a database (or file) to ensure that they are correct. For example, before an identification number is accepted, the database is queried to ensure that the number is valid. Because database checks are more "expensive" than the other types of checks (they require the system to do more work), most systems perform the other checks first and perform database checks only after the data have passed the previous checks.

FIGURE 9-15
Types of Input Validation

OUTPUT DESIGN

Outputs are the reports that the system produces, whether on the screen, on paper, or in other media, such as the Web. Outputs are perhaps the most visible part of any system, because a primary reason for using an information system is to access the information that it produces.

Basic Principles

The goal of the output mechanism is to present information to users so that they can accurately understand it with the least effort. The fundamental principles for output design reflect how the outputs are used and ways to make it simpler for users to understand them.

Understand Report Usage   The first principle in designing reports is to understand how they are used. Reports can be used for many different purposes. In some cases—but not very often—reports are read cover to cover because all information is needed. In most cases, reports are used to identify specific items or are used as references to find information, so the order in which items are sorted on the report or grouped within categories is critical. This is particularly important for the design of electronic or Web-based reports. Web reports that are intended to be read end to end should be presented in one long scrollable page, whereas reports that are primarily used to find specific information should be broken into multiple pages, each with a separate link. Page numbers and the date on which the report was prepared also are important for reference reports.

The frequency of the report may also play an important role in its design and distribution. *Real-time reports* provide data that are accurate to the second or minute at which they were produced (e.g., stock market quotes). *Batch reports* are those that report historical information that may be months, days, or hours old, and they often provide additional information beyond the reported information (e.g., totals, summaries, historical averages).

There are no inherent advantages to real-time reports over batch reports. The only advantages lie in the time value of the information. If the information in a report is time critical (e.g., stock prices, air traffic control information), then real-time reports have value. This is particularly important because real-time reports often are expensive to produce; unless they offer some clear business value, they may not be worth the extra cost.

Manage Information Load   Most managers get too much information, not too little (i.e., the *information load* confronting the manager is too great). The goal of a well-designed report is to provide all the information needed to support the task for which it was designed. This does not mean that the report should provide all the information available on the subject—just what the users decide they need to perform their jobs. In some cases, this may result in the production of several different reports on the same topics for the same users, because they are used in different ways. This is not bad design.

For users in Westernized countries, the most important information generally should be presented first, in the top left corner of the screen or paper report. Information should be provided in a format that is usable without modification. The user should not need to re-sort the report's information, highlight critical information to find it more easily amid a mass of data, or perform additional mathematical calculations.

Minimize Bias   No analyst sets out to design a biased report. The problem with *bias* is that it can be very subtle; analysts can introduce it unintentionally. Bias can be introduced by the way in which lists of data are sorted, because entries that appear first in a list may receive more attention than those appearing later in the list. Data often are sorted in alphabetic order, making those entries starting with the letter A more prominent. Data can be sorted in chronological order (or reverse chronological order), placing more emphasis on older (or most recent) entries. Data may be sorted by numeric value, placing more emphasis on higher or lower values. For example, consider a monthly sales report by state. Should the report be listed in alphabetic order by state name, in descending order by the amount sold, or in some other order (e.g., geographic region)? There are no easy answers to this, except to say that the order of presentation should match the way in which the information is used.

Graphic displays and reports can present particularly challenging design issues.[8] The scale on the axes in graphs is particularly subject to bias. For most types of graphs, the scale should always begin at zero; otherwise, comparisons among values can be misleading. For example, in Fig. 9-16, have sales increased by very much since 2003? The numbers in both charts are the same, but the visual images the two present are quite different. A glance at Fig. 9-16a would suggest only minor changes, whereas a glance at Fig. 9-16b might suggest that there have been some significant increases. In fact, sales have increased by a total of 15% over five years, or 3% per year. Fig. 9-16a presents the most accurate picture; Fig. 9-16b is biased because the scale starts very close to the lowest value in the graph and misleads the eye into inferring that there have been major changes (i.e., more than doubling from "two lines" in 2003 to "five lines" in 2008). Fig. 9-16b is the default graph produced by Microsoft Excel, so be aware of how easy it is to unintentionally introduce bias in graphs.

Types of Outputs

There are many different types of reports, such as *detail reports*, *summary reports*, *exception reports*, *turnaround documents*, and *graphs* (Fig. 9-17). Classifying reports is challenging because many reports have characteristics of several different types. For example, some detail reports also produce summary totals, making them summary reports.

**YOUR
TURN**

9-10 FINDING BIAS

Read through recent copies of a newspaper or popular press magazine such as *Time*, *Newsweek*, or *BusinessWeek* and find four graphs. How many are biased and how many are unbiased?

---

[8] Some of the best books on the design of charts and graphical displays are by Edward R. Tufte, *The Visual Display of Quantitative Information* (2001), *Envisioning Information* (1990), and *Visual Explanations* (1997), Cheshire, CT: Graphics Press. Another good book is by William Cleveland, *Visualizing Data*, Summit, NJ: Hobart Press, 1993.

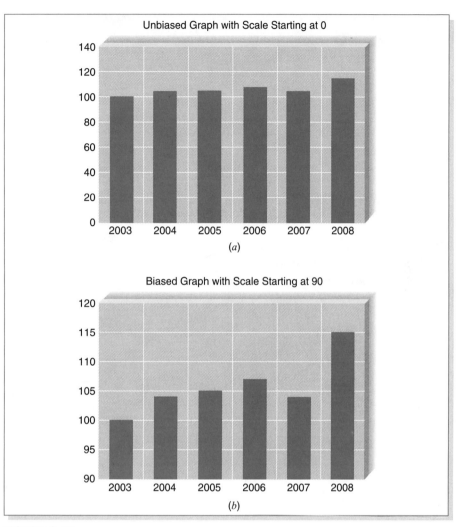

FIGURE 9-16
Bias in Graphs: (a) Unbiased Graph with Scale Starting at 0; (b) Biased Graph with Scale Starting at 90.

Media

There are many different types of media used to produce reports. The two dominant media today are paper and electronic. Paper is the more traditional medium and is relatively permanent, easy to use, and accessible in most situations. It also is highly portable, at least for short reports.

Paper also has several rather significant drawbacks. It is inflexible. Once the report is printed, it cannot be sorted or reformatted to present a different view of the information. Likewise, if the information on the report changes, the entire report must be reprinted. Paper reports are expensive, are hard to duplicate, and require considerable supplies (paper, ink) and storage space. Paper reports are also hard to quickly move long distances (e.g., from a head office in Toronto to a regional office in Bermuda).

Many organizations are therefore moving to electronic production of reports, whereby reports are "printed," but stored in electronic format on file servers or Web servers so that users can easily access them. Often, the reports are available in more

Type of Reports	When to Use	Notes
Detail report Lists detailed information about all the items requested.	When user needs full information about the items	This report is usually produced only in response to a query about items matching some criteria. This report is usually read cover to cover to aid understanding of one or more items in depth.
Summary report Lists summary information about all items.	When user needs brief information on many items	This report is usually produced only in response to a query about items matching some criteria, but it can be a complete database. This report is usually read for the purpose of comparing several items with each other. The order in which items are sorted is important.
Turnaround document Outputs that "turn around" and become inputs.	When a user (often a customer) needs to return an output to be processed	Turnaround documents are a special type of report that are both outputs and inputs. For example, most bills sent to consumers (e.g., credit card bills) provide information about the total amount owed and also contain a form that consumers fill in and return with payment.
Graphs Charts used in addition to and instead of tables of numbers.	When users need to compare data among several items	Well-done graphs help users compare two or more items or understand how one has changed over time. Graphs are poor at helping users recognize precise numeric values and should be replaced by or combined with tables when precision is important. Bar charts tend to be better than tables of numbers or other types of charts when it comes to comparing values between items. (But avoid three-dimensional charts that make comparisons difficult.) Line charts make it easier to compare values over time, whereas scatter charts make it easier to find clusters or unusual data. Pie charts show proportions or the relative shares of a whole.

FIGURE 9-17
Types of Reports

CONCEPTS

IN ACTION

9-C SELECTING THE WRONG STUDENTS

I helped a university department develop a small decision support system to analyze and rank students who applied to a specialized program. Some of the information was numeric and could easily be processed directly by the system (e.g., grade point average, standardized test scores). Other information required the faculty to make subjective judgments among the students (e.g., extracurricular activities, work experience). The users entered their evaluations of the subjective information via several data analysis screens in which the students were listed in alphabetical order.

In order to make the system "easier to use," the reports listing the results of the analysis were also presented in alphabetical order by student name, rather than in order from the highest ranked student to the lowest ranked student. In a series of tests prior to installation, the users selected the wrong students to admit in 20 percent of the cases. They assumed, wrongly, that the students listed first were the highest ranked students and simply selected the first students on the list for admission. Neither the title on the report, nor the fact that all the students' names were in alphabetical order made them realize that they had read the report incorrectly. *Alan Dennis*

QUESTION:

What concerns could this problem raise about the rest of the system?

9-D CUTTING PAPER TO SAVE MONEY

One of the Fortune 500 firms with which I have worked had an 18-story office building for its world headquarters. It devoted two full floors of this building to nothing more than storing "current" paper reports (a separate warehouse was maintained outside the city for "archived" reports such as tax documents). Imagine the annual cost of office space in the headquarters building tied up in these paper reports. Now imagine how a staff member would gain access to the reports, and you can quickly understand the driving force behind electronic reports, even if most users end up printing them. Within one year of switching to electronic reports (for as many reports as practical) the paper report storage area was reduced to one small storage room.

Alan Dennis

QUESTION:

What types of reports are most suited to electronic format? What types of reports are less suited to electronic reports?

predesigned formats than are their paper-based counterparts, because the cost of producing and storing different formats is minimal. Electronic reports also can be produced on demand as needed, and they enable the user to search more easily for certain words. Furthermore, electronic reports can provide a means to support ad hoc reports when users customize the contents of the report at the time the report is generated. Some users may still print the electronic report on their own printers. The reduced cost of electronic delivery over distance and improved user access to the reports usually offsets the cost of local printing.

APPLYING THE CONCEPTS AT TUNE SOURCE

In the Tune Source case, there are three different user interfaces to be designed: Process 1: Search and Browse Tunes; Process 2: Purchase Tunes; and Process 3: Promote Tunes. (See Fig. 5-15 in Chapter 5.) In this section, we focus only on Process 1, the Web portion used by customers to find tunes of interest.

Use Scenario Development

The first step in the interface design process was to develop the key use scenarios for the Digital Music Download system. Jason Wells, senior systems analyst at Tune Source and project manager for the Digital Music Download system, began by examining the DFD and thinking about the types of users and how they would interact with the system. As discussed previously, Jason identified two use scenarios: the browsing shopper and the hurry-up shopper. (See Fig. 9-6.) Jason also thought of several other use scenarios for the Web site in general, but he omitted them because they were not common. Likewise, he thought of several use scenarios that did not lead to sales (e.g., fans looking for information about their favorite artists and music), and he omitted them as well, as they were not important in the design of the Web site.

Interface Structure Design

Next, Jason created an ISD for the Web system. He began with the DFDs to ensure that all functionality defined for the system was included in the ISD. Fig. 9-18 shows

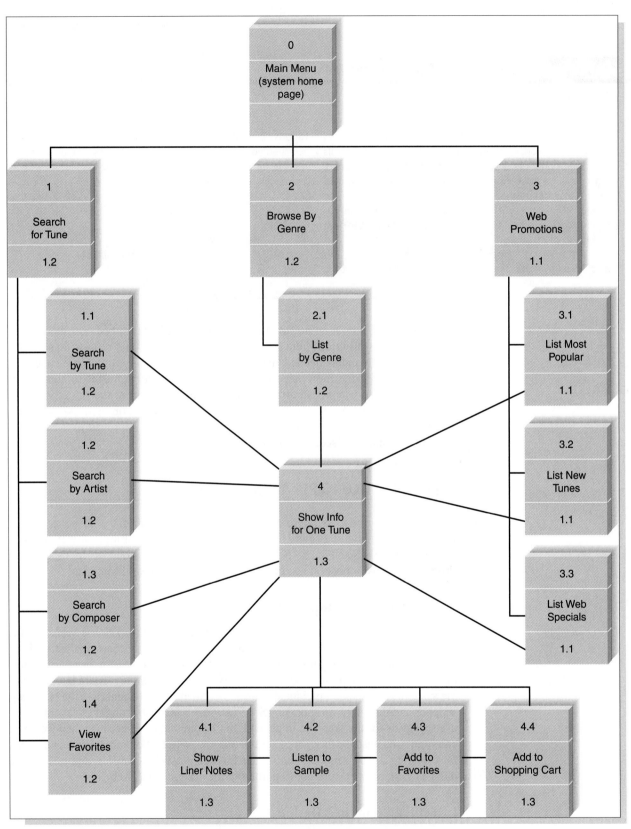

FIGURE 9-18
Tune Source ISD

the ISD for the Web portion of process 1. In practice, some of the processes on the level 1 DFD for this part of the system (Fig. 5-16) might be decomposed into several level 2 DFDs. However, to keep things simple, in this chapter we show an ISD that links to the level 1 DFD in Fig. 5-16, rather than attempting to create more DFDs and link the ISD to them.

The Initial Interface Structure Design   The Digital Music Download system will have a main menu or home page (interface number 0) that will enable the user to initiate a search (1), which would allow the user to enter search criteria to produce a list of tunes based on tune (1.1), artist (1.2), or composer (1.3), or to view the user's Favorites List (1.4). The home page would also have a browse feature (2) that would enable the user to select a music genre and produce a list of tunes within that genre (2.1). The home page would also have links to Web promotions (3) that would lead to lists of most popular tunes (3.1), newly added tunes (3.2), or Web special promotions (3.3).

Each of these lists of tunes would enable the user to click on a specific tune title and view detailed information about it (4), and listen to music samples. Jason decided to provide the additional marketing materials (e.g., reviews) on a separate page (4.1), rather than including them on the main entry for each tune, to prevent overcrowding and long time delays on the Web. Both the tune page (4) and additional material page (4.1) would let the user listen to a sample (4.2) and then put the tune on the user's Favorites List (4.3) and add to it the shopping cart (4.4). The user could then return to the home page (0) to enter a new search.

Reviewing the Interface Structure Design   Jason then examined the use scenarios to see how well the ISD enabled different types of users to work through the system. He started with the "browsing shopper" scenario and followed it through the ISD, imagining what would appear on each screen and pretending to navigate through the system. He found that the ISD worked well.

Jason next explored the "hurry-up shopper" scenario. In this case, the ISD did not work as well. Moving from the home page to the search page to the list of matching tunes to the tune info page with price and other information takes three mouse clicks. This falls within the three-clicks rule, but for someone in a hurry, this may be too many. Jason decided to add a "quick search" option to the home page (interface 0) that would enable the user to enter one search criterion (e.g., searching by just artist name or title, rather than doing a more detailed search, as would be possible on the search page) that, with one click, would take the user to the one tune that matched the criterion (interface 4) or to a list of tunes if there were more than one (interfaces 1.1, 1.2, 1.3). This would enable an impatient user to get to the tune of interest in one or two clicks

Interface Standards Design

Once the ISD was complete, Jason moved on to develop the interface standards for the system. The interface metaphor was straightforward: a Tune Source retail music store. The key interface objects and actions were equally straightforward, as was the use of the Tune Source logo icon (Fig. 9-19).

Interface Template Design

For the interface template, Jason decided on a simple, clean design that had the Tune Source logo in the upper left corner. The template had a navigation menu

---

Interface Metaphor: A Tune Source Music Store.

Interface Objects

- **Tune:** All items, whether single track or longer composition, unless it is important to distinguish among them.
- **Artist:** Person or group who records the tune.
- **Title:** Title or name of tune.
- **Composer:** Person or group who wrote the music for the tune (primarily used for classical music).
- **Music Genre:** Type of music. Current categories include Rock, Jazz, Classical, Country, Alternative, Soundtracks, Rap, Folk, Gospel.
- **Tune List:** List of tune(s) that match the specified criteria.
- **Favorites List:** A place for the customer to store tunes of interest.
- **Shopping Cart:** Place to store tunes until they are purchased.

Interface Actions

- **Search for:** Display a tune list that matches specified criteria.
- **Browse:** Display a tune list sorted in order by some criteria.
- **Buy:** Buy permission to download tune(s).
- **Download:** Transfer file to user's computer after purchase.

Interface Icons

- **Tune Source Logo** will be used on all screens.

FIGURE 9-19
Tune Source Interface Standards

across the top for navigation within the entire Web site (e.g., overall Web site home page, store locations) and one menu down the side of the page for navigation within the Digital Music Download system. The left-edge menu contained the links to the three top-level screens (interfaces 1, 2 and 3 in Fig. 9-18), as well as the "quick search" option. The center area of the screen is used for displaying forms and reports when the appropriate link is clicked. See Fig. 9-20. At this point, Jason decided to seek some quick feedback on the interface structure and standards before investing time in prototyping the interface designs. Therefore, he met with Carly Edwards, the project sponsor, to discuss the emerging design. Making changes at this point would be much simpler than waiting until after doing the prototype. Carly had a few suggestions, so, after the meeting, Jason made the changes and moved into the design prototyping step.

Design Prototyping

Jason decided to use Visio to create prototypes of the system. The Digital Music Download system was new territory for Tune Source and a strategic investment in a new business model, so it was important to make sure that no key issues were overlooked. The prototypes would provide the most detailed information and could be developed rapidly. Once satisfied with the layout, Jason planned to create HTML prototypes that could be used to test the interface interactively.

Jason began designing the prototype, starting with the home screen, and gradually worked his way through all the screens. The process was very iterative, and he

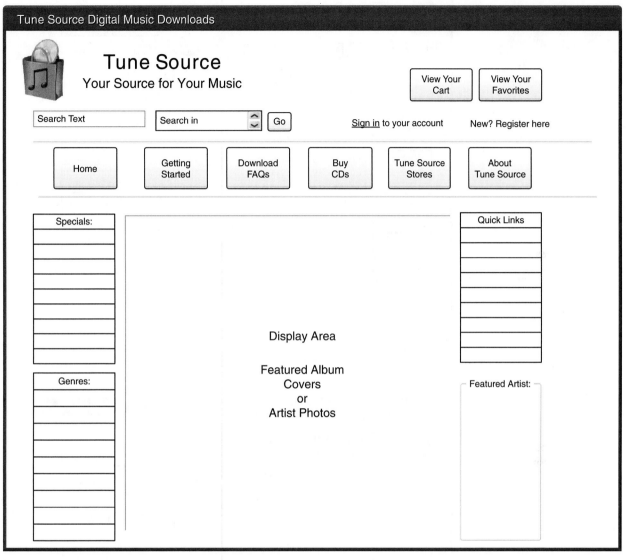

FIGURE 9-20
Tune Source User Interface Template

made many changes to the screens as he worked. Once he had an initial prototype designed, he posted it on Tune Source's internal intranet and solicited comments from several friends with lots of Web experience. He revised it according to the comments he received. Fig. 9-21 presents some screens from the prototype.

Interface Evaluation

The next step was interface evaluation. Jason decided on a two-phase evaluation. The first evaluation was to be an interactive one conducted by Carly Edwards, her marketing managers, selected staff members, and selected store managers. They worked hands-on with the prototype and identified several ways to improve it. Jason modified the HTML prototype to reflect the changes suggested by the group and asked Carly to review it again.

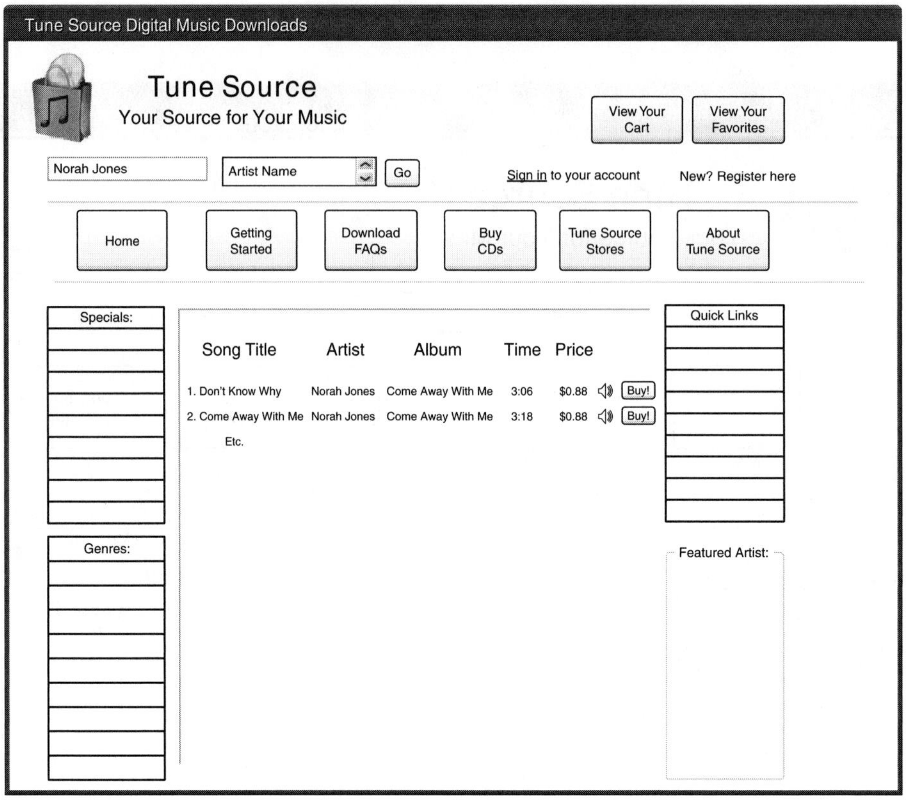

(a)

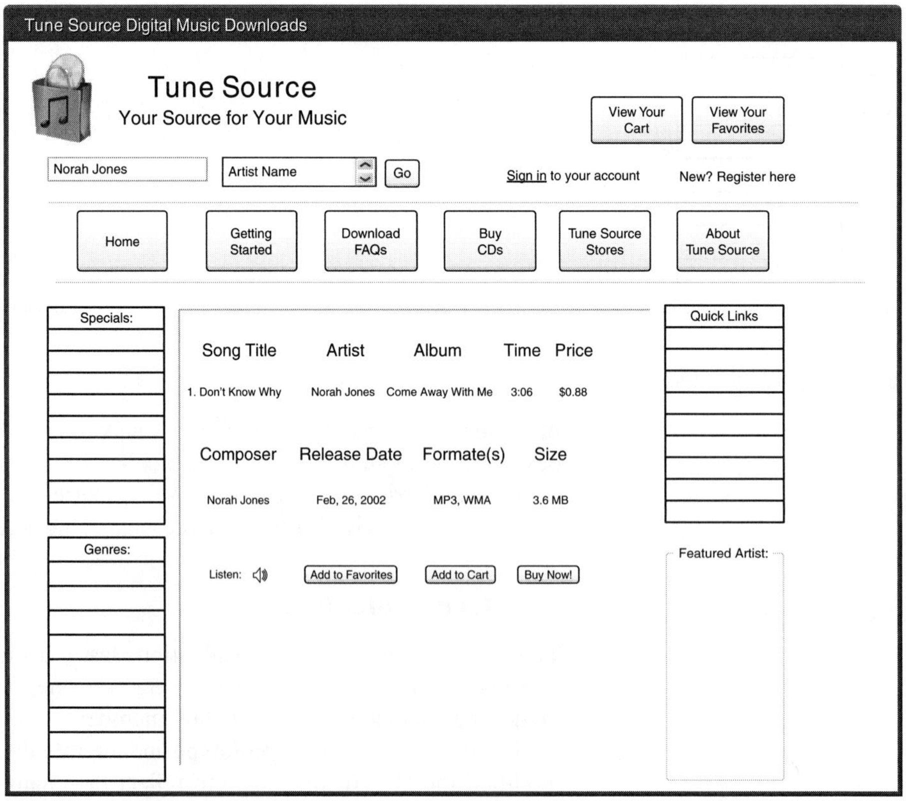

(b)

FIGURE 9-21

Sample interfaces from the Tune Source design prototype:
(a) list by artist (interface 1.2)
(b) information for one tune (interface 4)

The second evaluation was again interactive, this time performed by a series of two focus groups of potential customers, one with little Internet experience, the other with extensive Internet experience. Once again, several minor changes were identified. Jason again modified the HTML prototype and asked Carly to review it once more. When she was satisfied, the interface design was complete.

SUMMARY

User Interface Design Principles

The first element of the user interface design is the layout of the screen, form, or report, which is usually depicted by rectangular shapes with a top area for navigation, a central area for inputs and outputs, and a status line at the bottom. The design should help the user be aware of content and context, both between different parts of the system as they navigate through it and within any one form or report. All interfaces should be aesthetically pleasing (not necessarily works of art) and need to include significant white space, use colors carefully, and be consistent with fonts. Most interfaces should be designed to support both novice or first-time users as well as experienced users. Consistency in design (both within the system and across other systems used by the users) is important for the navigation controls, terminology, and layout of forms and reports. Finally, all interfaces should attempt to minimize user effort, for example, by requiring no more than three clicks from the main menu to perform an action.

The User Interface Design Process

First, analysts develop use scenarios describing commonly used patterns of actions that the users will perform. Second, they design the interface structure via an ISD based on the DFD. The ISD is then tested with the use scenarios to ensure that it enables users to quickly and smoothly perform these scenarios. Third, analysts define the interface standards in terms of interface metaphor(s), objects, actions, and icons. These elements are drawn together by the design of a basic interface template for each major section of the system. Fourth, the designs of the individual interfaces are prototyped, either through a simple storyboard, an HTML prototype, or a prototype in the development language of the system itself (e.g., Visual Basic). Finally, interface evaluation is conducted by heuristic evaluation, walk-through evaluation, interactive evaluation, or formal usability testing. This evaluation almost always identifies improvements, so the interfaces are redesigned and evaluated further.

Navigation Design

The fundamental goal of the navigation design is to make the system as simple to use as possible by preventing the user from making mistakes, simplifying the recovery from mistakes, and using a consistent grammer order (usually object–action order). Command languages, natural languages, and direct manipulation are used in navigation, but the most common approach is menus, (menu bar, drop-down menu, hyperlink menu, embedded hyperlinks, pop-up menu, tab menu, buttons and toolbars, and image maps). Error messages, confirmation messages, acknowledgment messages, delay messages, and help messages are common types of messages.

Input Design

The goal of input design is to simply and easily capture accurate information for the system, typically by using online or batch processing, capturing data at the source, and minimizing keystrokes. Input design includes both the design of input screens and all preprinted forms that are used to collect data before they are entered into the information system. There are many types of inputs, such as text fields, number fields, check boxes, radio buttons, on-screen list boxes, drop-down list boxes, and sliders. Most inputs are validated by some combination of completeness checks, format checks, range checks, check digits, consistency checks, and database checks.

Output Design

The goal of output design is to present information to users so that they can accurately understand it with the least effort, usually by understanding how reports will be used and designing them to minimize information overload and bias. Output design means designing both screens and reports in other media, such as paper and the Web. There are many types of reports, including detail reports, summary reports, exception reports, turnaround documents, and graphs.

KEY TERMS

Acknowledgment message
Action–object order
Aesthetics
Bar code reader
Batch processing
Batch report
Bias
Button
Check box
Check digit check
Combo box
Command language
Completeness check
Confirmation message
Consistency
Consistency check
Content awareness
Context-sensitive help
Database check
Data-entry operator
Default value
Delay message
Density
Detail report
Direct manipulation
Drop-down list box
Drop-down menu
Ease of learning
Ease of use
Edit check
Error message
Exception report
Field
Field label

Form
Format check
Grammar order
Graph
Graphical user interface (GUI)
Help message
Heuristic evaluation
Hot key
HTML prototype
Human-computer interaction (HCI)
Image map
Information load
Input mechanism
Interactive evaluation
Interface action
Interface design prototype
Interface evaluation
Interface icon
Interface metaphor
Interface object
Interface standards
Interface structure design
Interface structure diagram (ISD)
Interface template
Language prototype
Layout
Magnetic stripe readers
Menu
Menu bar
Natural language
Navigation mechanism
Number box
Object-action order
Online processing

On-screen list box
Optical character recognition
Output mechanism
Pop-up menu
Radio button
Range check
Real-time information
Real-time report
Report
RFID tag
Screen
Selection box
Slider
Smart card
Source data automation
Storyboard
Summary report
System interface
Tab menu
Text box
Three-clicks rule
Toolbar
Tool tip
Transaction processing
Turnaround document
Usability testing
Use scenario
User experience
User interface
Validation
Walk-through evaluation
Web page
White space

QUESTIONS

1. Explain three important user interface design principles.
2. What are three fundamental parts of most user interfaces?
3. Why is content awareness important?
4. What is white space, and why is it important?
5. Under what circumstances should densities be low? high?
6. How can a system be designed to be used by both experienced and first-time users?
7. Why is consistency in design important? Why can too much consistency cause problems?
8. How can different parts of the interface be consistent?
9. Describe the basic process of user interface design.
10. What are use scenarios, and why are they important?
11. What is an interface structure diagram (ISD), and why is it used?
12. Why are interface standards important?
13. Explain the purpose and contents of interface metaphors, interface objects, interface actions, interface icons, and interface templates.
14. Why do we prototype the user interface design?
15. Compare and contrast the three types of interface design prototypes.
16. Why is it important to perform an interface evaluation before the system is built?
17. Compare and contrast the four types of interface evaluation.
18. Under what conditions is heuristic evaluation justified?
19. What type of interface evaluation did you perform in the "Your Turn 9.1"?
20. Describe three basic principles of navigation design.
21. How can you prevent mistakes?
22. Explain the differences between object–action order and action–object order.
23. Describe four types of navigation controls.
24. Why are menus the most commonly used navigation control?
25. Compare and contrast four types of menus.
26. Under what circumstances would you use a drop-down menu versus a tab menu?
27. Describe five types of messages.
28. What are the key factors in designing an error message?
29. What is context-sensitive help? Does your word processor have context-sensitive help?
30. Explain three principles in the design of inputs.
31. Compare and contrast batch processing and online processing. Describe one application that would use batch processing and one that would use online processing.
32. Why is capturing data at the source important?
33. Describe four devices that can be used for source data automation.
34. Describe five types of inputs.
35. Compare and contrast check boxes and radio buttons. When would you use one versus the other?
36. Compare and contrast on-screen list boxes and drop-down list boxes. When would you use one versus the other?
37. Why is input validation important?
38. Describe five types of input validation methods.
39. Explain three principles in the design of outputs.
40. Describe five types of outputs.
41. When would you use electronic reports rather than paper reports, and vice versa?
42. What do you think are three common mistakes that novice analysts make in interface design?
43. How would you improve the form in Fig. 9-4?

EXERCISES

A. Develop two use scenarios for a Web site that sells some retail products (e.g., books, music, clothes).
B. Draw an ISD for a Web site that sells some retail products (e.g., books, music, clothes).
C. Describe the primary components of the interface standards for a Web site that sells some retail products (metaphors, objects, actions, icons, and templates).
D. Develop two use scenarios for the DFD in exercise C in Chapter 5.
E. Draw an ISD for the DFD in exercise C in Chapter 5.
F. Develop the interface standards (omitting the interface template) for the DFD in exercise C in Chapter 5.
G. Develop two use scenarios for the DFD in exercise E in Chapter 5.

H. Develop the interface standards (omitting the interface template) for the DFD in exercise E in Chapter 5.

I. Design an interface template for Exercise E.

J. Draw an ISD for the DFD in Exercise E in Chapter 5.

K. Design a storyboard for Exercise E in Chapter 5.

L. Develop an HTML, prototype for Exercise E in this chapter.

M. Develop an HTML prototype for Exercise F in this chapter.

N. Develop the interface standards (omitting the interface template) for the DFD in Exercise I in Chapter 5.

O. Draw an ISD for the DFD in Exercise I in Chapter 5.

P. Design a storyboard for Exercise I in Chapter 5.

Q. Develop two use scenarios for the DFD in Exercise I in Chapter 5.

R. Ask Jeeves (http://www.askjeeves.com) is an Internet search engine that uses natural language. Experiment with it and compare it with search engines that use key words.

S. Draw an ISD for "Your Turn 9.7," using the opposite grammar order from your original design. (If you didn't do the "Your Turn" exercise, draw two ISDs, one in each grammar order.) Which is "best"? Why?

T. In "Your Turn 9.7" you probably used menus. Design the navigation system again, using a command language.

MINICASES

1. Tots to Teens is a catalog retailer specializing in children's clothing. A project has been underway to develop a new order-entry system for the company's catalog clerks. The old system had a character-based user interface that corresponded to the system's COBOL underpinnings. The new system will feature a graphical user interface more in keeping with up-to-date PC products in use today. The company hopes that this new user interface will help reduce the turnover they have experienced with their order-entry clerks. Many newly hired order entry staff found the old system very difficult to learn and were overwhelmed by the numerous mysterious codes that had to be used to communicate with the system.

A user interface walk-through evaluation was scheduled for today to give the users a first look at the new system's interface. The project team was careful to invite several key users from the order-entry department. In particular, Norma was included because of her years of experience with the order-entry-system. Norma was known to be an informal leader in the department; her opinion influenced many of her associates. Norma had let it be known that she was less than thrilled with the ideas she had heard for the new system. Due to her experience and good memory, Norma worked very effectively with the character-based system and was able to breeze through even the most convoluted transactions with ease. Norma had trouble suppressing a sneer when she heard talk of such things as "icons" and "buttons" in the new user interface.

Cindy was also invited to the walk-through because of her influence in the order-entry department. Cindy has been with the department for just one year, but she quickly became known because of her successful organization of a sick-child day-care service for the children of the department workers. Sick children are the number-one cause of absenteeism in the department, and many of the workers could not afford to miss workdays. Never one to keep quiet when a situation needed improvement, Cindy has been a vocal supporter of the new system.

a. Drawing upon the design principles presented in the text, describe the features of the user interface that will be most important to experienced users like Norma.

b. Drawing upon the design principles presented in the text, describe the features of the user interface that will be most important to novice users like Cindy.

2. The members of a systems development project team have gone out for lunch together, and as often happens, the conversation has turned to work. The team has been working on the development of the user interface design, and so far, work has been progressing smoothly. The team should be completing work on the interface prototypes early next week. A combination of storyboards and language prototypes has been used in this project. The storyboards depict the overall structure and flow of the system, but the team developed language prototypes of the actual screens because they felt that seeing the actual screens would be valuable for the users.

Chris (the youngest member of the project team): *I read an article last night about a really cool way to evaluate a user interface design. It's called usability testing, and it's done by all the major software vendors. I think we should use it to evaluate our interface design.*

Heather (system analyst): *I've heard of that, too, but isn't it really expensive?*

Mark (project manager): *I'm afraid it is expensive, and I'm not sure we can justify the expense for this project.*

Chris: *But we really need to know that the interface works. I thought this usability testing technique would help us prove we have a good design.*

Amy (systems analyst): *It would, Chris, but there are other ways, too. I assumed we'd do a thorough walk-through with our users and present the interface to them at a meeting. We can project each interface screen so that the users can see it and give us their reaction. This is probably the most efficient way to get the users' response to our work.*

Heather: *That's true, but I'd sure like to see the users sit down and work with the system. I've always learned a lot by watching what they do, seeing where they get confused, and hearing their comments and feedback.*

Ryan (systems analyst): *It seems to me that we've put so much work into this interface design that all we really need to do is review it ourselves. Let's just make a list of the design principles we're most concerned about and check it ourselves to make sure we've followed them consistently. If we have, we should be fine.*

We want to get moving on the implementation, you know.

Mark: *These are all good ideas. It seems like we've all got a different view of how to evaluate the interface design. Let's try and sort out the technique that is best for our project.*

Develop a set of guidelines that can help a project team like the one discussed here select the most appropriate interface evaluation technique for their project.

3. The menu structure for Holiday Travel Vehicle's existing character-based system is shown here. Develop and prototype a new interface design for the system's functions, using a graphical user interface. Assume that the new system will need to include the same functions as those shown in the menus provided. Include any messages that will be produced as a user interacts with your interface (error, confirmation, status, etc.). Also, prepare a written summary that describes how your interface implements the principles of good interface design as presented in the textbook.

```
┌─────────────────────────────────────┐
│       Holiday Travel Vehicles       │
│                                     │
│             Main Menu               │
│                                     │
│         1 Sales Invoice             │
│         2 Vehicle Inventory         │
│         3 Reports                   │
│         4 Sales Staff               │
│                                     │
│ Type number of menu selection here:____ │
└─────────────────────────────────────┘
```

```
┌─────────────────────────────────────┐
│       Holiday Travel Vehicles       │
│                                     │
│          Sales Invoice Menu         │
│                                     │
│        1 Create Sales Invoice       │
│        2 Change Sales Invoice       │
│        3 Cancel Sales Invoice       │
│                                     │
│ Type number of menu selection here:____ │
└─────────────────────────────────────┘
```

```
┌─────────────────────────────────────┐
│       Holiday Travel Vehicles       │
│                                     │
│        Vehicle Inventory Menu       │
│                                     │
│   1 Create Vehicle Inventory Record │
│   2 Change Vehicle Inventory Record │
│   3 Delete Vehicle Inventory Record │
│                                     │
│ Type number of menu selection here:____ │
└─────────────────────────────────────┘
```

```
┌─────────────────────────────────────┐
│       Holiday Travel Vehicles       │
│                                     │
│            Reports Menu             │
│                                     │
│      1 Commission Report            │
│      2 RV Sales by Make Report      │
│      3 Trailer Sales by Make Report │
│      4 Dealer Options Report        │
│                                     │
│ Type number of menu selection here:____ │
└─────────────────────────────────────┘
```

```
┌─────────────────────────────────────┐
│       Holiday Travel Vehicles       │
│                                     │
│     Sales Staff Maintenance Menu    │
│                                     │
│       1 Add Salesperson Record      │
│       2 Change Salesperson Record   │
│       3 Delete Salesperson Record   │
│                                     │
│ Type number of menu selection here:____ │
└─────────────────────────────────────┘
```

4. One aspect of the new system under development at Holiday Travel Vehicles will be the direct entry of the sales invoice into the computer system by the salesperson as the purchase transaction is being completed. In the current system, the salesperson fills out the paper form shown here.

Design and prototype an input screen that will permit the salesperson to enter all the necessary information for the sales invoice. The following information may be helpful in your design process: Assume that Holiday Travel Vehicles sells recreational vehicles and trailers from four different manufacturers. Each manufacture has a fixed number of names and models of RVs and trailers. For the purposes of your prototype, use this format:

Mfg-A	Name-1 Model-X	Mfg-C	Name-1 Model-X
Mfg-A	Name-1 Model-Y	Mfg-C	Name-1 Model-Y
Mfg-A	Name-1 Model-Z	Mfg-C	Name-1 Model-Z
Mfg-B	Name-1 Model-X	Mfg-C	Name-2 Model-X
Mfg-B	Name-1 Model-Y	Mfg-C	Name-3 Model-X
Mfg-B	Name-2 Model-X	Mfg-D	Name-1 Model-X
Mfg-B	Name-2 Model-Y	Mfg-D	Name-2 Model-X
Mfg-B	Name-2 Model-Z	Mfg-D	Name-2 Model-Y

Also, assume that there are 10 different dealer options which could be installed on a vehicle at the customer's request. The company currently has 10 salespeople on staff.

Holiday Travel Vehicles
Sales Invoice

Invoice #: _____
Invoice Date: _____

Customer Name: _____
Address: _____
City: _____
State: _____
Zip: _____
Phone: _____

New RV/TRAILER
(Circle one)   Name: _____
Model: _____
Serial #: _____ Year: _____
Manufacturer: _____

Trade-in RV/TRAILER
(Circle one)   Name: _____
Model: _____
Year: _____
Manufacturer: _____

Options: Code   Description   Price
_____   _____   _____
_____   _____   _____
_____   _____   _____
_____   _____   _____

Vehicle Base Cost: _____
Trade-in Allowance: _____   _____
Total Options: _____   (Salesperson Name)
Tax: _____
License Fee: _____   _____
Final Cost: _____   (Customer Signature)

DESIGN

- ☑ **Select Design Strategy**
- ☑ **Design Architecture**
- ☑ **Select Hardware and Software**
- ☑ **Develop Use Scenarios**
- ☑ **Design Interface Structure**
- ☑ **Develop Interface Standards**
- ☑ **Design Interface Prototype**
- ☑ **Evaluate User Interface**
- ☑ **Design User Interface**
- ☐ Develop Physical Data Flow Diagrams
- ☐ Develop Program Structure Charts
- ☐ Develop Program Specifications
- ☐ Select Data Storage Format
- ☐ Develop Physical Entity Relationship Diagram
- ☐ Denormalize Entity Relationship Diagram
- ☐ Performance Tune Data Storage
- ☐ Size Data Storage

TASK CHECKLIST

CHAPTER 10

PROGRAM DESIGN

A nother important activity of the design phase is designing the programs that will perform the system's application logic. Programs can be quite complex, so analysts must create instructions and guidelines for programmers that clearly describe what the program must do. This chapter describes the activities that are performed when the program design is developed. First, the process of revising logical data flow diagrams into physical data flow diagrams is outlined. Then, two techniques typically used together for describing programs are presented. The structure chart depicts a program at a high level in graphic form. The program specification contains a set of written instructions in more detail. Together, these techniques communicate how the application logic for the system needs to be developed.

OBJECTIVES

- Be able to revise logical DFDs into physical DFDs.
- Be able to create a structure chart.
- Be able to write a program specification.
- Understand the use of pseudocode.
- Become familiar with event-driven programming.

CHAPTER OUTLINE

IMPLEMENTATION

INTRODUCTION

The application logic for a system will be expressed in programs that will be written during construction of the new system. Program design is the part of the design phase of the SDLC during which analysts determine what programs will be written, create instructions for the programmers about how the code should be written, and identify how the pieces of code will fit together to form a program.

Some people may think that program design is becoming less important, as project teams rely increasingly on packaged software or libraries of preprogrammed code to build systems. Program design techniques are still very important, however, for two reasons. First, even preexisting code needs to be understood, organized, and pieced together. Second, it is still common for the project team to have to write some (if not all) code and produce original programs that support the application logic of the system.

As analysts turn their attention to the programs that will need to be created for the new system, several things must be done. First, various implementation decisions will be made about the new system, such as what programming language(s) will be used. The data flow diagrams created during analysis are modified to show these implementation decisions, resulting in a set of *physical data flow diagrams*. The analysts then determine how the processes of the system will be organized, using a *structure chart* to depict their decisions. Finally, detailed instructions called *program specifications* are developed so that during construction, the programmers know exactly what they should be creating. These activities are the subject of this chapter.

MOVING FROM LOGICAL TO PHYSICAL PROCESS MODELS

During analysis, the systems analysts identified the processes and data flows that are needed to support the functional requirements of the new system. These processes and data flows are contained on the logical data flow diagrams for the to-be system. As we discussed in Chapter 5, the analysts avoid making implementation decisions during analysis, focusing first on the business requirements of the system. The logical DFDs do not contain any indication of how the system will actually be implemented when the information system is built; they simply state what the new system will do. In this way, developers do not get distracted by technical details and are not biased by technical limitations in the initial stages of system development. Business users better understand diagrams that show the "business view" of the system.

During design, *physical process models* are created to show implementation details and explain how the final system will work. These details can include references to actual technology, the format of information moving through processes, and the human interaction that is involved. In some cases, most often when packages are used, the use cases may need to be revised as well. These to-be models describe characteristics of the system that will be created, communicating the "systems view" of the new system.

The Physical Data Flow Diagram

The physical DFD contains the same components as the logical DFD (e.g., data stores, data flows), and the same rules apply (e.g., balancing, decomposition). The

Step	Explanation
Add implementation references.	Using the existing logical DFD, add the way in which the data stores, data flows, and processes will be implemented to each component.
Draw a human–machine boundary.	Draw a line to separate the automated parts of the system from the manual parts.
Add system-related data stores, data flows, and processes.	Add system-related data stores, data flows, and processes to the model (components that have little to do with the business process).
Update the data elements in the data flows.	Update the data flows to include system-related data elements.
Update the metadata in the CASE repository.	Update the metadata in the CASE repository to include physical characteristics.

CASE = computer-aided software engineering; DFD = data flow diagram.

FIGURE 10-1
Steps to Create the Physical Data Flow Diagram

basic difference between the two models is that a physical DFD contains additional details that describe how the system will be built. There are five steps to perform to make the transition to the physical DFD (Figure 10-1).

Step 1: Add Implementation References   The first step in creating a physical DFD is to begin with the existing logical DFD and add references to the ways in which the data stores, data flows, and processes will be implemented. Data stores on physical DFDs will refer to files and/or database tables; processes, to programs or human actions; and data flows, to the physical media for the data, such as paper reports, bar code scanning, input screens, or computer reports. The names for the various components on the physical DFD should contain references to these implementation details. By definition, external entities on the DFD are outside of the scope of the system and therefore remain unchanged in the physical diagram.

Figure 10-2 shows the physical DFD that was drawn to depict the physical details for the original logical DFD from Figure 5-16. Notice how the logical data store called Available Tunes that will store data in the Available Tunes table of a mySQL database has been renamed "mySQL: Available Tunes Table" and the logical data flow Requested Tunes now includes "mySQL: Requested Tunes Record" to show that this information will be in the form of a record from the Available Tunes table. Can you identify other changes that were made to the physical model to communicate how other components will be implemented?

Step 2: Draw a Human-Machine Boundary   The second step is to add a *human–machine boundary*. Physical DFDs differentiate human and computer interaction by a human-machine boundary, a line drawn on the model to separate human action from automated processes. For example, the search and browse tunes processes (i.e., processes 1.1–1.3) require the customer to interact with the Web by using an interface driven by system programs and processes. The physical model, therefore, contains a line separating the customer from the rest of the process to show exactly what is done by a person as opposed to a "machine." (See Figure 10-2.)

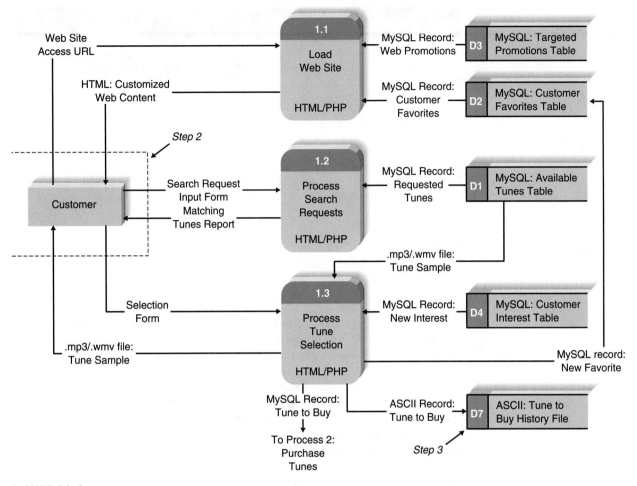

FIGURE 10-2
Physical DFD for Tune Source Process 1: Search and Browse Tunes (the How)

Every part of every process in the system may not be automated, so it is up to the project team to determine where to draw a human-machine boundary and how large to draw it. The project team will need to weigh the following criteria when drawing the boundary: cost, efficiency, and integrity. First, a piece of the system should be automated only if the cost of computerizing it is less than doing it manually. Next, the system should be more efficient with the mode that is selected. For example, if the project team must decide whether to store a paper copy of a document or to save an electronic file of information in a central file server, the team likely will find the latter option to be more efficient in terms of improving the users' ability to access and update the information.

Finally, the team should consider the integrity of the information that is handled by the system. It may be cheaper for a clerk to record orders by phone and deliver the order forms to the distribution area; however, errors could be made when the clerk takes the order, and a form could be misplaced en route to distribution. Instead, the project team may be more comfortable with an automated process that accepts a customer's order from the customer directly, using a Web form that is then directly transmitted to the distribution system.

Step 3: Add System-Related Data Stores, Data Flows, and Processes In step 3, you will add to the DFD additional processes, stores, or flows that are specific to the implementation of the system and have little (or nothing) to do with the business process itself. These additions can be due to technical limitations or to the need for audits, controls, or exception handling. Technical limitations occur when technology cannot support the way in which the system is modeled logically. For example, suppose that a data store exists on the logical DFD to hold customer information, but the database technology that will be used to build the system cannot handle the large volume of customers in one table. A physical DFD may need to have two data stores—one for current customers and one for old customers—so that the technology will work properly.

Audits, controls, or exception handling refers to putting checks and balances in place in the system in case something goes wrong. For instance, on rare occasions, customers might call and cancel an order that they placed. Instead of just having the system get rid of the information about that order, a process may be included for control purposes that records the deleted orders along with reasons for the cancellations. Or, consider the search and browse processes that we have been working with. Suppose that the project team is worried about the transfer of purchase records to the purchase tunes process. As a precaution, the team can place a data store on the physical DFD that captures information about each batch of records that is sent to the purchase tunes process. In this way, if problems were to occur, there would be a history of transactions that could be examined or used for backup purposes. (See Figure 10-2.)

Step 4: Update the Data Elements in the Data Flows The fourth step is to update the elements in the data flows. The data flows will appear to be identical in both the logical and physical DFDs, but the physical data flows may contain additional system-related data elements, for reasons similar to those described in the previous section. For example, most systems add system-related data elements to data flows that capture when changes were made to information (e.g., a last_update data element) and who made the change (e.g., an updated_by data element). Another physical data element is a system-generated number used to uniquely identify each record in a database. During step 4, the physical data elements are added to the metadata descriptions of the data flows in the CASE repository.

Step 5: Update the Metadata in the Computer-Aided Software Engineering Repository
Finally, the project team needs to make sure that the information about the DFD components in the CASE repository is updated with implementation-specific information. This information can include when batch processes will be run and how often, names of the actual tables or files that are represented by data flows, and the sizes and projected growth rates of the data stores.

Applying the Concepts at Tune Source

To better understand physical DFDs, we will now use an example based on the Tune Source promote tunes process. Figure 10-3 shows the logical DFD. We will perform each step to create the physical model, using the logical model as our starting point. Before we begin, see if you can identify how the data stores, data flows, and processes will need to change to reflect physical characteristics of the proposed system.

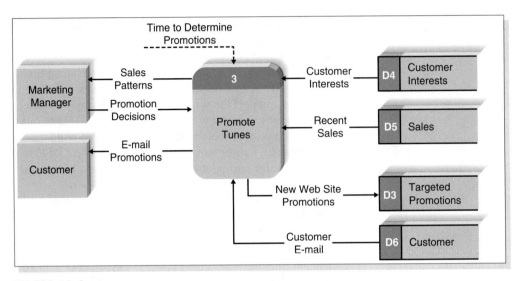

FIGURE 10-3
Logical Model of the Promote Tunes Process

First, we need to identify how the data flows, data stores, and processes will be implemented and add the implementation references on the DFD. From the original business requirements, we know that the marketing managers will receive reports on customer interests and tune sales via the Web. The marketing managers will submit information on promotions that will be displayed on the Web site. The marketing managers will also submit promotions that will be sent to customers via e-mail. On the physical DFD, each of the data flows is altered by renaming it appropriately, as shown in Figure 10-4.

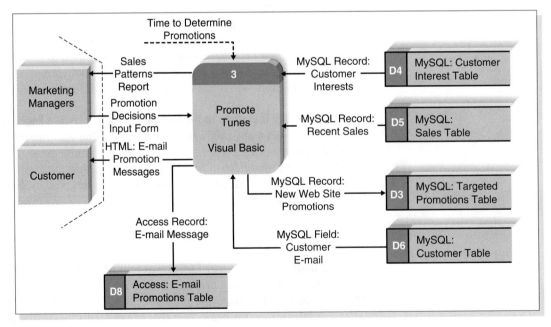

FIGURE 10-4
Physical Model for Promote Tunes Process

Let us assume that the data stores (i.e., customer interests, sales, targeted promotions, and customer) will refer to tables called customer interests, sales, targeted promotions, and customers, respectively, that are contained in a MySQL database; therefore, all four stores are updated with this information to indicate their physical qualities. Also, the promote tunes process will be written in Visual Basic (VB), and this information is added to the process model.

As a second step, a dotted line is drawn to represent the human-machine boundary and to communicate how much (and what parts) of the process is automated, and next we add system-related components to the model. Let us assume that a separate Access database is going to be maintained that includes records on e-mail promotion messages sent to customers. This database may be used by the marketing managers to analyze the effectiveness of their e-mail promotional campaigns. So, we add a data store to the diagram to reflect this decision. See Figure 10-4 for these changes.

Completion of the last two steps, 4 and 5, will not be apparent on the physical DFD. In step 4, we will add system-related data elements to the data flow entries in the CASE repository. For example, we will create a system-related data element called date-added and add it to the data flow that goes from process 3 to the targeted promotions data store. This field will capture the time a piece of promotional material was inserted in the system.

Step 5 requires that we add implementation-specific information in the metadata in the CASE repository. This can include such information as the actual field types and sizes of the data elements that will be stored in the tables, or the expected response time for a report to be created for the marketing manager.

DESIGNING PROGRAMS

It can be tempting to jump right into the implementation phase by coding without much thought or planning, but this can lead to disastrous results, such as inefficient programs, code that does not work with other code, and a system that doesn't do what it's supposed to do. Instead, analysts should first take time in the design phase to create a maintainable system. In other words, analysts should create a design that is modular and flexible. To do this, analysts can design programs in a *top-down modular approach*, using a variety of program design techniques.

Think about giving someone directions to your house (Figure 10-5). Before getting to the details, such as naming streets and identifying landmarks, it is best to first orient the person to your general location (e.g., the state you live in, the part of town). As he or she becomes comfortable with where to go at a high level, you can become more detailed in your instructions. This top-down approach helps orient the other person and conveys the big picture of where you live, making the detailed directions much easier to understand.

Also, directions can be communicated in *modules*:

First, drive from your house to the highway.
Then, drive from the highway to the appropriate exit.
Next, locate my neighborhood.
Finally, drive to my house.

Each line, or module, can change without affecting the rest of the directions. For example, if one friend is traveling to your house from the north and another is

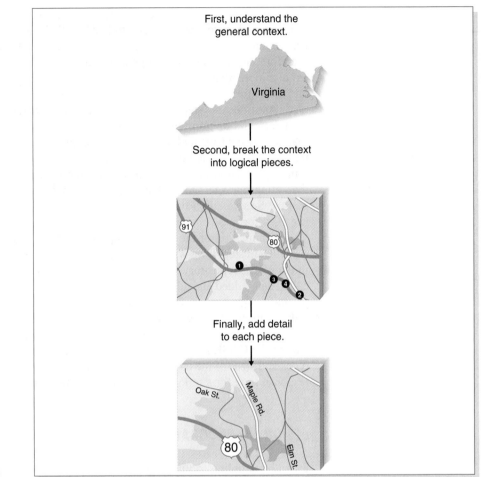

First, understand the
general context.

Virginia

Second, break the context
into logical pieces.

Finally, add detail
to each piece.

Oak St.

Maple Rd

Elm St.

FIGURE 10-5
Using a Top-Down Modular Approach

traveling from the south, it is likely that the last two modules of directions (i.e., to the neighborhood and to the house) will not change even though the first two modules will differ for each friend. The modular approach makes the directions much easier to develop and change.

Good program design is similar to the top-down modular approach that we described. First, analysts create a high-level diagram that shows the various components of a program, how the components should be organized, and how the components interrelate. This diagram, known as the *structure chart*, illustrates the organization and interactions of the different pieces of code within the program to the analysts and programmers so that the program can be developed by many programmers working independently. The diagram can be used when the project team plans to write code from scratch or when existing pieces of code will be assembled to build the system. The physical process models just described provide a good starting point for understanding what this structure chart needs to include.

Once the overall program is defined at a high level, with a structure chart, program specifications are written to describe exactly what needs to be included in each program module. The specifications include basic module information (e.g., a name, calculations that need to be performed, and the target programming language), special instructions for the programmer, and pseudocode. Pseudocode is

10-A WINNING BY DESIGN

The rapid development face-off was a competition between rapid application development (RAD) teams from the leading consulting firms in the United States. The goal was to see which team could develop a specific system in the least amount of time. Most teams used a very short program design step and quickly began programming.

The Ernst & Young (E&Y) team members used a different approach. They spent much more time in the program design step to ensure that the system was well designed before they moved into programming. At first, the E&Y team fell behind while its competitors jumped ahead. But E&Y ended up winning because the team spent much less time programming by following its well-designed blueprint.

QUESTION:

What are several reasons why planning ahead may have helped E&Y win?

a technique similar to structured English that is used to communicate what needs to be written, using programming structures and a generic language that is not program language specific. Program specifications leave the implementation details to the programmers, but they communicate the basic logic and programming structures to help reduce logical and syntactical errors during the implementation phase. Some RAD approaches deemphasize program specifications.

You will notice that the design techniques that are described here are based on information and techniques from earlier phases of the SDLC. For example, the components of the structure chart typically mirror the processes found on the data flow diagrams, and the process descriptions suggest the ways in which structure chart components should interrelate. Data models are used to explain the data that pass throughout the diagram. Also, analysts use the techniques and information to develop the program specifications, especially when writing pseudocode. Often during design, the analysts detect problems or inconsistencies with the analysis deliverables, and they must fine-tune or clarify previous work as they move forward.

In recent years, programmers have increasingly moved away from procedural programming languages and have migrated to event-driven programming. Programming languages such as Visual Basic are popular due to the fact that they combine features of procedural, event-driven, and object-oriented programming. Applications written in Visual Basic, for example, are "naturally" modularized because code procedures are written to prescribe the processing to perform when an event (e.g., a mouse click on a button object) occurs. These event procedures can be further decomposed to gain the advantages of modular design: code that is easier to understand, is reusable, has less redundancy, and is easier to maintain.

Therefore, the value of the modular design approaches we describe here has not truly diminished. The point is that planning before doing almost always improves the ultimate process when it comes to programming, and analysts should never begin writing code without having a complete understanding of what the code must do. Unfortunately, our experiences suggest that many project teams are much too quick at jumping into writing program code without first organizing and defining the basic program modules and how they interact.

At the end of program design, the project team compiles the *program design* document, which includes all of the structure charts and program specifications that will be used to implement the system. The program design is used by programmers to write code. We first describe the structure chart, a helpful tool that illustrates the overall organization of a program. Then we present the program specification, which contains detailed information about each module of code. Much of the information here is based on a classic book written by Meiler Page-Jones,[1] which we highly recommend that you read if you are interested in additional information on modular program design.

STRUCTURE CHART

The *structure chart* is an important technique that helps the analyst design the program for the new system. The structure chart shows all the components of code that must be included in a program at a high level, arranged in a hierarchical format that implies *sequence* (in what order components are invoked), *selection* (under what condition a module is invoked), and *iteration* (how often a component is repeated). The components are usually read from top to bottom, left to right, and they are numbered by a hierarchical numbering scheme in which lower levels have an additional level of numbering (e.g., the third level of modules would be numbered 1.1.1, 1.1.2, 1.1.3...).

Structure charts historically have been used to create transaction-based mainframe applications, which have many lines of code that must be carefully monitored. They help analysts create programs that are easy to understand and maintain, because the use of self-contained modules keeps changes from rippling throughout the programs. We believe that structure charts can be helpful in the building of many types of systems because they emphasize structure and reusability, characteristics of any good program.

Suppose that an academic system needs a program that will print a listing of students along with their grade point averages (GPAs), both for the current semester and overall. First, the program must retrieve the student grade records; then it must calculate the current and cumulative GPAs; finally, the grade list can be printed. The structure chart shown in Figure 10-6 communicates the basic components of this program and shows the interrelatedness of the modules. For example, by looking at this structure chart, a programmer can tell that there are four main code modules involved in creating a student grade listing: getting the student grade records, calculating current GPA, calculating cumulative GPA, and printing the listing. Also, there are various pieces of information that are either required by each module or created by it (e.g., the grade record, the cumulative GPA). The sections that follow use this example to describe each component of the structure chart.

Syntax

Module   A structure chart is composed of *modules* (lines of program code that perform a single function) that work together to form a program (Figure 10-7). The modules are depicted by a rectangle and connected by lines, which represent the passing of control. A *control module* is a higher-level component that contains the logic for performing other modules, and the components that it calls and controls are considered *subordinate modules*. For example, in Figure 10-6, module 1.0 is the control module that directs modules 1.1 through 1.4 as its subordinates.

---

[1] Meiler Page-Jones, *The Practical Guide to Structured Systems Design*, New York: Yourdon Press, 1980.

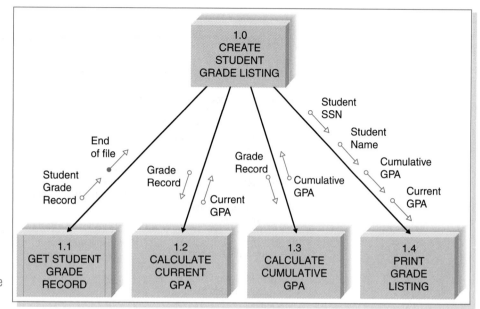

At times, modules are reused. These modules, called *library modules,* have
vertical lines on both sides of the rectangle to communicate that they will appear
several times on the structure chart (see Figure 10-7). The library module in Figure 10-6 is module 1.1, get student grade record, and this module is a generic module
that will be depicted several times in other parts of the diagram. Library modules
are highly encouraged because their reusability can save programmers from rewriting the same piece of code over and over again.

The lines that connect the modules communicate the passing of control. In
Figure 10-6, the control is linear, whereby all of the modules are performed in order
from top to bottom, left to right. There are two symbols that describe special types
of control that can appear on the structure chart. The curved arrow, or *loop,* indicates that the execution of some or all subordinate modules is repeated, and a *conditional line* (depicted by a diamond) denotes that execution of one or more of the
subordinate modules occurs in some cases but not in others. (See Figure 10-7.)

Look at the structure chart in Figure 10-8 and see how the loops and conditional line affect the meaning of the diagram. First, the loop through the lines to
modules 1.1, 1.2, and 1.3 means that, before the next two modules are invoked, the
first three modules will be repeated until their functionality is completed (i.e., all of
the student grades will be read and the two GPAs will be calculated before moving
to the print modules). Second, the lines connected by the conditional line convey
that both the dean's list report and grade listing are not printed each time this program is run, but instead are performed upon the basis of some condition. Therefore,
there are times when one or both of the print modules may not be invoked.

Another new symbol found on the structure chart in Figure 10-8 is the *connector.* (See Figure 10-7.) Structure charts can become quite unwieldy, especially
when they depict a large or complex program. A circle is used to connect parts of
the structure chart when there are space constraints and a diagram needs to be continued on another part of the page (i.e., an *on-page connector*), and a hexagon is
used to continue the diagram on another page entirely (i.e., an *off-page connector*).

Structure Chart Element	Purpose	Symbol
Every *module*: • Has a number. • Has a namec. • Is a control module if it calls other modules below it. • Is a subordinate module if it is controlled by a module at a higher level.	Denotes a logical piece of the program	**1.2 CALCULATE CURRENT GPA**
Every *library module* has: • A number. • A name. • Multiple instances within a diagram.	Denotes a logical piece of the program that is repeated within the structure chart	**1.1 GET STUDENT GRADE RECORD**
A *loop*: • Is drawn with a curved arrow. • Is placed around lines of one or more modules that are repeated.	Communicates that a module(s) is repeated	
A *conditional line*: • Is drawn with a diamond. • includes modules that are invoked on the basis of some condition.	Communicates that subordinate modules are invoked by the control module based on some condition	
A *data couple*: • Contains an arrow. • Contains an empty circle. • Names the type of data that are being passed. • Can be passed up or down. • Has a direction that is denoted by the arrow.	Communicates that data are being passed from one module to another	grade record
A *control couple*: • Contains an arrow. • Contains a filled-in circle. • Names the message or flag that is being passed. • Should be passed up, not down. • Has a direction that is denoted by the arrow.	Communicates that a message or a system flag is being passed from one module to another	end of file
An *off-page connector*: • Is denoted by the hexagon. • Has a title. • Is used when the diagram is too large to fit everything on the same page.	Identifies when parts of the diagram are continued on another page of the structure chart	**PRINT GRADE LISTING**
An *on-page connector*: • Is denoted by the circle. • Has a title. • Is used when the diagram is too large to fit everything in the same spot on a page.	Identifies when parts of the diagram are continued somewhere else on the same page of the structure chart	**PRINT GRADE LISTING**

FIGURE 10-7
Structure Chart Elements

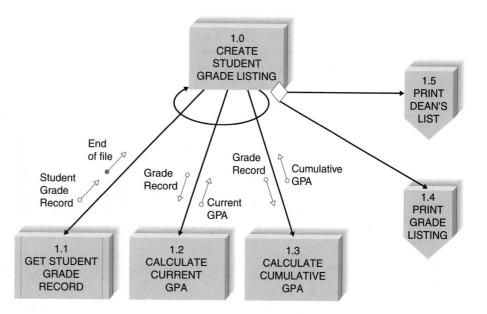

FIGURE 10-8
Revised Structure Chart Example

In Figure 10-8, notice that modules 1.4 and 1.5 are depicted on another page of the diagram.

Couples   *Couples*, shown by arrows, are drawn on the structure chart to show that information is passed between modules, with the arrowhead indicating which way the information is being sent. (See Figure 10-7.) *Data couples*, shown by arrows with empty circles, are used to represent the passing of pieces of data or data structures to other modules. For example, in Figure 10-8, a student grade record must be sent to module 1.2 for the GPA to be calculated, so a data couple is used to show the grade data structure being passed along.

Control couples, drawn with the use of arrows with filled-in circles, are used to pass parameters or system-related messages back and forth among modules. If some type of parameter needed to be passed (e.g., the customer is a new customer; the end of a file has been reached), a control couple (also called a *flag*) would be used. In Figure 10-8, module 1.1 sends an end-of-file parameter when the program reaches the end of the student grade file.

In general, control flags should be passed from subordinates to control modules, but not the other way around. Control flags are passed so that the control modules can make decisions about how the program will operate (e.g., module 1.1 passes the end-of-file marker to indicate that all records have been processed). Passing a control flag from higher to lower modules suggests that a lower-level module has control over the higher-level module.

The presence of couples signals that modules on the structure chart depend on each other in some way. A general rule is to be very conservative when applying couples to your diagram. In a later section, we will discuss style guidelines for couples to help you determine "good" from "bad" coupling situations.

Building the Structure Chart

Now that you understand the individual components of the structure chart, the next step is to learn how to put them together to form an effective design for the new system. Many times, process models are used as the starting point for structure charts. There are three basic kinds of processes on a process model: afferent, central, and efferent. *Afferent processes* are processes that provide inputs into the system, *central processes* perform critical functions in the operation of the system, and *efferent processes* deal with system outputs. Identify these three kinds of processes in Figure 10-9.

Each process of a DFD tends to represent one module on the structure chart, and if leveled DFDs are used, then each DFD level tends to correspond to a different level of the structure chart hierarchy (e.g., the process on the context-level DFD would correspond to the top module on the structure chart).

The difficulty comes when determining how the components on the structure chart should be organized. As we mentioned earlier, the structure chart communicates sequence, selection, and iteration, but none of these concepts is depicted explicitly in the process models. It is up to the analyst to make assumptions from

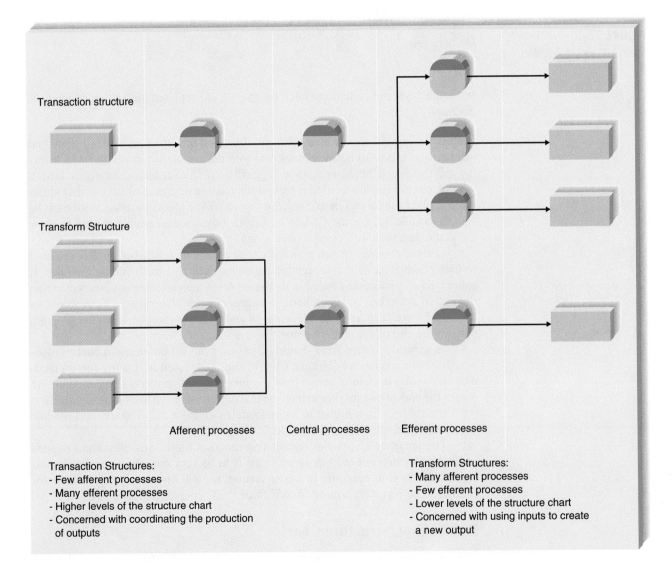

Transaction structure

Transform Structure

Afferent processes   Central processes   Efferent processes

Transaction Structures:
- Few afferent processes
- Many efferent processes
- Higher levels of the structure chart
- Concerned with coordinating the production
  of outputs

Transform Structures:
- Many afferent processes
- Few efferent processes
- Lower levels of the structure chart
- Concerned with using inputs to create
  a new output

FIGURE 10-9
Transform and Transaction Structures

the DFDs and read the process model descriptions to really understand how the structure chart should be drawn.

Transaction Structure   Luckily, there are two basic arrangements, or structures, for combining structure chart modules. The first arrangement is used when each module performs one of a group of individual transactions. This *transaction structure* contains a control module that calls subordinate modules, each of which handles a particular transaction. Pretend that Figure 10-10 illustrates the highest level of a student grade system. Module 1 is the control module that accepts a user's selection for what activity needs to be performed (e.g., maintain grade), and depending on the choice, one of the subordinate modules (1.1 through 1.4) is invoked. Transaction structures often occur where the actual system contains menus or submenus, and they are usually found higher up in the levels of a structure chart.

If the project team has used leveled DFDs to illustrate the processes for the system, the high levels of the DFD usually represent activities that belong in a transaction structure. In the current example, student grade system could correspond to the single process on the context-level DFD, and the four modules (1.1 through 1.4) would be the four processes on the level 0 diagram. If a leveled DFD approach is not used, then it may be a bit more difficult to differentiate a control module from its subordinates by using the process model. One hint is to look for points on the DFD in which a single data flow enters a process that produces multiple data flows as output—this usually indicates a transaction structure. See Figure 10-9 for an example of a process model that has transaction structure; notice how it contains many efferent processes and few afferent processes.

Transform Structure   A second type of module structure, called a *transform structure*, has a control module that calls several subordinate modules in sequence, after which something "happens." These modules are related because together they form a process that transforms some input into an output. Often, each module accepts an input from the module preceding it, works on the input, then passes it to the next module for more processing. For example, Figure 10-8 shows a control module that calls five subordinates. The control module describes what the subordinates will do

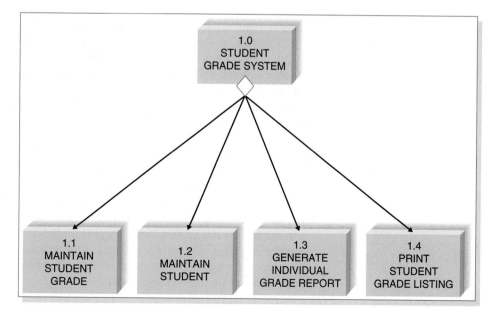

FIGURE 10-10
Transaction Structure

(e.g., create student grade listing), and the subordinates are invoked from left to right and transform the student grade records into two types of listings for student grades.

In a leveled DFD, the lowest levels usually represent transform structures. If a leveled DFD approach is not used, then you should look for the processes on the DFD for which an input is changed into an output of a different form. In this situation, the process in which the change is made likely will become a control module. All the processes leading up to the control module are subordinates that are performed first by the control module, followed by the processes that come after the control module. See Figure 10-9 for an example of transform structure; notice how there are many afferent processes and few efferent processes.

Applying the Concepts at Tune Source

Now that you are familiar with the basic components of the structure chart, the best way to learn how to build the diagram is to walk through an example that shows how to create one. Creating a structure chart is usually a four-step process. First, the analyst identifies the top-level modules and then decomposes them into lower levels. (This process is similar in some ways to identifying high-level processes in a DFD and then decomposing them into lower-level processes.) Second, the analyst adds the control connections among modules, such as loops and conditional lines that show when modules call subordinates. Third, he or she adds couples, the information that modules pass among themselves. Finally, the analyst reviews the structure chart and revises it again and again until it is complete.

The goal for this example is to create a structure chart that contains the modules of code that need to be programmed and shows how they need to be organized. The physical process model can be used as its starting point. Although it may neither map exactly into the future program nor contain enough levels of detail, the DFD will form a good rough-draft structure chart that can then be changed and improved. The requirements definition and use cases will provide additional detail. Let's walk through a structure chart example for Tune Source.

Step 1: Identify Modules and Levels First, identify the modules that belong on the diagram by converting the DFD processes into structure chart modules. Modules should perform only one function, so if, for some reason, a process contains more than one function, it should be broken into more than one module.

The various levels of the DFD generally translate into different levels of the structure chart. Look back at the DFDs that we created for Tune Source in Chapter 5 (Figures 5-13 and 5-15 through 5-18). The context-level DFD (the overall system) is placed at the top of the structure chart in Figure 10-11 to represent the overall control module of the system that manages the highest level of system functions. Then, the level 0 DFD processes are placed below it as subordinates. You should recognize that this particular structure of modules is a transaction structure, because the subordinates represent different functions that can be called by the control module.

This pattern continues through all the DFD levels. For example, the level 1 DFD that we created for the search and browse tunes process is placed below the search and browse tunes process control module. The subordinate modules are load Web site, process search requests, and process tune selection, the three processes from the search and browse tunes process level 1 DFD. Note that this structure of modules is a transform structure because the subordinate modules are carried out in a sequence to perform the process that is represented by the control module, search and browse tunes (Figure 10-11).

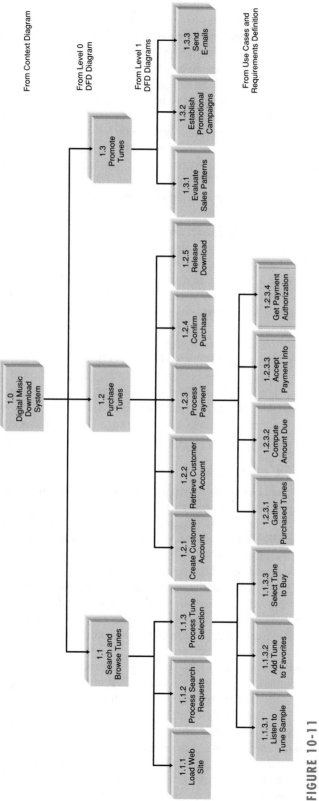

FIGURE 10-11

Step 1: Identify Modules and Levels for the Structure Chart

Likely, you will need to include additional levels of detail to the structure chart, until modules have enough detail so that they each perform only one function. Additional detail for the structure can be found within the use cases (Chapter 4) and requirements definition (Chapter 3) for the system. For example, if you read the use case for the search and browse tunes process in Figure 4-10, notice that step 3 includes listening to a sample, adding the tune to the Favorites list, and selecting the tune to buy. Modules have been added to the last row of Figure 10-11 to reflect our detailed understanding of these processes.

Finally, you must determine whether any modules on the diagram are reusable; if they are, they should be represented as library modules. In this particular portion of the structure chart, Jason has marked two modules as library modules, with vertical lines on the sides. He believes that these modules currently exist in the CD sales system and can be reused in this system.

Step 2: Identify Special Connections   The next step is to add loops and conditional lines to represent modules that are repeated or optional. For example, a customer of the Digital Music Download system can search for multiple tunes. Thus in Figure 10-12, we place a curved arrow around the line under the search and browse tunes process to show that modules 1.1.1 through 1.1.3 can be repeated several times. Can you think of other modules on the structure chart that will be iterated? According to Figure 10-12, one module under the *process payment* process also can happen several times before the system will accept payment information from the customer.

A diamond is placed below a control module that directs subordinates, which may or may not be performed. For example, customers may choose to listen to a tune sample, add it to the Favorites list, or buy it—they do not necessarily use all three alternatives. So a diamond is added below the process tune selection module to communicate this to the programmer. What other part of the structure chart contains subordinates that are invoked conditionally?

Step 3: Add Couples   Next, we must identify the information that has to pass among the modules. This information can be data attributes (denoted by an arrow with an empty circle) or special control parameters (denoted by an arrow with a filled-in circle). The arrowheads on the arrows indicate which way information is passed along. The DFD data flows provide us with some guidance about the couples to add, because the information that flows in and out of the DFD processes likely will also flow in and out of the corresponding structure chart modules.

We will illustrate the addition of couples to our structure chart by focusing just on the *purchase tunes* module and its subordinate modules. The DFD in Figure 5-17 shows that a new customer can provide customer information or can access existing customer information by signing in to his or her account. Therefore, one module on our structure chart (1.2.1) returns customer details for new customers, and one module (1.2.2) returns customer details for customers having existing accounts. The driver module (1.2 Purchase Tunes) calls the correct subordinate, depending on the existence of a customer account for the customer. The driver module then calls the *process payment* module (1.2.3). This module repeatedly calls its subordinate module, *gather purchased tunes* (1.2.3.1), to find all tunes the customer wants to purchase. These are then passed to the *compute amount due* module (1.2.3.2), which returns that result. Library module *accept payment info* (1.2.3.3) returns the customer's payment information, which is then used by the *get payment authorization* library module (1.2.3.4). A control couple is returned by that module,

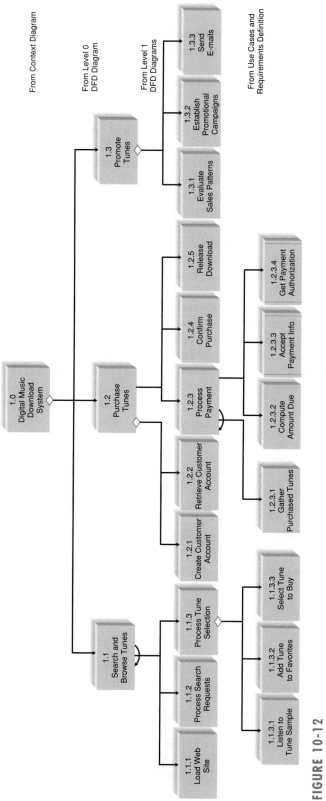

FIGURE 10-12

Step 2: Add Special Connections to the Structure Chart

indicating the result of the authorization step. The *process payment* module (1.2.3) returns the authorized payment data couple to its parent module, *purchase tunes* (1.2). The *purchase tunes* module calls the *confirm purchase* module (1.2.4) to obtain the customer's purchase confirmation, shown as a control couple. Finally, information about the purchased tune(s) is passed to the *release download* module (1.2.5) to complete the customer's purchase.

Revise Structure Chart   By now we have created the initial version of the structure chart based on the DFDs, use cases, and requirements definition, but rarely is a structure chart completed in one attempt. There are many gray areas and decisions that need to be confirmed by other information gleaned during analysis. There are several tools that can help when we are fine-tuning the structure chart. First, we can look at the process descriptions in the CASE repository to see whether there are any details of the processes that haven't yet been captured on the diagram. The process descriptions may uncover couples that were overlooked or explain more about how modules should be broken down. Second, we can examine the data model to confirm that the right records and specific fields have been passed using the data couples. This exercise also will confirm that data being passed are actually being captured by the system.

   As with most diagrams about which you have learned, the structure chart will evolve and contain more detail as new information is uncovered over the course of the project. Structure charts are not easy. The example that we have presented is much more straightforward than charts found in the real world. The following section explains some guidelines and good practices that you should apply to the chart as you work to improve it:

Design Guidelines

As you construct a structure chart, there are several guidelines that you can use to improve its quality. High-quality structure charts result in programs that are modular, reusable, and easy to implement. Measures of good design include cohesion, coupling, and appropriate levels of fan-in and/or fan-out.

Build Modules with High Cohesion   *Cohesion* refers to how well the lines of code within each structure chart module relate to each other. Ideally, a module should perform only one task, making it highly cohesive. Cohesive modules are easy to understand and build because their code performs one function, and they are built

---

YOUR TURN

10-1 STRUCTURE CHART

Using the structure chart in Figure 10-13 as a starting point, add modules that correspond to other parts of the Digital Music Download system. Use the data flow diagrams in Chapter 5 and the use case in Chapter 4 to help you.

QUESTION:

Do the modules that you added have a transform structure or a transaction structure—or both? Add any special connections to the chart as appropriate. Add necessary data and control couples.

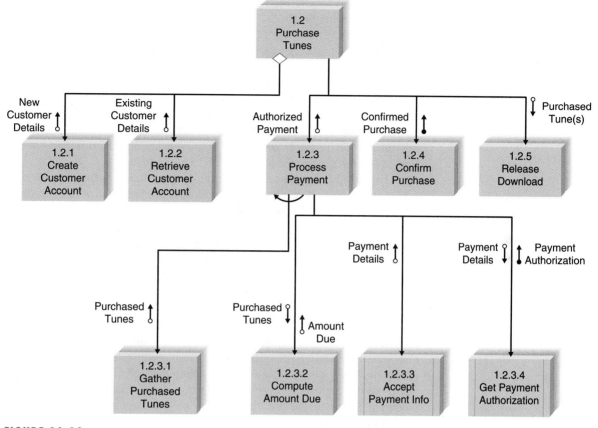

FIGURE 10-13
Step 3: Add Couples to the Structure Chart

to perform that function very efficiently. The more tasks that a module has to perform, the more complex the logic in the code must be to implement the tasks correctly. Typically, you can detect modules that are not cohesive from titles that have an *and* in them, signaling that the module performs multiple tasks.

Look back at the example in Figure 10.6. Currently, each module has good cohesion. Imagine, however, that module 1.3 actually said *calculate current and cumulative GPA* and that module 1.4 was *print grade listing and dean's list*. The *and* in both cases would signal a problem. These modules would not be considered cohesive, because they each perform two different tasks, limiting the flexibility of the modules and making the modules much more difficult to build and understand. If the program had to calculate only the current GPA while the module performed both functions, it would require much more complex logic in the code to make that happen.

Another signal of poor cohesion is the presence of control flags that are passed down to subordinate modules; their presence suggests that the subordinate has multiple functions from which one is chosen. Placing this kind of power in a subordinate module is not advisable, because it requires complex logic within the module to determine what functions to perform. In the previous example, if our subordinate module were *print grade listing and dean's list*, then a control flag would need to be sent to the subordinate module so that it could determine which report (or both) to print; the subordinate would have to make decisions regarding how to perform its functions.

There are various types of cohesion, some of which are better than others. For example, *functional cohesion* occurs when all elements of the module contribute to performing a single task, and this form of cohesion is highly desirable. By contrast, *temporal cohesion* takes place when functions within a module may not have much in common other than being invoked at the same time, and *coincidental cohesion* occurs when there is no apparent relationship among a module's functions (definitely something to avoid). Figure 10-14 lists seven types of cohesion, along with examples of each type. If you have difficulty differentiating different types of cohesion, use the decision tree in Figure 10-15 for guidance.

Factoring is the process of separating out a function from one module into a module of its own. If you find that a module is not cohesive or that it displays characteristics of a "bad" form of cohesion, you can apply factoring to create a better structure. For example, a more cohesive design for the *print grade listing and dean's list* example would be to factor out print dean's list and print grade listing into two separate modules. A control flag is not needed for this approach because subordinate modules would not have to make any kind of decision; each would perform one task—to print a report.

Build Loosely Coupled Modules *Coupling* involves how closely modules are interrelated, and the second guideline for good structure chart design states that modules should be loosely coupled. In this way, modules are independent from each other, which keeps code changes from rippling throughout the program. The numbers and kinds of couples on the structure chart reveal the presence of coupling between modules. Basically, the fewer the arrows on the diagrams, the easier it will be to make future alterations to the program.

Notice the coupling in the structure chart in Figure 10-8. The data couples (e.g., grade record) denote data that are passed among modules, and the control couple (e.g., end of file) shows that a message is being sent. Although the modules are communicating with one another, notice that the communication is quite limited (only one data couple passed in and out of the module) and there are no superfluous couples (data that are passed for no reason).

There are five types of coupling, each falling on different parts of a good-to-bad continuum. *Data coupling* occurs when modules pass parameters or specific pieces of data to each other, and this is a form of coupling that you want to see on your structure chart. A bad coupling type is *content coupling,* whereby one module actually refers to the inside of another module. Figure 10-16 presents the types of coupling and examples of each type.

Create High Fan-In *Fan-in* describes the number of control modules that communicate with a subordinate; a module with high fan-in has many different control modules that call it. This is a very good situation because high fan-in indicates that a module is reused in many places on the structure chart, which suggests that the module contains well-written generic code. (Fan-in also occurs when library modules are used.) Structures with high fan-in improve the reusability of modules and make it easier for programmers to recode when changes are made or mistakes are uncovered, because a change can be made in one place. Figures 10-17*a* and 10-17*b* show two different approaches for representing the functionality of reading an employee record. Example *a* is better.

	Type	Definition	Example
Good	Functional	Module performs one problem-related task.	Calculate Current GPA The module calculates current GPA only.
	Sequential	Output from one task is used by the next.	Format and Validate Current GPA Two tasks are performed, and the formatted GPA from the first task is the input for the second task.
	Communicational	Elements contribute to activities that use the same inputs or outputs.	Calculate Current and Cumulative GPA Two tasks are performed because they both use the student grade record as input.
	Procedural	Elements are performed in sequence but do not share data.	Print Grade Listing The module includes the following: housekeeping, produce report.
	Temporal	Activities are related in time.	Initialize Program Variables Although the tasks occur at the same time, each task is unrelated.
	Logical	List of activities; which one to perform is chosen outside of module.	Perform Customer Transaction This module will open a checking account, open a savings account, or calculate a loan, depending on the message that is sent by its control module.
Bad	Coincidental	No apparent relationship.	Perform Activities This module performs different functions that have nothing to do with each other: update customer record, calculate loan payment, print exception report, analyze competitor pricing structure.

FIGURE 10-14
Types of Cohesion (GPA = grade-point average)

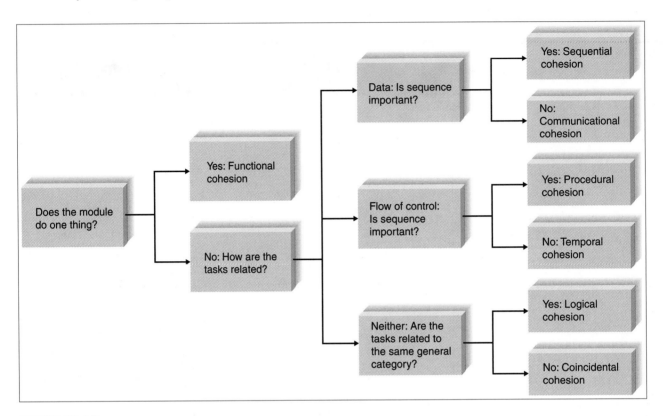

FIGURE 10-15
Cohesion Decision Tree (Adapted from Page-Jones, 1980)

Avoid High Fan-Out   Although we desire a subordinate to have multiple control modules, we want to avoid a large number of subordinates associated with a single control. Think of the management concept "span of control," which states that there is a limit to the number of employees that a boss can effectively manage. This concept applies to structure charts as well, in that a control module will become much less effective when given large numbers of modules to control. The general rule of thumb is to limit a control module's subordinates to approximately seven. One exception to this is a control module within a transaction structure. If a control module coordinates the invocation of subordinates, each of which performs unique functions, then it usually can handle whatever number of transactions exist. Figures 10-17*c* and 10-17*d* show high and low *fan-out* situations, respectively.

Assess the Chart for Quality   Finally, we have compiled a checklist (Figure 10-18) that may help you assess the quality of your structure chart. In addition, you should be aware that some CASE tools will critique the quality of your structure chart by using predetermined heuristics. Visible Analyst Workbench, for example, checks to make sure that all modules are labeled and connected and that data couples are labeled. It then reviews the connections between modules for correctness of connection, complexity of interface, and completeness of design. The analyzer gives warnings for low fan-in and high fan-out situations.

	Type	Definition	Example
Good ↓	Data	Modules pass fields of data or messages.	Update Student Record Student ID ↕ ⚲ Current GPA Calculate Current GPA All couples that are passed are used by the receiving module.
	Stamp	Modules pass record structures.	Update Student Record Student Record ↕ ⚲ Current GPA Calculate Current GPA Not all of the student record is used by the receiving module; only the *student ID* field is.
	Control	Module passes a piece of information that intends to control logic.	Update Student Record Student ID ↕ Current or Cumulative Flag ● ↕ ⚲ Current or Cumulative GPA Calculate Current or Cumulative GPA The receiving module has to determine which GPA to calculate.
	Common	Modules refer to the same global data area.	Typically, common coupling cannot be shown on the structure chart; it occurs when modules access the same data areas, and errors made in those areas can ripple through all the modules that use the data.
Bad	Content	Module refers to the inside of another module.	Module A: Update Student If student = new Then go to Module B Module B: Create Student At all costs, avoid modules referring to each other in this way.

FIGURE 10-16
Types of Coupling (GPA = grade-point average)

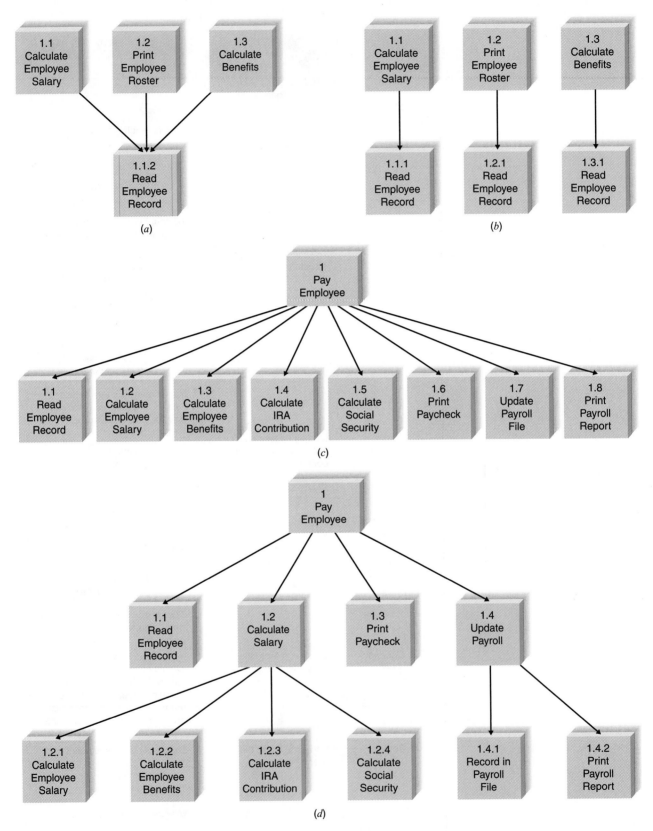

FIGURE 10-17
Examples of Fan-In and Fan-Out: *(a)* High Fan-In; *(b)* Low Fan-In; *(c)* High Fan-Out; *(d)* Low Fan-Out (IRA = individual retirement account)

✔ Library modules have been created whenever possible.
✔ The diagram has a high fan-in structure.
✔ Control modules have no more than seven subordinates.
✔ Each module performs only one function (high cohesion).
✔ Modules sparingly share information (loose coupling).
✔ Data couples that are passed are actually used by the accepting module.
✔ Control couples are passed from "low to high."
✔ Each module has a reasonable amount of code associated with it.

FIGURE 10-18
Checklist for Structure Chart Quality

PROGRAM SPECIFICATION

Once the analyst has communicated the big picture of how the program should be put together, he or she must describe the individual modules in enough detail so that programmers can take over and begin writing code. Modules on the structure chart are described by the use of *program specifications,* written documents that include explicit instructions on how to program pieces of code. Typically, project team members write one program specification for each module on the structure chart and then pass them along to programmers, who write the code during the implementation phase of the project. Specifications must be very clear and easy to understand, or else programmers will be slowed down trying to decipher vague or incomplete instructions.

Also, program specifications can pinpoint design problems that exist in the structure chart. At a high level, the structure chart may make sense, but when the analyst actually begins writing the detail behind the modules, he or she may find better ways for arranging the modules or may uncover missing or unnecessary couples.

Syntax

There is no formal syntax for a program specification, so every organization uses its own format, often a form like the one in Figure 10-19. Most program specification forms contain four components that convey the information that programmers will need to write the appropriate code.

Program Information   The top of the form in Figure 10-19 contains basic program information, such as the name of the module, its purpose, the deadline, the programmer, and the target programming language. This information is used to help manage the programming effort.

Events   The second section of the form is used to list the events that trigger the functionality in the program. An *event* is a thing that happens or takes place. Clicking the mouse generates a mouse event; pressing a key generates a keystroke event—in fact, almost everything the user does causes an event to occur.

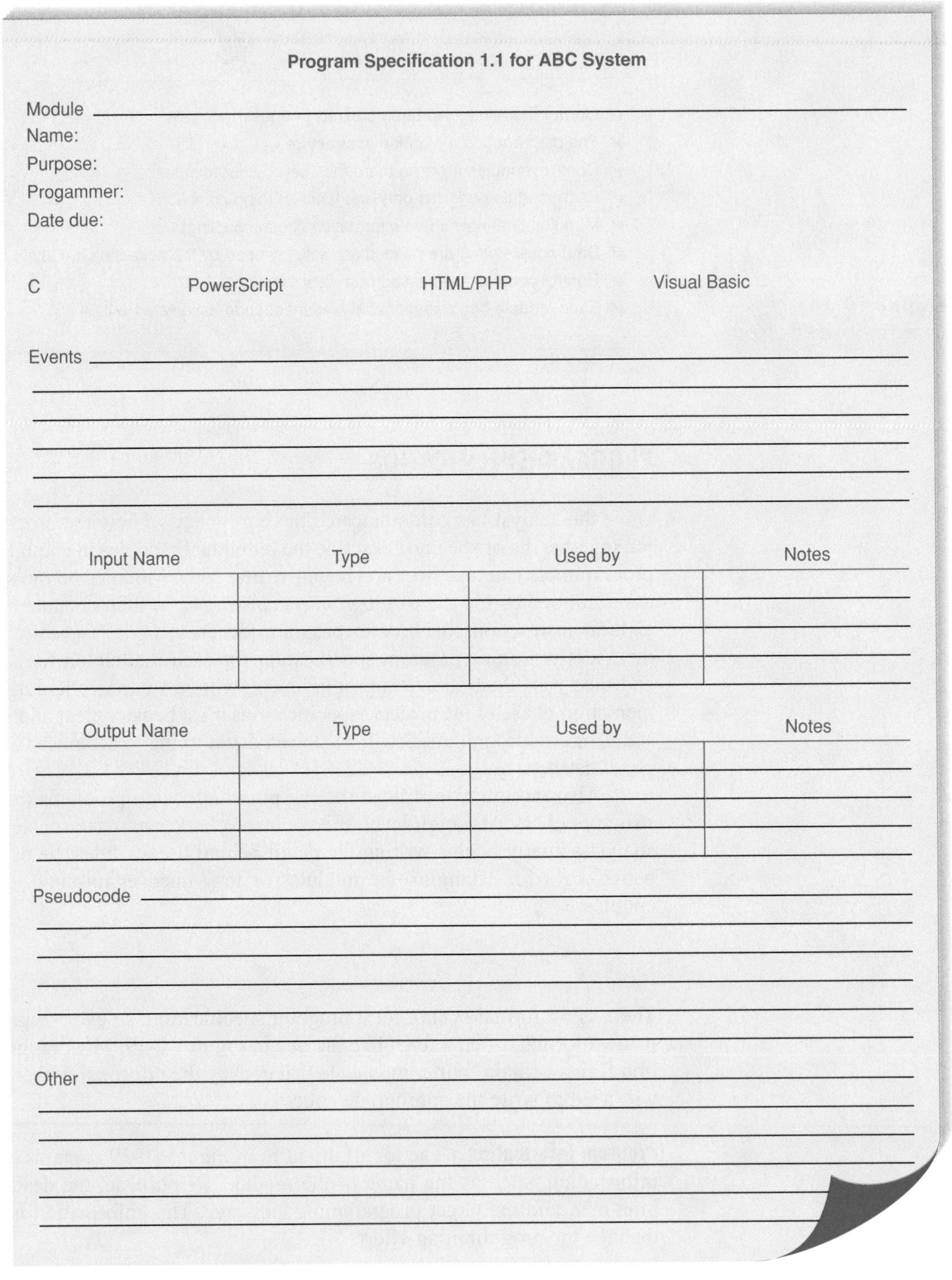

Program Specification 1.1 for ABC System

Module
Name:
Purpose:
Progammer:
Date due:

C   PowerScript   HTML/PHP   Visual Basic

Events _____

Input Name	Type	Used by	Notes

Output Name	Type	Used by	Notes

Pseudocode _____

Other _____

FIGURE 10-19
Program Specification Form

In the past, programmers used procedural programming languages (e.g., COBOL, C) containing instructions that were implemented in a predefined order, as determined by the computer system, and users were not allowed to deviate from the order. With structured programming, the event portion of the program specification is irrelevant. However, many programs today are *event-driven* (e.g., Visual Basic.Net, C++), and event-driven programs include procedures that are executed in response to an event initiated by the user, system, or program code. After initialization, the program waits for some kind of event to happen, and when it does, the program carries out the appropriate task, then waits once again.

We have found that many programmers still use program specifications when programming in event-driven languages, and they include the event section on the form to capture when the program will be invoked. Other programmers have switched to other design tools that capture event-driven programming instructions. One such tool, the behavioral state machine diagram, is described in detail in Chapter 14.

Inputs and Outputs   The next parts of the program specification describe the inputs and outputs to the program, which are identified by the data couples and control couples found on the structure chart. Programmers must understand what information is being passed and why, because that information ultimately will translate into variables and data structures within the actual program.

Pseudocode   *Pseudocode* is a detailed outline of the lines of code that need to be written, and it is presented in the next section of the form. If you remember, when we had to describe the processes on the DFDs, we used a technique called structured English, a language with syntax based on English and structured programming. These DFD descriptions in structured English are now used as the primary input to produce pseudocode.

Pseudocode is a language that contains logical structures, including sequential statements, conditional statements, and iteration. It differs from structured English in that pseudocode contains details that are programming specific, such as initialization instructions or linking, and it also is more extensive so that a programmer can write the module by mirroring the pseudocode instructions. In general, pseudocode is much more like real code, and its audience is the programmer as opposed to the analyst. Its format is not as important as the information it conveys. Figure 10-20 shows a short example of pseudocode for a module that is responsible for calculating a discount on a purchase transaction.

Writing good pseudocode can be difficult—imagine creating instructions that someone else can follow without having to ask for clarification or making a wrong

```
Calculate_discount_amount (total_price, discount_amount)
   If total_price < 50 THEN
      discount_amount = 0
   ELSE
   If total_price < 500 THEN
      discount_amount = total_price * .10
   ELSE
      discount_amount = total_price * .20
   END IF
END
```

FIGURE 10-20
Pseudocode

assumption. For example, have you ever given a friend directions to your house, but your friend ended up getting lost? To you, the directions might have been very clear, but that is because of your personal assumptions. To you, the instruction "take the first left turn" may really mean "take a left turn at the first stoplight." Someone else's interpretation might be "take a left turn at the first road, with or without a light." (Barbara has a very bad sense of direction and has been known to make a first left turn into a driveway!)

Therefore, when writing pseudocode, pay special attention to detail and readability.

The last section of the program specification provides space for other information that must be communicated to the programmer, such as calculations, special business rules, calls to subroutines or libraries, and other relevant issues. This also can point out changes or improvements that will be made to the structure chart on the basis of problems that the analyst detected during the specification process.

Some project teams do not create program specifications by using forms, but instead input the specification information directly into a CASE tool. In these cases, the information is added to the description for the appropriate module on the structure chart (or to its corresponding process on the DFD). Figure 10-21 illustrates how the CASE repository can be used to capture program design information.

Applying the Concepts at Tune Source

Refer to the structure chart in Figure 10-12 for the following example. Although not shown on the structure chart, there are subordinate modules associated with the *process search request* module (1.1.2) that perform searches for tunes by artist, by title, by genre, etc. Each module on the diagram should have an associated program specification, but for now let's create one for module 1.1.2.2, *find tunes by title*.

The first part of the form (Figure 10-22) contains basic information about the specification, such as its name and purpose. Because an event-driven programming language will be used, we list the events that will trigger the program to run (i.e., a mouse click, a menu selection).

The inputs and outputs for the program correspond to the two couples on the structure chart: title that is sent to module 1.1.2.2 and tune that is passed by the module. We added these to the input and output sections of the form, respectively.

Next, we used the structured English description for the module that is found in the process description to develop the pseudocode that will communicate the code that should be written for the program. However, as we wrote the pseudocode and examined the process description, we discovered a problem—the structure

---

YOUR TURN | **10-2 PROGRAM SPECIFICATION**

Create a program specification for module 1.2.3.2, compute amount due, on the structure chart shown in Figure 10-13.

QUESTION:
On the basis of your specification, are there any changes to the structure chart that you would recommend?

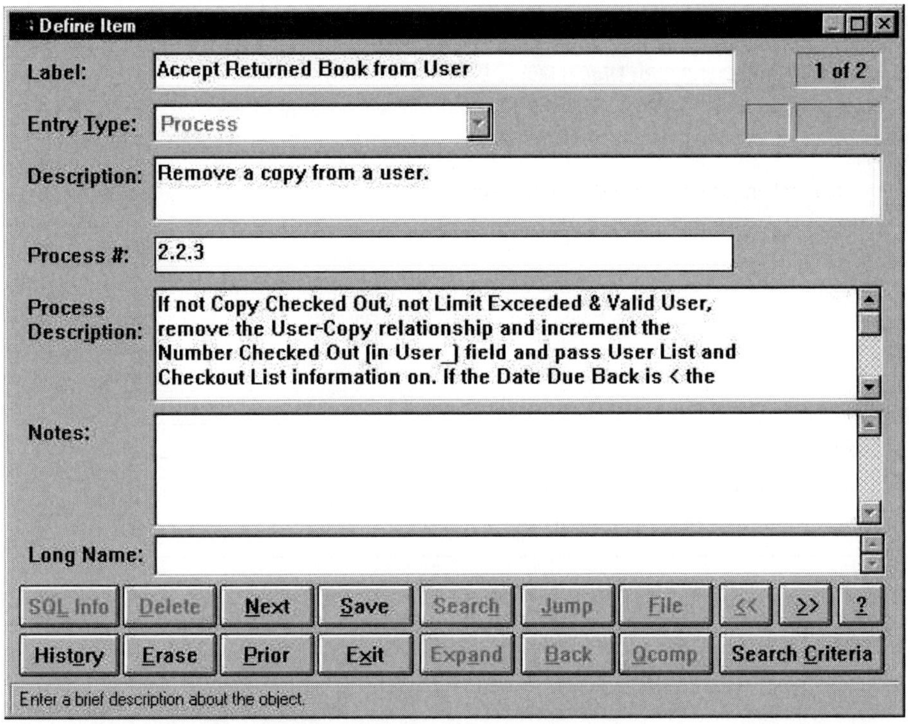

Analysis Phase Process Specification with structured English process description

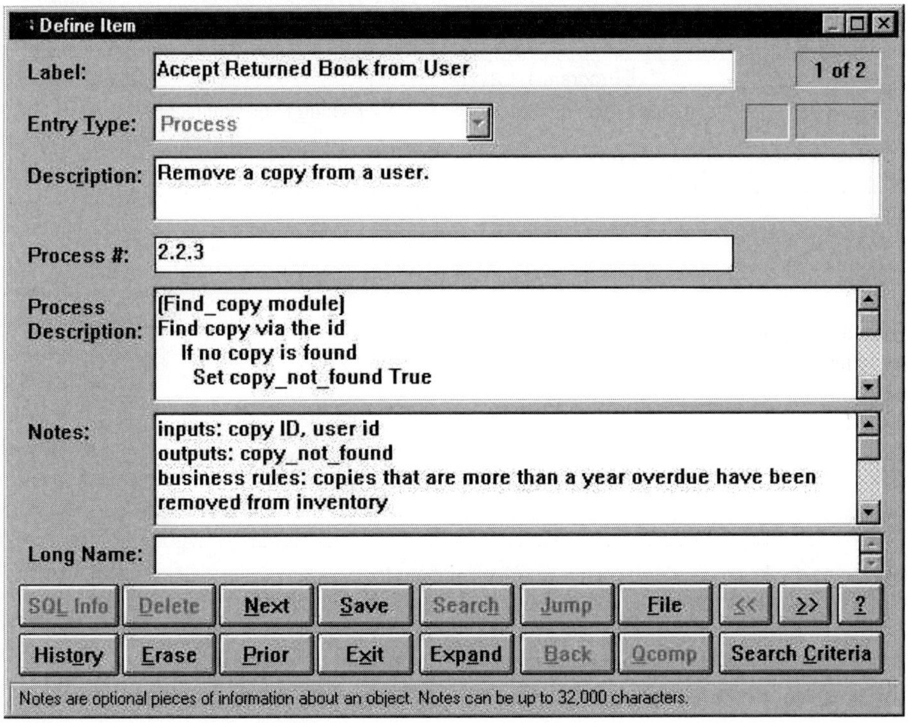

(First "Define Item" window)

Label:	Accept Returned Book from User	1 of 2
Entry Type:	Process	
Description:	Remove a copy from a user.	
Process #:	2.2.3	

Process Description: If not Copy Checked Out, not Limit Exceeded & Valid User, remove the User-Copy relationship and increment the Number Checked Out (in User_) field and pass User List and Checkout List information on. If the Date Due Back is < the

Notes:

Long Name:

SQL Info | Delete | Next | Save | Search | Jump | File | << | >> | ?

History | Erase | Prior | Exit | Expand | Back | Qcomp | Search Criteria

Enter a brief description about the object.

Design Phase Process Specification:
- Structured English has been changed to pseudocode.
- Relevant specification information like inputs, outputs, and business rules have been added to the Notes section.

(Second "Define Item" window)

Label:	Accept Returned Book from User	1 of 2
Entry Type:	Process	
Description:	Remove a copy from a user.	
Process #:	2.2.3	

Process Description:
```
[Find_copy module]
Find copy via the id
    If no copy is found
        Set copy_not_found True
```

Notes:
```
inputs: copy ID, user id
outputs: copy_not_found
business rules: copies that are more than a year overdue have been
removed from inventory
```

Long Name:

SQL Info | Delete | Next | Save | Search | Jump | File | << | >> | ?

History | Erase | Prior | Exit | Expand | Back | Qcomp | Search Criteria

Notes are optional pieces of information about an object. Notes can be up to 32,000 characters.

FIGURE 10-21
Process Description—Analysis and Design

Program Specification 1.1.2.2 for Digital Music Download System

Module _____

Name: Find_tune_by_Title

Purpose: Display basic tune information, using a title input by the user

Progammer: John Smith

Date due: April 26, 2009

☐ C   ■ HTML/PHP   ☐ Visual Basic   ☐ Javascript

Events _____

search by title push-button is clicked

search by title hyperlink is selected

Input Name:	Type:	Provided by:	Notes:
Tune title	String (50)	Program 1.1.2	

Output Name:	Type:	Used by	Notes:
Tune ID	String (10)	Program 1.1.2	
Not_found	Logical	Program 1.1.2	Used to communicate when tune is not found

Pseudocode _____

```
(Find_tune module)
not_found =True
  For all tune titles in Available Tunes table
      If user title matches tune title, save tune ID
      not-found = False
      End If
  End For
  Return
```

Other _____

Business rule: If no matching tunes are found, the "Artist of the week" will appear to the user.

Note: A control couple containing a not _found flag should be included from 1.1.2.2 to 1.1.2 to instruct 1.1.2 to display a not found message to the user and the Artist of the week.

FIGURE 10-22

Program Specification for Find Tune by Title

chart does not appear to handle the situation in which a user's search request cannot be located by the system. Although the pseudocode includes a "not found" condition, there is no mechanism for the program to pass this result back to its calling program. At this point, we made a note in the last section of the program specification to add a control couple to the structure chart that passes a "not found" flag, and a second output was added to the current specification form.

Finally, we added a business rule to the specification to explain to the programmer what will happen when a tune is not found; however, the functionality of this rule will be handled elsewhere in the program. The program specification is now ready for the implementation phase, when the form will be passed off to a programmer who will develop the code that meets its requirements.

SUMMARY

Moving from Logical to Physical Process Models
As the application logic of the information system is designed, the implementation decisions describing how the system will work are made. Physical data flow diagrams show these implementation details, including data stores that refer to files and database tables, programs or human actions that perform processes, and the physical transfer media for the data flows. The automated parts of the system are distinguished from the manual parts by the human-machine boundary.

Structure Chart
The structure chart shows all the functional components that must be included in the program at a high level, arranged in a hierarchical format that implies order and control. Lines that connect modules can contain a loop, which signifies that the subordinate module is repeated before other modules to its right are invoked. A diamond is placed over subordinate modules that are invoked conditionally. An arrow with a filled circle represents a control couple or flag, which passes system messages from one module to another. The data couple, an arrow with an empty circle, denotes the passing of records or fields.

Modules can be organized into one of two types of structures. The transaction structure contains a control module which calls subordinates that perform independent tasks. By contrast, transform structures convert some input into an output through a series of subordinate modules, and the control module describes the transformation that takes place.

Building Structure Charts
Creating a structure chart is usually a four-step process. First, the analyst identifies the top-level modules and then decomposes them into lower levels. Second, the analyst adds the control connections among modules, such as loops and conditional lines that show when modules call subordinates. Third, the analyst adds couples, the information that modules pass among themselves. Finally, the analyst reviews the structure chart and revises it again and again until it is complete.

Structure Chart Design Guidelines
There are several design guidelines that you should follow when designing structure charts. First, build modules with high cohesion so that each module performs only one function. There are seven kinds of cohesion, ranging from good to bad, and the instances of bad cohesion should be removed from the structure chart. Second,

modules should not be interdependent, but rather should be loosely coupled, using good types of coupling. There are five kinds of coupling, ranging from good to bad; as with cohesion, bad instances should be avoided. Finally, structure charts should display high fan-in and low fan-out, which means that modules should have many control modules but limited subordinates.

Program Specification

Program specifications provide more detailed instructions to the programmers about how to code the modules. The program specification contains several components that communicate basic module information (e.g., a name, calculations that must be performed, and the target programming language), inputs and outputs, special instructions for the programmer, and pseudocode.

Pseudocode

Pseudocode is a technique similar to structured English that communicates the code written with the use of programming structures and a generic language that is not program language specific. Pseudocode is much more like real code than is structured English, and its audience is the programmer as opposed to the analyst. Many programs today are event driven, meaning that their instructions are not necessarily invoked in a predefined order, as determined by the computer system. Instead, users control the order of modules through the way that they interact with the system. When event-driven programming is used, program specifications should include a section that describes the types of events that invoke the code.

KEY TERMS

Afferent process	Efferent processes	Physical data flow diagram
Central process	Event	Physical process model
Cohesion	Event driven	Procedural cohesion
Coincidental cohesion	Factoring	Program design
Common coupling	Fan-in	Program specification
Communicational cohesion	Fan-out	Pseudocode
Conditional line	Flag	Selection
Connector	Functional cohesion	Sequence
Content coupling	Human-machine boundary	Sequential cohesion
Control couple	Iteration	Stamp coupling
Control coupling	Library module	Structure chart
Control module	Logical cohesion	Subordinate module
Couple	Loop	Temporal cohesion
Coupling	Module	Top-down modular approach
Data couple	Off-page connector	Transaction structure
Data coupling	On-page connector	Transform structure

QUESTIONS

1. What is the purpose of creating a logical process model and then a physical process model?
2. What information is found on the physical DFD that is not included on the logical DFD?
3. What are some of the system-related data elements and data stores that may be needed on the physical DFD that were not a part of the logical DFD?
4. What is a human-machine boundary?
5. Why is using a top-down modular approach useful in program design?

6. Describe the primary deliverable produced during program design. What does it include and how is it used?

7. What is the purpose of the structure chart in program design?

8. Where does the analyst find the information needed to create a structure chart?

9. Distinguish between a control module, subordinate module, and library module on a structure chart. Can a particular module be all three? Why or why not?

10. What does a data couple depict on a structure chart? A control couple?

11. It is preferable for a control couple to flow in one particular direction on the structure chart. Which direction is preferred, and why?

12. What is the difference between a transaction structure and a transform structure? Can a module be a part of both types of structures? Why or why not?

13. What is meant by the characteristic of module cohesion? What is its role in structure chart quality?

14. List the seven types of cohesion. Why do the various types of cohesion range from good to bad? Give an example of good coupling and an example of bad coupling.

15. What is meant by the characteristic of module coupling? What is its role in structure chart quality?

16. List the seven types of coupling. Why do the various types of coupling range from good to bad? Give an example of good coupling and an example of bad coupling.

17. What is meant by the characteristics of fan-in and fan-out? What are their roles in structure chart quality?

18. List and discuss three ways to ensure the overall quality of a structure chart.

19. Describe the purpose of program specifications.

20. What is the difference between structured programming and event-driven programming?

21. Is program design more or less important when using event-driven languages such as Visual Basic?

EXERCISES

A. Draw a physical level 0 data flow diagram (DFD) for the following dentist office system, and compare it with the logical model that you created in Chapter 5: Whenever new patients are seen for the first time, they complete a patient information form that asks their name, address, phone number, and brief medical history, all of which are stored in the patient information file. When a patient calls to schedule a new appointment or change an existing appointment, the receptionist checks the appointment file for an available time. Once a good time is found for the patient, the appointment is scheduled. If the patient is a new patient, an incomplete entry is made in the patient file; the full information will be collected when the patient arrives for the appointment. Because appointments are often made so far in advance, the receptionist usually mails a reminder postcard to each patient two weeks before his or her appointment.

B. Create a physical level 0 DFD for the following, and compare it with the logical model that you created in Chapter 5: A Real Estate Inc. (AREI) sells houses. People who want to sell their houses sign a contract with AREI and provide information on the house. This information is kept in a database by AREI, and a subset of this information is sent to the citywide multiple listing service used by all real estate agents. AREI works with two types of potential buyers. Some buyers have an interest in one specific house.

In this case, AREI prints information from its database, which the real estate agent uses to help show the house to the buyer (a process beyond the scope of the system to be modeled). Other buyers seek AREI's advice in finding a house that meets their needs. In this case, buyers complete a buyer information form. Information from it is entered into a buyer database, and AREI real estate agents use its information to search AREI's database and the multiple listing service for houses that meet their needs. The results of these searches are printed and used to help the real estate agents show houses to the buyers.

C. Draw a physical level 0 DFD for the following system and compare it with the logical model that you created in Chapter 5. A Video Store (AVS) runs a series of fairly standard video stores. Before a video can be put on the shelf, it must be catalogued and entered into the video database. To rent a video, every customer must have a valid AVS customer card. Customers rent videos for three days at a time. Every time a customer rents a video, the system must ensure that he or she does not have any overdue videos. If so, the overdue videos must be returned and the customer must pay a fine before renting more videos. Likewise, if the customer has returned overdue videos, but has not paid the fine, the fine must be paid before new videos can be rented. Every morning, the store manager prints a report that lists overdue videos; if a video is two or more days overdue, the manager calls the customer to remind him or her to return the video. If a video is returned in damaged condition, the manager removes it from the video database and sometimes charges the customer.

D. What symbols would you use to depict the following situations on a structure chart?
  • A function occurs multiple times before the next module is invoked.
  • A function is continued on the bottom of the page of the structure chart.

• A customer record is passed from one part of the program to another.
• The program will print a record either on screen or on a printer, depending on the user's preference.
• A customer's ID is passed from one part of the program to another.
• A function cannot fit on the current page of the structure chart.

E. Describe the differences in the meanings between the two structure charts shown. How have the symbols changed the meanings?

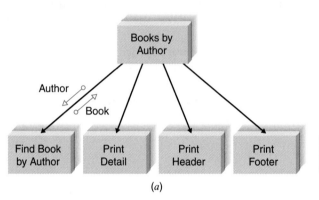

(a)

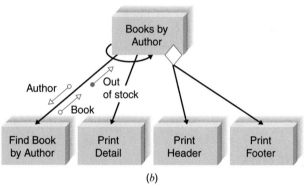

(b)

F. Create a structure chart based on the data flow diagrams (DFDs) that you created for the following exercises in Chapter 5:
  • Question D
  • Question E
  • Question F

  • Question G
  • Question H

G. Critique the structure chart shown, which depicts a guest making a hotel reservation. Describe the chart in terms of fan-in, fan-out, coupling, and cohesion. Redraw the chart to improve the design.

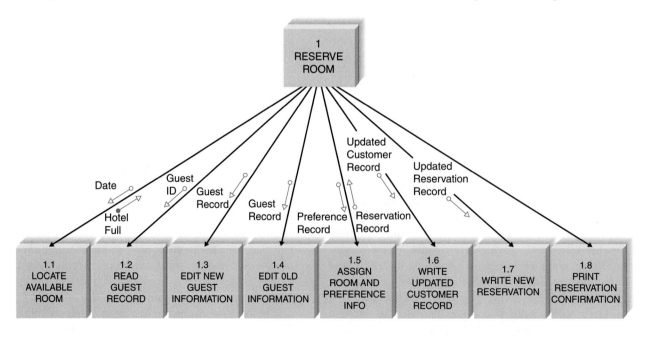

H. Identify the kinds of coupling that are represented in the following situations:

Customer Record	Customer Record, Order Record	Customer Address Record	Customer Name, Address, City, State, ZIP
PRINT MAILING LIST	PRINT MAILING LIST	PRINT MAILING LIST	PRINT MAILING LIST
(a)	(b)	(c)	(d)

I. Identify the kinds of cohesion that are represented in the following situations:
- accept customer address
- print mailing label record
- print customer address listing
- print marketing address report
- accept customer address
- validate zip code and state
- format customer address
- print customer address
- accept customer address
- print mailing label record

- accept customer address
- print mailing label record or
- print customer address listing or
- print marketing address report or
- validate customer address
- print mailing label record
- check customer balance
- print marketing address report
- record customer preference information

J. Identify whether the following structures are transaction or transform and explain the reasoning behind your answers.[2]

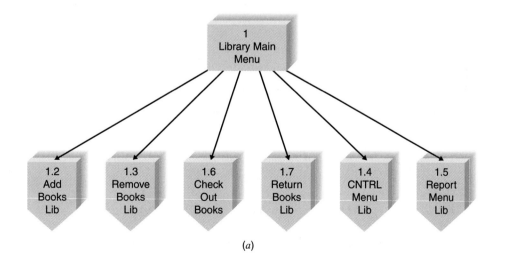

(a)

[2] The structure charts based on a library system are adapted from an example provided with the Visible Analyst Workbench software.

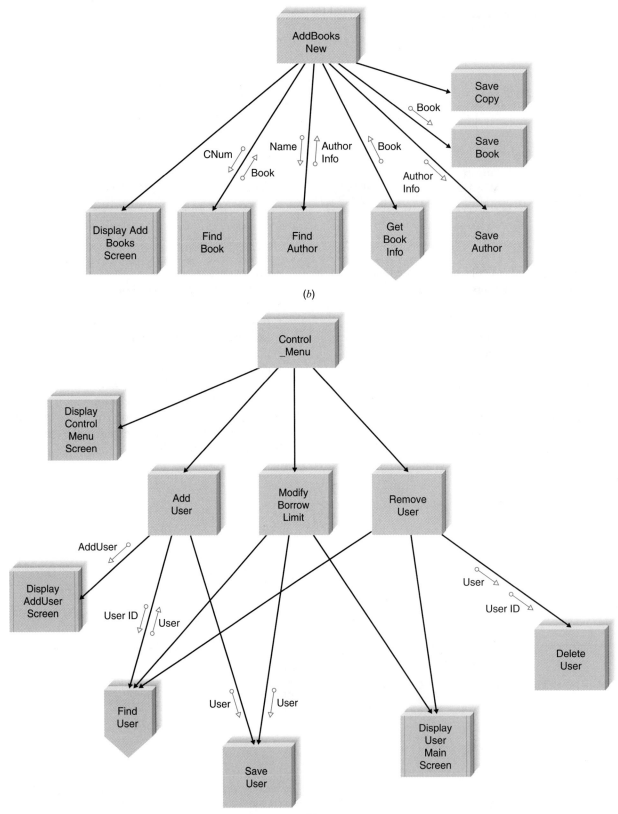

(b)

(c)

K. Create a program specification for module 1.1.3.1 on the structure chart in Figure 10-12.
L. Create a program specification for module 1.2.3.4 on the structure chart in Figure 10-12.
M. Create pseudocode for the program specification that you wrote in Exercise K.
N. Create pseudocode for the program specification that you wrote in Exercise L.
O. Create pseudocode that explains how to start the computer at your computer lab and open a file in the word processor. Exchange your pseudocode with a classmate and follow the instructions exactly as they appear. Discuss the results with your classmate. At what points were each set of instructions vague or unclear? How would you improve the pseudocode that you created originally?

MINICASES

1. In the new system for Holiday Travel Vehicles, the system users follow a two-stage process to record complete information on all of the vehicles sold. When an RV or trailer first arrives at the company from the manufacturer, a clerk from the inventory department creates a new vehicle record for it in the computer system. The data entered at this time include basic descriptive information on the vehicle such as manufacturer, name, model, year, base cost, and freight charges. When the vehicle is sold, the new vehicle record is updated to reflect the final terms of the sale and the dealer-installed options added to the vehicle. This information is entered into the system at the time of sale when the salesperson completes the sales invoice.

    When it is time for the clerk to finalize the new vehicle record, the clerk will select a menu option from the system, which is called "Finalize New Vehicle Record." The tasks involved in this process are described next.

    When the user selects the "Finalize New Vehicle Record" from the system menu, the user is immediately prompted for the serial number of the new vehicle. This serial number is used to retrieve the new vehicle record for the vehicle from system storage. If a record cannot be found, the serial number is probably invalid. The vehicle serial number is then used to retrieve the option records that describe the dealer-installed options that were added to the vehicle at the customer's request. There may be zero or more options. The cost of the option specified on the option record(s) is totaled. Then, the dealer cost is calculated, using the vehicle's base cost, freight charge, and total option cost. The completed new vehicle record is passed back to the calling module.

    a. Develop a structure chart for this segment of the Holiday Travel Vehicles system.
    b. What type of structure chart have you drawn, a transaction structure or a transform structure? Why?

2. Develop a program specification for Module 4.2.5 *(Calculate Dealer Cost)* in minicase 1.

PLANNING

ANALYSIS

DESIGN

☑ Select Design Strategy
☑ Design Architecture
☑ Select Hardware and Software
☑ Develop Use Scenarios
☑ Design Interface Structure
☑ Develop Interface Standards
☑ Design Interface Prototype
☑ Evaluate User Interface
☑ Design User Interface
☑ Develop Physical Data Flow Diagrams
☑ Develop Program Structure Charts
☑ Develop Program Specifications
☐ Select Data Storage Format
☐ Develop Physical Entity Relationship Diagram
☐ Denormalize Entity Relationship Diagram
☐ Performance Tune Data Storage
☐ Size Data Storage

T A S K C H E C K L I S T

PLANNING   ANALYSIS   DESIGN

CHAPTER 11

DATA STORAGE DESIGN

A nother important activity of the design phase is designing the data storage component of the system. This chapter describes the activities that are performed when developing the data storage design. First, the different ways in which data can be stored are described. Several important characteristics that should be considered when selecting the data storage format are discussed. The process of revising the logical data model into the physical data model is then outlined. Because one of the most popular data storage formats today is the relational database, optimization of relational databases from both storage and access perspectives is also included.

OBJECTIVES

- Become familiar with several file and database formats.
- Understand several goals of data storage.
- Be able to revise a logical ERD into a physical ERD.
- Be able to optimize a relational database for data storage and data access.
- Become familiar with indexes.
- Be able to estimate the size of a database.

CHAPTER OUTLINE

IMPLEMENTATION

INTRODUCTION

As explained in Chapter 8, the work done by any application program can be divided into four general functions: data storage, data access logic, application logic, and presentation logic. The data storage function is concerned with how data is stored and handled by the programs that run the system.

Applications are of little use without the data that they support. How useful is a multimedia application that can't support images or sound? Why would users log into a system to find information if it took them less time to locate the information manually? It is essential to ensure that data storage is designed so that inefficient systems, long response times, and difficult-to-access information (several hallmarks of failed systems) are avoided.

As analysts turn their attention to the data storage that will be needed for the new system, several things must be done. First, the data storage format for the new system must be selected. This chapter describes a variety of data storage formats and explains how to select the appropriate one for your application. There are two basic types of data storage formats for application systems: files and databases. There are multiple types of each storage format; for example, databases can be object-oriented, relational, multidimensional, and so on. Each type has certain characteristics that make it preferable for certain situations.

Following the selection of the data storage format, the data model created during analysis is modified to reflect this implementation decision. The logical data model will be converted into a *physical data model.* CASE repository information is expanded to include much more detailed information about specific implementation details. The analysts will also want to ensure that the DFDs and ERDs balance properly, so the CRUD matrix will be revised as necessary.

Finally, the selected data storage format must be designed to optimize its processing efficiency. One of the leading complaints by end users is that the final system is too slow. To avoid such complaints, project team members must allow time during the design phase to carefully make sure that the file or database performs as fast as possible. At the same time, the team must keep hardware costs down by minimizing the storage space that the application will require. The goals of maximizing access to data and minimizing the amount of space taken to store data can conflict, so designing data storage efficiency usually requires trade-offs. The team must carefully review the availability, reliability, and security nonfunctional requirements to identify issues that produce trade-offs in performance, cost, and storage space.

DATA STORAGE FORMATS

There are two main types of data storage formats: files and databases. *Files* are electronic lists of data that have been optimized to perform a particular transaction. For example, Figure 11-1 shows a patient appointment file with information about patient's appointments, in the form in which it is used, so that the information can be accessed and processed quickly by the system.

A *database* is a collection of groupings of information that are related to each other in some way (e.g., through common fields). Logical groupings of information could include such categories as customer data, information about an order, and product information. A *database management system* (*DBMS*) is software that creates

Appointment Date	Appointment Time	Duration	Reason	Patient ID	First Name	Last Name	Phone Number	Doctor ID	Doctor Last Name
11/23/2009	2:30	.25 hour	Flu	758843	Patrick	Dennis	548-9456	V524625587	Vroman
11/23/2009	2:30	1 hour	Physical	136136	Adelaide	Kin	548-7887	T445756225	Tantalo
11/23/2009	2:45	.25 hour	Shot	544822	Chris	Pullig	525-5464	V524625587	Vroman
11/23/2009	3:00	1 hour	Physical	345344	Felicia	Marston	548-9333	B544742245	Brousseau
11/23/2009	3:00	.5 hour	Migraine	236454	Thomas	Bateman	667-8955	V524625587	Vroman
11/23/2009	3:30	.5 hour	Muscular	887777	Ryan	Nelson	525-4772	V524625587	Vroman
11/23/2009	3:30	.25 hour	Shot	966233	Peter	Todd	667-2325	T445756225	Tantalo
11/23/2009	3:45	.75 hour	Muscular	951657	Mike	Morris	663-8944	T445756225	Tantalo
11/23/2009	4:00	1 hour	Physical	223238	Ellen	Whitener	525-8874	B544742245	Brousseau
11/23/2009	4:00	.5 hour	Flu	365548	Jerry	Starsia	548-9887	V524625587	Vroman
11/23/2009	4:30	1 hour	Minor surg	398633	Susan	Perry	525-6632	V524625587	Vroman
11/23/2009	4:30	.5 hour	Migraine	222577	Elizabeth	Gray	667-8400	T445756225	Tantalo
11/24/2009	8:30	.25 hour	Shot	858756	Elias	Awad	663-6364	T445756225	Tantalo
11/24/2009	8:30	1 hour	Minor surg	232158	Andy	Ruppel	525-9888	V524625587	Vroman
11/24/2009	8:30	.25 hour	Flu	244875	Rick	Grenci	548-2114	B544742245	Brousseau
11/24/2009	8:45	.5 hour	Muscular	655683	Eric	Meier	667-0254	T445756225	Tantalo
11/24/2009	8:45	1 hour	Physical	447521	Jane	Pace	548-0025	B544742245	Brousseau
11/24/2009	9:30	.5 hour	Flu	554263	Trey	Maxham	663-8547	V524625587	Vroman

FIGURE 11-1
Appointment File

and manipulates these databases (Figure 11-2). *End-user DBMS*s such as Microsoft Access support small-scale databases that are used to enhance personal productivity, and *enterprise DBMS*s, such as DB2, Jasmine, SQL Server, and Oracle, can manage huge volumes of data and support applications that run an entire company. An end-user DBMS is significantly less expensive and easier for novice users to use than its enterprise counterpart, but it does not have the features or capabilities that are necessary to support mission-critical or large-scale systems. Open-source DBMS's are also popular, such as MySQL.

The next section describes several different kinds of files and databases that can be used to handle a system's data storage requirements.

Files

A *data file* contains an electronic list of information that is formatted for a particular transaction, and the information is changed and manipulated by programs that are written for those purposes. Files created by older, legacy systems are frequently in a proprietary format, while newer systems use a standard format such as CSV (comma separated value) or tab-delimited. Typically, files are organized sequentially, and new records are added to the file's end. These records can be associated with other records by a pointer, which is information about the location of the related record. A pointer is placed at the end of each record, and it "points" to the next record in a series or set. Sometimes files are called *linked lists* because of the way the records are linked together by the pointers. There are several types of files that

Appointment Date	Appointment Time	Duration	Reason	Patient ID	Doctor ID
11/23/2009	2:30	.5 hour	Flu	758843	V524625587
11/23/2009	2:30	1 hour	Physical	136136	T445756225
11/23/2009	2:45	.25 hour	Shot	544822	V524625587
11/23/2009	3:00	1 hour	Physical	345344	B544742245
11/23/2009	3:00	.5 hour	Migraine	236454	V524625587
11/23/2009	3:30	.5 hour	Muscular	887777	V524625587
11/23/2009	3:30	.25 hour	Shot	966233	T445756225
11/23/2009	3:45	.75 hour	Muscular	951657	T445756225
11/23/2009	4:00	1 hour	Physical	223238	B544742245
11/23/2009	4:00	.5 hour	Flu	365548	V524625587
11/23/2009	4:30	1 hour	Minor surg	398633	V524625587
11/23/2009	4:30	.5 hour	Migraine	222577	T445756225
11/24/2009	8:30	.25 hour	Shot	858756	T445756225
11/24/2009	8:30	1 hour	Minor surg	232158	V524625587
11/24/2009	8:30	.25 hour	Flu	244875	B544742245
11/24/2009	8:45	.5 hour	Muscular	655683	T445756225
11/24/2009	8:45	1 hour	Physical	447521	B544742245
11/24/2009	9:30	.5 hour	Flu	554263	V524625587

Tables related by patient ID

Tables related by doctor ID

Patient ID	First Name	Last Name	Phone Number
136136	Adelaide	Kin	548-7887
222577	Elizabeth	Gray	667-8400
223238	Ellen	Whitener	525-8874
232158	Andy	Ruppel	525-9888
236454	Thomas	Bateman	667-8955
244875	Rick	Grenci	548-2114
345344	Felicia	Marston	548-9333
365548	Jerry	Starsia	548-9887
398633	Susan	Perry	525-6632
447521	Jane	Pace	548-0025
544822	Chris	Pullig	525-5464
554263	Trey	Maxham	663-8547
655683	Eric	Meier	667-0254
758843	Patrick	Dennis	548-9456
858756	Elias	Awad	663-6364
887777	Ryan	Nelson	525-4772
951657	Mike	Morris	663-8944
966233	Peter	Todd	667-2325

Doctor ID	Last Name
B544742245	Brousseau
T445756225	Tantalo
V524625587	Vroman

FIGURE 11-2
Appointment Database

differ in the way they are used to support an application: master files, look-up files, transaction files, audit files, and history files.

Master files store core information that is important to the business and, more specifically, to the application, such as order information or customer mailing information. They usually are kept for long periods, and new records are appended to the end of the file as new orders or new customers are captured by the system. If changes need to be made to existing records, programs must be written to update the old information.

Look-up files contain static values, such as a list of valid codes or the names of the U.S. states. Typically, the list is used for validation. For example, if a customer's mailing address is entered into a master file, the state name is validated against a look-up file that contains U.S. states to make sure that the operator entered the value correctly.

A *transaction file* holds information that can be used to update a master file. The transaction file can be destroyed after changes are added, or the file may be saved in case the transactions need to be accessed again in the future. Customer address changes, for one, would be stored in a transaction file until a program is run that updates the customer address master file with the new information.

For control purposes, a company might need to store information about how data changes over time. For example, as human resources clerks change employee salaries in a human resources system, the system should record the person who made the changes to the salary amount, the date, and the actual change that was made. An *audit file* records "before" and "after" images of data as the data are altered, so that an audit can be performed if the integrity of the data is questioned.

Sometimes files become so large that they are unwieldy, and much of the information in the file is no longer used. The *history file* (or archive file) stores past transactions (e.g., old customers, past orders) that are no longer needed by system users. Typically, the file is stored off-line, yet it can be accessed on an as-needed basis. Other files, such as master files, can then be streamlined to include only active or very recent information.

Databases

There are many different types of databases that exist on the market today. In this section, we provide a brief description of four databases with which you may come into contact: legacy, relational, object, and multidimensional. You will likely encounter a variety of ways to classify databases in your studies, but in this book we classify databases in terms of how they store and manipulate data.

Legacy Databases   The name *legacy database* is given to those databases which are based on older, sometimes outdated technology that is seldom used to develop new applications; however, you may come across them when maintaining or migrating from systems that already exist within your organization. Two examples of legacy databases include hierarchical databases and network databases. *Hierarchical databases* (e.g., IDMS) use hierarchies, or inverted trees, to represent relationships (similar to the one-to-many [1:M] relationships described in Chapter 6). The record at the top of the tree has zero or more child records, which in turn can serve as parents for other records (Figure 11-3). Hierarchical databases are known for rapid search capabilities and were used in the early systems in the airline industry.

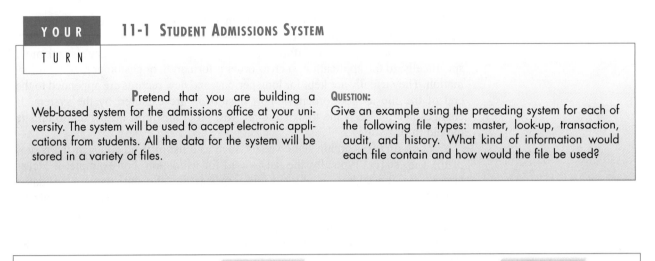

YOUR TURN

11-1 STUDENT ADMISSIONS SYSTEM

Pretend that you are building a Web-based system for the admissions office at your university. The system will be used to accept electronic applications from students. All the data for the system will be stored in a variety of files.

QUESTION:
Give an example using the preceding system for each of the following file types: master, look-up, transaction, audit, and history. What kind of information would each file contain and how would the file be used?

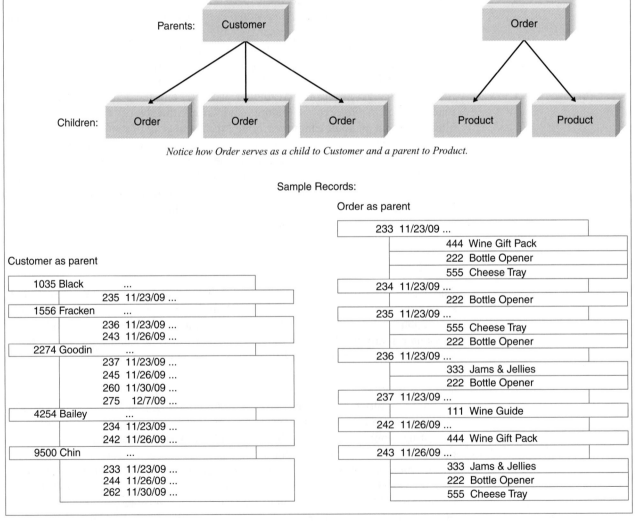

FIGURE 11-3
Hierarchical Database

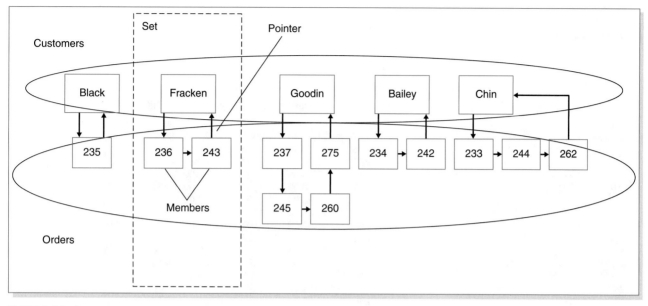

FIGURE 11-4
Network Database

Hierarchical databases cannot efficiently represent many-to-many (M:N) relationships or nonhierarchical associations—a major drawback—so network databases were developed to address this limitation (and others) of hierarchical technology. *Network databases* (e.g., IDMS/R, DBMS 10) are collections of records that are related to each other through *pointers*. Basically, a record is a *member* in one or more *sets,* and the pointers link the members in a set together (Figure 11-4).

Both kinds of legacy systems can handle data quite efficiently, but they require a great deal of programming effort. The application system software needs to contain code that manipulates the database pointers; in other words, the application program must understand how the database is built and be written to follow the structure of the database. When the database structure is changed, the application program must be rewritten to change the way it works, which makes the application using the databases difficult to build and maintain. The code required to maintain the pointers can be quite error prone, especially if bidirectional pointers were used. Years ago, when hardware was expensive and programmer time was cheap, hierarchical and network databases were good solutions for large systems; however, as hardware costs dropped and people costs skyrocketed, these solutions became much less cost effective.

Relational Databases   *The relational database* is the most popular kind of database for application development today. Although it is less "machine efficient" than its legacy counterparts, it is much easier to work with from a development perspective. A relational database is based on collections of tables, each of which has a *primary key*—a field(s) whose value is different for every row of the table. The tables are related to each other by the placement of the primary key from one table into the related table as a *foreign key* (Figure 11-5).

Most relational database management systems (RDBMSs) support *referential integrity*, or the idea of ensuring that values linking the tables together through the

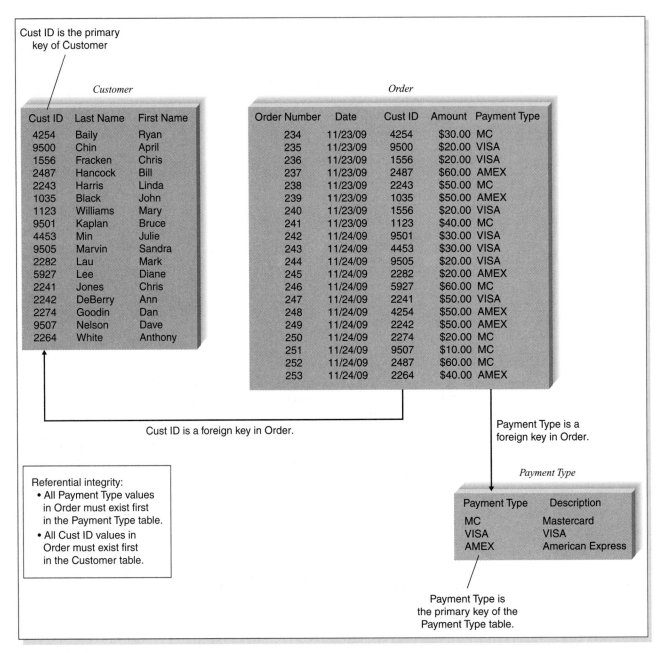

FIGURE 11-5
Relational Database

primary and foreign keys are valid and correctly synchronized. For example, if an order-entry clerk using the tables in Figure 11-5 attempted to add order 254 for customer number 1111, he or she would have made a mistake because no customer exists in the Customer table with that number. If the RDBMS supported referential integrity, it would check the customer numbers in the Customer table, discover that the number 1111 is invalid, and return an error to the entry clerk. The clerk would then go back to the original order form and recheck the customer information. Can you imagine the problems that would occur if the RDBMS let the entry clerk add the order with the wrong information? There would be no way to track down the name of the customer for order 254.

Tables have a set number of columns and a variable number of rows that contain occurrences of data. *Structured Query Language* (*SQL*) is the standard language for accessing the data in the tables, and it operates on complete tables, as opposed to the individual records in the tables. Thus, a query written in SQL is applied to all the records in a table all at once, which is different from a lot of programming languages that manipulate data record by record. When queries must include information from more than one table, the tables first are joined together on the basis of their primary key and foreign key relationships and treated as if they were one large table. Examples of RDBMS software are Microsoft Access, Oracle, DB2, Sybase, Informix, Microsoft SQL Server, and MySQL.

Object Databases The next type of database is the *object database*, or object-oriented database. (See Chapter 14 for more information on object-oriented approaches.) The basic premise of object orientation is that all things should be treated as objects that have both data (attributes) and processes (behaviors). An object changes or accesses its own attributes only through its behaviors. Objects may communicate with each other for information or certain actions. Changes to one object have no effect on other objects because the attributes and behaviors are self-contained, or encapsulated, within each one. This *encapsulation* allows objects to be reused to build many different systems, because they can be inserted and removed from applications with few ripple effects. For example, a customer object could be defined one time as having attributes (e.g., customer number, customer name) and behaviors (e.g., inserting a customer, deleting a customer), and then this customer object could be used to build any system that involves a customer.

In object databases, the combination of data and processes is represented by *object classes*, which are the major categories of objects in the system, and a class can contain a variety of *subclasses*, or special cases of that class. For example, a person class can have subclasses of employee and customer because employee and customer are special cases of person. An instance of data in object databases is referred to as an *instantiation* (e.g., *John Smith* is an instantiation of the *customer* object), and the relationships among classes are maintained by pointers (Figure 11-6).

Object-oriented database management systems (OODBMSs) are mainly used to support multimedia applications or systems that involve complex data (e.g., graphics, video, and sound). Telecommunications, financial services, health care, and transportation have been the most receptive to object databases. They are becoming a popular technology for supporting electronic commerce, online catalogs, and large Web multimedia applications.

Although pure OODBMSs like Jasmine exist, most organizations invest in *hybrid OODBMS* technology, which includes databases with both object and relational features. For instance, Oracle, a leader in the relational database market, incorporates object functionality and capabilities into its relational product.

Although the market for OODBMSs is expected to grow, the market for the technology is dwarfed by that for its relational and object-relational database counterparts ($13.8 billion).[1] For one, there are many more experienced developers and tools in the relational database arena. Also, relational users find that OODBMS technology comes with a very steep learning curve.

---

[1] Barbara Darrow, "Linux, SQL Server Drive Database Market: Report," *ChannelWeb*, May 24, 2006.

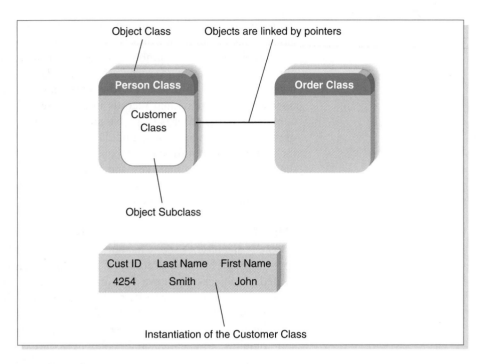

FIGURE 11-6
Object Database

Multidimensional Databases A multidimensional database is a type of relational database that is used extensively in data warehousing. *Data warehousing* is the practice of taking data from a company's transaction processing systems, transforming the data (e.g., cleaning them up, totaling them, aggregating them), and then storing the data for use in a data warehouse (i.e., a large database) that supports *decision support systems* (*DSS*). A data warehouse itself usually relies on relational technology as its storage format; however, companies can create *data marts*, which are smaller databases based on data warehouse data. Typically, a data mart receives downloads of data from the data warehouse regularly, and it supports DSS for a specific department or functional area of the company. For example, the marketing department may have a data mart that supports its campaign management DSS. Data marts are usually created with multidimensional databases.

In most cases, DSS is designed not to search for a particular record (e.g., "What did John Smith order on July 5, 2008?"), but rather to display information that is *aggregated* (e.g., totaled or averaged) across many records (e.g., "What was the average sales by quarter for product A?") Thus, data marts that support a DSS require that data be stored in a format in which they can be easily aggregated and manipulated across a variety of dimensions (e.g., time, product, region, sales rep). Unfortunately, legacy, object, and relational databases are designed and optimized to provide access to individual records, not to store data to support aggregations of data on multiple dimensions.

When data are first loaded into a multidimensional database, the database precalculates the data across multiple dimensions and stores the answers, using arrays or some other technique. Although the initial loading of the data can be quite slow because of all the calculations that must take place, data access is extremely fast because the "answers" already exist in the arrays. For example, the cube in Figure 11-7 represents a multidimensional database containing data that

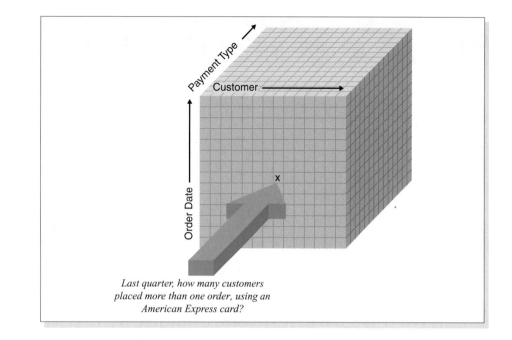

Last quarter, how many customers placed more than one order, using an American Express card?

FIGURE 11-7
Multidimensional Database

have been organized by customer, payment type, and order date. Precalculated quantitative information (e.g., totals, averages) is stored at the intersection of the dimensions (in each block), and the DSS directly accesses those blocks. Because blocks contain precalculated information, there is much less processing that needs to occur to provide the DSS with aggregated results.

Selecting a Storage Format

Each of the file and database data storage formats has its strengths and weaknesses, and no one format is inherently better than the others. In fact, sometimes, a project team will choose multiple data storage formats (e.g., a relational database for one data store, a file for another, and a multidimensional database for a third). Thus, it is important to understand the strengths and weaknesses of each format and when to use each one. Figure 11-8 summarizes the characteristics of each and the characteristics that can help identify when each type of storage is most appropriate.

Data Types   The first issue is the type of data that will need to be stored in the system. Most applications need to store simple data types, such as text, dates, and numbers, and all DBMSs are equipped to handle this kind of data. The best choice for simple data storage, however, usually is the relational database because the technology has matured over time and has continuously improved to handle simple data very effectively.

Increasingly, applications are incorporating complex data, such as video, images, or audio, and object databases are best able to handle data of this type. Complex data are stored as objects that can be manipulated much faster than with other storage formats. Other applications require aggregated data (i.e., information that has been summed, averaged, or combined in some way). Multidimensional databases are specially designed to store data so that they can be "sliced and diced"

	Files	Legacy DBMS	Relational DBMS	Object-Oriented DBMS	Multi-dimensional DBMS
Major strengths	Files can be designed for fast performance; good for short-term data storage.	Very mature products	Leader in the database market; can handle diverse data needs	Able to handle complex data	Configured to answer decision support questions quickly
Major weaknesses	Redundant data; data must be updated, using programs.	Not able to store data as efficiently; limited future	Cannot handle complex data	Technology is still maturing; skills are hard to find.	Highly specialized use; skills are hard to find
Data types supported	Simple	*Not recommended for new systems*	Simple	Complex (e.g., video, audio, images)	Aggregated
Types of application systems supported	Transaction processing	*Not recommended for new systems*	Transaction processing and decision making	Transaction processing	Decision making
Existing data formats	Organization dependent	Organization dependent	Organization dependent	Organization dependent	Organization dependent
Future needs	Limited future prospects	Poor future prospects	Good future prospects	Uncertain future prospects	Uncertain future prospects

DBMS = database management system.

FIGURE 11-8
Comparison of Data Storage Formats

and examined across important business dimensions. If the system is being built for analytical decision support, then this option likely will be most appropriate.

Type of Application System   There are many different kinds of application systems that can be developed. *Transaction processing systems* are designed to accept and process many simultaneous requests (e.g., order entry, distribution, payroll). In transaction processing systems, the data are continuously updated by a large number of users, and the queries that are asked of the systems typically are predefined or targeted at a small subset of records (e.g., "List the orders that were back-ordered today"; "What products did customer #1234 order on May 12, 2009?").

Another set of application systems comprises those designed to support decision making, such as business intelligence *management information systems* (MISs), *executive information systems* (EISs), and *expert systems* (ESs). These decision support systems (DSS) are built to support decision makers who need to examine large amounts of read-only historical data. The questions that they ask often are ad hoc, and they include hundreds or thousands of records at a time (e.g., "List all customers in the west region who purchased a product costing more than $500 at least three times"; "What products had increased sales in the summer months but have not been classified as summer merchandise?").

Transaction processing and DSSs thus have very different data storage needs. Transaction processing systems need data storage formats that are tuned for a lot of data updates and fast retrieval of predefined, specific questions. Files, relational databases, and object databases can all support these kinds of requirements.

By contrast, systems to support decision making are usually only reading data (not updating it), often in ad hoc ways. The best choices for these systems usually are relational databases and multidimensional databases because these formats can be configured specially for needs that may be unclear and less apt to change the data.

Existing Storage Formats   The data storage format should be selected primarily on the basis of the kind of data and application system being developed. Project teams should also consider the existing data storage formats in the organization when making design decisions. In this way, they can better understand the technical skills that already exist and how steep the learning curve will be when the data storage format is adopted. For example, a company that is familiar with relational databases will have little problem adopting a relational database for the project, whereas an object database may require substantial developer training. In the latter situation, the project team may have to plan for more time to integrate the object database with the company's relational systems.

Future Needs   The project team should be aware of current trends and technologies that are being used by other organizations. A large number of installations of a type of data storage format suggests that the selection of that format is "safe," in that needed skills and products are available. For example, it would probably be easier and less expensive to find relational database expertise when implementing a system than to find help with a multidimensional data storage format. Legacy database skills, too, would likely be difficult to find.

Applying the Concepts at Tune Source

The Tune Source Digital Music Download system needs to effectively present tune information to users and capture purchase data. Jason Wells, senior systems analyst and project manager for the Digital Music Download system, recognized that these goals were dependent on a good design of the data storage component for the new application.

The project team met to discuss two issues that would drive the data storage format selection: what kind of data would be in the system and how that data would be used by the application system. Using a white board, they listed the ideas presented in Figure 11-9. The project team agreed that the bulk of the data in the system would be text and numbers describing customers and purchases that are exchanged with Web users. A relational database would be able to handle the data effectively, and the technology would be well received because of its current use at Tune Source.

The team recognized, however, that relational technology may not be optimized to handle complex data such as the images, sound clips, and video clips associated with the application. Jason asked Kenji, a project team member, to investigate relational databases that offered object add-on products. It might be possible to invest in a relational database foundation and use its object functionality to handle the complex data.

The team noted that one transaction file must be designed to handle the interface with the Web shopping cart program. The team must design the file that stores temporary, purchase information on the Web server as customers navigate through the Web site.

Data	Type	Use	Suggested Format
Customer information	Simple (mostly text)	Transactions	Relational
Sales information	Simple (text and numbers)	Transactions	Relational
Tune information	Both simple and complex (the system will contain audio clips, video, etc.)	Transactions	Relational ?
Interests/Favorites	Simple (mostly text)	Transactions	Relational
Targeted promotion information	Simple text, formatted specifically for populating the Web site with customized content	Transactions	Relational
Temporary information	The system will likely need to hold information for temporary periods (e.g., the shopping cart will store purchase information before the purchase is actually completed)	Transactions	Transaction file

FIGURE 11-9
Types of Data in the Digital Music
Download System

Of course, Jason realized that other data needs would arise over time, but he felt confident that the major data issues were identified (e.g., the ability to handle complex data) and that the data storage design would be selected on the basis of the proper storage technologies.

MOVING FROM LOGICAL TO PHYSICAL DATA MODELS

During analysis, the analysts defined the data required by the application by creating *logical entity relationship diagrams* (*ERDs*). These logical models depict the "business view" of the data, but omit any implementation details. Now, having determined the data storage format, *physical data models* are created to show implementation details and to explain more about the "how" of the final system. These to-be models describe characteristics of the system that will be created, communicating the "systems view" of the new system.

The Physical Entity Relationship Diagram

Like the DFD, the ERD contains the same components for both the logical and physical models, including entities, relationships, and attributes. The difference lies in the fact that *physical ERDs* contain references to exactly how data will be stored in a file or database table and that much more metadata is added to the CASE repository to describe the data model components. The transition from the logical to physical data model is fairly straightforward; see the steps in Figure 11-10.

Step 1: Change Entities to Tables or Files The first step is to change all the entities in the logical ERD to reflect the files or tables that will be used to store the data.

Step	Explanation
Change entities to tables or files.	Beginning with the logical entity relationship diagram, change the entities to tables or files and update the metadata.
Change attributes to fields.	Convert the attributes to fields and update the metadata.
Add primary keys.	Assign primary keys to all entities.
Add foreign keys.	Add foreign keys to represent the relationships among entities.
Add system-related components.	Add system-related tables and fields.

FIGURE 11-10

Steps to Moving from Logical to Physical Entity Relationship Diagram

Usually, project teams adhere to strict naming conventions for such things as tables, files, and fields, so the physical ERD would use the names that the real components will have when implemented. Metadata for the tables and files, like the expected size of the table, are added to the CASE repository. See Figure 11-11 for a physical ERD from the Holiday Travel Vehicle system that was described in Chapters 5 and 6.

Step 2: Change Attributes to Fields   Second, change the attributes to fields, which are columns in files or tables, and add information like the field's length, data type, default value, and valid value to the CASE repository. There are a number of different data types that fields can have, such as number, decimal, longint, character, and variable character. The analyst inputs the data type along with the size of the field into the CASE tool so that the system can be designed for the right kind of information. A *default value* specifies what should be placed in a column if no value is explicitly supplied when a record is inserted into the table. A *valid value* is a fixed list of valid values for a particular column, or an expression to define some form of data validation code for a column or table. Figure 11-12 shows a variety of metadata describing the cust_id field in an Oracle Customer table.

Inputting complete information regarding the tables and columns into the CASE repository is very important. Many CASE tools will actually generate code to build tables and create files for the new system according to the information they contain for the physical models. By taking time to describe the physical data model in detail, the analyst can save a lot of time when the system is ready to be implemented.

Step 3: Add Primary Keys   As a third step, the attributes that served as identifiers on the logical ERD are converted into *primary keys*, which are fields that contain a unique value for each record in the file or table. For instance, Social Security Number would serve as a good primary key for a customer table if every customer record in the table will contain a unique value in the Social Security Number field. A unique identifier is mandatory for every table placed on the physical ERD; therefore, primary key fields must be created for entities that did not have identifiers previously. For example, if we did not choose an identifier for the customer entity on the logical ERD, we would now create a system-generated field (e.g., cust_id) that could serve as the primary key for the customer table. This field would have no meaning or purpose other than ensuring that each record has a field that contains a unique value.

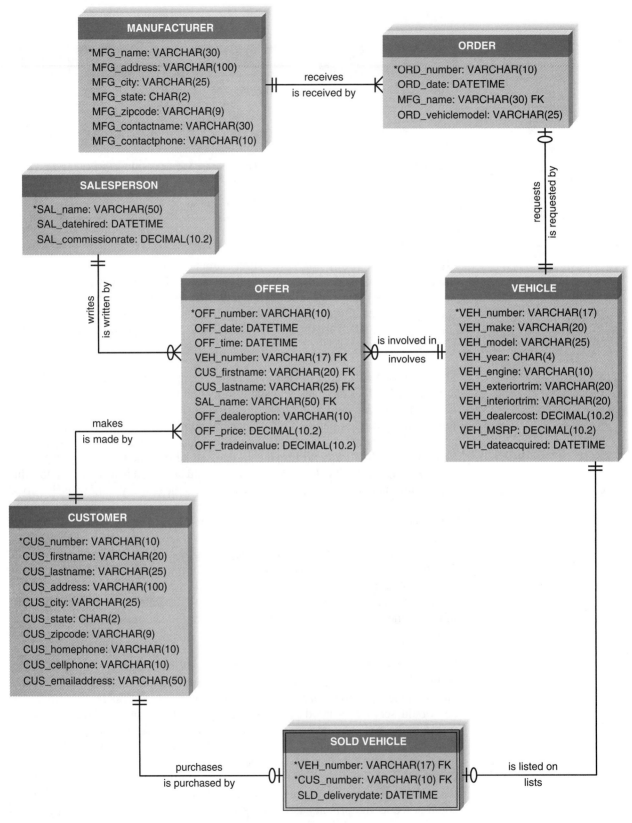

FIGURE 11-11
Holiday Travel Vehicle Physical ERD

Naming conventions
for fields: 4 digits of
table name followed
by the field name.

Notice that this will
be implemented
in Oracle.

No null, or blank,
values will be accepted
into the *cust_id* field.

The key signifies
that *cust_id* is a
primary key.

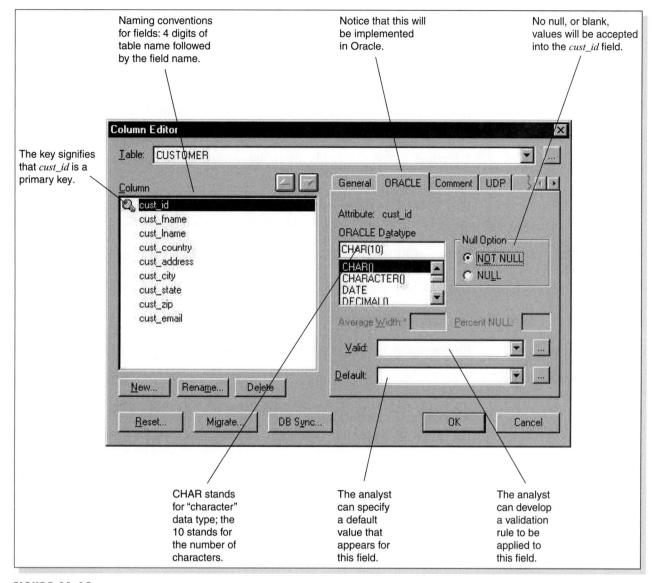

FIGURE 11-12
Metadata for a cust_id Field

CHAR stands
for "character"
data type; the
10 stands for
the number of
characters.

The analyst
can specify
a default
value that
appears for
this field.

The analyst
can develop
a validation
rule to be
applied to
this field.

Step 4: Add Foreign Keys   The relationships on the logical ERD show that pairs
of entities are associated with each other, and in step 4, the analyst specifies how
the associations are going to be maintained from a technical standpoint. In a
relational database, for example, an association between two tables is maintained by a technique referred to as a *foreign key*. A foreign key is the primary
key field(s) from one table that is repeated in another table to provide a common
field between the two tables. The common field contains values that match a
record in one table to a record in the other. For example, if we were to create two
tables called Customer and Order that were related to each other, we could
include the primary key field from Customer (cust_id) in the Order table as well.
In this way, if we want to find out customer information (e.g., name, address,

phone number) when looking at someone's order, we can use the value for cust_id that appears in the Order table to go back to the Customer table to locate the appropriate information.

Thus, on the physical ERD, the primary key fields in the parent tables (the "1" end of the relationship) are copied and placed as fields in the child tables (the "many" end of the relationship) and designated as foreign keys. The fields will contain values that are common between the two tables. Many times, the CASE tools that are used to draw ERDs will "migrate" foreign keys to the appropriate tables on the model automatically, and the database technology will ensure that the values in the two fields match appropriately, helping to ensure referential integrity.

Step 5: Add System-Related Components   As the fifth and final step, components are added to the physical ERD to reflect special implementation needs, including components that were included on the DFD. We have mentioned balance between DFDs and ERDs in earlier chapters, and this balance must be maintained in the physical models as well. Therefore, implementation-specific data stores and data elements from the physical DFD should be included on the ERD as tables and fields. For example, in Figure 10-2 we added the Tune to buy history data store to the physical DFD to serve as a "backup" for tunes that are sent to the purchase tunes process. Now we will need to add a tune to buy batch history file to the physical ERD model along with its fields and relationships.

Revisiting the CRUD Matrix

As discussed in Chapter 6, it is important to verify that the system's DFD and ERD models are balanced. In other words, we must ensure that data needed in the systems processes are stored and that all stored data are used by at least one process. The CRUD matrix was introduced in Chapter 6 as a tool showing how data are used by processes in the system.

Often the CRUD matrix is created during analysis on the basis of the logical process and data models. In design, as these models are converted to physical models, changes in the form of new processes, new data stores, and new data elements may occur. The CRUD matrix should be revised at this point to include the new components and ensure that balance is maintained between the physical ERD and DFDs.

If the CRUD matrix was not developed during analysis, it should be developed now prior to implementation. The matrix shows exactly how data are used and created by the major processes in the system, so it serves as a very useful component of the system design materials.

Applying the Concepts at Tune Source

Let us now apply some of the concepts that you have learned by creating a physical ERD, using the logical ERD that was created in Chapter 6.

When we use the logical model as a starting point, the first step is to rename the entities to match with the tables or files that will be used by the system (Figure 11-13). Outwardly, the data model does not look very different after this step, but notice that several entities have been renamed to be consistent with Tune Source's table naming

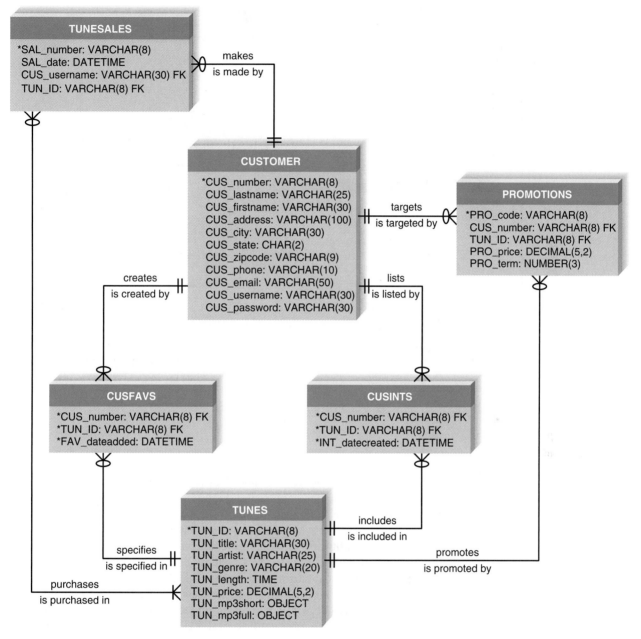

FIGURE 11-13
Tune Source Physical ERD

standards. At this time, we will need to include metadata for the tables, such as their estimated size.

Next, the attributes for the entities become fields with such characteristics as data type, length, and valid values, and this is recorded in the CASE repository. For example, CUS_state in the CUSTOMER table will be a text field with a size of two characters, and valid values are the 50 two-letter state abbreviations. If most customers at Tune Source live in the state of California, then it may be worthwhile to

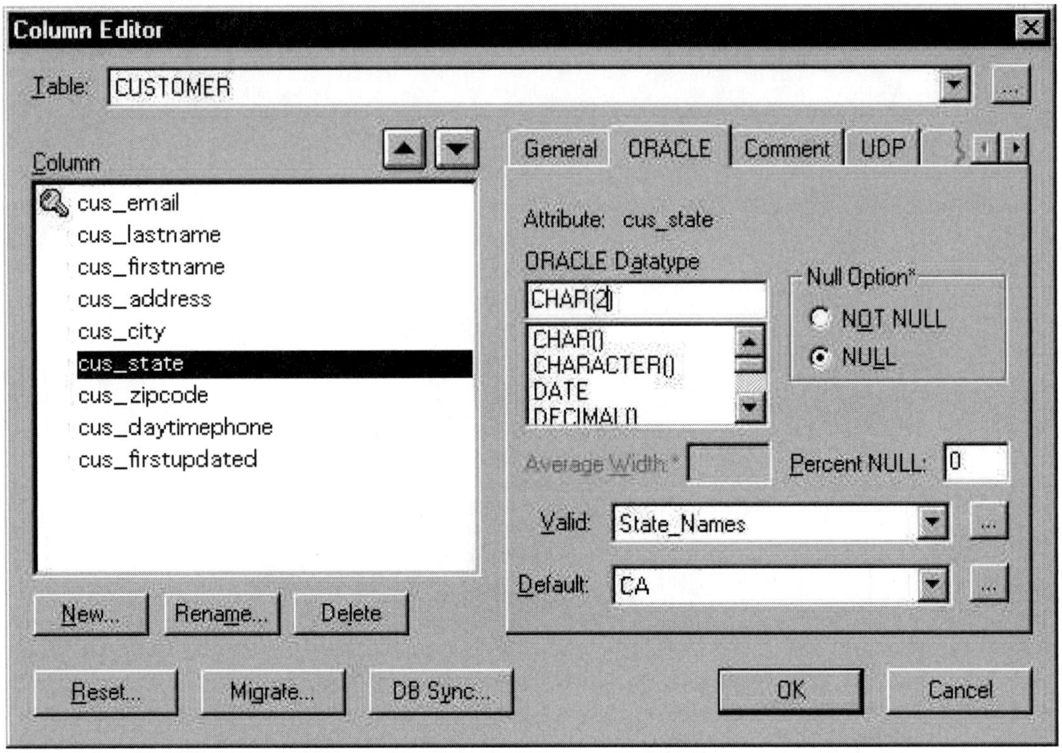

FIGURE 11-14
Computer-Aided Software Engineering Repository Entry for cus_state Field

make CA the default value for this field. However, since this is an Internet-based system, this assumption may not be valid. Figure 11-14 is an example of the CASE repository entry for the CUS_state field.

Step 3 suggests that we change the identifiers in the logical ERD to become primary keys, and entities without identifiers need to have a primary key created. At this time, we also can decide to use a system-generated primary key if it is more efficient than using logical attributes from the logical model.

The relationships on the logical ERD indicate where foreign key fields need to be placed. For example, CUS_number is placed as a field in TUNESALES to serve as the link between two entities, and TUNESALES gets the extra field because it is the child table (it exists at the "many" end of the relationship). Similarly, TUN_ID is placed in the TUNESALES table.

Finally, system-related components are included within the model. For example, fields that will capture when a record was last inserted or updated were added to many of the tables.

The project team also updated the CRUD matrix for the system. Figure 11-15 shows the CRUD matrix that was created for the Tune Source search and browse tunes process. Look at the original process models, and notice how the first process is merely reading information from data stores. This is illustrated on the CRUD matrix by an "R" placed in the relevant intersections of the matrix. Can you tell how data are used by the remaining processes?

	1.1 Load Web Site	1.2 Process Search Requests	1.3 Process Tune Selection
PROMOTIONS			
PRO_code	R		
CUS_number	R		
TUN_ID	R		
PRO_price	R		
PRO_term	R		
CUSFAVS			
CUS_number	R		C
TUN_ID	R		C
FAV_dateadded	R		C
TUNES			
TUN_ID		R	R
TUN_title		R	R
TUN_artist		R	R
TUN_genre		R	R
TUN_length		R	R
TUN_price		R	R
TUN_mp3short		R	R
TUN_mp3full		R	R
CUSINTS			
CUS_number			C
TUN_ID			C
INT_datecreated			C

FIGURE 11-15
CRUD Matrix for Search and Browse Tunes Process

OPTIMIZING DATA STORAGE

The selected data storage format is now optimized for processing efficiency. The optimization methods will vary with the format that you select; however, the basic concepts will remain the same. Once you understand how to optimize a particular type of data storage, you will have some idea as to how to approach the optimization of other formats. This section focuses on the optimization of the most popular data storage format: relational databases.

There are two primary dimensions in which to optimize a relational database: for storage efficiency and for speed of access. Unfortunately, these two goals often conflict because the best design for access speed may take up a great deal of storage space as compared with other less speedy designs. This section describes how to use normalization (Chapter 6) to optimize data storage for storage efficiency. The next section presents design techniques, such as denormalization and indexing, that will quicken the performance of the system. Ultimately, the project team will go through a series of trade-offs until the ideal balance between both optimization dimensions is reached. Finally, the project team must estimate the size of the data storage needed to ensure that there is enough capacity on the server(s).

11-2 ISLAND CHARTERS

In Chapter 6, you were asked to create a logical entity relationship diagram (ERD) for a charter company that owns boats that are used to charter trips to the islands ("Your Turn 6-8"). The company has created a computer system to track the boats it owns, including each boat's ID number, name, and seating capacity. The company also tracks information about the various islands, such as name and population. Every time a boat is chartered, it is important to know the data about the trip that takes place and the number of people on the trip. The company also keeps information about each captain, such as Social Security Number, name, birthdate, and how to contact next of kin. Boats travel to only one island per visit.

Create a physical ERD for this situation. Compare the diagram that you drew to the logical diagram that you created in Chapter 6.

Optimizing Storage Efficiency

The most efficient tables in a relational database in terms of storage space have no redundant data and very few null values, because the presence of these suggest that space is being wasted (and more data to store means higher data storage hardware costs). For example, notice that the sample order table in Figure 11-16 repeats customer information, such as name and state, each time a customer places an order, and it contains many null values in the last four columns. These null values occur whenever a customer places an order for less than three items (the maximum number on an order).

In addition to wasting space, redundancy and null values also allow more room for error and increase the likelihood that problems will arise with the integrity of the data. What if customer 1135 moves from Maryland to Georgia? In the case of Figure 11-16, a program must be written to ensure that all instances of that customer are updated to show "GA" as the new state of residence. If some of the instances are overlooked, then the table will contain an update anomaly whereby some of the records contain the correctly updated value for state and other records contain the old information.

11-3 DONATION TRACKING SYSTEM

A major public university graduates approximately 10,000 students per year, and its development office has decided to build a Web-based system that solicits and tracks donations from the university's large alumni body. Ultimately, the development officers hope to use the information in the system to better understand the alumni giving patterns so that they can improve giving rates.

QUESTION:
1. What kind of system is this?
2. Does it have characteristics of more than one?
3. What different kinds of data will this system use?
4. On the basis of your answers, what kind of data storage format(s) do you recommend for this system?

CUSTOMER ORDER

Order Number
Date
Cust ID
Last Name
First Name
State
Amount
Tax Rate
Product 1
Product Description 1
Product 2
Product Description 2
Product 3
Product Description 3

Redundant data   Null cells

Order Number	Date	Cust ID	Last Name	First Name	State	Amount	Tax Rate	Product	Product Desc	Product	Product Desc	Product	Product Desc
239	11/23/09	1135	Black	John	MD	$50.00	0.05	555	Cheese Tray				
260	11/24/09	1135	Black	John	MD	$40.00	0.05	444	Wine Gift Pack				
273	11/27/09	1135	Black	John	MD	$20.00	0.05	222	Bottle Opener				
241	11/23/09	1123	Williams	Mary	CA	$40.00	0.08	444	Wine Gift Pack				
262	11/24/09	1123	Williams	Mary	CA	$20.00	0.08	222	Bottle Opener				
287	11/27/09	1123	Williams	Mary	CA	$20.00	0.08	222	Bottle Opener				
290	11/30/09	1123	Williams	Mary	CA	$50.00	0.08	555	Cheese Tray				
234	11/23/09	2242	DeBerry	Ann	DC	$50.00	0.065	555	Cheese Tray				
237	11/7/09	2242	DeBerry	Ann	DC	$50.00	0.065	111	Wine Guide	444	Wine Gift Pack		
238	11/10/09	2242	DeBerry	Ann	DC	$40.00	0.065	444	Wine Gift Pack				
245	11/11/09	2242	DeBerry	Ann	DC	$20.00	0.065	222	Bottle Opener				
250	11/18/09	2242	DeBerry	Ann	DC	$20.00	0.065	222	Bottle Opener				
252	11/22/09	2242	DeBerry	Ann	DC	$60.00	0.065	222	Bottle Opener	444	Wine Gift Pack		
253	11/23/09	2242	DeBerry	Ann	DC	$60.00	0.065	222	Bottle Opener	444	Wine Gift Pack		
297	11/24/09	2242	DeBerry	Ann	DC	$30.00	0.065	333	Jams & Jellies				
243	11/11/09	4254	Bailey	Ryan	MD	$50.00	0.05	555	Cheese Tray				
246	11/18/09	4254	Bailey	Ryan	MD	$30.00	0.05	333	Jams & Jellies				
248	11/22/09	4254	Bailey	Ryan	MD	$60.00	0.05	222	Bottle Opener	333	Jams & Jellies	111	Wine Guide
235	11/17/09	9500	Chin	April	KS	$20.00	0.05	222	Bottle Opener				
242	11/23/09	9500	Chin	April	KS	$30.00	0.05	333	Jams & Jellies				
244	11/24/09	9500	Chin	April	KS	$20.00	0.05	222	Bottle Opener				
251	11/27/09	9500	Chin	April	KS	$10.00	0.05	111	Wine Guide				

FIGURE 11-16
Optimizing Data Storage

Null values threaten data integrity because they are difficult to interpret. A blank value in the customer order table's product fields could mean that (1) the customer did not want more than one or two products on his or her order, (2) the operator forgot to enter in all three products on the order, or (3) the customer canceled part of the order and the products were deleted by the operator. It is impossible to be sure of the actual meaning of the null values.

For both of these reasons—wasted storage space and data integrity threats—project teams should remove redundancy and null values from data storage design. During the design phase, the logical data model is used to examine the data storage design and optimize it for storage efficiency. If you follow the modeling instructions and guidelines that were presented in Chapter 6, you will have little trouble creating a design that is highly optimized in this way, because a well-formed logical data model does not contain redundancy or many null values.

Sometimes, however, a project team starts with a logical model that was poorly constructed or with a model that was created for files or a nonrelational type of data storage format. In these cases, the project team should follow the steps of the *normalization* process described in Chapter 6 (see Figure 6A-1). Normalization is the best way to optimize data storage for efficiency.

Optimizing Access Speed

After you have optimized your data model design for data storage efficiency, the end result is data that are spread out across a number of tables. When data from multiple tables must be accessed or queried, the tables first must be joined together. For example, in Figure 11-2, before the office manager can print out a list of appointments with patient and doctor names on it, the patient and doctor tables need to be joined with the appointment table on the basis of the patient ID and doctor ID fields. Only then can appointment, patient, and doctor information be included in the query's output. Joins can take a lot of time, especially if the tables are large or if many tables are involved.

Consider an order system that stores information about 10,000 different products, 25,000 customers, and 100,000 orders, each order containing three products, on average. If an analyst wanted to investigate whether there were regional differences in buying preferences, he or she would need to combine all of the tables to be able to look at products that have been ordered, while knowing the location of the customers placing the orders. A query of this information would result in a huge table with 300,000 rows (i.e., the number of products that have been ordered) and many columns representing columns from all three tables combined.

There are several techniques that the project team can use to try to speed up access to the data: denormalization, clustering, indexing, and estimating the size of the data for hardware planning purposes.

Denormalization After the logical data model is optimized in terms of data storage, the project team may decide to denormalize, or add redundancy back into the design that is depicted in the physical data model. *Denormalization* reduces the number of joins that must be performed in a query, thus speeding up data access. Figure 11-17 shows a denormalized physical data model for customer orders.

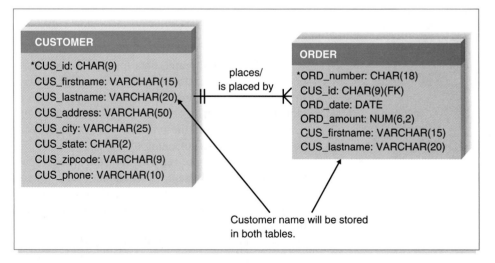

FIGURE 11-17
Denormalized Data Model

YOUR

TURN

11-4 DENORMALIZING A STUDENT ACTIVITY FILE

Consider the logical data model that you created in Chapter 6 for "Your Turn 6-7." Examine the model and describe possible opportunities for denormalization.

QUESTION:

How would you denormalize the physical data model, and what are the benefits of your changes?

The customer name was added back into the Order table because the project team learned during the analysis phase that queries about orders usually require the customer's name. Instead of joining the Order table repeatedly to the Customer table, the system now needs to access only the Order table because it contains all the relevant information.

Of course, denormalization should be applied sparingly, for the reasons described in the previous section, but it is ideal in situations in which information is queried frequently yet updated rarely. There are four cases in which you may rely on denormalization to reduce joins and improve performance (see Figure 11-18). First, denormalization can be applied in the case of *look-up tables*, which are tables that contain descriptions of values (e.g., a table of product descriptions, a table of payment types). Because descriptions of codes rarely change, it may be more efficient to include the description along with its respective code in the main table, to eliminate the need to join the look-up table each time a query is performed.

Second, 1:1 relationships are good candidates for denormalization. Although logically, two entities should be separated, from a practical standpoint the information from both entities may be regularly accessed together. Think about an order and its shipping information. Logically, it may make sense to separate the attributes related to shipping into a separate entity, but as a result, the queries regarding shipping likely will always need a join to the Order table. If the project team finds that certain shipping information, such as state and shipping method, are needed when orders are accessed, they may decide to combine the entities or include some shipping attributes in the order entity.

Third, at times it will be more efficient to include a parent entity's attributes in its child entity on the physical data model. For example, consider a customer table and an order table that share a 1:N relationship, with customer as the parent and order as the child. If queries regarding orders continuously require customer information, the most popular customer fields can be placed in order to reduce the required joins to the customer table, as was done with customer name in Figure 11-18.

Finally, denormalization is applied when a popular data modeling technique called *star schema design* is used.[2] Learning how to model with star schema is beyond the scope of this book, but there are a number of Web resources and books available that are listed on the textbook Web site. Basically, star schema is a way to model data whereby the data are denormalized to speed up data access for DSS. It uses two kinds of tables—fact tables and dimension tables—to store numerical, additive, and descriptive data, respectively. Star schema modeling is the way in

---

[2] A good book on star schema design is that by Claudia Imhoff, Nicholas Galemmo, and Jonathan Geiger, *Mastering Data Warehouse Design: Relational and Dimensional Techniques,* John Wiley & Sons, 2003.

Reason	Description	Example
Look-up Table	Include a code's description in the table using that code if the description is often used.	**ORDER** *ORD_number: CHAR(18) ORD_date: DATE ORD_amount: NUM(6,2) PAY_type: CHAR(2)(FK) PAY_description: VARCHAR(15) is paid by / pays **PAYMENT_TYPE** *PAY_type: CHAR(2) PAY_description: VARCHAR(15)
1:1 Relationships	Combine tables if they are related 1:1 and if they usually are accessed together.	**ORDER** *ORD_number: CHAR(18) ORD_date: DATE ORD_amount: NUM(6,2) SHI_state: CHAR(2) SHI_method: CHAR(4) is sent by / sends **SHIPMENT** *SHI_id: CHAR(9) ORD_num: CHAR(18) (FK) SHI_address: VARCHAR(50) SHI_city: VARCHAR(25) SHI_state: CHAR(2) SHI_zip: VARCHAR(9) SHI_method: CHAR(4)
1:N Relationships	Place fields from the parent (1) table into the child (N) table if the parent fields are used frequently with child information.	**CUSTOMER** *CUS_id: CHAR(9) CUS_firstname: VARCHAR(15) CUS_lastname: VARCHAR(20) CUS_address: VARCHAR(50) CUS_city: VARCHAR(25) CUS_state: CHAR(2) CUS_zipcode: VARCHAR(9) CUS_phone: VARCHAR(10) places / is placed by **ORDER** *ORD_number: CHAR(18) CUS_id: CHAR(9)(FK) ORD_date: DATE ORD_amount: NUM(6,2) CUS_firstname: VARCHAR(15) CUS_lastname: VARCHAR(20)
Star Schema Design	Data marts often are modeled with star schema design, which uses denormalization to maximaze DSS query performance.	**CUSTOMER** *CUS_id: CHAR(9) CUS_firstname: VARCHAR(15) CUS_lastname: VARCHAR(20) CUS_address: VARCHAR(50) CUS_city: VARCHAR(25) CUS_state: CHAR(2) CUS_zipcode: VARCHAR(9) CUS_phone: VARCHAR(10) CUS_gender: CHAR(1) CUS_birthdate: DATE **ORDER** *ORD_number: CHAR(18) ORD_paytype: CHAR(2) ORD_shipstate: CHAR(2) ORD_shipmethod: VARCHAR(8) dimension_1 dimension_3 **FACT** *FACT_id: CHAR(8) FACT_orderamount: NUM(6,2) FACT_ordercost: NUM(6,2) CUS_id: CHAR(9)(FK) TIM_date: DATE (FK) ORD_number: CHAR(18) **TIME** *TIM_date: DATE TIM_dayofweek: NUM(1) TIM_weeknumber: NUM(2) TIM_monthnumber: NUM(2) TIM_quarter: NUM(1) TIM_fiscalyear: NUM(4) TIM_holidayflag: CHAR(1) dimension_2

FIGURE 11-18
Reasons to Denormalize

which relational databases can be designed to emulate a multidimensional database. See Figure 11-18 for an example of a star schema design of a customer order database. The fact table contains order amount and cost (i.e., additive data), and the other tables contain information describing different dimensions of an order: the customer, the order itself, and time.

Clustering Speed of access also is influenced by the way in which the data are retrieved. Think about going shopping in a grocery store. If you have a list of items to buy, but you are unfamiliar with the store's layout, then you need to walk down every aisle to make sure that you don't miss anything from your list. Likewise, if records are arranged on a hard disk in no particular order (or in an order that is unrelated to your data needs), then any query of the records results in a *table scan* in which the DBMS has to access every row in the table before retrieving the result set. Table scans are the most inefficient of data retrieval methods.

One way to improve access speed is to reduce the number of times that the storage medium must be accessed during a transaction. This can be accomplished by *clustering* records together physically so that like records are stored close together. With *intrafile clustering*, similar records in the table are stored together in some way, such as in order by primary key or, in the case of a grocery store, by item type. Thus, whenever a query looks for records, it can go directly to the right spot on the hard disk (or other storage medium) because it knows in what order the records are stored, just as we can walk directly to the bread aisle in the store to pick up a loaf of bread. *Interfile clustering* combines records from more than one table that typically are retrieved together. For example, if customer information is usually accessed with the related order information, then the records from the two tables may be physically stored in a way that preserves the customer order relationship. Returning to the grocery store scenario, an interfile cluster would be similar to storing peanut butter, jelly, and bread next to each other in the same aisle because they are usually purchased together, not because they are similar types of items. Of course, each table can have only one clustering strategy because the records can be arranged physically in only one way.

CONCEPTS   **11-A MAIL-ORDER INDEX**

IN ACTION

A Virginia-based mail-order company sends out approximately 25 million catalogs each year, using a customer table with 10 million names. Although the primary key of the customer table is customer identification number, the table also contains an index of customer last names. Most people who call to place orders remember their last name, but not their customer identification number, so this index is used frequently.

An employee of the company explained that indexes are critical to reasonable response times. A fairly complicated query was written to locate customers by the state in which they lived, and it took over three weeks to return an answer. A customer state index was created, and that same query provided a response in 20 minutes; that's 1512 times faster!

QUESTION:

As an analyst, how can you make sure that the proper indexes have been put in place so that users are not waiting for weeks to receive the answers to their questions?

Indexing A time saver that you are familiar with is an index located in the back of a textbook, which points you directly to the page or pages that contain your topic of interest. Think of how long it would take to find all of the times that *relational database* appears in this textbook if you didn't have the index to rely on. An *index* in data storage is like an index in the back of a textbook; it is a minitable that contains values from one or more columns in a table and the location of the values within the table. Instead of paging through the entire textbook, you can move directly to the right pages and get the information you need. Indexes are one of the most important ways to improve database performance. Whenever you have performance problems, the first place to look is an index.

A query can use an index to find the locations of only those records that are included in the query answer, and a table can have an unlimited number of indexes. Figure 11-19 shows an index that orders records by payment type. A query that searches for all of the customers who used American Express can use this index to find the locations of the records that contain American Express as the payment type without having to scan the entire order table.

Project teams can make indexes perform even faster by placing them into the main memory of the data storage hardware. Retrieving information from memory is much faster than from another storage medium like a hard disk—think about how much faster it is to retrieve a phone number that you have memorized versus one that you need to look up in a phone book. Similarly, when a database has an index in memory, it can locate records very, very quickly.

Of course, indexes require overhead in that they take up space on the storage medium. Also, they need to be updated as records in tables are inserted, deleted, or changed. Thus, although indexes lead to faster access to the data, they slow down the update process. In general, you should create indexes sparingly for transaction systems or systems that require a lot of updates, but apply indexes generously when designing systems for decision support (Figure 11-20).

Usually, CASE tools allow you to define indexes and clustering strategies within the design of the physical data model. Figure 11-21 shows the index screen in one CASE tool (ER*win*) for the order table. In this example, three

PAYMENT TYPE INDEX

Payment Type	Pointer
AMEX	*
AMEX	*
AMEX	*
AMEX	*
AMEX	*
AMEX	*
MC	*
MC	*
MC	*
MC	*
MC	*
MC	*
MC	*
VISA	*
VISA	*
VISA	*
VISA	*
VISA	*
VISA	*
VISA	*

ORDER TABLE

Order Number	Date	Cust ID	Amount	Payment Type
234	11/23/09	4254	$30.00	MC
235	11/23/09	9500	$20.00	VISA
236	11/23/09	1556	$20.00	VISA
237	11/23/09	2487	$60.00	AMEX
238	11/23/09	2243	$50.00	MC
239	11/23/09	1035	$50.00	AMEX
240	11/23/09	1556	$20.00	VISA
241	11/23/09	1123	$40.00	MC
242	11/24/09	9501	$30.00	VISA
243	11/24/09	4453	$30.00	VISA
244	11/24/09	9505	$20.00	VISA
245	11/24/09	2282	$20.00	AMEX
246	11/24/09	5927	$60.00	MC
247	11/24/09	2241	$50.00	VISA
248	11/24/09	4254	$50.00	AMEX
249	11/24/09	2242	$50.00	AMEX
250	11/24/09	2274	$20.00	VISA
251	11/24/09	9507	$10.00	VISA
252	11/24/09	2487	$60.00	VISA
253	11/24/09	2264	$40.00	AMEX

FIGURE 11-19
Payment Type Index

- Use indexes sparingly for transaction systems.
- Use many indexes to improve response times in decision support systems.
- For each table, create a unique index that is based on the primary key.
- For each table, create an index that is based on the foreign key to improve the performance of joins.
- Create an index for fields that are used frequently for grouping, sorting, or criteria.

FIGURE 11-20
Guidelines for Creating Indexes

indexes have been designed for the table, and during the implementation phase, the CASE tool will generate the code that is necessary to construct these indexes in the DBMS.

Estimating Storage Size

Even if you have denormalized your physical data model, clustered records, and created indexes appropriately, the system will perform poorly if the database server cannot handle its volume of data. Therefore, one last way to plan for good performance is to apply *volumetrics*, which means estimating the amount of data that

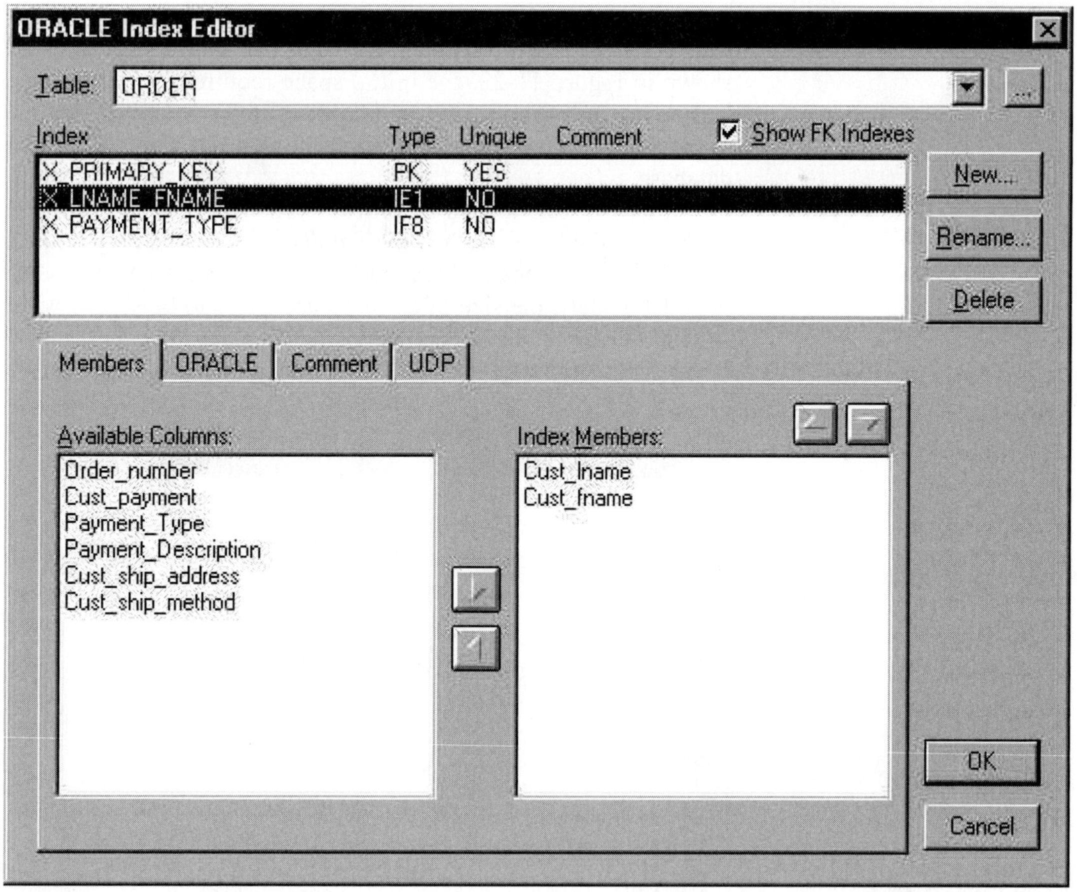

FIGURE 11-21
Indexes in ERwin

the hardware will need to support. You can incorporate your estimates into the database server hardware specification to make sure that the database hardware is sufficient for the project's needs. The size of the database will be determined by the amount of raw data in the tables and the *overhead* requirements of the DBMS. To estimate size, you will need to have a good understanding of the initial size of your data as well as its expected growth rate over time.

Raw data refers to all the data that are stored within the tables of the database, and it is calculated via a bottom-up approach. First, write down the estimated average width for each column (field) in the table and sum the values, yielding a total record size (Figure 11-22). For example, if a variable-width last name column is assigned a width of 20 characters, you can enter 13 as the average character width of the column. In Figure 11-22, the estimated record size is 49.

Next, calculate the overhead for the table as a percentage of each record. Overhead includes the room needed by the DBMS to support such functions as administrative actions and indexes, and it should be assigned on the basis of past experience, recommendations from technology vendors, or parameters that are built into software written to calculate volumetrics. For example, your DBMS vendor may recommend that you allocate 30% of the records' raw data size for overhead storage space, creating a total record size of 63.7 characters in the Figure 11-22 example.

Finally, record the number of initial records that will be loaded into the table, as well as the expected growth per month. This information should have been collected during the analysis phase as a nonfunctional data requirement. As shown in Figure 11-22, the initial space required by the first table is 3,185,000 characters, and future sizes can be projected on the basis of the growth figure. These steps are repeated for every table in order to get a total size for the entire database.

Many CASE tools will provide you with database size information on the basis of how you set up the physical data model, and they will calculate volumetrics estimates automatically. Figure 11-23 shows a volumetrics screen for ER*win*.

Ultimately, the size of the database needs to be shared with the design team so that the proper technology can be put in place to support the system's data, and

Field	Average Size (Characters)
Order number	8
Date	7
Cust ID	4
Last name	13
First name	9
State	2
Amount	4
Tax rate	2
Record size	49
Overhead	30%
Total record size	63.7
Initial table size	50,000
Initial table volume	3,185,000
Growth rate/month	1000
Table volume @ 3 years	5,478,200

FIGURE 11-22
Calculating Volumetrics

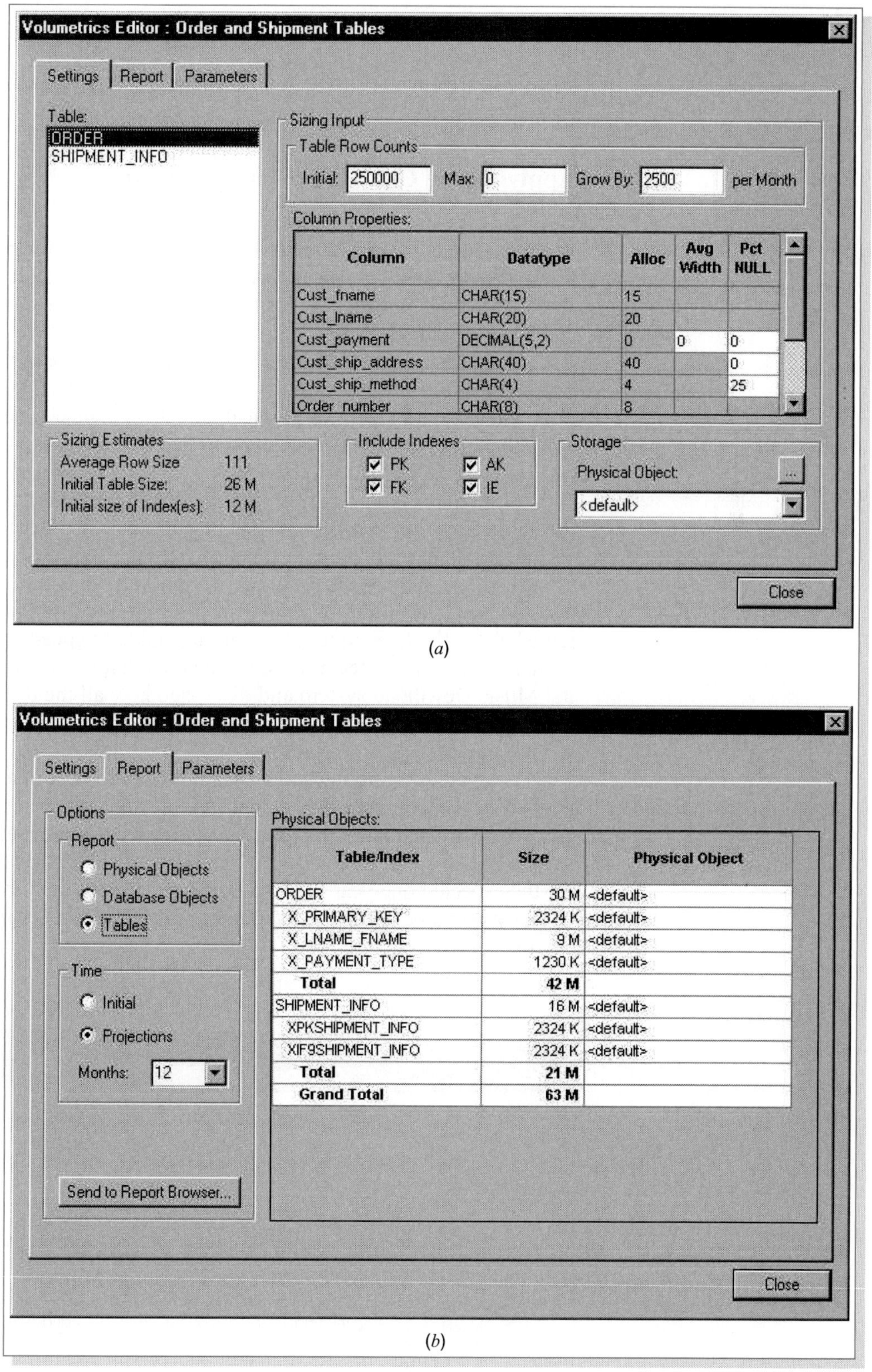

FIGURE 11-23

Volumetrics Screen in ERwin: (a) Information about Columns and Rows Is Entered into the ERwin; (b) Report Is Generated on the Basis of the Information.

potential performance problems can be addressed long before they affect the success of the system.

Applying the Concepts at Tune Source

Now that the team members had a good idea of the type of data storage formats that would be used, they were ready to optimize the data for performance efficiency. Kenji was the analyst in charge of the logical data model, and Jason wanted to be sure that the data model was optimized for storage efficiency before the team discussed access speed issues.

Kenji assured Jason that the current data model was in third normal form. He was confident of this because the project team followed the data modeling guidelines that led to a well-formed logical model. Of course, a week or so earlier, he did apply the three rules of normalization to the data model as a check to make sure that no design errors were overlooked.

Kenji then asked about the file formats for the transaction file identified in the earlier meeting. Jason suggested that he normalize the files to better understand the various tables that would be involved in the import procedure.

The last step of data storage design was to optimize the design for data access speed. Jason met with the analysts on the data storage design team and talked about the techniques that were available to speed up access to data in the system. Together, the team listed all the data that would be supported by the Digital Music Download system and discussed how all the data would be used. They developed the strategy laid out in Figure 11-24 to identify the specific techniques to put in place.

Ultimately, clustering strategies, indexes, and denormalization decisions were applied to the physical data model, and a volumetrics report was run from the CASE tool to estimate the initial and projected sizes of the database. The report suggested that an initial data storage capacity of about 5 gigabytes would be needed for the expected one-year life of the first version of the system. Additional storage capacity would be needed as the number of available tunes increases and for future versions of the system.

Target	Comments	Suggestions to Improve Data Access Speed
All tables	Basic table manipulation	Investigate whether records should be clustered physically by primary key. Create indexes for primary keys. Create indexes for foreign key fields.
All tables	Sorts and grouping	Create indexes for fields that are frequently sorted or grouped.
Tune information	Users will need to search Tune information by title, artist, and genre.	Create indexes for Tune title, artist, and genre.
Entire physical model	Investigate denormalization opportunities for all fields that are not updated very often.	Investigate 1:1 relationships. Investigate look-up tables. Investigate 1:M relationships.

FIGURE 11-24
Digital Music Download System Performance

Jason gave the estimates to the analyst in charge of managing the server hardware acquisition so that the person could ensure that the technology could handle the expected volume of data for the Digital Music Download system. The estimates would also go to the DBMS vendor during the implementation of the software so that the DBMS could be configured properly.

SUMMARY

File Data Storage Formats

There are two basic types of data storage formats: files and databases. Files are electronic lists of data that have been optimized to perform a particular transaction, and there are five different types: master, look-up, transaction, audit, and history. Master files typically are kept for long periods because they store important business information, such as order information or customer mailing information. Look-up files contain static values that are used to validate fields in the master files, and transaction files temporarily hold information that will be used for a master file update. An audit file records "before" and "after" images of data as they are altered so that an audit can be performed if the integrity of the data is questioned. Finally, the history file stores past transactions (e.g., old customers, past orders) that are no longer needed by the system.

Database Data Storage Formats

A database is a collection of groupings of information that are related to each other in some way, and a DBMS (database management system) is software that creates and manipulates these databases. There are four types of databases that are likely to be encountered during a project: legacy, relational, object, and multidimensional. The legacy databases (e.g., hierarchical databases and network databases) use older, sometimes outdated technology and are rarely used to develop new applications. The relational database is the most popular kind of database for application development today, and it is based on collections of tables that are related to each other through common fields known as foreign keys. Object databases contain data and processes that are represented by object classes, and relationships between object classes are shown by encapsulating one object class within another and are mainly used in multimedia applications (e.g., graphics, video, and sound). One of the newest members in the database arena is the multidimensional database, which has become popular with the increase in data warehousing. It stores precalculated quantitative information (e.g., totals, averages) at the intersection of dimensions (e.g., time, salesperson, product) to support applications that require data to be sliced and diced.

Selecting a Data Storage Format

The application's data should drive the storage format decision. Relational databases support simple data types very effectively, whereas object databases are best for complex data. Multidimensional databases are tuned to store aggregated, quantitative information. The type of system also should be considered when choosing among data storage formats. Relational databases have matured to support transactional systems, whereas multidimensional databases have been designed to perform best in decision support environments. Although less critical to the format selection decision, the project team needs to consider the kind of technology that exists within the organization and the kind of technology likely to be used in the future.

Physical Entity Relationship Diagrams

One important aspect of design is the movement from logical to physical entity relationship diagrams. Physical ERDs contain references to how data will be stored in a file or database table, and metadata are included to describe the data model components. The model reflects design decisions that will affect the physical implementation of the system.

The CRUD matrix should be modified to show exactly how data in the physical data model are created and used in the physical process model. The CRUD matrix helps ensure balance between the physical process and data models prior to implementation.

Optimizing Data Storage

There are two primary dimensions in which to optimize a relational database: for storage efficiency and for speed of access. The most efficient relational database tables in terms of data storage are those that have no redundant data and very few null values. Normalization is the process whereby a series of rules are applied to the logical data model to determine how well optimized it is for storage efficiency.

Once you have optimized your logical data design for storage efficiency, the data may be spread out across a number of tables. To improve speed, the project team may decide to denormalize—or add redundancy back into—the design that is depicted in the physical data model. Denormalization reduces the number of joins that must be performed in a query, thus speeding up data access. Denormalization is best in situations in which data are accessed frequently and updated rarely. There are three modeling situations that are good candidates for denormalization: look-up tables, entities that share one-to-one (1:1) relationships, and entities that share one-to-many (1:M) relationships. In all three cases, attributes from one entity are moved or repeated in another entity to reduce the joins that must occur during data access.

Clustering occurs when similar records are stored close together on the storage medium to speed up data retrieval. In intrafile clustering, similar records in the table are stored together in some way, such as in sequence. Interfile clustering combines records from more than one table that typically are retrieved together. Indexes also can be created to improve the access speed of a system. An index is a minitable that contains values from one or more columns in a table and information about where the values can be found. Instead of performing a table scan, which is the most inefficient way to retrieve data from a table, an index points directly to the records that match the requirements of a query.

Finally, the speed of the system can be improved if the right hardware is purchased to support its data. Analysts can use volumetrics to estimate the current and future size of data in the database and then share these numbers with the people who are responsible for buying and configuring the database hardware.

KEY TERMS

Aggregated	Database management system	End-user DBMS
Audit file	(DBMS)	Enterprise DBMS
Clustering	Decision support system (DSS)	Executive information system (EIS)
Data mart	Default value	Expert system (ES)
Data warehousing	Denormalization	File
Database	Encapsulation	Foreign key

Hierarchical database	Master file	Raw data
History file	Member	Referential integrity
Hybrid object-oriented DBMS	Multidimensional database	Relational database
Index	Network database	Set
Instantiation	Normalization	Star schema design
Interfile cluster	Object class	Structured Query Language
Intrafile cluster	Object database	(SQL)
Legacy database	Object-oriented DBMS	Subclass
Linked list	Overhead	Table scan
Logical entity relationship diagram	Physical data model	Transaction file
Look-up file	Physical entity relationship	Transaction processing system
Look-up table	diagram	Valid value
Management information system	Pointer	Volumetrics
(MIS)	Primary key	

QUESTIONS

1. Describe the two steps to data storage design.
2. How are a file and a database different from each other?
3. What is the difference between an end-user database and an enterprise database? Provide an example of each one.
4. Name five types of files, and describe the primary purpose of each type.
5. Name two types of legacy databases and the main problems associated with each type.
6. What is the most popular kind of database today? Provide three examples of products that are based on this technology.
7. What is referential integrity, and how is it implemented in a relational database?
8. What is the biggest strength of the object database? Describe two of its weaknesses.
9. How does the multidimensional database store data?
10. What are the two most important factors in determining the type of data storage format that should be adopted for a system? Why are these factors so important?
11. Why should you consider the storage formats that already exist in an organization when deciding on a storage format for a new system?

12. What are the differences between the logical and physical ERDS?
13. Describe the metadata associated with the physical ERD.
14. Describe the purpose of the primary and foreign keys.
15. Name three ways that null values in a database can be interpreted. Why is this problematic?
16. What are the two dimensions in which to optimize a relational database?
17. What is the purpose of normalization?
18. Describe three situations that can be good candidates for denormalization.
19. Describe several techniques that can improve performance of a database.
20. What is the difference between interfile and intrafile clustering? Why are they used?
21. What is an index, and how can it improve the performance of a system?
22. Describe what should be considered when estimating the size of a database.
23. Why is it important to understand the initial and projected size of a database during the design phase?
24. What are the key issues in deciding between using perfectly normalized databases and denormalized databases?

EXERCISES

A. Using the Web or other resources, identify a product that can be classified as an end-user database and a product that can be classified as an enterprise database. How are the products described and marketed? What kinds of applications and users do they support? In what kinds of situations would an organization choose to implement an end-user database over an enterprise database?

B. Visit a commercial Web site (e.g., CDnow, Amazon. com). If files were being used to store the data supporting the application, what types of files would be needed? What data would they contain?

C. Using the Web, review one of the products listed at the end of this exercise. What are the main features and functions of the software? In what companies has the database management system (DBMS) been implemented, and for what purposes? According to the information that you found, what are three strengths and weaknesses of the product?

- Relational DBMS
- Object DBMS
- Multidimensional DBMS

D. You have been given a file that contains fields relating to CD information. Using the steps of normalization, create a logical data model that represents this file in third normal form. The fields include the following:

- Musical group name
- Musicians in group
- Date group was formed
- Group's agent
- CD title 1
- CD title 2
- CD title 3
- CD 1 length
- CD 2 length
- CD 3 length

The assumptions are as follows:

- Musicians in group contains a list of the members in the musical group.
- Musical groups can have more than one CD, so both group name and CD title are needed to uniquely identify a particular CD.

E. Jim Smith's dealership sells Fords, Hondas, and Toyotas. The dealership keeps information about each car manufacturer with whom it deals so that employees can get in touch with manufacturers easily. The dealership staff also keeps information about the models of cars that the dealership carries from each manufacturer. They keep such information as list price, the price the dealership paid to obtain the model, and the model name and series (e.g., Honda Civic LX). They also keep information about all sales that they have made. (For instance, they will record the buyer's name, the car he or she bought, and the amount he or she paid for the car.) So that staff can contact the buyers in the future, contact information is also kept (e.g., address, phone number). Create a logical data model. (You may have done this already in Chapter 7.) Apply the rules of normalization to the model to check the model for processing efficiency.

F. Describe how you would denormalize the model that you created in question E. Draw the new physical model on the basis of your suggested changes. How would performance be affected by your suggestions?

G. Examine the physical data model that you created in question F. Develop a clustering and indexing strategy for this model. Describe how your strategy will improve the performance of the database.

H. Investigate the volumetric interface with the computer-aided software engineering (CASE) tool that you are using for class. What information do you as an analyst need to input into the tool? How are size estimates calculated? If your CASE tool does not accept volumetric information, how can you calculate the size of the database?

I. Calculate the size of the database that you created in question F. Provide size estimates for the initial size of the database as well as for the database in one year's time. Assume that the dealership sells 10 models of cars from each manufacturer to approximately 20,000 customers a year. The system will be set up initially with one year's worth of data.

J. How would the following ERD be changed to incorporate the design decision listed next?

- The analyst wants to keep track of the user ID of anyone who changes a grade for a course.
- A data store is added on the physical DFD so that information regarding the current semester's courses can be stored temporarily during the add/drop period before the courses become a part of the student's permanent record.
- The system would like to archive alumni into a table, once they graduate, so that only active students are stored in the student table.

K. Draw a physical process model (just the processes and data stores) for the following CRUD matrix:

	Register Student	Schedule Student	Create Transcript	Create Bill
Student				
Student Data Store	CRUD	R	R	R
Course Data Store		CRUD	R	
Billing Data Store		CRUD		CRUD
Grade Data Store			CRUD	

MINICASES

1. In the new system under development for Holiday Travel Vehicles, seven tables will be implemented in the new relational database. These tables are New Vehicle, Trade-in Vehicle, Sales Invoice, Customer, Salesperson, Installed Option, and Option. The expected average record size for these tables and the initial record count per table are given next.

Table Name	Average Record Size	Initial Table Size (records)
New Vehicle	65 characters	10,000
Trade-in Vehicle	48 characters	7,500
Sales Invoice	76 characters	16,000
Customer	61 characters	13,000
Salesperson	34 characters	100
Installed Option	16 characters	25,000
Option	28 characters	500

Perform a volumetrics analysis for the Holiday Travel Vehicles system. Assume that the DBMS that will be used to implement the system requires 35% overhead to be factored into the estimates. Also, assume a growth rate for the company of 10% per year. The systems development team wants to ensure that adequate hardware is obtained for the next three years.

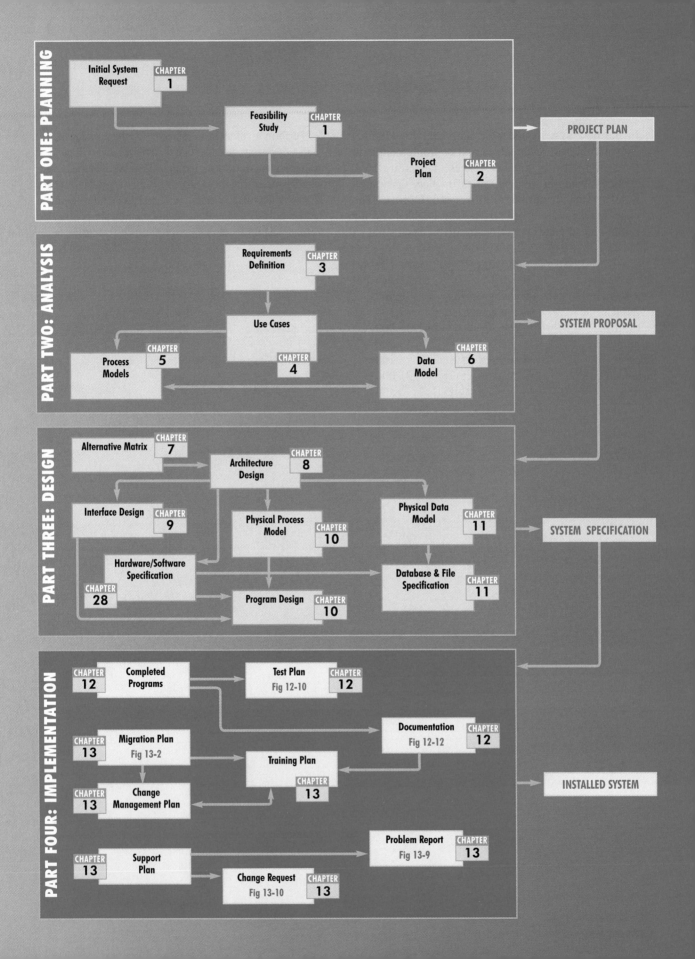

Programs

Test Plan

Documentation

Migration Plan

Change Management Plan

Training Plan

Support Plan

Problem Report

Change Request

Project Assessment

PART FOUR
IMPLEMENTATION
PHASE

PROJECT BINDER

Moving into Implementation

CHAPTER 12

The final phase in the SDLC
is the implementation phase,
during which the system is actually built
(or purchased, in the case
of a packaged software design).

At the end of implementation,
the final system is put into operation
and supported and maintained.

Transition to the New System

CHAPTER 13

PLANNING

ANALYSIS

DESIGN

IMPLEMENTATION

- [ ] **Program System**
- [ ] **Test Software**
- [ ] **Test Performance**
- [ ] Select System Conversion Strategy
- [ ] Train Users
- [ ] Select Support
- [ ] Maintain System
- [ ] Assess Project
- [ ] Conduct Post-Implementation Audit

T A S K C H E C K L I S T

PLANNING   ANALYSIS   DESIGN

CHAPTER 12

MOVING INTO IMPLEMENTATION

As the design phase is completed, the systems analyst begins to focus on the tasks associated with building the system, ensuring that it performs as designed and developing documentation for the system. Programmers will carry out the time-consuming and costly task of writing programs, while the systems analyst prepares plans for a variety of tests that will verify that the system performs as expected. Several different types of documentation will also be designed and written during this part of the systems development life cycle.

OBJECTIVES

- Be familiar with the system construction process.
- Understand different types of tests and when to use them.
- Understand how to develop user documentation.

CHAPTER OUTLINE

IMPLEMENTATION

INTRODUCTION

As the implementation phase begins, foremost on people's minds is *construction* of the new system. A major component of building the system is writing programs. In fact, some people mistakenly believe that programming is the focal point of systems development. We hope you agree that doing a good, thorough job on the analysis and design phases is essential to a smooth and successful implementation phase.

The implementation phase consists of developing and testing the system's software, documentation, and new operating procedures. These topics are presented in this chapter. Chapter 13 discusses additional issues that are essential to a successful system implementation, including installation of the new system, selection of the most suitable conversion approach, preparing the organization and the users to adapt to the new system, and ensuring that the system is supported after it is put into production.

Developing the system's software (writing programs) can be the largest single component of any systems development project in terms of both time and cost. It is generally also the best understood component and may offer the fewest problems of all the aspects of the SDLC. Since the systems analyst is usually not actually doing the programming (programmers are), in this chapter we concentrate our attention on managing the programming process.

While programmers are transforming program specifications into working program code, the systems analysts will be designing a variety of tests that will be performed on the new system. As the programs are finalized, the systems analysts may conduct these tests to verify that the system actually does what it was designed to do. Testing may be a major element of the implementation phase for the systems analysts. (In some organizations, testing is performed by specialized testers.)

During this phase, it is also the responsibility of the systems analysts to finalize the system documentation and develop the user documentation. The final section of this chapter discusses the various types of documentation that must be prepared.

MANAGING THE PROGRAMMING PROCESS

The programming process is quite well understood and generally flows smoothly. When system development projects fail, it is usually not because the programmers were unable to write the programs. Flaws in analysis, design, or project management are the leading contributors to project failure. In order to ensure that the process of programming is conducted successfully, we discuss several tasks that the project manager must do to manage the programming effort: assigning programming tasks, coordinating the activities, and managing the programming schedule.[1]

Assigning Programming Tasks

During project planning (Chapter 2), the project manager identified the programming support required for constructing the system in terms of the numbers and skill levels of programmers. Now the project manager must assign program modules to the programming staff. As discussed in Chapter 10, each programming module should be as separate and distinct as possible from the other modules. The project

---

[1] One of the best books on managing programming (even though it was first written in 1975) is that by Frederick P. Brooks Jr. *The Mythical Man-Month*, 20th anniversary ed., Reading, MA: Addison-Wesley, 1995.

CONCEPTS   **12-A THE COST OF A BUG**

IN ACTION

My first programming job in 1977 was to convert a set of application systems from one version of COBOL to another version of COBOL for the government of Prince Edward Island. The testing approach was to first run a set of test data through the old system and then run it through the new system to ensure that the results from the two matched. If they matched, then the last three months of production data were run through both to ensure they, too, matched.

Things went well until I began to convert the gas tax system that kept records on everyone authorized to purchase gasoline without paying tax. The test data ran fine, but the results using the production data were peculiar. The old and new systems matched, but rather than listing several thousand records, the report listed only 50. I checked the production data file and found it listed only 50 records, not the thousands that were supposed to be there.

The system worked by copying the existing gas tax records file into a new file and making changes in the new file. The old file was then copied to tape backup. There was a bug in the program such that if there were no changes to the file, a new file was created, but no records were copied into it.

I checked the tape backups and found one with the full set of data that was scheduled to be overwritten three days after I discovered the problem. The government was only three days away from losing all gas tax records.

Alan Dennis

QUESTION:

What might have happened if this bug hadn't been caught and all gas tax records were lost?

---

manager first groups together modules that are related. These groups of modules are then assigned to programmers on the basis of their experience and skill level. Experienced, skilled programmers will be assigned the most complex modules, while novice programmers will be given less complex ones.

It is quite likely that there will be a mismatch between the available programming skills and the programming skills that are needed to complete the programming. Consequently, the project manager must take steps at this time to ensure that skill deficiencies are eliminated through additional training or through mentoring arrangements with more experienced, skilled programmers. When the required skills are not readily available, the project manager must recognize the need for additional time in the project schedule.

While it will be tempting to speed up the programming process by adding more programming staff to the project, an ironic fact of system development is that the more programmers who are involved, the longer the project will take. As the size of the programming team increases, the need for coordination increases exponentially, and the more coordination that is required, the less time programmers can spend actually writing programs. The best size is the smallest possible programming team. When projects are so complex that they require a large team, the best strategy is to try to break the project into a series of smaller parts that can function as independently as possible.

Coordinating Activities

Coordination can be done through both high-tech and low-tech means. The simplest approach is to have a weekly project meeting to discuss any changes to the system that have arisen during the past week—or just any issues that have come up. Regular meetings, even if they are brief, encourage the widespread communication and discussion of issues before they become problems.

Another important way to improve coordination is to create and follow standards that can range from formal rules for naming files to forms that must be completed when goals are reached to programming guidelines. (See Chapter 2.) When a team forms standards and then follows them, the project can be completed faster because task coordination is less complex.

The project manager must put mechanisms in place to keep the programming effort well organized. Many project teams set up three "areas" in which programmers can work: a development area, a testing area, and a production area. These areas can be different directories on a server hard disk, different servers, or different physical locations, but the point is that files, data, and programs are separated on the basis of their status of completion. At first, programmers access and build files within the development area. Then they copy them to the testing area when they are "finished." If a program does not pass a test, it is sent back to development. Once all the programs are tested and ready to support the new system, they are copied into the production area—the location where the final system will reside.

Keeping files and programs in different places according to completion status helps manage *change control*, the action of coordinating a program as it changes through construction. Another change control technique is keeping track of what programs are being changed by whom, through the use of a *program log*. The log is merely a form on which programmers sign out programs to write, and sign in the programs when they are completed. Both the programming areas and program log help the analysts understand exactly who has worked on what and the program's status. Without these techniques, files can be put into production without the proper testing, two programmers can start working on the same program at the same time, files can be overlooked, and so on. Code management systems are available that facilitate the "checkout" of programs and maintain various versions of a module.

Many CASE tools are set up to track the status of programs and help manage programmers as they work. In most cases, maintaining coordination is not conceptually complex. It just requires a lot of attention and discipline to track small details.

Managing the Schedule

The time estimates that were produced during the initial planning phase and refined during the analysis and design phases must almost always be refined as the project progresses during construction, because it is virtually impossible to develop an exact assessment of the project's schedule. As we discussed in Chapter 2, a well-done set of time estimates will usually have a 10% margin of error by the time implementation is reached. It is critical that the time estimates be revised as the construction step proceeds. If a program module takes longer to develop than expected, then the prudent response is to move the expected completion date later by the same amount of time.

One of the most common causes for schedule problems is *scope creep*. Scope creep occurs when new requirements are added to the project after the system design has been finalized. Scope creep can be very expensive because changes made late in the SDLC can require much of the completed system design (and even programs already written) to be redone. Any proposed change during construction will require the approval of the project manager and should be addressed only after a quick cost–benefit analysis has been done.

Another common cause is the unnoticed day-by-day slippages in the schedule. One module is a day late here; another one, a day late there. Pretty soon these minor delays add up, and the project is noticeably behind schedule. Once again, the key to managing the programming effort is to watch these minor slippages carefully and update the schedule accordingly. It is especially critical to monitor slippage of all tasks on the critical path, since falling behind on these tasks will affect the final completion date for the project.

Typically, a project manager will create a risk assessment that tracks potential risks, along with an evaluation of their likelihood and potential impact. As programming progresses, the list of risks will change as some items are removed and others surface. The best project managers, however, work hard to keep risks from having an impact on the schedule and costs associated with the project.

TESTING

Writing programs is a fun, creative activity. Novice programmers tend to get caught up in the development of the programs themselves and are often much less enchanted with the tasks of testing and documenting their work. Testing and documentation aren't fun; consequently, they receive less attention than writing the programs.

Programming and testing are very similar to writing and editing, however. No professional writer (or serious student writing an important term paper) would stop

---

PRACTICAL TIP
12-1 AVOIDING CLASSIC IMPLEMENTATION MISTAKES

In previous chapters, we discussed classic mistakes and how to avoid them. Here, we summarize four classic mistakes in the implementation phase:

1. **Research-oriented development:** Using state-of-the-art technology requires research-oriented development that explores the new technology, because "bleeding-edge" tools and techniques are not well understood, are not well documented, and do not function exactly as promised.
   Solution: If you use state-of-the-art technology, you should significantly increase the project's time and cost estimates even if (some experts would say *especially if*) such technologies claim to reduce time and effort.

2. **Using low-cost personnel:** You get what you pay for. The lowest-cost consultant or staff member is significantly less productive than the best staff. Several studies have shown that the best programmers produce software six to eight times faster than the least productive (yet cost only 50% to 100% more).
   Solution: If cost is a critical issue, assign the best, most expensive personnel; never assign entry-level personnel in an attempt to save costs.

3. **Lack of code control:** On large projects, programmers must coordinate changes to the program source code (so that two programmers don't try to change the same program at the same time and one doesn't overwrite the other's changes). Although manual procedures appear to work (e.g., sending e-mail notes to others when you work on a program to tell them not to work on that program), mistakes are inevitable.
   Solution: Use a source code library that requires programmers to check out programs and prohibits others from working on them at the same time.

4. **Inadequate testing:** The number-one reason for project failure during implementation is ad hoc testing—in which programmers and analysts test the system without formal test plans.
   Solution: Always allocate sufficient time in the project plan for formal testing.

Source: Adapted from *Rapid Development*, Redmond, WA: Microsoft Press, 1996, pp. 29–50, by Steve McConnell.

after writing the first draft. Rereading, editing, and revising the initial draft into a good paper is the hallmark of good writing. Likewise, thorough testing is the hallmark of professional software developers. Most professional organizations devote more time and money to testing (and to revision and retesting) than to writing the programs in the first place.

The attention paid to testing is justified by the high costs associated with downtime and failures caused by software bugs.[2] Software bugs are estimated to cost the U.S. economy $59.5 billion annually.[3] One serious bug that causes an hour of downtime can cost more than one year's salary of a programmer—and how often are bugs found and fixed in an hour? Testing is therefore a form of insurance. Organizations are willing to spend a lot of time and money to prevent the possibility of major failures after the system is installed. Figure 12-1 lists some estimated income losses for companies or services that cannot function without their computer systems.

A program is not considered finished until it has passed its testing. For this reason, programming and testing are tightly coupled. Testing is frequently the primary focus of the systems analysts as the system is being constructed. The analysts must resist the temptation to rush into testing as soon as the very first program module is complete, however. Spontaneously testing different events and possibilities without spending time to develop a comprehensive test plan is dangerous, because important tests may be overlooked. If an error does occur, it may be difficult to reproduce the exact sequence of events that cause it. Instead, testing must be performed and documented systematically so that the project team always knows what has and has not been tested.

Brokerage operations	$6,450,000
Credit card authorization	2,600,000
eBay	225,000
Amazon.com	180,000
Package shipping services	150,000
Home Shopping Channel	113,000
Catalog sales center	90,000
Airline reservation system	89,000
Cellular service activation	41,000
Online network fees	25,000
ATM service fees	14,000
From *Internet Week*, 4/3/2000, and *FibreChannel: A Comprehensive Introduction*, R. Kembel, 2000, p. 8. Based on a survey done by Contingency Planning Research.	

FIGURE 12-1

Estimated Lost Income Resulting from One Hour of System Downtime

[2] When I was an undergraduate, I had the opportunity to hear Admiral Grace Hopper tell how the term *bug* was introduced. She was working on one of the early U.S. Navy computers when suddenly it failed. The computer would not restart properly, so she began to search for failed vacuum tubes. She found a moth inside one tube and recorded in the log book that a bug had caused the computer to crash. From then on, every computer crash was jokingly blamed on a bug (as opposed to programmer error), and eventually the term *bug* entered the general language of computing.

[3] See "Software Errors Cost U.S. Economy $59.5 Billion Annually," NIST Report 2002-10, www.nist.gov/public_affairs/releases/no2-10.htm.

The sections that follow describe a number of different types of tests that must be performed prior to installing the new system. Each type of test checks different features and/or scope of the system, until ultimately it is tested for acceptance by the users.

Test Planning

Testing starts with the tester's developing a *test plan* that defines a series of tests that will be conducted.[4] Figure 12-2 shows a typical test plan form. A test plan often has 20 to 30 pages, with a separate page for each individual test in the plan. Each individual test has a specific objective, describes a set of very specific *test cases* to examine, and defines the expected results and the actual results observed. The test objective is taken directly from the program specification or from the program source code. For example, suppose that the program specification stated that the order quantity must be between 10 and 100 cases. The tester would develop a series of test cases to ensure that the quantity is validated before the system accepts it.

It is impossible to test every possible combination of input and situation; there are simply too many possible combinations. In this example of an order quantity that must be between 10 and 100 cases, the test requires a minimum of 3 test cases: one with a valid value (e.g., 15), one with an invalid value too low (e.g., 7), and one with an invalid value too high (e.g., 110). Most tests would also include a test case with a non-numeric value to ensure that the data types were checked (e.g., ABCD). A really good test would include a test case with nonsensical, but potentially valid, data (e.g., 21.4).

In some cases, test cases cannot be conducted by entering data values, but must instead be handled by selecting certain combinations of commands or menu choices. The script area on the test plan is used to describe the sequence of keystrokes or mouse clicks and movements for this type of test.

Not all program modules are likely to be finished at the same time, so the programmer usually writes *stubs* for the unfinished modules to enable the modules around them to be tested. A stub is a placeholder for a module that usually displays a simple test message on the screen or returns some *hardcoded* value[5] when it is selected. For example, consider an application system that provides the five standard functions discussed in Chapter 5 for some data objects such as customers, vehicles, or employees: creating, changing, deleting, finding, and printing (whether on the screen or on a printer). Each of these functions could be a separate module that needs to be tested, and in fact, printing might be two separate modules, one for an on-screen list and one for the printer (Figure 12-3).

Suppose that the main menu module in Figure 12-3 was complete. It would be impossible to test it properly without the other modules, because the function of the main menu is to navigate to the other modules. In this case, a stub would be written for each of the other modules. These stubs would simply display a message on the screen when they were activated (e.g., "Delete item module reached"). In this way, the main menu module could pass module testing before the other modules were completed.

There are four general stages of tests: unit tests, integration tests, system tests, and acceptance tests. Although each application system is different, most errors are found during integration and system testing (Figure 12-4).

---

[4] For more information on testing, see William Perry, *Effective Methods for Software Testing*, "3d" ed. 2006.

[5] The word *hardcoded* means "written into the program." For example, suppose that you were writing a unit to calculate the net present value of a loan. The stub might be written to always display (or return to the calling module) a value of 100 regardless of the input values. In this case, we would say that the 100 was hardcoded.

Test Plan   Page ____ of ____

Program ID: _____   **Version number:** _____

Tester: _____   **Date designed:** _____   **Date conducted:** _____

Results: ☐ **Passed**   ☐ **Open items:**
_____

Test ID: _____   **Requirement addressed:** _____

Objective:
_____

Test cases

Interface ID	Data Field	Value Entered
1. _____	_____	_____
2. _____	_____	_____
3. _____	_____	_____
4. _____	_____	_____
5. _____	_____	_____
6. _____	_____	_____

_____

Script

_____

Expected results/notes

_____

Actual results/notes

FIGURE 12-2
Test Plan

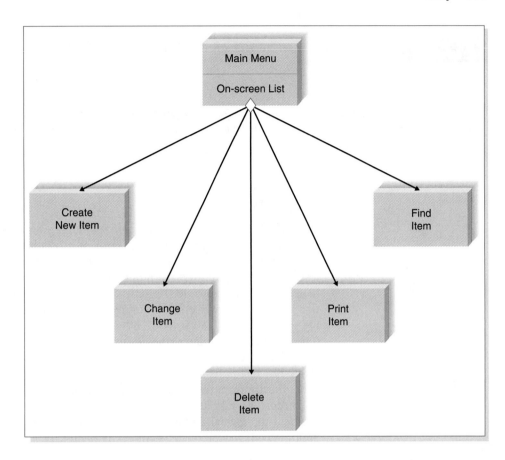

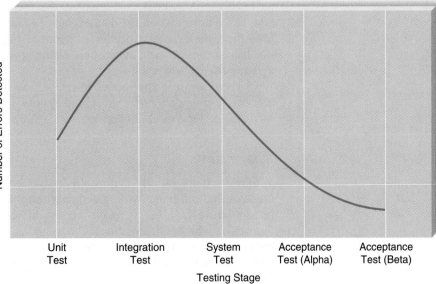

Pretend that you are a project manager for a bank developing software for automated teller machines (ATMs). Develop a unit test plan for the user interface component of the ATM.

Unit Tests

Unit tests focus on one unit—a program or a program module that performs a specific function that can be tested. The purpose of a unit test is to ensure that the module or program performs its function as defined in the program specification. Unit testing is performed after the programmer has developed and tested the code and believes it to be error free. These tests are based strictly on the program specification and may discover errors resulting from the programmer's misinterpretation of the specifications. Unit tests are often conducted by the systems analyst or, sometimes, by the programmer who developed the unit.

There are two approaches to unit testing: *black-box* and *white-box* (Figure 12-5). Black-box testing is the most commonly used. In this case, the test plan is developed directly from the program specification: Each item in the program specification becomes a test, and several test cases are developed for it. White-box testing is reserved for special circumstances in which the tester wants to review the actual program code, usually when complexity is high.

Integration Tests

Integration tests assess whether a set of modules or programs that must work together do so without error. They ensure that the interfaces and linkages between different parts of the system work properly. At this point, the modules have passed their individual unit tests, so the focus now is on the flow of control among modules and on the data exchanged among them. Integration testing follows the same general procedures as unit testing: the tester develops a test plan that has a series of tests. Integration testing is often done by a set of programmers and/or systems analysts.

There are four approaches to integration testing: user interface testing, use scenario testing, data flow testing, and system interface testing. (See Figure 12-5.) Most projects use all four approaches.

System Tests

System tests are usually conducted by the systems analysts to ensure that all modules and programs work together without error. System testing is similar to integration testing, but is much broader in scope. Whereas integration testing focuses on whether the modules work together without error, system tests examine how well the system meets business requirements and its usability, security, and performance under heavy load (see Figure 12-5). It also tests the system's documentation.

Stage	Types of Tests	Test Plan Source	When to Use	Notes
Unit Testing	Black-box testing: treats program as black box.	Program specifications	For normal unit testing	The tester focuses on whether the unit meets the requirements stated in the program specifications.
	White-box testing: looks inside the program to test its major elements.	Program source code	When complexity is high	By looking inside the unit to review the code itself, the tester may discover errors or assumptions not immediately obvious to someone treating the unit as a black box.
Integration Testing	User interface testing: The tester tests each interface function.	Interface design	For normal integration testing	Testing is done by moving through each and every menu item in the interface either in a top-down or bottom-up manner.
	Use scenario testing: The tester tests each use scenario.	Use scenario	When the user interface is important	Testing is done by moving through each use scenario to ensure that it works correctly. Use scenario testing is usually combined with user interface testing because it does not test all interfaces.
	Data flow testing: Tests each process in a step-by-step fashion.	Physical DFDs	When the system performs data processing	The entire system begins as a set of stubs. Each unit is added in turn, and the results of the unit are compared with the correct result from the test data; when a unit passes, the next unit is added and the test is rerun.
	System interface testing: tests the exchange of data with other systems.	Physical DFDs	When the system exchanges data	Because data transfers between systems are often automated and not monitored directly by the users, it is critical to design tests to ensure that they are being done correctly.
System Testing	Requirements testing: tests whether original business requirements are met.	System design, unit tests, and integration tests	For normal system testing	This test ensures that changes made as a result of integration testing did not create new errors. Testers often pretend to be uninformed users and perform improper actions to ensure that the system is immune to invalid actions (e.g., adding blank records).
	Usability testing: tests how convenient the system is to use.	Interface design and use scenarios	When user interface is important	This test is often done by analysts with experience in how users think and in good interface design. This test sometimes uses the formal usability testing procedures discussed in Chapter 9.
	Security testing: tests disaster recovery and unauthorized access.	Infrastructure design	When the system is important	Security testing is a complex task, usually done by an infrastructure analyst assigned to the project. In extreme cases, a professional firm may be hired.
	Performance testing: examines the ability to perform under high loads.	System proposal and infrastructure design	When the system is important	High volumes of transactions are generated and given to the system. This test is often done by the use of special-purpose testing software.
	Documentation testing: tests the accuracy of the documentation.	Help system, procedures, tutorials	For normal system testing	Analysts spot-check or check every item on every page in all documentation to ensure that the documentation items and examples work properly.
Acceptance Testing	Alpha testing: conducted by users to ensure that they accept the system.	System tests	For normal acceptance testing	Alpha tests often repeat previous tests, but are conducted by users themselves to ensure that they accept the system.
	Beta testing: uses real data, not test data.	No plan	When the system is important	Users closely monitor the system for errors or useful improvements.

DFD = data flow diagram.

FIGURE 12-5
Types of Tests

Acceptance Tests

Acceptance tests are done primarily by the users with support from the project team. The goal is to confirm that the system is complete, meets the business needs that prompted the system to be developed, and is acceptable to the users. Acceptance testing is done in two stages: *alpha testing*, in which users test the system using made-up data, and *beta testing*, in which users begin to use the system with real data and carefully monitor the system for errors. (See Figure 12-5.)

The users' perceptions of the new system will be significantly influenced by their experiences during acceptance testing. Since first impressions are sometimes difficult to change, analysts should strive to ensure that acceptance testing is conducted only following rigorous (and successful) system testing. In addition, listening to and responding to user feedback will be essential in shaping a positive reaction to and acceptance of the new system by the users.

DEVELOPING DOCUMENTATION

There are two fundamentally different types of documentation. *System documentation* is intended to help programmers and systems analysts understand the application software and enable them to build it or maintain it after the system is installed. System documentation is a by-product of the systems analysis and design process and is created as the project unfolds. Each step and phase produces documents that are essential in understanding how the system is built or is to be built, and these documents are stored in the project binder(s).

User documentation (such as user manuals, training manuals, and online help systems) is designed to help the user operate the system. Although most project teams expect users to have received training and to have read the user manuals before operating the system, unfortunately, this is not always the case. It is more common today—especially in the case of commercial software packages

---

CONCEPTS
IN ACTION

12-B Managing a Database Project

A consulting project involved a credit card "bottom feeder" (let's call it Credit Wonder). This company bought credit card accounts that were written off as uncollectable debts by major banks. Credit Wonder would buy the write-off accounts for 1 or 2 percent of their value and then would call the owners of the written-off accounts and "offer a deal" to the credit card account holders.

Credit Wonder wanted a database for these accounts. Legally, it did own them and so could contact the people who had owed the money—but as prescribed in credit law. For example, Credit Wonder could call only during certain hours and no more than once a week, and they had to speak to the actual account holder. Any

amount collected over the 1 to 2 percent of the original debt would be considered a gain. In its database, Credit Wonder wanted a history of what settlement was offered, the date the account holder was contacted, and additional notes.

QUESTIONS:
1. How might a systems analyst manage such a system project?
2. Who would the systems analyst need to interview to get the system requirements?
3. How would a database analyst help in structuring the database requirements?

for microcomputers—for users to begin using the software without training or reading the user manuals. In this section, we focus on user documentation.[6]

User documentation is often left until the end of the project, which is a dangerous strategy. Developing good documentation takes longer than many people expect, because it requires much more than simply writing a few pages. Producing documentation requires designing the documents (whether paper or online), writing the text, editing them, and testing them. For good-quality documentation, this process usually takes about 3 hours per page (single-spaced) for paper-based documentation or 2 hours per screen for online documentation. Thus, a "simple" set of documentation such as a 10-page user manual and a set of 20 help screens takes 70 hours. Of course, lower-quality documentation can be produced faster.

The time required to develop and test user documentation should be built into the project plan. Most organizations plan for documentation development to start once the interface design and program specifications are complete. The initial draft of documentation is usually scheduled for completion immediately after the unit tests are complete. This reduces—but doesn't eliminate—the chance that the documentation will need to be changed because of software changes, and it still leaves enough time for the documentation to be tested and revised before the acceptance tests are started.

Although paper-based manuals are still important, online documentation is becoming more important. Paper-based documentation is simpler to use because it is more familiar to users, especially novices who have less computer experience; online documentation requires the users to learn one more set of commands. Paper-based documentation also is easier to flip through to gain a general understanding of its organization and topics and can be used far away from the computer itself.

There are four key strengths of online documentation, however, which all but guarantee that it will be the dominant form for the fareseeable future. First, searching for information is often simpler (provided that the help search index is well designed). The user can type in a variety of keywords to view information almost instantaneously, rather than having to search through the index or table of contents in a paper document. Second, the same information can be presented several times in many different formats, so that the user can find and read the information in the most informative way. (Such redundancy is possible in paper documentation, but the cost and intimidating size of the resulting manual make it impractical.) Third, online documentation enables the user to interact with the documentation in many new ways that are not possible with static paper documentation. For example, it is possible to use links or "tool tips" (i.e., pop-up text; see Chapter 9) to explain unfamiliar terms, and programmers can write "show me" routines that demonstrate on the screen exactly what buttons to click and what text to type. Finally, online documentation is significantly less expensive to distribute and keep up to date than paper documentation.

Types of Documentation

There are three fundamentally different types of user documentation: reference documents, procedures manuals, and tutorials. *Reference documents* (also called the help system) are designed to be used when the user needs to learn how to

---

[6] For more information on developing documentation, see Thomas T. Barker, *Writing Software Documentation*, Boston: Allyn & Bacon, 1998.

perform a specific function (e.g., updating a field, adding a new record). Typically, people read reference information only after they have tried and failed to perform the function. Writing reference documents requires special care because users are often impatient or frustrated when they begin to read them.

Procedures manuals describe how to perform business tasks (e.g., printing a monthly report, taking a customer order). Each item in the procedures manual typically guides the user through a task that requires several functions or steps in the system. Therefore, each entry is typically much longer than an entry in a reference document.

Tutorials teach people how to use major components of the system (e.g., an introduction to the basic operations of the system). Each entry in the tutorial is typically longer still than the entries in procedures manuals, and the entries are usually designed to be read in sequence, whereas entries in reference documents and procedures manuals are designed to be read individually.

Regardless of the type of user documentation, the overall process for developing it is similar to the process of developing interfaces (see Chapter 9). The developer first designs the general structure for the documentation and then develops the individual components within it.

Designing Documentation Structure

In this section, we focus on the development of online documentation because we believe that it is the most common form of user documentation. The general structure used in most online documentation, whether reference documents, procedures manuals, or tutorials, is to develop a set of *documentation navigation controls* that lead the user to *documentation topics*. The documentation topics are the material that users want to read, whereas the navigation controls are the way in which users locate and access a specific topic.

Designing the structure of the documentation begins by identifying the different types of topics and navigation controls that must be included. Figure 12-6 shows a commonly used structure for online reference documents (i.e., the help system). The documentation topics generally come from three sources. The first and most obvious source of topics is the set of commands and menus in the user interface. This set of topics is very useful if the user wants to understand how a particular command or menu is used.

However, users often don't know what commands to look for or where they are in the system's menu structure. Instead, users have tasks they want to perform, and rather than thinking in terms of commands, they think in terms of their business tasks. Therefore, the second and often more useful set of topics focuses on how to perform certain tasks, usually those in the use scenarios from the user interface design. (See Chapter 9.) These topics walk the user through the set of steps (often involving several keystrokes or mouse clicks) needed to perform some task.

The third set of topics are definitions of important terms. These terms are usually the entities and data elements in the system, but sometimes they also include commands.

There are five general types of navigation controls for topics, but not all systems use all five types. (See Figure 12-6.) The first is the table of contents that organizes the information in a logical form, as though the users were to read the reference documentation from start to finish. The second, the index, provides access into the topics via important keywords, in the same way that the index at the back

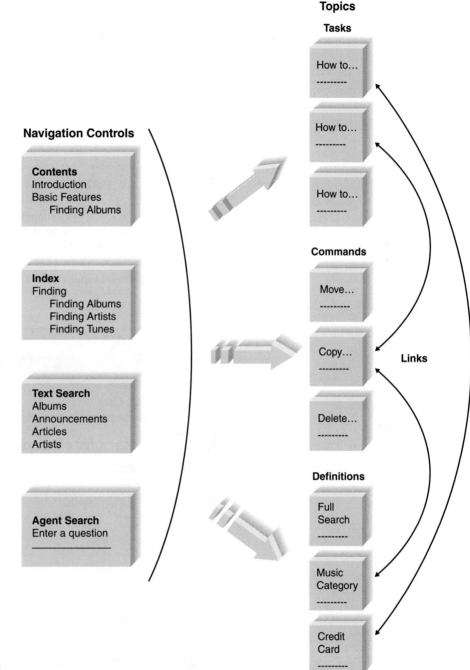

FIGURE 12-6
Organizing Online Reference Documents

of a book helps you to find topics. Third, text search provides the ability to search through the topics either for any text the user types or for words that match a developer-specified set of words that is much larger than the list of words in the index. Unlike the index, text search typically provides no organization to the words (other than alphabetic). Fourth, some systems provide the ability to use an intelligent agent to help in the search. The fifth and final navigation control to topics are the Web-like links between topics that enable the user to click and move among topics.

Procedure manuals and tutorials are similar, but often simpler in structure. When the new system significantly changes the way things are done, these resources are very important. Topics for procedures manuals usually come from the use scenarios developed during interface design and from other basic tasks the users must perform. Topics for tutorials are usually organized around major sections of the system and the level of experience of the user. Most tutorials start with basic, most commonly used commands and then move into more complex and less frequently used commands.

Writing Documentation Topics

The general format for topics is fairly similar across application systems and operating systems (Figure 12-7). Topics typically start with very clear titles, followed by some introductory text that defines the topic, and then provide detailed, step-by-step instructions on how to perform what is being described (where appropriate). Many topics include screen images to help the user find items on the screen; some also have "show me" examples in which the series of keystrokes and/or mouse movements and clicks needed to perform the function

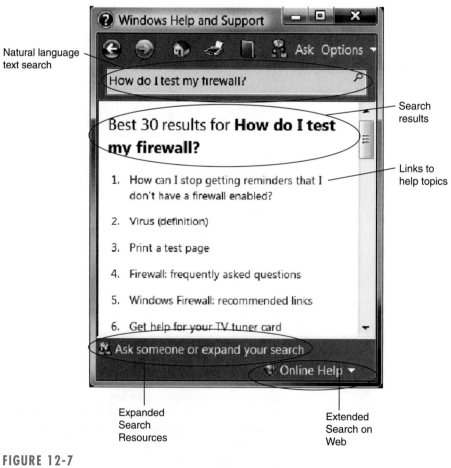

FIGURE 12-7
A Help Topic in Microsoft Word

are demonstrated to the user. Most also include navigation controls to enable movement among topics, usually at the top of the window, plus links to other topics. Some also have links to related topics that include options or other commands and tasks the user may want to perform in concert with the topic being read.

Writing the topic content can be challenging. It requires a good understanding of the users (or, more accurately, the range of users) and a knowledge of what skills the users currently have and can be expected to import from other systems and tools they are using or have used (including the system the new system is replacing). Topics should always be written from the viewpoint of the user and describe what the user wants to accomplish, not what the system can do. Figure 12-8 provides some general guidelines to improve the quality of documentation text.[7]

Identifying Navigation Terms

As you write the documentation topics, you also begin to identify the terms that will be used to help users find topics. The table of contents is usually the most straightforward, because it is developed from the logical structure of the documentation topics, whether reference topics, procedure topics, or tutorial topics. The items for the index and search engine require more care because they are developed from the major parts of the system and the users' business functions. Every time you write a topic, you must also list the terms that will be used to find the topic. Terms for the index and search engine can come from four distinct sources.

The first source for index terms is the set of the commands in the user interface, such as *open file*, *modify customer*, and *print open orders*. All commands contain two parts (action and object). It is important to develop the index for both parts because users could search for information by using either part. A user looking for more information about saving files, for example, might search by using the term *save* or the term *files*.

The second source is the set of major concepts in the system, which are often the entities, data stores, and data elements in the data flow diagrams. In the case of Tune Source, for example, this might include *music genre*, *artist*, and *tune*.

A third source is the set of business tasks the user performs, such as ordering replacement units or making an appointment. Often these will be contained in the

---

[7] One of the best books to explain the art of writing is that by William Strunk, Jr., and E. B. White, *Elements of Style*, 3d ed., Needham Heights, MA: Allyn & Bacon, 1995.

Guideline	Before the Guideline	After the Guideline
Use the active voice: The active voice creates more active and readable text by putting the subject at the start of the sentence, the verb in the middle, and the object at the end.	Finding tunes is done by using the tune title, the artist's name, or a genre of music.	Find a tune by the tune title, the artist's name, or a music genre.
Use e-prime style: E-prime style creates more active writing by omitting all forms of the verb *to be*.	The text you want to copy must be selected before you click on the *copy* button.	Select the text you want to copy before you click on the *copy* button.
Use consistent terms: Always use the same term to refer to the same items, rather than switching among synonyms (e.g., change, modify, update).	Select the text you want to copy. Pressing the *copy* button will copy the marked text to the new location.	Select the text you want to copy. Press the copy button to copy the selected text. Press the *paste* button to place the text into the new location.
Use simple language: Always use the simplest language possible to accurately convey the meaning. This does not mean that you should "dumb down" the text, but that you should avoid artificially inflating its complexity. Avoid separating subjects and verbs and try to use the fewest words possible. (When you encounter a complex piece of text, try eliminating words; you may be surprised at how few words are really needed to convey meaning.)	The Georgia Statewide Academic and Medical System (GSAMS) is a cooperative and collaborative distance learning network in the state of Georgia. The organization in Atlanta that administers and manages the technical and overall operations of the currently more than 300 interactive audio and video teleconferencing classrooms throughout the Georgia system is the Department of Administrative Service (DOAS). (56 words)	The Department of Administrative Service (DOAS) in Atlanta manages the Georgia Statewide Academic and Medical System (GSAMS), a distance learning network with more than 300 teleconferencing classrooms throughout Georgia. (29 words)
Use friendly language: Too often, documentation is cold and sterile because it is written in a very formal manner. Remember, you are writing for a person, not a computer.	Blank disks have been provided to you by the operations department. It is suggested that you make backup copies of all essential data to ensure that your data are not lost.	Make a backup copy of all data that is important to you. If you need more diskettes, contact the operations department.
Use parallel grammatical structures: Parallel grammatical structures indicate the similarity among items in lists and help the reader understand content.	Opening files Saving a document How to delete files	Opening a file Saving a file Deleting a file
Use steps correctly: Novices often intersperse actions and the results of actions when describing a step-by-step process. Steps are always actions.	1. Press the *customer* button. 2. The customer dialogue box will appear. 3. Type the customer ID and press the *submit* button and the customer record will appear.	1. Press the *customer* button. 2. Type the customer ID in the customer dialogue box when it appears. 3. Press the *submit* button to view the customer record for this customer.
Use short paragraphs: Readers of documentation usually quickly scan text to find the information they need, so the text in the middle of long paragraphs is often overlooked. Use numerous separate paragraphs to help readers find information more quickly.		

Source: Adapted from *Writing Software Documentation*, Boston: Allyn & Bacon, 1998, by T. T. Barker.

FIGURE 12-8
Guidelines for Crafting Documentation Topics

CONCEPTS

IN ACTION

12-C SYSTEMS FOR COMPLEX ELECTRICAL SYSTEMS

Systems integration across platforms and companies grows more complex with time. In a case study from Florida in 2008, an electrical company real-time system detected a minor problem in the power grid and shut down the entire system, plunging over two million people into the dark. The system experts placed the blame on a substation software system that detected the minor fluctuation, but had the ability to immediately shut the entire system down. Although there may be times when such a rapid response is vital (such as the nuclear disasters in Chernobyl Ukraine and Three Mile Island), this was a case where such a response was not warranted.

QUESTIONS:
1. Since software controls substation operations, how might a systems analyst approach this problem as a systems project?
2. Are there special considerations that a systems analyst needs to think about when dealing with real-time systems?

command set, but sometimes they require several commands and use terms that do not always appear in the system. A good source for these terms is the use scenarios developed by interface design. (See Chapter 9.)

A fourth, often controversial, source is the set of synonyms for the three sets of items mentioned previously. Users sometimes don't think in terms of the nicely defined terms used by the system. They may try to find information on how to *stop* or *quit* rather than *exit*, or on how to *erase* rather than *delete.* Including synonyms in the index increases the complexity and size of the documentation system but can greatly improve the value of the system to the users.

APPLYING THE CONCEPTS AT TUNE SOURCE

Managing Programming

Three programmers were assigned by Tune Source to develop the three major parts of the Digital Music Download system. The first was the Web interface, both the client side (browser) and the server side. The second, the purchase transaction system, was client–server based. The third was the sales analysis and promotions portion of the system. Programming went smoothly and, despite a few minor problems, according to plan.

Testing

While the programmers were working, Jason—senior systems analyst and project manager for Tune Source's Digital Music Download system—began developing the test plans and user documentation. The test plans for the three components were similar, but slightly more intensive for the Web interface component (Figure 12-9). Unit testing by black-box testing from program specifications was planned for all components. Figure 12-10 shows part of one unit test for the Web interface component.

Integration testing for the Web interface and system management components would encompass all user interface and use scenario tests to ensure that the

Test Stage	Web Interface	System Management	System Interfaces
Unit tests	Black-box tests	Black-box tests	Black-box tests
Integration tests	User interface tests; use scenario tests	User interface tests; use scenario tests	System interface tests
System tests	Requirements tests; security tests; performance tests; usability tests	Requirements tests; security tests	Requirements tests; security tests; performance tests
Acceptance tests	Alpha test; beta test	Alpha test; beta test	Alpha test; beta test

FIGURE 12-9
Tune Source's Test Plan

interface worked properly. The system interface component would undergo system interface tests to ensure that the system performed calculations properly and was capable of exchanging data with external systems used for credit card authorization.

Systems tests are by definition tests of the entire system—all components together. However, not all parts of the system would receive the same level of testing. Requirements tests would be conducted on all parts of the system to ensure that all requirements were met. Security was a critical issue, so the security of all aspects of the system would be tested. Security tests would be developed by Tune Source's infrastructure team, and once the system passed those tests, an external security consulting firm would be hired to attempt to break into the system.

Performance was an important issue for the parts of the system used by the customer (the Web interface and the system interfaces for payment processing), but not as important for the promotions component that would be used by staff, not customers. The customer-facing components would undergo rigorous performance testing to see how many transactions (whether searching or purchasing a download) they could handle before they were unable to provide a response time of 2 seconds or less. Jason also ensured that the architecture design included an upgrade plan so that, as demand on the system increased, there was a clear plan for when and how to increase the processing capability of the system.

Finally, formal usability tests would be conducted on the Web interface portion of the system, with six potential users (both novice and expert Internet users).

Acceptance tests would be conducted in two stages, alpha and beta. Alpha tests would be done during the training of Tune Source's store staff in the use of the in-store kiosks. Carly would work together with Jason to develop a series of tests and training exercises to train staff on how to use the system. They would then load the real music data into the system. These same staff and other Tune Source staff members would also pretend to be customers and test the Web interface.

Beta testing would begin by "going live" with the in-store kiosks. In-store shoppers would be offered a free download in return for evaluating the system. Then, the Web site would go live, but announced only to Tune Source employees. As an incentive to try the Web site, employees would be offered five free downloads from the Web site. The site would also have a prominent button on every screen that would enable employees to e-mail comments to the project team, and the announcement would encourage employees to report problems, suggestions,

Test Plan

Page: _12_ of _32_

Program ID: _ORD56_   Version Number: _3_

Tester: _Smith_   Date Designed: _9/9_   Date Conducted: _9/9_

Results: ☑ Passed   ☐ Open Items

Test ID: _12_   Requirement Addressed: _Verify purchase information_

Objective:

Ensure that the information entered by customer on the purchase tunes form
is valid.

Test Cases

	Interface ID	Data Field	Value Entered
1)	REQ56-3.5	Zip code	Blank
2)	REQ56-3.5	Zip code	9021
3)	REQ56-3.5	Zip code	90210
4)	REQ56-3.5	Zip code	C1A 2C6
5)			
6)			

Script

Expected Results/Notes

Test 3 is a valid zip code. All others should be rejected.

Actual Results/Notes

Test 3 accepted. Tests 1, 2, and 4 were rejected with correct error message.

FIGURE 12-10
Tune Source Unit Test Plan Example

and compliments to the project team. After one month, assuming that all went well, the beta test would be completed and the site would be linked to the main Web site and advertised to the general public.

Developing User Documentation

There were three types of documentation (reference documents, procedures manuals, and tutorials) that could be produced for the Web interface and the promotion component. Since the number of Tune Source staff using the promotion component would be small, Jason decided to produce only the reference documentation (an online help system). He believed that an intensive training program and a one-month beta-test period would be sufficient without tutorials and formal procedure manuals. Likewise, he felt that the process of purchasing tunes and the user interface itself were simple enough not to require a tutorial on the Web—a help system would be sufficient, and a procedure manual didn't make sense.

Jason decided that the reference documents for both the Web interface and promotion components would contain help topics for user tasks, commands, and definitions. He also decided that the documentation component would contain four types of navigation controls: a table of contents, an index, a finder, and links to definitions. He did not think that the system was complex enough to benefit from a search agent.

After these decisions were made, Jason assigned the development of the reference documents to a technical writer assigned to the project team. Figure 12-11 shows examples of the topics the writer developed. The tasks and commands were taken directly from the interface design. The list of definitions was put together, once the tasks and commands were developed, on the basis of the writer's experience in understanding what terms might be confusing to the user.

Once the topic list was developed, the technical writer then began writing the topics themselves and the navigation controls to access. Figure 12-12 shows an example of one topic taken from the task list: how to place a request. This topic presents a brief description of what it is and then leads the user through the step-by-step process needed to complete the task. The topic also lists the navigation controls that will be used to find the topic, in terms of the table of contents entries, index entries, and search entries. It also lists what words in the topic itself will have links to other topics (e.g., shopping cart).

Tasks	Commands	Terms
Find tune.	Find	Tune
Add a tune to my shopping cart.	Browse	Artist
Add a favorite.	Quick search	Genre
Checkout.	Full search	Special deals
What's in my shopping cart?		Cart
		Shopping cart

FIGURE 12-11
Sample Help Topics for Tune Source

Help Topic	Navigation Controls
How to Place a Request	**Table of Contents** list:
	How to Buy a Tune
There are four steps when you are ready to check-out and download the tunes you have selected (the items in your shopping cart):	**Index** list:
	Finding Tunes
1. Move to the Purchase Tunes Page.	Listening to Samples
	Purchasing a Tune
Click on the (Purchase Tunes) button to move to the purchase tunes page.	**Search** find by:
	Checkout
2. Make sure you are buying what you want.	Delete Items
	Favorites
The purchase tunes screen displays all the items in your shopping cart. Read through the list to make sure these are what you want, because once you submit your purchase you cannot change it.	Listen
	Paying
	Purchase Tune
You can delete a tune by	Shopping Cart
	Links:
	Shopping Cart

FIGURE 12-12
Example Documentation Topic for Tune Source

SUMMARY

Managing Programming
Programming is done by programmers, so systems analysts have other responsibilities during this stage. The project manager, however, is usually very busy. The first step is to assign tasks to the programmers—ideally, the fewest possible to complete the project, because coordination problems increase as the size of the programming team increases. Coordination can be improved by having regular meetings, ensuring that standards are followed, implementing change control, and using computer-aided software engineering (CASE) tools effectively. One of the key functions of the project manager is to manage the schedule and adjust it for delays. Two common causes of delays are scope creep and minor slippages that go unnoticed.

Testing
Tests must be carefully planned because the cost of fixing one major bug after the system is installed can easily exceed the annual salary of a programmer. A test plan contains several tests that examine different aspects of the system. A test, in turn, specifies several test cases that will be examined by the testers. A unit test examines a module or program within the system; test cases come from the program specifications or the program code itself. An integration test examines how well several modules work together; test cases come from the interface design, use scenarios, and the physical data flow diagrams (DFDs). A system test examines the system as a whole and is broader than the unit and integration tests; test cases come from the system design, the infrastructure design, the unit tests, and the integration. Acceptance testing is done by the users to determine whether the system is acceptable to them; it draws on the system test plans (alpha testing) and the real work the users perform (beta testing).

Documentation

Documentation, both user documentation and system documentation, is moving away from paper-based documents to online documentation. There are three types of user documentation: Reference documents are designed to be used when the user needs to learn how to perform a specific function (e.g., an online help system); procedures manuals describe how to perform business tasks; and tutorials teach people how to use the system. Documentation navigation controls (e.g., a table of contents, index, a "find" function, intelligent agents, or links between pages) enable users to find documentation topics (e.g., how to perform a function, how to use an interface command, an explanation of a term).

KEY TERMS

Acceptance test	Integration test	System test
Alpha test	Performance testing	Test case
Beta test	Procedures manual	Test plan
Black-box testing	Program log	Tutorial
Change control	Reference document	Unit test
Construction	Requirements testing	Usability testing
Data flow testing	Scope creep	Use scenario testing
Documentation navigation control	Security testing	User documentation
Documentation testing	Stub	User interface testing
Documentation topic	System documentation	White-box testing
Hardcoded	System interface testing	

QUESTIONS

1. Discuss the issues the project manager must consider when assigning programming tasks to the programmers.
2. If the project manager feels that programming is falling behind schedule, should more programmers be assigned to the project? Why or why not?
3. Describe the typical way that project managers organize the programmers' work storage areas. Why is this approach useful?
4. What is meant by change control? How is it helpful to the programming effort?
5. Discuss why testing is so essential to the development of the new system.
6. Explain how a test case relates to a test plan.
7. What is the primary goal of unit testing?
8. How are test cases developed for unit tests?
9. What is the primary goal of integration testing?
10. Describe the four approaches to integration testing.
11. How are the test cases developed for integration tests?
12. Compare and contrast black-box testing and white-box testing.
13. Compare and contrast system testing and acceptance testing.
14. Describe the five approaches to systems testing.
15. Discuss the role users play in testing.
16. What is the difference between alpha testing and beta testing?
17. Explain the difference between user documentation and system documentation.
18. What are the reasons underlying the popularity of online documentation?
19. Are there any limitations to online documentation? Explain.
20. Distinguish between these types of user documentation: reference documents, procedures manuals, and tutorials.
21. Describe the five types of documentation navigation controls.
22. What are the commonly used sources of documentation topics? Which is the most important? Why?
23. What are the commonly used sources of documentation navigation controls? Which is the most important? Why?
24. What do you think are three common mistakes made by novice systems analysts during programming and testing?

25. What do you think are three common mistakes made by novice systems analysts in preparing user documentation?

26. In our experience, documentation is left to the very end of most projects. Why do you think this happens? How could it be avoided?

27. In our experience, few organizations perform as thorough testing as they should. Why do you think this happens? How could it be avoided?

28. Create several guidelines for developing good documentation. Hint: Think about behaviors that might lead to developing poor documentation.

EXERCISES

A. Develop a unit test plan for the calculator program in Windows (or a similar program for the Mac or UNIX).

B. Develop a unit test plan for a Web site that enables you to perform some function (e.g., make travel reservations, order books).

C. If the registration system at your university does not have a good online help system, develop one for one screen of the user interface.

D. Examine and prepare a report on the online help system for the calculator program in Windows (or a similar program for the Mac or Unix). (You may be surprised at the amount of help that is available for such a simple program).

E. Compare and contrast the online help resources at two different Web sites that enable you to perform the same function (e.g., make travel reservations, order books).

MINICASES

1. A new systems development project is Pete's first experience as a project manager, and he has led his team successfully to the programming phase of the project. The project has not always gone smoothly, and Pete has made a few mistakes, but he is generally pleased with the progress of his team and the quality of the system being developed. Now that programming has begun, Pete has been hoping for a little break in the hectic pace of his workday.

   Prior to beginning programming. Pete recognized that the time estimates made earlier in the project were too optimistic. However, he was firmly committed to meeting the project deadline because of his desire for his first project to be a success. In anticipation of this time-pressure problem, Pete arranged with the human resources department to bring in two new college graduates and two college interns to beef up the programming staff. Pete would have liked to find some staff with more experience, but the budget was too tight and he was committed to keeping the project budget under control.

   Pete made his programming assignments, and work on the programs began about two weeks ago. Now, Pete has started to hear some rumbles from the programming team leaders that may signal trouble. It seems that the programmers have reported several instances where they wrote programs, only to be unable to find them when they went to test them. Also, several programmers have opened programs that they had written, only to

   find that someone had changed portions of their programs without their knowledge.

   a. Is the programming phase of a project a time for the project manager to relax? Why or why not?

   b. What problems can you identify in this situation?

   c. What advice do you have for the project manager?

   d. How likely does it seem that Pete will achieve his desired goals of being on time and within budget if nothing is done?

2. The systems analysts are developing the test plan for the user interface for the Holiday Travel Vehicles system. As the salespeople are entering a sales invoice into the system, they will be able to either enter an option code into a text box or select an option code from a drop-down list. A combo box was used to implement this, since it was felt that the salespeople would quickly become familiar with the most common option codes and would prefer entering them directly to speed up the entry process.

   It is now time to develop the test for validating the option code field during data entry. If the customer did not request any dealer-installed options for the vehicle, the salesperson should enter "none"; the field should not be blank. The valid option codes are four-character alphabetic codes and should be matched against a list of valid codes.

   Prepare a test plan for the test of the option code field during data entry.

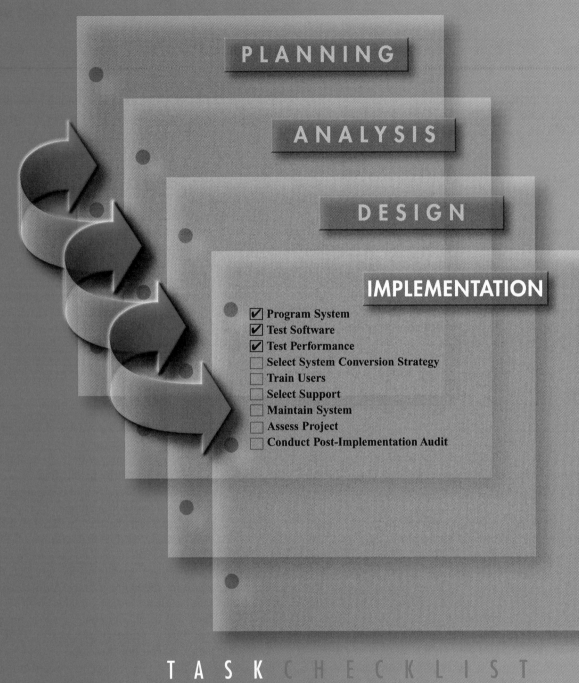

PLANNING

ANALYSIS

DESIGN

IMPLEMENTATION

- ☑ **Program System**
- ☑ **Test Software**
- ☑ **Test Performance**
- ☐ **Select System Conversion Strategy**
- ☐ **Train Users**
- ☐ **Select Support**
- ☐ **Maintain System**
- ☐ **Assess Project**
- ☐ **Conduct Post-Implementation Audit**

T A S K C H E C K L I S T

PLANNING

ANALYSIS

DESIGN

CHAPTER 13

TRANSITION TO THE NEW SYSTEM

T his chapter examines the activities needed to install the information system and successfully convert the organization to using it. It also discusses postimplementation activities, such as system support, system maintenance, and project assessment. Installing the system and making it available for use from a technical perspective is relatively straightforward. However, the training and organizational issues surrounding the installation are more complex and challenging because they focus on people, not computers.

OBJECTIVES

- Be familiar with the system installation process.
- Be familiar with the elements of a migration plan.
- Understand different types of conversion strategies and when to use them.
- Understand several techniques for managing change.
- Be familiar with postinstallation processes.

CHAPTER OUTLINE

IMPLEMENTATION

INTRODUCTION

It must be remembered that there is nothing more difficult to plan, more doubtful of success, nor more dangerous to manage than the creation of a new system. For the initiator has the animosity of all who would profit by the preservation of the old institution and merely lukewarm defenders in those who would gain by the new.

—Machiavelli, *The Prince*, 1513

Although written nearly 500 years ago, Machiavelli's comments are still true today. Managing the change to a new system—whether or not it is computerized—is one of the most difficult tasks in any organization. There are business issues, technical issues, and people issues that must be addressed in order to prepare for and successfully adapt to the change. Because of these challenges, planning for the transition from old to new systems begins while the programmers are still developing the software. Leaving this planning to the last minute is a recipe for failure.

This chapter discusses the transition from the as-is system to the to-be system and ways to successfully manage this process. The migration plan encompasses activities that will be performed to prepare for the technical and business transition, and to prepare the people for the transition. We also present several important support and follow-up activities that should be performed following the installation of the new system.

MAKING THE TRANSITION TO THE NEW SYSTEM

In many ways, using a computer system or set of work processes is much like driving on a dirt road. Over time with repeated use, the road begins to develop ruts in the most commonly used parts of the road. Although these ruts show where to drive, they make change difficult. As people use a computer system or set of work processes, those system/work processes begin to become habits or norms; people learn them and become comfortable with them. These system or work processes then begin to limit people's activities and make it difficult for them to change because they begin to see their jobs in terms of these processes rather than in terms of the final business goal of serving customers.

One of the earliest models for managing organizational change was developed by Kurt Lewin.[1] Lewin argued that change is a three-step process: unfreeze, move, refreeze (Figure 13-1). First, the project team must *unfreeze* the existing habits and norms (the as-is system) so that change is possible. Most of the SDLC to this point has laid the groundwork for unfreezing. Users are aware of the new system being developed, some have participated in an analysis of the current system (and so are aware of its problems), and some have helped design the new system (and so have some sense of the potential benefits of the new system). These activities have helped to unfreeze the current habits and norms.

The second step of Lewin's three-step model is to *move*, or *transition,* from the old system to the new. The *migration plan* incorporates many issues that must be addressed to facilitate this transition. First, the *conversion strategy* needs to be

---

[1] Kurt Lewin, "Frontiers in Group Dynamics," *Human Relations*, 1947, 1:5–41; and Kurt Lewin, "Group Decision and Social Change" in E. E. Maccoby, T. M. Newcomb, and E. L. Hartley, eds., *Readings in Social Psychology*, New York: Holt, Rinehart & Winston, 1958, pp. 197–211.

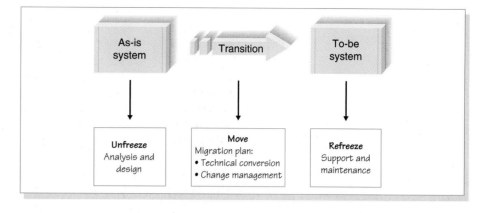

FIGURE 13-1

Implementing Change

selected, determining the style of the switch from the old to the new system, what parts of the organization will be converted when, and how much of the system is converted at a time. Plans to handle potential business disruption due to technical problems during conversion should be outlined in the *business contingency plan.* Arrangements for the hardware and software installation should be completed, and decisions about how the data will be converted into the new system will be made. The final major segment of the migration plan involves helping the people who are affected by the new system understand the change and motivating them to adopt the new system. The next section of this chapter discusses these aspects of the migration plan.

Lewin's third step is to *refreeze* the new system as the habitual way of performing the work processes—ensuring that the new system successfully becomes the standard way of performing the business functions it supports. This refreezing process is a key goal of the postimplementation activities discussed in the final section of this chapter. By providing ongoing support for the new system and immediately beginning to identify improvements for the next version of the system, the organization helps solidify the new system as the new habitual way of doing business. Postimplementation activities include *system support*, which means providing help desk and telephone support for users with problems; *system maintenance*, which means fixing bugs and improving the system after it has been installed; and *project assessment*, which is the process of evaluating the project to identify what went well and what could be improved for the next system development project.

THE MIGRATION PLAN

The transition from the old business processes and computer programs to the new business processes and computer programs will be facilitated by ensuring that a number of business, technical, and people issues are addressed. The decisions, plans, and procedures that will guide the transition are outlined in the *migration plan.* (See Figure 13-2.) The migration plan specifies what activities will be performed when and by whom as the transition is made from the old to the new system.

In order to ensure that business is ready to make the transition, the project team must determine the best conversion strategy to use as the new system is introduced to the organization. Also, plans should be made to ensure that the business

Migration Plan		
Preparing the Business	**Preparing the Technology**	**Preparing the People**
☑ Select a conversion strategy.	☑ Install hardware.	☑ Revise management policies.
☑ Prepare a business contingency plan.	☑ Install software.	☑ Assess costs and benefits.
	☑ Convert data.	☑ Motivate adoption.
		☑ Conduct training.

FIGURE 13-2

Elements of a Migration Plan

can continue its operations even in the event of technical glitches in the new system. These plans are termed *business contingency plans.*

Technical readiness is achieved by arranging for and installing any needed hardware and software, and converting data as needed for the new system. These arrangements, while essential, are usually the least difficult of all the issues dealt with in the migration plan.

Ensuring that the people who will be affected by the new system are ready and able to use it is the most complex element of the migration plan. Managing the "people" side of change requires the team to understand the potential for resistance to the new system, develop organizational support and encouragement for the change, and prepare the users through appropriate training activities.

Selecting the Conversion Strategy

The process by which the new system is introduced into the organization is called the conversion strategy. Those implementing this strategy must consider three different aspects of introducing the system: how abruptly the change is made (the conversion *style*), the organizational span of the introduction (conversion *locations*), and the extent of the system that is introduced (conversion *modules*). The choices made in these three dimensions will affect the cost, time, and risk associated with the transition, as explained in the sections that follow. (See Figure 13-3.)

Conversion Style   The switch from the old system to the new system can be made abruptly or gradually. An abrupt change is called *direct conversion*, and, as the name implies, involves the instant replacement of the old system with the new system. In essence, the old system is turned off and the new is turned on, often coinciding with a fiscal-year change or other calendar event.

Direct conversion is simple and straightforward, but also risky. Any problems with the new system that have not been detected during testing may seriously disrupt the organization's ability to function.

A more gradual introduction is made with *parallel conversion*, in which both the old and the new systems are used simultaneously for a period of time. The two systems are operated side by side, and users must work with both the old and new systems. For example, if a new accounting system is introduced with a parallel conversion style, data must be entered into both systems. Output from both systems is carefully compared to ensure that the new system is performing correctly. After some period (often one to two months) of parallel operation and intense comparison between the two systems, use of the old system is discontinued.

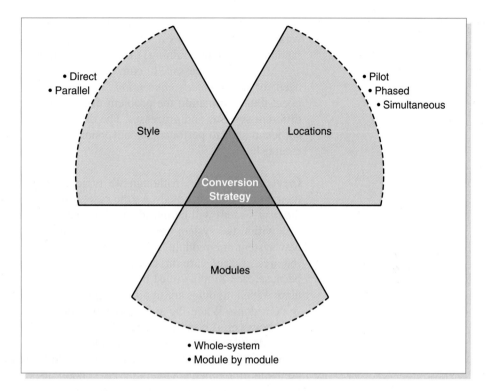

FIGURE 13-3
Conversion Strategies

Parallel conversion reduces risk by providing the organization with a fallback position if major problems are encountered with the new system. It adds expense, however, as users are required to do their job tasks twice: once with each system that performs the same function.

Conversion Locations   The new system can be introduced to different parts of the organization at different times, or it can be introduced throughout the organization at the same time. A *pilot conversion* selects one or more locations (or units or work groups within a location) to be converted first as a part of a pilot test. If the conversion at the pilot location is successful, then the system is installed at the remaining locations.

Pilot conversion has the advantage of limiting the effect of the new system to just the pilot location. In essence, an additional level of testing is provided before the new system is introduced organizationwide. This type of conversion can be done only in organizations that can tolerate different locations using different systems and business processes for a certain length of time. It also obviously requires a considerable time before the system is installed at all organizational locations.

In some situations, it is preferable to introduce the system to different locations, in phases. With *phased conversion*, a first set of locations is converted, then a second set, then a third set, and so on, until all locations are converted. Sometimes there is a deliberate delay between the phases, so that any problems with the system are detected before too much of the organization is affected. In other circumstances, the project team may begin a new phase immediately following the completion of the previous phase.

Phased conversion has the same advantages and disadvantages as pilot conversion. It also involves a smaller set of people to perform the actual conversion (and any associated training) than if all locations were converted at once.

It may be necessary to convert all locations at the same time, suggesting the need for *simultaneous conversion*. The new system is installed at all locations at once, thus eliminating the problem of having different organizational units using different systems and processes. The drawback of this option is that there must be sufficient staff to perform the conversion and train the users at all locations simultaneously.

Conversion Modules   Although we typically expect that systems are installed in their entirety, this is not always the case. It may be desirable to decide how much of the new system will be introduced into the organization at a time. When the modules within the system are separate and distinct, organizations may convert to the new system one module at a time, using *modular conversion*. Modular conversion requires special care in developing the system (and usually adds extra cost), because each module must be written to work with both the old and the new systems. When modules are tightly integrated, this is very challenging and is therefore seldom done. When the software is written with loose association between modules, however, it becomes easier.

Modular conversion reduces the amount of training needed for people to begin using the new system, since users need to be trained only for the new module being implemented. Modular conversion does require significant time to introduce each module of the system in sequence.

Whole-system conversion, installing the entire system at one time, is most common. This approach is simple and straightforward and is required if the system consists of tightly integrated modules. If the system is large and/or extremely complex, however (e.g., an enterprise resource planning system such as SAP or Oracle), the whole system may prove too difficult for users to learn in one conversion step.

Evaluating the Strategy Choices   Each of the segments in Figure 13-3 are independent, so a conversion strategy can be developed by combining any of the options just discussed.

CONCEPTS

IN ACTION

13-A CONVERTING TO THE EURO (PART 1)

When the European Union decided to introduce the euro, the European Central Bank had to develop a new computer system (called Target) to provide a currency settlement system for use by investment banks and brokerages. Prior to the introduction of the euro, settlement was performed between the central banks of the countries involved. After the introduction, the Target system, which consists of 15 national banking systems, would settle trades and perform currency conversions for cross-border payments for stocks and bonds.

Source: "Debut of Euro Nearly Flawless," *Computerworld*, 33(2) p. 16, January 11, 1999, by Thomas Hoffman.

QUESTION:
Implementing Target was a major undertaking for a number of reasons. If you were an analyst on the project, what kinds of issues would you have to address to make sure the conversion happened successfully?

Characteristic	Conversion Style		Conversion Location			Conversion Modules	
	Direct Conversion	**Parallel Conversion**	**Pilot Conversion**	**Phased Conversion**	**Simultaneous Conversion**	**Whole-System Conversion**	**Modular Conversion**
Risk	High	Low	Low	Medium	High	High	Medium
Cost	Low	High	Medium	Medium	High	Medium	High
Time	Short	Long	Medium	Long	Short	Short	Long

FIGURE 13-4
Characteristics of Conversion Strategies

For example, one commonly used approach is to begin with a pilot conversion of the whole system, using parallel conversion in a handful of test locations. Once the system has passed the pilot test at these locations, it is then installed in the remaining locations by phased conversion with direct cutover. There are three important factors to consider in selecting a conversion strategy: risk, cost, and the time required (Figure 13-4).

Risk The introduction of the new system exposes the organization to *risk* associated with problems and errors that may impede business operations. After the system has passed a rigorous battery of unit, integration, system, and acceptance testing, it should be bug free—maybe. Because humans make mistakes, undiscovered bugs may exist. Depending on the choices made, the conversion process provides one last step in which bugs can be detected and fixed before the system is in widespread use.

The parallel conversion strategy is less risky than direct conversion because of the security of continuing to operate the old system. If bugs are encountered, the new system can be shut down and fixed while the old system continues to function. Converting a pilot location is less risky than phased conversion or simultaneous conversion because the effects of bugs are limited to the pilot location. Those involved, knowing the installation is a pilot test, expect to encounter bugs. Finally, converting by modules is less risky than simultaneous conversion. The number of bugs encountered at any one time should be fewer when a few modules at a time are converted, making it easier to deal with problems as they occur. If numerous bugs are experienced together during simultaneous conversion, the total effect may be more disruptive than if the bugs were encountered gradually.

The significance of the risk factor in selecting a conversion strategy depends on the system being implemented. The team must weigh the probability of undetected bugs remaining in the system against the potential consequences of those undetected bugs. If the system has undergone extensive methodical testing, including alpha and beta testing, then the probability of undetected bugs is lower than if testing were less rigorous. There remains the chance, however, that mistakes were made in analysis and that the new system may not properly fulfill the business requirements.

Assessing the consequences (or cost) of a bug is challenging. Most analysts and senior managers are capable of making a reasonable guess at the relative significance of a bug, however. For example, it is obvious that the importance of negative consequences of a bug in an automated stock market trading system or a medical life-support system is much greater than in a computer game or word processing program. (Recall Figure 12-1.) Therefore, risk is likely to be a very important factor in the selection of a conversion strategy if the system has had limited testing and/or if the significance of bugs is high. If the system has been thoroughly tested and/or the cost of bugs is not too high, then risk becomes less important to the conversion strategy decision.

Cost   The various conversion strategies have different costs. These costs can include salaries for people who work with the system (e.g., users, trainers, system administrators, external consultants), travel expenses, operation expenses, communication costs, and hardware leases. Parallel conversion is more expensive than direct cutover because it requires that two systems (the old and the new) be operated at the same time. Employees must now perform twice the usual work and also cross-check the results of the two systems.

Pilot conversion and phased conversion have somewhat similar costs. Simultaneous conversion has higher costs because more staff are required to support all the locations as they simultaneously switch from the old to the new system. Modular conversion is more expensive than whole system conversion because it requires more programming. The old system must be updated to work with selected modules in the new system, and modules in the new system must be programmed to work with selected modules in both the old and new systems.

Time   The final factor is the amount of time required to convert between the old and the new system. Direct conversion is the fastest because it is immediate. Parallel conversion takes longer because the full advantages of the new system do not become available until the old system is turned off. Simultaneous conversion is fastest because all locations are converted at the same time. Phased conversion generally takes longer than pilot conversion because usually (but not always), once the pilot test is complete, all remaining locations are simultaneously converted. Phased conversion proceeds in waves, often requiring several months before all locations are converted. Likewise, modular conversion takes longer than whole-system conversion because the modules are introduced one after another.

Preparing a Business Contingency Plan

It is tempting to believe that doing careful and thorough work in analysis and design and managing the IT project correctly will produce a successful system implementation. It is common for the team to view their prospects for success with optimism. With new systems, however, it may be more appropriate to always expect the worst.

YOUR TURN

13-1 DEVELOPING A CONVERSION STRATEGY

Suppose that you are leading the conversion from one word processor to another at your university. Develop a conversion strategy. You have also been asked to develop a conversion strategy for the university's new Web-based course registration system. How would the second conversion strategy be similar to or different from the one you developed for the word processor?

CONCEPTS   13-B U.S. ARMY INSTALLATION SUPPORT

IN ACTION

Throughout the 1960s, 1970s, and 1980s, the U.S. Army automated its installations ("army bases," in civilian terms). Automation was usually a local effort at each of the more than 100 bases. Although some bases had developed software together (or borrowed software developed at other bases), each base often had software that performed different functions or performed the same function in different ways. In 1989, the army decided to standardize the software so that the same software would be used everywhere. This would greatly reduce software maintenance and also reduce training when soldiers were transferred between bases.

The software took four years to develop. The system was quite complex, and the project manager was concerned that there was a high risk that not all requirements of all installations had been properly captured. Cost and time were less important, since the project had already run four years and cost $100 million.

Therefore, the project manager chose a modular pilot conversion using parallel conversion. The manager selected seven installations, each representing a different type of army installation (e.g., training base, arsenal, depot) and began the conversion. All went well, but several new features were identified that had been overlooked during the analysis, design, and construction. These were added and the pilot testing resumed. Finally, the system was installed in the rest of the army installations using a phased direct conversion of the whole system. *Alan Dennis*

QUESTION:
1. Do you think the conversion strategy was appropriate?
2. Regardless of whether you agree, what other conversion strategy could have been used?

Keeping small technology glitches in the new system from turning into major business disasters is known as *business contingency planning.* Contingency plans help the business withstand relatively small problems with the new system so that major business disruptions are prevented.

Some might say that business disasters are prevented with good project management and migration planning; therefore, developing contingency plans to cope with disasters is unnecessary. Large projects spanning multiple business processes and involving huge amounts of code, however, provide numerous combinations of relatively small technical problems that together can have devastating consequences. Enterprise resource planning software projects are good examples. In 2004, Hewlett-Packard experienced an estimated $160 million financial impact when a $30-million SAP project in the Industry Standard Server division experienced relatively minor programming problems. In 2001, Nike experienced small IT problems in an SAP installation that cost the company $100 million in

YOUR   13-2 COMPARING CONVERSION STRATEGIES

TURN

■ Develop the combination of conversion strategy dimensions that produces the least risk; the most risk.
■ Develop the combination of conversion strategy dimensions that produces the least cost; the most cost.
■ Develop the combination of conversion strategy dimensions that requires the least time; the most time.

Now, compare these strategies. Do you see any relationships? Based on your analysis, what advice might you give a team selecting a conversion strategy?

lost revenue.[2] It may be less risky to plan for how to cope with system failure (contingency plan) than to try to prevent failure purely through project management techniques.

Choosing parallel conversion is one approach to contingency planning. Operating the old and new systems together for a time ensures that a fallback system is available if problems occur with the new system. Parallel conversion is not always feasible, however. Consequently, the worst-case outcome—*no system at all*—should be imagined and planned for, potentially going back to simple manual procedures.

One of the limitations of problem prevention through perfect project management techniques is the constant pressure of budget constraints and limited time that most projects face. With no budget or time pressure, it might be possible to prevent problems from occurring, but this is rarely the situation. Therefore, during the development of the migration plan, the project team should devote some attention to identifying the worst-case scenarios for the project, understanding the total business impact of those worst-case scenarios, and developing procedures and work-arounds that will enable the business to withstand those events. Since the contingency plan focuses on keeping the business up and running in the event of IT problems, it will be important to involve key business managers and users in the plan development.

Preparing the Technology

There are three major steps involved in preparing the technical aspects of the new system for operations: install the hardware, install the software, and convert the data. (See Figure 13-2.) Although it may be possible to do some of these steps in parallel, they usually must be performed sequentially at any one location.

The first step is to buy and install any needed hardware. In many cases, no new hardware is needed, but sometimes the project requires new servers, client computers, printers, and networking equipment. The new hardware requirements should have been defined in the hardware and software specifications during design (see Chapter 8) and used to acquire the needed resources. It is now critical to work closely with vendors who are supplying needed hardware and software to ensure that the deliveries are coordinated with the conversion schedule so that the equipment is available when it is needed. Nothing can stop a conversion plan in its tracks as easily as the failure of a vendor to deliver needed equipment.

Once the hardware is installed, tested, and certified as being operational, the second step is to install the software. This includes the to-be system under development, and sometimes, additional software that must be installed to make the system operational. For example, the Tune Source Digital Music Download system needs Web server software. At this point, the system is usually tested again to ensure that it operates as planned.

The third step is to convert the data from the as-is system to the to-be system. Data conversion is usually the most technically complicated step in the migration plan. Often, separate programs must be written to convert the data from the as-is system to the new formats required in the to-be system and store it in the to-be system files and databases. This process is often complicated by the fact that the files and databases in the to-be system do not exactly match the files and databases in the as-is system (e.g., the to-be system may use several tables in a database to store customer data that was contained in one file in the as-is system). Formal test plans are always required for data conversion efforts. (See Chapter 12.)

---

[2] Christopher Koch, "When Bad Things Happen to Good Projects," *CIO Magazine*, December 1, 2004.

Preparing People for the New System

In the context of a systems development project, people who will use the new system need help to adopt and adapt to the new system. The process of helping them adjust to the new system and its new work processes without undue stress is called *change management*.[3] There are three key roles in any major organizational change. The first is the *sponsor* of the change—the person who wants the change. This person is the business sponsor who first initiated the request for the new system. (See Chapter 1.) Usually the sponsor is a senior manager of the part of the organization that must adopt and use the new system. It is critical that the sponsor be active in the change management process, because a change that is clearly being driven by the sponsor, not by the project team or the IS organization, has greater legitimacy in the eyes of the users. The sponsor has direct management authority over those who will adopt the system.

The second role is that of the *change agent*—the person(s) leading the change effort. The change agent, charged with actually planning and implementing the change, is usually someone outside of the business unit adopting the system and therefore has no direct management authority over the potential adopters. Because the change agent is an outsider from a different organizational culture, he or she has less credibility than do the sponsor and other members of the business unit. After all, once the system has been installed, the change agent usually leaves and thus has no ongoing impact.

The third role is that of *potential adopter*, or target of the change—the people who actually must change. These are the people for whom the new system is designed and who will ultimately choose to use or not use the system.

In the early days of computing, many project teams simply assumed that their job ended when the old system was converted to the new system at a technical level. The philosophy was "build it and they will come." Unfortunately, that happens only in the movies. Resistance to change is common in most organizations. Therefore, the change management plan is an important part of the overall migration plan that glues together the key steps in the change management process. Successful change requires that people want to adopt the change and are able to adopt the change. The change management plan has four basic steps: revising management policies, assessing the cost and benefit models of potential adopters, motivating adoption, and enabling people to adopt through training. (See Figure 13-2.) Before we can discuss the change management plan, however, we must first understand why people resist change.

Understanding Resistance to Change

People resist change—even change for the better—for very rational reasons.[4] What is good for the organization is not necessarily good for the people who work there. For example, consider an order-processing clerk who used to receive orders to be shipped on paper shipping documents, but now uses a computer to receive the same information. Rather than typing shipping labels with a typewriter, the clerk now

---

[3] Many books have been written on change management. Some of our favorites are the following: Patrick Connor and Linda Lake, *Managing Organizational Change*, 2d ed., Westport, CT: Praeger, 1994; Douglas Smith, *Taking Charge of Change*, Reading, MA: Addison-Wesley, 1996; and Daryl Conner, *Managing at the Speed of Change*, New York: Villard Books, 1992.

[4] This section benefited from conversations with Dr. Robert Briggs, research scientist at the Center for the Management of Information at the University of Arizona.

clicks on the print button on the computer and the label is produced automatically. The clerk can now ship many more orders each day, which is a clear benefit to the organization. The clerk, however, probably doesn't really care how many packages are shipped. His or her pay doesn't change; it's just a question of whether the clerk prefers a computer or typewriter. Learning to use the new system and work processes—even if the change is minor—requires more effort than continuing to use the existing, well-understood system and work processes.

So why do people accept change? Simply put, every change has a set of costs and benefits associated with it. If the benefits of accepting the change outweigh the costs of the change, then people change. And sometimes the benefit of change is avoidance of the pain that you would experience if you did not adopt the change (e.g., if you don't change, you are fired, so one of the benefits of adopting the change is that you still have a job).

In general, when people are presented with an opportunity for change, they perform a cost–benefit analysis (sometimes consciously, sometimes subconsciously) and decide the extent to which they will embrace and adopt the change. They identify the costs of and benefits from the system and decide whether the change is worthwhile. However, it is not that simple, because most costs and benefits are not certain. There is some uncertainty as to whether a certain benefit or cost will actually occur; so both the costs of and benefits from the new system will need to be weighted by the degree of certainty associated with them (Figure 13-5). Unfortunately, most humans tend to overestimate the probability of costs and underestimate the probability of benefits.

There are also costs and benefits associated with the actual transition process itself. For example, suppose that you found a nicer house or apartment than your current one. Even if you liked it better, you might decide not to move, simply because the cost of moving outweighed the benefits of the new house or apartment itself. Likewise, adopting a new computer system might require you to learn new skills, which could be seen as a cost by some people, but as a benefit by others who perceive that those skills may somehow provide other benefits beyond the use of the system itself. Once again, any costs and benefits from the transition process must be weighted by the certainty with which they will occur. (See Figure 13-5.)

Taken together, these two sets of costs and benefits (and their relative certainties) affect the acceptance of change or resistance to change that project teams encounter when installing new systems in organizations. The first step in change

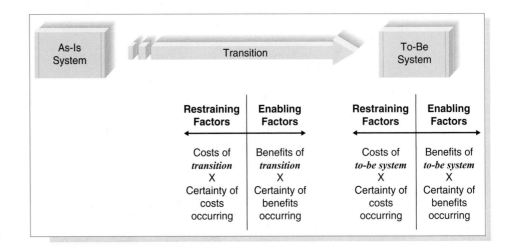

FIGURE 13-5
The Costs and Benefits of Change

management is to understand the factors that inhibit change—the factors that affect the *perception* of costs and benefits and certainty that they will be generated by the new system. It is critical to understand that the "real" costs and benefits are far less important than the perceived costs and benefits. People act on what they *believe* to be true, not on what *is* true. Thus, any understanding of how to motivate change must be developed from the viewpoint of the people expected to change, not from the viewpoint of those leading the change.

Revising Management Policies

The first major step in the change management plan is to change the management policies that were designed for the as-is system to new management policies designed to support the to-be system. *Management policies* provide goals, define how work processes should be performed, and determine how organizational members are rewarded. No computer system will be successfully adopted unless management policies support its adoption. Many new computer systems bring changes to business processes; they enable new ways of working. Unless the policies that provide the rules and rewards for those processes are revised to reflect the new opportunities that the system permits, potential adopters cannot easily use it.

Management has three basic tools for structuring work processes in organizations.[5] The first is the *standard operating procedures* (*SOPs*) that become the habitual routines for how work is performed. The SOPs are both formal and informal. Formal SOPs define proper behavior. Informal SOPs are the norms that have developed over time for how processes are actually performed. Management must ensure that the formal SOPs are revised to match the to-be system. The informal SOPs will then evolve to refine and fill in details absent in the formal SOPs.

The second aspect of management policy is defining how people assign meaning to events. What does it mean to "be successful" or "do good work"? Policies help people understand meaning by defining *measurements* and *rewards*. Measurements explicitly define meaning because they provide clear and concrete evidence about what is important to the organization. Rewards reinforce measurements because "what gets measured gets done" (an overused, but accurate, saying). Measurements must be carefully designed to motivate desired behavior. The IBM credit example ("Your Turn 3-3" in Chapter 3) illustrates the problem when flawed measurements drive improper behavior. (When the credit analysts became too busy to handle credit requests, they would "find" nonexistent errors so that they could return the requests unprocessed.)

A third aspect of management policy is *resource allocation*. Managers can have a clear and immediate impact on behavior by allocating resources. They can redirect funds and staff from one project to another, create an infrastructure that supports the new system, and invest in training programs. Each of these activities has both a direct and a symbolic effect. The direct effect comes from the actual reallocation of resources. The symbolic effect shows that management is serious about its intentions. There is less uncertainty about management's long-term commitment to a new system when potential adopters see resources being committed to support it.

---

[5] This section builds on the work of Anthony Giddons, *The Constitution of Society: Outline of the Theory of Structure*, Berkeley: University of California Press, 1984. A good summary of Giddons' theory that has been revised and adapted for use in understanding information systems is an article by Wanda Orlikowski and Dan Robey, "Information Technology and the Structuring of Organizations," *Information Systems Research*, 1991, 2(2):143–169.

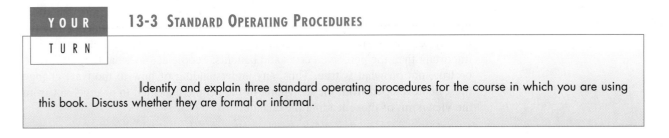

Assessing Costs and Benefits

The next step in developing a change management plan is to develop two clear and concise lists of costs and benefits provided by the new system (and the transition to it), compared with the as-is system. The first list is developed from the perspective of the organization, which should flow easily from the business case developed during the feasibility study and refined over the life of the project. (See Chapter 1.) This set of organizational costs and benefits should be distributed widely so that everyone expected to adopt the new system clearly understands why the new system is valuable to the organization.

The second list of costs and benefits is developed from the viewpoints of the different potential adopters expected to change, or stakeholders in the change. For example, one set of potential adopters may be the front-line employees, another may be the first-line supervisors, and yet another might be middle management. Each of these potential adopters or stakeholders may have a different set of costs and benefits associated with the change—costs and benefits that can differ widely from those of the organization. In some situations, unions may be key stakeholders that can make or break successful change.

Many systems analysts naturally assume that front-line employees are the ones whose set of costs and benefits are the most likely to diverge from those of the organization and thus are the ones who most resist change. However, these employees usually bear the brunt of problems with the current system. When problems occur, they often experience them firsthand. Middle managers and first-line supervisors are the most likely to have a divergent set of costs and benefits; therefore, they resist change because new computer systems often change how much power those individuals have. For example, a new computer system may improve the organization's control over a work process (a benefit to the organization), but reduce the decision-making power of middle management (a clear cost to middle managers).

An analysis of the costs and benefits for each set of potential adopters or stakeholders will help pinpoint those who will likely support the change and those who may resist the change. The challenge at this point is to try to change the balance of the costs and benefits for those expected to resist the change so that they support it (or at least do not actively resist it).

This analysis may uncover some serious problems that have the potential to block the successful adoption of the system. It may be necessary to reexamine the management policies and make significant changes to ensure that the balance of costs and benefits is such that important potential adopters are motivated to adopt the system.

Figure 13-6 summarizes some of the factors that are important to successful change. The first and most important is a compelling personal reason to change. All change is made by individuals, not organizations. If there are compelling reasons

The Migration Plan **473**

	Factor	Examples	Effects	Actions to Take
Benefits of to-be system	*Compelling* personal reason(s) for change	Increased pay, fewer unpleasant aspects, opportunity for promotion, most existing skills remain valuable	If the new system provides clear personal benefits to those who must adopt it, they are more likely to embrace the change.	Perform a cost–benefit analysis from the viewpoint of the stakeholders, make changes where needed, and actively promote the benefits.
Certainty of benefits	*Compelling* organizational reason(s) for change	Risk of bankruptcy, acquisition, government regulation	If adopters do not understand why the organization is implementing the change, they are less certain that the change will occur.	Perform a cost–benefit analysis from the viewpoint of the organization and launch a vigorous information campaign to explain the results to everyone.
	Demonstrated top management support	Active involvement, frequent mentions in speeches	If top management is not seen to actively support the change, there is less certainty that the change will occur.	Encourage top management to participate in the information campaign.
	Committed and involved business sponsor	Active involvement, frequent visits to users and project team, championing	If the business sponsor (the functional manager who initiated the project) is not seen to actively support the change, there is less certainty that the change will occur.	Encourage the business sponsor to participate in the information campaign and play an active role in the change management plan.
	Credible top management and business sponsor	Management and sponsor who do what they say instead of being members of the "management fad of the month" club	If the business sponsor and top management have credibility in the eyes of the adopters, the certainty of the claimed benefits is higher.	Ensure that the business sponsor and/or top management has credibility so that such involvement will help; if there is no credibility, involvement will have little effect.
Costs of transition	Low personal costs of change	Few new skills needed	The cost of the change is not borne equally by all stakeholders; the costs are likely to be higher for some.	Perform a cost–benefit analysis from the viewpoint of the stakeholders, make changes where needed, and actively promote the low costs.
Certainty of costs	Clear plan for change	Clear dates and instructions for change, clear expectations	If there is a clear migration plan, it will likely lower the perceived costs of transition.	Publicize the migration plan.
	Credible change agent	Previous experience with change, does what he or she promises to do	If the change agent has credibility in the eyes of the adopters, the certainty of the claimed costs is higher.	If the change agent is not credible, then change will be difficult.
	Clear mandate for change agent from sponsor	Open support for change agent when disagreements occur	If the change agent has a clear mandate from the business sponsor, the certainty of the claimed costs is higher.	The business sponsor must actively demonstrate support for the change agent.

FIGURE 13-6
Major Factors in Successful Change

for the key groups of individual stakeholders to want the change, then the change is more likely to be successful. Factors such as increased salary, reduced unpleasantness, and—depending on the individuals—opportunities for promotion and personal development can be important motivators. If the change makes current skills less valuable, however, individuals may resist the change because they have

13-C MANAGING GLOBAL PROJECTS

Shamrock Foods is a major food distributor centered in Tralee, Ireland. Originally a dairy cooperative, Shamrock branched into various food components (dried milk, cheese solids, flavorings [or flavourings, as the Irish would spell it]) and has had substantial growth in the past 10 years, most of which came by way of acquisition of existing companies or facilities. For example, Iowa Soybean in the United States is now a subsidiary of Shamrock Foods, as is a large dairy cooperative in Wisconsin.

Shamrock has processing facilities in over 12 countries and distribution and sales in over 30 countries. With the rapid growth by acquisition, the company has generally adopted a "hands-off" policy keeping the systems separated and not integrated into a unified ERP system. Thus, each acquired company is still largely autonomous, although it reports to Shamrock Foods and is managed by Shamrock Foods.

This separation concept has been a problem for Conor Lynch, CFO of Shamrock Foods. The board of directors would like some aggregated data for direction and analysis of acquired businesses. Conor has the reports from the various subsidiaries, but has to have his staff convert the figures reported in them to a consistent basis (generally, either Euros or American dollars).

QUESTIONS:
1. When should a multinational/multisite business consolidate data systems?
2. There are costs associated with consolidating data systems that have a variety of hardware and software systems. For example, the various acquired companies already had their own functioning accounting systems. What justification should Conor use to push for a consolidated, unified ERP system?
3. At times, Conor has to deal with incomplete and incompatible data. For instance, inventory systems might be FIFO for some of the subsidiaries and LIFO for other subsidiaries. How might a CFO with multinational interests deal with incomplete and incompatible data?

invested a lot of time and energy in acquiring those skills and anything that diminishes those skills may be perceived as diminishing the individual (because important skills bring respect and power).

There must also be a compelling reason for the organization to need the change; otherwise, individuals become skeptical in regard to whether the change is important and are less certain that it will in fact occur. Probably the hardest organization to change is an organization that has been successful, because individuals come to believe that what worked in the past will continue to work. By contrast, in an organization that is on the brink of bankruptcy, it is easier to convince individuals that change is needed. Commitment and support from credible business sponsors and top management are also important in increasing the certainty that the change will occur.

The likelihood of successful change is increased when the cost of the transition to individuals who must change is low. The need for significantly different new skills or disruptions in operations and work habits may create resistance. A clear migration plan developed by a credible change agent who has support from the business sponsor is an important factor in increasing the certainty about the costs of the transition process.

Motivating Adoption

The single most important factor in motivating a change is providing clear and convincing evidence of the need for change. Simply put, everyone who is expected to adopt the change must be convinced that the benefits from the to-be system outweigh the costs of changing.

There are two basic strategies to motivating adoption: informational and political. Both strategies are often used simultaneously. With an *informational strategy*, the goal is to convince potential adopters that the change is for the better. This strategy works when the cost–benefit set of the target adopters has more benefits than costs. In other words, there really are clear reasons for the potential adopters to welcome the change.

Using this approach, the project team provides clear and convincing evidence of the costs and benefits of moving to the to-be system. The project team writes memos and develops presentations that outline the costs and benefits of adopting the system from the perspective of the organization and from the perspective of the target group of potential adopters. This information is disseminated widely throughout the target group, much like an advertising or public relations campaign. It must emphasize the benefits as well as increase the certainty in the minds of potential adopters that these benefits will actually be achieved. In our experience, it is always easier to sell painkillers than vitamins; that is, it is easier to convince potential adopters that a new system will remove a major problem (or other source of pain) than that it will provide new benefits (e.g., increase sales). Therefore, informational campaigns are more likely to be successful if they stress the reduction or elimination of problems, rather than focus on the provision of new opportunities.

The other strategy to motivate change is a *political strategy*. With a political strategy, organizational power, not information, is used to motivate change. This approach is often used when the cost–benefit set of the target adopters has more costs than benefits. In other words, although the change may benefit the organization, there are no reasons for the potential adopters to welcome the change.

The political strategy is usually beyond the control of the project team. It requires someone in the organization who holds legitimate power over the target group to influence the group to adopt the change. This may be done in a coercive manner (e.g., "adopt the system or you're fired") or in a negotiated manner, in which the target group gains benefits in other ways that are linked to the adoption of the system (e.g., linking system adoption to increased training opportunities). Management policies can play a key role in a political strategy by linking salary to certain behaviors desired with the new system.

In general, for any change that has true organizational benefits, about 20% to 30% of potential adopters will be *ready adopters*. They recognize the benefits, quickly adopt the system, and become proponents of the system. Another 20% to 30% are *resistant adopters*. They simply refuse to accept the change, and they fight against it, either because the new system has more costs than benefits for them personally or because they place such a high cost on the transition process itself that no amount of benefits from the new system can outweigh the change costs. The remaining 40% to 60% are *reluctant adopters*. They tend to be apathetic and will

---

YOUR
TURN

13-4 OVERCOMING RESISTANCE TO A NEW EXECUTIVE INFORMATION SYSTEM

How would you motivate adoption if you were the developer of a new executive information system designed to provide your organization's top executives with key performance measures and economic trend information?

Sponsor	Change Agent	Potential Adopters
The sponsor wants the change to occur.	The change agent leads the change effort.	Potential adopters are the people who must change.
		20%–30% are ready adopters.
		20%–30% are resistant adopters.
		40%–60% are reluctant adopters.

FIGURE 13-7

Actors in the Change Management Process

go with the flow to either support or resist the system, depending on how the project evolves and how their coworkers react to the system. Figure 13-7 illustrates the actors who are involved in the change management process.

The goal of change management is to actively support and encourage the ready adopters and help them win over the reluctant adopters. There is usually little that can be done about the resistant adopters because their set of costs and benefits may be divergent from those of the organization. Unless there are simple steps that can be taken to rebalance their costs and benefits or the organization chooses to adopt a strong political strategy, it is often best to ignore this small minority of resistant adopters and focus on the larger majority of ready and reluctant adopters.

Enabling Adoption: Training

Potential adopters may want to adopt the change, but unless they are capable of adopting it, they won't. Adoption is enabled by providing employees the skills needed to adopt the change through careful *training*. Training is probably the most self-evident part of any change management initiative. How can an organization expect its staff members to adopt a new system if they are not trained? We have found that training is one of the most commonly overlooked parts of the process, however. Many organizations and project managers simply expect potential adopters to find the system easy to learn. Since the system is presumed to be so simple, it is taken for granted that potential adopters should be able to learn with little effort. Unfortunately, this is usually an overly optimistic assumption.

Every new system requires new skills, either because the basic work processes have changed (sometimes radically in the case of business process reengineering [BPR]; see Chapter 3) or because the computer system used to support the processes is different. The more radical the changes to the business processes, the more important it is to ensure that the organization has the new skills required to operate the new business processes and supporting information system. In general, there are three ways to get these new skills. One is to hire new employees who have the needed skills that the existing staff does not. Another is to outsource the processes to an organization that has the skills that the existing staff does not. Both of these approaches are controversial and are usually considered only in the case of BPR when the new skills needed are likely to be the most different from the set of skills of the current staff. In most cases, organizations choose the third alternative: training existing staff in the new business processes and the to-be system. Every training plan must consider what to train and how to deliver the training.

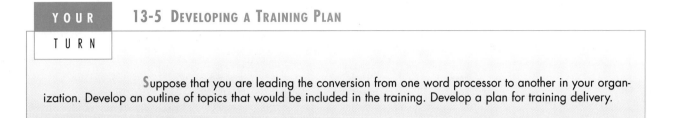

13-5 DEVELOPING A TRAINING PLAN

Suppose that you are leading the conversion from one word processor to another in your organization. Develop an outline of topics that would be included in the training. Develop a plan for training delivery.

What to Train   What training should you provide to the system users? It's obvious: how to use the system. The training should cover all the capabilities of the new system, so that users understand what each module does, right?

Wrong. Training for business systems should focus on helping the users to accomplish their jobs, not on how to use the system. The system is simply a means to an end, not the end in itself. This focus on performing the job (i.e., the business processes), not using the system, has two important implications. First, the training must focus on those activities around the system, as well as on the system itself. The training must help the users understand how the computer fits into the bigger picture of their jobs. The use of the system must be put in the context of the manual and computerized business processes, and it must also cover the new management policies that were implemented along with the new computer system.

Second, the training should focus on what the user needs to do, not on what the system can do. This is a subtle—but very important—distinction. Most systems will provide far more capabilities than the users will need to use (e.g., when was the last time you wrote a macro in Microsoft Word?). Rather than attempting to teach the users all the features of the system, training should instead focus on the much smaller set of activities that users perform on a regular basis and ensure that users are truly expert in those. When the focus is on the 20% of functions that the users will use 80% of the time (instead of attempting to cover all functions), users become confident about their ability to use the system. Training should mention the other little-used functions, but only so that users are aware of their existence and know how to learn about them when their use becomes necessary.

One source of guidance for designing training materials is the use cases and use scenarios. The use cases and use scenarios outline the common activities that users perform and thus can be helpful in understanding the business processes and system functions that are likely to be most important to the users.

How to Train   There are many ways to deliver training. The most commonly used approach is *classroom training*. This has the advantage of training many users at one time with only one instructor and creates a shared experience among the users.

It is also possible to provide *one-on-one training* in which one trainer works closely with one user at a time. This is obviously more expensive, but the trainer can design the training program to meet the needs of individual users and can better ensure that the users really do understand the material. This approach is typically used only when the users are very important or when there are very few users.

Another approach that is becoming more common is to use some form of *computer-based training* (*CBT*), in which the training program is delivered via computer,

FIGURE 13-8
Selecting a Training Method

	One-on-One Training	Classroom Training	Computer-Based Training
Cost to develop	Low–medium	Medium	High
Cost to deliver	High	Medium	Low
Impact	High	Medium–high	Low–medium
Reach	Low	Medium	High

either on CD or over the Web. CBT programs can include text slides, audio, and even video and animation. CBT is typically more costly to develop, but is cheaper to deliver because no instructor is needed to actually provide the training.

Figure 13-8 summarizes four important factors to consider in selecting a training method. CBT is typically more expensive to develop than one-on-one or classroom training, but it is less expensive to deliver. One-on-one training has the most impact on the user because it can be customized to the user's precise needs, knowledge, and abilities, whereas CBT has the least impact. However, CBT has the greatest reach—the ability to train the most users over the widest distance in the shortest time—because it is so much simpler to distribute, compared with classroom and one-on-one training, since no instructors are needed.

Figure 13-8 suggests a clear pattern for most organizations. If there are only a few users to train, one-on-one training is the most effective. If there are many users to train, many organizations turn to CBT. We believe that the use of CBT will increase in the future. Quite often, large organizations use a combination of all three methods. Regardless of which approach is used, it is important to leave the users with a set of easily accessible materials that can be referred to long after the training has ended (usually a quick reference guide and a set of manuals, whether on paper or in electronic form).

CONCEPTS **13-D FINISHING THE PROCESS**

IN ACTION

As a great analyst, you've planned, analyzed, and designed a good solution. Now you need to implement it. As part of implementation, do you think that training is just a wasted expense?

Stress is common in a help-desk call center. Users of computing services call to get access to locked accounts, get help when technology isn't working as planned, and frequently can become very upset. Employees of the help-desk call center can get stressed out, and this can result in a greater number of sick days, less productivity, and higher turnover. Max Productivity Incorporated (MPI) is a training company that works with people in high-stress jobs. MPI's training program helps employees

learn how to relax, how to "shake off" tough users, and how to create "win–win" scenarios. MPI claims to be able to reduce employee turnover by 50 percent, increase productivity by 20 percent, and reduce stress, anger, and depression by 75 percent.

QUESTIONS:

1. How would you challenge MPI to verify its claims regarding reducing turnover, increasing productivity, and decreasing stress and anger?
2. How would you conduct a "cost–benefit" analysis aimed at deciding whether to hire MPI to do ongoing training for your help-desk call center employees?

POSTIMPLEMENTATION ACTIVITIES

The goal of postimplementation activities is to *institutionalize* the use of the new system—that is, to make it the normal, accepted, routine way of performing the business processes. The postimplementation activities attempt to refreeze the organization after the successful transition to the new system. Although the work of the project team naturally winds down after implementation, the business sponsor and, sometimes, the project manager are actively involved in refreezing. These two—and, ideally, many other stakeholders—actively promote the new system and monitor its adoption and usage. They usually provide a steady flow of information about the system and encourage users to contact them to discuss issues.

In this section, we examine three key postimplementation activities; support (providing assistance in the use of the system), maintenance (continuing to refine and improve the system), and project assessment (analyzing the project to understand what activities were done well—and should be repeated—and what activities need improvement in future projects).

System Support

Once the project team has installed the system and performed the change management activities, the system is officially turned over to the *operations group*. This group is responsible for the operation of the system, whereas the project team is responsible for the development of the system. Members of the operations group usually are closely involved in the installation activities because they are the ones who must ensure that the system actually works. After the system is installed, the project team leaves but the operations group remains.

Providing system support means helping the users to use the system. Usually, this means providing answers to questions and helping users understand how to perform a certain function; this type of support can be thought of as *on-demand training.*

Online support is the most common form of on-demand training. This includes the documentation and help screens built into the system, as well as separate Web sites that provide answers to *frequently asked questions (FAQs)* that enable users to find answers without contacting a person. Obviously, the goal of most systems is to provide sufficiently good online support so that the user doesn't need to contact a person, because providing online support is much less expensive than is providing a person to answer questions.

Most organizations provide a *help desk* that provides a place for a user to talk with a person who can answer questions (usually over the phone, but sometimes in person). The help desk supports all systems, not just one specific system, so it receives calls about a wide variety of software and hardware. The help desk is operated by *level 1 support* staff who have very broad computer skills and are able to respond to a wide range of requests, from network problems and hardware problems to problems with commercial software and with the business application software developed in house.

The goal of most help desks is to have the level 1 support staff resolve 80% of the help requests they receive on the first call. If the issue cannot be resolved by level 1 support staff, a *problem report* (Figure 13-9) is completed (often using a special computer system designed to track problem reports) and passed to a *level 2 support* staff member.

> - Time and date of the report
> - Name, e-mail address, and telephone number of the support person taking the report
> - Name, e-mail address, and telephone number of the person who reported the problem
> - Software and/or hardware causing the problem
> - Location of the problem
> - Description of the problem
> - Action taken
> - Disposition (problem fixed or forwarded to system maintenance)

FIGURE 13-9
Elements of a Problem Report

The level 2 support staff members are people who know the application system well and can provide expert advice. For a new system, they are usually selected during the implementation phase and become familiar with the system as it is being tested. Sometimes, the level 2 support staff members participate in training during the change management process to become more knowledgeable with the system, the new business processes, and the users themselves.

The level 2 support staff works with users to resolve problems. Most problems are successfully resolved by the level 2 staff. In the first few months after the system is installed, however, the problem may turn out to be a bug in the software that must be fixed. In this case, the problem report becomes a *change request* that is passed to the system maintenance group. (See the next section.)

System Maintenance

System maintenance is the process of refining the system to make sure it continues to meet business needs. Substantially more money and effort are devoted to system maintenance than to the initial development of the system, simply because a system continues to change and evolve as it is used. Most beginning systems analysts and

---

CONCEPTS   **13-E CONVERTING TO THE EURO (PART 2)**

IN ACTION

When the European Union decided to introduce the euro, the European Central Bank had to develop a new computer system (called Target) to provide a currency settlement system for use by investment banks and brokerages. The euro opened at an exchange rate of U.S. $1.167. However, a rumor that the Target system malfunctioned sent the value of the euro plunging two days later.

That evening, it was determined that the malfunction was not due to system problems. Instead, operators at some German banks had misunderstood how to use the system and had entered incorrect data. Once the problems were identified and the operators quickly retrained, the Target system continued to operate and the euro quickly regained its lost value.

Source: "Debut of Euro Nearly Flawless," *Computerworld,* January 11, 1999, 33(2), p. 16, by Thomas Hoffman.

QUESTION:

Target could be considered a high-risk system because of its effects on the European economy. What kinds of system support activities could be put in place to mitigate problems with Target?

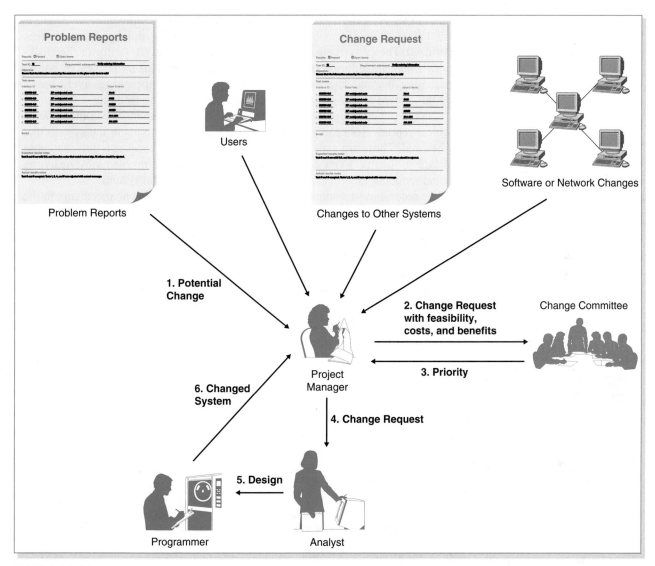

FIGURE 13-10
Processing a Change Request

programmers work first on maintenance projects; usually only after they have gained some experience are they assigned to new development projects.

Every system is "owned" by a project manager in the IS group (Figure 13-10). This individual is responsible for coordinating the systems maintenance effort for that system. Whenever a potential change to the system is identified, a change request is prepared and forwarded to the project manager. The change request is a "smaller" version of the *system request* discussed in Chapters 1 and 2. It describes the change requested and explains why the change is important.

Changes can be small or large. Change requests that are likely to require a significant effort are typically handled in the same manner as system requests: They follow the same process as the project described in this book, starting with project initiation in Chapter 1 and following through installation in this chapter.

Minor changes typically follow a "smaller" version of this same process. There is an initial assessment of feasibility and of costs and benefits, and the change request is prioritized. Then a systems analyst (or a programmer/analyst) performs the analysis, which may include interviewing users, and prepares an initial design before programming begins. The new (or revised) program is then extensively tested before the system is converted from the old system to the revised one.

Change requests typically come from five sources. The most common source is problem reports from the operations group that identify bugs in the system that must be fixed. These are usually given immediate priority because a bug can cause significant problems. Even a minor bug can cause major problems by upsetting users and reducing their acceptance of and confidence in the system.

The second most common source of change requests is enhancements to the system from users. As users work with the system, they often identify minor changes in the design that can make the system easier to use or identify additional functions that are needed. These enhancements are important in satisfying the users and are often key in ensuring that the system changes as the business requirements change. Enhancements are often given second priority after bug fixes.

A third source of change requests is other system development projects. For example, as part of Tune Source's Digital Music Download project, Tune Source likely had to make some minor changes to its existing Web-based CD sales system to ensure that the two systems would work together. These changes, required by the

---

CONCEPTS **13-F SOFTWARE BUGS**

IN ACTION

The awful truth is that every operating system and application system is defective. System complexity, the competitive pressure to hurry applications to market, and simple incompetence contribute to the problem.

Will software ever be bug free? Not likely. Microsoft Windows Group General Manager Chris Jones believes that bigger programs breed more bugs. Each revision is usually bigger and more complex than its predecessor, which means that there will always be new places for bugs to hide. Former Microsoft product manager Richard Freedman agrees that the potential for defects increases as software becomes more complex, but he believes that users ultimately win more than they lose. "I'd say the features have gotten exponentially better, and the product quality has degraded a fractional amount."

Still, the majority of users who responded to our survey said they'd buy a software program with fewer features if it were bug free. This sentiment runs counter to what most software developers believe. "People buy features, plain and simple," explains Freedman. "There have been attempts to release stripped-down word processors and spreadsheets, and they don't sell." Freed-

man says a trend toward smaller, less-bug-prone software with fewer features will "never happen."

Eventually, the software ships and the bug reports start rolling in. What happens next is what separates the companies you want to patronize from the slackers. While almost every vendor provides bug fixes eventually, some companies do a better job of it than others. Some observers view Microsoft's market dominance as a roadblock to bug-free software. Todd Paglia, an attorney with the Washington, D.C.-based Consumer Project on Technology, says, "If actual competition for operating systems existed and we had greater competition for some of the software that runs on the Microsoft operating system, we would have higher quality than we have now."

Source: "Software Bugs Run Rampant," *PC World*, January 1999 17(1): p. 46, by Scott Spanbauer.

QUESTION:

If commercial systems contain the amount of bugs that this article suggests, what are the implications for systems developed in house? Would in-house systems be more likely to have a lower or higher quality than commercial systems? Explain.

need to integrate two systems, are generally rare, but are becoming more common as system integration efforts become more common.

A fourth source of change requests is those that occur when underlying software or networks change. For example, a new version of Windows often will require an application to change the way it interacts with Windows or enable application systems to take advantage of new features that improve efficiency. While users may never see these changes (because most changes are inside the system and do not affect its user interface or functionality), these changes can be among the most challenging to implement because analysts and programmers must learn about the new system characteristics, understand how application systems use (or can use) those characteristics, and then make the needed programming changes.

The fifth source of change requests is senior management. These change requests are often driven by major changes in the organization's strategy (e.g., the Tune Source Digital Music Download project) or operations. These significant change requests are typically treated as separate projects, but the project manager responsible for the initial system is often placed in charge of the new project.

Project Assessment

The goal of *project assessment* is to understand what was successful about the system and the project activities (and therefore should be continued in the next system or project) and what needs to be improved. Project assessment is not routine in most organizations, except for military organizations, which are accustomed to preparing after-action reports. Nonetheless, assessment can be an important component in organizational learning because it helps organizations and people understand how to improve their work. It is particularly important for junior staff members because it helps promote faster learning. There are two primary parts to project assessment— project team review and system review.

Project Team Review   *Project team review* focuses on the way the project team carried out its activities. Each project member prepares a short two- to three-page document that reports on and analyzes his or her performance. The focus is on performance improvement, not penalties for mistakes made. By explicitly identifying mistakes and understanding their causes, project team members will, it is hoped, be better prepared for the next time they encounter a similar situation—and less likely to repeat the same mistakes. Likewise, by identifying excellent performance, team members will be able to understand why their actions worked well and how to repeat them in future projects.

The documents prepared by each team member are assessed by the project manager, who meets with the team members to help them understand how to improve their performance. The project manager then prepares a summary document that outlines the key learnings from the project. This summary identifies what actions should be taken in future projects to improve performance, but is not intended to identify team members who made mistakes. The summary is widely circulated among all project managers to help them understand how to manage their projects better. Often, it is also circulated among regular staff members who did not work on the project so that they, too, can learn from projects outside their scope.

System Review   The focus of the *system review* is understanding the extent to which the proposed costs and benefits from the new system that were identified during

PRACTICAL	**13-1 Beating Buggy Software**
TIP	

How do you avoid bugs in the commercial software you buy? Here are six tips:

1. **Know your software:** Find out if the few programs you use day in and day out have known bugs and patches, and track the Web sites that offer the latest information on them.
2. **Back up your data:** This dictum should be tattooed on every monitor. Stop reading right now and copy the data you can't afford to lose onto a CD, second hard disk, or Web server. We'll wait.
3. **Don't upgrade—yet:** It's tempting to upgrade to the latest and greatest version of your favorite software, but why chance it? Wait a few months, check out other users' experiences with the upgrade on Usenet newsgroups or the vendor's own discussion forum, and then go for it. But only if you must.

4. **Upgrade slowly:** If you decide to upgrade, allow yourself at least a month to test the upgrade on a separate system before you install it on all the computers in your home or office.
5. **Forget the betas:** Installing beta software on your primary computer is a game of Russian roulette. If you really have to play with beta software, get a second computer.
6. **Complain:** The more you complain about bugs and demand remedies, the more costly it is for vendors to ship buggy products. It's like voting—the more people participate, the better are the results.

Source: "Software Bugs Run Rampant," *PC World*, January, 1999, 17(1): p. 46, Scott Spanbauer.

project initiation were actually recognized from the implemented system. Project team review is usually conducted immediately after the system is installed, while key events are still fresh in team members' minds, but system review is often undertaken several months after the system is installed, because it often takes a while before the system can be properly assessed.

System review starts with the system request and feasibility analysis prepared at the start of the project. The detailed analyses prepared for the expected business value (both tangible and intangible), as well as the economic feasibility analysis, are reexamined, and a new analysis is prepared after the system has been installed. The objective is to compare the anticipated business value against the actual realized business value from the system. This helps the organization assess whether the system actually provided the value it was planned to provide. Whether or not the system provides the expected value, future projects can benefit from an improved understanding of the true costs and benefits.

A formal system review also has important behavioral implications for project initiation. Since everyone involved with the project knows that all statements about business value and the financial estimates prepared during project initiation will be evaluated at the end of the project, they have an incentive to be conservative in their assessments. No one wants to be the project sponsor or project manager for a project that goes radically over budget or fails to deliver promised benefits.

APPLYING THE CONCEPTS AT TUNE SOURCE

Installation of the Digital Music Download system at Tune Source was somewhat simpler than the installation of most systems because the system was new; there was no as-is system. Most changes would be felt by the staff in the stores who might need to assist customers using the in-store kiosks to buy music downloads. Jason did not expect any major problems in this area.

Implementation Process

The team was faced with the problem of installing the in-store kiosks and training the staff in all 50 of Tune Source's stores. Because the new in-store kiosks were new and not changing any old functions, it was less important to make sure that the conversion was completely synchronized across all stores. Because the risk associated with the system was low, and because both cost and time were somewhat important, Jason chose to use direct conversion with a whole-system conversion, but with a pilot phase first. You will recall from the last chapter that the system was beta tested with employees. Jason chose to use the beta test as the pilot conversion.

The in-store kiosks were installed in the 18 stores in a greater Los Angeles area for the beta test. The manager and the employees in each of these 18 stores were trained in the use of the new in-store kiosks.

Conversion during the pilot phase went smoothly. First, the new hardware was purchased and installed. Then the software was installed on the Web server of the company intranet. Data were loaded into the MySQL database by several temporary employees contracted for the job. Since this system contains new data, there was no data conversion to manage.

At the end of the beta test and pilot conversion phase, the kiosks were then installed in the remaining 32 stores in the Tune Source chain and their staffs were trained. Once the in-store kiosks were operating smoothly, the system was ready for general use by the public on the Internet.

Preparing the People

There were few change management issues because there were few existing staff members who had to change. New staff were hired, most by internal transfer from other groups within Tune Source. The most likely stakeholders to be concerned by the change would be managers and employees in the traditional retail stores who might see the Digital Music Download system as a threat to their stores. Jason therefore developed an information campaign (distributed through the employee newsletter and internal Web site) that discussed the reasons for the change and explained that the Digital Music Download system should be seen as a complement to the existing stores, not as a competitor. The system was instead targeted at Web-based competitors such as Amazon.com.

The new management policies were developed, along with a training plan that encompassed both the manual work procedures and computerized procedures. Jason decided to use classroom training for the marketing personnel who would be using the promotion system component, because there was a small number of them and it was simpler and more cost effective to train them all together in one classroom session.

Postimplementation Activities

Support of the system was turned over to the Tune Source operations group, who had hired four additional support staff members with expertise in networking and Web-based systems. System maintenance began almost immediately, with Jason designated as the project manager responsible for maintenance of this version of the system plus the development of the next version. Jason began planning to develop the next version of the system.

Project team review uncovered several key learnings, mostly involving Web-based programming and the difficulties in optimizing searches and providing fast, flawless file transfer protocols. The project was delivered on budget, with the exception that more was spent on programming than was anticipated.

A preliminary system review was conducted after two months of operations. Thanks to an advertising campaign, sales via the Internet system were $120,000 for the first month and $162,000 for the second, showing a gradual increase. (Remember that the goal for the first year of operations was $2.6 million.) Operating expenses averaged $47,000 per month, a bit higher than the projected average, owing to startup costs. Nonetheless, Carly Edwards, vice president of marketing and the project sponsor, was quite pleased. She approved the feasibility study for the follow-on project to develop the second version of the Internet system, and Jason began the SDLC all over again.

SUMMARY

Making the Transition to the New System

Transitioning to the new system is facilitated by following Lewin's three-step model of organizational change: Unfreeze, move, and refreeze. Activities during systems analysis and design will help unfreeze attachment to the existing system. The migration plan guides the movement from the as-is system to the to-be system. The support and maintenance provided for the new system helps to refreeze the new system into everyday use in the organization.

The Migration Plan

The migration plan encompasses a number of elements that will guide the transition from the old to the new system. The organization's readiness can be developed by the conversion strategy that is selected and business contingency planning. The technology is prepared through installation of the hardware and software and conversion of the data. The people are prepared to accept and use the new system through many channels, including management policies, adoption motivation techniques, and training. Understanding the sources of resistance to change and the costs and benefits that the users perceive will help analysts develop a successful migration plan.

Postimplementation Activities

System support is performed by the operations group, which provides online and help-desk support to the users. System support has both a level 1 support staff, which answers the phone and handles most of the questions, and level 2 support staff, which follows up on challenging problems and sometimes generates change requests for bug fixes. System maintenance responds to change requests (from the system support staff, users, other development project teams, and senior management) to fix bugs and improve the business value of the system. The goal of project assessment is to understand what was successful about the system and the project activities (and therefore should be continued in the next system or project) and what needs to be improved. Project team review focuses on the way in which the project team carried out its activities and usually results in documentation of key lessons learned. System review focuses on understanding the extent to which the proposed costs and benefits from the new system that were identified during project initiation were actually recognized from the implemented system.

KEY TERMS

Business contingency plan
Change agent
Change management
Change request
Classroom training
Computer-based training (CBT)
Conversion
Conversion location
Conversion modules
Conversion strategy
Conversion style
Direct conversion
Frequently asked questions (FAQs)
Help desk
Informational strategy
Installation
Institutionalization
Level 1 support

Level 2 support
Management policies
Measurements
Migration plan
Modular conversion
On-demand training
One-on-one training
Online support
Operations group
Parallel conversion
Phased conversion
Pilot conversion
Political strategy
Postimplementation
Potential adopter
Problem report
Project assessment
Project team review

Ready adopters
Refreeze
Reluctant adopters
Resistant adopters
Resource allocation
Rewards
Simultaneous conversion
Sponsor
Standard operating procedures
   (SOPs)
System maintenance
System request
System review
System support
Training
Transition
Unfreeze
Whole-system conversion

QUESTIONS

1. What are the three basic steps in managing organizational change?
2. What are the major components of a migration plan?
3. Compare and contrast direct conversion and parallel conversion.
4. Compare and contrast pilot conversion, phased conversion, and simultaneous conversion.
5. Compare and contrast modular conversion and whole-system conversion.
6. Explain the trade-offs among selecting between the types of conversion in Questions 3, 4, and 5.
7. What are the three key roles in any change management initiative?
8. Why do people resist change? Explain the basic model for understanding why people accept or resist change.
9. What are the three major elements of management policies that must be considered when implementing a new system?
10. Compare and contrast an information change management strategy with a political change management strategy. Is one better than the other?
11. Explain the three categories of adopters you are likely to encounter in any change management initiative.

12. How should you decide what items to include in your training plan?
13. Compare and contrast three basic approaches to training.
14. What is the role of the operations group in the systems development life cycle (SDLC)?
15. Compare and contrast two major ways to provide system support.
16. How is a problem report different from a change request?
17. What are the major sources of change requests?
18. Why is project assessment important?
19. How is project team review different from system review?
20. What do you think are three common mistakes that novice analysts make in migrating from the as-is to the to-be system?
21. Some experts argue that change management is more important than any other part of the SDLC. Do you agree or not? Explain.
22. In our experience, change management planning often receives less attention than conversion planning. Why do you think this happens?

EXERCISES

A. Suppose that you are installing a new accounting package in your small business. What conversion strategy would you use? Develop a conversion plan (i.e., technical aspects only).

B. Suppose that you are installing a new room reservation system for your university that tracks which courses are assigned to which rooms. Assume that all the rooms in each building are "owned" by one college or department and only one person in that college or department has permission to assign them. What conversion strategy would you use? Develop a conversion plan (i.e., technical aspects only).

C. Suppose you are installing a new payroll system in a very large multinational corporation. What conversion strategy would you use? Develop a conversion plan (i.e., technical aspects only).

D. Consider a major change you have experienced in your life (e.g., taking a new job, starting a new school). Prepare a cost–benefit analysis of the change in terms of both the change and the transition to the change.

E. Suppose that you are the project manager for a new library system for your university. The system will improve the way in which students, faculty, and staff can search for books by enabling them to search over the Web, rather than using only the current text-based system available on the computer terminals in the library. Prepare a cost–benefit analysis of the change in terms of both the change and the transition to the change for the major stakeholders.

F. Prepare a plan to motivate the adoption of the system described in Exercise E.

G. Prepare a training plan that includes both what you would train and how the training would be delivered for the system described in Exercise E.

H. Suppose that you are leading the installation of a new decision support system to help admissions officers manage the admissions process at your university. Develop a change management plan (i.e., organizational aspects only).

I. Suppose that you are the project leader for the development of a new Web-based course registration system for your university that replaces an old system in which students had to go to the coliseum at certain times and stand in line to get permission slips for each course they wanted to take. Develop a migration plan (including both technical conversion and change management).

J. Suppose that you are the project leader for the development of a new airline reservation system that will be used by the airline's in-house reservation agents. The system will replace the current command-driven system designed in the 1970s that uses terminals. The new system uses PCs with a Web-based interface. Develop a migration plan (including both conversion and change management) for your telephone operators.

K. Suppose that you are the project leader for the scenario described in Exercise J. Develop a migration plan (including both conversion and change management) for the independent travel agencies who use your system.

MINICASES

1. Nancy is the IS department head at MOTO Inc., a human resources management firm. The IS staff at MOTO Inc. completed work on a new client management software system about a month ago. Nancy was impressed with the performance of her staff on this project because the firm had not previously undertaken a project of this scale in house. One of Nancy's weekly tasks is to evaluate and prioritize the change requests that have come in for the various applications used by the firm.

Right now, Nancy has on her desk five change requests for the client system. One request is from a system user who would like some formatting changes made to a daily report produced by the system. Another request is from a user who would like the sequence of menu options changed on one of the system menus to more closely reflect the frequency of use for those options. A third request came in from the billing department. This department performs billing through the use of a billing software package. A major upgrade of this software is being planned, and the interface between the client system and the billing system will need to be changed to accommodate the new software's data structures. The fourth request seems to be a system bug that occurs whenever a client cancels a contract (a rare occurrence, fortunately). The last request came from Susan, the company president. This request confirms the rumor that MOTO Inc. is about to acquire another new business. The new business specializes in the temporary placement of skilled professional and scientific employees, and represents a new business area for MOTO Inc. The client management software system will need to be modified to incorporate the special client arrangements that are associated with the acquired firm.

How do you recommend that Nancy prioritize these change requests for the client/management system?

2. Sky View Aerial Photography offers a wide range of aerial photographic, video, and infrared imaging services. The company has grown from its early days of snapping pictures of client houses to its current status as a full-service aerial image specialist. Sky View now maintains numerous contracts with various governmental agencies for aerial mapping and surveying work. Sky View has its offices at the airport where its fleet of specially equipped aircraft are hangared. Sky View contracts with several freelance pilots and photographers for some of its aerial work and also employs several full-time pilots and photographers.

The owners of Sky View Aerial Photography recently contracted with a systems development consulting firm to develop a new information system for the business. As the number of contracts, aircraft flights, pilots, and photographers increased, the company experienced difficulty keeping accurate records of its business activity and the utilization of its fleet of aircraft. The new system will require all pilots and photographers to swipe an ID badge through a reader at the beginning and conclusion of each photo flight, along with recording information about the aircraft used and the client served on that flight. These records would be reconciled against the actual aircraft utilization logs maintained and recorded by the hangar personnel.

The office staff was eagerly awaiting the installation of the new system. Their general attitude was that the system would reduce the number of problems and errors that they encountered and would make their work easier. The pilots, photographers, and hangar staff were less enthusiastic, being unaccustomed to having their activities monitored in this way.

   a. Discuss the factors that may inhibit the acceptance of this new system by the pilots, photographers, and hangar staff.

   b. Discuss how an informational strategy could be used to motivate adoption of the new system at Sky View Aerial Photography.

   c. Discuss how a political strategy could be used to motivate adoption of the new system at Sky View Aerial Photography.

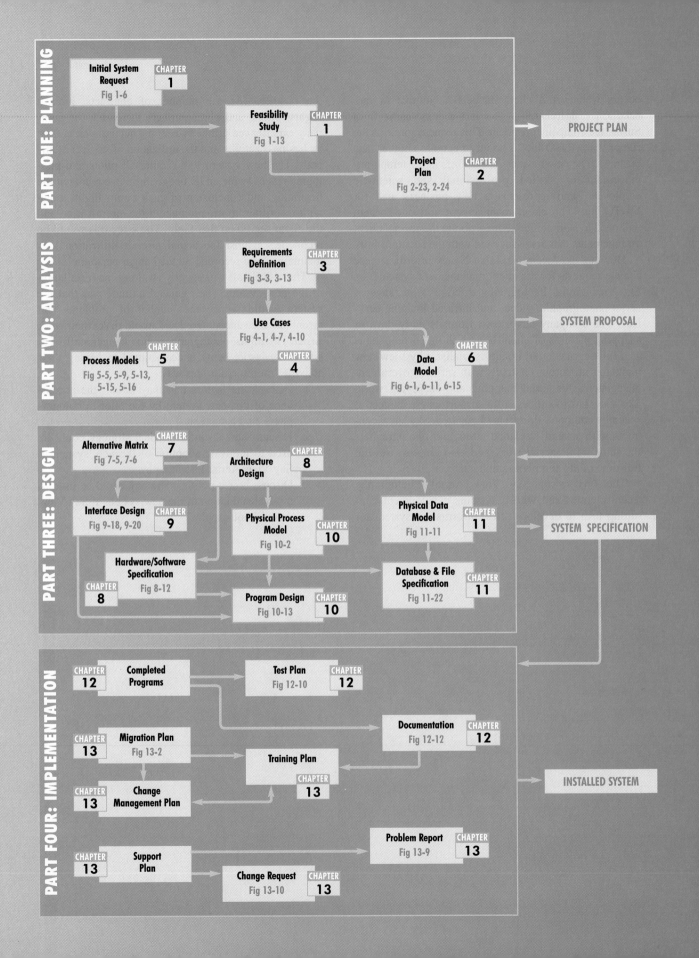

CHAPTER 14

THE MOVEMENT
TO OBJECTS

T he field of systems analysis and design now incorporates object-oriented concepts and techniques, by which a system is viewed as a collection of self-contained objects that include both data and processes. Objects can be built as individual pieces and then put together to form a system, leading to modular, reusable project components. In 1997, the Unified Modeling Language (UML) was accepted as the standard language for object development. This chapter describes the four most effective UML models: the use case diagram, class diagram, sequence diagram, and behavioral state machine diagram.

OBJECTIVES

- Understand basic concepts of the object approach and UML.
- Be able to create a use case diagram.
- Be able to create a class diagram.
- Be able to create a sequence diagram.
- Be able to create a behavioral state machine diagram.

CHAPTER OUTLINE

INTRODUCTION

By this point, we have presented the important skills that you will need for a real-world systems development project. You can be certain that all projects move through the four phases of planning, analysis, design, and implementation; all projects require you to gather requirements, model the business needs, and create blueprints for how the system should be built; and all projects require an understanding of organizational behavior concepts like change management and team building. This is true for large and small projects; custom built and packaged; local and global.

These underlying skills remain largely unchanged over time, but the actual techniques and approaches that analysts and developers use do change—often dramatically—over time. As we implied in Chapter 1, the field of systems analysis and design still has a lot of room for improvement: Projects still run over budget, users often cannot get applications when they need them, and some systems still fail to meet important user needs. Thus, the state of the systems analysis and design field is one of constant transition and continuous improvement. Analysts and developers learn from past mistakes and successes and evolve their practices to incorporate new techniques and new approaches that work better.

Today, an exciting enhancement to systems analysis and design is the application of the *object-oriented approach.* The object-oriented approach views a system as a collection of self-contained objects, including both data and processes. As you know, traditional systems analysis and design methodologies are either data-centric or process-centric. (See Chapter 1.) Until the mid-1980s, developers had to keep the data and processes separate in order to build systems that could run on the mainframe computers of that era. Due to the increase in processor power and the decrease in processor cost, object-oriented approaches became feasible. Consequently, developers focused on building systems more efficiently by enabling the analyst to work with a system's data and processes simultaneously as objects. These objects can be built as individual pieces and then put together to form a system. The beauty of objects is that they can be reused over and over in many different systems and changed without affecting other system components.

Although some people feel that the move to objects will radically change the field of systems analysis and design and the SDLC, we see the incorporation of objects as an evolving process in which object-oriented techniques are gradually integrated into the mainstream SDLC. Therefore, it is important for you as an analyst to understand what object orientation is and why it is causing such a stir in the industry, as well as to become familiar with some popular object-oriented techniques that you may need to use on projects.

One of the major hurdles of learning object-oriented approaches to developing information systems is the volume of new terminology. In this chapter, we will provide an overview to the basic characteristics of an object-oriented system, introduce basic object-oriented systems analysis and design and the Unified Process, and provide an overview of the Unified Modeling Language (UML Version 2.0). We will then explain how to draw four of the fundamental diagrams in the UML: the use case diagram, the class diagram, the sequence diagram, and the behavioral state machine diagram.

BASIC CHARACTERISTICS OF OBJECT-ORIENTED SYSTEMS

Object-oriented systems focus on capturing the structure and behavior of information systems in little modules that encompass both data and processes. These little modules are known as objects. In this section of the chapter, we describe the basic characteristics of object-oriented systems.

Classes and Objects

A *class* is the general template we use to define and create specific *instances*, or objects. Every object is associated with a class. For example, all of the objects that capture information about patients could fall into a class called Patient, because there are attributes (e.g., names, addresses, and birth dates) and methods (e.g., insert new instances, maintain information, and delete entries) that all patients share. (See Figure 14-1.)

An *object* is an instantiation of a class. In other words, an object is a person, place, event, or thing about which we want to capture information. If we were building a sales system for an RV dealer, classes might include vehicle, customer, and offer. The specific customers like Jim Maloney, Mary Wilson, and Theresa Marks are considered instances, or objects, of the customer class.

Each object has *attributes* that describe information about the object, such as a customer's name, address, e-mail, and phone number. The state of an object is defined by the value of its attributes and its relationships with other objects at a particular point in time. For example, a vehicle might have a state of "new" or "pre-owned."

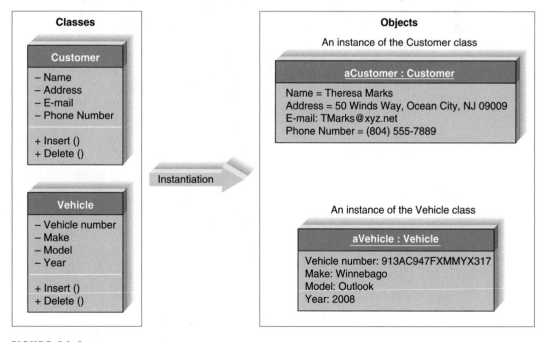

FIGURE 14-1
Classes and Objects

One of the more confusing aspects of object-oriented systems development is the fact that in most object-oriented programming languages, both classes and instances of classes can have attributes and methods. Class attributes and methods tend to be used to model attributes (or methods) that deal with issues related to all instances of the class. For example, to create a new customer object, a message is sent to the customer class to create a new instance of itself. However, from a systems analysis and design point of view, we will focus primarily on attributes and methods of objects, and not of classes.

Methods and Messages

Methods implement an object's *behavior*. A method is nothing more than an action that an object can perform. Methods are very much like a function or procedure in a traditional programming language such as C, COBOL, or Pascal. *Messages* are information sent to objects to trigger methods. A message is essentially a function or procedure call from one object to another object. For example, if a customer is new to the RV dealership, the system will send an insert message to the customer object. The customer object will receive a message (instruction) and do what it needs to do to insert the new customer into the system (execute its method). (See Figure 14-2.)

Encapsulation and Information Hiding

The ideas of *encapsulation* and *information hiding* are interrelated in object-oriented systems. Neither of the concepts is new, however. Encapsulation is simply the combining of process and data into a single entity. Object-oriented approaches combine process and data into holistic entities (objects).

Information hiding was first promoted in structured systems development. The principle of information hiding suggests that only the information required to use a software module be published to the user of the module. Typically, this implies that the information required to be passed to the module and the information returned from the module are published. Exactly how the module implements the required functionality is not relevant. We really do not care how the

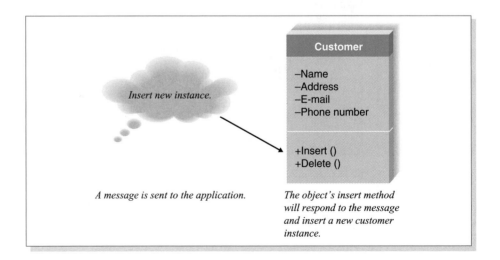

FIGURE 14-2
Messages and Methods

object performs its functions, so long as the functions occur. In object-oriented systems, combining encapsulation with the information hiding principle suggests that the information hiding principle be applied to objects instead of merely applying it to functions or processes. As such, objects are treated like black boxes.

The fact that we can use an object by calling methods is the key to reusability, because it shields the internal workings of the object from changes in the outside system and it keeps the system from being affected when changes are made to an object. In Figure 14-2, notice how a message (insert new customer) is sent to an object, yet the internal algorithms needed to respond to the message are hidden from other parts of the system. The only information that an object needs to know is the set of operations, or methods, that other objects can perform and what messages need to be sent to trigger them.

Inheritance

Inheritance, as an information systems development characteristic, was proposed in data modeling in the late 1970s and early 1980s. The data modeling literature suggests using inheritance to identify higher level, or more general, classes of objects. Common sets of attributes and methods can be organized into *superclasses*. Typically, classes are arranged in a hierarchy whereby the superclasses, or general classes, are at the top, and the *subclasses*, or specific classes, are at the bottom. In Figure 14-3,

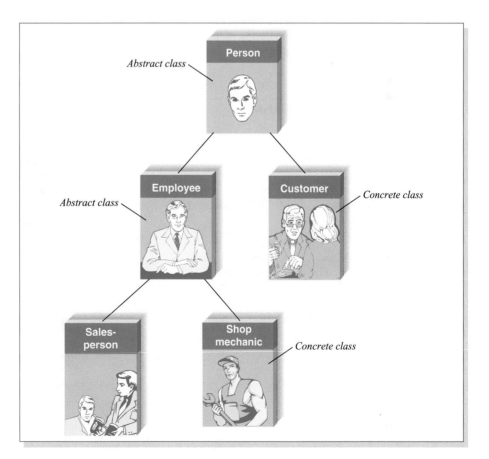

FIGURE 14-3
Class Hierarchy

person is a superclass to the classes employee and customer. Employee, in turn, is a superclass to salesperson and shop mechanic. Notice how a class (e.g., employee) can serve as a superclass and a subclass concurrently. The relationship between the class and its superclass is known as the *A-Kind-Of* (*AKO*) relationship. For example, in Figure 14-3, a salesperson is A-Kind-Of employee, which is A-Kind-Of person.

Subclasses *inherit* the attributes and methods from the superclass above them. That is, each subclass contains attributes and methods from its parent superclass. For example, Figure 14-3 shows that both employee and customer are subclasses of person and therefore will inherit the attributes and methods of the person class. Inheritance makes it simpler to define classes. Instead of repeating the attributes and methods in the employee and customer classes separately, the attributes and methods that are common to both are placed in the person class and inherited by those classes below it. Notice how much more efficient hierarchies of object classes are than are the same objects without a hierarchy, in Figure 14-4.

Most classes throughout a hierarchy will lead to instances; any class that has instances is called a *concrete class.* For example, if Mary Wilson and Jim Maloney were instances of the customer class, customer would be considered a concrete class. Some classes do not produce instances, because they are used merely as templates for other, more specific classes (especially those classes located high up in a hierarchy). They are *abstract classes.* Person would be an example of an abstract class. Instead of creating objects from person, we would create instances representing the more specific classes of employee and customer, both types of person. (See Figure 14-3.) What kind of class is the salesperson class? Why?

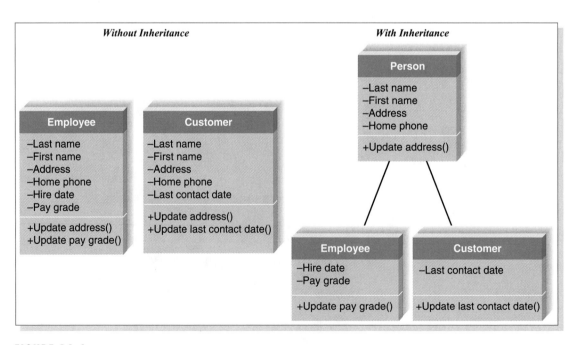

FIGURE 14-4

Inheritance

Polymorphism and Dynamic Binding

Polymorphism means that the same message can be interpreted differently by different classes of objects. For example, inserting a patient means something different than inserting an appointment. As such, different pieces of information need to be collected and stored. Luckily, we do not have to be concerned with *how* something is done when using objects. We can simply send a message to an object, and that object will be responsible for interpreting the message appropriately. For example, if we sent the message "Draw yourself" to a square object, a circle object, and a triangle object, the results would be very different, even though the message is the same. Notice in Figure 14-5 how each object responds appropriately (and differently), even though the message is identical.

Polymorphism is made possible through *dynamic binding.* Dynamic, or late, binding is a technique that delays identifying the type of object until run-time. As such, the specific method that is actually called is not chosen by the object-oriented system until the system is running. This is in contrast to *static binding.* In a statically bound system, the type of object would be determined at compile time. Therefore, the developer would have to choose which method should be called, instead of

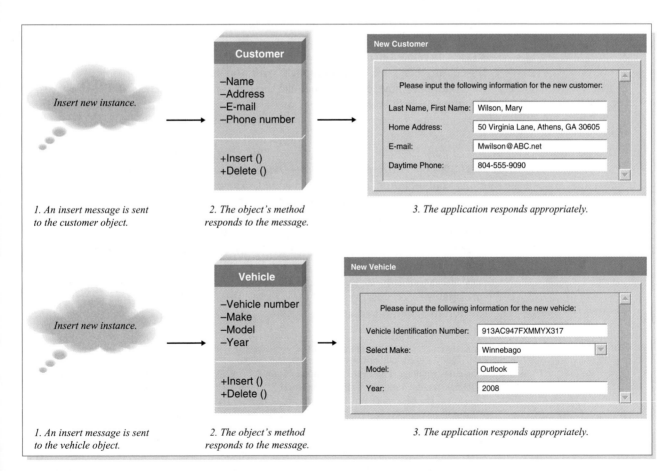

FIGURE 14-5
Polymorphism and Encapsulation

allowing the system to do it. This is why in most traditional programming languages you find complicated decision logic based on the different types of objects in a system. For example, in a traditional programming language, instead of sending the message "Draw yourself" to the different types of graphical objects mentioned earlier, you would have to write decision logic by using a case statement or a set of "if" statements to determine what kind of graphical object you wanted to draw, and you would have to name each draw function differently (e.g., draw-square, draw-circle, or draw-triangle). This obviously makes the system much more complicated and more difficult to understand.

OBJECT-ORIENTED SYSTEMS ANALYSIS AND DESIGN

Object-oriented approaches to developing information systems, technically speaking, can use any of the traditional methodologies presented in Chapter 2 (waterfall development, parallel development, V-model, iterative development, system prototyping, and throwaway prototyping). The object-oriented approaches are most associated with an *iterative development RAD* methodology, however. The primary difference between a traditional approach like structured design and an object-oriented approach is how a problem is decomposed. In traditional approaches, the problem decomposition is either process-centric or data-centric. When modeling real-world systems is involved, however, processes and data are so closely related that it is difficult to pick one or the other as the primary focus. Based on this lack of congruence with the real world, new object-oriented methodologies have emerged that use the RAD-based sequence of SDLC phases, but attempt to balance the emphasis between process and data. This is done by focusing the decomposition of problems on objects that contain both data and processes.

Until 1995, object concepts were popular, but implemented in many different ways to different developers. Each developer had his or her own methodology and notation (e.g., Booch, Coad, Moses, OMT, OOSE, and SOMA[1]). Then, in 1995, Rational Software brought three industry leaders together to create a single approach to object-oriented systems development. Grady Booch, Ivar Jacobson, and James Rumbaugh worked with others to create a standard set of diagramming techniques known as the *Unified Modeling Language* (*UML*).[2] The current version of UML, Version 2.0, will be described briefly in a later section. According to its creators, any object-oriented approach to developing information systems must be (1) use case driven, (2) architecture centric, and (3) iterative and incremental.

---

[1] See Grady Booch, *Object-Oriented Analysis and Design with Applications*, 2d ed., Redwood City, CA: Benjamin/Cummings, 1994; Peter Coad and Edward Yourdon, *Object-Oriented Analysis*, 2d ed., Englewood Cliffs, NJ: Yourdon Press, 1991; Brian Henderson-Sellers and Julian Edwards, *Book Two of Object-Oriented Knowledge: The Working Object*, Sydney, Australia: Prentice Hall, 1994; James Rumbaugh, Michael Blaha, William Premerlani, Frederick Eddy, and William Lorensen, *Object-Oriented Modeling and Design*, Englewood Cliffs, NJ: Prentice Hall, 1991; Ivar Jacobson, Magnus Christerson, Patrik Jonsson, and Gunnar Overgaard, *Object-Oriented Software Engineering: A Use Case Approach*, Wokingham, England: Addison-Wesley, 1992; Ian Graham, *Migrating to Object Technology*, Wokingham, England: Addison-Wesley, 1994.

[2] Grady Booch, Ivar Jacobson, and James Rumbaugh, *The Unified Modeling Language User Guide*, Reading, MA: Addison-Wesley, 1999. For a complete description of all UML diagramming techniques, see http://www-306.ibm.com/software/rational/uml/.

Use Case Driven

Use case driven means that use cases are the primary modeling tool employed to define the behavior of the system. A *use case* describes how the user interacts with the system to perform some activity, such as placing an order, making a reservation, or searching for information. The use cases are used to identify and to communicate the requirements for the system to the programmers who must write the system.

Use cases are inherently simple because they focus on only one activity at a time. In contrast, the process models we have learned about in this book are far more complex because they require the developers to create models of the entire system. In traditional process models, each business activity is decomposed into a set of subprocesses, which are further decomposed into more subprocesses, and so on. In contrast, use cases focus on only one activity at a time, so developing models is much simpler.

As we have seen, traditional systems development can utilize the use case (see Chapter 4), but they emphasize the decomposition of the complete business process into subprocesses and sub-subprocesses. Object-oriented approaches stress focusing on just one use case activity at a time and distributing that use case over a set of communicating and collaborating objects. This single focus helps make analysis and design simpler.

Architecture Centric

Any modern approach to systems analysis and design should be architecture centric. *Architecture centric* means that the underlying architecture of the evolving system drives the specification, construction, and documentation of the system. There are three separate, but interrelated, architectural views of a system: functional, static, and dynamic. The *functional view* describes the external behavior of the system from the perspective of the user. On the surface, this view is closely related to process-modeling approaches in structured analysis and design. There are important differences between them, however. The *static view* describes the structure of the system in terms of attributes, methods, classes, relationships, and messages. This view is very similar to data-modeling approaches in structured analysis and design. The *dynamic view* describes the internal behavior of the system in terms of messages passed between objects and state changes within an object. This view in many ways combines the process and data-modeling approaches, because the execution of a method can cause state changes in the receiving object.

Iterative and Incremental

Object-oriented approaches emphasize *iterative* and *incremental* development that undergoes continuous testing throughout the life of the project. Each iteration of the system brings the system closer and closer to the final needs of the users.

Benefits of Object-Oriented Systems Analysis and Design

So far, we have described several major concepts that permeate any object-oriented approach to systems development, but you may be wondering how these concepts affect the performance of a project team. The answer is simple. Concepts like polymorphism, encapsulation, and inheritance taken together allow analysts to break a complex system into smaller, more manageable components, to work on the components individually, and to more easily piece the components back together to form a system. This modularity makes system development easier to grasp, easier to share among members of a project team, and easier to communicate to users who are needed throughout the SDLC to provide requirements and confirm how well the system meets the requirements.

By modularizing system development, the project team is actually creating reusable pieces that can be plugged into other systems efforts, or used as starting points for other projects. Ultimately, this can save time, because new projects do not have to start from scratch and learning curves are not as steep.

Finally, many people argue that "object think" is a much more realistic way to think about the real world. Users typically do not think in terms of data or process; instead, they see their business as a collection of logical units that contain both—so communicating in terms of objects improves the interaction between the user and the analyst or developer. Figure 14-6 summarizes the major concepts of the object approach and how each contributes to the benefits that have just been described.

Concept	Supports	Leads to
Classes, objects, methods, and messages	• A more realistic way for people think about their business • Highly cohesive units that contain both data and processes	• Better communication between user and analyst or developer • Reusable objects • Benefits from having a highly cohesive system (See cohesion in Chapter 10)
Encapsulation and information hiding	• Loosely coupled units	• Reusable objects • Fewer ripple effects from changes within an object or in the system itself • Benefits from having a loosely coupled system design (See coupling in Chapter 10)
Inheritance	• Allows us to use classes as standard templates from which other classes can be built	• Less redundancy • Faster creation of new classes • Standards and consistency within and across development efforts • Ease in supporting exceptions
Polymorphism	• Minimal messaging that is interpreted by objects themselves	• Simpler programming of events • Ease in replacing or changing objects in a system • Fewer ripple effects from changes within an object or in the system itself
Use case driven	• Allows users and analysts to focus on how a user will interact with the system to perform a single activity	• Better understanding and gathering of user needs • Better communication between user and analyst
Architecture centric and functional, static, and dynamic views	• Viewing the evolving system from multiple points of view	• Better understanding and modeling of user needs • More complete depiction of information system
Iterative and incremental development	• Continuous testing and refinement of the evolving system	• Meeting real needs of users • Higher quality systems

FIGURE 14-6

Benefits of the Object Approach

UNIFIED MODELING LANGUAGE, VERSION 2.0

The objective of the Unified Modeling Language is to provide a common vocabulary of object-based terms and diagramming techniques that is rich enough to model any systems development project from analysis to design. The current version of UML, version 2.0, was accepted by the Object Management Group (OMG) in 2003. This version of UML defines a set of 14 diagramming techniques for modeling a system. Figure 14-7 provides an overview of these diagrams.

The diagrams are broken into two major groupings: one for modeling the structure of a system and one for modeling behavior. *Structure diagrams* are used for representing the data and static relationships that are in an information system. *Behavior diagrams* provide the analyst with a way to depict the dynamic relationships among the instances or objects that represent the business information system. They also allow the modeling of dynamic behavior of individual objects throughout their lifetime. The behavior diagrams support the analyst in modeling the functional requirements of an evolving information system.

Diagram Name	Used to	Primary Phase
Structure Diagrams		
Class	Illustrate the relationships between classes modeled in the system.	Analysis, Design
Object	Illustrate the relationships between objects modeled in the system.	
	Function when actual instances of the classes will better communicate the model.	Analysis, Design
Package	Group other UML elements together to form higher level constructs.	Analysis, Design, Implementation
Deployment	Show the physical architecture of the system. Can also be used to show software components being deployed onto the physical architecture.	Physical Design, Implementation
Component	Illustrate the physical relationships among the software components.	Physical Design, Implementation
Composite Structure	Illustrate the internal structure of a class—i.e., the relationships among the parts of a class.	Analysis, Design
Behavioral Diagrams		
Activity	Illustrate business work flows independent of classes, the flow of activities in a use case, or detailed design of a method.	Analysis, Design
Sequence	Model the behavior of objects within a use case. Focuses on the time-based ordering of an activity.	Analysis, Design
Communication	Model the behavior of objects within a use case. Focuses on the communication among a set of collaborating objects of an activity.	Analysis, Design
Interaction Overview	Illustrate an overview of the flow of control of a process.	Analysis, Design
Timing	Illustrate the interaction that takes place among a set of objects and the state changes that they go through along a time axis.	Analysis, Design
Behavioral State Machine	Examine the behavior of one class.	Analysis, Design
Protocol State Machine	Illustrate the dependencies among the different interfaces of a class.	Analysis, Design
Use Case	Capture business requirements for the system and to illustrate the interaction between the system and its environment.	Analysis

FIGURE 14-7
UML 2.0 Diagram Summary

Depending on where in the development process the system is, different diagrams play a more important role. In some cases, the same diagramming technique is used throughout the development process. In that case, the diagrams start off as very conceptual and abstract. As the system is developed, the diagrams evolve to include details that ultimately lead to code generation and development. In other words, the diagrams move from documenting the requirements to laying out the design. Overall, the consistent notation, integration among the diagramming techniques, and the application of the diagrams across the entire development process make the UML a powerful and flexible language for analysts and developers.

Note that UML is not a methodology; it does not formally mandate *how* to apply the diagramming techniques. Many organizations are experimenting with UML and trying to understand how to incorporate its techniques into their systems analysis and design methodologies. In many cases, the UML diagrams simply replace the older structured techniques (e.g., class diagrams replace ERD diagrams). The basic SDLC stays the same, but one step is performed by a different diagramming technique. Methodologies that are suited to the object-oriented approach are available, however, such as the rational unified process (RUP).

The Rational Unified Process (RUP)

Rational Software Corporation has created a methodology called the *rational unified process* (*RUP*) that defines *how* to apply UML. RUP is a rapid application development approach to building systems that is similar to the iterative development approach or extreme programming described in Chapter 2. (See Figure 14-8 and Figure 2-5.) The first step of the methodology is building use cases for the system, which identify and communicate the high-level business requirements for the system. This step drives the rest of the SDLC. Next, analysts draw analysis diagrams, later building on the analysis efforts through design and development. The UML diagrams start off conceptual and abstract, and then include details that ultimately will lead to code generation and development. The diagrams move from showing the *what* to showing the *how*.

RUP emphasizes iterative, incremental development and prototyping that undergo continuous testing throughout the life of the project. In Figure 14-8, each iteration of the system brings the system closer and closer to the real needs of the users. The 14 UML diagrams are drawn and changed throughout the process.

Four Fundamental UML Diagrams

One could spend an entire book explaining how to use UML to develop systems,[3] but we don't have that much space here. Fortunately, four UML diagramming techniques have come to dominate object-oriented projects: use case diagrams, class diagrams, sequence diagrams, and behavioral state machine diagrams. The other diagramming techniques are useful for their particular purposes, but these four techniques form the core of UML as used in practice today and will be the focus of this chapter.

The four diagramming techniques are integrated and used together to replace DFDs and ERDs in the traditional SDLC. (See Figure 14-9.) The use case diagram

---

[3] In fact, we have: See Alan Dennis, Barbara Haley Wixom, David Tegarden, *Systems Analysis & Design: An Object-Oriented Approach with UML, Version 2.0*, 2d ed. New York: John Wiley & Sons, 2005.

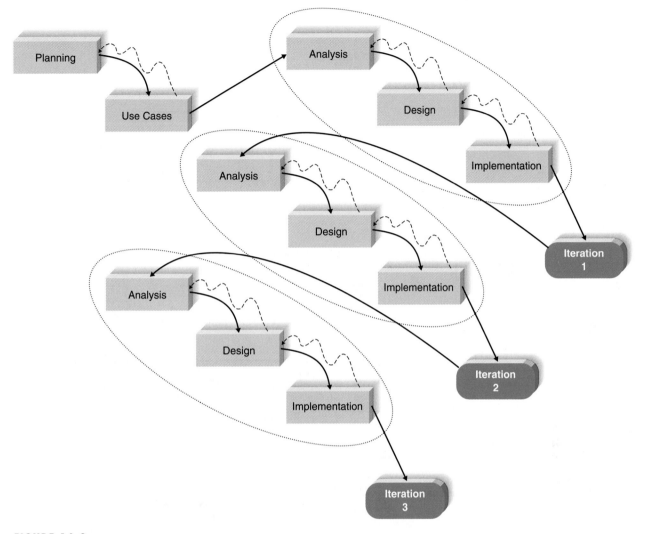

FIGURE 14-8
An Adaptation of the Unified Process Phased Development Methodology

is typically used to summarize the set of use cases for a logical part of the system (or the whole system). Then class diagrams, sequence diagrams, and behavioral state machine diagrams are used to further define the evolving system from various perspectives. The use case diagram is always created first, but the order in which the other diagrams are created depends upon the project and the personal preferences of the analysts. Most analysts start either with the class diagrams (showing what objects contain and how they are related, much like ERDs) or the sequence diagrams (showing how objects dynamically interact, much like DFDs), but in practice, the process is iterative. Developing sequence diagrams often leads to changes in the class diagrams and vice versa, so analysts often move back and forth between the two, refining each in turn as they define the system. Generally speaking, behavioral state machine diagrams are developed later, after the class diagrams have been refined. In this chapter, we will start with the use case diagram, move to the class diagrams, and finish up with the sequence diagrams and behavioral state machine diagrams.

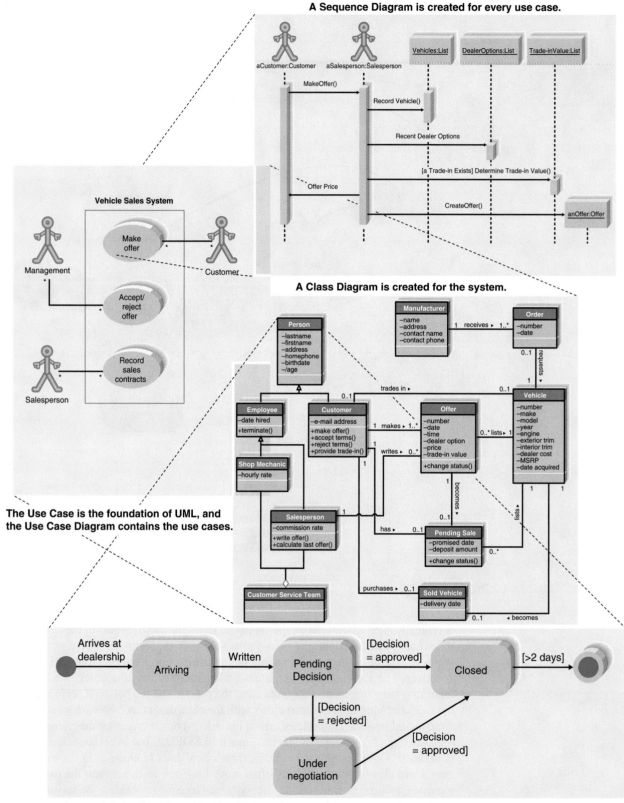

A Sequence Diagram is created for every use case.

A Class Diagram is created for the system.

The Use Case is the foundation of UML, and the Use Case Diagram contains the use cases.

A Behavioral State Machine Diagram is created for every complex class on the Class Diagram.

FIGURE 14-9
The Integration of Four Unified Modeling Language (UML) Diagrams

USE CASE DIAGRAM

Use cases are the primary drivers for all of the UML diagramming techniques. The use case communicates at a high level what the system needs to do, and each of the UML diagramming techniques build upon this by presenting the functionality in different ways, each view having a different purpose (as described in Figure 14-7). In the early stages of analysis, the analyst first identifies one use case for each major part of the system and creates accompanying documentation, the use case report, to describe each function in detail. A use case may represent several "paths" that a user can take while interacting with the system; each path is referred to as a *scenario.* Use cases and use case diagrams support the functional view just described. You may want to take a moment and review Chapter 4 on use cases before continuing with the rest of this chapter.

For now, we will learn how the use case is the building block for the *use case diagram*, which summarizes all of the use cases (for the part of the system being modeled) together in one picture. An analyst can use the use case diagram to better understand the functionality of the system at a very high level. Typically, the use case diagram is drawn early on in the SDLC, when the analyst is gathering and defining requirements for the system, because it provides a simple, straightforward way of communicating to the users exactly what the system will do (i.e., at the same point of the SDLC as we would create a DFD).

This section will first describe the syntax for the use case diagram and then demonstrate how to build one, using an example from Tune Source.

Elements of a Use Case Diagram

A use case diagram illustrates in a very simple way the main functions of the system and the different kinds of users who will interact with it. For example, Figure 14-10 presents a use case diagram for the Holiday Travel Vehicles sales system. We can see from the diagram that customers, salespersons, and management personnel will use the Sales System to make offers, accept/reject offers, and record sales contracts, respectively.

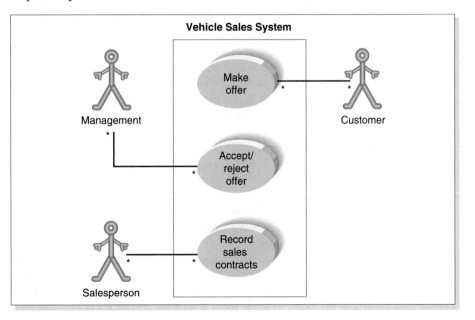

FIGURE 14-10

Use Case Diagram for Vehicle Sales System

Term and Definition	Symbol
An actor ■ Is a person or system that derives benefit from and is external to the system. ■ Is labeled with its role. ■ Can be associated with other actors by a specialization/superclass association, denoted by an arrow with a hollow arrowhead. ■ Is placed outside the system boundary.	Actor role name
A use case ■ Represents a major piece of system functionality. ■ Can extend another use case. ■ Can use another use case. ■ Is placed inside the system boundary. ■ Is labeled with a descriptive verb–noun phrase.	Use case name
A system boundary ■ Includes the name of the system inside or on top. ■ Represents the scope of the system.	System name
An association relationship ■ Links an actor with the use case(s) with which it interacts.	* *

FIGURE 14-11
Syntax for Use Case Diagram

Actor The labeled stick figures on the diagram represent actors. (See Figure 14-11.) An *actor* is similar to an external entity found in DFDs—it is a person or another system that interacts with and derives value from the system. An actor is not a specific user, but a *role* that a user can play while interacting with the system. Actors are external to the system and initiate a use case. If we were modeling a doctor's office appointment system, a data-entry clerk (or a nurse entering patient information) would not be considered an actor, because he or she would fall within the scope of the system itself. (This is the same rule for DFD external entities.) The diagram in Figure 14-10 shows that three actors will interact with the appointment system (a customer, a salesperson, and management).

Sometimes an actor plays a specialized role of a more general type of actor. For example, there may be times when a new customer interacts with the system in a way that is somewhat different from a returning customer. In this case, a *specialized actor* (i.e., *new customer*) can be placed on the model, shown by a line with a hollow triangle at the end of the more general superclass of actor (i.e., *customer*). The specialized actor will inherit the behavior of the superclass and extend it in some way. (See Figure 14-12). Can you think of some ways in which a new customer may behave differently than an existing customer?

Association Relationship Use cases are connected to actors through *association relationships*. These show with which use cases the actors interact. (See Figure 14-11.) A line drawn from an actor to a use case depicts an association. The association typically represents two-way communication between the use case and the actor. The "*" shown at either end of the association represents multiplicity; in Figure 14-10, we see that a customer instance can execute the make offer use case as many times

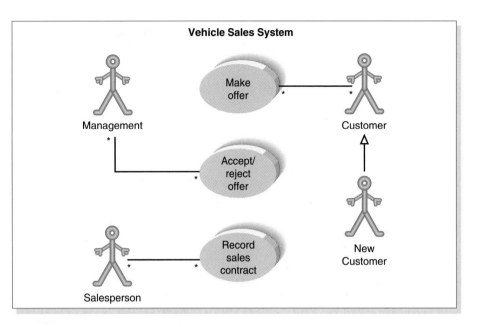

FIGURE 14-12
Use Case Diagram with Specialized Actor

as they wish, and it is possible for the make offer use case to be executed by many customers.

Use Case   A use case, depicted by an oval, is a major process that the system will perform that benefits an actor(s) in some way (see Figure 14-11), and it is labeled by a descriptive verb phrase (much like a DFD process). We can tell from Figure 14-12 that the system has three primary use cases: make offer, accept/reject offer, and record sales contract.

There are times when one use case will either use the functionality or extend the functionality of another use case on the diagram, and these are shown by *includes* or *extends relationships.* It may be easier to understand these relationships with the help of examples. Let's assume that every time customers make an offer, they are asked to confirm their contact and basic customer information to ensure that the system always contains the most up-to-date information on its customers. Therefore, we may want to include a use case called *update customer information* that extends the *make offer* use case to include the functionality just described. Notice how a dotted-line arrow in Figure 14-13, between "update customer information" and "make offer," denotes the *extends* relationship.

Similarly, there are times when a single use case contains common functions that are used by other use cases. For example, suppose that there is a use case called *manage offers* that performs some routine tasks needed to maintain the dealership's offers, and the two use cases *record sales contract* and *accept/reject offer* both perform the routine tasks. Figure 14-13 shows how we can design the system so that *manage offers* is a shared use case that is used by others. A dotted-line arrow again is used to denote the *includes* relationship.

System Boundary   The use cases are enclosed within a *system boundary*, which is a box that represents the system and clearly delineates what parts of the diagram are external or internal to it. (See Figure 14-11.) The name of the system can appear either inside or on top of the box.

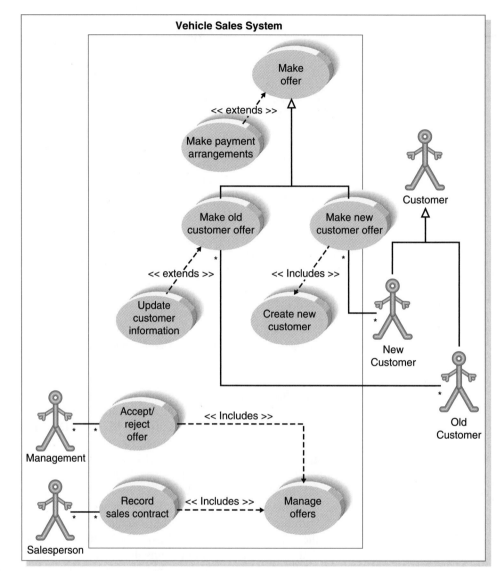

FIGURE 14-13
Extends and Includes Associations

Creating a Use Case Diagram

Let's demonstrate how to draw a use case diagram by using the Tune Source Digital Music Download system. You should note that the use case diagram communicates information that is similar to information found in DFD context and level 0 diagrams. In fact, you may want to compare the use case diagram that we are about to draw with the diagrams that were created in Chapter 5.

Identify Use Cases   Before a use case diagram can be created, it is helpful to go through the process of identifying the use cases that correspond to the system's major functionality and putting together the use case documentation for each of them. The way to create use cases was explained in Chapter 4, and we refer you to that chapter now if you would like to refresh your memory. If you recall, we found that the Tune Source Digital Music Download system needs to support the three use cases that are presented in Figure 14-14.

Use case name: Search and Browse Tunes		ID: 1	Importance level: High
Primary actor: Customer			

Short description: This use case handles customers who search and browse the tunes on the Web site.

Trigger: Customer arrives at Web site to search and browse tune selections.

Type: (External)/ Temporal

Major Inputs		Major Outputs	
Description	Source	Description	Destination
Customer request	Customer	Tune sample	Customer
Web promotions	Targeted promotions file	New interests entry	Interests file
Customer tune selection	Customer	New favorites entry	Favorites file
		Selected tune to buy	Purchase Tune
			use case

Use case name: Purchase Tunes		ID: 2	Importance level: High
Primary actor: Customer			

Short description: This use case handles the purchase and download of tunes.

Trigger: Customer selects tune to buy and download.

Type: (External)/ Temporal

Major Inputs		Major Outputs	
Description	Source	Description	Destination
Selected tune to buy	Search and browse	New customer record	Customer file
	tunes use case	Total cost of purchase	Customer
Customer details	Customer	New purchase record	Sales file
Tune price	Tune information file	Downloaded tune	Customer
Payment details	Customer		

Use case name: Promote Tunes		ID: 3	Importance level: High
Primary actor: Marketing Department Staff			

Short description: This use case handles the periodic creation of targeted promotions.

Trigger: Time for marketing department to update current promotions/specials.

Type: External / (Temporal)

Major Inputs		Major Outputs	
Description	Source	Description	Destination
Customer favorites	Favorites file	New Web promotions	Targeted promotions file
Customer purchases	Sales file	Promotional e-mails	Customer

FIGURE 14-14
Use Cases for Tune Source

Draw the System Boundary First, place a box on the use case diagram to represent the system, and place the system's name either inside or on top of the box. This will form the border of the system, separating use cases (i.e., the system's functionality) from actors (i.e., the roles of the external users).

Place the Use Cases on the Diagram The next step is to add the use cases inside the system boundary. There should be no more than six to eight use cases on the model, so if you identify more than eight, you should group together the use cases into *packages* (i.e., logical groups of use cases) to make the diagrams easier to read and keep the models at a reasonable level of complexity.

At this point, special use case relationships (includes or extends) should be added to the model. These are identified by looking for use cases that may include common functionality that other use cases require (i.e., includes relationships) or use cases that add additional functionality to others (i.e., extends relationships). The current model does not include examples of these relationships.

Identify the Actors Once the use cases are placed on the diagram, you will need to identify the actors. We recommend that you look at the sources and destinations to major inputs and outputs that you identified in the use cases. Although some sources and destinations refer to internal system components (e.g., *Targeted Promotions database*, *Available Tunes database*), others refer to actors (e.g., *Customer*, *Marketing Manager*). Look at the use case reports in Figure 14-14 and see whether you can identify the actors that belong on the use case diagram. At this point, there are no specialized actors that need to be included.

Add Association Relationships The last step is to draw lines connecting the actors with the use cases with which they interact. No order is implied by the diagram, and the items you have added along the way do not have to be placed in a particular order; therefore, you may want to rearrange the symbols a bit to minimize the number of lines that cross so that the diagram is less confusing. Figure 14-15 is the use case diagram that we have created.

CLASS DIAGRAM

The next major diagramming technique is the *class diagram*. The class diagram is a *static model* that supports the static view of the evolving system. It shows the classes and the relationships among the classes that remain constant in the system

---

YOUR TURN **14-1 IDENTIFYING USE CASE RELATIONSHIPS AND SPECIALIZED ACTORS**

The use case diagram for the Digital Music Download system does not include special use case relationships (e.g., extends or includes) or specialized actors. See whether you can come up with one example for each of these special cases that may be helpful for Tune Source to add to the use case diagram. Describe how the development effort may benefit from including your examples.

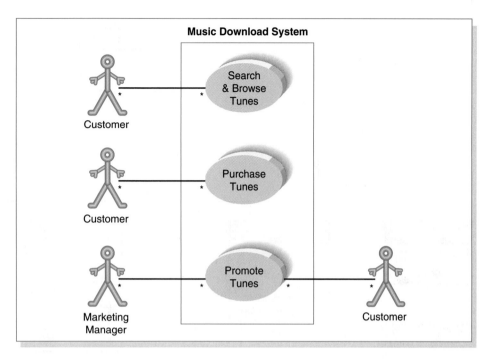

FIGURE 14-15
Tune Source Digital Music Download System Use Case Diagram

over time. The class diagram is very similar to the entity relationship diagram (ERD) in Chapter 6; however, the class diagram depicts classes, which include attributes, behaviors, and states, while entities in the ERD include only attributes. The scope of a class diagram, like the ERD, is systemwide. The sections that follow will first present the syntax of the class diagram and then the way in which a class diagram is drawn.

Elements of a Class Diagram

Figure 14-16 shows a class diagram that was created to reflect the classes and relationships needed for the set of use cases which describe the RV sales system in Chapters 4 and 5.

YOUR TURN   **14-2 DRAWING A USE CASE DIAGRAM**

Create a use case diagram for the system described next:

Owners of apartments fill in information forms about the rental units they have available (e.g., location, number of bedrooms, monthly rent), which are entered into a database. Students can search through this data-base via the Web to find apartments that meet their needs (e.g., a two-bedroom apartment for $800 or less per month within ¹/₂ mile of campus). They then contact the apartment owners directly to see the apartment and possibly rent it. Apartment owners call the service to delete their listing when they have rented their apartment(s).

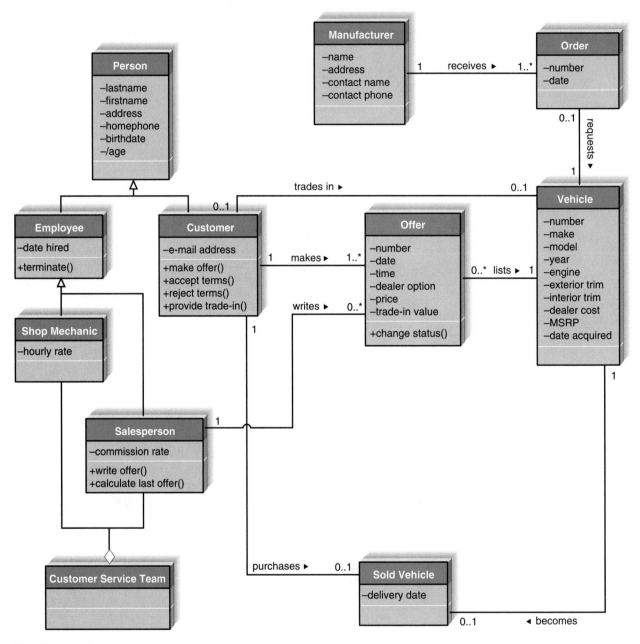

FIGURE 14-16
Class Diagram for Holiday Travel Vehicles

Class The main building block of a class diagram is the *class*, which stores and manages information in the system. (See Figure 14-17.) During analysis, classes refer to the people, places, events, and things about which the system will capture information. Later, during design and implementation, classes can refer to implementation-specific artifacts like windows, forms, and other objects used to build the system. Each class is drawn by using three part-rectangles with the class's name at the top, attributes in the middle, and methods (also called operations) at the bottom. You should be able to identify that *Person*, *Employee*, *Shop Mechanic*,

Term and Definition	Symbol
A class ▪ Represents a kind of person, place, or thing about which the system must capture and store information. ▪ Has a name typed in bold and centered in its top compartment. ▪ Has a list of attributes in its middle compartment. ▪ Has a list of operations in its bottom compartment. ▪ Does not explicitly show operations that are available to all classes.	**Class name** –Attribute name –/derived attribute name +Operation name ()
An attribute ▪ Represents properties that describe the state of an object. ▪ Can be derived from other attributes, shown by placing a slash before the attribute's name.	Attribute name /derived attribute name
A method ▪ Represents the actions or functions that a class can perform. ▪ Can be classified as a constructor, query, or update operation. ▪ Includes parentheses that may contain special parameters or information needed to perform the operation.	Operation name ()
An association ▪ Represents a relationship between multiple classes, or a class and itself. ▪ Is labeled by a verb phrase or a role name, whichever better represents the relationship. ▪ Can exist between one or more classes. ▪ Contains multiplicity symbols, which represent the minimum and maximum times a class instance can be associated with the related class instance.	1..* verb phrase 0..1

FIGURE 14-17
Class Diagram Syntax

Salesperson, *Customer*, *Manufacturer*, *Order*, *Offer*, *Vehicle*, and *Sold Vehicle* are classes in Figure 14-16. The attributes of a class and their values define the state of each object that is created from the class, and the behavior is represented by the methods.

Attributes are properties of the class about which we want to capture information. (See Figure 14-17.) Notice that the *Person* class in Figure 14-16 contains the attributes lastname, firstname, address, phone, birthdate, and age. At times, you may want to store *derived attributes*, which are attributes that can be calculated or derived from other attributes and therefore are not stored. Derived attributed are indicated by placing a slash (/) in front of the attribute's name. Notice how the *Person* class contains a derived attribute called "/age," which can be derived by subtracting the person's birthdate from the current date. It is also possible to show the *visibility* of the attribute on the diagram. Visibility relates to the level of information hiding to be enforced for the attribute. The visibility of an attribute can either be public ($+$), protected (#), or private ($-$). A *public* attribute is one that is not hidden from any other object. As such, other objects can modify its value. A *protected* attribute is one that is hidden from all other classes except its immediate subclasses. A *private* attribute is one that is hidden from all other classes. The default visibility for an attribute normally is private.

Operations are actions or functions that a class can perform. (See Figure 14-17.) The functions that are available to all classes (e.g., *create a new instance*, *return a value for a particular attribute*, *set a value for a particular attribute*, or *delete an instance*) are not explicitly shown within the class rectangle. Instead, only those operations that are unique to the class are included, such as the "terminate" and "make offer" operations in Figure 14-16. Notice that both of the operations are followed by parentheses. Operations should be shown with parentheses that are either empty, or filled with some value which represents a parameter that the operation needs for it to act. As with attributes, the visibility of an operation can be designated as public, protected, or private. The default visibility for an operation is normally public.

There are three kinds of operations that a class can contain: constructor, query, and update. A *constructor operation* creates a new instance of a class. For example, the vehicle class may have an operation called *insert ()* that creates a new vehicle instance. Because an operation available to all classes (e.g., create a new instance) is not shown on class diagrams, you will not see constructor methods in Figure 14-16.

A *query operation* makes information about the state of an object available to other objects, but it will not change the object in any way. For instance, the "calculate last offer ()" operation that determines when a salesperson last wrote an offer will result in the object being accessed by the system, but it will not make any change to its information. If a query operation merely asks for information from attributes in the class (e.g., a customer's name, address, or phone), then it is not shown on the diagram, because we assume that all objects have operations that produce the values of their attributes.

An *update operation* will change the value of some or all of the object's attributes, which may result in a change in the object's state. Consider changing the status of an offer from open to closed with a operation called "change status ()," or associating a customer with a particular offer with *make offer* (*offer*).

Associations A primary purpose of the class diagram is to show the associations, or relationships, that classes have with one another. These are depicted on the diagram by lines drawn between classes. (See Figure 14-17.) These associations are very similar to the relationships that are found on the ERD. Associations are maintained by *references*, which are similar to pointers and maintained internally by the system (unlike in the relational models where relationships are maintained by foreign and primary keys).

When multiple classes share an association (or a class shares an association with itself), a line is drawn and labeled with either the name of the association or the roles that the classes play in the association. For example, in Figure 14-16, the two classes *customer* and *offer* are associated with one another whenever a customer makes an offer. Thus, a line labeled *makes* connects *customer* and *offer*, representing exactly how the two classes are associated with each other. Also, notice that there is a small solid triangle beside of the name of the association. The triangle allows a direction to be associated with the name of the association. In Figure 14-16, the makes association includes a triangle, indicating that the association is to be read as *customer makes offer*. Inclusion of the triangle simply increases the readability of the diagram.

Associations also have *multiplicity*, which shows how an instance of an object can be associated with other instances. Numbers are placed on the association path to denote the minimum and maximum instances that can be related through the association in the format *minimum number maximum number*. (See Figure 14-18.) This is identical to the modality and cardinality of a relationship on an ERD. The numbers specify the association from the class at the far end of the association line to the end with the number. For example, in Figure 14-16, there is a "1.." on the offer end of the *customer makes offer* association. This means that a customer can be associated with one through many different offers. At the customer end of this same association there is a "1," meaning that an offer must be associated with one and only one (1) customer.

There are times when an association itself has associated properties, especially when its classes share a many-to-many relationship. In these cases, a class is formed called an *association class* that has its own attributes and methods. This is very similar to the intersection entity that is placed on an ERD. It is shown as a rectangle attached by a dashed line to the association path, and the rectangle's name matches the label of the association. Figure 14-16 does not show any association

Instance(s)	Representation of Instance(s)	Diagram Involving Instance(s)	Explanation of Diagram
Exactly one	1	Department —1— Boss	A department has one and only one boss.
Zero or more	0..*	Employee —0..*— Child	An employee has zero to many children.
One or more	1..*	Boss —1..*— Employee	A boss is responsible for one or more employees.
Zero or one	0..1	Employee —0..1— Spouse	An employee can be married to zero or one spouse.
Specified range	2..4	Employee —2..4— Vacation	An employee can take between two to four vacations each year.
Multiple, disjoint ranges	1..3, 5	Employee —1..3, 5— Committee	An employee is a member of one to three or five committees.

FIGURE 14-18
Multiplicity

classes. Most times, classes are related through a "normal" association, but there are two special cases of an association that you will see appear quite often: generalization and aggregation.

Generalization and Aggregation *Generalization* shows that one class (subclass) inherits from another class (superclass), meaning that the properties and operations of the superclass are also valid for objects of the subclass. The generalization path is shown with a solid line from the subclass to the superclass and a hollow arrow pointing at the superclass. For example, Figure 14-16 communicates that *shop mechanics*, and *salespeople* are all kinds of *employees* and those *employees* and *customers* are kinds of *persons*. The generalization association occurs when you need to use words like "is a kind of" to describe the relationship.

Aggregation is used when classes actually comprise other classes. For example, think about a vehicle dealership that has decided to create customer care teams that include shop mechanics and salespeople. As customers visit the dealership, they are assigned to a customer care team that cares for their needs during their visits. Figure 14-16 shows how this relationship is denoted on the class diagram. A diamond is placed nearest the class representing the aggregation (*customer care team*), and lines are drawn from the arrow to connect the classes that serve as its parts (*shop mechanics* and *salespeople*). Aggregation associations are typically identified when you need to use words like "is a part of" or "is made up of" to describe the relationship.

Simplifying Class Diagrams

When a class diagram is drawn with all of the classes and associations for a real-world system, the class diagram can become very complex. When this occurs, it is sometimes necessary to simplify the diagram by using a *view* to limit the amount of information displayed. Views are simply subsets of information contained in the entire model. For example, a use case view shows only the classes and relationships that are needed for a particular use case. Another view could show only a particular type of relationship, such as aggregation, association, or generalization. A third type of view could restrict the information shown to just that associated with a specific class, such as its name, attributes, and/or methods.

A second approach to simplifying class diagrams is through the use of packages (i.e., logical groups of classes). To make the diagrams easier to read and keep the models at a reasonable level of complexity, you can group related classes together into *packages*. Packages are general constructs that can be applied to any of the elements in UML models. We discussed them previously as a way to simplify use case diagrams, and they can also be used to simplify class diagrams.

Creating a Class Diagram

Creating a class diagram (like any UML diagram) is an iterative process whereby the analyst starts by drawing a rough version of the diagram and then refines it over time. We will take you through one iteration of class diagram creation, but we would expect that the diagram would change dramatically as you communicate with users and fine-tune your understanding of the system.

Identify Classes   The steps for creating a class diagram are quite similar to the steps that we learned to create an ERD. First, you will need to identify what classes should be placed on the diagram. Remember, like ERDs, class diagrams show the classes that are needed for the system as a whole. However, for demonstration purposes, we investigate only a single use case: search and browse tunes.

Many different approaches have been suggested to aid the analyst in identifying a set of candidate classes for the class diagram. The most common approach is *textual analysis*, the analysis of the text in the use cases. The analyst starts by reviewing the use cases and the use case diagrams. The text descriptions in the use cases are examined to identify potential objects, attributes, methods, and associations. The nouns in the use case suggest possible classes, while the verbs suggest possible operations or associations. Figure 14-19 presents a summary of guidelines that we have found useful.

Identify Attributes and Operations   Hopefully, you determined that the class diagram will need to include classes that represent *Available Tunes*, *Favorites*, *Interests*, *Promotions*, and *Customer*. The next step is to define the kinds of information that we want to capture about each class. The use case also provides insight into the kind of

Guideline	Example
Nouns → imply *objects* or *classes*. A common or improper noun implies a class of objects. A proper noun or direct reference implies an instance of a class. A collective noun implies a class of objects made up of groups of instances of another class.	"An employee serves the customer" implies two classes of objects, employee and customer. "John addressed the issues raised by Susan" implies two instances of an object, John and Susan. "The list of students was not verified" implies that a list of students is an object that has its own attributes and methods.
Verbs → imply *associations* or *operations*. A doing verb implies an operation. A being verb implies a classification association between an object and its class. A having verb implies an aggregation or association relationship. A transitive verb implies an operation. A predicate or descriptive verb phrase implies an operation.	"Don files purchase orders" implies a "file" operation. "Joe is a dog" implies that Joe is an instance of the dog class. "The car has an engine" implies an aggregation association between car and engine. "Frank sent Donna an order" implies that Frank and Donna are instances of some class that has an operation related to sending an order. "If the two employees are in different departments, then ..." implies an operation to test whether employees are or are not in different departments.
Adjectives → imply *attributes* of a class. An adjective implies an attribute of an object.	"All 55-year-old customers are now eligible for the senior discount" implies that age is an attribute.
Adverbs → imply an attribute of an *association* or *operation*. An adverb implies an attribute of an association or an attribute of an operation.	"John drives very fast" implies a speed attribute associated with the driving operation.

These guidelines are based on Russell J. Abbott, "Program Design by Informal English Descriptions," *Communications of the ACM*, 26(11), 1983, pp. 882–94; Peter P-S Chen, "English Sentence Structure and Entity-Relationship Diagrams" *Information Sciences: An International Journal*, 29(2–3), 1983, pp. 127–149; and Ian Graham, *Migrating to Object Technology*, Reading, MA: Addison-Wesley, 1995.

FIGURE 14-19
Textual Analysis Guidelines

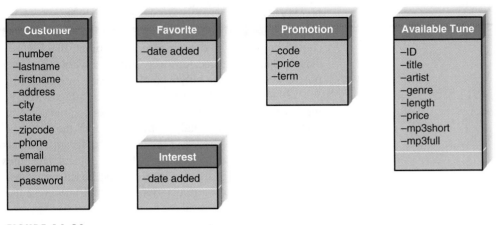

FIGURE 14-20
Initial Attributes for Class Diagram

information that needs to be captured, under the section labeled "Information for Steps." Sometimes additional requirements-gathering techniques from Chapter 3 are also needed. At this point, try to list some pieces of information that we likely will want to capture for each class—it may help to reread the description of the Search and Browse Tunes use case in Chapter 4 (Figure 4-10) and the purchase tunes use case in Figure 4-11. One issue, of course, is that the use case reports in Chapter 4 were written to be used in a structured environment, not an object-oriented environment, but you should be able to make the translation. Take a moment and add attributes to the classes.

At this point, we also want to consider what special operations each class will need to contain. (Remember that all classes can perform basic operations like inserting a new instance, so these are *not* placed on the diagram.) Figure 14-20 shows a "first cut" at the attributes for the class diagram. Can you think of other attributes that we could have included in any of these classes?

Draw Associations between the Classes   Associations are added to the class diagram by drawing association lines. Go through each class and determine other classes to which it is associated, the name of the association (or the role it plays), and the number of instances that can participate in the association. For example, the *promotion* class is associated to the *customer* class because a promotion *targets a customer*. A customer can be targeted by a zero or many promotions (multiplicity = 0..*), and

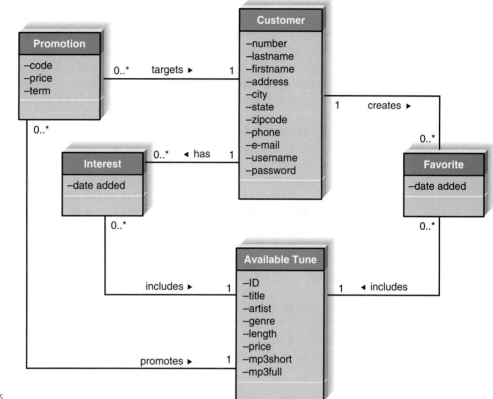

FIGURE 14-21
Revised Attributes and Associations

a promotion can be associated with one and only one customer (multiplicity = 1). Take time now to formulate the associations for *Interest, Favorite,* and *Available Tunes.* Figure 14-21 shows the diagram that we have created so far. Notice that we included associations between *Customer* and *Favorite, Customer and Interest, Favorite* and *Available Tune, Interest* and *Available Tune,* and *Promotion* and *Available Tune.* Finally, you should examine the model for opportunities to use aggregation or generalization associations.

SEQUENCE DIAGRAM

The next major UML diagramming technique is the *sequence diagram.* A sequence diagram illustrates the objects that participate in a use case and the messages that pass between them over time for *one* use case. A sequence diagram is a *dynamic model* that supports a dynamic view of the evolving systems. It shows the explicit sequence of messages that are passed between objects in a defined interaction. Since sequence diagrams emphasize the time-based ordering of the activity that takes place among a set of objects, they are very helpful for understanding real-time specifications and complex use cases.

The sequence diagram can be a *generic sequence diagram* that shows all possible scenarios[4] for a use case, but usually each analyst develops a set of *instance*

---

[4] Remember that a scenario is a single executable path through a use case.

sequence diagrams, each of which depicts a single scenario within the use case. If you are interested in understanding the flow of control of a scenario by time, you should use a sequence diagram to depict this information. The diagrams are used throughout both the analysis and design phases; however, the design diagrams are very implementation specific, often including database objects or specific GUI components as the classes. The following sections first present the syntax of a sequence diagram and then demonstrate how one should be drawn:

Elements of a Sequence Diagram   Figure 14-22 presents an instance sequence diagram that depicts the objects and messages for the "make offer" use case that describes the process by which a customer creates a new offer for the Holiday Travel Vehicle system. In this specific instance, the create offer process is portrayed.

Actors and objects participating in the sequence are placed across the top of the diagram, depicted by actor symbols from the use case diagram or unlabeled rectangles. (See Figure 14-23.) Notice that the objects in Figure 14-22 are *aCustomer*, *aSalesperson*, *Vehicles*, *Dealer Options*, *Trade-in Value*, and *anOffer*. They are not placed in any particular order, although it is nice to organize them in some logical way, such as the order in which they participate in the sequence. For each of the objects, the name of the class that they are an instance of is given after the object's name (e.g., *Vehicles:List* means that *Vehicles* is an instance of the *List* class that contains individual vehicle objects).

A dotted line runs vertically below each actor and object to denote the *lifeline* of the actors/objects over time. (See Figure 14-22.) Sometimes an object creates a

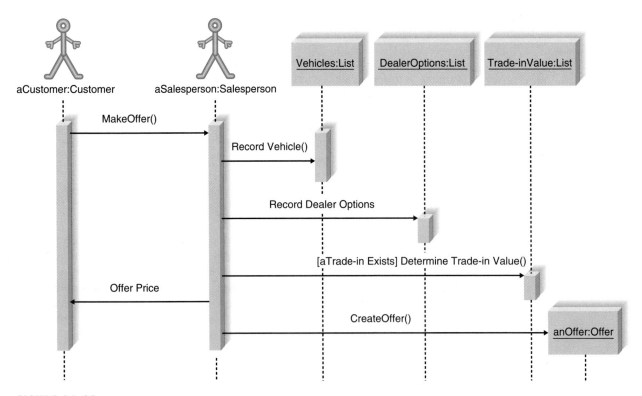

FIGURE 14-22
Sequence Diagram

Term and Definition	Symbol
An actor: ■ Is a person or system that derives benefit from and is external to the system. ■ Participates in a sequence by sending and/or receiving messages. ■ Is placed across the top of the diagram.	 anActor
An object: ■ Participates in a sequence by sending and/or receiving messages. ■ Is placed across the top of the diagram.	anObject:aClass
A lifeline: ■ Denotes the life of an object during a sequence. ■ Contains an X at the point at which the class no longer interacts.	
A focus of control: ■ Is a long narrow rectangle placed atop a lifeline. ■ Denotes when an object is sending or receiving messages.	
A message: ■ Conveys information from one object to another one.	aMessage()
Object destruction: ■ An *X* is placed at the end of an object's lifeline to show that it is going out of existence.	X

FIGURE 14-23
Sequence Diagram Syntax

temporary object, and in this case an X is placed at the end of the lifeline at the point the object is destroyed (not shown). For example, think about a shopping cart object for a Web commerce application. The shopping cart is used for temporarily capturing line items for an order, but once the order is confirmed, the shopping cart is no longer needed. In this case, an X would be located at the point at which the shopping cart object is destroyed. When objects continue to exist in the system after they are used in the sequence diagram, the lifeline continues to the bottom of the diagram. (This is the case with all of the objects in Figure 14-22.)

A thin, rectangular box, called the *execution occurrence*, is overlaid onto the life-line to show when the classes are sending and receiving messages. (See Figure 14-23.) A *message* is a communication between objects that conveys information, with the expectation that activity will ensue, and messages passed between objects are shown by solid lines connecting two objects, called *links*. (See Figure 14-23.) The arrow on the link shows which way the message is being passed, and any argument values for the message are placed in parentheses next to the message's name. The order of messages goes from the top to the bottom of the page, so messages located higher on the diagram represent messages that occur earlier in the sequence, versus the lower messages that occur later. Messages may also be numbered to enforce sequence. In Figure 14-22, *Record Vehicle* is a message sent from the object *aSalesperson* to the object *Vehicles*, which is a container for the current vehicle to record information about the vehicle under offer.

There are times that a message is sent only if a *condition* is met. In those cases, the condition is placed between a set of [], such as *[a Trade-in Exists] Determine Trade-in Value()*. The condition is placed in front of the message name. However, when a sequence diagram is used to model a specific scenario, conditions typically are not shown on any single sequence diagram. Instead, conditions are implied only through the existence of different sequence diagrams. Finally, it is possible to explicitly show the return from a message, with a return link, a dashed message. However, adding return links tends to clutter the diagram. Therefore, unless the return links add a lot of information to the diagram, they should be omitted.

Sometimes, an object will create another object. This is shown by the message being sent directly to an object instead of its lifeline. In Figure 14-22, the object *aSalesperson* creates the object *anOffer*.

Creating a Sequence Diagram

The best way to learn how to create a sequence diagram is to draw one. We will use the scenario of buying a tune immediately from the use case "Purchase Tunes" that was created in Chapter 4 and illustrated in Figure 4-11. Figure 14-24 lists the main steps that this "purchase a tune" sequence diagram will need to communicate. The steps followed when creating a sequence diagram are somewhat similar to the steps that we learned to create a DFD.

Identify Objects   The first step is to identify instances of the classes that participate in the sequence being modeled; that is, the objects that interact with each other during the use case sequence. Think of the major kinds of information that need to be captured by the system. Objects typically can be taken from the use case report created during the development of the use case diagram. (See Chapter 4.) The sources and destinations on the use case (i.e., the external entities or data stores) are usually a good starting point for identifying the classes. Also, classes can be external actors that are represented on the use case diagram.

For example, the instances of classes used for the Purchase A Tune scenario include *Customer* and *Tune*. These should be placed in boxes and listed across the top of the drawing. (See Figure 14-25.) The instances of *Customer* and *Tune* correspond to data stores that we ultimately will need in the system, whereas the instances of *Shopping Cart* and *Payment Approval* represent external actors who appeared on the use case diagram. Because the latter instances interact in the sequence, we want to include them in the diagram.

---

1. User requests tune information.
2. User inserts tune into shopping cart.
3. User checks out and provides payment information.
4. Payment is authorized.
5. Tune released for download.

FIGURE 14-24
Steps of the Customer Buys
Tune Scenario

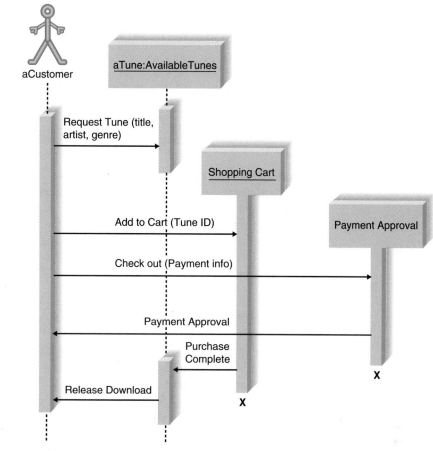

Remember, at this point in time, you are trying to identify only the objects that take part in a specific scenario of a use case. As such, don't worry too much about perfectly identifying all the objects of the use case. Other scenario-based sequence diagrams may uncover additional objects. Also, the class diagram created in the previous section of this chapter described how the classes are defined and refined. However, based on the sequence diagrams created, the class diagram usually is revised, since analysts have a better understanding of the classes after they develop them.

Add Messages   Next, draw arrows to represent the messages being passed from object to object, with the arrow pointing in the message's transmission direction. The arrows should be placed in order from the first message (at the top) to the last (at the bottom) to show time sequence. Any parameters passed along with the messages should be placed in parentheses next to the message's name. If a message is expected to be returned as a response to a message, then the return message is not explicitly shown on the diagram. Examine the steps in Figure 14-24 and see whether you can determine the way in which the messages should be added to the sequence diagram. Figure 14-25 shows our results. Notice how we did not include messages back to Customer in response to *Request Tune.* In this case, it is assumed that the customer will receive response messages about the requested tune.

In "Your Turn 14-3" you were asked to draw a use case diagram for the campus housing system. Select one of the use cases from the diagram and create a sequence diagram that represents the interaction among objects in the use case.

Place Lifeline and Execution Occurrences   Last, you will need to show when objects are participating in the sequence. A vertical dotted line is added below each object to represent the object's existence during the sequence, and an X should be placed below objects at the point on the lifeline where they are no longer interacting with other objects. You should draw a narrow rectangular box over top of the lifelines to represent when the objects are sending and receiving messages. See Figure 14-25 for the completed sequence diagram.

BEHAVIORAL STATE MACHINE DIAGRAM

Some of the classes in the class diagrams are quite dynamic in that they pass through a variety of states over the course of their existence. For example, a vehicle can change over time from being "new" to "pre-owned," on the basis of its status with the dealership. A *behavioral state machine diagram* is a dynamic model that shows the different states that a single class passes through during its life in response to events, along with its responses and actions. Typically, behavioral state machine diagrams are not used for all classes, but just to further define complex classes to help simplify the design of algorithms for their methods. The behavioral state machine diagram shows the different states of the class and what events cause the class to change from one state to another. In comparison to the sequence diagrams, behavioral state machine diagrams should be used if you are interested in understanding the dynamic aspects of a single class and how its instances evolve over time, and not with how a particular use case scenario is executed over a set of classes.

Elements of a Behavioral State Machine Diagram

Figure 14-26 presents an example of a behavioral state machine diagram representing the offer class in the context of a vehicle dealership. From this diagram, we can tell that an offer is brought to the dealership and is written. If the owner finds the offer to be acceptable, it is closed and is no longer considered an offer after two days elapse. If an offer is rejected, it may be renegotiated until it is acceptable.

State   A *state* is a set of values that describes an object at a specific point in time, and it represents a point in an object's life in which it satisfies some condition, performs some action, or waits for something to happen. (See Figure 14-27.) In Figure 14-26, states include *arriving*, *pending*, *closed*, and *under negotiation*. A state is depicted by a *state symbol*, which is a rectangle with rounded corners with a

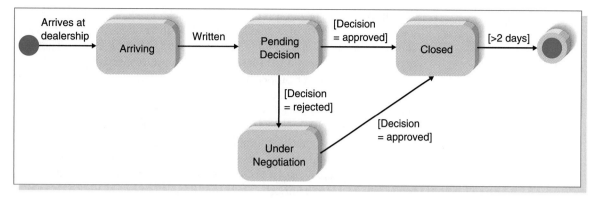

FIGURE 14-26
Behavioral State Machine Diagram for an Offer for a Vehicle

Term and Definition	Symbol
A state ▪ Is shown as a rectangle with rounded corners. ▪ Has a name that represents the state of an object.	
An initial state ▪ Is shown as a small filled-in circle. ▪ Represents the point at which an object begins to exist.	●
A final state ▪ Is shown as a circle surrounding a small, solid filled-in circle (bull's-eye). ▪ Represents the completion of activity.	◉
An event ▪ Is a noteworthy occurrence that triggers a change in state. ▪ Can be a designated condition becoming true, the receipt of an explicit signal from one object to another, or the passage of a designated period. ▪ Is used to label a transition.	Event name
A transition ▪ Indicates that an object in the first state will enter the second state. ▪ Is triggered by the occurrence of the event labeling the transition. ▪ Is shown as a solid arrow from one state to another, labeled by the event name.	⟶

FIGURE 14-27
Behavioral State Machine Syntax

descriptive label that communicates a particular state. There are two exceptions. An *initial state* is shown by a small, solid, filled-in circle, and an object's *final state* is shown as a circle surrounding a small, solid, filled-in circle. These exceptions depict when an object begins and ceases to exist, respectively.

The attributes or properties of an object affect the state that it is in; however, not all attributes or attribute changes will make a difference. For example, think about the address of the customer making the offer. In Figure 14-26, those attributes make very little difference as to changes in an offer's state. However, if states were based upon a customer's geographic location (e.g., in-town customers were treated differently than out-of-town customers), changes to the customer's address may influence state changes. In the current diagram, the attribute that influences state transitions is the offer price.

Event   An *event* is something that takes place at a certain point in time and changes a value(s) that describes an object, which in turn changes the object's state. It can be a designated condition becoming true, the receipt of the call for a method by an object, or the passage of a designated period. The state of the object determines exactly what the response will be. In Figure 14-26, arriving at the dealership, an approved decision, and a 2-day time lapse are events that cause changes to the offer's state.

Arrows are used to connect the state symbols, representing the transitions between states. A *transition* is a relationship that represents the movement of an object from one state to another state. Some transitions will have a guard condition. A *guard condition* is a Boolean expression that includes attribute values, which allows a transition only if the condition is true. Each arrow is labeled with the appropriate event name and with any parameters or conditions that may apply. For example, the two transitions from *pending* to *closed* and *under negotiation* contain guard conditions.

Creating a Behavioral State Machine Diagram

Behavioral state machine diagrams are drawn to depict a single class from a class diagram. Typically, the classes are very dynamic and complex, requiring a good understanding of their states over time and events triggering changes. You should examine your class diagram to identify which classes will need to undergo a complex series of state changes and draw a diagram for each of them. Let us investigate the state of the *selected tune* class from the Tune Source Digital Music Download system.

YOUR TURN

14-5 Drawing a Behavioral State Machine Diagram

You have been working with the system for the campus housing service that helps students find apartments. One of the dynamic classes in this system likely is the apartment class. Draw a behavioral state machine diagram to show the various states that an apartment class transitions to throughout its lifetime. Can you think of other classes that would make good candidates for a behavioral state machine diagram?

1. The customer adds items into the shopping cart.
2. The customer checks out and submits the purchase once he or she is finished.
3. The purchase is pending while payment is authorized.
4. The payment is approved.
5. The purchase is pending for final customer approval.
6. The customer confirms the purchase.
7. The download is released.

FIGURE 14-28
The Life of a Tune Download

Identify the States The first step is to identify the various states that a selected tune will have over its lifetime. This information is gleaned from reading the use case reports, talking with users, and relying on the requirements-gathering techniques that you learned about in Chapter 3. You should begin by writing the steps of what happens to a selection over time, from start to finish, similar to how you would create the "major steps performed" section of a use case report. Figure 14-28 shows order from start to finish, from a selected tune's perspective.

Identify the Transitions The next step is to identify the sequence of states that a selected tune object will pass through during its lifetime and then determine exactly what causes each state to occur. Place state figures on the diagram to represent the states and label the transitions to describe the events that are taking place to cause state changes. For example, the event *Customer adds tune to cart* moves the order from the *initial* state to the *in cart* state. (See Figure 14-29.) During the *in cart* state, the selected tune awaits the customer's decision to buy the tune. At that point, the tune awaits the payment approval. Once that is received, the tune awaits the customer's final purchase confirmation. When confirmation is received, the tune is released for download.

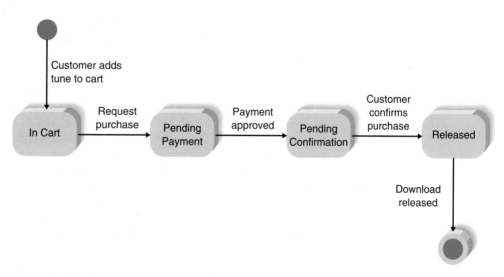

FIGURE 14-29
Behavioral State Machine Diagram for a Customer Purchase

SUMMARY

Today, the most exciting change to systems analysis and design is the move to object-oriented techniques, which view a system as a collection of self-contained objects that have both data and processes. However, the ideas underlying object-oriented techniques are simply ideas that have either evolved from traditional approaches to systems development or they are old ideas that have now become practical due to the cost–performance ratios of modern computer hardware in comparison to the ratios of the past. Today, the cost of developing modern software is composed primarily of the cost associated with the developers themselves and not the computers. Therefore, object-oriented approaches to developing information systems hold out much promise in controlling these costs.

An object is a person, place, or thing about which we want to capture information. Each object has attributes that describe information about it and its behaviors, which are described by methods that specify what an object can do. Objects are grouped into classes, which are collections of objects that share common attributes and methods. The classes can be arranged in a hierarchical fashion in which low-level classes, or subclasses, inherit attributes and methods from superclasses above them, to reduce the redundancy in development. Objects communicate with each other by sending messages, which trigger methods. Polymorphism allows a message to be interpreted differently by different kinds of objects. This form of communication allows us to treat objects as black boxes and ignore the inner workings of the objects. Encapsulation and information hiding allow an object to conceal its inner processes and data from the other objects.

Object-oriented analysis and design using UML allows the analyst to decompose complex problems into smaller, more manageable components through a commonly accepted set of notation. UML is a standard set of diagramming techniques that provide a graphical representation rich enough to model any systems development project, from analysis through implementation. Typically, today most object-oriented analysis and design approaches use the UML to depict an evolving system. Finally, many people believe that users do not think in terms of data or processes, but instead in terms of a collection of collaborating objects. As such, object-oriented analysis and design using UML allows the analyst to interact with the user, employing objects from the user's environment instead of a set of separate processes and data.

Use Case Diagram

A use case diagram illustrates the main functions of a system and the different kinds of users that interact with it. The diagram includes actors, which are people or things that derive value from the system, and use cases that represent the functionality of the system. The actors and use cases are separated by a system boundary and connected by lines representing associations. At times, actors are specialized versions of more general actors. Similarly, use cases can extend or include other use cases. Building use case diagrams is a five-step process whereby the analyst identifies the use cases, draws the system boundary, adds the use cases to the diagram, identifies the actors, and, finally, adds appropriate associations to connect use cases and actors together.

Class Diagram

The class diagram shows the classes and relationships among classes that remain constant in the system, over time. The main building block of the class diagram is a class, which stores and manages information in the system. Classes have attributes that capture information about the class and about operations, which are actions that a class can perform. There are three kinds of operations: constructor, query, and update. The classes are related to each other through an association, which has a name and a multiplicity that denotes the minimum and maximum instances that participate in the relationship. Two special associations, aggregation and generalization, are used when classes comprise other classes or when one subclass inherits properties and behaviors from a superclass, respectively. Class diagrams are created by first identifying classes, along with their attributes and operations. Then relationships are drawn among classes to show associations. Special notations are used to depict the aggregation and generalization associations.

Sequence Diagram

The sequence diagram is a dynamic model that illustrates instances of classes that participate in a use case and messages that pass between them over time. Objects are placed horizontally across the top of a sequence diagram, each having a dotted line, called a lifeline, vertically below it. The focus of control, represented by a thin rectangle, is placed over the lifeline to show when the objects are sending or receiving messages. A message is a communication between objects that conveys information with the expectation that activity will ensue, and the messages are shown by an arrow connecting two objects that points in the direction that the message is being passed. To create a sequence diagram, first identify the classes that participate in the use case and then add the messages that pass among them. Finally, you will need to add the lifeline and focus of control. Sequence diagrams are helpful for understanding real-time specifications and for complex scenarios of a use case.

Behavioral State Machine Diagram

The behavioral state machine diagram shows the different states that a single instance of a class passes through during its life in response to events, along with responses and actions. A state is a set of values that describes an object at a specific point in time, and it represents a point in an object's life in which it satisfies some condition, performs some action, or waits for something to happen. An event is something that takes place at a certain point in time and changes a value(s) that describes an object, which in turn changes the object's state. As objects move from state to state, they undergo transitions. When drawing a behavioral state machine diagram, rectangles with rounded corners are first placed on the model to represent the various states that the class will take. Next, arrows are drawn between the rectangles to denote the transitions, and event labels are written above the arrows to describe the event that causes the transition to occur.

KEY TERMS

A-Kind-Of (AKO)	Attribute	Constructor operation
Abstract class	Behavior	Derived attribute
Actor	Behavior diagram	Dynamic binding
Aggregation	Behavioral state machine diagram	Dynamic model
Architecture centric	Class	Dynamic view
Association relationship	Class diagram	Encapsulation
Association class	Concrete class	Event

Execution occurrence	Method	State symbol
Extends relationship	Multiplicity	Static binding
Final state	Object	Static model
Functional view	Object-oriented approach	Static view
Generalization	Operation	Structure diagram
Generic sequence diagram	Package	Subclass
Guard condition	Phased development RAD	Superclass
Includes relationship	Polymorphism	System boundary
Incremental	Private attribute	Temporary object
Information hiding	Protected attribute	Textual analysis
Inherit	Public attribute	Transition
Inheritance	Query operation	Unified Modeling Language
Initial state	Rational Unified Process (RUP)	(UML)
Instance	Reference	Update operation
Instance sequence diagram	Role	Use case
Iterative	Scenario	Use case diagram
Lifeline	Sequence diagram	Use case driven
Links	Specialized actor	View
Message	State	Visibility

QUESTIONS

1. Contrast the items in the following sets of terms:
   - Object; class; instance; entity relationship diagram (ERD) entity
   - Property; method; attribute
   - State; behavior
   - Superclass; subclass
   - Concrete class; abstract class
   - Method; message
   - Encapsulation; inheritance; polymorphism
   - Static binding; dynamic binding
2. How is the object approach different from the data and process approaches to systems development?
3. How can the object approach improve the systems development process?
4. Describe how the object approach supports the program design concepts of cohesion and coupling that were presented in Chapter 10.
5. What is the Unified Modeling Language (UML)? How does it support the object approach to systems development?
6. Describe the steps in creating a use case diagram.
7. How can you employ the use case report to develop a use case diagram?
8. How is the use case diagram similar to the context and level 0 data flow diagrams (DFDs)? How is it different?

9. Give two examples of the extends associations on a use case diagram. Give two examples for the includes association.
10. Which of the following could be an actor found on a use case diagram? Why?
    - Ms. Mary Smith
    - Supplier
    - Customer
    - Internet customer
    - Mr. John Seals
    - Data-entry clerk
    - Database administrator
11. Consider a process called *validate credit history*, which is used to validate the credit history for customers who want to take out a loan. Explain how it can be an example of an includes association on a use case diagram. Describe how it is an example of an extends association. As an analyst, how would you know which interpretation is correct?
12. Give examples of a static model and a dynamic model in UML. How are the two kinds of models different?
13. Describe the main building blocks for the sequence diagram and how they are represented on the model.
14. Do lifelines always continue down the entire page of a sequence diagram? Explain.
15. Describe the steps used to create a sequence diagram.

16. How is a class diagram different from an ERD?

17. Give three examples of derived attributes that may exist on a class diagram. How would they be denoted on the model?

18. Identify the operations that follow as constructor, query, or update. Which operations would not need to be shown in the class rectangle?
    - Calculate employee raise (raise percent)
    - Insert employee ()
    - Insert spouse ()
    - Calculate sick days ()
    - Locate employee name ()
    - Find employee address ()
    - Increment number of employee vacation days ()
    - Change employee address ()
    - Place request for vacation (vacation day)

19. Draw the associations that are described by the business rules that follow. Include the multiplicities for each relationship.
    - A patient must be assigned to only one doctor, and a doctor can have one or many patients.
    - An employee has one phone extension, and a unique phone extension is assigned to an employee.
    - A bookstore sells at least one book, and a book can be sold at up to 10 other bookstores around town.
    - A movie either has one star, two costars, or more than 10 people starring together. A star must be in at least one movie.

20. What are the two kinds of labels that a class diagram can have for each association? When is each kind of label used?

21. Why is an association class used for a class diagram? Give an example of an association class that may be found in a class diagram that captures students and the courses that they have taken.

22. Give two examples of aggregation associations and generalization associations. How is each type of association depicted on a class diagram?

23. Are states always depicted by rounded rectangles on a behavioral state machine diagram? Explain.

24. What three kinds of events can lead to state transitions on a behavioral state machine diagram?

25. Describe the type of class that is best represented by a behavioral state machine diagram. Give two examples of classes that would be good candidates for behavioral state machine diagrams.

26. Compare and contrast the rational unified process (RUP) with UML.

27. Describe the way in which the RUP is implemented on a systems project.

28. Identify the model(s) that contains each of the following components:
    - Aggregation association
    - Class
    - Derived attributes
    - Extends association
    - Execution occurrence
    - Guard condition
    - Initial state
    - Links
    - Message
    - Multiplicity
    - Specialized actor
    - System boundary
    - Update method

29. What do you think are three common mistakes that novice analysts make in using UML techniques?

30. Do you think that UML will become more popular than the traditional structured techniques discussed previously? Why or why not?

31. Some experts argue that object-oriented techniques are simpler for novices to understand and use than are DFDs and ERDs. Do you agree? Why or why not?

EXERCISES

A. Investigate the Web site for Rational Software (www-306.ibm.com/software/rational/) and its repository of information about Unified Modeling Language (UML). Write a paragraph news brief on the current state of UML (the current version and when it will be released, future improvements, etc.).

B. Investigate the Object Management Group (OMG). Write a brief memo describing what it is, its purpose, and its influence on UML and the object approach to systems development. (Hint: A good resource is: www.omg.org.)

C. Investigate the rational unified process (RUP). Describe the major benefits of RUP and the steps that it contains. Compare the methodology with one of the other methodologies described in Chapter 2.

D. Investigate computer-aided software engineering (CASE) tools that support UML (e.g., Rational Software's Rational Rose, Microsoft's VISIO) and describe how well they support the language. What CASE tool would you recommend for a project team about to embark on a project by using the object approach? Why?

E. Consider a system that is used to run a small clothing store. Its main functionality is maintaining inventory of stock, selling items to customers, and producing sales reports for management. List examples for each of the following items that may be found on a use case diagram that models such a system: use case; extends use case; includes use case; actor; specialized actor.

F. Create a use case diagram that would illustrate the use cases for the following dentist office system: Whenever new patients are seen for the first time, they complete a patient information form that asks their name, address, phone number, and brief medical history, which is stored in the patient information file. When a patient calls to schedule a new appointment or change an existing appointment, the receptionist checks the appointment file for an available time. Once a good time is found for the patient, the appointment is scheduled. If the patient is a new patient, an incomplete entry is made in the patient file; the full information will be collected when the patient arrives for the appointment. Because appointments are often made far in advance, the receptionist usually mails a reminder postcard to each patient two weeks before his or her appointment.

G. Create a use case diagram that would illustrate the use cases for the following online university registration system: The system should enable the staff members of each academic department to examine the courses offered by their department, add and remove courses, and change the information about courses (e.g., the maximum number of students permitted). It should permit students to examine currently available courses, add and drop courses to and from their schedules, and examine the courses for which they are enrolled. Department staff should be able to print a variety of reports about the courses and the students enrolled in them. The system should ensure that no student takes too many courses and that students who have any unpaid fees are not permitted to register. (Assume that a fees data store is maintained by the university's financial office, which the registration system accesses but does not change.)

H. Create a use case diagram that would illustrate the use cases for the following system: A Real Estate

Inc. (AREI) sells houses. People who want to sell their houses sign a contract with AREI and provide information on their house. This information is kept in a database by AREI, and a subset of this information is sent to the citywide multiple listing service used by all real estate agents. AREI works with two types of potential buyers. Some buyers have an interest in one specific house. In this case, AREI prints information from its database, which the real estate agent uses to help show the house to the buyer (a process beyond the scope of the system to be modeled). Other buyers seek AREI's advice in finding a house that meets their needs. In this case, the buyer completes a buyer information form that is entered into a buyer database, and AREI real estate agents use its information to search AREI's database and the multiple listing service for houses that meet their needs. The results of these searches are printed and used to help the real estate agent show houses to the buyer.

I. Create a sequence diagram for each of the following scenario descriptions for a video store system: A Video Store (AVS) runs a series of fairly standard video stores:
- Every customer must have a valid AVS customer card in order to rent a video. Customers rent videos for three days at a time. Every time a customer rents a video, the system must ensure that he or she does not have any overdue videos. If there are overdue videos, they must be returned and an overdue fee must be paid before the customer can rent more videos.
- If the customer has returned overdue videos, but has not paid the overdue fee, the fee must be paid before new videos can be rented. If the customer is a premier customer, the first two overdue fees can be waived, and the customer can rent the video.
- Every morning, the store manager prints a report that lists overdue videos; if a video is two or more days overdue, the manager calls the customer to remind him or her to return the video.

J. Create a sequence diagram for each of the following scenario descriptions for a health club membership system:
- When members join the health club, they pay a fee for a certain length of time. The club wants to mail out reminder letters to members, asking them to renew their memberships one month before their memberships expire. About half of the members do not renew their memberships. These members

are sent follow-up surveys to complete about why they decided not to renew so that the club can learn how to increase retention. If the member did not renew because of cost, a special discount is offered to that customer. Typically, 25% of accounts are reactivated because of this offer.

- Every time a member enters the club, an attendant takes his or her card and scans it to make sure that the person is an active member. If the member is not active, the system presents the amount of money it costs to renew the membership. The customer is given the chance to pay the fee and use the club, and the system makes note of the reactivation of the account so that special attention can be given to this customer when the next round of renewal notices is dispensed.

K. Create class diagrams that describe the classes and relationships depicted in the following scenarios:

- Researchers are placed into a database that is maintained by the state of Georgia. Information of interest includes researcher name, title, position, date began current position, number of years at current position; university name, location, enrollment; and research interests. Researchers are associated with one institution, and each researcher can have up to five research interests. More than one researcher can have the same interest, and the system tracks the ranking of the best researchers for each interest. The system should be able to insert new researchers, universities, and research interests; produce information, such as the number of researchers at each university, contact information for the researchers, and research interests that do not have associated researchers; and change researcher rankings for the various research interests.

- A department store has a bridal registry. This registry keeps information about the bride, the products that the store carries, and the products for which each customer registers. Some products include several related items; for example, dish sets include plates, specialty dishes, and serving bowls. Customers typically register for a large number of products, and many customers register for the same products. Draw the class diagram and give at least two examples of query and update operations that could be placed somewhere on the model.

- Jim Smith's dealership sells Fords, Hondas, and Toyotas. The dealership keeps information about

each car manufacturer with whom employees deal so that they can get in touch with manufacturers easily. The dealership also keeps basic information about the models of cars that it carries from each manufacturer. The dealership keeps such information as list price, the price the dealership paid to obtain the model, and the model name and series (e.g., Honda Civic LX). It also keeps information about all sales that employees have made. (For instance, the dealership will record the buyer's name, the car he or she bought, and the amount the buyer paid for the car.) To contact the buyers in the future, the dealership also keeps contact information (e.g., address, phone number).

L. Think about sending a first-class letter to an international pen pal. Describe the process that the letter goes through to get from your initial creation of the letter to being read by your friend, from the letter's perspective. Draw a behavioral state machine diagram that depicts the states that the letter moves through.

M. Consider the video store described in question I. Draw a behavioral state machine diagram that describes the various states that a video goes through from the time it is placed on the shelf through the rental and return processes.

N. Draw a behavioral state machine diagram that describes the various states that a travel authorization can have through its approval process. A travel authorization form is used in most companies to approve travel expenses for employees. Typically, an employee fills out a blank form and sends it to his or her boss for a signature. If the amount is fairly small (under $300), then the boss signs the form and routes it to accounts payable to be input into the accounting system. The system cuts a check that is sent to the employee for the right amount, and after the check is cashed, the form is filed away with the canceled check. If the check is not cashed within 90 days, the travel form expires. When the amount of the travel voucher is large (over $300), the boss signs the form and sends it to the chief financial officer (CFO) along with a paragraph explaining the purpose of the travel, and the CFO will sign the form and pass it along to accounts payable. Of course, both the boss and the CFO can reject the travel authorization form if they do not feel that the expenses are reasonable. In this case, the employee can change the form to include more explanation or decide to pay the expenses.

O. Identify the use cases for the following system: Picnics R Us (PRU) is a small catering firm with five employees. During a typical summer weekend, PRU caters 15 picnics for 20 to 50 people each. The business has grown rapidly over the past year, and the owner wants to install a new computer system for managing the ordering and buying processes. PRU has a set of 10 standard menus. When potential customers call, the receptionist describes the menus to them. If the customer decides to book a picnic, the receptionist records the customer information (name, address, phone number, etc.) and the information about the picnic (e.g., place, date, time, which one of the standard menus, total price) on a contract. The customer is then faxed a copy of the contract and must sign and return it along with a deposit (often by credit card or check) before the picnic is officially booked. The remaining money is collected when the picnic is delivered. Sometimes, the customer wants something special (e.g., birthday cake). In this case, the receptionist takes the information and gives it to the owner, who determines the cost; the receptionist then calls the customer back with the price information. Sometimes, the customer accepts the price; other times, the customer requests some changes, which have to go back to the owner for a new cost estimate. Each week, the owner looks through the picnics scheduled for that weekend and orders the supplies (e.g., plates) and food (e.g., bread, chicken) needed to make them. The owner would like to use the system for marketing as well. It should be able to track how customers learned about PRU and to identify repeat customers, so that PRU can mail special offers to them. The owner also wants to track the picnics on which PRU sent a contract, but the customer neither signed the contract nor actually booked a picnic.
- Create the use case diagram for the PRU system.
- Choose one use case diagram and create a sequence diagram.
- Create a class diagram for the PRU system.
- Create a behavioral state machine diagram to depict one of the classes on the previous class diagram.

P. Identify the use cases for the following system: Of-the-Month Club (OTMC) is an innovative young firm that sells memberships to people who have an interest in certain products. People pay membership fees for one year and each month receive a product by mail. For example, OTMC has a coffee-of-the-month club that sends members one pound of special coffee each month. OTMC currently offers six memberships (coffee, wine, beer, cigars, flowers, and computer games), each of which costs a different amount. Customers usually belong to just one, but some belong to two or more. When people join OTMC, the telephone operator records the name, mailing address, phone number, e-mail address, credit card information, start date, and membership service(s) (e.g., coffee). Some customers request a double or triple membership (e.g., two pounds of coffee, three cases of beer). The computer game membership operates a bit differently from the others. In this case, the member must also select the type of game (action, arcade, fantasy/science fiction, educational, etc.) and age level. OTMC is planning to greatly expand the types of memberships it offers (e.g., video games, movies, toys, cheese, fruit, vegetables), so the system must accommodate this future expansion. OTMC is also planning to offer three-month and six-month memberships.
- Create the use case diagram for the OTMC system.
- Choose one use case diagram and create a sequence diagram.
- Create a class diagram for the OTMC system.
- Create a behavioral state machine diagram to depict one of the classes on the previous class diagram.

Q. Think about your school or local library and the processes involved in checking out books, signing up new borrowers, and sending out overdue notices, all from the library's perspective. Describe three use cases that represent these three functions.
- Create the use case diagram for the library system.
- Choose one use case diagram and create a sequence diagram.
- Create a class diagram for the library system.
- Create a behavioral state machine diagram to depict one of the classes on the previous class diagram.

R. Think about the system that handles student admissions at your university. The primary function of the system should be to track a student from the request for information through the admission process until the student is either admitted or rejected for attendance at the school. Write the use case report that can describe an "admit student" use case.
- Create the use case diagram for the one use case. Pretend that students of alumni are handled differently from other students. Also, a generic *update student information* use case is available for your system to use.

- Choose one use case diagram and create a sequence diagram. Pretend that a temporary student object is used by the system to hold information about people before they send in an admission form. After the form is sent in, these people are considered students.
- Create a class diagram for the student admission system. An admissions form includes the contents of the form, SAT information, and references. Additional information is captured about students of alumni, such as their parents' graduation year(s), contact information, and college major(s).
- Create a behavioral state machine diagram to depict a person as he or she moves through the admissions process.

MINICASES

1. The new information system at Jones Legal Investigation Services will be developed, using objects. The data to be managed by this system will be complex, consisting of large amounts of text, dates, numbers, graphical images, video clips, and audio clips. The primary functions of the system will be to establish an investigation when requests come in from client-attorneys, record the investigative procedures that are conducted and the information that is gathered during an investigation, and produce bills for investigative services. Develop a use case diagram for this new system.

2. The case investigation undergoes several states in the Jones Legal Investigation Services system. The case investigation is first established when the attorney requests that an investigation be conducted. When the investigator begins to perform the various investigative techniques, the case investigation becomes active. The client-attorney can begin settlement negotiations, or the case can go to trial. Settlement negotiations may result in a settlement, or the case may have to go to trial if settlement negotiations fail. Ultimately, the case investigation is closed when the case is closed by settlement agreement or judicial verdict. Develop a behavioral state machine diagram for this situation.

INDEX